New Testament Commentary

Romans

New Testament Commentary

Romans

VOLUME I: CHAPTERS 1–8

William Hendriksen

THE BANNER OF TRUTH TRUST

THE BANNER OF TRUTH TRUST
3 Murrayfield Road, Edinburgh EH12 6EL

*

© 1980 William Hendrikson
First Banner of Truth edition 1980
ISBN 0 85151 324 7
Library of congress Catalog Card Number 80:1869
Reprinted as combined volume with volume 2 1982
ISBN 0 85151 365 4

*

*

Printed and bound in Great Britain at
The Camelot Press Ltd, Southampton

FOREWORD

A heart-warming book is Romans. It is filled with instruction touching both life and doctrine. It imparts comfort in life and, as every faithful pastor knows, and ever so many other people have testified, also in the hour of death.

However, this book is very controversial. On many passages high-ranking interpreters differ. In connection with issues in dispute I have not tried to avoid taking a position. Among them, as concern chapters 1-8, are the following:

1. Paul writes, "to all in Rome who are beloved of God" (1:7). Were those addressed predominantly Jews or Gentiles? See pp. 20-23.

2. When the apostle uses the verb *to justify* or the noun *justification* in such passages as 3:24; 4:25; 5:1, 16, 18, is he using these words in (a) a causative sense, or (b) a declarative (forensic) sense? See pp. 130, 245.

3. In 5:1 did Paul say: (a) "We have peace," (b) "Let us have (or: continue to have) peace," or (c) "Let us enjoy the peace we have"? See pp. 168, footnote 140.

4. Who is the person described in Rom. 7:14-25? Is he: (a) an unbeliever, (b) an immature believer, or (c) Paul himself, the believer, and by extension, the believer generally? See pp. 225-230.

5. When, in 8:26b, the apostle states that "the Spirit himself (αὐτὸ τὸ πνεῦμα) intercedes for us with unspoken groanings," does he mean that it is indeed *the Spirit* who groans, or does he mean that *we* groan, repeating the thought of verse 23? See pp. 273-277.

It will become clear that here and there I differ with those for whom I have the highest respect, and whose writings I warmly recommend. May the cause of the gospel prosper even through differences in interpretation!

William Hendriksen

TABLE OF CONTENTS

COMMENTARY

LIST OF ABBREVIATIONS

A. *Book Abbreviations*

A.R.V.	American Standard Revised Version
A.V.	Authorized Version (King James)
Gram. N.T.	A. T. Robertson, *Grammar of the Greek New Testament in the Light of Historical Research*
Gram. N.T. (Bl.-Debr.)	F. Blass and A. DeBrunner, *A Greek Grammar of the New Testament and Other Early Christian Literature*
Grk. N.T. (A-B-M-W)	*The Greek New Testament*, edited by Kurt Aland, Matthew Black, Bruce M. Metzger, and Allen Wikgren
I.S.B.E.	*International Standard Bible Encyclopedia*
L.N.T. (Th.)	Thayer's *Greek-English Lexicon of the New Testament*
L.N.T. (A. and G.)	W. F. Arndt and F. W. Gingrich, *A Greek-English Lexicon of the New Testament and Other Early Christian Literature*
M.M.	*The Vocabulary of the Greek New Testament Illustrated from the Papyri and Other Non-Literary sources*, by James Hope Moulton and George Milligan
N.A.S. (N.T.)	New American Standard Bible (New Testament)
N.E.B.	New English Bible
N.I.V.	New International Version
N.T.C.	W. Hendriksen, *New Testament Commentary*
R.S.V.	Revised Standard Version
S.BK.	Strack and Billerbeck, *Kommentar zum Neuen Testament aus Talmud und Midrasch*
S.H.E.R.K.	*The New Schaff-Herzog Encyclopedia of Religious Knowledge*
Th.D.N.T.	*Theological Dictionary of the New Testament*, edited by G. Kittel and G. Friedrich, and translated from the German by G. W. Bromiley

LIST OF ABBREVIATIONS

Please Note

In order to differentiate between the second person plural (see Rom. 1:11: "I am yearning to see y o u") and the second person singular (see Rom. 2:1: "Therefore you have no excuse"), the letters in "y o u pl." are spaced, those in "you sing." are not.

Introduction

to

The Epistle to the Romans

I. Its Applicability Always and Everywhere

The church of Rome consisted of Jews and Gentiles. Which group predominated? See Section IV of this Introduction; also see on the following passages: 1:5, 6, 13; 2:17ff.; 7:1-6; 11:13; 15:15f. There was the danger that one group would look down with *disdain* on the other: the Jews on the Gentiles (2:1f.), the Gentiles on the Jews (11:18). Paul therefore emphasizes that "there is no distinction between Jew and Greek, for the same Lord is Lord of all" (10:12).

Today, too, this truth needs to be stressed, for the fact that, in a certain sense, "before God all men are equal" is by no means universally acknowledged. Even the church, sad to say, has not always taken to heart the full implications of this principle.

The people addressed in this epistle were also being exposed to another evil, namely, the heresy of concluding that since salvation is not dependent upon works, but rests entirely on grace, therefore the performance of good deeds is unnecessary; in fact, might even become an obstacle to full spiritual development. If salvation is the product of grace, why not, by means of living in sin, offer grace ample scope to operate? Why not "continue in sin that grace may bound"? See 6:1.

Most decisively does Paul refute this line of reasoning. He argues that for those who "have become united with Christ" (6:5) such a course is simply impossible, and that those who think otherwise are laboring under a pernicious *delusion*, "For the wages of sin is death, but the free gift of God is life in Christ Jesus our Lord" (6:23).

Today, too, especially in certain fundamentalistic circles, a kind of antinomianism is being propagated. We are being told that the believer is not under the law in any sense whatever. Therefore, as long as he trusts in Christ as his personal Savior he can more or less do whatever he pleases. Works are of no account. Did not Paul say, "For by grace y o u have been saved through faith; and this not of yourselves; (it is) the gift of God; not of works, lest anyone should boast"?

The answer is: Shortquoting Paul is unjustified. Paul continues, "For his handiwork are we, created in Christ Jesus *for good works,* which God prepared beforehand that we should walk in them." He who quotes Eph. 2:8, 9 should also quote verse 10. He who appeals to Titus 3:5a must accord equal weight to verses 5b, 14.

Here in Romans Paul's denunciation of antinomianism is scorching, withering, "We who died to sin, how can we any longer live in it?" (6:2)

And as to not being in any sense under the law, Rom. 13:8, 9 teaches the opposite. So do I Cor. 9:21; Gal. 5:14.

The Greek and Roman world of Paul's day was indeed a hopeless world. It was a realm filled with *despair*. According to the Greek (and afterward also the Roman) conception, at the moment of death there is no hope for the body, nor even for the soul. Reluctantly the latter departs from the body either with the dying breath or through open wounds. It enters the very dismal realm of the shades. Or else it simply ceases to exist. The Stoics mostly thought that it is the rational universe that persists; individuals do not. The Iliad ends with funeral rites.

Today among many people a somewhat similar attitude prevails. With respect to any life after this life, uncertainty reigns supreme. And with respect to mankind's future here on earth, pessimism is more and more gaining the upper hand. There is little talk now of "making the world safe for democracy" or of "waging a war to end all wars." Even in certain religious circles concerted Christian action in order to promote the glory of God in every sphere is frowned upon.

Also in this respect the study of the book of Romans is rewarding. This book offers hope. In fact, the subject of hope—for which see also the books of Psalms, Acts, Hebrews, and especially I Peter—is mentioned more often in Romans than in any other New Testament book. The apostle even tells us, "It was in hope that we were saved" (8:24), a hope well-founded (8:26-39). He calls the Divine Being "the God of hope" (15:13). From start to finish this book proclaims good tidings (3:24; 4:16-25; 7:24, 25; chapter 8 in its entirety; 11:33-36; 13:8-14; 16:25-27). And it encourages Christian action (12:9-21; 13:7; 14:19; 15:30; 16:1, 2).

At the root of every question is the question of man's guilt. "How can a man be righteous before God" (Job 9:2; 25:4). Paul, too, asked this question. So did Luther, and so does everybody, consciously or unconsciously. Romans answers it.

It is, accordingly, a book for every age, including our own.

II. Its Author

With few exceptions scholars agree that it was indeed the apostle Paul who wrote Romans. The evidence favoring this conclusion may, without exaggeration, be called overwhelming. The arguments that have been advanced against it—for example, "Luke, in the book of Acts, never mentions the establishment of a church in Rome; so Paul could not have written a letter to the Romans"—are so absurd that they merit no further comment.

For the sake of climactic effect the evidence in favor of Pauline authorship will be traced in reverse chronological order (from later to earlier).

INTRODUCTION TO THE EPISTLE

Eusebius, the great church historian, writing at the beginning of the fourth century, refers to "the fourteen [sic!] letters of Paul," and in the same context (*Ecclesiastical History* III.iii.4, 5) makes mention of Romans as being one of them. Origen (fl.210-250), Tertullian (fl.193-216), and Clement of Alexandria (fl.190-200) are in full agreement.

The Muratorian Fragment (about 180-200), so named because it was published by Cardinal Ludovico A. Muratori (1672-1750), who had discovered it in the Ambrosian Library at Milan, contains the oldest extant list of New Testament writings. It is incomplete, is written in poor Latin and includes titles of books that were read in the church of Rome during the early days. In connection with Romans this Fragment reads:

"Now the epistles of Paul, what they are, whence and for what reason they were sent, they themselves make clear to him who is willing to understand. First of all he wrote at length to the Corinthians ... then to the Galatians ... and to the Romans on the order of the Scriptures, intimating also that Christ is the chief matter in them."

Irenaeus (fl. about 182-188) states, "Paul, speaking to the Romans, declares, 'Much more they who receive abundance of grace and righteousness will reign in life by the one, Christ Jesus'" (*Against Heresies* III.xvi), freely quoting Rom. 5:17. In this and several other statements Irenaeus clearly ascribes the authorship of Romans to Paul.

Going back even farther we reach the days of Marcion, who came to Rome shortly before the year 144. His canon of sacred writings consists of ten Pauline epistles plus Luke, all edited to suit the heretic's personal theology. He recognizes Romans as one of Paul's chief works.

The early apostolic fathers were not in the habit of mentioning the names of the holy men of God whom they quoted. Nevertheless, the fact that they are quoting, whether literally or (as often) freely, is frequently very clear, as is also the identity of the one whom they are quoting.

This is true, for example, with respect to Polycarp, bishop of Smyrna. This valiant Christian hero, "a disciple of John," suffered martyrdom in the year 155. In his letter *To The Philippians* VI.ii he shows that he is well acquainted with Paul's epistles, including Romans. In a sentence which reflects both Rom. 14:10, 12 and II Cor. 5:10 he writes, "If, then, we beseech the Lord to forgive us, we ourselves ought also to forgive, for we stand before the eyes of the Lord God, and we must all appear before the judgment seat of Christ, and each must give an account of himself." The following quotation from this same letter shows that the mind and heart of this devout early martyr were immersed in the writings of Paul:

"These things, brothers, I write to y o u concerning righteousness. I do so not on my own initiative, but because y o u first invited me. For neither am I, nor is any other like me, able to rival the wisdom of the blessed and glorious Paul, who, when he was living among y o u, in the presence of his contemporaries taught accurately and steadfastly the word of truth, and who also, when he was absent, wrote letters to y o u. By means of the study of these letters y o u will be able to build yourselves up in the faith given to y o u . . ." III.i, ii.

Ignatius, bishop of Antioch, while on his way to Rome and martyrdom, in the beginning of the second century A.D., wrote a number of letters, mostly to churches. These letters again clearly show that he was acquainted with, and highly regarded, Paul's epistles, including the one to the Romans. Note, for example, the following resemblances:

Romans		Cf. Ignatius *To The Ephesians*
1:3	of the seed of David	XVIII.ii
4:20	was strengthened in faith	X.ii
8:5, 8	carnal versus spiritual people	VIII.ii
6:4	newness of life	XIX.iii

A great admirer of Paul was Clement, bishop of Rome during the final decades of the first century. In his letter *To The Corinthians* he writes, "Take the epistle of the blessed Paul the apostle . . . With true inspiration he charged y o u concerning himself and Cephas and Apollos, because even then y o u were given to partisan discord." Cf. I Cor. 3:1–9. That he was also thoroughly acquainted with another epistle written by the same apostle, namely Romans, is clear from XXXV.v, vi. Cf. Rom. 1:29–32. In this case not only does he use many of Paul's words, but he even arranges some of them in the same order: "unrighteousness, wickedness, greed (or covetousness)." And at the close of this little paragraph compare Clement's "Not only those who do them are hateful to God but also those who approve of them," with Paul's "They not only continue to do these very things but also approve of those who practice them."

This brings us, finally, to the apostles and their own writings. II Peter 3:15, 16 reads as follows:

"Bear in mind that the patience of our Lord means salvation, just as our beloved brother Paul, according to the wisdom given him, wrote y o u, as also (he writes) in all his letters, speaking in them of these matters. . . ."

It is not surprising, therefore, that there is a close resemblance between Peter's letters and Paul's, as is evident especially when Romans and I Peter are placed side by side:

Romans		Cf. I Peter
12:1	a sacrifice acceptable to God	2:5
12:2	be not fashioned	1:14
12:3	as God has allotted to each	4:10
12:9	love without hypocrisy (see the original)	1:22 (see the original)
12:10	love of the brothers	2:17

In conclusion, whoever rejects the Pauline authorship of Romans must also reject the Pauline authorship of I and II Corinthians, Galatians, Ephesians, Colossians, etc. The writer who in Rom. 3:20-24; 4:3 proclaims the deeply satisfying doctrine of "justification not by human merit but by faith" does so also in Gal. 2:16; 3:6, 11; Titus 3:5-7. The inspired artist who in Rom. 12:5 pictures the church as Christ's body with its many members has not changed his identity in I Cor. 10:17; 12:12-14, 27; Eph. 1:22, 23; Col. 2:19. The exhorter who in Rom. 12:6-8 insists that these members shall use their respective talents for the benefit of the entire body emphasizes the same duty in I Cor. 12:15-26, 28-31; Eph. 4:11-16. And the warm-hearted enthusiastic philanthropist of Rom. 15:15-28 is also the gift collector and benefactor of II Cor. 8 and 9. He calls himself "Paul, servant of Jesus Christ, apostle" (Rom. 1:1). We have every reason to believe him.

Saul, whose Roman name was *Paul*[1] was born at Tarsus, a center of Greek culture, a university city located in Cilicia, near the northeastern corner of the Mediterranean Sea. He received his early training in Jerusalem under that most distinguished doctor of the Law, Gamaliel, grandson of the famous Hillel. The witnesses who stoned Stephen laid their garments at the feet of Paul (Acts 7:58). Immediately after Stephen's death Paul took a leading part in the persecution of Christians. He put his whole soul into this task. He "breathed threatening and slaughter against the disciples of the Lord" (Acts 9:1). Not satisfied with waging the persecution in Jerusalem, he even asked of the high priest letters to the synagogues in Damascus that he might bring bound to Jerusalem "any that were of the Way, whether men or women" (Acts 9:2).

Then something happened that would bring about a radical change not only in the life of Saul of Tarsus but in the course of all future history.

It was the hour of noon and the sun was shining in all its strength. Paul was approaching Damascus to destroy the Christian community in that city. Suddenly, a light from heaven, brighter than the sun, shone around him. "And he fell upon the earth, and heard a voice saying to him, Saul, Saul, why do you persecute me? And he said, Who art thou, Lord?" The voice answered, "I am Jesus whom you are persecuting; but rise and enter into the city, and you will be told what you must do" (Acts 9:3-6).

The men who accompanied Paul saw the light but could not distinguish the Person. They heard the voice or sound, but could not understand the words. Paul, on the other hand, saw the Lord and heard his words. Arriving in Damascus, he received his sight through the ministry of Ananias, who also baptized him. He began his evangelistic work in Damascus:

> And at once in the synagogues he proclaimed Jesus, that he is the Son of God. And all who heard him were amazed and asked, "Is not he the man who in Jerusalem raised havoc among those who call on this name? And has he not come here for the purpose of bringing them bound before the chief priests?" But Saul increased the more in strength, and confounded the Jews who dwelt in Damascus, proving that this is the Christ (Acts 9: 20-22).

---

1. For more information on these names see N.T.C. on I and II Thessalonians, p. 38.

Paul spent some time in Arabia, but Scripture does not tell us what he did there. When he returned to Damascus, his preaching aroused such opposition that he had to flee for his life, for the Jews were plotting to kill him. They had the co-operation of the civil authorities. Paul's report is as follows:

> In Damascus the governor under Aretas the king guarded the city of the Damascenes in order to take me: and through a window was I let down in a basket by the wall, and escaped his hands (II Cor. 11:32, 33).

Fully three years after his conversion Paul arrived in Jerusalem (Gal. 1:18). He tried to join the disciples but they were all afraid of him, for they did not believe that he was really a disciple. But Barnabas, a big-hearted Levite of Cyprus who had been converted earlier (Acts 4:36, 37), removed their apprehension and introduced Paul to Peter and to James, the Lord's brother. "To visit Cephas [Peter]" had been Paul's purpose when he started out from Damascus (Gal. 1:18). While in Jerusalem, the former persecutor preached fearlessly to the Greek-speaking Jews (Acts 9:28, 29). They immediately plotted to kill him. Hence, the brothers decided to send Paul away. In a vision the Lord himself confirmed this decision.

Paul had spent only fifteen days with Peter, as he himself states in Galatians 1:18. This is in complete harmony with the account which we find in Acts 22:17-21:

> And it happened that, when I had returned to Jerusalem and was praying in the temple, I fell into a trance, and saw him [the Lord] saying to me, Make haste and quickly get out of Jerusalem; because they will not accept your testimony concerning me . . . Depart: for I will send you far away to the Gentiles.

Accordingly, the apostle left Jerusalem before he had seen the rest of the apostles and before he had become known by sight to the churches in Judea. Nevertheless, believers everywhere had heard the good news. "The man who once persecuted us is now preaching the faith he formerly tried to destroy." They glorified God (Gal. 1:23).

Paul's friends brought him to Caesarea and sent him off to Tarsus.

It is probable that the apostle labored in Tarsus and the surrounding territory for several years, founding the churches that are mentioned in Acts 15:41. When Barnabas, who had been sent to Antioch in Syria, saw the progress of the gospel in that great city and the need of an additional worker, he went to Tarsus to seek Paul and brought him to Antioch. Together they labored here for a year. The church grew rapidly and became the starting point for Paul's mission to the pagan world (Acts 9:30; 11:20-26).

About this time a great famine occurred "over all the world," just as had been predicted by the prophet Agabus. Luke tells us that this famine took place in the days of Claudius (Acts 11:28). He was emperor during the years 41-54. At Antioch contributions for the relief of the Christians in

Judea were made. By the hands of Barnabas and Paul these were sent to Jerusalem. This trip probably occurred about the year 44, shortly before the death of Herod Agrippa I (Acts 12:1). The two men, having accomplished their mission, returned to Antioch.

The extension of the church from Antioch by means of *three great missionary journeys* began at this time. The Holy Spirit directed the church to set apart Barnabas and Paul for the work to which God had called them. So, "when they had fasted and prayed and laid their hands on them, they sent them away" (Acts 13:1-3). We do not know how long a time this first missionary journey occupied. All we can say is that it must be assigned, in general, to the period 44-50. For the details of this journey, followed by the Jerusalem Conference, see Acts 13:1—15:35. It is clear that on this trip Paul and his companions did not travel very far to the west. The journey was confined to the island of Cyprus and the southern part of the Roman province of Galatia.

The second journey is described in Acts 15:36—18:22. Its probable date is 50/51-53/54. It covered far more territory than did the first trip. In fact, this time the missionaries did not stay in Asia but actually entered Europe. Evangelistic work was carried on in Macedonia (Northern Greece) and Achaia (Southern Greece). The cities visited were respectively (a) Philippi, Thessalonica, Berea; and (b) Athens and Corinth. In the latter city Paul remained a long time (Acts 18:11, 18), preaching and supporting himself by working at his trade of making tents. It was also from this city that the apostle sent his epistle to the Galatians, and, perhaps a little later, the two epistles to the Thessalonians. On the homeward stretch of this tour Paul stopped at Ephesus but did not remain there very long. He promised, however, to return (Acts 18:20, 21). By way of Caesarea he came back to Antioch.

On his third journey (53/54-57/58; Acts 18:23—21:16) Paul, "having passed through the upper country," came to Ephesus, thus fulfilling his promise (Acts 19:1). He remained here a long time (Acts 19:8, 10; 20:31) and was very successful. It is probable that all or most of "the seven churches of Asia" (Rev. 1:4) were founded during this period. Also, it would seem that before writing I Corinthians the apostle made a second visit to Corinth (II Cor. 12:14; 13:1), returning shortly afterward to Ephesus. A little later he wrote a letter to the Corinthians, the one we call I Corinthians.

When he finally left Ephesus Paul went to Macedonia. It was here (in Philippi perhaps?) that he wrote II Corinthians. And so the apostle came at last to Corinth, his third visit to that city. It was when he was about to depart from Corinth that he wrote Romans (Rom. 15:22-25; cf. Acts 20:3).

The triumph of the gospel during the period of Paul's three missionary journeys was truly amazing. It has been estimated that by the close of the apostolic period the total number of Christians in the world had reached half a million. Ever so many missionaries and lay witnesses contributed to bring about this result. Undoubtedly the most effective worker of them all was "God's chosen vessel," the apostle Paul. He was "a *Hebrew* of the Hebrews," a *Roman* citizen by birth, and versed in the "wisdom" of the *Greeks*.

There were certain external factors which favored Paul and his message, such as

1. a world government
2. world peace
3. a world language (Greek)
4. famous Roman roads linking the various parts of the world
5. world skepticism with respect to pagan deities
6. the dispersion of the Jews and of their monotheistic religion among the nations of the world
7. the translation of the Old Testament into Greek, in a sense the world language.

Nevertheless, there were also formidable obstacles. Journeying up and down the Roman Empire in order to blaze a trail for the gospel was a task beset with great dangers (II Cor. 11:23-28). Moreover, the enemies were many and relentless. Therefore, although we do not wish to detract in the least from the significance of the aforementioned favorable circumstances, *more* than this was needed if the gospel were to triumph. *More* was also divinely provided.

God, in his wonderful providence, prepared not only external conditions which favored the spread of Christianity, but also *the man* who was going to make use of these conditions. Paul had been "separated from his mother's womb" in order to proclaim the gospel to the Gentiles (Gal. 1:15-17).

What kind of person, then, was Paul?

He was a man with a *brilliant intellect,* an *iron will,* and a *compassionate heart.*

1. *brilliant intellect*

Paul was a thinker of the first order, a man with a penetrating mind, well-versed in the Old Testament, and able to grasp the connection between its precious passages and the doctrine of salvation in Christ. Far from being the creator of a brand-new theological system, as some seem to think, he discovered the doctrine of justification by faith in such Old Testament passages as Gen. 15:6; Ps. 32:1f.; Hab. 2:4. See Rom. 1:17; 3:21f.; 4:3. He also understood that what made this marvelously gracious solution of man's guilt-problem possible was Messiah's vicarious sacrifice, as Isaiah's fifty-third chapter teaches. That Paul was indeed well acquainted with the contents of that chapter is clear from Rom. 10:16 (cf. Isa. 53:1), and is probably also indicated in I Cor. 15:3 (cf. Isa. 53:5-12). And may not the following references point in the same direction: Rom. 4:25 (cf. Isa. 53:4, 5); Rom. 5:19 (cf. Isa. 53:11); Rom. 8:34 (cf. Isa. 53:12); and I Cor. 5:7 (cf. Isa. 53:7)?

This plan of salvation is in harmony with the words of Jesus recorded in Matt. 20:28; Mark 10:45; John 6:51; 10:11, 14, 16, 28; and also with those spoken by the Lord in connection with the institution of the Lord's Supper, and recorded by both Paul (I Cor. 11:23-26) and his close friend and frequent travel companion Luke (22:19, 20, on which see N.T.C. on Luke, pp. 961-964).

Several passages in Paul's epistles reveal consummate literary skill. In this connection reference is generally made to Rom. 8, I Cor. 13, and I Cor. 15. But are not the language and the style of the following passages equally superb: Rom. 2:17-29; 5:1-11; chapter 12; I Cor. 4:11-13; II Cor. 5:1-10; 11:22-33; Gal. 2:19-21; Eph. 2:8-10; 2:14-21; 6:10-20; Phil. 3:7-21; 4:4-9; I Tim. 3:16?

A combination of astuteness and wisdom is evident in what may be called Paul's *Mission Strategy,* embracing such points as the following:

a. Work in the great urban centers, so that from there the message may spread to the surrounding towns and villages.

b. Make use of the synagogue, in order to reach not only Jews but also Gentile proselytes.

c. Show that new-dispensation events are the fulfilment of old-dispensation prophecies.

d. Adapt the gospel message to the culture and the needs of the hearers.

e. Do follow-up work by means of return visits, letters, and special envoys.

f. Promote unity between rich and poor, Gentile and Jew, by asking the more prosperous churches to help the poorer ones.

2. *iron will*

Coupled with his penetrating mind was Paul's invincible determination to be a channel of blessing for men. His slogan was: "Woe to me if I do not preach the gospel . . . I have become all things to all men that by all possible means I may save some" (I Cor. 9:22), to the glory of God (I Cor. 10:31).

This indomitable purpose and resolution must certainly be considered an element in the explanation of the apostle's willingness to endure persecution for the sake of the cause to which he was so ardently devoted. How tremendous his sacrifice! How unlimited his willingness to suffer for the sake of Christ and his kingdom! Here are Paul's own words, II Cor. 11:23-28:

> In labors far greater,
> In prisons more often,
> In scourgings above measure,
> In exposure to death often.
> Of the Jews five times I received forty lashes minus one.
> Three times I was beaten with rods,
> Once I was stoned,
> Three times I suffered shipwreck,

A night and a day have I been in the deep;
In journeyings often,
In perils of rivers,
In perils of robbers,
In perils from my countrymen,
In perils from the Gentiles,
In perils in the city,
In perils in the wilderness,
In perils at sea;
In perils among false brothers,
In labor and toil,
In watchings often,
In hunger and thirst,
In fastings often,
In cold and nakedness.
Besides everything else
There is that which presses upon me daily,
Anxiety for all the churches.

Even when we limit ourselves to the story concerning Paul as recorded in the book of Acts we stand amazed at the amount of suffering which this hero of faith, *in order to accomplish his unwavering and consuming purpose,* was willing to endure. But when we add to the record of Acts what Paul himself tells us here in II Cor. 11, words fail to express our admiration for this great gift of God to the church! Cf. J. D. Quin, "Seven Times he wore chains," *JBL,* Dec. 1978, pp. 574, 575.

Moreover, it should be borne in mind that II Cor. 11 was written *before* the apostle's imprisonment in Jerusalem, Caesarea, and Rome (Acts 20:22, 23; 21:11, 27-28:31). This also means, of course, that *Paul had already experienced all the trials mentioned in II Cor. 11 before he composed his epistle to the Romans!* Keeping this in mind will make the study of Romans even more interesting and profitable.

In speaking about the apostle's iron will, his hewing to the line no matter what the cost, this resoluteness must not be misconstrued. It did not amount to bullheadedness. The beauty of Paul's philosophy was exactly this, that when principle was at stake—for example, that of Christ's all-sufficiency for salvation—he was unbending, but in matters not involving principle he could be very accommodating, flexible, conciliatory. Therefore, instead of charging the apostle with inconsistency, we should credit him with kindness. When the Judaistic party in Jerusalem demanded that *Titus* be circumcised, Paul did not yield to its clamor (Gal. 2:3). Yet, he circumcised *Timothy* (Acts 16:3). It was one thing to circumcise a person of mixed parentage, as was Timothy, and to do this in order to make him a more effective witness among the Jews; it was an entirely different matter to force circumcision on Titus (both of whose parents were Gentiles) and, in general, on all the Gentiles, *with the implication that unless they received this sacrament they could not be saved* (Acts 15:1).

Paul's flexibility probably also explains his willingness, after his arrival in Jerusalem from his third missionary journey, to yield to the suggestion that he join four men who had taken a temporary Nazirite vow and pay for their offerings (Acts 21:17-26). The question whether this concession on his part was wise does not concern us at this point. The fact that must be emphasized is this: Paul, while taking a firm position on matters of principle, was always willing to yield on matters neither forbidden or enjoined. He followed this course purposely and consistently, as I Cor. 9:20, 21 shows.

Of the American poet John Greenleaf Whittier it has been said that he "yielded in smaller matters, that he might win in the greater."[2] The same could be said of Paul.

3. compassionate heart

The apostle's "drive" would not have been so keen had it not been activated by this third factor. Various phases of the apostle's intensely emotional personality are exhibited in the book of Acts and in the epistles. Here was a *marvelously loving heart,* a truly great soul!

Having formerly persecuted the followers of Jesus, after his conversion Sorrow, hearty and profound, walked with Paul (I Cor. 15:9; I Tim. 1:15). That to such a bitter persecutor Christ had revealed himself as a loving Savior baffled him. He just could not get over it (Eph. 3:8; I Tim. 1:16). It caused his heart to overflow with lasting, humble gratitude! For this and for other reasons his epistles are full of magnificent doxologies (Rom. 9:5; 11:36; 16:25-27; Eph. 1:3f.; 3:20f.; Phil. 4:20; I Tim. 1:17; 6:15; II Tim. 4:18), which are the spontaneous utterances of the man who wrote, "*For the love of Christ constrains us*" (II Cor. 5:14). Having been "laid hold on" by Christ, the apostle in turn was eager to burn himself out for the salvation of others (I Cor. 9:22; 10:33; II Cor. 12:15).

His heart ached intensely because so many of his own people (Israelites) were not saved (Rom. 9:1-3; 10:1). Anxiety for all his churches pressed upon him daily (II Cor. 11:28). How fervent and touching were his prayers for them (Eph. 3:14-19; I Thess. 3:9-13). *How he loved them,* so that he could write, "We were gentle in the midst of y o u as a nurse cherishes her own children. So, being affectionately desirous of y o u, we gladly shared with y o u not only the gospel of God but also our own souls ... For now we really live if y o u stand fast in the Lord" (I Thess. 2:7, 8; 3:8). How earnest were his pleadings (II Cor. 5:20; Gal. 4:19, 20; Eph. 4:1), and how tactful! Though for their own good he was able to rebuke the wayward very sharply (Gal. 1:6-9; 3:1-4), even this was a manifestation of the love of his great, throbbing heart. Is it any wonder that, when occasion demanded it, out of the eyes of a man with an ebullient spirit and loving heart there welled forth fountains of tears (Acts 20:19, 31), so that both in II Cor. 2:4 and in Phil. 3:18 these are mentioned? And is it at all surprising that, on the

---

2. A. H. Strong, *American Poets and Their Theology,* Philadelphia, etc., 1916, p. 124.

other hand, on one occasion the tears of his friends, because of his imminent departure and the afflictions in store for him, well-nigh broke his
heart (Acts 21:13)? Truly Paul's *weeping* when he writes about the enemies
of the cross of Christ is as glorious as is the *joy, joy, joy* that sings its way
through his epistle to the Philippians!

III.   Its Place and Date of Composition

The following facts point to Corinth as *the place* where the apostle composed the epistle to the Romans:

1. He commends to the church Phoebe whom he calls "a servant of the
church of Cenchrea." Now Cenchrea was the eastern port of Corinth. It is
generally, and probably correctly, assumed that Phoebe carried Paul's letter
to its destination.

2. He calls Gaius his "host." This person may well have been the one of
that name mentioned in I Cor. 1:14, where the apostle informs the Corinthians that he had baptized this member of their congregation. In Rom.
16:23 Gaius is sending greetings.

3. Also extending a salutation is Erastus. Cf. II Tim. 4:20, "Erastus
remained *at Corinth.*" An inscription discovered on a paving-block *at
Corinth* reads, "Erastus laid this pavement at his own expense." *If* these
references are to the Erastus of Rom. 16:23, they confirm the theory that
Romans was composed in Corinth.

Determination of *the time* of composition is perhaps somewhat more
difficult. At least opinions differ rather widely. The question must be answered, "When was Paul in Corinth under circumstances that harmonized
with the situation as pictured in his letter to the Romans?"

His *first* stop in that place was during the second missionary journey
(Acts 15:36—18:22). According to Acts 15 this journey began soon after
the close of the Jerusalem Conference, though exactly how soon afterward
has not been revealed. See Acts 15:30, 36. If the date A.D. 50 is assigned to
that gathering, as is generally done, the somewhat flexible date 50/51–53/
54 for the entire second missionary journey may well be correct. Nevertheless, it cannot have been during *this* stay at Corinth that the apostle wrote
Romans. That letter clearly belongs to a considerably later time period,
when Paul's missionary labors in the eastern part of the empire were nearing their completion. Note the following: "From Jerusalem and round
about, as far as Illyricum, I have fully preached the gospel of Christ" (Rom.
15:19); "I no longer have any room for work in these regions" (15:23). Cf.
1:10: "... now *at last.*"

Shall we then link Romans with Paul's *second* journey to Corinth, the
painful visit implied in II Cor. 12:14; 13:1? But this trip must have been of
short duration and made under circumstances unfavorable for the composition of this great epistle. As indicated earlier, it was probably made during
Paul's very lengthy stay at Ephesus, and *before* he wrote I Corinthians.

Everything points to the probability that Paul wrote Romans toward the close of his three-month ministry in Achaia (Greece), mentioned in Acts 20:3; hence during his *third* recorded visit to Corinth on his *third* missionary journey (Acts 18:23—21:16).

On his subsequent *departure* from Corinth Paul's original plan had been to sail directly from Greece to Syria, in order from there to travel to Jerusalem with gifts for its poor saints, charitable contributions made by their fellow-Christians in Macedonia and Achaia. But the timely discovery of a plot against the apostle's life changed this plan, so that, instead, he returned to Jerusalem by way of Macedonia (Philippi) and Mysia (Troas). See Acts 20:3–6; Rom. 15:25.

The third missionary journey had already lasted a long time before Paul left Corinth. This is clear from the fact that even before reaching Corinth on this trip the apostle had spent "two months" and "two years" at Ephesus (Acts 19:8, 10). In fact, all in all he seems to have worked there for a period of "three years" (Acts 20:31). The date for his entire third missionary journey was therefore probably 53/54–57/58, and the date for the composition of the epistle to the Romans, just before his departure from Corinth, was probably 57 or 58. Since it was Paul's intention to reach Jerusalem by Pentecost (Acts 20:16), we can perhaps be even more specific and say that the letter was probably written *toward the close* of the winter and/or *during the beginning* of the spring.

A considerably earlier date for the third missionary journey and for Romans brings the story into conflict with the date for Paul's accusation before Gallio (Acts 18:12-17) during the apostle's second missionary journey. It has been established that Gallio's consulship fell within the period 51-53.[3] Also, such an early date would result in the necessity of moving back the dates of Paul's arrival in Jerusalem, his arrest, and his imprisonment in Caesarea during the administration of Felix (and later on, of Festus). And since Felix probably did not become governor until the year 52,[4] it would then be difficult to explain how Paul, in his defense before this governor, could say, "Knowing that *for many years* you have been a judge over this nation, I cheerfully make my defense."

IV. Its Addressees

Under this heading an attempt will be made to answer two questions: How did the church of Rome originate? Which group predominated numerically: Jews or Gentiles?

During Christ's earthly ministry (A.D. 26-30) people were brought out of the darkness into the light (John 3:26; 12:19). However, not all "followers"

---

3. See J. J. Foakes Jackson and Kirsopp Lake, *The Beginnings of Christianity,* Grand Rapids, 1966, Vol. V, pp. 460-464.
4. See Josephus, *Antiquities* XX.137; *Jewish War* II.247.

possessed "saving faith" (Matt. 13:1-7, 18-22; John 6:66), though some did (Matt. 13:8, 23; Luke 12:32; John 17:6-8). Included in the group of those who were genuine believers were not only Jews (Matt. 19:28) but also Gentiles (Matt. 8:10, 11; cf. 21:41) and Samaritans (John 4). Moreover, on and after Pentecost the number of disciples increased by leaps and bounds (Acts 2:41; 4:4). Gospel activity was resumed in Samaria. Philistia and probably even Ethiopia heard the message (Acts 8).

What was taking place in all these regions did not go unnoticed elsewhere, for, although modern methods of communication—radio, television, telephone, etc.—were nonexistent, people traveled extensively, thereby keeping each other informed about happenings in all parts of the Roman Empire. Soon, too, Damascus and Syria counted believers among their inhabitants. One of them was Ananias (Acts 9; for an even earlier reference to Syria see Matt. 4:24).

Travel was heavy in those days and, notwithstanding dangers, was relatively safe because of the still prevailing Pax Romana (reign of peace enforced by the Roman Empire).

There were ships. Admittedly they were not as luxurious as those of today. In fact, they were not even primarily intended for passenger service or tourism. Many of them were cargo vessels that brought grain to various places, especially to Rome; that is, to its ports or harbors. Rome's huge population—estimated variously at 1,000,000 to 1,500,000—needed to be fed.

In addition to these freighters there were also many smaller vessels. However, ships and boats were not always available. Navigation generally took place between the beginning of March and the middle of November. But when these vessels were plying the waters, their owners and/or captains were willing, for a consideration, to take aboard passengers. As the book of Acts indicates, Paul made frequent use of this mode of travel.

There were also those famous Roman roads: Via Appia, Via Cornelia, Via Aurelia, Via Valeria, etc. They were of sturdy and durable construction and were furnished with distance markers. Twenty main highways issued from Rome's "Golden Milestone," each diverging into numerous branches, so that the various parts of the empire were bound together by a huge network of arteries.[5] To go from one city to another, people would often make use of both means of travel: they would get to their destinations by sea and land. Thus, in order to reach Rome a Philippian might take the Egnatian Way from Philippi to Dyrrachium. Then by ship he would cross the Adriatic to Brundisium. From there the Appian Way would take him to Rome.

From the New Testament and from other sources one gains the impression that there were many great travelers. So, for example, Aquila and Priscilla (or Prisca) at different intervals in their lives must have traveled

---

5. See W. V. Von Hagen, *The Roads That Led to Rome,* Cleveland and New York, 1967.

from Pontus to Rome and from there to Corinth (Acts 18:2); later to Ephesus (Acts 18:18, 19; I Cor. 16:19), then to Rome (Rom. 16:3), and subsequently back to Ephesus (II Tim. 4:19). Luke too traveled extensively. So did Timothy, Titus, and especially Paul! See II Cor. 11:25, 26.

Why did people go to Rome? For any one of the following reasons, or for a combination of two or more of them: to settle there, to conduct business, to ply a trade, to pursue a profession, to study, to escape arrest (it was easy to "get lost" in this big city), to satisfy their curiosity concerning the metropolis on the Tiber about which so many rumors had been circulating, to visit friends and relatives, and best of all, to bring the gospel to the Romans. There must have been other incentives that led people to this city. Also, thousands of individuals had actually been *deported* to Rome. Others were involved in the movements of military forces.

Why do I mention all this? To emphasize the fact, often overlooked, that there is every reason to believe that the gospel must have reached Rome at an early date. In their fear of indulging in "wild speculation" some forget that "realistic historical imagination" is not only justifiable but necessary. This is sometimes overlooked. So, for example, there are those who minimize the importance of Pentecost (Acts 2) for the establishment of the church in Rome. Because they can find no record of any connection between Pentecost and conversions taking place in Rome at such an early date, they reject the idea that there was such a relationship. Or they will say that the visitors from Rome who attended the Feast in Jerusalem and later on returned to their homes were not in a position to start a church.

But the evangelist Luke has definitely reported that among those who witnessed the astounding miracles attending the outpouring of the Holy Spirit there were "visitors from Rome, both Jews and proselytes" (Gentile converts to Judaism). See Acts 2:10. Is it not reasonable to believe that at least some of these visitors from Rome were among the three thousand converts (Acts 2:41)? Having returned to their homes, would they have failed to tell their friends and relatives in Rome what they had seen and heard in Jerusalem? And must we indeed believe that from that moment on they would have ignored the opportunity to pelt newly arrived or returning travelers with questions about the "Jesus is the Christ" movement and the outpouring of the Holy Spirit as proof of Christ's exaltation to the position at the Father's right hand?

Not many years after the great Pentecost described in Acts 2 friends may also have come to Rome from mission-minded Antioch in Syria. Even before A.D. 44 the gospel had been proclaimed in that city, where "the disciples were first called *Christians*" (Acts 11:26). The church at Antioch contained several men who were qualified to spread the good tidings (Acts 13:1). So, since all roads led to Rome and travel back and forth was heavy, it is at least conceivable that some of these mission-minded Antiochians at an early date proclaimed the gospel in Rome, adding strength to the very young church. Soon members of other churches—for example, those in

Philippi, Corinth, and Ephesus—may well have co-operated, for between each of them and Rome communication was constant.

It will have become evident that in its earliest beginnings the Roman church was probably started not (except indirectly) by any apostle but by the rank and file of those Jews and proselytes who had witnessed the miracles of Pentecost and had afterward returned to their homes in Rome. It should be stressed that these "lay" people were *Jews* or, in some cases had at one time been converted to the *Jewish* religion. It should not cause surprise therefore if we discover that in its very beginnings the church in Rome revealed this Jewish character.

Are there any records that lend further support to this theory? A fourth century A.D. Latin father, known as "Ambrosiaster," in the Introduction to his *Commentary on Romans,* informs us that the Roman church was founded not by the apostles but by certain Jewish Christians who imposed a "Judaic form" on it. Does not this Judaic form remind us of what is recorded in Acts 15:1; 21:17-24 with reference to the church at *Jerusalem?*

In its subsequent history did the establishment or further growth of the church in Rome leave any traces in historical records? There is nothing of a very clear and substantial nature. But Suetonius (*Life of Claudius* XXV.ii), has handed down this statement: "Claudius expelled the Jews from Rome because they were constantly making disturbances at the instigation of Chrestus." The spelling *Chrestus* to indicate *Christus* (= Christ) was not unusual. So interpreted, this bit of information could shed light on Acts 18:2, which similarly reports a banishment of the Jews from Rome during the reign of emperor Claudius (date of his reign A.D. 41-54). Suetonius, then, might be saying that with the introduction of Christianity into Rome quarrels broke out between those Jews who had accepted the Christian religion and the others of their race who remained hostile to the new faith. Erroneously (if Chrestus = Christus), yet understandably, Suetonius regarded Christ as the instigator. But though this interpretation—Chrestus=Christus—is possible, it is not necessarily correct, and has not been accepted by all expositors.[6]

Aside from his sermon on the day of Pentecost did the apostle *Peter* contribute anything to the establishment of the Roman church? Two extremes must be avoided. On the one hand that of the Roman Catholic Church, which, on the basis of an early tradition, ascribed to Peter a twenty-five year episcopacy (A.D. 42-67) over the church in Rome; on the other, the position of those who deny or at least cast doubt on *any* connection between Peter and that church.

As to the first extreme, if it were factual, Peter would have occupied the position of supreme authority in the Roman church during a period includ-

---

6. Lenski is among those who reject the identification. See his *Interpretation of The Acts of the Apostles,* Columbus, 1944, p. 745. See, however, also F. J. Foakes Jackson and Kirsopp Lake, *op. cit.,* Vol. V, p. 295.

ing the very year when Paul sent his epistle to that body of believers. Yet in his list of greetings, addressed to individual believers in Rome, Paul never even mentions Peter. See Rom. 16:3-15. Is it at all possible that Paul would have been guilty of such neglect and breach of etiquette? And as to the second extreme, an appeal is often made to Rom. 15:20, which is then interpreted to imply that, before Paul wrote Romans, Christ had not yet been named in Rome; at least no apostle as yet had entered that city. However, that interpretation of Rom. 15:20 is not necessarily correct.

It would seem that when Paul was released from his first Roman imprisonment and was traveling to various congregations of his far-flung spiritual domain (see N.T.C. on I and II Timothy and Titus, pp. 39, 40), Peter was in Rome. He wrote the letter that came to be known as "the First Epistle of Peter." It was addressed to "the elect who are sojourners in Pontus, Galatia, etc." Note its closing salutation: "The church [literally *she*] that is in Babylon, elect together with y o u, greets y o u" (I Peter 5:13). In all probability this "Babylon" is Rome. Is not this identification the starting point from which one should proceed in the explanation of the same designation in Rev. 17:5? However, these events—Paul's release, Peter's writing—occurred *after* Paul wrote Romans.

We know therefore that, at least toward the close of his life, Peter labored in the church of Rome. Had he perhaps been there before? Did his Pentecost sermon, heard and transmitted by the visitors from Rome, indirectly qualify him for the title "founder" of the Roman church?

These questions cannot be answered with any degree of certainty. The book of Acts leaves many gaps. It makes allowance for many years, from A.D. 33 on, during which Peter *may* have been strengthening the church of Rome. Clement of Alexandria writes that Peter "had publicly preached the word in Rome" (*Hypotuposeis*, as quoted by Eusebius VI.xiv.6). And even somewhat earlier Irenaeus made the statement, "Peter and Paul went westward and founded the church in Rome" (*Against Heresies* III.i.1; cf. Eusebius V.viii.3). But of these statements of Clement and of Irenaeus there are various interpretations and evaluations. We probably do well to reserve our judgment. We should add, however, that according to tradition Mark's Gospel was composed to satisfy the urgent request of the people of Rome for a written summary of Peter's preaching in that city.

As to *Paul's* part in the establishment of this church, it is clear from Rom. 1:10; cf. 15:28, that at the time of the writing of this letter the apostle, though being himself a Roman citizen by birth (Acts 22:28), had not yet set foot in Rome. It is also clear, however, that he had met, at least had become acquainted (whether directly or indirectly) with several of the people belonging to Rome's church (16:3-15). He was eager to see Rome, and even more, to meet his friends there. He was actually going to reach the capital of the Roman Empire, but in a manner that had not been included in *his* plan but in *God's* (Acts 25:11, chapters 27, 28). In Rome Paul, *the prisoner*, was going to be very effective in proclaiming the gospel (Phil. 1:12-14). But at the time when this epistle was being written these future developments had not been revealed to him.

In the church of Rome which group predominated numerically: Jews or Gentiles? In the main there are three views:

1. The Roman church consisted mainly of Jews.[7]

Arguments used in support of this theory:

a. Paul was a Jew. In Rom. 3:9 he writes, "Are *we* better than they?" Moreover, note the preceding context: "the Jew" (verse 1) and "the Jews" (verse 2). Accordingly some of the modern translations have even inserted the word "Jews" into the text of Rom. 3:9; hence "we Jews."

Answer. In its continuation verse 9 shows that the author is now no longer thinking exclusively of Jews. He now proceeds from the fact that "all men," both Jews and Greeks, are by nature "under sin." That this is true with respect to the Greeks or Gentiles he has demonstrated in 1:18-32. That it holds also in the case of the Jews he has made clear in 2:1-3:8. So he now specifically turns his attention to himself and the church he is addressing, as a pastor who is facing his "congregation," and he asks, "What then? Are we—*y o u and I*—any better?" He means, "better than humanity (Jews and Greeks) in general?" His answer amounts to, "Not at all, for we too belong to this entity (the entire human race) on which God's judgment rests. No one is righteous, not even one."[8] Or somewhat wider: "we" = *I and all other true believers.* See also on 3:9.

b. In 7:1 Paul says, "I am speaking to men who know *the law* [or simply *law*]." He must be addressing especially the Jews, for they alone had been trained in the knowledge of God's holy law.

Answer. He is addressing the Jewish contingent of the church to be sure, but not necessarily *especially* the Jews. If Paul is thinking of the law of God, found in the Old Testament and summarized in the ten commandments, the answer might be as follows: Many a believer from among the Gentiles had entered the church by way of the synagogue. Even as a proselyte to the Jewish faith he had become acquainted with the law of God. And as a Christian he had come to understand that law far better. Conclusion: what Paul says here in Rom. 7:1 does not prove that most of the members of the Roman church were Jews by race.

Also, room must be left for the possibility that *law* here in Rom. 7:1 means "law in general." See on that passage. If so, then too, Rom. 7:1 fails to prove that most of the addressees were Jews by race.

---

7. T. Zahn, *Introduction to the New Testament,* English tr. Edinburgh, 1909, Vol. I, p. 422; and before him F. C. Bauer, *Paul, the Apostle of Jesus Christ,* English tr. 1873, Vol. I, pp. 321 ff. Other defenders of this view: W. Manson, N. Krieger, J. A. C. Van Leeuwen and D. Jacobs, etc.

8. In this connection see especially A. F. N. Lekkerkerker, *De Prediking van het Nieuwe Testament, De Brief van Paulus aan de Romeinen,* Nijkerk, 1971, p. 129.

c. Rom. 9–11 pertains especially to the Jews. It concerns *Israel*. *Answer*. To a considerable extent this must be granted. But this does not mean that most of the addressed were Jews. In fact, it is exactly this section which shows that most of the addressees were converts from the Gentile world, for Paul regards the Jews as being, by and large, distinct from the people to whom he is directing his remarks. The apostle is thinking of two groups: Gentiles and Jews. When he is describing the condition and destiny of the Jews, he deliberately employs the pronouns *they, their, them*. Examples: "*Theirs* is the adoption" (9:4); "My heart's desire for *them* is that *they* may be saved" (10:1). Note especially the distinction the apostle makes between the third person, referring to the Jews, and the second, referring to the addressed: "*They* were broken off because of *their* unbelief, and *you* are established through faith" (11:20). Similarly in 11:24 Paul makes a distinction between "you" and "these natural branches" (obviously the Jews). This use of the third person to indicate Israel continues through verse 31.

d. The dialectical method of argumentation employed here shows that the writer is addressing Jews, for that was the method they appreciated. Their former teachers, the rabbis, were in the habit of resorting to this form of lecturing.

Answer. Greeks—for example, Socrates—were not unfamiliar with this stylistic device. Besides, Paul was conscious of the objections his opponents might advance against his doctrines. So, very effectively, he anticipates their objections, and by means of the question-and-answer method clinches his argument. See 9:14; 9:19; 10:18, 19; 11:1; 11:11; 11:19f. More on this under heading V of this Introduction.

2. The Roman church consisted mainly of Gentiles.[9]
Proof:

a. In Rom. 1:5, 6 the apostle states ". . . we received grace and apostleship (to call) people from among all the Gentiles to the obedience that springs from faith, among whom y o u are also . . ."

b. 1:13 ends with the words, "in order that I might obtain some fruit among y o u also, as I have among the rest of the Gentiles."

c. In 11:13 Paul says, "I am talking to y o u Gentiles. Inasmuch as I am the apostle to the Gentiles, I magnify my ministry."

d. 15:15 reads, "I have written to y o u rather boldly on some points, so as to remind y o u of them again, because of the grace God gave me to be a

---

9. Among those who favor this view are the following: W. Sanday and A. C. Headlam, *A Critical and Exegetical Commentary on the Epistle to the Romans (International Critical Commentary)*, Edinburgh, 1902, p. xxxiif.; M.-J. Lagrange, *Saint Paul, Épître aux Romains*, Paris, 1950, pp. xxi–xxiv; H. Ridderbos, *Aan De Romeinen, (Commentaar Op Het Nieuwe Testament)*, Kampen, 1959, pp. 6–10; and John Murray, *The Epistle to the Romans*, Grand Rapids, 1959, Vol. I, pp. xxi, xxii.

minister of Christ Jesus to the Gentiles . . . that the Gentiles might become an offering acceptable to God." Note also how very frequently the word "Gentiles" occurs in 15:9–18.

e. The fact that in the list of greetings Paul singles out certain individuals (see verses 7, 11, and 21) as being his fellow-countrymen also confirms the conclusion that not the Jews but the Gentiles constituted the majority of the church in Rome.

3. These arguments would seem to be unanswerable. Nevertheless, an attempt has been made to refute them. In what in many respects is a splendid commentary—I would urge the readers by all means to study it—C. E. B. Cranfield[10] attempts to prove that it is not possible to establish whether most of the members of the church at Rome were Jews or were Romans. In my opinion his *refutation* of the position that *Jewish* Christians formed the majority is adequate, and his view that at the time of Paul there must, nevertheless, have been a considerable number of Jews in the Roman church is well argued. But when he states that the expression "among whom y o u are also" may mean no more than that the Roman church was situated in the midst of the Gentile world, and that in 1:13 the expression "as among the rest of the Gentiles" may be considered slightly inexact, I must dissent.

My conclusion, therefore, is that theory No. 2, namely, that most of the members of the Roman Church were Christians from the Gentiles, is correct, though the exact proportion of Jews to Gentiles is unknown.

A few facts should be added, however. First of all, since in the first and second centuries church buildings in the sense in which we think of them today were not yet in existence, families would hold services in their own homes. Such services would be attended by the members of the household: perhaps father, mother, children, sometimes other close relatives (cf. Luke 12:53), servants. If the house was large enough to accommodate others, they too were invited. The early church numbered many hospitable members, ready and eager to offer their facilities for religious use: meetings, services, etc. Thus, in Jerusalem "many were gathered together and were praying" in the house of Mary, the mother of John Mark (Acts 12:12). Lydia graciously invited Paul, Silas, Timothy, and Luke to use her home as their headquarters (Acts 16:15, 40). WhereverAquila and Prisca went they would if at all possible welcome the worshipers to their home. Hence, both at Ephesus (I Cor. 16:19) and at Rome (Rom. 16:3–5) there was "a church at their house." Laodicea too had a house-church (Col. 4:15). Corinth may have had a house-church at the home of Gaius. In Laodicea Nympha performed the duty of hostess to the members of the church of which she was a member.

---

10. *The Epistle To The Romans (International Critical Commentary)*, Edinburgh, 1975, Vol. I, pp. 18-21.

How many of these house-churches there were in Rome we do not know. The house-church mentioned in Rom. 16:5 may not have been the only one; 16:14 ("the brothers with them") and 16:15 ("all the saints with them") may indicate others. And there may have been more, especially in such a large city.

In connection with the present subject—whether the Jews or the Gentiles predominated in the Roman church, while fully maintaining that most of the members had been gathered into the church from the Gentiles (whether directly or indirectly), can we not leave open the possibility that, among the various units composing this church, there may have been at least one, a house-church, in which not the Gentiles but the Jews predominated numerically?

Far more important, however, is the fact that the author of Romans is not mainly interested in the question whether there were more Jews or more Gentiles among those whom he was addressing. *His* emphasis is on the fact that both Jew and Gentile are by nature "under sin" (Rom. 3:9); in other words, that "all have sinned and fall short of the glory of God" (3:23); that the way of salvation through faith in Christ is open to all (3:24); that Abraham is the father of all that believe (4:11, 12); and that for all who are in Christ Jesus there is no condemnation (8:1 f.). *We* may talk about Jew versus Gentile. *Romans stresses the idea of unity.* One of its most precious passages is 10:12, 13:

"For there is no distinction between Jew and Greek; for the same Lord is Lord of all, and abounds in riches for all who call on him. For whoever calls on the name of the Lord will be saved."

V.   Its Occasion and Purpose

On this subject there is considerable difference of opinion. Much has been written about it, especially in recent years.[11]

As was pointed out earlier, Paul had reached the end of his mission work in the *eastern* part of the Roman Empire. He had "planted" (I Cor. 3:6) the gospel in the large centers (and in some of the smaller towns besides). From

---

11. From the almost endless number of books and articles on this subject I wish to call attention merely to the following:

K. P. Donfried (editor and contributor), *The Romans Debate*, Minneapolis, 1977. In this book the question, "Why did Paul write Romans?" is explored by nine American and European scholars.

John Knox and C. R. Cragg, *The Epistle to the Romans* (Vol. IX in *The Interpreter's Bible*), New York and Nashville, 1954, pp. 358–363.

E. F. Harrison, *Romans* (Vol. X. in *The Expositor's Bible Commentary*), Grand Rapids, 1976, pp. 5, 6. An excellent summary!

G. W. Barker, W. L. Lane, J. R. Michaels, *The New Testament Speaks*, New York, Evanston, and London, 1969, pp. 192, 193. Excellent mission emphasis!

H. Ridderbos, *Aan De Romeinen*, pp. 10–14.

these centers—such as Syrian Antioch, Philippi, Corinth, Ephesus—the word of the Lord was spreading widely (cf. Acts 19:20, 26; Rev. 1:4, 11). In fact Paul himself had proclaimed the good tidings of salvation from Jerusalem all the way to present-day Yugoslavia and Albania (Rom. 15:19). The gospel had even reached Rome, though Paul himself had never visited this city. He did, however, have many friends there, intimate acquaintances whom he loved dearly.

So now he hopes that the yearning he has cherished for many years, namely, to go to Rome (Rom. 15:23; cf. 1:10, 11; Acts 19:21) may at last be satisfied.

He realizes, however, that he cannot immediately sail to Rome by way of the Corinthan Gulf and Ionian Sea, for he has been conducting a campaign for the benefit of the poor saints in Jerusalem. Since this drive has been successful Paul, according to a previous promise (I Cor. 16:4), intends, the Lord willing, to go to Jerusalem, so that, in person, he, accompanied by others, may present the gifts that have been collected for the poor (Acts 24:17). And then he will wend his way to Rome! That was the plan.

But why does Paul want to visit Rome's church? What, exactly, is his purpose?

The initial answer must be that Paul, being an intensely warm and loving person, desires to go to Rome in order to be a blessing to his friends (Rom. 1:10, 11) and to be refreshed by them (15:32). Moreover, it is for this same reason that he, now that it is impossible for him to go to Rome *immediately,* communicates with the Roman church by means of this letter. He writes to the Romans because he loves them. They are his friends "in Christ," and by means of this letter he imparts his love to them, praises them (1:8), informs them about his constant prayers for them (1:9), asks them to pray for him (15:30), and informs them about his traveling plans (1:10-12; 15:24 f.).

It is strange that this deeply personal reason (desire for fellowship, etc.), a reason clearly brought out by the apostle himself, is often overlooked. At times the emphasis is placed entirely on theological motivation or on mission incentive: Paul wants to correct the errors of the antinomians and/or wants to make Rome the headquarters for the evangelization of Spain. To be sure, these matters are important, but we should *begin* with the reason first stated by Paul himself in this very epistle.

All the more does Paul feel the necessity of writing this letter and by means of it asking the Roman church to remember him in prayer, because he is not at all sure that he will ever reach Rome. Rom. 1:10 introduces this fear, and 15:31 clarifies what the apostle has in mind. There are two things he fears: (a) that the Jews may kill him; (b) that the Jerusalem "saints" may not even be willing to accept the bounteous gift coming to them from the *Gentiles.*

As to the first misgiving, that it was not groundless is clear from such a passage as Acts 20:3 (because of a plot by the Jews Paul had to change his traveling plan), and from Acts 14:19; 17:5, 13; 18:6, 12 f.; 23:12-21; II

Cor. 11:24, 32, 33. Moreover, Paul's misgiving was not entirely subjective. He was constantly receiving intimations from the Holy Spirit, hints of impending hardships (Acts 20:22, 23). See also 21:10, 11, 27f.

As to the second fear, though the brothers welcomed Paul and his companions warmly (Acts 21:17), to what extent this warm welcome also included appreciation for the "collection" on which Paul had spent so much time and effort is not made clear.

The fact here mentioned, namely, that to the mind of Paul the possibility was real, the prospect formidable, that he might never get to see his dear friends in Rome, explains why he had to write *this* type of letter, one which, in its first seven chapters is characterized by argumentative style. Note, for example, the series of expressions such as, "What then shall we say?" See 4:1; 6:1; 7:7; 8:31; 9:14, 30. Not only is this kind of style reminiscent of the manner in which Paul, *the missionary,* had during his many travels been arguing with his bitter opponents, the unbelieving Jews, but it also shows that he is conscious of the fact that Rome's little church is surrounded by a huge army of such unbelievers. Paul, therefore, in this letter to the Romans, is showing the Roman church how it should defend itself against the constant onslaught of these opponents; yes, how it might even win some of them for Christ! If the addressees can no longer contact Paul himself, they will at least be able to read and reread this precious letter.

This also indicates that the epistle to the Romans is not really "a complete compendium of Christian Doctrine." If it had been Paul's intention to draw up such a document, he would surely have included far more material. *Paul is a very practical man. He knows exactly what the Roman church needs. Guided by the Holy Spirit, he fulfils that need. Moreover, since the doctrine at stake, namely, that concerning the manner in which sinners are saved, is basic, what is presented in 1:16–8:39 is urgently needed not only by the church in Rome but by every church, every believer, every sinner, down through the ages.*

By and large the condition of the Roman church must have been very encouraging (1:8; 15:14; 16:19). But that cannot mean that the intellectual maturity of its membership was complete and/or that its moral and spiritual development left nothing to be desired. On the contrary, this church too had its weaknesses. It was in need of instruction with respect to God's promises to Israel. So one of the purposes of this epistle was to supply that instruction (chapters 9-11). More light was also needed on the question of clean versus unclean foods. That light too is richly supplied (14:13-18).

Not only *information* but also *exhortation* or *admonition* was needed, and this especially with respect to such matters as obedience to civil authority (chapter 13) and the proper attitude of "the strong" toward "the weak" (14:1-12; 15:1-4). And in connection with the need—then, now, always—of such virtues as unity, humility, and above all love, who will wish to deny that Rom. 12 is one of the finest not only in Scripture but in all of literature?

What has been said so far clearly indicates that the ardent desire to be a blessing to the church in Rome was definitely included in Paul's purpose in writing this letter. The view according to which the apostle intended *merely* to pass through Rome in order to make it a base of operations for mission activity in Spain is incorrect. Rom. 15:24 ("I hope to visit y o u while passing through") is balanced by 1:15 ("I am eager to preach the gospel also to y o u who are in Rome").

For the rest, it remains true that one of the items included in Paul's aim was securing the co-operation of the Roman church in connection with his contemplated journey to Spain, as 15:24 clearly shows.

In conclusion, to arrive at a complete answer to the question, "Why did Paul write Romans?" the following two Pauline passages should not be ignored:

> "*I have become all things to all men, in order that, by any and all means, I might save some*" (I Cor. 9:22).

> "*Whether therefore y o u eat or drink, or whatever y o u do, do all to the glory of God*" (I Cor. 10:31).

A great missionary indeed was Paul. His heart burned with love for people, and even more with love for God, the One who had rescued him, even him, formerly a bitter persecutor of God's precious children! He just "could not get over it!" It seems as if across the span of the centuries we can still hear him say, "I have been crucified with Christ; and it is no longer I who lives, but Christ who lives in me, and that (life) which I now live in flesh I live in faith, (the faith) which is in the Son of God, who loved me and gave himself up for me" (Gal. 2:20).

But one does not need to be a famous missionary like Paul to render service in God's kingdom, a service recognized by God himself. There was, for example, sister Phoebe of Cenchrea, a harbor of Corinth, located a little to the east of that great cosmopolitan center. Always she was ready to render service to the Lord and his cause. When she heard that the great missionary was composing a letter addressed to his dear friends in Rome, did she volunteer her willingness to deliver it? Or did Paul himself take the initiative in asking her to render this service? However this may have been, it is clear that she was standing ready, *always* ready to do whatever she could do out of love for her Lord and Savior.

I believe that the purpose and the occasion of Paul's epistle to the Romans have now been made clear.

VI. Its Text

A few words should be written about the integrity of the text of Romans. Does the Greek text on which our translations are based faithfully represent what Paul actually wrote *to the church in Rome?*

There are those who doubt it, and this for the following reasons:

1. Not every manuscript contains the reading "in Rome" in 1:7 and 1:15. In 1:7 a variant substitutes "all who are in the love of God" for "all who are in Rome, beloved of God." Also in verse 15 "in Rome" is then omitted.

2. The strikingly beautiful doxology, "Now to him who is able to establish y o u . . . be glory forever through Jesus Christ. Amen," which in our Bibles is found at the close of chapter 16, is in some sources found at the close of chapter 14; in others, at the close of chapters 14 and 16; and in one very early papyrus (Chester Beatty) at the close of chapter 15.

3. As to the greetings (16:3-15), there are those who maintain that they point to the church of Ephesus rather than to that of Rome, as the group for which they were intended; for

a. How could Paul have known so many persons in Rome? He himself had never been there. But he had spent a long time in Ephesus.

b. Prisca (or Priscilla) and Aquila were living in Ephesus shortly before this (Acts 18:18, 19; I Cor. 16:19), and Epaenetus is called "the first-fruits" (= first convert to Christ) in *Asia*. This again reminds us of Ephesus, not of Rome.

c. The sharp reprimand of 16:17, 18 is out of line with the words of praise the apostle addresses to those whom he has in mind in 1:8; 15:14. Sharp condemnation and warm commendation do not go together. Therefore chapter 16 must have been addressed to another audience than those to whom Paul is speaking in the preceding chapters.

Though it must be admitted that not every problem can be solved, the following answers to these doubts about the integrity of the text deserve consideration:

As to 1: The omission of "in Rome" is a rare exception. The phrase "in Rome" has decisive manuscript support. Besides, the context favors reference to a definite place. Note especially verse 10, "I keep pleading that somehow by God's will now at last the way may be opened for me to come to y o u." Could it be that the heretic Marcion, who was rejected by the Roman church, had something to do with the omission of this phrase in 1:7, 15?

As to 2: The *best* manuscripts favor 16:25-27 as the proper place for this doxology. According to the testimony of Origen it was Marcion who deleted everything in Romans following 14:23. His negative attitude toward the Old Testament and its "god" or "demi-urge" is well-known. So there were too many statements in chapter 15 he did not like. See especially verse 4. Nevertheless, Romans must have a proper conclusion. It is therefore not surprising that the doxology at the close of chapter 16 was transferred to chapter 14. Once the process of moving a passage from one place to another begins, where will it end? It must be admitted, however, that the exact reason why the Chester Beatty manuscript has placed the doxology at the close of chapter 15 is not known. But this does not in any way cancel the fact that its place at the close of chapter 16 is favored by the strongest manuscript evidence.

As to 3:

a. Because of the heavy and constant traffic between Rome and other cities, it is reasonable to suppose that the apostle had met these people on his journeys. In a few cases he may have received ample information about them from friends. Moreover, the very reason that he had not been in Rome himself makes it all the more probable that by warmly greeting those he did know he desired to gain an entrance into the hearts of the entire Roman church.

b. As has been indicated previously, Prisca and Aquila were great travelers. Besides, what is so unreasonable about supposing that they went back to the place where they had lived before, namely, Rome? Together with ever so many others they returned when the edict of expulsion was no longer in effect. And as to Epaenetus, the fact that he was "the first-fruits of Asia" surely does not mean that he had to remain in Asia for the rest of his life.

c. The warning of 16:17, 18 concerns certain definite individuals, "false teachers" perhaps, who are always and everywhere trying to destroy God's kingdom. That Paul is not withdrawing his favorable estimate of Rome's church is very clear from the context. See verse 19.

It has become clear, therefore, that the arguments against the integrity of the text of Paul's epistle to the Romans are very weak indeed!

For more on the arrangement of the text of Romans 16, in connection with Harry Gamble's study, see Vol. II of the present commentary.

VII.   Its Theme and Summary

Does Romans have a theme? If by "theme" is meant a subject from which the author never digresses, the answer is *No.* This letter touches on a variety of subjects: Paul's desire to visit Rome (1:10), God's wrath (1:18), Adam versus Christ (5:12–21), antinomianism (6:1), soul struggle (7:15–24), present suffering contrasted with future glory (8:18), Israel (chapters 9–11), love (12:9), taxes (13:6), vegetarianism (14:2), the strong and the weak (14:1; 15:1), philanthropy (15:25–27), Spain (15:28), Phoebe (16:1), Satan (16:20).

On the other hand, if by "theme" is meant a central topic, which, having been announced, is subsequently taken up again and again, either as a whole or in part, the answer is *Yes.*

This theme was the product not of human excogitation but of divine implantation in the heart and mind of struggling Saul of Tarsus.

Applicable to him are these poetic lines:

> O long and dark the stairs I trod
> With trembling feet to find my God,
> Gaining a foothold bit by bit,

Then slipping back and losing it.
Never progressing; striving still
With weakening grasp and faltering will,
Bleeding to climb to God, while he
Serenely smiled, unnoting me.
Then came a certain time when I
Loosened my hold and fell thereby;
Down to the lowest step my fall,
As if I had not climbed at all.
Now when I lay despairing there,
Listen . . . a footfall on the stair,
On that same stair where I afraid,
Faltered and fell and lay dismayed.
And lo, when hope had ceased to be,
My God came down the stairs to me.

Anonymous

". . . justified freely by his grace, through the redemption which is in Christ Jesus" (Rom. 3:24).

The theme of Romans, introduced in 1:16, 17 . . . "The righteous shall live by faith . . .", expressed more fully in 3:21-24, 28, reflected in such passages as 5:1; 8:30-34; 9:30-32; 11:23-26; 16:26, is never absent from the writer's mind.

Justification by faith (Rom. 5:1), spread out into "justification by grace through faith" (see 3:22-24; cf. Eph. 2:8), is clearly the theme of Romans. It is also the theme of Galatians. There is a close resemblance between the larger and the smaller epistle. Gen. 15:6, "Abraham believed God, and it was credited to him as righteousness," is quoted in both letters (Rom. 4:3, 9, 22; Gal. 3:6). Cf. James 2:23. Among other verbal resemblances are:

Rom. 1:17 and Gal. 2:16; 3:11	Rom. 13:8 and Gal. 5:14
Rom. 6:6-8 and Gal. 2:20	Rom. 13:13, 14 and Gal. 5:16, 17
Rom. 8:14-17 and Gal. 4:5-7	Rom. 14:12 and Gal. 6:5

Nevertheless, there is also a striking difference between the two. Not only does this difference refer to size and subject matter—the larger epistle containing much material that is not found in the smaller—it pertains also and especially to the manner in which the apostle speaks to the addressees.

Romans sets forth calmly that for every sinner, whether Jew or Gentile, there is salvation full and free through faith in Christ, apart from law works. Galatians, in a tone that is not nearly as calm and at times becomes fiery, defends this glorious gospel against its detractors. Its denunciations are withering.

Chapter
1:1-15   Here in Romans, after a *Prologue,* in which Paul *greets* the Christians in Rome (1:1-7), and informs them that he is *thanking* God

for the fact that their faith is being proclaimed everywhere, and that he is *asking* God to grant him the opportunity to visit and preach the gospel among them (verses 8-15), he announces and develops *the theme* of that gospel as follows:

JUSTIFICATION BY FAITH

1:16—3:31 Justification by faith, apart from the works of the law, is:

1—3   A. Real and Necessary
1. Theme: "The gospel is the power of God for salvation to everyone who exercises faith, . . . as it is written, But the righteous shall live by faith" (1:16, 17).
2. The *Gentiles* need this justification (1:18-32).
3. The *Jews* also need it (2:1—3:8).
4. Accordingly, "there is none righteous, not even one" (3:9-20).
5. "But now, apart from law, a righteousness from God has been revealed, a righteousness through *faith* in Jesus Christ . . ." (3:21-31).

4   B. Scriptural
1. The Example of Abraham (4:1-12).
2. This Example Shows that God's Promise is Realized Through Faith, not Works (4:13-25).

5—8   C. Effective; that is, Producing the Desired Results; Such As:
1a. *Peace and its Concomitants,* including Assurance of Complete Salvation (5:1-11).
1b. The Certainty and Copiousness of Salvation Confirmed by the Parallel Adam—Christ (5:12-21).
2a. *Holiness* (6:1-14).
2b. Who is Y o u r Master? Sin or God? (6:15-23).
3a. *Liberty:* Freedom from the Law (7:1-6).
3b. The Sinner's Relation to God's Law, in the Light of Paul's Own Experience and That of Others Like Him (7:7-13).
3c. Paul's Own Experience and That of Others Like Him (continued): The Wretched Man's Struggle and Victory (7:14-25).
4a. "No Condemnation" for Those in Christ Jesus (8:1-30).
4b. *Super-invincibility,* that is, Being More Than Conquerors (8:31-39).

Having shown that the doctrine of justification—hence salvation—by faith is Real and Necessary (chapters 1-3), Scriptural (chapter 4), and Effective, i.e., fruit-producing (chapters 5-8), Paul proceeds to prove, in chapters 9-11, that it is also Historical, in the sense that in the course of history God's most precious promises were ever intended for, and realized in, the *believing* remnant, that this is true today (while Paul was writing), and will so continue.

Chapters 12–16 contain the *Practical Application* of all this. In other words, these concluding chapters show how those who have been justified (and therefore saved) by God-given faith, should reveal their gratitude in lives of love toward their fellowmen and devotion to their gracious Triune God.

Further details with respect to chapters 9—16—Outline and Explanation of the text—is reserved for N.T.C. on Paul's Epistle to the Romans, Volume II, which is now being prepared.

Commentary

on

The Epistle to the Romans

Chapter 1:1-15

Prologue

Outline

Salutation.
1:1–7

Paul's thanksgiving and desire to visit Rome.
1:8–15

CHAPTER 1:1-15

1 1 Paul, a servant of Christ Jesus, a called apostle, one set apart for the gospel of God, 2 which he promised beforehand through his prophets in (the) sacred Scriptures, 3 concerning his Son, who, according to the flesh was born of the seed of David, 4 but by virtue of[12] the Spirit of holiness, was, by means of the resurrection from the dead, appointed to be the Son of God *invested with power,* namely, Jesus Christ our Lord, 5 through whom and for whose sake we received the gift of apostleship, in order to bring about obedience of faith,[13] among all the Gentiles, 6 including also y o u, the called of Jesus Christ;

7 to all in Rome who are beloved of God, saints by virtue of having been called: Grace to y o u and peace from God our Father and the Lord Jesus Christ.

Salutation
1:1-7

1. Paul, a servant of Christ Jesus, a called apostle, one set apart for the gospel of God . . .

This is the beginning of Paul's lengthiest opening salutation. For a comparison note the following list which, in an ascending series, indicates the number of words *in the original* for each salutation:

I Thessalonians	19	II Corinthians	41
II Thessalonians	27	Philemon	41
Colossians	28	I Corinthians	55
Ephesians	28 (or 30)	Titus	65
II Timothy	29	Galatians	75
Philippians	32	Romans	93
I Timothy	32		

As in his epistle to Titus so here in Romans Paul introduces himself as a *doulos* (pl. *douloi* in Phil. 1:1) of Christ Jesus. As the English equivalent of *doulos* some prefer—some even insist on—*slave.* It must be granted that such traits as the slave's required absolute submission to his master and thorough dependence on him, as also the master's ownership of and unrestricted authority over his slave, can be applied, though in a far more exalted sense, to the relation between Christ and believers. See, for exam-

---

12. Or: in accordance with
13. Or: based on faith; or: springing from faith

37

ple, I Cor. 3:23; 6:19b, 20. Nevertheless, since with the concept *slave* we generally associate such ideas as involuntary service, forced subjection, and (frequently) harsh treatment, many have, probably correctly, concluded that "slave" is not the best English equivalent in *this* context.

Besides, it should be borne in mind that Paul was "a Hebrew of Hebrews" (Phil. 3:5), thoroughly at home in the Old Testament. Therefore when he calls himself "a *doulos* of Christ Jesus," he is probably reflecting on passages in which Abraham (Gen. 26:24), Moses (Num. 12:7), Joshua (Josh. 24:29), David (II Sam. 7:5), Isaiah (Isa. 20:3), etc., are called Jehovah's *servants*. Is it not even possible that the figure of the wholeheartedly committed Servant described in Isa. 49:1-7; 52:13; 53:11 contributed to the meaning of the word *doulos* here in Rom. 1:1?

Paul presents himself as a servant *of Christ Jesus*.[14] The personal name *Jesus*, meaning either "he will certainly save" (cf. Matt. 1:21), or "Jehovah is salvation," which ultimately amount to the same thing, is preceded by the official designation *Christ* (Anointed). Of this Christ Jesus, Paul is a servant, completely surrendered to his Master.

This servant is at the same time "a called apostle."

Now in the broadest sense an *apostle* (Greek *apostolos*, a term derived from a verb which means *to send, to send away on a commission, to dispatch*) is anyone who is sent or by whom a message is sent; hence, an ambassador, envoy, messenger. In classical Greek the term could refer to a naval expedition, and "an apostolic boat" was a cargo vessel. In later Judaism "apostles" were envoys sent out by the Jerusalem patriarchate to collect tribute from the Jews of the Dispersion. In the New Testament the term takes on a distinctly religious sense. In its widest meaning it refers to any gospel-messenger, anyone who is sent on a spiritual mission, anyone who in that capacity represents his Sender and brings the message of salvation. Thus used, Barnabas, Epaphroditus, Apollos, Silvanus, and Timothy are all called "apostles" (Acts 14:14; I Cor. 4:6, 9; Phil. 2:25; I Thess. 2:6; cf. 1:1; and see also I Cor. 15:7). They all represent God's cause, though in doing so they may also represent certain definite churches whose "apostles" they are called (cf. II Cor. 8:23). Thus Paul and Barnabas represent the church of Antioch (Acts 13:1, 2), and Epaphroditus is Philippi's "apostle" (Phil. 2:25).

But in determining the meaning of the term *apostle* here in Rom. 1:1 it will be far better to study those passages in which it is used in its more usual sense. Occurring ten times in the Gospels, almost thirty times in Acts, more than thirty times in the Pauline epistles (including the five occurrences in the Pastorals), and eight times in the rest of the New Testament, it generally (but note important exception in Heb. 3:1 and the exceptions already indicated) refers to the Twelve and Paul.

---

14. Why "Christ Jesus" instead of "Jesus Christ"? For a possible answer to this question see N.T.C. on I Tim. 1:1, p. 51.

In that fullest, deepest sense a man is an apostle *for life* and *wherever he goes.* He is clothed with *the authority of* the One who sent him, and that authority concerns both *doctrine and life.* The idea, found in much present-day religious literature, according to which an apostle has no real office, no authority, lacks scriptural support. Anyone can see this for himself by studying such passages as Matt. 16:19; 18:18; 28:18, 19 (note the connection); John 20:23; I Cor. 5:3-5; II Cor. 10:8; I Thess. 2:6.

Paul, then, was an apostle in the richest sense of the term. His apostleship was the same as that of the Twelve. Hence, we speak of "the Twelve and Paul." Paul even stresses the fact that the risen Savior had appeared to *him* just as truly as he had appeared to Cephas (I Cor. 15:5, 8). That same Savior had assigned to him a task so broad and universal that his entire life was henceforth to be occupied with it (Acts 26:16-18).

Yet Paul was definitely *not* one of the Twelve. The idea that the disciples had made a mistake when they had chosen Matthias to take the place of Judas, and that the Holy Spirit later designated Paul as the real substitute, hardly merits consideration (see Acts 1:24). *But if he was not one of the Twelve yet was invested with the same office, what was the relation between him and the Twelve?* The answer is probably suggested by Acts 1:8 and Gal. 2:7-9. On the basis of these passages this answer can be formulated thus: The Twelve, by recognizing Paul as having been specially called to minister to the Gentiles, were in effect carrying out through him their calling to the Gentiles.

The characteristics of full apostleship—the apostleship of the Twelve and Paul—were as follows:

In the first place, the apostles have been chosen, called, and sent forth by Christ himself. They have received their commission directly from him (John 6:70; 13:18; 15:16, 19; Gal. 1:6).

Secondly, they are qualified for their tasks by Jesus, and have been ear-and-eye witnesses of his words and deeds; specifically, they are the witnesses of his resurrection (Acts 1:8, 21, 22; I Cor. 9:1; 15:8; Gal. 1:12; Eph. 3:2-8; I John 1:1-3). Note: though Acts 1:21, 22 does not apply to Paul, the other passages do apply to him. Paul too had seen the Lord!

Thirdly, they have been endowed in a special measure with the Holy Spirit, and it is this Holy Spirit who leads them into all the truth (Matt. 10:20; John 14:26; 15:26; 16:7-14; 20:22; I Cor. 2:10-13; 7:40; I Thess. 4:8).

Fourthly, God blesses their work, confirming its value by means of signs and miracles, and giving them much fruit upon their labors (Matt. 10:1, 8; Acts 2:43; 3:2; 5:12-16; Rom. 15:18, 19; I Cor. 9:2; II Cor. 12:12; Gal. 2:8).

Fifthly, their office is not restricted to a local church, neither does it extend over a short period of time; on the contrary, it is for the entire church and for life (Acts 26:16-18; II Tim. 4:7, 8).

Note "a *called* apostle." This surely is much better than either "called an apostle" or "called to be or to become an apostle." What the original means is that Paul was an apostle by virtue of having been effectively called by God to this office. Similarly the people he addresses were *saints* by virtue of having been called, "saints by (divine) vocation." See on verse 7.

As a called apostle, Paul had been "set apart for the gospel of God." From the beginning he had been designed by God for the proclamation of the gospel. Note especially Gal. 1:15, where the apostle expresses himself as follows, ". . . it pleased him who separated me from my mother's womb and called me through his grace, to reveal his Son in me, in order that I might preach his gospel among the Gentiles. . . ."

Paul speaks of "the gospel *of God*" or "*God's* gospel." And it is indeed the God-spell, the *spell* or *story* that tells us what *God* has done to save sinners. For that very reason it is an *evangel* or *message of good tidings*. It is the glad news of salvation which God addresses to a world lost in sin. Not what *we* must do but what *God* in Christ has done for us is the most prominent part of that good news. This is clear from the manner in which the noun *evangel* and the related verb, *to proclaim an evangel, to bring good news*, are used in the Old Testament. See LXX on Ps. 40:9; 96:2; Isa. 40:9; 52:7; 61:1; and Nah. 1:15.

Here in Rom. 1 the term "gospel of God" (verse 1) has two modifiers, one in verse 2, the other in verse 3 f.

2. . . . which he promised beforehand through his prophets in (the) sacred Scriptures . . .

This passage is indeed very important. It shows us how Paul, inspired by the Holy Spirit, wants us to regard the Old Testament. He clearly views the old and the new dispensation as belonging together. He regards (a) the Old Testament and (b) the good news of salvation as proclaimed by Jesus and his messengers, as being a unit. Speaking by and large we can say that the Old Testament contains the promises; the New Testament shows how these promises had been, were being, and were going to be fulfilled.

When Paul says "his prophets" he has reference, of course, not only to such holy men of God as Isaiah, Jeremiah, etc., but also to Moses, Samuel, David, etc. To speak in language which even children can understand:

> The Old is by the New explained,
> The New is in the Old contained.

or similarly:

> The New is in the Old concealed,
> The Old is by the New revealed.

What Paul writes here is exactly what Jesus also proclaimed; and this not only in those well-known passages: Luke 24:25-32, 44-48, to which reference is often made in this connection, but certainly also in Luke 4:21 (in the context 4:16-30), "Today, in y o u r very hearing, this passage of Scripture is being fulfilled," and in Luke 22:37, "For I tell y o u, what has been written must be fulfilled in me: 'And he was numbered with the transgressors.' Yes, that passage about me is reaching its fulfillment." For more on this subject see N.T.C. on Luke, p. 977, and on Philippians, pp. 81-85.

The point to be emphasized here is that both Jesus (see John 10:35; 17:17) and Paul esteemed the Old Testament very highly. They deemed it to be *sacred*. When a person rejects the Old Testament, he is therefore also rejecting Jesus and Paul!

We now proceed to the second modifier of the term "the gospel of God." It is this:

3, 4. ... concerning his Son, who, according to the flesh was born of the seed of David, but by virtue of [or: in accordance with] the Spirit of holiness, was, by means of the resurrection from the dead, appointed to be the Son of God *invested with power,* **namely, Jesus Christ our Lord ...**

Interpreters differ rather sharply in their explanation of these lines. My own interpretation is based, to a large extent, on my conclusions with respect to the meaning of the original. So, I invite students of the Greek to study the footnote.[15]

---

15. The following questions should be asked and answered:
   a. What is the meaning of the acc. of σάρξ as here used?
   b. Does the verb ὁρίζω (of which the gen. s. m. aor. pass. participle appears here) have the meaning *to declare* (as in certain translations) or *to appoint?*
   c. Does the phrase ἐν δυνάμει modify υἱοῦ θεοῦ or ὁρισθέντος?
   d. What is the meaning of πνεῦμα ἁγιωσύνης?
   e. What is the meaning of κατά before πνεῦμα ἁγιωσύνης?
   f. Do κατὰ σάρκα and κατὰ ἁγιωσύνης form a contrast between two elements within Christ's human nature? Do they refer to Christ's human versus his divine nature?
   g. What is the meaning of ἐξ in verse 4?
   Answers:
   a. This word has a variety of meanings in Paul's epistles. For the list see footnote 187, p. 217. Meaning f. seems to be intended here, for it was according to his human nature (not his divine nature) that Jesus was a descendant of David.
   b. Elsewhere in the New Testament this verb uniformly has the sense *to determine, decree, appoint.* See also NT.C. on Luke 22:22, p. 969. There is no good reason to weaken this meaning to "to declare." Nevertheless, *to declare, make known,* may well be included in *to appoint,* as here used.
   c. This phrase probably modifies the immediately preceding words; hence, "Son of God invested with power." But even if it is construed with the verb, the resultant meaning would be almost the same.
   d. The term "the Spirit of holiness" is derived from Isa. 63:10 f. Cf. Ps. 51:11. The reference here in Rom. 1:4 is to the Holy (divine, exalted) Spirit.
   e. As one of the meanings of κατά, followed by the acc., L.N.T.(Th.), p. 328 gives *through, by virtue of.* This connotation of *agency* became especially widespread in later Koine Greek. Perhaps there is a combination here of agency and standard of measurement. The rendering "by virtue of" may be as good as any.
   f. Definitely not. There is indeed a contrast, but that contrast is between (a) what Christ *was* as to his human nature, and (b) what he *became* by virtue of the Spirit of holiness. In other words, the contrast is between Christ's state of humiliation and his state of exaltation. One cannot very well place an *element* of Christ's human nature over against the third *Person* of the Holy Trinity.
   g. We must be very careful here. The meaning "since" (hence, "since the resurrection from the dead") cannot be entirely ruled out. It may be correct. See Mark 10:20 "since (or from) my youth." However, the meaning "because of," for which see Rev. 16:10 ("They gnawed their tongues because of pain") would seem to be somewhat more natural here.

Paul confesses Jesus to be God's Son. He means that the Savior was God's Son entirely apart from and antecedently to his assumption of the human nature. *He is the Son of God from all eternity; hence, he is God.* This confession harmonizes with what the apostle says elsewhere. Thus, in Rom. 9:5, according to what is probably the best reading and interpretation, Paul calls Jesus "over all God blest forever." In Titus 2:13 he describes him as "our great God and Savior." He is, in fact, "the One in whom all the fulness of the godhead is concentrated" (Col. 2:9). Cf. Phil. 2:6.

Now it is this Son who, without laying aside his divine nature, assumed the human nature. Though he was rich, yet for our sake he became poor, in order that we through his poverty might become rich (II Cor. 8:9). In the fulness of time he was born of a woman (Gal. 4:4). Throughout his earthly sojourn he was indeed "a man of sorrows and acquainted with grief" (Isa. 53:3). Exactly how it was possible for the completely intact and glorious divine nature of the Savior to dwell in intimate union with his human nature, the latter burdened with the load of our guilt and all the unspeakable agonies this condition implied, surpasses human comprehension.

Our passage also informs us that with respect to this human nature Jesus "was born of the seed of David." This was in fulfilment of the oft repeated promise. See II Sam. 7:12, 13, 16; Ps. 89:3, 4, 19, 24; 132:17; Isa. 11:1-5, 10; Jer. 23:5, 6; 30:9; 33:14-16; Ezek. 34:23, 24; 37:24; Matt. 1:1; Luke 1:27, 32, 33, 69; 3:23-31; John 7:42; Acts 2:30; II Tim. 2:8; Rev. 5:5; 22:16. Had he not been a descendant of David he could not have been the Messiah, for prophecy concerning him must be fulfilled.

His state of humiliation, however, could not last forever. As a reward for his willingness to endure it, he was, by virtue of the Spirit of holiness, appointed to be the Son of God "in power" or "invested with power."

With respect to Christ's "appointment" from eternity, effectuated in time, see Ps. 2:7, 8; Acts 13:33; Heb. 1:5; 5:5. The implied exaltation took place by means of his resurrection from the dead; that is, his glorious resurrection was the first important step in his journey to glory. It was followed by Christ's ascension, coronation, and act of pouring out the Holy Spirit.

In the expression "he was appointed to be the Son of God *invested with power,*" all emphasis falls on the words in italics. As has already been pointed out, from all eternity he was the Son of God, but during his period of humiliation his power, in its fullest degree, was, as it were, hidden from view. By means of his glorious resurrection his investiture with power not only was enhanced but also began to shine forth in all its glory. The expression here used reminds us of Peter's statement, made in a very similar context, namely, "Without a shadow of doubt, therefore, let all the house of Israel be assured that God has made him both Lord and Christ, this Jesus whom y o u crucified" (Acts 2:36). That statement did not imply that before his resurrection Jesus was not Lord and Christ. It meant that the power, majesty, and glory of his exalted office was now beginning to shine forth in all its augmented brilliance.

Now Rom. 1:4 informs us that this manifestation of Christ's investiture with power was brought about by "the Spirit of holiness." This "Spirit of holiness" must not be identified with the *spiritual* over against the *physical* element in Christ's human nature, or with his *divine* as contrasted with his *human* nature, but with the Holy Spirit, the third person in the divine Trinity.

But though the third person is distinct from the second, the two, the Holy Spirit and Christ, are most intimately related. Says Dr. H. Bavinck (my translation from the Dutch):

"To be sure, the Spirit of holiness was already dwelling in Christ before his resurrection; in fact, from the moment of his conception, for he was conceived by the Holy Spirit (Luke 1:35), was filled with the Holy Spirit (Luke 4:1), received him without measure (John 3:34)... But this glory which Christ possessed inwardly, was not able to reveal itself outwardly. He was flesh, and because of the weakness of the flesh he was put to death on the cross (II Cor. 13:4). But in death he laid aside this weakness, and severed every connection with sin and death. God, who, for our sake, delivered up to death his own Son, also raised him from death, through his Spirit, who, as Spirit of holiness, dwells in Christ and in all believers (Rom. 8:11). He raised him in order that from that moment on he would no longer live in the weakness of the flesh but in the power of the Spirit."[16]

It was because of this great power that the exalted divine-and-human Savior from his heavenly throne poured out the Spirit upon his church, imparting strength, conviction, courage, and illumination to those who previously had been very weak. Also it was this energy that enabled him to bring about conversions by the thousands, so that even according to the testimony of enemies "the world was being turned upside down" (Acts 17:6). Moreover, it was as a result of the exertion of this mighty influence that the barrier between Jew and Gentile, a wall so formidable that its removal must have seemed impossible, was actually broken down. And it was on account of this force that the glorious gospel of the risen and exalted Savior began to penetrate every sphere of life and is still doing this today.

The impartation of *life* is generally ascribed to the Holy Spirit:

> Thy Spirit, O Lord, makes life to abound,
> The earth is renewed, and fruitful the ground;
> To God ascribe glory and wisdom and might,
> Let God in his creatures forever delight.
>
> See Ps. 104:30, 31

---

16. *Gereformeerde Dogmatiek*, Kampen, 1918, third edition, Vol. III, pp. 488, 489.

If, then, the *impartation* of life is ascribed to the Holy Spirit, is it not logical that here in Rom. 1:4 the *renewal* of life—Christ's resurrection—is also ascribed to him?

Paul concludes this summary of names of the One who is the heart and center of "the gospel of God" (verse 1) by adding, "Jesus Christ our Lord." This meaningful title shows what the One who is being described means to the apostle; in fact, to the church in general, and to that of Rome in particular. Note "*God's* Son" (verses 3, 4a) "... our Lord" (verse 4b). Observe also the combination of the personal name Jesus=Savior with the official name Christ=Anointed One. Adoration: *Lord* (Owner, Ruler, Provider) is placed side by side with Appropriation: *our* Lord. It is by means of "Jesus Christ our Lord" that the true gospel reaches its climax. Apart from him salvation is impossible. With him as our joyfully recognized Sovereign, the object of our trust and love, damnation is unthinkable. See Rom. 8:1.

Having already introduced himself in verse 1, Paul now adds some more information about himself; that is, about himself in relation to "Jesus Christ our Lord" from whom he had received his important commission:

5. ... through whom and for whose sake we received the gift of apostleship, in order to bring about obedience of faith, among all the Gentiles ...

Literally the passage reads, "through whom and for whose sake we received *grace and apostleship*." Many translators have retained these words, in that order, in their versions. So interpreted, Paul would be saying that he had received two things: (a) grace; that is, God's unmerited favor, imparting salvation, plus (b) apostleship.[17] This interpretation may be correct.

Personally I favor the other view, namely, that what we have here in verse 5 is an instance of *hendiadys* (the "*one* by means of *two*" figure of speech; that is: *one* concept is expressed by *two* nouns connected by *and*), and that the meaning is, accordingly, "the gift (or grace) of apostleship." I favor this interpretation and translation for the following reasons:

1. In the present context it is hard to see why Paul would have to emphasize that he is a man saved by grace.

2. Also in Rom. 15:15, 16 the "grace" mentioned is Paul's ministry, his apostolic office.[18] And cf. 12:6.

When Paul says, "*We* received," he is in all probability using the literary or writer's plural.[19] If so, he is referring to himself, not also to others.

When did Paul receive from "Jesus Christ our Lord" the gift of apostle-

---

17. This view is defended by J. Murray, *op. cit.*, Vol. I, p. 13; also by S. Greijdanus, in another precious work, *De Brief van den Apostle Paulus aan de Gemeente te Rome (Kommentaar op het Nieuwe Testament)*, Amsterdam, 1933, Vol. I, p. 67. It is favored by many other commentators and by most translators.

18. This view (heniadys) is also favored by the following commentators, among others: Bruce, Cranfield, Ridderbos, Van Leeuwen and Jacobs; and by such translations as: Berkeley Version, Good News for Modern Man, Knox, Moffat, N.E.B., etc.

19. See Gram. N.T., pp. 406, 407.

ship, with the implied mandate to exercise it? Many passages occur to the mind; for example: Acts 9:1–19 (note especially verse 15); 18:9, 10; 22:6–21; 26:12–18; Rom. 15:15, 16. Among all of them there are two that deserve more than passing notice:

In the first, Jesus is represented as addressing Paul in connection with the unforgettable vision the latter received while as a relentless persecutor he was on his way to Damascus. In answer to Paul's question, "Who art thou, Lord?" the Lord answered, "I am Jesus, whom you are persecuting. But arise and stand on your feet, for I have appeared to you for this purpose, to appoint you (to be) a servant and a witness of what you have seen of me and what I will show you. I will rescue you from your own people and from the Gentiles, to whom I am sending you, to open their eyes in order that they may turn from darkness to light and from the dominion of Satan to God, so as to receive forgiveness of sins and a place among those who are sanctified by faith in me" (Acts 26:15b–18).

In the second, which reports what happened shortly afterward, while Paul was praying in the temple, it is stated that he fell into a trance and heard the Lord saying to him, "Depart, for I will send you far away to the Gentiles" (Acts 22:21).

In both of these passages the apostle is described as a man who received his apostolic mission from Jesus Christ. See also N.T.C. on Gal. 1:1.

Note "through whom and for whose sake." This means that not only is it true that Paul received his apostleship from or through Christ, but it is also a fact that he received it in order that by means of it he might proclaim the name of Christ and promote his cause.

The purpose for which Paul was appointed was to bring about *obedience of faith.* Such obedience is based on faith and springs from faith. In fact, so very closely are faith and obedience connected that they may be compared to inseparable identical twins. When you see the one you see the other. A person cannot have genuine faith without having obedience, nor vice versa.[20]

A striking illustration of this fact is offered by the apostle himself in two synonymous passages, the one concerning *faith;* the other, concerning *obedience:*

Rom. 1:8, ". . . I thank my God through Jesus Christ for y o u all, because y o u r faith is being proclaimed throughout the entire world."

Rom. 16:19, "For the fame of y o u r obedience has reached everyone." It is by means of obedience of faith that a person embraces Christ.

After Paul has written ". . . in order to bring about obedience of faith among all the Gentiles," he continues:

6. . . . including also y o u, the called of Jesus Christ . . .

It is clear that Paul, who in verses 1–5 has been speaking not only about

---

20. In the Dutch language the two are sometimes combined into one word: *geloofsgehoorzaamheid.*

himself and his apostolic office but also about the Christ-centered gospel, now turns specifically to those whom he is addressing. To be sure, they had never been absent from his mind. But he now mentions them as those who were definitely included in the number of people for whom the gospel was intended.

Speaking by and large, the apostle rejoices in being able to state that Rome's membership had not only been *invited* to embrace Jesus Christ as Lord and Savior, but had also, by God's sovereign grace, *responded favorably* to the invitation. Paul is speaking therefore about what is often termed "the effectual call" (Rom. 8:28, 30; 9:24 I Cor. 1:9, 24, 26, etc.).

Implied in these words is also the fact that Paul is deeply conscious of the fact that he has a definite, a very special, right to address these people. Is he not "the apostle (par excellence) to the Gentiles"? In addition to the immediately preceding verse (verse 5) see also Rom. 11:13; 15:16; Gal. 2:8, 9; Eph. 3:8; I Tim. 2:7. And is not the most natural implication of the words "among all the Gentiles, including also y o u" (or "among whom y o u are also") this, that those whom Paul here addresses were mostly Gentiles by race, and had at one time been Gentiles also by religion? See *Introduction*, Section IV.

When Paul names those he is addressing "the called of Jesus Christ," he means "those who by virtue of having been effectively called belong to Jesus Christ, are his people." They are even now his very own, having been given to him by the Father. See John 10:27, 28. Cf. John 17:6, 9, 24; Titus 2:14; I Peter 2:9. See also I Cor. 6:19, 20. This inclusion in God's family is also implied in the words:

7. ... to all in Rome who are beloved of God, saints by virtue of having been called: ...

By means of the phrase "to all in Rome who are beloved of God" Paul continues what he had begun in verse 6, namely, to describe those whom he addresses. This time he includes in his description the name of the place where they are living, *Rome*. For the reason why we believe that the words "in Rome" are a genuine part of the text see *Introduction VI*, under *As to 1*, p. 27.

As to the expression "beloved of God" (or "loved by God"), a study of the book of Romans in its entirety reveals that for Paul these words indicate not only that God *now* loves the believers in Rome but also that he had loved them from all eternity (cf. Jer. 31:3), and would never stop loving them (Rom. 8:31–39). We know that this is the apostle's view, for, as he sees it, God's concern for his children is an unbreakable chain (Rom. 8:29, 30). It reaches from one eternity to the next. It is a love that *precedes, accompanies, and follows* their love for God. And, of course, even men's love for God must not be viewed as an independent entity. Rather, "We love because he first loved us" (I John 4:19). The same idea is certainly implied in *Paul's* teaching on this subject. See Rom. 5:5–11; 8:28.

Paul adds, "saints by virtue of having been called."

Though *interpreters* have spared no efforts in calling attention to *this* meaning of the original,[21] *translators* continue to offer: "called to be saints." But that is not what Paul says. He is telling the Roman Christians what, by grace, they *are* even now. He is stating that something has happened to them: they have been effectively called. *By this inner or effective call is meant that operation of the Holy Spirit whereby he so applies the gospel to the minds and hearts of sinners that they become aware of their guilt, begin to understand their need of Jesus Christ, and embrace him as their Lord and Savior.* Thus these people become *saints,* that is, people who have been "set apart" in order to live lives to the glory of the Triune God as revealed in Christ Jesus.

As mentioned earlier, Paul had been thoroughly drilled in the contents of what we today call the Old Testament. He knew that during the old dispensation there were certain places, objects, and people that had been "set apart" and "consecrated" for the service of God; for example, the holy place (I Kings 8:10) and the holy of holies (Exod. 26:33), the tithe of the land (Lev. 27:30), the priests (Lev. 21:6, 7), and even the Israelites as a whole, viewed in distinction from the other nations (Exod. 19:6; Lev. 20:26; Deut. 7:6; Dan. 7:22). It is this idea which in the New Testament is applied to Christians generally. *They* are the "elect race, royal priesthood, holy nation, people for God's own possession" of the new dispensation, chosen to declare God's praises (I Peter 2:9). A saint, then, is a person whose guilt has been blotted out on the basis of Christ's substitutionary atonement, and who, consequently, by means of the power of the indwelling Spirit, strives to live to God's glory. He is one who has been *set apart* and *consecrated* for service.

Paul, then, is stating that the addressees are such people. They are saints by virtue of having been effectively called.

But now, having rejected the rendering "called *to be* saints," because it is wrong, it is but fair to point out that this very translation, though far from satisfactory, does contain one element of value. It points to the fact that a person who, by God's sovereign grace and power, has become a saint cannot rest on his laurels. On the contrary, now being a saint, he should endeavor day after day after day to live as a saint should live. This is true all the more because as long as he is still on this earth, he remains a sinner. He should do his utmost—not by his own power, for he has none, but by the power of the Holy Spirit—*to be* "holy and without blemish before him" (Eph. 1:4). If he is indeed a saint, he will also actually do this. Thus we see that even a faulty translation of Rom. 1:7 can point in the right direction.

Paul has called these Romans "the called of Jesus Christ, beloved of God, saints." "Why," we may well ask, "is he so generous in his praise for these

---

21. With minor variations one finds this translation in the commentaries on Romans authored by the following, among others: Bruce, Coltman, Cranfield, Denney, Erdman, Greijdanus, Hobbs, Murray, Ridderbos.

people and so eager to assure them that he loves them ... and even better, that God loves them?" Probably because he knows, and they know, that he, Paul, has not founded this church. So he is, as it were, saying, "I love y o u as sincerely and deeply as if I myself had been the founder of y o u r church. And I consider myself y o u r apostle; yes, y o u r very own."

Grace to y o u and peace from God our Father and the Lord Jesus Christ.

This is the form of the salutation found in most of Paul's epistles. In Colossians and in I Thessalonians there is an abbreviation; in I and II Timothy there is an expansion, the word "mercy" having been inserted between "grace" and "peace." In Titus the word "our Savior" has been substituted for "our Lord."

What we see here in Romans, etc., is that the Greek greeting form has been combined with the Jewish form. The Greek says *Chaire!* = "Joy to you!" The Jew says *Shalom!* = "Peace!" Not only, however, have these two greetings been joined by Paul but they have at the same time been transformed into one distinctively *Christian* salutation. Note, in this connection, that *chaire* has been changed into *charis* = *grace*.

Grace, as here used, is God's spontaneous, unmerited favor in action, his freely bestowed lovingkindness in operation, bestowing salvation upon guilt-laden sinners who turn to him for refuge. It is, as it were, the rainbow round about the very throne out of which proceed flashes of lightning, rumblings, and peals of thunder (Rev. 4:3, 5). We think of the Judge who not only remits the penalty but also cancels the guilt of the offender and even adopts him as his own son.

Grace brings *peace.* The latter is both a *state,* that of reconciliation with God, and a *condition,* the inner conviction that consequently all is well. It is the great blessing which Christ by his atoning sacrifice bestowed upon the church (John 14:27), and it surpasses all understanding (Phil. 4:7). It is not the reflection of an unclouded sky in the tranquil waters of a picturesque lake, but rather the cleft of the rock in which the Lord hides his children when the storm is raging (think of the theme of Zephaniah's prophecy); or, to change the figure somewhat but with retention of the main thought, it is the hiding place under the wings, to which the hen gathers her brood, so that the little chicks are safe while the storm bursts loose in all its fury upon herself.

Now this grace and this peace have their origin in God *our* (precious word of appropriation and inclusion!) Father, and have been merited for believers by him who is the great Master-Owner-Conqueror ("Lord"), Savior ("Jesus"), and Office-Bearer ("Christ"), and who, because of his threefold anointing "is able to save to the uttermost them that draw near to God through him" (Heb. 7:25).

For further details about certain aspects of Paul's opening salutations see N.T.C. on I and II Thessalonians, pp. 37–45; on Philippians, pp. 43–49; and on I and II Timothy and Titus, pp. 49–56; 339–344.

8 To begin with, I thank my God through Jesus Christ for y o u all, because y o u r faith is being talked about throughout the entire world. 9 For God, whom I serve from the heart[22] in the gospel of his Son, is my witness, how unceasingly I make mention of y o u 10 at all times in my prayers, asking if perhaps now at last, by God's will, the way may be opened for me to come to y o u. 11 For I am yearning to see y o u, in order that I may impart some spiritual gift to y o u, so that y o u may be strengthened—12 I mean that while (I am) among y o u, we may be mutually encouraged by each other's faith, both y o u r s and mine. 13 I do not want y o u to be unaware, brothers, that many times I planned to come to y o u—but have been prevented until now—in order that I might have some fruit among y o u also, just as (I have had) among the rest of the Gentiles. 14 To both Greeks and barbarians, to both learned and unlearned,[23] I am a debtor; 15 hence my eagerness to preach the gospel also to y o u in Rome.

Paul's thanksgiving and desire to visit Rome
1:8-15

8. To begin with, I thank my God through Jesus Christ for y o u all, because y o u r faith is being talked about throughout the entire world.
The Prologue proceeds in the usual manner; that is, with the apostle's thanksgiving. See also I Cor. 1:4-9; Eph. 1:15, 16; Phil. 1:3-8; Col. 1:3-8; I Thess. 1:2-10; II Thess. 1:3-10; I Tim. 1:12-17; II Tim. 1:3-5; Philem. 4, 5.

"I thank my God." For this author God was not a philosophical abstraction but a real Friend. Cf. Ps. 25:14; James 2:23. God was the object of Paul's trust and love, the One to whom he owed everything. Was it not God who had changed this bitter persecutor into an enthusiastic promoter of the gospel? Therefore, to appreciate the meaning of the designation "*my* God" and the emotions that must have surged through the apostle's heart when he wrote this, one should read such passages as Acts 9:3-8; 27:23 ("the God whose I am, whom also I serve"); I Cor. 15:9; Gal. 1:13 f.; Eph. 3:8; and I Tim. 1:12-17.

". . . through Jesus Christ." It was through him that blessings had been received (see the preceding context, verses 4-6). Therefore also through him thanksgiving must be returned. This circle must never be broken! Divine blessings descending from heaven should ascend back to heaven in the form of grateful acknowledgment. See Ps. 50:15.

". . . for y o u all," not only for those whom Paul had met or with whom he had become acquainted and whom he mentions by name in 16:3-15, but for the entire congregation.

". . . because y o u r faith is being talked about throughout the entire world." Cf. Col. 1:6, I Thess. 1:8. This is understandable, especially in view of the fact that Rome was the capital, the metropolis, of "the world" known to Paul. Ever so many people had contact with Rome, either directly or

---

22. Literally: in my spirit
23. Or: to both wise and foolish

through friends, relatives, business associates, etc. The fact that in the very heart of pagan Rome there were those who worshiped the true God was indeed a worthy topic for conversation, an adequate reason for joyful thanksgiving.

9, 10. For God, whom I serve from the heart [or: in my spirit] in the gospel of his Son, is my witness, how unceasingly I make mention of y o u at all times in my prayers, asking if perhaps now at last, by God's will, the way may be opened for me to come to y o u.

"God . . . is my witness." In order that the believers in Rome may know how earnestly Paul prays for them and how deeply he yearns to see them, he, for confirmation of what he writes, appeals to the omniscient God, who cannot lie, and who judges human hearts and motives. Cf. I Sam. 15:29; Jer. 11:20; II Tim. 2:13; Titus 1:2; Heb. 6:18.

"God, whom I serve from the heart." The word used in the original refers to service of a distinctly religious kind. Often it amounts to *worship* (Matt. 4:10; Luke 1:74; Heb. 9:9, 14; Rev. 7:15; 22:3), though the object of such service or worship is not always the true God who has revealed himself in Jesus Christ. In a few cases the indicated activity amounts to *idolatry* (Acts 7:42; Rom. 1:25). With Paul the object of this service is the One he calls "my God" (verse 8), or, as here in verse 9, simply "God." When the apostle states "whom I serve *in my spirit*" (thus literally), he probably means "from the heart," that is, "with sincere devotion of heart" (Calvin).

. . . (whom I serve) . . . "in the gospel of his Son." Several interpreters insert the word "preaching" or "proclaiming" between "in" and "the gospel." If questioned about this, they might appeal to verse 15: "hence my eagerness *to preach the gospel* also to y o u in Rome." Undoubtedly also here in verse 9 the reference is mainly to gospel preaching. Nevertheless, the expression "I serve God in the gospel" may well have a somewhat broader connotation. Does not Paul serve God in the gospel of his Son also *when he prays* that the seed sown may fall into good soil, *when he comforts an individual,* and, above all, *when he dedicates his entire life and all his talents to God?*

Note "the gospel *of his Son,*" for it is by means of the latter's incarnation, life, death, resurrection, ascension, coronation, intercession, and pouring out of the Spirit (Acts 2:33), that believers obtain the promised blessings.

With respect to the rest of the sentence, it is probably advisable to read this first without insertion of any comma (reserving the phrase "by God's will" for later comment). Note, therefore, the following:

". . . how unceasingly I make mention of y o u at all times in my prayers asking if perhaps now at last . . . the way may be opened for me to come to y o u."

Where shall we place the comma? Our first inclination is probably to place it after the words "how unceasingly I make mention of y o u." Our reason for wishing to place it there is that otherwise the sentence results in an apparent redundance: "unceasingly . . . at all times." With the comma placed after ". . . of y o u," the sentence would read: "God is my witness

50

how unceasingly I make mention of y o u, at all times in my prayers asking if perhaps now at last . . . the way may be opened for me to come to y o u."[24]

Though I respect those who favor this construction, and highly regard their books, I cannot agree. By apparently solving one problem, are they not creating a bigger one? It is difficult to believe that Paul meant to convey the thought that whenever he prayed he was always asking the Lord to lead him to Rome! Besides, so construed, does not the expression "how unceasingly I make mention of y o u" hang in the air? This unceasingly making mention of these people would then be introduced by an expression that almost amounts to an oath, as if merely mentioning them, without the modifier "in my prayers," were that important!

I believe, therefore, that the comma should be placed after "in my prayers." What the apostle *is* emphasizing is that his habit of constantly including the Roman believers in his prayers has not suffered any letup.[25]

"asking if perhaps," etc. As pointed out in *Introduction V*, Paul is not at all sure that he will ever reach Rome. See also 15:31.

". . . now at last." The restless eagerness of a heart filled with love and longing causes Paul to write as he does.

". . . by God's will." It is clear from Acts 18:21; Rom. 15:32; I Cor. 1:1; 4:19; 16:7 that for Paul *Deo volente* was not an empty phrase. The constant and voluntary act of subjecting himself to God's sovereign intention for his (Paul's) life and labors was that which sustained him in all his trials. II Cor. 12:7-10 contains a striking illustration of this attitude of wholehearted, unconditional submission. The phrase sometimes heard, namely, "God willing *or not willing*," would never have proceeded from Paul's lips or occurred to his mind. The truth expressed so beautifully in passages like Rom. 8:28-39 prevented this from ever happening. *How Christ-like this attitude!* See Matt. 26:39, 42; Mark 14:36; Luke 22:41, 42.

". . . the way may be opened," that is, the opportunity may, by divine arrangement, present itself.

Why was Paul so eager to visit the church in Rome? The answer is found in verses 11-15; also in 15:24. Since this matter has been discussed in the *Introduction, Section V,* it is not necessary to elaborate.

11, 12. For I am yearning to see y o u, in order that I may impart some spiritual gift to y o u, so that y o u may be strengthened—I mean that while (I am) among y o u, we may be mutually encouraged by each other's faith, both y o u r s and mine.

" . . . some spiritual gift." Paul expresses himself very modestly here. He is

---

24. For this construction see the following, slightly varying, translations: A.R.V., N.A.S., Phillips, N.E.B.; and consult the commentaries written by (respectively): Greijdanus, Hodge, Murray, Lekkerkerker, to mention only a few.
25. For this interpretation, again with variations, see the following translations: A.V., R.S.V., N.I.V., and commentaries by Lange, Cranfield, Ridderbos, etc.

referring to spiritual strengthening in general, not to the impartation of any specific charismatic gift, such as speaking in tongues, etc.

This modesty or humility on the part of the author is also evident from the use of the passive voice: "that y o u may be strengthened," that is, by *God*.

And especially does this attractive trait—namely humility, "that low sweet root, from which all heavenly virtues shoot" (Moore)—reveal itself in the final line, in which the apostle places himself on a level with the Roman believers, by stating that his presence in Rome will mean *mutual* encouragement; as if to say, "My faith, as well as y o u r s, is in need of strengthening. Y o u will be a blessing to me; I to y o u." Says Calvin, "Note to what degree of modesty his pious heart submitted itself, so that he did not disdain to seek confirmation from inexperienced beginners. He means what he says, too, for there is no one so void of gifts in the Church of Christ who is unable to contribute something to our benefit. Ill will and pride, however, prevent our deriving such fruit from one another."

13. I do not want y o u to be unaware, brothers, that many times I planned to come to y o u—but have been prevented until now—in order that I might have some fruit among y o u also, just as (I have had) among the rest of the Gentiles.

"I do not want y o u to be unaware." This expression occurs also in Rom. 11:25; I Cor. 10:1; 12:1; II Cor. 1:8; and I Thess. 4:13. It is a kind of litotes; i.e., a figure of speech in which something is expressed and even emphasized by the negation of its opposite. For example, "not a few" probably means "many" or even "very many." So what Paul means in the present connection is, "I want y o u to take special note of the fact that...."

" ... brothers." "All men are brothers" is a common saying. Though in a certain sense this cannot be denied, it is not what Paul had in mind. He is speaking about "brothers *in Christ*," about "those who together belong to *The Family of God*." See N.T.C. on Ephesians, pp. 165-170. In the vocabulary of Paul the word "brothers" occurs with great frequency; in fact, slightly more than 100 times. In Romans it is found 14 times. The fact that what the apostle generally has in mind when he uses the term is "those who are united in a common bond of Christian fellowship" is especially clear from such passages as I Cor. 15:58; Col. 1:2; I Tim. 6:2.

Also at this point, the recognition of *The Family of God*, whose members are "brothers" and "sisters," Paul is following the teaching and example of Christ. See Matt. 12:50; Mark 3:35; Heb. 2:11.

" ... that many times I planned to come to y o u." This can mean no less than that there had actually been several occasions when Paul had made serious plans to visit the church in Rome. When had this happened? During a previous stay in Corinth? In connection with the apostle's lengthy ministry in Ephesus? We do not know. What we do know, however, is that Paul, by writing this, is revealing to the believers in Rome that his interest in and love for them was not born yesterday. On the contrary, he has heard many reports about them, has repeatedly remembered them in his prayers, is still doing this (verse 9), is filled with tenderness toward them, and is again (as often previously) planning to visit them.

It is clear that "but have been prevented until now" is a parenthesis. What was it that had blocked these planned trips? It is possible that 15:22—especially in view of its immediately following context—points in the direction of an answer.

The sentence, "I do not want y o u to be unaware, brothers, that many times I planned to come to y o u" continues as follows: "in order that I might have some fruit among y o u also . . ." In Paul's thinking what was included in this *fruit?* Growth in spiritual knowledge? That the apostle considered this important is clear from such passages as Eph. 1:17; 4:13; Col. 1:9, 10. And certainly the fruit he himself mentions in Gal. 5:22, 23—love, joy, peace, longsuffering (or patience), kindness, goodness, faithfulness, meekness (or gentleness), self-control, and similar graces—should be added.

When Paul mentioned "fruit," could he also have been thinking about conversions to the Christian religion, whether directly from paganism, or from paganism via Judaism? Some commentators deny this. Yet, in view of I Cor. 9:22, is it at all possible to exclude this type of fruit from the harvest Paul had in mind?

What is important in this connection is to note, once again, how very close is the relationship between the mind of Christ and the mind of Paul. Did not also our Lord emphasize the necessity of fruitbearing? See John 15:1-8. Add Matt. 9:36-38; 11:28; John 4:35; 7:37, 38.

" . . . in order that I might have some fruit among y o u also, just as (I have had) among the rest of the Gentiles." It will never do to skip this statement, as if it were of no importance. Nor is it satisfactory to dismiss it after having commented that evidently the church in Rome consisted for the most part of Gentiles, though that inference is probably warranted. See *Introduction, IV.* It would appear to me that the real lesson conveyed by verse 13 is once again Paul's modesty. "Some fruit . . . among the rest of the Gentiles." What a humble manner of describing the rich and abundant harvest of families and individuals which through the instrumentality of Paul had been won for the Lord from among the Gentiles! Read Acts 13:48; 14:21-23; 16:14, 15, 31-34; 17:4, 12, 34; 18:14; 19:10, 18-20. Some of these Gentiles had been won for the Lord from the darkness of heathendom; others had been transferred out of the kingdom of darkness to that of light after having tarried first, for a little while, at the depot of Judaism, a way station where the deepest needs of the soul had failed to find ultimate satisfaction. The totality of the harvest had been enormous. And this was true without even counting *the Jews* who had been converted. "Some fruit among y o u also just as among the rest of the Gentiles!" *Paul's humility was indeed profound, an example to us all.* And of whom does that meekness, humility, and kindness remind us? See Isa. 42:1-4; Matt. 12:18-21.

Paul has just now referred to "the Gentiles" (". . . just as I have had among the rest of the Gentiles"). With respect to the Gentiles, then, he now continues:

14, 15. To both Greeks and barbarians, to both learned and unlearned, I am a debtor; hence my eagerness to preach the gospel also to y o u in Rome.

The wide variety of explanations of these words may come as somewhat of a surprise.[26] As I see it, what we have here is an example of the type of parallelism in which the second member, though repeating the thought of the first, adds something to it by way of explanation. In other words

learned and unlearned

explains

Greeks and barbarians.

Paul is writing to believers living in Rome. It is understandable, therefore, that when he uses the term *Greeks* he does not limit himself to people born in Greece. What he means is: Gentiles who were either of Greek descent or were in the habit of speaking Greek and had, at least to a certain extent, assimilated Greek culture. The very fact that the apostle is writing this epistle in Greek and takes for granted that the addressees can understand it, proves that, in the sense already indicated, the people to whom he writes could be called "Greeks."

Now, whenever a Greek-speaking person was listening to conversation carried on by a foreigner, the latter's unintelligible chatter sounded to him like *brrrbrrr*. So he would call the stranger a *barbarian*. Some of these barbarians were undoubtedly people of low intelligence or *were so regarded by the "Greeks."* However, the gospel reaches out to all, educated and uneducated, cultured and uncultured. What Paul is saying, then, is this: "It is my divine calling to preach the gospel to both Greeks and barbarians; that is, to both learned and unlearned."

There was and is *one* message for both, *one* and the same way of salvation for both. The people of Lystra were used to speaking in the Lycaonian language (Acts 14:11). Paul had brought the gospel to them. Believers in Rome were fluent in Greek. They too must hear the gospel from the lips of Paul. Had not the Lord appointed him to be "the apostle to the Gentiles" regardless of their real or assumed degree of culture? Was it not true that they *needed* to hear this gospel? Those who were still in darkness needed to hear it. Those who had been brought out of darkness into the light also needed it. To all of them Paul considered himself to be a debtor; first, because of the commission God had given him; secondly, because he him-

---

26. Though one may or may not agree with the interpretation presented by Cranfield, *op. cit.,* p. 83, his summary of five different views is both interesting and helpful.

self had been a persecutor and had been rescued by the Lord in such an unforgettably gracious manner. And so to both Greeks and barbarians, that is, to both learned and unlearned, hence also to those living in Rome, the apostle must bring the good tidings.

It is as if also at this point we hear him saying, "Woe to me if I do not preach the gospel" (I Cor. 9:16). Not only was it his inescapable duty to do this. He himself was also *eager* to do it.

Chapters 1:16—8:39

Justification by Faith

Outline

Justification by Faith

A. *Real and Necessary.*
1. *Theme.*
"The gospel is the power of God for salvation
to everyone who exercises faith."
1:16, 17

2. *The Gentiles need this justification.*
"Although they knew God, they did not glorify
him as God, or give thanks."
1:18–32

CHAPTER 1:16-32

16 For I am not ashamed of the gospel, for it is (the) power of God for salvation to everyone who exercises faith; to the Jew first, and also to the Greek. 17 For in it a righteousness from God is revealed from faith to faith; as it is written, "But the righteous shall live by faith."

A. *Real and Necessary.*
1. *Theme.*
"The gospel is the power of God for salvation
to everyone who exercises faith."
1:16, 17

It is of the utmost importance that this thematic passage be interpreted correctly. With a few necessary exceptions, I shall not take the time to discuss, in detail, the various views with which I cannot agree. The reader can find these conflicting theories for himself. I shall simply try to interpret the terms and/or phrases one by one, and afterward summarize the whole.

16. For I am not ashamed of the gospel ...

The apostle was not reluctant to preach the gospel, for he loved that good news. In the preceding context Paul had made mention of "learned" (as well as unlearned) people. There must have been many philosophers in such cities as Athens, Corinth, Ephesus, and, last but not least, *Rome*. Has the apostle perhaps delayed his coming to Rome because he was ashamed of meeting these highly educated individuals?

His answer amounts to, "No, indeed!" When he writes, "I am not ashamed," etc., he probably means, "I am proud and overjoyed to receive the opportunity to preach the gospel." And why should he not be eager to proclaim the message of salvation through Christ, the news concerning "Christ Crucified ... the power of God and the wisdom of God" (I Cor. 1:23, 24)?

... for it is (the) power of God for salvation to everyone who exercises faith ...

The word "for" is again definitely in place. It is logical to say, "I am not ashamed of the gospel, *for it reveals the saving power of God.*"

Are the Romans always boasting about their power, the force by which they have conquered the world? "The gospel I proclaim," says Paul, as it were, "is superior by far. It has achieved and offers something far better, namely,

59

(everlasting) *salvation,* and this not for the people of one particular nation—for example Rome—but for everyone who exercises faith." The most urgent and imperative need of the soul is not earthly renown, but peace, joy, glory for today, tomorrow, and the never-ending future. Compared with "the power of God" how feeble the power of Rome or of any earthly host. Earthly armies *destroy.* The gospel *saves.* It is the power of God "for salvation." And what is salvation? What does *to save* mean? In Paul's writings it means:

NEGATIVELY	POSITIVELY
to rescue men from sin's:	to bring men into the state of:
a. guilt (Eph. 1:7; Col. 1:14)	a. righteousness (Rom. 3:21-26; 5:1)
b. pollution (Rom. 6:6, 17; 7:21-25a)	b. holiness (Rom. 6:1-4; 12:1, 2)
c. slavery (Rom. 7:24, 25; Gal. 5:1)	c. freedom (Gal. 5:1; II Cor. 3:17)
d. punishment:	d. blessedness:
(1) alienation from God (Eph. 2:12)	(1) fellowship with God (Eph. 2:13)
(2) the wrath of God (Eph. 2:3)	(2) the love of God "shed abroad" in the heart (Rom. 5:5)
(3) everlasting death (Eph. 2:5, 6)	(3) everlasting life (Eph. 2:1, 5; Col. 3:1-4)

Note that over against each evil stands a corresponding blessing. To be saved, then, means to be emancipated from the greatest evil, and to be placed in possession of the greatest good. The promised blessings pertain to the past, present, and never-ending future. Justification, sanctification, and glorification are all included. The state of salvation is opposed to the state of "perishing" or being "lost." Cf. Luke 19:10; John 3:16.

". . . to everyone," regardless, therefore, of race, nationality, age, sex, social rank, degree of education or culture, etc. Cf. Isa. 45:22; John 4:42; I Tim. 1:15.

But note the significant qualification "(to everyone) *who exercises faith.*"[27] Cf. John 3:16.

And what is meant by faith? It is trust, confidence, leaning on the everlasting arms, the conviction (Heb. 11:1) that through Christ and his atoning sacrifice, my sins are forgiven, my debt is canceled; and that, having now been adopted as a child of The King,

> I am in my Father's keeping,
> I am in his tender care;

---

27. As far as the meaning is concerned, the far more usual rendering, "to everyone *who believes*" is certainly correct. However, it fails to retain the harmony of the original, in which the participle in verse 16 (πιστεύοντι) and the two forms of the noun in verse 17 (πίστεως, πίστιν) are cognate; that is, derived from the same stem. Moreover, when this harmony is retained in the translation, is not the meaning of the entire passage (verses 16, 17) grasped more quickly?

One encounters the same difficulty (lack of harmony) in the Latin, and naturally also in the French, Spanish, etc., translations. On the other hand, everything runs very smoothly in the German, Dutch, Frisian, Swedish, Danish, and South African renderings.

Whether waking, whether sleeping,
I am in his care.

Mrs. C. H. Morris, lines from
"When the Early Morning Breaking"

Faith is the trunk of the tree whose roots represent grace, and whose fruit symbolizes good works. It is the coupling that connects man's train with God's engine. It is the sinner's empty hand stretched out to God, the Giver. It is, from start to finish, *God's gift.* See N.T.C. on Ephesians (2:8), pp. 121-123.

... to the Jew first, and also to the Greek.

That was the divinely planned historical order. As Paul shows in chapter 4 (and to a certain extent already here in verse 16) the gospel of salvation is essentially the same in both dispensations. However, in the divine economy it was revealed first of all to the Jews. During the old dispensation they were the highly privileged nation. See Ps. 147:19, 20; Amos 3:2. Naturally that "advantage" did not immediately cease when the new dispensation was ushered in (Rom. 3:1, 2; 9:4, 5). When Jesus for the first time charged his twelve disciples, he sent them only "to the lost sheep of the house of Israel" (Matt. 10:5, 6). And when Paul carried out his mission mandate, he and his companions, wherever possible, first of all brought the gospel to the Jews.

But there came a change. It is useless to deny this, for on this subject Scripture expresses itself very clearly. Even during the old dispensation God had made it clear that salvation was not going to be limited to one nation. See Gen. 12:3; 22:18; Ps. 72; 87; Isa. 60:1-3; 61:1-3 (in the light of Luke 4); Mal. 1:11. Jesus himself opened the door more and more widely (Matt. 8:10-12; 28:19, 20; Luke 14:23; 17:11-19; 20:9-16; 24:45-47; John 3:16; 4:35-42; 10:16). Similarly, by divine direction, when the Jews refused to accept the gospel, the apostles proclaimed it to the Gentiles (Acts 13:46; 18:5, 6; 19:8, 9). By divine inspiration Paul teaches that the wall of separation between Jew and Gentile has been completely broken down (Eph. 2:11-22), and that there is no longer any distinction (Rom. 10:11, 12). Thus "also to the Greek," that is, to the person(s) influenced by Greek culture, hence to the Gentile(s), the door was opened wide. The gospel became the power of God for salvation to *every* true believer.

The question arises, "How does Paul prove that the gospel is indeed the power of God for salvation *to everyone who exercises faith?*" The answer is given in verse **17. For in it a righteousness from God is revealed from faith to faith; as it is written, "But the righteous shall live by faith."**

Taken by itself, without reference to context, the expression here rendered "righteousness from God" could be translated "righteousness of God" (see A.V.). The question then is, "What does this mean?"

How Luther struggled with this problem! How it bothered him ... until one day, rather suddenly, by divine illumination he realized that what was meant here was not God's retributive justice but the righteousness freely imputed to the sinner by God's sovereign grace, on the basis of Christ's

61

substitutionary atonement, and made the sinner's own possession by means of God-given faith. When the great Reformer made the discovery that Rom. 1:17 speaks about God's gracious verdict of righteousness pronounced upon the believer, he experienced the happiest day in his life. In what may be termed his "Commentary on Romans" he writes:

"The sum and substance of this letter is: to pull down, to pluck up, and to destroy all wisdom and righteousness of the flesh . . . and to affirm and enlarge [prove to be large] the reality of sin, however unconscious we may be of its existence." He continues by pointing out that there have always been people, both Jews and Gentiles, who believed in the possibility of inner goodness. Of these the apostle says, "Professing themselves to be wise, they became foolish" (Rom. 1:22). Luther then shows that in Romans the apostle teaches the very opposite, namely, that the only way in which a person becomes really good is the one provided by God's righteousness. He states, "For God does not want to save us by our own but by an extraneous righteousness, one that does not originate in ourselves but comes to us from beyond ourselves, which does not arise on earth but comes from heaven."[28]

Luther's experience changed his view of the Bible. From this point on Scripture became a book of light and joy for him. It was as if he had been delivered from a dark dungeon and brought into beautiful daylight, where he could inhale the fresh, invigorating, exhilarating air. The peace of God which transcends all understanding now filled his heart and mind.

And was not Luther's experience a replica of Paul's? Read Phil. 3:1-14. What makes Romans so fascinating is the fact that it is not only the product of divine inspiration but also the precipitate of the apostle's conversion experience.

Both Luther and Calvin defined the term which in the A.V. is rendered "the righteousness of God" as indicating *the righteousness that avails before God*. And there can be no question about the fact that this kind of righteousness is indeed indicated. The question remains, "Should not something be added?" Both Reformers, in their discussions, have indeed added something. They have added that the righteousness to which Paul refers is by God freely granted or imputed to the sinner who, by the power of the Holy Spirit, accepts it—that is, appropriates Christ and all his benefits—*by faith*.

That this position is correct becomes clear when Paul is allowed to be his own interpreter. In Phil. 3:8, 9, in discussing the same subject, he writes, ". . . that I may gain Christ, and be found in him, not having a righteousness of my own, legal righteousness, but that (which is) *from* God (and rests) on faith." It is clear then that also here in Rom. 1:17 the term in question should be rendered "righteousness *from* God," meaning that God, its Au-

---

28. Martin Luther, *Lectures on Romans*, tr. of *Römerbriefvorlesung* (Vol. 56 of the Weimar edition of Luther's Works), Philadelphia, 1961, pp. 3, 4.

thor, imputes this right standing to the sinner, who accepts it by faith. *From start to finish* this righteousness is *sola fide;* that is, by faith alone. This also explains the expression "from faith to faith."[29] See Rom. 3:28. And even that faith is God's gift. It is all a matter of sovereign grace, not of works. See N.T.C. on Eph. 2:8-10.

This should not be interpreted as if *the exercise* of faith is the operation of God. *We ourselves* must accept the Triune God, as revealed in Christ Jesus. It is *we* who must exercise faith. God does not believe for us. This position is in harmony with Scripture. See John 3:16; Phil. 2:12, 13; II Thess. 2:13.[30] We should bear in mind, moreover, that not only the gift of faith is from God but so is also the power to exercise it. To him alone be the glory!

"As it is written, But the righteous shall live by faith."

In presenting this comforting doctrine Paul is not introducing something new. The words "as it is written" show that he is basing his presentation on the Old Testament. And it is indeed in that book, which for the apostle as well as for his addressees was the Bible, that *righteousness,* and therefore *salvation,* is repeatedly presented as a treasure which belongs to Jehovah. By sovereign grace he bestows it as a gift on all who *trust* in him. A few precious passages will make this clear. One of the most familiar and outstanding is surely Isa. 12:2:

"Behold, God is my salvation. I will trust and will not be afraid, for Jehovah, even Jehovah, is my strength and song; and he has become my salvation."

Note also the following:

"For thy salvation I am waiting, O Lord" (Gen. 49:18).

"Salvation belongs to the Lord" (Ps. 3:8).

"Thou art the God of my salvation" (Ps. 25:5).

"The Lord is my light and my salvation. Whom shall I fear?" (Ps. 27:1). Fear is the opposite of trust.

"O sing to the Lord a new song, for he has done marvelous things. His right hand and his holy arm have achieved salvation for him. The Lord has

---

29. The expression "from faith to faith" is too short and simple to allow for complicated interpretations. So, for example, I cannot accept Barth's view that it means "from God's faithfulness to man's faith"; or Murray's that by means of this brief phrase the apostle would be saying "only by faith are we the beneficiaries of this righteousness and every believer is the beneficiary." The most simple interpretation of such a brief expression is usually the best. According to this rule the meaning is in all probability: "from start to finish (or: from first to last) by faith." In agreement with this interpretation are also the following: Cranfield, Erdman, Harrison, Hodge, and Ridderbos.

30. Would it not seem, therefore, that Lenski, who in his commentaries has enriched the church with much excellent material, expresses himself somewhat injudiciously in his *Interpretation of St. Paul's Epistle to the Romans,* Columbus, p. 83? Read also his comments on what he calls "false Calvinistic exegesis" (p. 9).

made known his salvation. He has revealed his righteousness in the sight
of the nations" (Ps. 98:1, 2).

Note close relation between *salvation* and *righteousness* both here and
elsewhere.

"The Lord is my strength and my song. And he has become my salvation" (Ps. 118:14).

"I long for thy salvation, O Lord" (Ps. 119:174).

"I bring near my righteousness, and my salvation shall not tarry" (Isa.
46:13).

"My righteousness is near. My salvation has gone forth. And my arms will
judge the peoples . . . My salvation will be forever. And my righteousness
will not diminish . . . My righteousness will be forever, and my salvation to
all generations" (Isa. 51:5–8).

"Their righteousness [or vindication] is from me, says the Lord" (Isa.
54:17).

"He has clothed me with the garments of salvation. He has wrapped me
in a garment of righteousness (Isa. 61:10).

"For Zion's sake I will not be silent. And for Jerusalem's sake I will not
keep quiet, until her righteousness goes forth like brightness, and her
salvation like a torch that is burning" (Isa. 62:1).

Here in Rom. 1:17, "But the righteous shall live by faith," the apostle
is almost literally quoting Hab. 2:4b. There are those who insist on the rendering (here in Rom. 1:17), "But the righteous by faith shall live." In other
words, they connect "by faith" with "the righteous" instead of with "shall
live." I have not been convinced by their arguments. Those who are interested in this question should read the footnote.[31]

---

31. The reasons that have convinced me that ἐκ πίστεως should be connected with ζήσεται,
not with δίκαιος, are as follows:
   a. In the Habakkuk passage (the original) the phrase "by his faithfulness" or "by his faith" is
most logically connected with "he lives." See I. Lesser's rendering (in *Twenty-Four Books of the
Holy Scriptures*, New York, n.d., Vol. II, p. 959), "But the righteous ever liveth in his (trustful)
faith."
   b. If Paul had intended to connect "by faith" with "the righteous" he would probably have
written ὁ δὲ ἐκ πίστεως δίκαιος instead of ὁ δὲ δίκαιος ἐκ πίστεως.
   c. The phrase ἐκ πίστεως here in verse 17b corresponds to the same phrase in the earlier
part of the verse. There too it belongs to the predicate, not to the subject.
   d. In Paul's epistles there is no parallel to "righteous by faith." Rom. 5:1 is not really a
parallel.
   e. If here in Rom. 1:17 we connect ἐκ πίστεως with δίκαιος, should we not also do this in
Gal. 3:11, where the identical Old Testament passage is quoted by the same writer and for the
same purpose? Now in Galatians the context makes it very clear that "shall live by faith" and
not "the righteous by faith" is the meaning. This is shown by the preceding and also by the

The prophet Habakkuk appeared upon the scene of history during the reign of wicked Jehoiakim (608-597 B.C.). What bothered him was that it seemed as if wicked men were getting away with their wickedness. Jehovah apparently tolerated such evils as the exploitation of the needy, strife, contention, violence, etc. So the prophet begins to ask questions. He addresses these questions to Jehovah. He complains, objects, and waits for an answer. Habakkuk's first question amounted to this, "Why does Jehovah allow the wicked in Judah to oppress the righteous?" Jehovah answers, "Evil-doers will be punished. The Chaldeans (Babylonians) are coming." But this answer does not quite satisfy the prophet. So he asks another one, which was tantamount to this: "Why does Jehovah allow the Chaldeans to punish the Jews, who at least are more righteous than these foreigners?" The prophet stations himself upon his watch-tower and awaits an answer. The answer arrives: "The Chaldeans, too, will be punished. In fact *all sinners* will be punished . . . but the righteous shall live by his *faith*." It is his duty and privilege to *trust*, and to do this even then when he is not able to "figure out" the justice of Jehovah's doings. In this humble trust and quiet confidence he shall truly *live*, prosper.

But Jehovah does more than merely tell the prophet that he must *exercise* faith. He also *strengthens* that faith by means of a marvelous, progressive vision. Habakkuk sees the symbol of Jehovah's presence, descending from Mt. Paran. Having descended he stands firm and shakes the earth. The tent-hangings of Cushan and Midian are trembling and are being torn to shreds. One question worries the prophet: "Upon whom is Jehovah's wrath going to fall? Merely upon the realm of nature? Upon Judah perhaps?" Finally, the answer arrives; Jehovah destroys the Chaldeans and delivers his people.

So fearful and terrifying had been the appearance of Jehovah, so alarming the sound of the tempest, of crumbling mountains, etc., that the prophet is trembling in every part of his body. Nevertheless, having witnessed that Jehovah had descended for the defense of his own people, Habakkuk no longer questions the ways of God's providence. From now on he "waits quietly." He expresses his feelings in a beautiful psalm of *trust:* "For though the fig tree shall not flourish . . . Yet I will rejoice in Jehovah, I will joy in the God of my salvation."

Paul, accordingly, could not have chosen a better prophecy from which

---

following context; for "live by faith" is there contrasted with "justified by law" and is also contrasted with "live by (doing) them." We cannot very well adopt one grammatical construction for Gal. 3:11, and another for Rom. 1:17.

f. If we translate, "He who is justified by faith (or: The righteous by faith) shall live" we are placing the emphasis where it does not belong. The entire context indicates that Paul's emphasis is on "live *by faith*" instead of "live by the works of the law."

Having carefully read and studied Cranfield's arguments in favor of the opposite position I am unable to agree. But, for the sake of fairness, I hope everyone will by all means read Cranfield, *op. cit.*, pp. 101, 102.

to quote than that of Habakkuk. The passage fits the situation exactly! In every age and in all circumstances, hence also in connection with the question, "What must I do to be accepted by God?" it remains true that "The righteous shall live by faith." "In quietness and confidence shall be y o u r strength" (Isa. 30:15).

But not only is Paul's doctrine in line with the teaching of the Old Testament—a subject on which the apostle is going to dwell in far more detail in chapter 4—it is also in harmony with the teaching of Christ during his earthly ministry. See N.T.C. on Luke 18:9-14, pp. 818-821.

To summarize, what Paul teaches here in Rom. 1:16, 17 and in Gal. 3:11 amounts to this:

> Not the labors of my hands,
> Can fulfil thy law's demands;
> Could my zeal no languor know,
> Could my tears forever flow,
> All for sin could not atone;
> Thou must save, and thou alone.

> Lines from "Rock of Ages"
> by A. M. Toplady

---

18 For the wrath of God is being revealed from heaven against all ungodliness and unrighteousness of people who are constantly attempting to suppress the truth by (their) unrighteousness, 19 because what can be known of God is plain to them, for God has made it plain to them. 20 For since the creation of the world his invisible qualities—his eternal power and divine nature—have been clearly seen, being understood through (his) works, so that these people are without excuse.

21 For although they knew God, they neither glorified him as God nor gave thanks to him, but became futile in their speculations, and their foolish hearts were darkened. 22 Although they claimed to be wise, they became fools 23 and exchanged the glory of the immortal God for an image in the shape of mortal man and of birds, four-footed animals, and reptiles.[32]

24 Therefore God, letting them follow the sinful cravings of their own hearts, gave them over to sexual immorality, so that their bodies were dishonored among themselves; 25 since they had indeed exchanged God, (who is) the truth, for a lie, and worshiped and served the creature rather than the Creator, who is blessed forever. Amen.

26 Because of this, God gave them over to passions that bring dishonor. For as well as their females [or women] exchanged natural intercourse for that (which is) contrary to nature, 27 so likewise also the males [or men] having abandoned natural intercourse with the female [or woman], were consumed by flaming passion for one another, males with males [or men with men] perpetrating shamelessness, and receiving in their own persons the due return for their deviation.

28 And since they did not deem it worthwhile to retain the knowledge of God, he gave them over to (their) worthless disposition, to do what is improper; 29 having become filled with every kind of unrighteousness, wickedness, greed, depravity; being full of envy, murder, strife, deceit, and malice. (They are) gossips, 30 slanderers, haters of God, insolent, arrogant, boastful, inventors of (novel forms of) evil, disobedient to (their) parents, 31 senseless, faithless, loveless, pitiless. 32 And although they know the ordinance of God that those who

---

32. Or: creeping things, crawling creatures.

practice such things are worthy of death, they not only continue to do them but also approve of those who practice them.

---

2. The Gentiles need this justification.
"Although they knew God, they did not glorify
him as God, or give thanks"
1:18-32

18. For the wrath of God is being revealed from heaven against all ungodliness and unrighteousness of people who are constantly attempting to suppress the truth by (their) unrighteousness...

What kind of people is Paul describing in 1:18-32? There are those who maintain that since the word *Gentiles* is never mentioned in this section and since at least some of the sins here catalogued were committed by Jews as well as by Gentiles, we must conclude that the apostle is here referring to unregenerate men in general, not just to Gentiles.

There is some truth in this. See on 2:1. On the other hand, is it not also true that several traits here mentioned are far more character ic of Gentiles than of Jews? Note, for example, image worship (verse 23), and see also verses 26, 27. Moreover, to a large extent the people here described derive their knowledge of God not from special but from general revelation (verses 19, 20). Besides, 2:1 clearly marks a transition to the discussion of another group of people, namely, the Jews (see 2:17). This too seems to indicate that up to this point Paul has been speaking chiefly about Gentiles. Finally, does not 3:9 prove that the apostle had been speaking about two groups, namely, Gentiles and Jews (there mentioned in reverse order)? We conclude therefore that in 1:18-32 the reference is *mainly* to Gentiles, though it is true that not all Gentiles were guilty (or equally guilty) of the enumerated vices.

The word "For" should not be left untranslated. It indicates the relation between verses 16, 17, on the one hand, and verse 18 on the other. The reasoning is probably along this line: No other way to be saved is available than that of accepting the gospel by faith, *for* since the wrath of God rests by nature upon man, the latter is completely unable to save himself, whether by performing the works of the law or by any other means.

What is meant by God's wrath? See also John 3:36; Rom. 9:22; Eph. 5:6; Col. 3:6; I Thess. 1:10. God's *wrath* is his settled indignation. It differs from *fury*, which generally points in the direction of *rage*, sudden outbursts of anger.[33] Whenever God's wrath is mentioned in the New Testament the final manifestation of divine vengeance is either indicated or, as here, is at least in the background.

"... is being revealed..." What is meant is that this wrath is revealed *in*

---

33. For more on this see R. C. Trench, *Synonyms of The New Testament*, Grand Rapids, 1948 (reprint), par. 37. See also below, on 2:8.

action; for example, by means of the deluge (Gen. 6-8), the destruction of Sodom and Gomorrah (Gen. 19), the plagues upon Egypt (Exod. 6-12), and the bowls of wrath (Rev. 16). In each case Scripture shows that these manifestations of wrath have their origin in *heaven.* It is God, dwelling in heaven, who vents his wrath upon the perpetrators of "ungodliness and unrighteousness."

These two concepts—ungodliness and unrighteousness—must not be viewed as completely separate entities; as if, for example, the first pertains exclusively to the religious sphere; the second only to the moral realm; or as if the first concerns merely the first table of the law; the second, the remainder of the law. Both represent sin, rebellion against God. The first views sin as want of reverence for God; the second, as want of reverence for his ordinances, his holy law. That the relation between these two is very close is shown by the fact that at the close of verse 18 *one* term, unrighteousness, covers both concepts.

"... of people who are constantly attempting to suppress[34] the truth by their unrighteousness ..."

Elsewhere too Scripture teaches that the wicked make an attempt to suppress the truth. The fool is constantly trying to convince himself that "there is no God." To Ps. 14:1 and 53:1 add Ps. 73:11; Rom. 2:15. Even when he is confronted with the voice of God addressing him by means of special revelation, he still refuses to capitulate. See Mark 6:20, 26, 27. In fact, as it was in the case of Herod Antipas, so generally, the more conscience warns, the more the sinner hardens himself.

But do the Gentiles really have sufficient knowledge of the truth to be considered guilty of constantly attempting to suppress it? The answer is found in the next verse:

19. ... because what can be known of God is plain to them, for God has made it plain to them.

Even entirely apart from special revelation through the gospel, which ever so many Gentiles have never heard, God has made himself known and continues to do so by means of his general revelation in nature, history, and conscience; here, as the sequel indicates, with emphasis on God's revelation

---

34. In favor of the conative force of this pres. act. participle (κατεχόντων) are the following facts:

a. A verb which by itself suggests effort, when used in a context that implies action in progress (for example, progression in the present, or in the past as in Luke 4:42), points in the direction of *attempted* action. See E. De Witt Burton, *Syntax of the Moods and Tenses in New Testament Greek,* Chicago, 1923, p. 8.

b. Even some of those exegetes who in their *translation* have adopted the English equivalent "who suppress," etc., in their *interpretation* speak about the *efforts* of the ungodly to suppress the truth.

c. The conotative force of the participle is clear also from this fact that no less than three times (verses 19, 20, and 21) the immediate context assures us that the ungodly do not succeed in holding down or blotting out the truth. They sin against better knowledge. See also on verses 28 and 32.

In favor of the conative force of this present participle is also Cranfield, *op. cit.,* p. 112.

in *nature;* that is, in "creation." Not as if men, acting on their own initiative, could have discovered God, but, as the passage states, *God* has made known to them[35] whatever in the area of creation can be made known about him.

20. For since the creation of the world his invisible qualities—his eternal power and divine nature—have been clearly seen, being understood through (his) works, so that these people are without excuse.[36] The little word "For" is again very meaningful. It is not only continuative but also supportive, showing that what was said in verse 19 is indeed a fact.

The sentence introduced by "For" may even reflect on what was said earlier, namely, in verse 18; that is, it may be viewed as indicating why the wrath of God is being revealed against the wicked: their wicked deeds are inexcusable!

In verses 16, 17 Paul had been speaking about God's revelation *in the gospel* unto salvation. It is clear that here, in verses 19, 20 he has made the transition from special to general revelation. He is now speaking about "the things that are made," that is, about God's revelation "in his works," meaning, in *creation* or *nature.*

Note the expression "God's invisible qualities." That God is indeed invisible is taught everywhere in Scripture. Note especially the following passages:

"God himself no one has ever seen" (John 1:18).

"(the Son of his love, who is) the image of the invisible God" (Col. 1:15).

"the King of the ages, the imperishable, invisible, only God" (I Tim. 1:17).

"... seeing him who is invisible" (Heb. 11:27).

A further explanation of these invisible qualities or attributes is given in the words "his eternal power and divine nature."

---

35. ἐν αὐτοῖς can be used instead of the ordinary dative; so probably here; hence "to them." See L.N.T. (A. and G.), p. 260.

36. Several items in the Greek text require comment:

a. ἀόρατα ... καθορᾶται. The oxymoron is probably intentional.

b. καθορᾶται, third per. s. pres. pass. indicat. of καθοράω, (κατά, perfective, plus ὁράω, to see), to see clearly.

c. νοούμενα, nom. pl. n. pres. pass. participle of νοέω, to perceive, understand. The participial form is related to the noun νοῦς, which, depending on the context, can have any one of the following meanings: mind, intellect, intelligence, thought, understanding, attitude, disposition. In the present passage νοῦς must be viewed as *intellect plus* (or including) *sense of responsibility.* Man's entire mental and moral state of being is indicated. It is in that sense that νοούμενα can here be interpreted as meaning "being perceived" or "understood." As an adverbial modifier of καθορᾶται, the participle νοούμενα shows that more than merely physical vision is indicated by καθορᾶται.

d. ἀΐδιος (from ἀεί), ever-enduring, eternal.

e. εἰς τὸ εἶναι does not necessarily always introduce a purpose clause. A result clause is far more reasonable in the present connection. See Gram. N.T., p. 1003; L.N.T. (A. and G.), p. 228 (under 4e).

69

As to this eternal power or never-failing omnipotence, it is evident in all God's works (Ps. 111:2; 118:17; 119:27; 139:14; 145:10); in Israel's deliverance from Egypt (Exod. 20:1, 2) and in God's tender care bestowed on his people (Deut. 33:27). Again and again psalmists and prophets refer to God's mighty deeds. No one is able to stay his hand (Dan. 4:35). He does whatever he pleases, for nothing is too difficult for him (Gen. 18:14; Jer. 32:27).

In the present context, however, it is not—at least not primarily—God's mighty deeds in history that are being contemplated. The reference is rather to the works of *creation:* the works of God which *for a very long time,* in fact *ever since the creation of the universe,* have been visible to men and have made their indelible impression upon their minds.

Paul is thinking of the God who created the heavens and the earth and who establishes them by perpetual decrees (Gen. 1; Ps. 104). He is reflecting on the One who made "the Pleiades and the Orion, who turns the shadow of death into the morning, and makes the day dark with night" (Amos 5:8).

The term "his divine nature" indicates the sum of all God's glorious attributes, in the present connection especially those attributes which make and leave an impression on everybody's mind: the exhibition of God's power, wisdom, and goodness in the created universe. Such passages as Ps. 8, Ps. 19:1–6, and Isa. 40:21, 22, 26 shed further light on the subject.

The rendering "His invisible qualities . . . have been clearly seen" correctly reproduces the sense of the original, but fails to do justice to its beauty. The original (Greek), even somewhat more clearly than the usual English translation, employs a pair of words which, though resembling each other in form, express a seeming contradiction. Call it a paradox or an oxymoron if you prefer. A closer approach to the original would be: "his *unseeable* qualities . . . *are clearly seen."*

But how is it possible to see the unseeable? Is it not true that physical eyes are unable to see God's invisible qualities? True; yet, while these eyes are observing the glories of the universe which God created, the soul, with its invisible eye, is being deeply impressed. It *clearly sees* God's power displayed in "the things that were made," that is, in God's works.

The Belgic Confession, Article I, commenting on Rom. 1:20, speaks about "the creation, preservation, and government of the universe; which is before our eyes as a most elegant book, wherein all creatures, great and small, are as so many characters leading us *to see clearly the invisible things of God, even his everlasting power and divinity,* as the apostle says, 'All these things are sufficient to convince men and to leave them without excuse.'"

". . . so that these people are without excuse." Even though they have been constantly surrounded by the evidences not only of God's existence but also of his infinite power, adorable goodness, and incomparable wisdom, they have refused to acknowledge him as *their* God, and to worship him.

Even without the benefit of such products of human invention as *microscope* and *telescope*, they were able to reflect on the vastness of the universe, the fixed order of the heavenly bodies in their courses, the arrangement of the leaves around a stem, the cycle of the divinely created water-works (evaporation, cloud formation, distillation, pool formation), the mystery of growth from seed to plant—not just any plant but the particular kind of plant from which the seed originated, the thrill of the sunrise from faint rosy flush to majestic orb, the skill of birds in building their "homes" without ever having taken lessons in home building, the generous manner in which food is supplied for all creatures, the adaptation of living creatures to their environment (for example, the flexible soles of the camel's feet to the soft desert sands), etc., etc. In addition to this voice of God in the works of creation there was also the voice of that same God in conscience (2:15). The evidence was overwhelming. And still no response of adoration and gratitude. Then surely their conduct is inexcusable!

21. For although they knew God, they neither glorified him as God nor gave thanks to him, but became futile in their speculations, and their foolish hearts were darkened.

Verse 21 is a clarification and amplification of verse 18 (final clause) and verse 20. It confirms the statement that by their unrighteousness these wicked people are constantly attempting to suppress the truth that has been and is continually being revealed to them, and that they are accordingly without excuse.

For, although they knew God from his works in creation, they did not glorify him: did not acknowledge him as their God and did not bestow upon him the honor and praise they owed him. Nor did they return thanks to him for the blessings they were constantly receiving. That they were the recipients of blessings in abundance is clear (Matt. 5:45; Luke 6:35; Acts 14:17). But though there are indeed *blessings* that are *common, gratitude* in return for them is not. A striking example is Luke 17:11–19.

Instead of praising God for all his benefits, these people became futile in their speculations. Instead of following the advice incorporated in a hymn:

> Lift now hearts and voices
> While our soul rejoices
> In our God above,

the minds and hearts of these people remained on a horizontal plane: they carried on a dialog with themselves. Their minds were arguing, speculating. Their hearts were void of thanksgiving and adoration. Such hearts are useless; in fact, worse than useless. Whenever people, in their conceit and ingratitude, begin to reason on their own, without constantly checking the results of their speculations with God's revelation in nature, history, conscience, and especially, whenever possible, with the Word of God, their *foolish* hearts are darkened.

Such darkness indicates mental dullness, emotional despair, and spiritual depravity.

Note the expression "their foolish hearts." In Paul's epistles the word *heart* (s. and pl.) occurs more than fifty times. The heart, according to Paul and Scripture in general, is the hub of the wheel of man's existence, the mainspring of all his thoughts, words, and deeds. It is the motive power hidden away deeply within man; so deeply, in fact, that God, he alone, knows its secrets. See Prov. 4:23; 23:7; Jer. 17:9, 10; Matt. 12:34; 15:18, 19; Luke 6:45; Rom. 8:27; I Cor. 14:25; I Thess. 2:4.

Of course, the word's exact shade of meaning in each case depends on the context. Sometimes, in Paul, when the word *heart(s)* is used, the emphasis is on the emotions or feelings (Rom. 1:24; 9:2); sometimes on the intellect (Rom. 10:6–9); and sometimes on the will (Rom. 2:5).

Now when, according to the present passage (1:21), men's hearts are darkened, it follows that whatever they feel, think, say, or do is detrimentally affected. Their minds cannot reason straight; their emotions cannot function properly, imparting peace and joy to their lives; and their wills do not even try to be in harmony with God's holy law. Note the tragic result:

22, 23. Although they claimed to be wise, they became fools and exchanged the glory of the immortal God for an image in the shape of mortal man and of birds, four-footed animals, and reptiles [or crawling creatures].

What a contrast between the *claim* and the *reality*. For a striking example read John 9:40, 41. However, the present passage refers especially to the blindness of *heathendom* and of all who imitate its foolish practices. As has been indicated, such blindness is inexcusable. It amounts to sinful folly. It is illustrated in such passages as the following:

"Let us build for ourselves a city, and a tower whose top will reach into heaven" (Gen. 11:4).

"The Syrians said, 'Jehovah is a god of the hills, but he is not a god of the valleys'" (I Kings 20:28; see also verse 23).

"Those who lavish gold . . . hire a goldsmith, who makes a god of it. They bow down; indeed, they worship it. Then they lift it upon (their) shoulders and carry it. They set it in its place, and there it stands! It does not move from its place. Though a person may cry to it, it cannot answer. It cannot rescue him from his distress" (Isa. 46:6, 7).

What stupendous folly! Said Aaron, "The people gave the gold to me. I threw it into the fire, and out came this calf!" (Exod. 32:24). Cf. verse 4: "This is your God, O Israel, that brought you up out of the land of Egypt."

And to think that people would actually give up their faith in the glory of God—the excellence of his attributes, with all this implies in blessings for those who rely on him—in exchange for the worship of idols. They exchange *the One who carries* for *those who must be carried* (contrast Isa. 63:9 with Isa. 46:1). What *fools* they have made of themselves![37]

In the enumeration: man, birds, quadrupeds, reptiles or crawling creatures ("creeping things"), *man* is mentioned first. Throughout the ages people have paid homage to *man, mortal* man at that, and have prostrated themselves before his *image* (see Dan. 3; and N.T.C. on Matthew, p. 857). The slogan has been, and in many circles is even today, "No God for a gift God gave us; mankind alone must save us."

By adding "an image in the shape of . . . birds, quadrupeds, and creeping things (reptiles, etc.)," Paul is following the order of the Creation Account (Gen. 1:20-25). Here again it is the *image* of the animal that is mentioned as the object of worship. Think of the golden calf at Sinai (Exod. 32) and the golden calves at Bethel and Dan (I Kings 12:28f.). As to birds, think of the veneration accorded by the Romans to the image of the eagle. See N.T.C. on Matthew, pp. 187, 188. And even "creeping things" were reproduced in the idolatrous imagery of the Gentiles and at one time or another were worshiped by Jewish imitators (Ezek. 8:10).

All this in spite of the fact that:

a. Such worship had been strictly forbidden by the Lord (Exod. 20:4, 5; Deut. 4:15-19; 5:8, 9). Every worship of the creature, whether directly or through an image, whether in the heavens (worship of sun, moon, stars) or on earth, had been warned against again and again.

b. By bowing down before any object other than the true and only God, those wicked and foolish enough to do this were losing much. That is brought out by the very wording of the present passage: "they became fools and exchanged the glory of the immortal God for an image," etc. This reminds us of

Ps. 106:20: "They exchanged their glory—God was Israel's glory—for the image of an ox that munches grass"; and also of

Jer. 2:11: "Has any nation ever changed (its) gods, though they were not (even) gods? But my people have changed their glory for something that is of no benefit whatever."

Even in the apocrypha such sin and folly was held up to scathing ridicule:

"An experienced woodcutter will cut down a tree that is easy to handle. Skillfully he strips off all its bark. And then, with pleasing workmanship, he makes a useful article that serves life's needs . . . But he takes a castoff piece, one that is good for nothing, a stick crooked and full of knots. He carves it with care . . . and causes it to resemble a man. Or he makes it to look like some worthless animal, giving it a coat of red paint, and with paint covering every blemish . . . Then he makes for it a suitable niche, sets it in

---

37. The *possibility* that Paul meant, "By pretending to be wise they made themselves fools," must be granted.

the wall, and fastens it with iron. He takes care that it does not fall, because he knows that it cannot help itself, for it is only an image and in need of help. Then he prays (to it) about possessions and his marriage and children . . . For health he appeals to a thing that is weak. For life he prays to a thing that is dead. For aid he entreats an object that is thoroughly inexperienced . . . He asks strength of a thing whose hands have no strength" (Wisd. of Solomon 13:11-19, abbreviated). Cf. Isa. 40:19f.

Indeed, they exchanged "the glory of the immortal God" for a mere image!

Here, in Rom. 1:23, the word *glory* does not have exactly the same meaning as it has in Ps. 106:20; Jer. 2:11, though the two connotations are not far apart. In these two Old Testament passages the designation "glory" indicates God himself. In Paul's passage it refers to God's absolute perfection and splendor, the sum-total of all his marvelous attributes. For more on this very interesting term *glory* read the footnote.[38]

God's response to the wicked course chosen by sinful men (verses 22, 23) is indicated in the next verse.

24. Therefore God, letting them follow the sinful cravings of their own hearts, gave them over to sexual immorality, so that their bodies were dishonored among themselves . . .

Note the close connection between idolatry (verse 23) and immorality

---

38. Paul uses the word δόξα, *glory*, more than seventy-five times in his epistles. Since it is a word with many different, though related, meanings, a closer study is profitable. The noun is related to the verb δοκέω; hence, has the primary meaning *opinion* (IV Macc. 5:18). It is but a small step to the meaning *good opinion* concerning someone; hence, *praise, honor, homage*.

The Hebrew *kābhōdh*, which is the most common word for *glory* in the Old Testament, has the primary meaning *weight, heaviness, burden* (Isa. 22:24); hence, *substance, wealth, dignity*. It is used to describe Jacob's *substance*, his flocks and herds (Gen. 31:1). At times the element of brightness, radiance, splendor is added to that of substance. Thus, the word is used to indicate *the brilliant physical manifestation of Jehovah's presence* (Exod. 16:7; Isa. 1-5).

In a study of the meaning of δόξα in Paul's epistles both the Greek derivation and use and the Hebrew background must be borne in mind. Accordingly, the different senses in which the word is used by Paul may be summarized as follows:

a. *praise, honor, bestowed on creatures or belonging to them, approbation, approval, reputation*. Here the antonym is *dishonor* (II Cor. 6:8) or *shame* (Phil. 3:19). The synonym of δόξα, so used, is τιμή (Rom. 2:7, 10).

b. *adoration or homage rendered to God*. Thus the word is used in Phil. 1:11, as is shown by its synonym *praise*. See also Rom. 3:7; 4:20; 11:36; I Cor. 10:31; etc.

c. *the thing which reflects honor or credit on someone, or the person whose virtues redound to the glory of another* (I Cor. 11:7, 15; II Cor. 8:23; I Thess. 2:20).

d. *external splendor, brightness, brilliance, or radiance* (of the heavenly bodies, I Cor. 15:40, 41).

e. *the bright cloud by which God made himself manifest, the shekinah* (Rom. 9:4).

f. *the manifested excellence, absolute perfection, royal majesty, splendor or sublimity of God* (here in Rom. 1:23, cf. verses 19, 20; II Cor. 4:6), *or of Christ* (II Cor. 3:18; 4:4), *particularly also at his second coming* (Titus 2:13; II Thess. 1:9).

g. *God's majestic power* (Rom. 6:4).

h. *the light that surrounds those who are, or have just been, in contact with God* (II Cor. 3:7).

i. *the state and/or place of blessedness into which believers will enter* (Rom. 8:18); *and Christ has already entered* (I Tim. 3:16).

j. in general, *the pre-eminently excellent or illustrious condition of something or of someone, manifested excellence, either now or in the future.*

(verse 24). Similarly in the apocryphal book Wisd. of Solomon we read: "For the idea of making idols was the beginning of fornication, and their invention was the corruption of life" (14:12).

In this connection we should bear in mind that Paul is writing this epistle from Corinth, a city notorious for its sexual immorality and debauchery. The expression "to live like a Corinthian" meant "to live a life of moral degradation." Corinth's temple counted more than a thousand lust-promoting priestesses.

The fact that no less than three times (verses 24, 26, 28) we are told that "God gave them over" is significant. In the interpretation of this shocking statement extremes should be avoided. One extreme position would be to say that as soon as these sins—idolatry and immorality—started to appear God *immediately* said, "Let them perish!" That, however, is not what Scripture teaches with respect to the manner in which God deals with sinners. Read especially Gen. 4:6, 7, and note the tender manner in which God dealt with Cain!

The woman "Jezebel" seems to have been the very embodiment of the sins mentioned in the present context (cf. Rev. 2:20 with Rom. 1:23, 24), namely, idolatry and immorality. Nevertheless, God gave her "time to repent." And even in the days of Noah, "when the wickedness of man was great on the earth, and every imagination of the thoughts of his heart was only evil continually" (Gen. 6:5), "the patience of God waited" (I Peter 3:20). Other examples of patience shown to sinners, "handing them over to Satan" *in order that this disciplinary action might lead them to repentance,* are found in I Cor. 5:5 and I Tim. 1:20. And the fact that also in the Romans 1 context God had revealed himself to the wicked, so that they might turn to him, is clear not only from the immediate context (Rom. 1:19-21) but also from 2:15.

It is not surprising, therefore, that it has been suggested that also here in Rom. 1:24, 26, 28, the divine relinquishment is of the same merciful character, a smiting *in order to heal* (Isa. 19:22).[39]

Unquestionably recognition of this divine patience is proper in connection with the study of Rom. 1:18-25. Nevertheless, justice must be done also to the other side of the picture. Mercy unrequited produces wrath. Divine patience without favorable response on the part of man results in the outpouring of divine indignation. Honesty in exegesis compels one to admit that verse 24 is part of a paragraph that is introduced by a reference to "the wrath of God" (verse 18). What the present verse (24) holds before us, therefore, is the fact that at the proper time—known only to God— impenitent sinners are by that wrath allowed to be swept away by their own sins into the pit of their vile passions. *By a positive action of God's will they are finally abandoned.*

39. So, for example, Cranfield, *op. cit.,* p. 121.

Speaking about the uncleanness or "impurity" (II Cor. 12:21; Gal. 5:19; Eph. 5:3; I Thess. 4:7) into which these sinners have plunged themselves "so that their bodies were dishonored among themselves" (for explanation see on verses 26, 27), Col. 3:5, 6 states, "Put to death therefore y o u r members that (are) upon the earth: immorality, impurity, passion, evil desire, and greed, which is idolatry, *on account of which things the wrath of God is coming.*" Though the outpouring of this wrath in all its fulness is a matter of the future ("eschatological"), a foretaste is by the impenitent experienced even here and now. God finally abandons them, allowing them to perish in their own wickedness.

25. ... **since they had indeed exchanged God, (who is) the truth, for a lie, and worshiped and served the creature rather than**[40] **the Creator, who is blessed forever. Amen.**

Verse 25, which must probably be considered a modifier of verse 24, resumes the thought of verse 23. Similarly verse 26 is an elaboration of verse 24.

The fact that in verses 21-23 a reason had already been given for the divine abandonment mentioned in verse 24, by no means rules out the possibility that this reason is in essence repeated here in verse 25, especially since this verse is not a *mere* repetition but an elaboration in which a new thought is added (see the final clause of verse 25).[41]

The translation as here proposed[42] brings out the chiastic parallelism of the original:

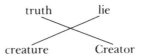

That God, the Creator, should be called "the truth" is not strange. See John 14:6(cf. Ps. 31:5; Isa. 65:16). Neither is it strange that an idol, or any creature (sun, moon, stars, etc.) that is regarded as an object of worship, should be called "a lie." Isa. 44:20 describes a sculptor, who has made for himself a "god." He reaches out and takes hold of it, but fails to ask himself, "Is there not *a lie* in my right hand?" The LXX equivalent of the Hebrew word for "lie" is ψεῦδος. The idol is "a lie" because (in the imagination of the worshiper) it promises much; however, it provides nothing!

---

40. παρά, alongside of; i.e., compared to; here: rather (than), the idea being that they worshiped and served the creature *and not* the Creator. For a similar use of παρά see Luke 18:14.

41. This, it would seem to me, is better than starting a new paragraph with verse 25. The doxology at the close of that verse is a fitting conclusion of the little paragraph—but see also Cranfield, who favors the opposite view, stating his reasons on p. 123 of his commentary.

42. Note "God (who is) the truth." (One might also say "the true God." See N.E.B.) This is better than "the truth of (or about) God," for it is clear that in this chiastic parallelism τὴν ἀλήθειαν τοῦ θεοῦ is a synonym of τὸν κτίσαντα; as is τῷ ψεύδει of τῇ κτίσει. The genitive τοῦ θεοῦ is one of *apposition*. It is not possessive.

What Paul is saying, then, is this: they (the Gentiles, etc.) *worshiped* (i.e., adored, revered) and *served* (rendered cultic service to) the creature rather than the Creator, and therefore deserved the punishment described in verse 24.

At the mention of God, the Creator, the apostle adds a doxology, strictly speaking a benediction: "who is blessed forever. Amen." Commentators remind us that this was a Jewish custom when God's name was mentioned. Nevertheless, anyone who has made a study of Paul's life, as revealed to us in his epistles and in the book of Acts, is bound to agree that for this apostle a benediction, or in general a doxology, was not uttered merely out of custom. Rather, when Paul reflects on God, to whom he owes so very much, he shrinks back in revulsion at the thought that there are those who, in their religious practices, substitute a mere creature for that wonderful God who has done so much for him, the former bitter persecutor. Every reported Pauline benediction or doxology is sincere and soulful. In addition to the benediction reported in Rom. 1:25 study also those found in Rom. 9:5; II Cor. 1:3, 11:31; Eph. 1:3f. And see Luke 1:68, I Peter 1:3. For other praise exclamations or doxologies see Rom. 11:36; 16:25-27; II Cor. 9:15; Eph. 3:20, 21.

The apostle concludes this little paragraph by adding a wholehearted and worshipful *Amen* to the benediction he has uttered just now. It is a word of solemn affirmation and enthusiastic approval. For more about this word *Amen* see N.T.C. on Matthew, pp. 290, 291, and on John, Vol. I, pp. 110, 111.

26, 27. Because of this, God gave them over to passions that bring dishonor. For as well as their females [or women] exchanged natural intercourse for that (which is) contrary to nature, so likewise also the males [or men], having abandoned natural intercourse with the female [or woman], were consumed by flaming passion for one another, males with males [or men with men] perpetrating shamelessness, and receiving in their own persons the due return for their deviation.[43]

---

43. Note τε ... τε: as ... so; not only ... but also; as well as ... so likewise. The rendering "even their women" (A.V. and some commentators) cannot be recommended.

θήλειαι, nom. pl. f. of θῆλυς, female. See also Matt. 19:4; Mark 10:6; Gal. 3:28. In certain contexts the word, however, can be rendered "woman."

χρῆσις (here acc. s. -v), use, usefulness, but in the present context: sexual intercourse. Secular Greek also employs the term in that sense. For example Xenophon, in his ΣΥΜΠΟΣ-ΙΟΝ (*Banquet*) 8.28, writes, "Not only human beings but also gods and demigods set a higher value on friendship of the spirit than on τὴν τοῦ σώματος χρῆσιν, "use of the body," that is, sexual intercourse. Similar examples of χρῆσις in the sense of "sexual relations" can be found in the writings of Plato, Plutarch, Isocrates, etc.

ἐξεκαύθησαν, third per. pl. aor. indicat. pass. of ἐκκαίομαι, to be inflamed; only here in the New Testament. But compare I Cor. 7:9, though the "burning" mentioned there is of a different character: in a sense it is not "contrary to nature."

ὀρέξει, dat. s. of ὄρεξις, ardent longing, lust; cf. ὀρέγω, to desire eagerly, reach out after (I Tim. 3:1; I Tim. 6:10; Heb. 11:16).

ἀσχημοσύνη (here acc. s. -v), in the New Testament used only here and in Rev. 16:15. The

The connection between verse 26 and verse 25 is the same as that between verse 24 and verses 22, 23. In each case the sin is mentioned first, then the result. Now Paul no longer dwells on sexual immorality in general, as in verse 24, but becomes specific, and focuses the attention on one of its most disgusting manifestations, namely, wilful homosexuality.

For "God gave them over" see on verse 24.

". . . to passions that bring dishonor." Here we find an echo of verse 24b: "so that their bodies were dishonored among themselves."

". . . their females exchanged natural intercourse for that (which is) contrary to nature." This "exchange" reminds us of the "exchange" mentioned in verses 23 and 25: ". . . the glory of the immortal God for an image . . ."; "God (who is) the truth, for a lie."

It is clear that the apostle is censuring the wilful practice of homosexuality or sodomy. And, indeed, Scripture does not make light of this vice. In Lev. 20:13 the death penalty is pronounced upon its perpetrators. For more information on this horrible evil read Gen. 19:4-9; Lev. 18:22; 20:13; Deut. 23:17, 18; Judg. 19:22-24; I Kings 14:24; 15:12; 22:46; II Kings 23:7; Isa. 3:9; Lam. 4:6; and see also I Cor. 6:9, 10; Eph. 4:19; I Tim. 1:10; II Peter 2:6; Jude 7.

A person's sexual orientation, whether heterosexual or homosexual is not the point at issue. What matters is what a person does with his sexuality!

According to the plain teaching of Scripture sexual intercourse was intended for a husband and his wife, for no one else! (Gen. 2:24). See also Matt. 19:5; Mark 10:7, 8; I Cor. 6:16; Eph. 5:31. All else is "contrary to God's will." It is in conflict with the Creator's intention.

It is not clear why homosexual relations between females (lesbianism) is condemned *before* illicit relations between males (pederasty). The only explanation that has any merit, as far as I can see, is the one according to which the apostle wanted to place special emphasis on the male-with-male perversion; hence, kept the condemnation of this vice for the close of the sentence, so that he would then be able to enlarge on it, since, of the two homosexual sins it was probably the most prevalent.

". . . males with males perpetrating shamelessness." Throughout the

---

word is derived from ἀ and σχῆμα; hence, "without (proper) form," deformed, shameful; and the noun as here used means shamelessness, indecent acts, improper behavior. In Rev. 16:15 it refers to a person's *shame:* that is, "private parts."

ἀντιμισθία (here acc. s. -v). From my dissertation on *The Meaning of the Preposition ἀντί in the New Testament,* p. 81, I quote the following:

"This word is used in a favorable sense in II Cor. 6:13; in an unfavorable sense in Rom. 1:27, the only two New Testament passages in which it occurs. The fact that the ἀντιμισθία is here regarded as a "return" or requital for a certain kind of action is clearly brought out by the addition of the words ἥν ἔδει in Rom. 1:27. The ἀντιμισθία is that which was due. Moreover, the base-word itself already suggests the idea of a return. Therefore the meaning of the preposition is clear."

πλάνης, gen. s. of πλάνη, wandering; cf. *planet:* "wandering star." What is meant in the present context is, accordingly, a wandering away (or deviation) from the proper course, a perversion.

apostle uses the terms *males* and *females* (thus literally). He stresses the distinction between the sexes, as is also done in the following passages: Gen. 1:27; 5:2; Lev. 12:7; 27:3-7; Num. 5:3; Matt. 19:4; Mark 10:6; Gal. 3:28. The rendering "men" and "women" is also possible. Nevertheless, the sins here condemned are committed not only by men and women, but also, at times, by "boys" and "girls."

". . . receiving in their own persons the due return for their deviation."

That this wicked practice results in a harvest of bitterness has been proved again and again and is being demonstrated every day of the year. Some of the fruits are: a guilty conscience, sleeplessness, emotional stress, depression. Moreover, such mental discord does not leave *the body* untouched. In his very interesting book *None of These Diseases*, Westwood, New Jersey, 1963, p. 60, Dr. S. M. McMillen informs us that according to a report published in 1948 two-thirds of the patients who went to a physician had symptoms caused or aggravated by mental stress.

Truly "God is not mocked. Whatever a person sows, that also he will reap. For he who sows to his own flesh [i.e., allows his old nature to have its own way] will from the flesh reap corruption, and he who sows to the Spirit [allowing the Spirit to rule over him] will from the Spirit reap life everlasting" (Gal. 6:7, 8. See also I Cor. 3:17; 6:19, 20; 10:31).

The best of all remedies against reaping the fruits of corruption is the practice of the kind of life described beautifully in such passages as Rom. 12; I Cor. 13; Gal. 5:22, 23; and Eph. 5.

28. And since they did not deem it worthwhile to retain the knowledge of God, he gave them over to (their) worthless disposition, to do what is improper...[44]

Here for the third and last time our attention is focused on the correlation between man's rejection of God and God's rejection of man. For the two previous references to this correlation see verses 24 and 26. Men's arrogance comes to the fore in the expression, "They did not deem it worthwhile to retain the knowledge of God," the very knowledge to which reference was made in verses 18-21; note especially, "For although they knew God" (verse 21). Instead of regarding this knowledge about God which they were deriving from his revelation in nature to be a precious

---

44. ἐδοκίμασαν, 3rd per. pl. aor. indicat. act. of δοκιμάζω. In certain contexts this verb means: to prove, test, examine (Rom. 12:2; I Peter 1:7; etc.). It may also mean: to approve (after testing), see fit; consider worthwhile. For this meaning see Rom. 14:22; I Cor. 16:3; and our present passage, Rom. 1:28.

ἀδόκιμον, not approved; hence, rejected, unable to pass the test, worthless, disqualified, unfit (Rom. 1:28; I Cor. 9:27; II Cor. 13:5-7; II Tim. 3:8; Titus 1:16; Heb. 6:8).

Note word-play: οὐκ ἐδοκίμασαν... ἀδόκιμον νοῦν: they did not approve, did *not* deem (it) *worthwhile... worthless* disposition.

On the meaning of the noun ἐπίγνωσις and the cognate verb ἐπιγινώσκω see the article by R. E. Picerelli in *E.Q.*, Vol. XLVII, April-June, 1975, pp. 85-93.

καθήκοντα, acc. pl. n. pres. participle of καθήκω (κατά plus ἥκω), to come down (to), to be becoming, proper; hence here τὰ μὴ καθήκοντα indicates the things that are not becoming, not proper; hence improper, indecent, immoral.

treasure, they were constantly attempting to suppress it (verse 18) and, as is stated here in verse 28, regarded it as a negligible entity. They did not deem it to be worthwhile to pay any attention to God and to his revelation. So they continued on their sinful way, as described in verses 21-27 (the way of idolatry and immorality). In fact, the improper things the apostle has in mind probably also covered those mentioned in verses 29-32. Note that an evil "disposition" or "mind" or "attitude" results in evil *deeds*.

29-31. ... having become filled with every kind of unrighteousness, wickedness, greed, depravity; being full of envy, murder, strife, deceit, and malice.

(They are) gossips, slanderers, haters of God, insolent, arrogant, boastful, inventors of (novel forms of) evil, disobedient to (their) parents, senseless, faithless, loveless, pitiless.

The list of vices mentioned in Rom. 1:29-31 should be compared with similar lists elsewhere in Paul's writings: Rom. 13:13; I Cor. 5:9-11; 6:9, 10; II Cor. 12:20, 21; Gal. 5:19-21; Eph. 4:19; 5:3-5; Col. 3:5-9; I Thess. 2:3; 4:3-7; I Tim. 1:9, 10; 6:4, 5; II Tim. 3:2-5; and Titus 3:3, 9, 10.

Whether there were factors other than identity of authorship (for example, already existing lists) that account for this resemblance is difficult to ascertain.

The most simple and logical way to divide the twenty-one vices mentioned in Rom. 1:29-31 is to list them in three groups:

a. one group of four vices (in the original each in the dat. s.), these four being introduced by the words "having become filled with every kind of";

b. one group of five vices (all in the gen. s.), introduced by "being full of"; and

c. one group of twelve items, beginning with "gossips."[45]

The final four items in this group of twelve form a kind of sub-group, each member beginning with ἀ-privative (equal to English prefix *un, dis-*, or suffix *-less*).

The 4-5-12 grouping is also accepted by Cranfield, Murray, Ridderbos, Robertson, etc.

It will be noticed that no longer is there any specific reference to sins of sex, since that subject has been fully treated in the preceding verses.[46]

GROUP OF FOUR

unrighteousness. See on verse 18.

wickedness. This describes those people who take delight in doing what is wrong.

---

45. In the original πεπληρωμένους is in apposition with αὐτούς in verse 28. Also in apposition is the entire third group, beginning with *gossips* (literally "whisperers").
46. There is no textual justification for the insertion of the word πορνείᾳ ("fornication" A.V.) in verse 29.

greed. This is covetousness, over-reaching, the craving for more and more and still more possessions, no matter how they are obtained. At times, as in Eph. 5:3, the word applies to ravenous self-assertion in matters of sex, at the expense of others.

depravity. This is badness in general. It is hard to distinguish it from wickedness.

GROUP OF FIVE

envy.[47] This is the keen displeasure aroused by seeing someone having something which you begrudge him.

murder. Envy often leads to murder. This was true in the case of Cain who murdered Abel (Gen. 4:1-8; I John 3:12). It was true also with respect to those who demanded Christ's crucifixion (Matt. 27:18; Mark 15:10). And was it not envy that caused the brothers of Joseph to plan his death? See Gen. 37:4, 18.

strife. This refers to a quarrelsome disposition and its consequences.

deceit. This is cunning, treachery.

malice. This indicates malignity, spite, the desire to harm people.

GROUP OF TWELVE

gossips. The "whispering" slanderers are meant. They do not—perhaps do not dare to—come out in the open with their vilifying chatter, but whisper it into someone's ear.

slanderers. What the gossips do *secretly,* the slanderers do *openly.*

haters of God. The word used in the original more often refers to those who are hated by God. However, the word is also used at times, as it is here, to indicate those who hate God.

insolent. See also I Tim. 1:13. This marks overweening individuals. They treat others with contempt, as if *they* (these insolent ones) and *they alone,* amounted to anything, and all others amounted to nothing.

arrogant. These fellows consider themselves "supermen."

boastful. Such people are constantly bragging about themselves. Think of Lamech (Gen. 4:23, 24), of Sennacherib (II Chron. 32: 10-14); and of those described in Isa. 10:8-11; 14:13, 14.

inventors of (novel forms of) evil. The reference is to those who take special delight in inventing "original" methods of destroying their fellowmen.

disobedient to (their) parents. Read Exod. 20:12; Lev. 19:3; Prov. 20:20; Matt. 15:4; 19:19; Eph. 6:2.

And now the little sub-group of four:

senseless.[48] These are the people that are "void of understanding." But this is not merely a mental weakness; it is also a moral blemish. They are

---

47. Note the sound-similarity in the original between φθόνου (envy) and φόνου (murder).

48. Note assonance (in the original) between this and the next item: ἀσυνέτους, ἀσυνθέτους.

stupid because they have all along been unwilling to listen to God! See
Matt. 15:16; Mark 7:18; Rom. 10:19 (cf. Deut. 32:2).

faithless. They are "not true to the covenant," hence are perfidious, not to
be trusted. See Ps. 73:15; 78:57; 119:158.

loveless. The meaning is: without natural affection. It was not at all unusual
for pagans to drown or in some other way to destroy unwanted offspring. In this connection think of present-day *abortion,* for which all
kinds of excuses are being invented.

pitiless. The reference is to people without mercy, cruel persons, ruthless
ones. Think not only of *the robbers* in the parable of *The Samaritan Who
Cared* (Luke 10), but also of *the priest* and *the Levite,* the two who "passed
by on the other side."

**32. And although they know the ordinance of God that those who
practice such things are worthy of death, they not only continue to do
them but also approve of those who practice them.**

What Paul is saying is that the perpetrators of the crimes, either implied
or expressed in verses 29-31, must not be regarded as being so innocent
that they cannot distinguish between right and wrong. On the contrary,
they know—have an awareness of the fact—that according to God's ordinance, his decree, those who practice such vices are worthy of death.

How do they know this? They know it because a righteous and holy God
has revealed himself to them in nature (1:21) and in conscience (2:14, 15);
in fact, is constantly doing this. Accordingly, they sense the fact that God
will call them to account, and that continuing in their evil way will result in
perdition for them. Nevertheless, in spite of this awareness, they not only
continue to practice these vices and to perpetrate these crimes but even
applaud others who do the same.

There are those who see a problem here; as if the apostle were saying
that rejoicing to see other people engage in wickedness while you yourself
abstain is even more wicked than taking part in such evil practices yourself.
Having created this problem, they then try to solve it.

But is it not true that what Paul is actually saying is that those who *not only*
practice these vices *but also* applaud others who engage in them are even
worse than those who simply practice them? For example, a person might
commit a wicked deed. Afterward he is sorry. Perhaps he even warns
others. But here is another person who not only commits evil and continues
to do so, but who *in addition* encourages others to copy his example,
applauding them when they do so. Certainly such an individual has
reached the climax of perversity.

Having reached the close of the chapter, and looking back, we should not
forget that Paul's real purpose in writing it was to show that man's (here
particularly the Gentile's) wickedness is so great that only God is able to
rescue him. Only when man accepts the divinely appointed way of salvation, namely, that of embracing God by faith, can he be saved. To God
alone be the glory!

Practical Lessons Derived from Romans 1

Verse 1

"Paul . . . a called apostle, one set apart for the gospel of God." It was God who called Paul and who set him apart for his special task. Does not this prove that, in the final analysis, Romans is *God's* letter addressed to the church and individual believer in every age? And does not this knowledge make the epistle even more precious?

Verse 4

"the Son of God *invested with power,* namely, Jesus Christ our Lord."
The fact that there are no limits to that power, and the additional fact that it is exercised in our interest—note "*our* Lord"—should comfort us in every trial, so that, with the author of Hebrews (2:9), we exclaim, " . . . But we see Jesus . . . crowned with glory and honor."

Verse 7

"Grace to y o u and peace," etc.
When a person becomes a Christian everything changes. Even the manner in which he greets people is transformed. See the explanation of this verse.

Verses 8, 9, 11, 15

" . . . *my* God . . . whom I serve *from the heart* . . . I *am yearning* to see y o u . . . hence my *eagerness* to preach the gospel also to y o u in Rome."
Many people get "all excited" about picnics or sports. Paul is "excited" about God. Note his enthusiasm and eagerness in the quoted expressions.

Verse 11

" . . . in order that I may impart . . ."
Paul knew that the Christian's business in life is "to impart," that is, to be a blessing.

Verse 12

"I mean that . . . we may be mutually encouraged by each other's faith, both y o u r s and mine."
The apostle is also convinced that even the lowliest child of God can impart something to him (Paul).

Verses 16, 17

" . . . to everyone who exercises faith . . . from faith to faith . . . shall live by faith."
Again and again Paul mentions faith, looking away from oneself for salvation, and looking to God to receive it as a gift.
From the Translator's Preface of my translation of Dr. Herman Bavinck's work on *The Doctrine of God* (published by that title, in paperback, Grand Rapids, 1977) I quote the following:

" 'My learning does not help me now; neither does my Dogmatics; faith alone saves me.'

"These remarkable words, uttered by one of the greatest Reformed theologians, Dr. Herman Bavinck, should not be misinterpreted. They were uttered on his death-bed and did not imply that this humble child of God retracted anything that he had written, or that he was trying to express regrets. The statement simply means that a system of doctrine, however necessary and valuable, is of no avail in and by itself. It must be translated into Christian living. There must be genuine faith in the Triune God as manifested in Jesus Christ. Now, Dr. Bavinck was, indeed, a man of faith, a faith which in his case was working through love."

Verse 18

"For the wrath of God is being revealed from heaven against all ungodliness and unrighteousness . . ."

The attempt to downgrade God's wrath is foolish. That wrath should fill our hearts with joy and satisfaction, for if God's wrath did not blaze against sin, how could he be a holy God? And how would it be possible for a God lacking the quality of holiness to save us?

Besides, we insist on drastic measures against crime, and on the appointment or election of judges and officers who do not think lightly of crime. Is it consistent, then, to expect that the evil practice which fills the minds and hearts of decent men with horror and indignation should leave *God* untouched? Therefore, instead of trying to minimize the reality of God's wrath, should we not rather thank him for his marvelous plan whereby the Son of God bore the wrath of God in our stead?

Verses 21–32

"For although they knew God, they neither glorified him as God nor gave thanks to him . . . they exchanged the glory of God for an image . . . Therefore God . . . gave them over to sexual immorality . . . to passions that bring dishonor . . . They not only practice such (wicked) things but also approve of those who practice them."

Notice that sin begets sin. Apart from God's grace the sinner descends lower and lower on the ladder of evil. The lesson: *Avoid the first downward step.* By God's grace and power, keep clinging to God and to his will for our lives, as revealed in Scripture.

Summary of Chapter 1

In what may be called a Prologue or Introduction, Paul, a servant of Christ Jesus, and a called apostle, pronounces his official salutation upon the members of the church located in Rome, the empire's capital (verses 1–7).

The apostle expresses his elation over the fact that the faith of these Romans is being proclaimed everywhere, and he tells them that he is asking God to grant him the opportunity to visit them soon (verses 8–15).

He then announces what may, in a qualified sense, be termed his *theme,* namely, "the gospel is the power of God for salvation to everyone who exercises faith." In other words, justification, which is basic to salvation, is by faith alone. This great truth was by divine direction proclaimed first of all to the Jews, and is now also to be made known to the Gentiles. In confirmation of the theme Paul adds the words found in Hab. 2:4b, "But the righteous shall live by faith." All this is found in Rom. 1:16, 17.

Having stated that the way of salvation is the same for everyone, namely, by faith alone, Paul now divides the human race into two groups: Gentiles and Jews.

He first of all describes the conditions existing in the Gentile world. He shows that although God, by means of his general revelation, made himself known to the Gentiles, "they neither glorified him as God nor gave thanks to him" (verses 18-21). Instead of worshiping the one true God, they became idol worshipers (verses 22, 23). As a result God at last abandoned them (verses 24, 26, 28) to their own sinful practices, including not only wilful homosexuality (verses 24-27) but also many other vices, twenty-one of which are mentioned in verses 29-31.

The chapter closes on this dismal note: "And although they know the ordinance of God that those who practice such things are worthy of death, they not only continue to do them but also approve of those who practice them" (verse 32).

Outline (continued)

Justification by Faith

3. *The Jews also need this justification.*
"Therefore you have no excuse, O man, whoever you are,
when you pass judgment (on someone else), . . . because you,
the judge, are practicing the same things."
2:1—3:8

CHAPTER 2:1—3:8

2 1 Therefore you have no excuse, O man, whoever you are, when you pass judgment (on someone else), for at whatever point you judge the other person, you are condemning yourself, because you, the judge, are practicing the same things.

2 Now we know that God's judgment is justly pronounced[49] against those who practice such things. 3 And do you imagine—you who, though you pass judgment on those who practice these things, do the same things yourself—that you will escape God's judgment? 4 Or do you look down on the riches of his kindness, forbearance, and patience, not realizing that God's kindness seeks to bring you to conversion?

5 But by your hard and unconverted heart[50] you are storing up for yourself wrath in the day of wrath and of the revelation of the righteous judgment of God, 6 who will render to every person according to his deeds. 7 To those who, by perseverance in doing what is right, are seeking glory, honor, and immortality (he will give) life everlasting, 8 but for those who are filled with selfish ambition and who disobey the truth but obey unrighteousness (there will be) wrath and anger. 9 (There will be) affliction and distress for every human being who is an evil-doer; first for the Jew, also for the Greek; 10 but glory, honor, and peace for everyone who does what is good; first for the Jew, also for the Greek; 11 for God does not show partiality.[51]

12 For all who have sinned in ignorance of the law [or: apart from the law] will perish even though they do not know the law [or: will perish apart from the law]; and all who have sinned knowing the law [or: under the law] will be judged by the law. 13 For it is not the hearers of the law who are righteous in God's sight, but it is the doers of the law who will be pronounced righteous. 14 For when Gentiles who do not possess the law do by nature things required by the law, they are a law for themselves, even though they do not have the law, 15 since they show that the work required by the law is written on their hearts, their consciences also bearing witness, and their thoughts between themselves now accusing, now even defending them. 16 (All this will become clear) on the day when, according to my gospel, God, through Jesus Christ, will judge men's secrets.

17 Now you, if you call yourself a Jew, and rely on (the) law, and brag about your relationship to God, 18 and, being instructed out of the law, know (his) will, and approve the things that really matter;[52] 19 and if you are convinced that you are a guide for the blind, a light for those in darkness, 20 an instructor of the foolish, a teacher of the immature,[53] because in the law you have the embodiment of knowledge and truth—21 you, then, who teach someone else, don't you teach yourself? You who preach that people should not steal, do you steal? 22 You who say that people should not commit adultery, do you commit adultery? You who

---

49. Literally: is according to truth.
50. Or: hardness and unconverted heart.
51. Literally: for there is no partiality with God.
52. Or: the things that are excellent.
53. Or: of infants.

abhor idols, do you rob temples? 23 You who brag about the law, do you dishonor God by (your) transgression of the law? 24 As it is written,
"Because of y o u the name of God is being
blasphemed among the Gentiles."
25 Circumcision does indeed profit, but only if you put the law into practice. But if you are a transgressor of the law, your circumcision has become uncircumcision. 26 Therefore, if the uncircumcised man keeps the requirements of the law, will not his uncircumcision be regarded as circumcision? 27 Indeed, he who is physically uncircumcised but keeps the law will condemn you, who, though provided with the written code and circumcision, are a transgressor of the law. 28 For he is not a (real) Jew who is one only on the outside, nor is (true) circumcision something external and physical. 29 But he is a (real) Jew who is one inwardly; and (real) circumcision is a matter of the heart, by the Spirit, not by the written code. Such a person's praise is not from man but from God.

3:1 What advantage, then, does the Jew have, or what is the value of circumcision?
2 Much in every respect. First of all, they have been entrusted with the oracles of God. 3 And what if some (of them) were unfaithful? Their unfaithfulness does not nullify God's faithfulness, does it? 4 By no means! Let God be true, and every person a liar. As it is written:
"That thou mayest be proved right in thy words
And prevail in thy judging."
5 But if our unrighteousness confirms God's righteousness, what shall we say? The God who inflicts wrath is not unrighteous, is he? (I speak from a human standpoint.) 6 By no means! For then how could God judge the world? 7 (Someone might object) "If through my falsehood God's truthfulness is enhanced to his glory, why am I still being condemned as a sinner?" 8 Why not say—as we are being slanderously reported and some claim that we say—"Let us do evil that good may result"? Their condemnation is deserved.

---

3. *The Jews also need this justification.*
"Therefore you have no excuse, O man, whoever you are,
when you pass judgment (on someone else), . . . because you,
the judge, are practicing the same things."
2:1—3:8

1. Therefore you have no excuse, O man, whoever you are, when you pass judgment (on someone else), for at whatever point you judge the other person, you are condemning yourself, because you, the judge, are practicing the same things.

Many are puzzled by the word "Therefore" (or "Wherefore"). It must be admitted that its meaning is not immediately clear. The following interpretation, however, seems to be supported by the preceding context: "Since it has been established (1:18-32) that the immoral practices of the Gentiles are an abomination to God, *therefore* you, too, whoever you may be, are without excuse when you practice these same evils, the very vices you condemn in others."

The question might be asked, "But does not the description of the evil practices of the Gentiles prove that Jew and Gentile differed considerably in their manner of life?" It has already been admitted that, on the whole, that is true. See on 1:18. It is true, however, only in a certain sense. For example, the Gentiles were idolaters. But many a Jew, by means of his self-righteousness, was making an idol of *himself.* Many a Gentile refused to repent. But so, in his own way, did many a Jew. Besides, as the apostle shows in 2:21-23, many specific sins were committed by both Jew and Gentile, by each in his own way.

We now understand what the apostle means when he says, ". . . at whatever point you judge the other person, you are condemning yourself, for you, the judge, are practicing the same things." Before we leave this passage (to which we shall return again in our Practical Lessons) we must not fail to notice how closely Paul's reasoning approaches that of Jesus. See Matt. 7:1-4; Luke 6:41, 42.

2. Now we know that God's judgment is justly pronounced [or: is according to truth] against those who practice such things.

For the expression "*we* know" or "*we* agree"—that is, "y o u, who read or hear this, and *I,* the writer, agree"—see also 3:19; 7:14; 8:22, 28; II Cor. 5:1; I Tim. 1:8.

Though this statement is, of course, meant for everyone who reads or listens to the reading of Romans, as, in a sense, is true of everything in Scripture, it was intended especially for the Jews, specifically mentioned in verses 9, 10, 17, 28, 29; 3:1, 9. They were the very people who were always bragging about the fact that they *possessed* the "law" (God's special revelation reduced to writing, what we today call the Old Testament), as if mere *possession* made them better than any other people. So the apostle reminds them of the fact that self-righteous people will not escape the judgment. What God requires is that we *do* the things he commands.

Do these people think, perhaps, that because the hour of the final accounting has not yet arrived, they can afford to ignore the divine warnings?

"God's judgment is justly pronounced," that is, it is ever in line with absolute truth and justice. That is by no means always the case with respect to human evaluations. "I'm six feet tall," exclaimed the little boy. When his father asked him how he had arrived at this conclusion, he replied, "I found a stick as big as myself, and I divided it into six equal parts, calling each part a foot. That makes me just as tall as you are: six feet." We smile about the argumentation of the little fellow, but do we not often make ourselves guilty of similar reasoning: measuring ourselves and others by our own measuring rod? The result is often a too favorable estimate of ourselves, and a too harsh judgment of others.

The point Paul makes is that in the final analysis human judgments, whether about ourselves or about others, do not count. God's judgment, on the other hand, is inescapable:

3. And do you imagine—you who, though you pass judgment on those who practice these things, do the same things yourself—that you will escape God's judgment?

The implication is clear. II Cor. 5:10 expresses it in these words, "For we must all appear in our true character before the judgment seat of Christ, so that each one may receive what is due him for the things done (while he was) in the body, whether it be good or whether it be worthless." It is clear that no one can escape this judgment.

Paul continues **4. Or do you look down on the riches of his kindness, forbearance, and patience, not realizing that God's kindness seeks to bring you to conversion?**

One reason for a sense of security—false security, of course—has been given, namely, "Being a Jew, I am in possession of God's holy law." Now a second reason for this baseless tranquility is added, namely, "I have not been abandoned by God to a life of scandalous immorality (1:22-32); therefore it must be that God's kindness (or goodness, generosity), forbearance, and patience (or longsuffering) are still smiling upon me. He must be very pleased with me." For more on "forbearance" see on 3:25 and compare 8:32.

The apostle, on the other hand, reminds the self-righteous Jew that the purpose of God's *kindness*—here probably representing all the three previously mentioned qualities—is not at all to make him feel self-satisfied but rather to bring him to *conversion*. When the Jew reflects on the vices of the Gentiles he should bear in mind that even if it should be true that he does not have any of them, he has nothing to brag about. The absence of any number of pagan vices does not constitute even a single virtue. Not even a billion zeros make a single plus. What the Jew should do is this: he should constantly remember that God's aim in being so kind to him is to bring him to *conversion*.

The rendering *repentance* is not the best, although sorrow for sin is certainly included in what Paul has in mind. Repentance may be called the negative aspect of conversion. The positive aspect is reaching out to God by means of genuine trust and wholehearted surrender. Conversion indicates a complete turnabout: from Satan to God; from sin to holiness. See II Cor. 7:8-10; II Tim. 2:25. It is the frame of mind, heart, and will of the person who says,

> Other refuge have I none;
> Hangs my helpless soul on thee.[54]

> Lines from "Jesus Lover of My Soul"
> by Charles Wesley

Note the piquant contrast between the arrogant disposition of the self-righteous Jew, who resists conversion, and the kindness of God that seeks to bring him to conversion. For the divine qualities here mentioned see also the following passages: Gen. 18:22-33; Exod. 34:6; Num. 14:18; Neh. 9:17; Ps. 86:15; 103:8; 145:8; Isa. 1:18; 55:6, 7; Ezek. 18:23, 32; 33:11;

---

54. On μετάνοια (verse 4) and ἀμετανόητος (verse 5) see J. Behm's article in Th.D.N.T., Vol. IV, pp. 975-1009; B. B. Warfield, *Biblical and Theological Studies*, Philadelphia, 1954, p. 366; and W. D. Chamberlain, *The Meaning of Repentance*, Philadelphia, 1943, p. 22.

Hos. 11:8; Joel 2:13; Jon. 4:2; Mic. 7:18, 19; Nah. 1:3; Luke 13:8; II Peter 3:9. Also see N.T.C. on Luke, pp. 76, 696, 697.

5-8. But by your hard and unconverted heart you are storing up for yourself wrath in the day of wrath and of the revelation of the righteous judgment of God, who will render to every person according to his deeds. To those who, by perseverance in doing what is right, are seeking glory, honor, and immortality (he will give) life everlasting, but for those who are filled with selfish ambition and who disobey the truth but obey un-righteousness (there will be) wrath and anger.

Over against the delusion of those who were constantly condemning others but refusing to be converted (verses 3, 4) the apostle now reveals the true situation. He informs them that even though the wrath of God may not as yet have reached the Jew in the manner in which it had already been revealed to the Gentile, this does not mean that it will never be poured out on him. It merely indicates that for a while his (the Jew's) punishment is being suspended. All the while, however, that wrath is, as it were, piling up. This must be true, for the sin of the Jew is very grievous. To describe it the apostle uses the expression, "your hardness and unconverted heart." But in this case we must probably link "hardness" with "heart," as Scripture does so often. For the Old Testament see Deut. 10:16; Prov. 28:14; Ezek. 3:7; and for the New Testament Matt. 19:8; Mark 3:5; 6:52; 8:17; 10:5; John 12:40; Heb. 3:8, 15; 4:7. Thus we arrive at the phrase "your hard and unconverted heart."[55]

It should be noted that the person whom Paul addresses is himself the agent in piling up wrath for himself. Moreover, the wrath is that of God, as in 1:18, but in the present case the pouring out of this wrath is connected with, and takes place on, "the day of wrath and of the revelation of the righteous judgment of God," that is, on *the day of the final judgment.* Though some (for example, K. Barth) reject this explanation, it is supported by the following arguments.

a. The broader context (verse 16) favors it. Note, "(All this will become clear) on the day when, according to my gospel, God, through Jesus Christ, will judge men's secrets."

b. In fact, the *immediate* context (verse 6) describes this day as the one in which God "will render to every person according to his deeds." This reminds one of Matt. 16:27, "For the Son of man shall come in the glory of his Father, with his angels, and then shall he render to each according to his deeds."

c. See also the following passages:

I Cor. 3:13 ("the day")

I Cor. 4:3-5

---

55. For this construction see also Behm in the article to which reference was made in the preceding footnote; p. 1009, footnote 3.

I Thess. 5:4 ("that day")

II Thess. 1:7-10

II Tim. 4:8.

The day of *wrath* (see on 1:18) is the same time the day of "the revelation of the *righteous* judgment of God." Here the truth mentioned in verse 2, namely, that God's judgment is "according to truth" is essentially repeated. Among men judgments are by no means always "righteous."

The fact that every person will be judged "according to his deeds" is taught throughout Scripture (Eccl. 11:9; 12:14; Matt. 16:27; 25:31-46; John 5:28, 29; I Cor. 3:12-15; 4:5; II Cor. 5:10; Gal. 6:7-9; Eph. 6:8; Rev. 2:23; 11:18; 20:12, 13).

The question has been asked, however, "If God judges people 'according to their deeds,' how can salvation be 'by grace alone'?" Now it should be emphasized that the line "Naught have I gotten but what I received" (James M. Gray) is thoroughly scriptural. Salvation is indeed by grace alone (Ps. 115:1; Isa. 48:11; Jer. 31:31-34; Ezek. 36:22-31; Dan. 9:19; Acts 15:11; Rom. 3:24; 5:15; Eph. 1:4-7; 2:8-10; I Tim. 1:15, to mention only a few passages). Nevertheless, again and again when Paul emphasizes divine sovereignty or saving activity he immediately links it with human responsibility (Eph. 2:8-10; Phil. 2:12, 13; II Thess. 2:13; II Tim. 2:19). Granted that man cannot perform his duties or discharge his responsibilities in his own strength, it is nevertheless he to whom a task is assigned. God does not assume this task for him. But, in his sovereign grace and love, God rewards man for his faithfulness in accomplishing what has been assigned to him. Moreover, both rewards and punishments are distributed *in accordance with the degree of faithfulness or unfaithfulness* shown by anyone. In the final analysis it is the person who makes light of the thoroughly biblical doctrine of human responsibility who has any real problem.

In verses 7, 8 Paul divides mankind into two large groups, as Jesus had done again and again (Matt. 7:24-29; 10:39; 11:25, 26; 12:35; 13:41-43; 18:5, 6; 21:28-32; 23:12; 25:29, 46; etc.).

The first group consists of all who *persevere* (Matt. 24:13; Col. 1:23; Heb. 3:14; Rev. 2:10) in doing what is right; not *right* merely in the eyes of other people, a standard of measurement which the apostle has just now condemned (verses 1-3), but right in God's eyes. These are people whose aim is high (Phil. 3:8-14). By persevering in God-glorifying deeds they are aiming to obtain *glory* (see above on 1:23, item "a" in the list of Meanings), *honor,* and *immortality,* that is, incorruptible and indestructible resurrection life in never-ending bliss, that of the new heaven and earth (Rom. 8:23; I Cor. 15:42, 50-57; I Peter 1:4; II Peter 3:13; Rev. 21:1—22:5).

On them God will bestow *life everlasting,* the totality of that life which was already in principle their portion before death. On the day of the final judgment they receive this blessing in full measure for both soul and (as far as applicable) body.

And what is life everlasting? According to Scripture it is fellowship with God in Christ (John 17:3), possession of the peace of God that transcends all understanding (Phil. 4:7), joy inexpressible and full of glory (I Peter 1:8), the light of the knowledge of the glory of God in the face of Christ (II Cor. 4:6), and the love of God poured out into one's heart (Rom. 5:5), all of this to continue forever and ever.

The second group consists of those who are filled with selfish ambition. Instead of obeying the truth, they lend their ears to whatever is God-dishonoring. For them there will be wrath and anger; that is, on the day of the final judgment and forever afterward they will be the objects of God's keen displeasure and indignation. They will always be conscious of this, and will never be able to get out from under it.[56]

The sharp contrast between the everlasting destiny of the two groups, as portrayed here in Rom. 2:7, 8, can be compared with the similarly contrasting descriptions found in the book of Revelation:

A. The Blessedness of the Saved

"Never again shall they be hungry, and never again shall they be thirsty. The sun shall not beat down on them nor any heat, for the Lamb, sitting in the center of the throne, shall be their shepherd. He shall guide them to springs of living water, and God shall wipe away every tear from their eyes" (Rev. 7:16, 17).

B. The Wretchedness of the Lost

"The sound of harpists, musicians, flute players, and trumpeters shall be heard in you never again.

A workman in any trade shall be found in you never again.

The sound of a millstone shall be heard in you never again.

---

56. For ἐριθεία see L.N.T. (A. and G.), p. 309. In addition to its occurrence here in Rom. 2:8 this word is also found in II Cor. 12:20; Gal. 5:20; Phil. 1:17; 2:3; James 3:14, 16. Its meaning is disputed. If there is a connection between this word and ἔρις, the meaning might be strife, contentiousness, faction. On the other hand, if the word is derived from ἔριθος, a hireling, the meaning would be: the spirit of a hireling; hence, selfish ambition, selfishness (cf. John 10:12). In the present passage (Rom. 2:8), since man's everlasting destiny is at stake, the concept *selfishness* or *selfish ambition,* more basic than *contention,* may well be the meaning. In support of this theory it is generally pointed out that Aristotle in a couple passages of his work *Politics* uses the word in that more basic sense.

What may well be an even stronger argument in favor of the view that ἐριθεία = *selfish ambition* is the fact that both in Gal. 5:20 and in II Cor. 12:20 ἐριθεία is used in addition to ἔρις, which would probably not be the case if the meaning were identical. Also, it has been shown (see N.T.C. on Galatians, pp. 218, 220, and on Philippians, pp. 72, 100) that the rendering "selfish ambition" suits the context in Gal. 5:20 and Phil 1:17; 2:3. It also is in line with the context in II Cor. 12:20 and James 3:14, 16.

For the difference between ὀργή and θυμός see on 1:18. If, when these two words are used in connection with *God,* there is a difference in meaning, it would probably be that ὀργή stresses the *presence* or *feeling* of keen divine displeasure or indignation, while θυμός places the emphasis on its *effusion.*

The light of a lamp shall shine in you never again.
And the voice of bridegroom and bride shall be heard in you never
again" (Rev. 18:22, 23).

**9-11. (There will be) affliction and distress for every human being
who is an evil-doer; first for the Jew, also for the Greek; but glory, honor,
and peace for everyone who does what is good; first for the Jew, also for
the Greek; for God does not show partiality [or: for there is no partiality
with God].**

First a comment about the form, then about the meaning of this passage.

As to *form,* it is clear that the antithesis found in verses 7, 8 is reproduced
here in inverted order. This is true in two respects:

a. In verses 7, 8 the obedient were mentioned before the disobedient; in
verses 9, 10 the opposite is true.

b. In verses 7, 8 the description of the person (whether obedient or
disobedient) precedes the mention of the reward (7b) or punishment (8b).
The reverse is true with respect to verses 9, 10.

As to *meaning,* here in verses 9, 10 the fact is stressed that not what a
person imagines himself to be but what he actually is in God's sight, as
demonstrated by his life, his works, determines what will happen to him in
the final judgment. This holds for every "soul of man," that is, for every
living person.

For the evil-doer (verse 9) there will be *outward affliction* and *inward distress.* Cf. 8:35.

In connection with well-doers (verse 10), note that what according to
verse 7 God's people were seeking, namely, "glory and honor and *immortality,*" is also what they receive, namely, "glory and honor and *peace.*"
Here the terms "immortality" and "peace" may be viewed as being, at least
to a considerable extent, synonymous. See what was said in the preceding
about "immortality." The word "peace" should be interpreted in its
broadest sense, as indicating salvation full and free, joyful and never-
ending participation, with renewed soul and body, in all the blessings of the
new heaven and earth. This, of course, includes sweet fellowship with God
Triune and with all the redeemed. All this to God's glory!

Since in the order of history the Jews had received the gospel before the
Greeks or Gentiles, this order—first the Jew; then the Greek—will also be
taken into account in the final judgment. Neither with respect to punishment nor with respect to reward will the fact be lost sight of that the Jews
had been privileged far above the Gentiles (1:16; 3:1, 2; 9:4, 5).

This, however, must not be interpreted to mean that God will deal more
generously with the Jew than with the Gentile. On the contrary "God does
not show favoritism" (verse 11), a lesson Peter had to learn (Acts 10:34).

We are reminded of a passage from the lips of Jesus:

"From every one who has been given much, much will be required; and
from the one who has been entrusted with much, all the more will be
demanded" (Luke 12:48).

12, 13. For all who have sinned in ignorance of the law [or: apart from the law][57] will perish even though they did not know the law [or: will perish apart from the law]; and all who have sinned knowing the law [or: under the law] will be judged by the law. For it is not the hearers of the law who are righteous in God's sight, but it is the doers of the law who will be pronounced righteous.

The statement that every person will be judged according to his deeds (verses 6-11) receives clarification and augmentation in the present passage. The apostle underscores the fact that what counts both now and in the day of the Grand Assize is not whether people have possessed the law or have heard it read to them in the synagogue or elsewhere, but whether they have conducted their lives in harmony with its requirements.

Those who have sinned in ignorance of the law—cf. I Cor. 9:21—in other words, the Gentiles, will perish even though they did not know the law. That by using the word "law" the apostle is thinking especially of the Pentateuch, even more precisely, of the law of the Ten Commandments, is clear from verses 21, 22. Cf. Rom. 13:8-10. They will perish because of their *sins*. And, on the other hand, those who were privileged to possess and/or to hear the law must not think that this fact as such will be of any benefit to them before God. On the contrary, disobeying the law which is being constantly dinned into one's ears will make condemnation so much more severe. Not those who merely hear, but those who hear *and do* will be pronounced righteous.

A word of caution is necessary at this point. It must be borne in mind that at this juncture the apostle is not drawing a contrast between justification *by faith* and justification *by the works of the law.* Those who would so interpret

---

57. Twice in one verse the original uses the word ἀνόμως. It is related to the noun ἀνομία and to the adjective ἄνομος.

The noun, as it occurs in Matt. 7:23; 13:41; 23:28; 24:12; Rom. 6:19; II Cor. 6:14; Titus 2:14; Heb. 1:9 can be rendered "lawlessness" or "wickedness." In Rom. 4:7 it has reference to lawless deeds, offenses. "The man of lawlessness" (Antichrist) is mentioned in II Thess. 2:3, and "the mystery of lawlessness" in II Thess. 2:7. I John 3:4 states that "sin is lawlessness."

The adjective ἄνομος, in the sense of *lawless*, occurs in Luke 22:37 (gen. pl.): "He was numbered with the lawless ones," that is, "with the transgressors." Note also "By the hands of lawless (or wicked) men . . ." (Acts 2:23), and cf. I Tim. 1:9. II Peter 2:8 mentions "lawless deeds."

Nevertheless, with respect to Rom. 2:12 the rendering "All who have sinned *lawlessly*" would be the worst kind of tautology, since "sin is lawlessness," as has been indicated.

How, then, must we render the *adverb* ἀνόμως? It is clear that the meaning of the noun ἀνομία or of the adjective ἄνομος, as it is used in the passages cited in the preceding, does not help any. What will help is the use of the *adjective* in I Cor. 9:21. Here the rendering "I (became) lawless [that is wicked]" would be wrong. Paul cannot have meant that he became wicked to those who were wicked. The meaning must be, "To those without law (or: not having the law) I became as one without law (or: not having the law)." That passage supplies the key to the correct translation of the adverb ἀνόμως here in Rom. 2:12. The meaning is: "All who have sinned in ignorance of the law will perish even though they did not know the law; and all who have sinned knowing the law will be judged by the law." Here the first ἀνόμως (apart from the law) can be rendered "in ignorance of the law," and the second ἀνόμως must mean, and can be freely translated "though they did not know the law."

what he is saying would be making Paul contradict himself, for the very purpose of this letter is to show that a person is not justified by the works of the law but by faith in Christ. No, the antithesis he is discussing here in 2:12, 13 is that between two groups of people: (a) those who not only hear but also obey, and (b) those who merely hear. Cf. Matt. 7:24-29. It is, of course, the former who are pronounced righteous by God. Cf. Lev. 18:5, "If you obey them [my statutes] you shall live."

So interpreted, that rule holds even for those believers who are living in the new dispensation. Precisely because they have been delivered from the curse of the law, they are all the more deeply obliged not only to hear but also to obey the gospel. By their good deeds, resulting from gratitude, they show that by God's sovereign grace and power they have given their hearts to him. In him alone do they place their trust. From him they have received their status of being righteous in God's eyes.

When Paul discusses the antithesis: justification *by faith* or *by works* he will make very clear that it is not by works but by faith that a person is justified (Rom. 3:20, 28; 4:2; Gal. 2:16; 3:11, 12). See on 3:20, 28.

14, 15. For when Gentiles who do not possess the law do by nature things required by the law, they are a law for themselves, even though they do not have the law, since they show that the work required by the law is written on their hearts, their consciences also bearing witness, and their thoughts between themselves now accusing, now even defending them.

Some translators and commentators consider verses 14, 15 to be a parenthesis.[58] One of the reasons for this construction is that verse 15 does not seem to link naturally with verse 16.

The *objections* to the idea of a parenthesis beginning with verse 14 are:

a. The connection between verses 13 and 14 is too close to justify their arbitrary separation which such a parenthesis would bring about.[59]

b. Placing parentheses around verses 14, 15 does not solve the difficulty of getting rid of the seemingly unnatural connection—or lack of connection—between verses 15 and 16.

As I see it, the solution to the problem lies in the direction pointed out by J. Denney in his comments on verse 16; *The Expositor's Greek Testament* (on Romans), Vol. II, Grand Rapids, n.d., p. 598, and by Ridderbos on the page to which reference was made in the preceding footnote. Verse 16 should be linked with the main verbs of the entire little paragraph: God's righteous judgment *will be revealed* (verse 5); all who sin under the law *will be judged* (verse 12); while those who obey the law *will be declared righteous* (verse 13), all this is to take place and to become clear "on the day when . . . God will judge men's secrets" (verse 16). Somewhat similarly Rid-

---

58. A.V. includes even verse 13 in this parenthesis.
59. So also Ridderbos, *op. cit.*, p. 62. He describes the connection between verses 13 and 14 as a *natural* one.

derbos states that for the proper understanding of verse 16 one should preface its statement with "All this will become clear." See my translation. Similar is also the rendering of verse 16 found in Phillips, namely, "We may be sure that all this will be taken into account in the day," etc. What we have in verse 16 is almost surely a case of "abbreviated expression." On this subject see N.T.C. on John, Vol. I, p. 206.

So much for *the construction* of these verses. As to *the meaning* of verses 14, 15, note the following:

Paul has just now stated that whether a person sinned in ignorance of the law or knew the law—hence, whether he be Gentile or Jew—he will be treated as a transgressor if he conducts himself in a manner contrary to God's holy law. Every person will receive a penalty or a reward commensurate with his deeds (see verse 6). This does not cancel the fact that the measure of light one has received will be taken into account. See Amos 3:2; Luke 12:47, 48.

The objection might be raised, "But is this fair to the Gentile? After all, he does not have the faintest notion about God's law. Why, then, should he be punished at all?"

As shown in verses 14, 15, this objection is not valid. Even though the Gentile does not have the law as originally written on tablets of stone (Exod. 24:12), God wrote on his heart—for this idiom see Jer. 31:33; II Cor. 3:3—what was the work required by the law. He equipped him with a sense of right and wrong. He did not permit even the Gentile to remain altogether without a testimony concerning God. Cf. Ps. 19:1-4; Acts 17:26-28; Rom. 1:28, 32. This accounts for the fact that Gentiles are "a law for themselves." By nature—that is, without prompting or guidance coming from any written code, therefore in a sense spontaneously—a Gentile will at times do certain things required by God's law. For example, he is kind to his wife and children, has a heart for the poor, promotes honesty in government, shows courage in fighting crime, etc.

What God has written on his heart finds a response in this man's conscience. As the etymology of the word, both in Greek and in English (from Latin) implies, conscience is a *knowledge along with* (or shared with) the person. It is that individual's inner sense of right and wrong; his (to a certain extent divinely imparted) moral consciousness viewed in the act of pronouncing judgment upon himself, that is, upon his thoughts, attitudes, words, and deeds, whether past, present, or contemplated. As the passage states, the resulting *thoughts* or *judgments* are either condemnatory or, in certain instances, even commendatory. For more on conscience see 9:1; 13:5.[60]

---

60. τὸ ἔργον τοῦ νόμου. For similar construction see John 6:29, where "the work of God" means the work required by God, the work that is in harmony with his will.

Note the gen. absolute συμμαρτυρούσης αὐτῶν τῆς συνειδήσεως. The question has been asked, "What is the significance of the prefix σύν in the gen. s. fem. pres. participle συμμαρτυρούσης? Does conscience bear witness along with the thoughts? Along with the people? Or

16. (All this will become clear) on the day when, according to my gospel, God, through Jesus Christ, will judge men's secrets.

The connection between this verse and the preceding context has already been discussed. The meaning of verse 16, then, is along this line, that on Judgment Day "all this"—men's thoughts, words, actions, motivations, God's evaluations—will become clear. It is on that day that God will judge not only men's open deeds but even their secrets (Eccl. 12:14; Luke 12:3; I Cor. 4:5).

A few additional matters require our attention:

a. God will judge "through Jesus Christ."

It is true that in the original the modifier "through Jesus Christ" is far removed from "God will judge," and is much closer to "according to my gospel." It is for this reason that some commentators link "my gospel" with "through Jesus Christ." They reach the conclusion that what the apostle is really saying is that it was Jesus Christ who had entrusted him with the gospel. Now the fact as such that Paul had received the gospel from Christ is not only true but is even worthy of emphasis. See N.T.C. on Gal. 1:1. But this is definitely not the thought here in Rom. 2:16. Here, as frequently, the emphasis is on the fact that God will judge mankind through his Son, Jesus Christ. A passage which, in more than one respect, parallels Rom. 2:16 is I Cor. 4:5, "Therefore judge nothing before the appointed time. Wait until the Lord comes, who will both bring to light the things hidden in darkness and will expose the motives of men's hearts." Other passages in which the truth that God judges through Jesus Christ is taught, either directly or by implication, are Matt. 25:31-36; John 5:22; Acts 17:31; II Cor. 5:10.

b. Since "the darkness and the light are both alike to God" (Ps. 139:12), it should not sound strange that God, through Christ, will judge both what was done in the darkness and what was performed in open daylight.

c. Paul adds "according to my gospel." It was the apostle's gospel because in its fulness it had been conveyed to him by the Lord, and because he, Paul, loved it. Ponder his words, "Woe to me if I preach not the gospel (I Cor. 9:16)!" The good news is not complete without the very important

---

must we assume that although originally the prefix strengthened the meaning of the verbal form, its added strength gradually faded, as happened frequently in such cases, with the result that what Paul is saying is simply this, that the conscience of these people bore witness to that which God had written on their hearts?" This explanation probably deserves the preference.

Another gen. absolute is καὶ μεταξὺ ἀλλήλων τῶν λογισμῶν κτλ. Does this have reference to thoughts between Gentile and Gentile, or to thoughts between (or among) themselves? Probably the latter, for

a. The modifier "between themselves" stands closer to "thoughts" than to Gentiles. Unless there is a sound reason to do otherwise—as is sometimes the case; see on verse 16—it is generally best to link modifiers with words that stand closest to them, especially when, as in the present case, the resulting idea makes good sense.

b. It is indeed a fact that the thoughts that fill the mind as a result of the operation of conscience operate independently; in fact, so very independently that at times the involved person *hates* these thoughts or judgments. He may even rise in rebellion against them. He may curse the thoughts with which his conscience tortures him.

item with respect to the glorious day of Christ's Return unto Judgment, a day of supreme joy for every child of God. To mention a few examples of the importance the apostle attached to that second coming note the following: Rom. 8:18-23; I Cor. 15:20-58; Phil. 3:20, 21; I Thess. 1:10; 2:19, 20; 3:3:13; 4:13-18; 5:1-11, 23, 24; II Thess. 1:5-10; 2:1 f.; Titus 2:11-14.

Before leaving this important passage (Rom. 2:14-16) there is one more lesson to which I wish to call the reader's attention. That lesson is: *in our doctrinal views we should try to avoid extremes.*

Note how, by implication, Paul is teaching us this principle. He is in the process of establishing the thesis that there is only one way in which the sinner, whether Gentile or Jew, can attain to the status of being accepted by God. That way was opened by God himself. Gentiles need this "justification by faith" because "although they knew God, they did not glorify him as God, or give thanks." Jews also need it, for "they practice the same things." Both Gentile and Jew are by nature bad . . . bad . . . bad.

Yet, in the midst of this section the statement occurs, "Gentiles who do not possess the law do by nature the things required by the law." In other words, Paul is not forgetting that there is a sense in which it is legitimate to say that the unregenerate can do good.[61] God's image in man has not been completely destroyed.

This reminds us of Calvin, who similarly avoided extremes in writing about this same subject. In his *Institutes of the Christian Religion* (tr. by John Allen, Philadelphia, 1928, Vol. I, p. 264) he speaks about "the universal state of human depravity." Note also ". . . man is so enslaved by sin, as to be of his own nature incapable of an effort, or even an aspiration, toward that which is good" (p. 278). Nevertheless, he also states, "in all ages there have been some persons who, from the mere dictates of nature, have devoted their whole lives to the pursuit of virtue. . . . Some men have not only been eminent for noble actions, but have uniformly conducted themselves in a most virtuous manner throughout the whole course of their lives. But here we ought to remember that amidst the corruption of human nature there is some room for divine grace, not to purify it, but internally to restrain its operations" (pp. 262, 263).

When Aristotle gave the advice that people should eagerly render service to those in need (*The Nicomachean Ethics* IX. 6), and when he ordered that at

---

61. This follows unless one adopts the theory favored by K. Barth (going back even to Augustine), according to which the reference here in Rom. 2:14 is to Gentile Christians. See Barth's *Kirchliche Dogmatik*, Zollikon-Zurich, 1932, Vol. I, p. 332; and his *Shorter Commentary on Romans*, London, 1959, p. 36. Others who defend this view are F. Flückiger, in his article "Die Werke des Gesetzes bei den Heiden (nach Röm. 2:14ff.)," *ThZ* 1952, pp. 17-42; and Cranfield, *op. cit.,* p. 56.

Objections:

1. The passage clearly states that the Gentiles "by nature" perform these "things required by the law." This expression "by nature" must mean "before conversion."

2. The passage refers to Gentiles "who do not possess the law." This too, as 13:8, 9 and many other references indicate, cannot refer to Christians.

his death some of his slaves should be set free, was he not, in a sense, doing good? Does not the Old Testament record generous deeds performed by such Gentiles as Cyrus (Ezra 1:1-4; 5:13-17), Darius (6:1-12), and Artaxerxes (7:11-26)? Note what Ezra says about the deed of the latter (7:27, 28). II Chron. 24:20-22 does not leave the impression that King Joash was a child of God. Nevertheless, II Chron. 24:2 states, "And Joash did that which was right in the eyes of Jehovah all the days of Jehoiada the priest."

When the city clerk of Ephesus quieted the rioters (Acts 19:35-41), was not that to a certain extent a good deed? When Romans of high standing protected the apostle Paul (Acts 23:12-30; 27:43), was not that commendable? And the deed of those "barbarians" who "showed unusual kindness to Paul and those with him, building a fire and welcoming all because it was raining and cold" (Acts 28:2), was not also that a manifestation of "goodness"?

To be sure, man is by nature "totally depraved," in the sense that depravity has invaded every part of his being: mind, heart, and will. If he is to be saved it is God who must save him. Man cannot save himself. This, however, does not and cannot mean that he is "*absolutely* depraved," as bad as he can be, as bad as the devil himself. Did not also Jesus teach that there is a sense in which even the unconverted "do good"? See Luke 6:33.

The lesson Paul teaches—namely, *Avoid Extremes!*, should be taken to heart.

The remainder of chapter 2 can be divided into the following units:

a. A description of Jewish self-exaltation (verses 17-20), leading to:

b. A series of questions for self-examination. Paul asks how the Jews dare to accuse the Gentiles of sins they themselves commit (verses 21-23).

c. A grave accusation (verse 24).

d. A portrayal of the contrast between the true and the merely nominal Jew; and between heart circumcision and literal circumcision (verses 25-29).

A. *A Description of Jewish Self-Exaltation*

17-20. Now you, if you call yourself a Jew, and rely on (the) law, and brag about your relationship to God, and, being instructed out of the law, know (his) will, and approve the things that really matter [or: the things that are excellent]; and if you are convinced that you are a guide for the blind, a light for those in darkness, an instructor of the foolish, a teacher of the immature [or: of infants], because in the law you have the embodiment of knowledge and truth . . .

Although the Jews were uniquely privileged, enjoying advantages above all others, they did not seem to realize that these blessings implied obligations. Many of these people, instead of using their superior endowments to help those in need, merely bragged about their prerogatives. This attitude of boastfulness found expression in various ways, as will be indicated.

First of all, they bragged about the very fact that they were Jews, probably thinking, "Since we are Jews, we are better than everybody else." Was it not true that a Jew had a right to consider himself a member of the chosen race? Read Exod. 19:6; Deut. 10:15; Isa. 43:20, 21.

Now Paul is not altogether condemning pride of race or of nationality. Did not Mordecai, probably with a feeling of pride, proclaim, "I am a Jew"? See Esther 3:4. However, it makes a universe of difference in what spirit and with what purpose a person says this. Does he mean, "By God's sovereign, unmerited grace I am a worshiper of the only true God, and I regard it my high privilege to make all my wants and wishes known to him, and to dedicate my life completely to him and his cause. Therefore I cannot and will not bow down before, and pay homage to, anyone or to anything else"? That was undoubtedly the spirit in which Mordecai told people that he was a Jew. But when a person says, "I am a Jew," implying, "Therefore I am better than you. Listen carefully to me, and do whatever I say," he is *placing confidence in himself,* not in God.

"... and rely on (the) law." Here again we must bear in mind that there is a sense in which relying or resting on God's law is the right thing to do. Is not God's law the standard according to which a person's conduct should be regulated? And did not the Psalmist "take delight" in God's law? Read Ps. 119. However, the Jews whom Paul had in mind were committing a twofold error with respect to relying on the law: (1) the mere possession of, and instruction in, the law gave them a sense of security and superiority; and (2) they believed that by means of a strenuous and continued effort to obey that law they could, as it were, earn salvation.

"... and brag about your relationship to God," as if this relationship—if, in any given case, it even existed—had been brought about by good deeds!

Here, for the first time in Romans the apostle uses the verb *to boast* or *to brag.* The word used in the original[62] is in the New Testament almost confined to the writings of Paul. It occurs five times in Romans (2:17, 23; 5:2, 3, 11), twice in Galatians (6:13, 14); once in Ephesians (2:9); once in Philippians (3:3); but by far most frequently in the Corinthian correspondence: five (perhaps six) times[63] in I Corinthians, and no less than twenty times in II Corinthians. So all in all Paul uses this verb 34 or 35 times. It is also found in James 1:9; 4:16.[64]

At times this verb is used in a favorable sense; for example, "... far be it for me *to glory* except in the cross of our Lord Jesus Christ" (Gal. 6:14).

---

62. Here καυχᾶσαι, 2nd per. s. pres. indicat. (for καυχᾷ) of καυχάομαι, to boast or brag (about), exult, glory, or take pride in.

63. Six times if this verb is authentic in I Cor. 13:3.

64. The cognate noun καύχημα occurs ten times in Paul's letters; once in Heb. 3:6; while καύχησις also is found ten times in the writings of Paul; once in James 4:16. The compound κατακαυχάομαι is found only in Rom. 11:18; James 2:13; 3:14. See also R. Bultmann, Th.D.N.T., Vol. III, pp. 648-654.

There is such a thing as glorying in the Lord (II Cor. 10:17) or in Christ Jesus (Phil. 3:3). The apostle is even able to glory in his weaknesses, for when he is weak, then (in the Lord) he is strong (II Cor. 12:9, 10).

Often, however, the verb is used in an unfavorable sense. For example, the Corinthians were *boasting* or *bragging* about *men,* almost as if they owed their salvation to *them* (I Cor. 1:12, 29). So Paul tells them, "No more boasting about men!" (I Cor. 3:21; cf. 4:7). "Let him who boasts, boast in the Lord" (II Cor. 10:17). But although glorying or exulting in the Lord is wonderful, bragging about one's close relationship to God, as if its attainment had been a human achievement, is very sinful. And this is what the Jews whom Paul had in mind were doing.

". . . and being instructed out of the law, know (his) will, and approve the things that really matter . . ."

Though it is possible to construct "being instructed out of the law" solely with "approve the things that really matter," I can see no reason why this *instruction out of* (hence, based on) *the law* should not also be linked with "know (his) will." Certainly both the knowledge of God's will and the ability and desire to rank essentials above non-essentials, resulted from being "catechized" in the law. On "being catechized" or "instructed" see also N.T.C. on Luke 1:4, p. 62.[65]

As a result of being catechized in the law, the Jew was supposed to be able and desirous to approve the things that really mattered. He regarded himself as a person who knew the difference between essentials and non-essentials, preferring the former. Instead of "and approve the things that really matter" or "the essential things," the rendering "and approve the things that are excellent" is also possible. In *meaning* these two translations differ only slightly. See N.T.C. on Phil. 1:10.

What Paul is saying, then, is this, "If you call yourself a Jew, and rely on the law . . . and, being instructed out of the law, know (his) will, and approve the things that really matter. . . ." He now adds, "and if you are convinced that you are a guide for the blind," etc.

Note the four parallel items:

(1) *a guide for the blind.*

Physical blindness is mentioned with great frequency in Scripture. See, for example, Lev. 21:18; 22:22; Deut. 15:21; 28:28, 29; II Sam. 5:6; Zeph. 1:17; John 5:3. It was due to various causes, among which may well have been unsanitary environment, venereal disease, lack of eye care immediately after birth. During the days of Christ's sojourn on earth he restored sight to many a blind person (Matt. 9:27-30; 11:5; 12:22; 20:30-34; Mark 8:22-26; 10:46-52; Luke 7:21; John 11:37). Jesus also instructed his audiences to treat blind people with special kindness, inviting them to their banquets, etc. (Luke 14:13, 21).

---

65. The verb κατηχέω is used also with reference to instruction in *the gospel.* See Acts 18:25; Gal. 6:6. In Acts 21:21 the sense is *to inform.*

Guides were needed to lead the blind (II Kings 6:19; Matt. 12:22). They must be *reliable* guides. See Deut. 27:18.

It is understandable that by an easy transition, probably already evident in Deut. 27:18, physical blindness became the symbol of intellectual, moral, and spiritual blindness (Isa. 42:19; 56:10; Rom. 11:7, 8; II Cor. 4:4; I John 2:11). Note especially the impressive transition from the one (physical) to the other (spiritual) in John 9:1, 7, 39–41.

Very sad indeed was the condition of spiritually blind *people* if they were being led by similarly blind *guides* (Matt. 15:14; 23:16–24; and cf. Luke 6:39).

When, therefore, Paul now writes, "If you are convinced that you are a guide for the blind," is he not implying, "Be sure that you are a reliable guide!"? We can understand that many a Jew, instructed in temple and/or synagogue, must have regarded himself as being indeed a capable guide for those not equally *privileged* (?).

(2) *a light for those in darkness*

The Bible of the Jews was and is a mission book, from beginning—"In your seed shall all the nations of the earth be blessed" (Gen. 22:18)—to end—"From the rising of the sun even to its setting my name shall be great among the Gentiles" (Mal. 1:11). And in between beginning and end we read "I have appointed you as a light for the Gentiles" (Isa. 42:6). See also Isa. 9:2; 49:6; 58:8; 60:3.

To a certain extent the Jews understood this. Living in the midst of a pagan environment—especially during the captivity, but to some extent even earlier and in a sense also again during the days of Christ's sojourn on earth—they not only defended themselves against heathen attacks upon their monotheism but even carried the war into the enemy's camp by attacking the polytheism and the wickednesses, especially sexual perversity, of the Gentiles. The holy books too were translated into languages which the Gentiles could understand. To a certain extent, therefore, the Jews were a blessing for the surrounding nations. Many a pagan found Christ by means of the stepping stone of the synagogue, for it was here that Jesus and later on his apostles, especially Paul, proclaimed the gospel of salvation. See N.T.C. on Mark, *The Synagogue During New Testament Times*, pp. 74-77.

That is one side of the picture. The other side is described by Jesus in Matt. 23:15, in these words, "Woe to y o u, scribes and Pharisees, hypocrites! because y o u travel about on sea and land to make a single proselyte, and when he has become one, y o u make him twice as much a son of hell as y o u are yourselves." It was not so much the purpose of scribes and Pharisees to change a Gentile into a Jew; no, he must become a full-fledged, legalistic, ritualistic, hair-splitting Pharisee, one filled with fanatic zeal for his new salvation-by-works religion. As Jesus implies, soon this new convert would even out-Pharisee the Pharisees in bigotry, for it is a fact that new converts frequently outdo themselves in becoming fanatically devoted to their new faith.

With all this in mind, it will be easier to understand Paul's remark, "and *if you are convinced that you are . . . a light for those in darkness. . . .*"

(3) *an instructor of the foolish*

What Paul probably meant was, "If you are convinced that you have been endowed with so much wisdom and knowledge that you are thoroughly qualified to teach those (in your estimation) foolish know-nothings . . ."

(4) *a teacher of the immature*

A rendering that merits consideration and may well be correct is "a teacher of *babes* [or infants]." See I Cor. 3:1; Eph. 4:14; Heb. 5:13. It is easy to understand that a Jew, having been drilled in the knowledge of the law from his youth might deem himself thoroughly capable of imparting instruction to Gentiles; or, if he considered that a task for his teachers, the scribes (cf. Matt. 23:15), and would prefer not to approach too closely to those who in his eyes were unclean, he could at least teach recent converts (to Judaism) from paganism. Paul adds, "having in the law the embodiment [or repository] of knowledge and truth." That the law of God, minus the load of man-made restrictions and modifications, was indeed a priceless and inexhaustible treasure cannot be denied. The law of the Ten Commandments, the entire Pentateuch, even better the entire Old Testament, was indeed a source of knowledge (Ps. 119:66) and truth (Ps. 119:142).

If now for a moment we summarize what Paul is saying—"If you are convinced that you are a guide for the blind, a light for those in darkness, an instructor of the foolish, a teacher of infants, because in the law you have the embodiment of knowledge and truth . . . ," does it not seem that Calvin was right when he characterized this part of Paul's sentence as being tinged with ridicule? The apostle is probably saying, "If you think you are really so learned and wise and capable, is it not high time that you begin to examine *yourself?*"

B. *A Series of Questions for Self-Examination*

21-23. . . . you, then, who teach someone else, don't you teach yourself? You who preach that people should not steal, do you steal? You who say that people should not commit adultery, do you commit adultery? You who abhor idols, do you rob temples? You who brag about the law, do you dishonor God by (your) transgression of the law?

First a word about the *construction* of this passage. It is held by some that verses 17-23 contain a number of anacolutha, that is, statements in which the grammatical construction with which the sentence begins is not completed: the condition (or protasis) does not have the expected conclusion (or apodosis). The answer is that though, strictly speaking, there is some truth in this assertion, in the broader sense the charge is untrue. What Paul is saying amounts to this, "If you present yourself as a person who relies on God and his law, and even teach others the meaning of this law and impress upon them that they should live in harmony with it, how is it that you yourself do not practice what you preach?"

Another matter touching on construction is this, "Should verse 23 be translated as a *statement* (so, for example, N.E.B. and Cranfield), or as a *question?*" The original allows either. Those who favor the first alternative base their opinion on the fact that verse 24 is a confirmation—note γάρ—of that which precedes. But how can it be a *confirmation* of a *question?*

On the surface this reasoning sounds convincing. But is it? Verse 23 can still be regarded as a question if in connection with verse 24 the very real possibility of abbreviated discourse is kept in mind. See N.T.C. on John, Vol. I, p. 206. The sense of verse 24 would then be, "(I ask this question) for because of y o u the name of God is being blasphemed among the Gentiles."

Moreover, the reason I, along with most translators, favor the idea that verse 23 is a question is that both in form and content it harmonizes with the four preceding lines (about teaching, stealing, committing adultery, and robbing temples).

It is interesting to note how precisely Jewish sources agree with the implied charges made here by Paul. The question, "You who teach others, don't you teach yourself?" is found again and again in rabbinical writings. Note the following: "You have many a man who teaches himself but does not teach others, many a man who teaches others but does not teach himself, many a man who teaches himself and others, and many a one who teaches neither himself nor others" (S.BK. III, p. 107).

For instances of stealing that occurred among the "learned ones" see the same source, again p. 107; for adultery, pp. 109-111—sometimes of a very scandalous nature among the rabbis!—; and for the robbing of temples, pp. 113-115.

That the life of many a scribe and/or Pharisee was not in keeping with his teaching, and certainly not in harmony with God's holy law as found in Scripture, is brought out clearly by Jesus (Matt. 23; Mark 7:9-13; Luke 11:37-52).

It is asserted at times that there is no proof in Scripture that Jews could be legitimately charged with the crime of robbing temples. However, is there not certain evidence which might indirectly point to its actual occurrence? Note the following:

If something resembling this evil had never occurred or had never been in danger of occurring, why would it have been so sternly forbidden in Deut. 7:25? Moreover, does not the fact that according to Acts 19:37 the city clerk at Ephesus, in quieting a tumultuous crowd, asserted, "Y o u have brought these men [Paul and his traveling companions] here, *though they have neither robbed temples* nor blasphemed our goddess," indicate that such *sacrilege* (temple robbery) was not altogether unheard of? Besides, why would Paul have mentioned it here in 2:22 if in this respect the Jews were completely innocent?[66]

---

66. Add to all this the reference to temple robbery in Josephus, *Antiquity* IV.207. Without corroborative value but too interesting to pass by in silence is the mention of temple robbery in

Paul's final question is, "You who brag about the law, do you dishonor God by (your) transgression of the law?" The very question shows that the apostle realized that among his Jewish opponents there was a sharp contrast between theology and practice, between doctrine and life. To attain acceptance with God on the basis of obedience to his law, such obedience must, of course, be perfect, a goal unattainable here on earth. In fact, with respect to Paul's opponents the very opposite was true, as he now indicates by means of

C. A Grave Accusation

24. As it is written, "Because of y o u the name of God is being blasphemed among the Gentiles."

The quotation is based on Isa. 52:5. It is an adaptation of the LXX version[67] of that passage. The context, however, is somewhat different in the two cases. The Old Testament passage takes into consideration the assumption on the part of the Gentiles that when a nation is conquered and deported, its god has also been conquered. So the conquered nation is blasphemed along with its god. Cf. Ezek. 36:20. Here in Rom. 2:24 the Gentiles are represented as reasoning: the people (Israel) behave wickedly; therefore their god must be wicked also, for people resemble their god.

The two instances are alike, however, in this respect: in both cases Israel had failed to be what according to Rom. 2:19 it pretended to be, namely, a light for those in darkness. It was for that reason that Israel was deported and its God mocked. It was also for that reason that God's name was in Paul's day being blasphemed among the Gentiles.

D.   *A portrayal of the contrast between the true and the merely nominal Jew;*
and between heart circumcision and literal circumcision

25-27. Circumcision does indeed profit, but only if you put the law into practice. But if you are a transgressor of the law, your circumcision has become uncircumcision. Therefore, if the uncircumcised man keeps the requirements of the law, will not his uncircumcision be regarded as circumcision? Indeed, he who is physically uncircumcised but keeps the law will condemn you, who, though provided with the written code and circumcision, are a transgressor of the law.

Paul has already shown that the Jews cannot build the castle of their confidence on the fact that they, and not the Gentiles, were in possession of

---

a fictitious story fabricated by an anti-Semite. According to this fairy tale, reported by Josephus (*Against Apion* 1.310, 311), a group of condemned Jewish lepers, having been sent to the desert so that they might perish there, start out on a trip to the land that was later called Judea. Arrived, they build here a city which was called *Ierosyla* (Jerusalem), that is, according to this thoroughly corrupt etymology, "the town of temple robbers!"

On the serious side see the treatment of the verb ἱεροσυλέω and of the noun ἱερόσυλος by G. Schrenk in Th.D.N.T., Vol. IV, pp. 255-257.

67. δι' ὑμᾶς διὰ παντὸς τὸ ὄνομά μου βλασφημεῖται ἐν τοῖς ἔθνεσιν.

the law, in which they had received instruction. He now proceeds to prove that neither can they base their sense of security on the circumstance that they, and not the Gentiles, have been circumcised. Paul argues that circumcision unaccompanied by obedience to God's holy law is of no value. The same is true, of course, with respect to the water of baptism and with respect to the bread and wine in holy communion. As signs and seals these things have value, but only when accompanied by obedience. A circumcised person who is a transgressor of the law is equal to an uncircumcised individual.

The converse is also true: an uncircumcised man who in a certain sense (see on 2:14) keeps God's law is, in God's sight, equal to a circumcised person.

This causes Paul to address his Jewish opponent as follows: "Indeed, he who is physically uncircumcised but keeps the law *will condemn* you, who, though provided with the written code and circumcision, are a transgressor of the law."[68] Here again, as always, Paul agrees with Jesus. See Matt. 12:41, 42; Luke 11:31, 32.

Paul is summarizing here. What he is saying is that neither of the two grounds on which Jews often based their confidence—the possession of the law or the fact of having been circumcised—sufficed for salvation. He has already enlarged on the first point, having shown that the Jews he has in mind have not kept the law (see verses 13, 17-24). In fact, *no one* can keep the law in all its details. No one is by nature even true to its underlying principles.

Now the apostle shows that also the second ground of confidence is insecure: a circumcision that is merely outward is not any better than is the observation of the mere letter of the law. The letter kills; the Spirit imparts life (Rom. 7:6; II Cor. 3:6).

---

68. Note καὶ κρινεῖ ἡ ἐκ φύσεως ἀκροβυστία τὸν νόμον τελοῦσα σὲ (2:27a); meaning: "and the physically uncircumcised keeping the law will condemn [or judge] you," which can be interpreted as an elliptical conditional sentence: "and if the physically uncircumcised person keeps the law, he will condemn you," which, in turn, can be transposed into, "And [or Indeed], he who is physically uncircumcised but keeps the law will condemn you." See also footnote 119.

διὰ γράμματος καὶ περιτομῆς. Note various interpretations that have been given to διὰ as used here:
(1) because, while Gram. N.T. (Bl.-Debr.), par. 223, p. 119.
(2) manner and means shading off into one another, Gram. N.T., p. 583.
(3) accompanied by, with the advantage of, A. T. Robertson, *Word Pictures*, New York and London, 1933, Vol. IV. p. 340.
(4) attendant circumstance, Cranfield, p. 174.
It would seem that *means* (or *agency*) and *concession* (though) are both implied in this sentence. The thought is somewhat compressed, as happens often both in writing and in speaking. A.R.V. reads, "you, who *with* the letter and circumcision art a transgressor of the law." Notice "with" (hence, attendant circumstance). But, again, does not such a "with" imply "though"? We sometimes hear the expression, "*With* all his learning, he can be so foolish." Does not this "with" have the meaning "in spite of having" or "though he has"? So also in Rom. 2:27b many translations have adopted "though" or "even though" as being the best rendering of the Greek in this particular case. I agree.

Is it not clear that what Paul is actually doing is preparing the reader or hearer for the foreceful affirmation or re-affirmation of the *theme,* "Apart from the righteousness freely granted by God no one can ever attain to the state of being accepted by God"? See Rom. 1:17; 3:21-24; 5:1; etc. A very important conclusion and climax follow:

28, 29. For he is not a (real) Jew who is one only on the outside, nor is (true) circumcision something external and physical. But he is a (real) Jew who is one inwardly; and (real) circumcision is a matter of the heart, by the Spirit, not by the written code. Such a person's praise is not from man but from God.[69]

Paul's opponents among the Jews were building their hope for eternity on the mere fact that they were Jews, and therefore, as they thought, God's chosen people. This reminds us of the days of John the Baptist when these people were similarly resting their case on the parallel circumstance that they were "Abraham's seed" (Matt. 3:9; John 8:33, 39).

Paul, on the other hand, draws a sharp distinction between Jew and Jew: (a) the person who is a Jew outwardly only; that is, a Jew by virtue of physical or biological descent, nothing more; and (b) the individual who is a Jew not only outwardly but also inwardly; that is, a Jew to the eyes of the One before whom the secrets of men's hearts and lives are an open book (Ps. 139:1-6; Rom. 2:16; Heb. 4:13).

Similarly he draws a distinction between (a) merely physical circumcision, the excision of the male's prepuce, in strict compliance with "the written code," the letter of the law (cf. Gen. 17: 10-13; Lev. 12:3); and (b) circumcision that concerns the heart: the removal (in principle) from that heart of whatever is evil; heart renewal (cf. Lev. 26:41; Deut. 10:16; 30:6; Jer. 4:4; 9:26; Ezek. 44:7), which is the work of the Holy Spirit (Rom. 7:6; II Cor. 3:6, 18; Gal. 5:16-23).[70]

Concerning the Jew who is one also on the inside, and whose heart has accordingly been circumcised by the Holy Spirit, Paul says, "Such a person's praise is not from man but from God." This is a play on words, one that goes back all the way to the book of Genesis:

"She [Leah] conceived again and gave birth to a son, and she said, 'This time I will *praise* the Lord.' Therefore she named him Judah" (Gen. 29:35).

"*Judah,* your brothers will *praise* you." (Gen. 49:8).

---

69. This is surely a striking example of abbreviated discourse. The words printed in brackets are *implied.* I agree here with Cranfield, p. 175.

οὐ γὰρ ὁ ἐν τῷ φανερῷ ['Ιουδαῖος] 'Ιουδαῖός ἐστιν, οὐδὲ ἡ ἐν τῷ φανερῷ ἐν σαρκὶ [περιτομὴ] περιτομή [ἐστιν]. ἀλλ᾽ ὁ ἐν τῷ κρυπτῷ 'Ιουδαῖος ['Ιουδαῖός ἐστιν], καὶ περιτομὴ καρδίας ἐν πνεύματι οὐ γράμματι [περιτομή ἐστιν], οὗ ὁ ἔπαινος οὐκ ἐξ ἀνθρώπων [ἐστιν] ἀλλ᾽ ἐκ τοῦ θεοῦ.

70. Verse 29 should not be rendered "by the spirit," as if the human spirit were meant: for:
(1) after "of the heart" this would be redundant; and
(2) as has been indicated, such renewal is in Scripture ascribed to the Holy Spirit.

The word JEW, derived from JUDAH, means PRAISED.[71]
As is clear from Scripture, many of the Jews praised *themselves* (Rom. 2:17-20) and were eager to receive praise from *men* (Matt. 6:1-8, 16-18; 23:5-12). Therefore, they did not deserve to be called "Jews," for, according to Rom. 2:29, a genuine Jew is one whose praise does not come from men but from God.

At this point in the explanation of Romans some commentators hurry to point out that when Paul places such emphasis on the fact that the only real Jew is the one who is a Jew inwardly, he cannot mean that there are no rich blessings in store for the Jews as a people, believers and unbelievers alike. To substantiate their position they refer to Rom. 9:1—11:36. Would it not be better to wait with drawing conclusions from that remote section until we come to it? For the present all we know is that the apostle affirms that "he is not a (real) Jew who is one only on the outside . . . but he is a Jew who is one inwardly . . . whose praise is not from men but from God." That Paul also uses the term *Jew* in a more general, physical sense is clear. He has done this in 1:16; 2:9, 10, 17, 28, is about to do it again (3:1), and will do it once more in 10:12.

Accordingly, using the term "Jew" in that more general sense, the apostle continues:

3:1. What advantage, then, does the Jew have, or what is the value of circumcision?

At this point Paul seems to be hearing an objection. It is as if someone is saying, "If, in order to amount to something, one has to be a Jew inwardly, and must have experienced the circumcision of the heart, then is there any advantage in being a Jew in the broader literal sense, or in having been physically circumcised?" Is there *any* advantage at all in belonging to the Jewish nation?

Paul answers, **2. Much, in every respect. First of all,[72] they have been entrusted with the oracles of God.**

Among the many passages showing that the Jews as a people received privileges above all other nations are the following: Ps. 147:20; Isa. 5:5, 6; Amos 3:2, 3; Matt. 22:1-8; Luke 13:6; 14:16, 17, 24; *and especially Rom. 9:4, 5, where the apostle returns to this subject and enlarges on it.*

When Paul mentally calls the roll of Jewish prerogatives, one item tops all others, namely, the fact that to the Jews, and to no other nation, was accorded the unique privilege, the high honor, of being the custodians of the *oracles* of God, that entire special revelation to Israel which consisted not only of commandments, but also of predictions and promises.

All of this had been entrusted to the Jews, to be accepted by faith, obeyed (as far as applicable), held in honor, and transmitted to others.

---

71. The Hebrew word for Judah is יְהוּדָה and for Jew יְהוּדִי. These forms are clearly connected with the Hiph'il of יָרָה, to throw, though the nature of the connection is obscure.
72. It is impossible to determine whether γάρ is authentic.

Privileges imply duties; honors go hand in hand with responsibilities. Could it be truthfully stated that Israel had shouldered these responsibilities? That it had been faithful to its trust? If not, what then? Says Paul: **3, 4. And what if some (of them) were unfaithful?**[73] **Their unfaithfulness does not nullify God's faithfulness, does it? By no means. Let God be true, and every person a liar.** As it is written:

    "**That thou mayest be proved right in thy words**
    And prevail in thy judging."

That Israel as a people had been blessed with many advantages cannot be questioned. But does this fact, considered by itself, guarantee a rosy future? Not necessarily. If the Jews expect God's special blessing, they better be faithful to their trust. If they fail to be a blessing to the nations, a light to the Gentiles, their future is dark.

Illustration: A youth enrolls in college. He has the following advantages over many others: he comes from a rich family, so that paying room and board, tuition, etc., is no problem. He enjoys excellent health, and is even blessed with above average intelligence. The college he attends rates very high. His teachers are the best. In spite of all these advantages he never graduates. Why not? Because he does not make the most of his opportunities. He fritters away his time, is lazy, unfaithful to his trust.

As 2:21–23 has shown, something similar was true with respect to Israel. It too, in spite of all its special privileges, had become unfaithful to its trust, and because of this disloyalty God's name was being blasphemed among the Gentiles (2:24). As a people, therefore, unless it should experience a radical change of heart, it could not look forward to a glorious future.

Does Paul mean that *all* the Jews were doomed? He does not. Very tactfully and mercifully he states (here in Rom. 3:3) that "some" of them

---

73. Granted that in this passage τὴν πίστιν τοῦ θεοῦ means God's faithfulness, there is considerable difference of opinion with respect to the meaning of the verb ἠπίστησαν and the noun ἀπιστία. Some believe that in this passage the noun means both lack of faith and lack of faithfulness (Greijdanus). Others accept "lack of faith" (Sanday and Headlam). Among translators who have adopted this view are A.V., A.R.V., N.A.S., Berkeley, Norlie, N.I.V. Among those who favor "were unfaithful" (=untrustworthy) for the verb, and "unfaithfulness" for the noun are, among commentators, etc.: Bultmann, Th.D.N.T., Vol. VI, p. 208; L.N.T. (A. and G.), p. 84, Bruce, Hodge, Lenski, Ridderbos, Van Leeuwen and Jacobs. Among translators who support this view are Beck, Williams, Phillips, R.S.V., N.E.B., Weymouth, Moffatt, Good News for Modern Man, Jerusalem Bible, Dutch (Nieuwe Vertaling).

There is certainly room for difference of opinion, and, as Cranfield and others have pointed out, there is a very close connection between "lack of faith" and "lack of faithfulness." He who lacks faithfulness also lacks faith. Yet, I too favor the translation "were unfaithful . . . unfaithfulness." Reason: it agrees best with the present context in which God's faithfulness is contrasted with human ἀπιστία.Though the meaning of the same word in other passages of the same epistle is important, is not the immediate context even more important? Besides, not only does verse 3 point in this direction, because here the unfaithfulness of men is contrasted with God's faithfulness, but so does also verse 4, where divine veracity is synonymous with the preceding divine faithfulness, and where human mendacity reminds one of similar human unfaithfulness.

were unfaithful. It would seem that even now he is distinguishing between "Israel" and "Israel" (cf. 9:6). In another passage where the apostle uses the word "*some*" once in each of four successive verses, this indefinite designation seems to amount to "most" (I Cor. 10:7–10; cf. verse 5). But here in Rom. 3:3 he does not indicate the proportion. He simply writes, "What if some of them were unfaithful?" And he adds, "Their unfaithfulness does not nullify God's faithfulness, does it?"

Does he mean then, "In spite of their unfaithfulness God will still grant them a glorious future, because they are Jews"? Probably not. His real meaning seems to be this: "Since God is faithful, those Jews who are faithful to him, and therefore to that which has been entrusted to them, will certainly receive the fulfilment of his promises."

But the God who is faithful to his *promises* is also faithful to his *threats*. Divine faithfulness is a priceless comfort for the faithful, an earnest warning for those in danger of becoming unfaithful, and a harbinger of doom for those who continue to be untrustworthy. Cf. II Tim. 2:11–13.

The very suggestion that God might become unfaithful causes the apostle to shudder. He exclaims, "By no means" (or "Let it not be," "Perish the thought," "God forbid"). This expression occurs often in Paul's epistles— including Rom. 3:31; 6:2, 15; 7:7; 9:14; 11:1, 6— and elsewhere.

By adding, "Let God be true (cf. Ps. 119:9, 160; Jer. 10:10) and every person a liar (Ps. 116:11)," Paul places divine veracity (akin to faithfulness) and human mendacity (an ally of unfaithfulness) over against each other, in sharp contrast, and prays that full recognition be accorded to the former. *Human mendacity and unfaithfulness, far from nullifying divine faithfulness, causes it to stand out in bold relief.*

Paul adds words taken from Ps. 51:4b (=LXX 50:6b).

In order to understand the relevancy of this quotation for Paul's purpose we should see it on the basis of its background.

David had sinned grievously. He had committed adultery with Bathsheba, the wife of Uriah. When he had discovered that Bathsheba had become pregnant, he had, in a very deceitful manner, brought about the death of Uriah, and married Bathsheba. Then the Lord had sent Nathan the prophet to David. By means of a parable about a rich man who had deprived a poor man of his one and only "little ewe lamb," he had elicited from the lips of David the words, "As the Lord lives, the man who has done this deserves to die." Nathan's response had been, "You are the man." Result: David's deep sorrow and his admission, "I have sinned against the Lord." See II Sam. 11, 12.

In Psalm 51 David again confesses his sins and says,
"Against thee only have I sinned and done that which is evil in thy sight."
In the words quoted here in Rom. 3:4b he adds, "(I confess this in order)
That thou mayest be proved right in thy words
And prevail in thy judging" (Ps. 51:4b).

It is clear, therefore, that David's aim was to make his confession as frank, open, and unconditional as possible, in order that on the dark background of his own unrighteousness God's righteousness in judging him would stand out the more clearly. David wants God to triumph! Faulty and perverse human reasoning now registers an objection which Paul, almost apologizing for even paying attention to it, immediately knocks down:

5, 6. But if our unrighteousness confirms God's righteousness, what shall we say? The God who inflicts wrath is not unrighteous, is he? (I speak from a human standpoint.)[74] By no means! For then how could God judge the world?

It is clear that not only the words of Paul in Rom. 3:4a but also those of David in 3:4b quoted from Ps. 51, make God's righteousness stand out on the dark background of human sin. As the dark shadows in Rembrandt's (misnamed) *Night Watch* causes the spots of light to explode all the more brilliantly, so man's unrighteousness accentuates God's righteousness.

The opponent now raises an objection which amounts to this: "On the basis of your doctrine, Paul, since man's unrighteousness brings out more sharply God's righteousness, should not the Almighty be happy about that turn of events? Is he not unfair when, instead, he inflicts wrath on man?"

With another "Perish the thought" (or "By no means") the apostle, filled with holy indignation, crushes this wicked type of reasoning. It is as if he were saying, "What? God unfair? How do you even dare to suggest this? It is agreed, is it not, that God is qualified to judge and actually will judge the world? Well, then, how could he be unfair? Shall not the Judge of all the earth deal justly?" (Gen. 18:25).

7, 8. (Someone might object) If through my falsehood God's truthfulness is enhanced to his glory, why am I still being condemned as a sinner? Why not say—as we are being slanderously reported and some claim that we say—Let us do evil that good may result? Their condemnation is deserved.

Here are two rhetorical questions followed by a brusque appraising answer.[75]

---

74. The Greek reads κατὰ ἄνθρωπον λέγω, both here and in Gal. 3:15, "I speak from a human standpoint." I Cor. 9:8 (with λαλῶ for λέγω) has the same meaning. Note also ἀνθρώπινον λέγω, "I speak in human terms" (Rom. 6:19). With respect to the meaning of somewhat similar phrases in I Cor. 3:3 and I Cor. 15:32 opinions vary.

75. The grammatical construction of verse 8, beginning with "Why not say" is probably as follows:
    a. After the opening words καὶ μὴ insert λέγομεν or something similar.
    b. The parenthesis enclosed within the rhetorical question of verse 8 begins with the first καθὼς and ends with λέγειν.
    c. ὅτι is recitative. For various ways in which this little word is used see N.T.C. on John, Vol. I, p. 54.
    d. ὧν refers to τινες.

There is a close connection between verses 5, 6 and verses 7, 8. Compare:
"If our unrighteousness confirms God's righteousness . . ." (vs. 5)
with
"If through my falsehood God's truthfulness is enhanced . . ." (vs. 7).
In both cases the attack upon God's rectitude or righteousness is repulsed, his honor maintained.

However, there are also minor differences:

(1) Note the change from *our* unrighteousness (verse 5) to *my* falsehood . . . why am *I*, etc. However, the first person plural returns in verse 8.

(2) In verses 7, 8 the attention shifts from the condemnation of the attack on God's righteousness to the condemnation of the perversion of the doctrine of salvation by grace. Hence there is also a close connection between 3:7, 8 and 6:1.

Compare:
"Let us do evil that good may result" (3:8)
with
"Let us continue in sin that grace may increase" (6:1).

The opponents speak as if, when Paul taught that a person is saved by grace, he meant, "Go ahead and sin to y o u r heart's content, in order that grace may have a chance to do its work!"

For more on this terribly destructive perversion of sound doctrine see on 6:1 f.

The apostle concludes by saying, "Their condemnation is deserved." He means, "Those who flaunt this slogan will receive a just retribution. The people who so wickedly misrepresent the doctrine we proclaim will get what they deserve."

Practical Lessons Derived from Romans 2:1—3:8
A. From Chapter 2

Verse 1

"At whatever point you judge the other person, you are condemning yourself." According to a Dutch proverb,[76] "He who compares himself with another person is generally easy on himself."

Verse 3

"Do you imagine that you will escape God's judgment?"
There are all kinds of ways in which the guilty person tries to escape punishment: (a) fleeing to another country and living there under an assumed name; (b) instead

---

76. "Die zich aan een ander spiegelt, spiegelt zich zacht."

of making an excuse, immediately changing the subject so that the opponent in his excitement begins to defend himself; (c) placing himself in the hands of "a lawyer who has never lost a case." At times such tricks work, at least for a while. But one can never escape *God's* judgment, and that is what counts. Is "escape" then entirely impossible? The only real way is, "Confess. Ask forgiveness. If possible, make restitution. By God's grace begin a new life."

Verse 4

Verse 4 mentions "the riches of God's kindness, tolerance, and patience." Who can read the following passages without being overcome with emotion and gratitude? See Gen. 4:6, 7; 18:22, 23; 39:5; Ps. 36:6; 145:9, 15, 16; Isa. 1:18; 55:1, 6, 7; 57:15; Jer. 31:31–35; Lam. 3:22, 33; Ezek. 18:23, 32; 33:11; Hos. 11:8; Jonah 4:10, 11; Mic. 7:18, 19; Zeph. 3:17; Matt. 5:43–45; 11:25–30; Luke 6:35 (see also N.T.C. on Luke, p. 76); John 3:16; 7:37; Acts 14:16, 17; Rom. 8:31–39; II Cor. 5:20, 21; 8:9; I Tim. 4:10; Heb. 4:16; Rev. 22:17. The reading of this or a similar list of passages has often helped children of God while they were passing through valleys of doubt, as every pastor can testify.

Verse 5

"You are storing up for yourself wrath." If the national debt of the United States of America would be reduced by a billion dollars a year, how long would it take to pay it off? Each hour, minute, and even second the sinner is increasing the pile of his debt . . . unless, by God's sovereign grace and power, he surrenders himself to Christ and discovers that "Jesus paid it all." What a "joy unspeakable and full of glory!"

Verse 13

"It is the doers of the law who will be pronounced righteous." Good works have never saved anybody. Yet without them no one has a right to claim that he is a Christian. The believer does the works of the law "out of gratitude for salvation received as God's free gift."

Verse 15

". . . their conscience also bearing witness . . ." If conscience forbids you to do something, you should not do it. But be sure to send conscience to school, the school of the Bible. If conscience allows you to do something, does that necessarily mean that the contemplated action is right?

Verse 16

"God, through Jesus Christ, will judge men's secrets." By means of wiretapping, concealed microphones, hidden cameras, and many other devices secrets are being uncovered. Potential enemies are discovering that the nature and extent of their armor is no longer a secret. Yet, in spite of all detection equipment some secrets remain undiscovered. Not, however, before the eyes of God. Read Ps. 139. Add Heb. 4:13. Is this a dreadful thought? Could it be a source of comfort? Read John 21:17.

Verses 17-23

The apostle urges the Jews to examine themselves. Yet, again and again certain psychologists tell us that self-examination is "morbid," may lead to a dangerous guilt complex, etc. *To a certain extent* these psychologists are right. What is the solution? Study Psalm 51.

Verses 28, 29

Following the example of Matthew Henry, we can read these verses as follows, "For he is not a Christian who is one only on the outside, nor is (real) baptism something external and physical. But he is a Christian who is one inwardly; and (real) baptism is a matter of the heart, by the Spirit, not by the written code. Such a person's praise is not from man but from God."

B. From 3:1-8

Verse 3

"Their unfaithfulness does not nullify God's faithfulness, does it?" Comment on:
1. God's faithfulness ... a frightening thought.
2. God's faithfulness, a source of comfort.

Verses 5-8

In a certain state an amendment was proposed that would have legalized casino gambling (in a specified district). The proponents argued that if this amendment passed, huge profits would result for the benefit of education, etc. These people argued as did those whom Paul denounces in Rom. 3:5-8. In what respect? See Commentary.

Summary of Chapter 2:1—3:8

Having shown that *the Gentiles* are the objects of God's wrath because of their sinful practices, the apostle now directs his attention to *the Jews*, and states that they are without excuse when they practice some of the very evils they condemn in others. Let not the Jew think that because he has not been abandoned by God to a life of most scandalous immorality, God must be very pleased with him. Rather, let him take to heart the fact that God's kindness toward him should bring him to conversion (2:1-4).

Paul continues, "But by your hard and unconverted heart you are storing up for yourself wrath in the day of wrath and of the revelation of the righteous judgment of God, who will render to every person according to his deeds ... and who does not show partiality" (verses 5-11).

"All who have sinned in ignorance of the law will perish even though they did not know the law, and all who have sinned knowing the law will be judged by the law. For it is not the hearers of the law who are righteous in God's sight but it is the doers...."

The apostle then reveals that even the Gentiles, who do not have the written law, do have a conscience which at times condemns and at times commends them. God will take all this into consideration. He will judge with absolute fairness, not showing any partiality. All this will become clear on the day of the final judgment, when God, through Jesus Christ, will judge men's secrets (verses 12-16).

The next paragraph may be condensed into this one big question, "Do you, who are a Jew, really practice what you preach?" More in detail, Paul asks, "Do you, who call yourself a Jew and rely on (the) law . . . and consider yourself a light for those in darkness, try to live in accordance with the law?" . . . "You, then, who teach someone else, don't you teach yourself; you who preach that people should not steal, do you steal?" etc. He concludes this section with the accusation, "As it is written [see Isa. 52:5] 'Because of y o u [i.e., y o u r wickedness] the name of God is being blasphemed among the Gentiles" (verses 17-24).

The Jew was of the opinion that because he had the law and had been circumcised, all was well for time and eternity. Paul answers, "Circumcision does indeed profit, but only if you put the law into practice . . . He is not a (real) Jew who is one only on the outside, nor is (true) circumcision something external and physical. But he is a (real) Jew who is one inwardly; and (real) circumcision is a matter of the heart, by the Spirit, not by the written code. Such a person's praise is not from man but from God." (verses 25-29).

At this point the apostle seems to hear an objection. It is as if someone is saying, "But Paul, do you mean that the Jews have no advantages, the most priceless of them being that the oracles of God have been entrusted to them?" (3:1, 2).

The question naturally arises, "But what if some of the Jews are unfaithful to that trust? Their unfaithfulness will not nullify God's faithfulness, will it?" Paul answers, "By no means. Let God be true, and every person a liar. As it is written,

" 'That thou mayest be proved right in thy words
And prevail in thy judging.' "

Since God is faithful, those Jews who are faithful to him and to their trust will certainly receive the promised goods. Human unfaithfulness, far from invalidating divine faithfulness, causes it to stand out in bold relief; just as, for example, David, by means of his wholehearted confession (Ps. 51), caused God's righteousness in judging him to shine forth all the more brilliantly on the dark background of the adulterer's own sinfulness. See II Sam. 11, 12.

This answer, however, leads to the question, "Since this is true, namely, that man's unrighteousness brings out more sharply God's righteousness, should not God be happy about that turn of events, instead of inflicting wrath on man for his sins?" This question is asked first in 3:5 and then, in a slightly different form, in verse 7. In both cases it amounts to, "Does not the end—namely, the revelation of God's glorious attributes—justify the means, namely, man's sinfulness?"

Paul's answer is, "Perish the thought, and let the people who so wickedly misrepresent our gospel receive the punishment they deserve" (verses 3-8).

Outline (continued)

Justification by Faith

4. *Accordingly,*
"There is no one righteous, not even one."
"All have turned aside."
3:9–20

5. "But now, apart from law, a righteousness from God has been
revealed . . . a righteousness through faith in Jesus Christ."
3:21–31

CHAPTER 3:9-31

9 What then? Are we any better? Not at all, for we just previously made the charge that Jews and Greeks alike are all under (the power of) sin. 10 As it is written:

"There is no one righteous, not even one;   *Eccl. 7:20*
11   there is no one who understands;
      there is no one who is searching for God.
12   All have turned aside; together they have become worthless;
      there is no one who does what is right;
      there is not even one."   *Ps. 14:3; 53:1-3.*
                                                LXX:13:1, 3; 52:2-4.
13   "An open grave is their throat;
      with their tongues they practice deception."   *Ps. 5:9; LXX:5:10.*
   "The poison of vipers is under their lips."   *Ps. 140:3; LXX:139:4.*
14   "Their mouth is full of cursing and bitterness."   *Ps. 10:7; LXX:9:28.*

15   "Swift (are) their feet to shed blood;
16   ruin and misery mark their ways,
17   and the way of peace they have not known."   *Isa. 59:7, 8.*
18   "There is no fear of God before their eyes."   *Ps. 36:1; LXX:35:2.*

19 Now we know that whatever the law says, it speaks to those (who are) within the pale of the law, that every mouth may be silenced, and the entire world may be exposed to the judgment of God.[77] 20 Therefore by law works no flesh[78] will be justified in his sight, for through law (comes) consciousness of sin.

4. *Accordingly*,
"There is no one righteous, not even one."
"All have turned aside."
3:9-20

9a. What then? Are we any better?
These words present problems. Interpretations vary widely.[79]

---

77. Or: may stand guilty before God.
78. Or: mortal being.
79. First, there is the question of the Greek text. Should we read προεχόμεθα or προεχώμεθα? Since the former has by far the strongest textual support, and there are no reasons to reject it, I accept it as being authentic. In view of οὐ πάντως, it is clear that both Τί οὖν and προεχόμεθα should be followed by the Greek question mark (;).
    The next question is, "What does the verb προεχόμεθα (not to be confused with

The meaning, "Do we excel?" or "Are we any better?" suits the present context, in view of the fact that the status of both Gentiles (1:18-32) and Jews (2:1-3:8), a very deplorable status indeed, has been described.

The next question is, "What does *we* mean?"

As many translators and interpreters see it, the meaning is, "We Jews." But this position is vulnerable:

a. The apostle has already indicated, and this in some detail, that Jews are not better than Gentiles. See 2:1, 17-24. Why, then, should he now be raising this question again?

b. Paul has been referring to the Jew(s) in the *third* person (1:16; 2:9; 3:1), and will do so again (9:4; 10:1; 11:20; etc.); and see above, p. 21. He has also *addressed* the typical Jew, using the second person (2:17f.). In the entire preceding discussion (1:1-3:8) he has never identified himself with the Jews. Never has he said, "we Jews." What sound reason is there for supposing that he does so here in 3:9?

Moreover, he probably does not mean, "In comparison with others, do the Jews have any outward advantages or privileges?" for on this subject he has already made himself very clear (3:1, 2). The present context indicates that the reference now is to *superior standing with God*.

Accordingly, the true meaning must be, "Do we—I, Paul, and y o u, believers in Rome—excel?" Or, more broadly, "Do we, believers in Christ (in general), excel? Are we better than all other people? Do we have a superior standing with God?"

This interpretation is supported also by the following considerations:

a. It is clear that the pronoun "we" implied in the immediately preceding sentence (verse 8: ". . . as *we* are being slanderously reported, and as some claim that *we* say") refers to the believer, Paul, and those associated with him; therefore refers to "believers."

b. It is also clear that in the immediately following line (verse 9b: ". . . for *we* just previously made the charge") this "we" refers to Paul, the believer.

The conclusion would seem to be clear. What the apostle is asking is this,

---

προερχόμεθα) mean?" Very little help is available from other sources. In the New Testament this verb occurs nowhere else. See, however, Josephus, *Against Apion* II. 186. But Rom. 3:9 uses the middle voice. Is the meaning then "Do we *hold* something *in front* of ourselves for protection?" "Do we have a defense?"

Or should we ascribe a *passive* meaning to this middle; hence, "Are we being excelled?" It would be very difficult to fit either of these meanings into the present context.

Is it possible, then, that this middle form must be given an active meaning? The answer sometimes given is, "No example has been found that this verb, in its middle form, has an active meaning." But when the applicable examples are so few and far between, such a verdict has little, if any, value. More significant is the fact that use of a middle form in an active sense is by no means infrequent in Koine Greek or in Paul's epistles. See Gram. N.T. (Bl.-Debr.), par. 316, p. 165. The sense may therefore very well be "Do we excel?" "Are we any better?" So interpreted, the prefix πρό is that of *precedence*. The total meaning, justifiable also from the point of view of etymology, may well be, "Do we possess any priority?" In the present context this would amount to, "In the eyes of God do we hold a superior standing of righteousness?" Or more simply, "Are we any better?"

"*By nature*—or *of ourselves*—are we, Christians, better than all other people?" We have a right *in our explanation* to add the words "by nature," for the apostle has not yet expounded, in any detail, what we become "by grace." For that doctrine see 3:21f. The fact that *by nature* everyone is a "child of wrath" is clear from Eph. 2:1-3.[80]

Continued: **9b. Not at all, for we just previously made the charge that Jews and Greeks alike are all under (the power of) sin.**

Paul's "Not at all" is decisive.[81] He has indeed shown that the Jews are sinners, and as such are lying under the sentence of condemnation (2:1-3:8). He has proved this also with respect to the Greeks or Gentiles (1:18-32). Accordingly, the entire human race is condemnable before God. That means, therefore, that basically the same applies to the apostle himself and to all those who serve the Lord with him, for[82] they too belong to this sin-laden, guilt-burdened human race. *By nature* all are under (the power of) sin.

For additional substantiation of this charge the apostle, in a manner that is both artistic and convincing, introduces a chain of Old Testament passages. If he has borrowed this mode of argumentation from the rabbis, that surely cannot be held against him. Fact is that the material he quotes is relevant, well-chosen, inspired.

On the formal side, it is clear that the quotation-chain (verses 10b-18) has three strophes or stanzas. The first strophe (verses 10b-12) consists of two sets of three lines; the second (verses 13, 14) has two sets of two lines, and so does the third (verses 15-18).

The quotations are not all *ad verbum* (literal) but are all *ad sensum* (according to meaning).

By far the most of the quoted material is from the Psalms, though the Prophets (Isaiah) and the Writings (Ecclesiastes) are also represented. Does not this indicate that Paul regarded not only the historical but also the poetical and the prophetical books of the Old Testament as being inspired?

Turning now to the material contents of this chain of proof, we note that the opening strophe is as follows:

10-12.   As it is written:
"There is no one righteous, not even one;
    there is no one who understands;
    there is no one who is searching for God.

---

80. In this interpretation I agree with Greijdanus, *op. cit.*, p. 171, against Ridderbos, *op. cit.*, p. 76. As mentioned previously, in essence I agree also with Lekkerkerker. See p. 20.

81. Though it is true that οὐ πάντως can mean either (a) not altogether, not in every respect; or (b) not at all, the *radical nature of the explanatory and confirmatory quotations in verses 10-18 favors the latter sense*. Here I agree with Ridderbos (*op. cit.*, p. 76), as against Cranfield (*op. cit.*, p. 190), Greijdanus (*op. cit.*, p. 171) and J. A. C. Van Leeuwen and D. Jacobs, *Korte Verklaring der Heilige Schrift*, Kampen, 1932, p. 43.

82. I can see no good reason for interpreting γάρ as here used in any other sense than as meaning *for*.

**All have turned aside; together they have become worthless;
there is no one who does what is right;
there is not even one."**

It is clear that the argument which intends to demonstrate the universality of sin builds up to a climax.

The very first strophe shows that Paul is not describing this or that particular race or class of people but men in general. The picture he draws is dismal: no one is righteous; in fact, no one understands his deplorable condition. And no one is even trying to understand, is even searching for God, the Source of all wisdom and knowledge.

But are there no exceptions? Paul answers, "There is no one . . . no one . . . no one . . . no one . . . not even one."

He makes all this even more emphatic by interspersing the five negatives with one positive statement, "*All* have turned aside" (from God and his law), etc. Is not this *all* an echo of the one in verse 9 ("Jews and Greeks alike are *all* under the power of sin")?

To make his argument convincing the apostle now descends to particulars. He speaks about the evil *throat* (voice), *tongue, lips, mouth:*

**13, 14.   "An open grave is their throat;
With their tongue they practice deception."
"The poison of vipers is under their lips.
Their mouth is full of cursing and bitterness."**

It must be borne in mind that Paul is attempting to prove that *by nature* all people, without exception, are under the power of sin. In order to do so, what specific type of sinfulness will he select as an illustration? Will he remind his listeners or readers of the gross immorality that marked the heathen world? Cf. 1:24, 26, 27. He will not, for in that case many a Jew and perhaps even this or that Gentile might object, "But I, for one, am not guilty!"

Guided by the Holy Spirit, the apostle wisely selects *the sin of the tongue* to illustrate the universality of human sinfulness, for with respect to *this* evil who can truthfully say, "I am not guilty?"[83] On this subject of sinful human speech see also Ps. 39:1; Prov. 10:19; 17:27; Matt. 5:22, 37; 10:19, 20 (and parallels); Titus 3:2; James 1:19, 26; 3:1-12; I Peter 3:10.

Since a tree is known by its fruit, and a man by his deeds, Paul stresses the viciousness of the evil throat by showing how it operates. Quoting from Ps. 5:9 he describes the throat as "an open grave." He is probably thinking of a huge, cruel monster, ready to devour its victims; yes, even to devour them *unawares.* On a human plane this destruction may even take place by means of flattery, "the smooth tongue" of Ps. 5:9, the one that practices deception.

The final line of verse 13, "The poison of vipers is under their lips" is an

---

83. In this connection I wish to call the reader's attention to L. B. Flynn's book, *Did I Say That?*, Nashville, 1959. It is very interesting and instructive.

exact quotation of the LXX version of Ps. 140:3 (LXX 139:4).[84] The emphasis continues to be on the perfidious manner in which people, *acting from motives that lie outside of the sphere of God's sovereign grace*, try to destroy their intended victims. Their words may be very flattering, but watch out: the speakers cannot be trusted. They resemble vipers which "under their lips," at the base of their fangs, are equipped with sacs filled with deadly poison. Examples: Saul (I Sam. 18:17); David; *yes even David* (II Sam. 11).

Still continuing in the same vein, that is, emphasizing the deceitful nature of human speech, the "chain" continues in verse 14, with a quotation from Ps. 10:7 (LXX 9:28), "Their mouth is full of cursing and bitterness." In the Psalm from which these words are quoted the context again very definitely stresses *the treacherous manner* in which a person will at times try to "use" and abuse his fellowmen. Note such expressions as "he lurks in secret, lies in wait, crouches." Truly, deceptive is man's heart! See Jer. 17:9.

Thus interpreted, the reference to "cursing and bitterness" may well mean that in the process of attempting to deceive their neighbors people will at times perjure themselves; that is, they will pronounce *bitter curses* upon themselves, to be poured out if what they say turns out not to have been true. For example, a merchant will say to a potential customer, "May I drop dead on this very spot if I have not shelled out more for this article than I ask you to pay for it." In expressing this wish he is, of course, insincere.[85]

Since the second strophe dealt with men's *speech*, it is logical that the final one, in its first three lines, would describe men's life and conduct, their *actions*.

15-18. **"Swift (are) their feet to shed blood;**
      ruin and misery mark their ways,
      and the way of peace they have not known.
      There is no fear of God before their eyes."[86]

A long and still continuing series of wars and murders proves that the first three lines of this final stanza are true today as well as in Isaiah's time.

---

84. In both places—LXX and here in Rom. 3:13—the original reads: ἰὸς ἀσπίδως ὑπὸ τὰ χείλη αὐτῶν.

85. Another interpretation, favored by several commentators, divides the *cursing* and the *bitterness* between the perpetrator and the victim: the former utters curses, the latter experiences bitterness. But at this point is not this separation of two nouns connected by *and* rather unnatural?

86. ὀξεῖς, nom. pl. m. of ὀξύς, sharp (cf. *acute*); Rev. 1:16; 2:12; 14:14, 17, 18; 19:15; and in connection with time: quick, swift.

In the New Testament σύντριμμα occurs only here. The cognate verb συντρίβω means *to rub together;* hence, to bruise, crush, destroy. See N.T.C. on Luke 9:39 (p. 524). We use the expression "to rub each other the wrong way." It is understandable that the noun σύντριμμα means destruction, ruin.

With respect to the derivation of the word ταλαιπωρία unanimity is lacking, though to *tol*erate (bear, endure) that which is *por*otic (in the sense of forming a hardness or callus) may point in the right direction. The word occurs also in James 5:1. It means hardship, suffering, distress, misery. The related adjective ταλαίπωρος is found in Rom. 7:24; Rev. 3:17.

See Isa. 59:7, 8. The ruin and misery brought about by these explosions of human wrath are evident everywhere.

The basic reason for this deplorable situation is expressed in the final line, "There is no fear of God before their eyes" (Ps. 36:1). The *consistent* operation of the fear of God in human hearts would have brought about a yearning for the reconciliation of man with God and with his fellowmen.

The conclusion of this section is found in verses 19, 20, beginning as follows:

19. Now we know that whatever the law says, it speaks to those (who are) within the pale of the law ...

Since in the preceding series of quotations the apostle has never quoted from the Decalog or even, in general, from the Pentateuch, but only from the Psalms, Prophets, and Writings, it is clear that the term "the law" must refer to the Old Testament as a whole. Such passages as John 10:34; 15:25; and I Cor. 14:25 illustrate a similar use of the expression "the law."

If, in the present case, there is any real difference in meaning between "says" and "speaks," it would be that "says" refers to what is said, and "speaks" draws attention to the act of speaking.

With respect to the phrase "those (who are) within the pale of the law" there is a wide difference of interpretation. Here are a few samples:

a. *the Jews.* Thus J. P. Lange, *Commentary on the Holy Scriptures,* (translated and edited by P. Schaff), Grand Rapids (reprint), 1869, p. 121; also Ridderbos, *op. cit.,* p. 79.

b. *all who have the Old Testament,* including the believers in Rome. That view is expressed by Lenski, *op. cit.,* pp. 239, 240, who correctly stresses the fact that Paul is not just writing to Jews, but to the Roman Christians.

c. *everybody, the whole world.* Thus Greijdanus, *op. cit.,* p. 177; and Murray, *op. cit.,* p. 106.

d. *everybody, but with special application to the Jews.* For this interpretation see, for example, C. R. Erdman, *Epistle of Paul to the Romans,* Phila., n.d., p. 50; and G. B. Wilson, *Romans, A Digest of Reformed Comment,* Edinburgh, 1977, p. 56.

I believe c.—everybody, the whole world—most adequately expresses what Paul had in mind. It is true that the phrase "those (who are) within the pale of the law" might cause us to think exclusively of the Jews. However, does not the law, God's Word, have a message for all? And does it not have authority over, and a claim on all, whether they be believers or unbelievers? And does it not concern all, without exception, whether they be Jews or Gentiles by race?

Besides, words must be interpreted in light of their context, which is as follows: **that every mouth may be silenced, and the entire world may be exposed to the judgment of [or: may stand guilty before] God.**

It is clear that the apostle is no longer thinking exclusively about Gentiles or Jews. No, he is summarizing his argument, combining the conclusions to which he has arrived in connection with Gentiles (1:32), Jews (2:21-24), everybody, including even believers (3:9) as they are by nature. He repeats the verdict expressed earlier. See especially 3:9-12.

The figure used is dramatic, fear-inspiring, unforgettable. Everybody is standing in front of God, the Judge. The records are read, and as it were one by one the accused are given an opportunity to answer the charges made against them. However, their guilt having been exposed, they have no answer. Their mouths are silenced, stopped.

Conclusion: **20. Therefore by law-works no flesh [or: mortal being] will be justified in his sight, for through law (comes) consciousness of sin.**

In somewhat different phraseology the thought of Ps. 143:2 ("Do not bring thy servant into judgment, for no one living is righteous before thee") is here reproduced.[87] Cf. Job 9:2.

Paul's argument is irrefutable. By the works of the law no one can ever be justified in God's sight. Why not? Consider, for a moment, what the law demands. Nothing less than this, that a person love God "with all" his heart, soul, mind, and strength, and that he love his neighbor as he loves himself (Matt. 22:37-40; Mark 12:29-31; Luke 10:27). The apostle has shown that it is exactly this love that was lacking on the part of both Gentile (note: "neither gave thanks," Rom. 1:21) and Jew (note: "hard and unconverted heart," 2:5). He has made clear that *every person* stands condemned before God (3:19).

He stands condemned because of his sins of commission, but also because of his sins of omission (1:21, 28; 2:21; 3:11; cf. Matt. 25:41-43); not only because of his sins open and public, but also because of the evil he commits in secret (Rom. 2:16). He is damnable in God's sight not only because of what he says and does (Rom. 3:13-17), but even because of what he *is* (3:9, 10); that is, because of his sinful *state*.

Only one conclusion is possible therefore. Man is doomed, doomed, doomed. His condition is one of thorough hopelessness and despair. And the law, with its demand of nothing less than moral and spiritual *perfection* (cf. Lev. 19:2), a state to which man, in his own power, can never attain, creates in him a dreadful, mortifying sense of sin; hence, a presentiment of doom, total and everlasting.

---

21 But now, apart from law, a righteousness from God, attested by the law and the prophets, has been revealed, 22 namely, a righteousness from God which, through faith in

---

87. Note the Hebraisms: (a) A word for word rendering of the Hebrew text would be, "... for not is righteous before thy face all living being." The LXX version (of Ps. 142:2b) is: ὅτι οὐ δικαιωθήσεται ἐνώπιόν σου πᾶς ζῶν. Note "not ... all" in the sense of "no." (b) For "all living being" Paul has substituted "all flesh," which is frequently used in the Hebrew text of the Old Testament to indicate mankind considered in its frailty and insignificance, as contrasted with God viewed in his greatness and majesty.

The various meanings of the word σάρξ in Paul's epistles are summarized on p. 217.

For δικαιωθήσεται πᾶσα σάρξ see also Gal. 2:16, where the same expression is used without the addition ἐνώπιον αὐτοῦ ("before him" or "in his sight").

Jesus Christ, (comes) to *all* who exercise faith—for there is no distinction,   23 since all have sinned and fall short of the glory of God—   24 being justified freely by his grace through the redemption (accomplished) in Christ Jesus;   25 whom God designed to be, by the shedding of his blood, a wrath-removing[88] sacrifice, (effective) through faith. (God did this) to demonstrate his justice, because in his forbearance he had treated past sins with indulgence.[89]   26 (So he did it) to demonstrate his justice in the present time, that he might be just and the One who justifies the person who has faith in Jesus.

27 What room, then, is left for boasting?[90] It is excluded. On what basis? Of works? No, but on the basis of faith.   28 For we maintain that it is by faith that a person is justified, apart from law works.   29 Or is God (the God) of Jews only? Is he not (the God) of Gentiles also? Certainly, of Gentiles also; 30 seeing that there is only one God, who will justify the circumcised by faith, and the uncircumcised through that same faith.   31 Do we then invalidate the law through our (insistence on)[91] faith? By no means. On the contrary, we uphold the law.

---

5. "But now, apart from law, a righteousness from God has been revealed . . . a righteousness through faith in Jesus Christ."
3:21–31

21. But now, apart from law, a righteousness from God, attested by the law and the prophets, has been revealed . . .

Dark and dismal is man's condition. This darkness and despair is unfathomable and universal. It envelops all.

Then suddenly a light, the very light which previously had flickered for a brief moment (1:16, 17), comes streaming in. Hope revives.

This light, this ray of optimism, comes not from below but from above. It is "a righteousness from God." It is he who comes to the rescue. It is he who condescends to save those who had made themselves thoroughly unworthy of being saved. And, being God, he does this—of course!—without sacrificing his righteousness or lifting the demands of his law. This is the *light* of his glorious gospel. Study such passages as Isa. 9:1 (cf. Matt. 4:16); 49:6b; 58:8; 60:1, 3, 19, 20; Mic. 7:8; Luke 1:78, 79; 2:32; John 1:9; 8:12; Acts 13:47; Eph. 5:8, 9; Rev. 22:5.

Why God did this is a mystery we shall never be able *fully* to understand. Such love is infinite and incomprehensible. See what the apostle says about it in Rom. 5:6–8, and how in II Cor. 9:15 he pours out his heart in gratitude and adoration by exclaiming, "Thanks be to God for his indescribably precious gift!" What took place when (to speak in human terms) in the quiet recess of eternity God Triune decided to deliver man from the greatest evil and to place him in possession of the greatest good, to do this at *such* a price (II Cor. 5:21), is a matter so marvelous and sublime that in his epistle to the Ephesians the apostle prays that the readers (or hearers), being rooted and established in love, may be strong, in unison with all the

---

88. Or: propitiatory.
89. Or: had overlooked past sins.
90. Literally: Where, then, is boasting?
91. Or: teaching about.

saints, *to grasp* the breadth, length, height, and depth of *the love of Christ which* (in all its dimensions) *can never be grasped* (3:14-19)! This too is a matter "angels desire to look into" (I Peter 1:12). It is the most glorious paradox one can imagine.

Here in Rom. 3:21 Paul states, "But now"—that is, at this present time (verse 26; cf. 5:9), this very strategic moment in the history of redemption, in Gal 4:4 called *the fulness of the time*—"*a righteousness from God* has been revealed." This righteousness goes into effect "apart from the law," which can only mean that it was not, and cannot be, earned by men's obedience to God's law. It was and is a righteousness "apart from *the works* of the law." Cf. Rom. 3:28; 4:6-8; Gal. 2:16, 21; 3:10-13; Eph. 2:9; Phil. 3:9; II Tim. 1:9; Titus 3:5.[92]

Is Paul presenting a new doctrine, something never heard of? On the contrary, he is speaking about "a righteousness attested by the law and the prophets."[93] The apostle has already quoted Hab. 2:4; see Rom. 1:17. Undoubtedly he also has in mind other passages; such as Gen. 15:6; Ps. 32:1, 2; see Rom. 4:3, 7, 8. And see N.T.C. on Luke, p. 125.

Continued: **22, 23. namely, a righteousness from God which, through faith in Jesus Christ, (comes) to *all* who exercise faith—for there is no distinction, since all have sinned and fall short of the glory of God—** ...

In substance Paul here repeats what he has stated in 1:16, 17. He is not forgetting his *theme*. In the former passage he had declared, "The gospel . . . is (the) power of God for salvation to everyone who exercises faith . . . For in it a righteousness from God is revealed from faith to faith . . ." He now adds that the object of this faith is *Jesus Christ*. Cf. Matt. 1:21; John 3:16; 14:6; Acts 4:12.

With great emphasis the apostle repeats the thought of 1:16b, namely, that this righteousness is granted to *all* those—and *only* to those—who put this faith into practice; that is, to all true believers in Jesus Christ. It makes no difference whether a person is rich or poor, young or old, male or female, educated or uneducated, Jew or Gentile. All need this righteousness and can obtain it only through faith in the Savior, in and through whom the Triune God reveals himself.

There is no distinction. Since *all,* everybody in the entire world, have sinned and therefore fall short of or lack the glory of God, no one should base his hope for acceptance with God on his own goodness. God's law demands perfection, and no one is any longer perfect in God's sight. The apostle has explained this in some detail; first with respect to the Gentiles (1:18-32); next with respect to the Jews (2:1-3:8). He has summarized it in 3:9-20.

All people have sinned and fall short—or are falling short—of God's

---

92. This does not mean that the law has no place in the plan of redemption. See on 3:31.
93. For this designation of what we today call the Old Testament see also Matt. 5:17; 7:12; 22:40; Luke 16:16; Acts 24:14; 28:23.

glory. When man transgressed God's command he lost the earlier blessings; specifically, the divine *approval* resting upon him, hence also freedom of access to God. See Gen. 3:8.[94]

24, 25a. ... being justified freely by his grace through the redemption (accomplished) in Christ Jesus; whom God designed to be, by the shedding of his blood, a wrath-removing sacrifice, (effective) through faith.

---

94. With respect to the meaning of καὶ ὑστεροῦνται τῆς δόξης τοῦ θεοῦ commentators differ widely. Here are four views:

a. All men fail to render to God the glory they owe him. The divine standard for human life, the ideal of perfection, remains far above and beyond the reach of anyone. See W. H. G. Thomas, *St. Paul's Epistle to the Romans*, Grand Rapids, 1946, p. 112.

Though the thought here expressed is true, as has been indicated previously (3:10–18), and in his very practical and devotional commentary Thomas adds a valuable illustration, this is probably not what Rom. 3:23b means, for in that case would not Paul have inserted an additional verbal form? Would he not have written, "All fall short of *doing* everything to God's glory"? See I Cor. 10:31.

b. The term "glory of God" refers to the future heavenly glory. So sure is Ridderbos (*op. cit.*, p. 84) that this is the correct interpretation that he states, "Nothing else can be meant by it."

It is true that there are several Pauline passages in which "glory" or "glory of God" refers to the believers' future reward. See, for example, Rom. 2:7; 5:2; 8:18, 30; I Cor. 15:43; II Cor. 4:17; Col. 1:27; 3:4; II Tim. 2:10. Nevertheless, it is important to take note of the fact that here in Rom. 3:23b Paul uses the present tense. He says that because of the entrance of sin all men *are falling short* of God's glory. If he had been thinking of the glory awaiting God's children in heaven, would he not have used the future tense?

c. Just as by redemption a person is transformed into the image of God (II Cor. 3:18), so previously by means of the fall he became destitute of that perfection which is the reflection of God's glory. He lost what he once possessed. The term "the glory of God" as used in Rom. 3:23b therefore means "conformity to God's image." See Murray, *op. cit.*, p. 113; and John Knox, *The Interpreter's Bible*, Vol. IX, p. 430. Closely related is the view of E. F. Harrison, *The Expositor's Bible Commentary*, Grand Rapids, 1976, p. 41, according to which the term in question refers to the privilege man originally enjoyed of having direct communion with God. What man originally enjoyed in Paradise was lost through sin. Or, as Van Leeuwen-Jacobs (*op. cit.*, p. 53) point out, because of the fall man can no longer approach God directly but must stand from afar (Exod. 20:18, 21; Num. 4:15; 17:13, etc.). See also U. Wilckens, Th.D.N.T., Vol. VIII, p. 596. According to that article Paul may be referring to the glory with which Adam was originally invested.

Insofar as this theory interprets the phrase "glory of God" as a reference to a privilege (or privileges) man enjoyed in the state of rectitude but has lost through the entrance of sin, I agree with it. The words "All have sinned *and*—probably meaning *and as a result*—are falling short of the glory of God" certainly seem to point in that direction.

Is it possible, however, that the apostle may have been thinking first of all of something else which man once had but now lacks? This introduces us to the next theory:

d. The term "glory of God" means "glory imparted by God." It refers to "glory" in the sense of *approval, approbation, praise*. (For the various senses in which the term δόξα is used by Paul see above, p. 74.) Supporting this theory are C. Hodge, *A Commentary on the Epistle to the Romans*, Grand Rapids, 1886, p. 140; J. Denney, *op. cit.*, p. 610; C. R. Erdman, *op. cit.*, p. 52; and in a sense R. C. H. Lenski, *op. cit.*, p. 249. Also R. Knox, who translates, ". . . all alike are unworthy of God's praise."

The objection raised against this theory, namely, that in that case Paul would have used a preposition, would have written παρὰ θεοῦ (cf. John 5:44; II Peter 1:17) is not very convincing; for:

(1) Without using a preposition *John* can refer to "praise coming from God" (12:43). If John, why not Paul?

(2) When Paul refers to "*righteousness* coming from God," he at times does this without

Note the various elements of this important passage:

a. *being justified*
Here, for the first time in Romans, the verb *to justify* is used in a positive context in order to set forth the doctrine of justification by faith.[95]

It is easy to go astray here in interpreting Paul's thought. By combining the beginning of verse 24 with the closing words of verse 23 the result is, "... all have sinned and fall short of the glory of God, being justified freely by his grace," etc. Is Paul actually saying, then, that all sinners are being justified; therefore, are being saved? Has Paul suddenly become a universalist?

The writer of this commentary remembers hearing a minister say from the pulpit, "In the end everybody will be saved. I have hope even for the devil." Omitting the part about the devil, was that minister in line with Paul?

But this cannot be, for in 1:16, 17 and 3:22 the apostle insists that the "righteousness from God" is a blessing bestowed on those who exercise faith, on no one else.

What is the solution? Probably this: when in verse 22a Paul declares that God's righteousness extends to all who exercise faith, there is, as it were, an interruption. It is as if someone (a Jew perhaps?) is asking, "Only to those, Paul? Not also to us who, though we do not share your faith in Jesus Christ, have tried very hard to please God by means of our effort to live in harmony with his law? Are we no better than other people? *Is there no distinction between us and others?*"

The answer to this parenthetical question—as has already been shown—is, "There is no distinction, since all have sinned and fall short of the glory of God" (22b, 23).

Returning now to the main line of thought, "a righteousness from God which, through faith in Jesus Christ (comes) to *all* who exercise faith" (verse 22a), the apostle continues, "being justified freely by his grace through the

---

using a preposition (Rom. 1:17; 3:21, 22). If he can do this with the word "righteousness," why not with "glory"?

(3) What may well be the strongest argument in favor of interpreting Paul to mean that as a result of man's sin he is falling short of, or lacking, the divine approbation or praise is this, that in these earlier chapters of the epistle, and to some extent even later, the apostle is operating with a series of concepts such as sin, condemnation, righteousness, justification. Into this series—think especially of justification—the concept *approbation* fits very naturally.

I therefore believe that verse 23 means "All have sinned and as a result are now in a state in which they are falling short of (or are lacking) what they possessed before the fall, namely, the inestimable blessing of having the approval of God resting upon them."

This implies the truth mentioned under theory c, for how can I say, "God approves of me" without at the same time also saying, "Therefore I have freedom of access to him"? Hence, while, as I see it, theory d. is to be preferred, theory c. comes very close and is probably implied.

95. Earlier use of the verb δικαιόω in Romans:
2:13, in connection with a contrast between doers and merely hearers.
3:4, in the sense of divine vindication ("that thou mayest be proved right").
3:20, negatively, to indicate the impossibility of salvation by works.

redemption (accomplished) in Christ Jesus" (verse 24). Not everybody but only those who exercise faith, the genuine believers, receive the great blessing of justification.[96]

When used, as here in Rom. 3:24, in the dominant forensic sense, *to justify* means *to declare righteous;* and *justification* may be defined as *that gracious act of God whereby, on the basis solely of Christ's accomplished mediatorial work, he declares the sinner just, and the latter accepts this benefit with a believing heart.* In defense of this definition see not only the present context (Rom. 3:24-30) but also 4:3, 5; 5:1, 9; 8:30; Gal. 2:15, 16; 3:8, 11, 24; 5:4; Titus 3:7. *Justification stands over against condemnation.* See Rom. 8:1, 33, 34.

Justification is a matter of *imputation* (reckoning, charging): the sinner's guilt is imputed to Christ; the latter's righteousness is imputed to the sinner (Gen. 15:6; Ps. 32:1, 2; Isa. 53:4-6; Jer. 23:6; Rom. 5:18, 19). While *justification* is a matter of *imputation, sanctification* is a matter of *transformation.* In justification the Father takes the lead (Rom. 8:33); in sanctification the Holy Spirit does (II Thess. 2:13). The first is a "once for all" verdict, the second a lifelong process. Nevertheless, although the two should never be identified, neither should they be separated. They are distinct but not separate.

b. *freely*

The word used in the original means "as a gift"; in other words, without payment made by the one who receives it; without any human merit. See I Tim. 1:9; Titus 3:4. If the sinner is to be *declared righteous* at all, it will have to be *freely,* for, as has been shown in the preceding, as measured by the standard of God's requirement (Lev. 19:2; Matt. 22:37 and parallels), human merit is impossible. Man cannot earn the great and basic blessing of justification. He can only accept it as a gift (Isa. 55:1).

c. *by his grace*

Grace is God's love directed toward the *guilty*, just as his *mercy* is that same love directed toward *those in misery.*[97] It is easy to understand that "freely" and "by his grace" go together.

d. *through the redemption (accomplished) in Christ Jesus*

The word *redemption* (Greek ἀπολύτρωσις) occurs ten times in the New Testament (Luke 21:28; Rom. 3:24; 8:23; I Cor. 1:30; Eph. 1:7, 14; 4:30; Col. 1:14; Heb. 9:15; 11:35). In those passages in which the term is used, as here in Rom. 3:24, in its full spiritual sense, it indicates deliverance, by

---

96. The fact that δικαιούμενοι is in the nominative but πάντας is in the accusative is no valid objection to the proposed construction, for this is not at all unusual when the modifier is so far away from the word or phrase it modifies, especially when such a nominative introduces a new clause.

97. For more on *grace* see N.T.C. on Luke, pp. 181, 182.

means of the payment of a ransom, from the guilt, punishment, and power of sin.[98]

This redemption was accomplished *in*, probably meaning "in connection with," Christ Jesus, the Anointed Savior. Most translators have adopted this or a very similar translation, namely, "*in* Christ Jesus." Some, however, prefer "*by* Christ Jesus." The Greek allows either. In favor of "in" or "in connection with" is the fact that in verses 23, 24 "God" is clearly mentioned as the Author of the believers' redemption. Not to Jesus alone but to God Triune should be accorded the praise and glory for man's deliverance from sin and its consequences. It was accomplished or brought about in and through Christ Jesus; that is, by means of his voluntary suffering and death on the cross.

e. *whom God designed to be . . .*[99]

This *design* points back to the divine eternal counsel. In that counsel or decree Christ Jesus was designed to be the One through whom the plan of

---

98. It must be granted that in such a passage as, for example, Rom. 8:23 the deliverance indicated by this noun does not in and by itself include the idea of the payment of a ransom.

99. The root meaning of the verb προτίθημι, of which the form here used, προέθετο, is the third per. s. 2nd. aor. indicat. middle, is *to set before;* which, in the middle voice becomes *to set before oneself.* It is easy to understand that one may set something before oneself in a twofold sense: (1) for public display; (2) for mental consideration; to plan (something) for oneself; Dutch: *zich (iets) voornemen.* Most translators prefer (1). However, in favor of (2) *to plan, purpose, design,* the following facts should be borne in mind:

In both of the other instances in which this verb is used in the New Testament, Rom. 1:13 ("many times *I planned* to come to y o u") and Eph. 1:9 ("which *he purposed* for himself") the sense is clearly telic. If there, why not here? Also note that wherever in the New Testament the cognate *noun* πρόθεσις is used, except when it occurs in connection with showbread (the consecrated unleavened loaves placed on a table in the Holy Place), the meaning is *purpose:* "with steadfast purpose" (Acts 11:23); "supposing that they had obtained their purpose" (Acts 27:13); "called according to his purpose" (Rom. 8:28); "in order that God's purpose according to election might stand" (Rom. 9:11); "having been foreordained according to the purpose of him who accomplishes all things according to the counsel of his will" (Eph. 1:11); "according to the eternal purpose which he formed in Christ" (Eph. 3:11); "who saved us . . . according to his own purpose and grace" (II Tim. 1:9); and "You, however, followed my purpose" (II Tim. 3:10).

In favor of a telic rendering here in Rom. 3:25a are also Origen, Ambrosiaster, Chrysostom, Oecumenius, Lagrange, Fritzsche, Robertson, Phillips ("appointed," cf. Jerusalem Bible), N.E.B. ("designed") and Cranfield.

In support of the rendering *presented, set forth, put forward,* or something similar, it has been argued that this meaning fits better into a context which speaks of the *demonstration* of God's justice (3:25, 26), and that it parallels the words of Paul in Gal. 3:1 ("Jesus was openly displayed"). But it is not clear how it can be convincingly argued that a verb indicating the demonstration of *God's* justice parallels a verb referring to the shedding of *Christ's* blood. Besides, the grammatical construction in the two cases differs radically. And Gal. 3:1 certainly belongs to a different type of context than the first clause in Rom. 3:25.

In order to justify a meaning for the Greek verb which it has nowhere else in the New Testament, and which differs substantially from the sense of the cognate noun in *all* comparable New Testament instances of its use, stronger arguments will have to be presented. On this question see also the fine remarks of Cranfield, *op. cit.,* Vol. I, pp. 208-210.

salvation would be realized. Christ Jesus and his people can never be separated. Note such parallel passages as Eph. 1:4, 7, 10, 11.

f. *by the shedding of his blood, a wrath-removing or propitiatory sacrifice*[100]
Blood represents life (Lev. 17:11; Matt. 20:28, cf. 26:28; John 10:11, 15). The words "by the shedding of his blood" refer to Messiah's voluntary sacrifice of his life in the place of those whom he came to save. Cf. Isa. 53:10–12.

Though it is being constantly denied, there is indeed such a thing as the wrath of God that rests on the sinner and must be removed if he is to be saved. See Rom. 1:18; 2:5, 8; 3:5; 5:9; 9:22; Eph. 2:3; 5:6; Col. 3:6, I Thess. 1:10; 2:16; 5:9; Rev. 6:16, 17; 11:18; 14:10; 16:19; 19:15.

When atonement is rendered, God's wrath is removed. Rom. 3:25a mentions a wrath-removing or propitiatory sacrifice, namely, Christ Jesus himself. It was he who *gave*—voluntarily offered—his blood; hence his life; hence himself (I Tim. 2:6) for his sheep, bearing the wrath of God *in their stead,* thereby causing them to be reconciled to God.

There are many passages which teach this truth, either as a whole or in part: Isa. 53:4–8, 12; Matt. 20:28; 26:28; Mark 10:45; 14:24; Luke 22:20; Acts 20:28; I Cor. 10:16; 11:25; II Cor. 5:20, 21; Eph. 1:7; 2:13; Col. 1:20; I Peter 1:18, 19; 2:24; I John 1:7; 5:6; Heb. 9:11, 12, 15, 23–28; Rev. 1:5; 5:9; 7:14; 12:11; 13:8.

The Greek word for which I have chosen the English equivalent "wrath-removing (or propitiatory) sacrifice," in the LXX (Greek translation of the Old Testament) indicates the blood-sprinkled lid of the ark of the covenant. This is the "mercy seat" (A.V.) or "atonement cover" (N.I.V.). See Exod. 25:17, 18; Lev. 16:2, 3; etc. In all, the word occurs more than twenty times in the Pentateuch, most often in Exodus. In the description of tabernacle furniture (Heb. 9:1–5) it is logical to believe that verse 5 similarly refers to this *cover*. However, although the same Greek word is found also in Rom. 3:25, it is understandable that most translators—there are exceptions—hesitate to call Christ Jesus either a "mercy seat" or an "atonement cover." "Wrath-removing sacrifice," "sacrifice of atonement" (N.I.V.),[101] or simply "propitiation" (A.V., A.R.V.) is better. See also I John 2:2; 4:10.

g. *(effective) through faith*
Christ's propitiatory sacrifice does not go into effect automatically. If a person wishes to obtain this great blessing—the turning away of God's

---

100. The phrase "by the shedding of his blood" should probably not be construed with "faith," resulting in the rendering "faith in his blood." It is true that ἐν τῷ αὐτοῦ αἵματι directly follows πίστεως; and it is also true that grammatically (ἐν plus the dative to indicate faith's object) is not as unusual as some maintain. (See, for example, Gal. 3:26; Eph. 1:15; Col. 1:4; I Tim. 3:13; II Tim. 1:13). But it is also a fact that a modifier does not always stand close to the word it modifies. Moreover, with Paul the object of faith is a person, not a thing.

101. To help the reader the N.I.V. adds this valuable footnote: "(God presented him) as the one who would turn away his wrath, taking away sin."

wrath, forgiveness, acceptance with God—he must exercise genuine faith in Christ, in and through whom God Triune reveals himself.

The indispensability of faith has been pointed out before (1:8, 16, 17; 3:22) and will be emphasized again (3:26, 28, 30; 4:3, etc.). Without faith no one can please God (Heb. 11:6). To be saved a person needs faith, *God-given* faith (Eph. 2:8).

By works, human effort, or earnings no one has ever been saved or will ever reach everlasting, heavenly glory (3:9–20).

> Not what my hands have done
> Can save my guilty soul;
> Not what my toiling flesh has borne
> Can make my spirit whole.
> Not what I feel or do
> Can give me peace with God;
> Not all my prayers and sighs and tears
> Can bear my awful load.
>
> Thy grace alone, O God,
> To me can pardon speak;
> Thy power alone, O Son of God,
> Can this sore bondage break.
> No other work save thine,
> No other blood will do;
> No strength save that which is divine
> Can bear me safely through.
>
> Horatius Bonar

By way of summary it can be pointed out, therefore, that justification, as taught by Paul, is in no sense whatever the work of man. On the contrary, it is:

a. God's gift (Rom. 5:15–18)
b. the product of his grace (3:24; 4:16; 5:15)
c. free (5:16)
d. not of works (3:20)
e. the opposite of condemnation (8:1, 33, 34)
f. that which deprives man of every reason for boasting (3:27)
g. appropriated by faith, even that faith being God-given (Eph. 2:8).

That this doctrine of justification by faith is in accord with the teaching of the Old Testament will be shown in Romans 4.

That it also is in harmony with the teaching of Christ will be indicated in a moment (see the next paragraph). Add Luke 18:14.

All this is contrary to Rome's doctrine, for while Rome certainly teaches that Christ, by means of his atonement, supplied the meritorious basis for our justification, the predisposing cause must be supplied by ourselves; that is, by our hope, faith, love, contrition, etc. In his doctoral dissertation *Attrition and Contrition at the Council of Trent,* Kampen, 1955, p. 227, G. J. Spykman made the following excellent observation:

"Trent in effect made saving grace dependent upon what the penitent does or fails to do, be it in ever so refined form. . . . Not only grace but also good works contributed to justification, it held." He further points out that this "flatly contradicts Christ's invitation, 'Come to me all ye that labor and are heavy laden, and I will give y o u rest'" (Matt. 11:28-30).

25b, 26. (God did this) to demonstrate his justice, because in his forbearance he had treated past sins with indulgence. (So he did it) to demonstrate his justice in the present time, that he might be just and the One who justifies the person who has faith in Jesus.

How did it happen that, according to God's plan from eternity, nothing could keep Jesus from shedding his blood as a propitiatory sacrifice? The answer is: This happened in order to prove or demonstrate that God had not been unfair or unjust when, in his *forbearance* (cf. 2:4, and see on 8:32), he had treated with indulgence—had "passed over," "overlooked"—for the time being the sins of his people committed in earlier days; that is, during the old dispensation. When God's Son suffered and died, he did so to atone for the sins of *all* who had accepted or were going to accept him by a living faith; that is, for *all* believers in *both* dispensations. The merits of the cross reach backward as well as forward. By not allowing the earlier sins to be left forever unpunished but loading them on Christ (Isa. 53:6), God demonstrated that he was, is, and forevermore will be *just*. And since he is just, who can deny that he, he alone, has a right to be, and actually is, the justifier of all who repose their trust in *Jesus*?[102]

Note the following:

a. Again, as frequently in Romans, we are told that the wonderful blessing of justification is for that person, for him (her) alone, who has *faith* in Jesus.

b. "In *Jesus*." That must mean the Jesus of history, the One who was born in Bethlehem, was crucified, rose again, and ascended to heaven. The claim that it is possible to believe in a Christ who is not the Jesus of history to which Scripture bears testimony is false!

27. What room, then, is left for boasting? It is excluded. On what basis?[103] Of works? No, but on the basis of faith.

Paul has made clear that no one, whether Gentile or Jew, can achieve acceptance with God, hence salvation, by means of his own works or boasting (see on 2:17) or on the basis of the privileges he has received (3:3, 4, 9). Nevertheless, it is characteristic of certain people to boast or brag. See Mic.

---

102. For a different translation and interpretation of the closing words of verse 26: δι-καιοῦντα τὸν ἐκ πίστεως 'Ιησοῦ, see Cranfield, *op. cit.*, pp. 201, 213.

103. Or: principle.

The word νόμος does not always have the same meaning. In Rom. 2:12f. it refers to *the Pentateuch*, with emphasis on the Decalog, as is clear from 2:21, 22. In 3:19 the reference is to *the Old Testament* as a whole. In 8:2 (cf. 7:23) the apostle is thinking of an *actuating principle.* Here in 3:27 the meaning seems to be *basis, norm, standard, principle.*

3:11; Matt. 3:9; Rom. 2:17, 23; 4:2; I Cor. 1:29; Phil. 3:3. Paul may have been thinking especially of the Jews in this connection. All such boasting is senseless and sinful, for "no one is righteous, not even one" (Rom. 3:10). "All have sinned and fall short of the glory of God" (3:23). So, there simply is no room for boasting. Very decisively Paul states. "It is excluded," meaning, "Once for all it has been banished."[104]

On what basis has it been thrown out? On the basis of works perhaps? Of course not. Constant reflection on meritorious (?) accomplishments makes a person proud, not humble. This sinful habit *en*courages rather than *dis*courages boasting.

It is the doctrine of justification, hence salvation, *by faith,* which implies that there is no room whatever for bragging. For faith is a *gift* of God, as is also salvation considered in its entirety. Not even the tiniest part of it is a product of man's ingenuity. See Eph. 2:8, 9. This truth, when applied to the heart by the Holy Spirit, convinces a person that whatever good he possesses has been received (I Cor. 4:7), and that he who boasts should boast in the Lord (I Cor. 1:31).

The right to brag has been excluded. On the basis of faith it has been ruled out. So, in support of verse 27, and to summarize, Paul again states what *in essence* he has said before (1:17; 3:22-24, 26) and is going to reiterate (5:1; 9:30-33; 10:5-13):

28. For we maintain that it is by faith that a person is justified, apart from law works.

Here, by implication, the two conceivable methods of being saved are set over against each other in a sharp antithesis. According to the first, a person is saved by obeying God's law (which to the Jew meant: as interpreted and expanded by tradition). According to the second, he is saved by faith. All "glorying" is excluded. It is by faith that it has been excluded. According to the first, justification, therefore also salvation, is the product of human merit; according to the second, of divine grace.

Paul here, as well as everywhere else, definitely endorses the second proposition. He rejects the first. No wonder, for he who stresses *works* expects salvation to come from within; that is, *from below.* He who emphasizes *faith* looks away from himself to God, and expects salvation to come from him; that is, *from above.*

When, in his translation of the New Testament Luther reached this passage he rendered it as follows, "So halten wir nun dafür, dass der Mensch gerecht werde ohne des Gesetzes Werke, allein durch den Glauben," that is, "So we hold that a person is justified without works of the law, through faith alone." For this addition of the word *alone* he was severely criticized. His answer was:

"If your papist makes much useless fuss about the word *sola, alone,* tell

---

104. Note ἐξεκλείσθη, third per. s. aor. indicat. pass. of ἐκκλείω, to shut out, exclude.

him at once: Doctor Martin Luther will have it so ... Are they [the Papists]
doctors? So am I. Are they learned? So am I. Are they preachers? So am I.
Are they theologians? So am I ... Therefore the word *alone* shall remain in
my New Testament, and though all papal donkeys get furious, they shall
not take it out."[105]

Luther should not have inserted this word. And the critics should not
have raised such a storm of protest about it, for, after all, when Paul states
that it is by faith that a person is justified, apart from law works, does he not
actually mean "by faith alone"?

This position, of course, does not exclude works of gratitude, *the fruit* of
faith, as the apostle makes very clear, both in Romans (6:1-14; 7:4-6;
8:12-14; ch. 12, etc.), and in other epistles (Gal. 5:22-26; Eph. 2:8-10; I
Tim. 2:1-6; Titus 2:11-14).

Hymn writers have caught the true meaning of Rom. 3:28 and similar
passages:

> My hope is built on nothing less
> Than Jesus' blood and righteousness;
> I dare not trust the sweetest frame,
> But wholly lean on Jesus' name.
> On Christ, the solid Rock, I stand;
> All other ground is sinking sand.
>
> Edward Mote

In close connection with the thought of verse 28 Paul continues:

**29, 30. Or is God (the God) of Jews only? Is he not (the God) of Gen-
tiles also? Certainly, of Gentiles also; seeing that there is only one God,
who will justify the circumcised by faith, and the uncircumcised through
that same faith.**

If it were true that works in conformity with the law were required as a
condition upon the fulfilment of which salvation was based, then Gentiles,
living apart from the law, would have no chance to be saved. God would be
the God of the Jews only. The Gentiles would have to look elsewhere for
salvation; perhaps to some other God? The apostle definitely rejects this
suggestion. He affirms that there are not two Gods, one for the Jews, and
one for the Gentiles. In harmony with what he has said previously (see
especially such passages as 2:25f.; 3:22) and is going to say a little later
(10:12, 13), and in thorough agreement also with the teachings of Jesus
(Matt. 8:10-12; John 3:16; 10:14-16; 17:20, 21), the apostle here strongly
affirms that there is only *one* God (cf. Deut. 6:4; Isa. 45:5) and only *one* way
of salvation for both Jew and Gentile, for circumcised and uncircumcised
(Gen. 22:18; Isa. 45:22; Rom. 4:9-12). See also footnote 119.

It is hard to see how, by inspiration of the Holy Spirit, Paul could have
expressed the "no distinction" truth in clearer language. It takes but little

---

105. See Luther's *Sendbrief vom Dolmetschen,* Erl.-Frkf. ed. Vol. LXV, p. 107f.

imagination to sense how the entire Roman congregation, gathered for worship, whether in one meeting place or in several, must have rejoiced when this epistle, with its emphasis on unity (cf. Eph. 2:11-17) was read. The notion according to which even today God recognizes two groups in which he takes special delight—the Jews and the church—finds no support either here or anywhere else in Scripture. What *does* find support is Paul's passage found in Eph. 4:4-6:

"There is one body and one Spirit, just as also y o u were called in one hope which y o u r calling brought y o u; one Lord, one faith, one baptism; one God and Father of all, who is over all and through all and in all."[106]

The apostle closes this section with the words of verse

31. Do we then invalidate the law through our (insistence on) faith? By no means. On the contrary, we uphold the law.

There are those who say that 3:31 should have been 4:1; in other words, that it belongs to and introduces the material of the fourth chapter. They take the term "the law" as used here in 3:31, to be the equivalent of "Scripture" in 4:3. Moreover, it has already been admitted that the term *law* does at times have that significance.

However, there are two main objections against directly connecting with chapter 4:

a. No clear connection can be shown between the substance of 3:31 and the opening paragraph of chapter 4.

b. The very wording of 3:31—Note "Do we, *then*," etc.—clearly indicates that this passage reflects on that which *precedes*.

What the apostle is saying amounts to this: "Since by law-works no mortal will ever be justified (3:20), and since it was *apart from the law* that a righteousness from God has been revealed (verse 21), and since, therefore, a person is justified *by faith, apart from the works of the law* (verse 28), are we depriving the law of its value?"

"Do we then invalidate the law through our (insistence on) faith?"

Paul's answer is very abrupt and decisive, "By no means. On the contrary, we uphold the law."

The forceful character of the answer must probably be explained in light of the fact that there were those who were saying, "Let us do away with the law. All we need is faith. Let us continue in sin, that grace may abound." See on 3:8 and 6:1.

If anyone should ask the further question, "In which way, Paul, do you uphold the law by your emphasis on justification by faith?," he would undoubtedly refer that individual to the contents of Rom. 3:20; 7:7, 8, 13; Gal. 2:19; 3:21, 24.

The doctrines of (a) justification, hence salvation, by faith and (b) that of the usefulness of God's law, coincide beautifully; for "through law comes

---

106. Though it is true that in verse 30 ἐx indicates source; and διά probably intermediate agency, the distinction should be considered a rhetorical device, with no further significance.

consciousness of sin." And this very consciousness, when it is sanctified by
the Holy Spirit, causes one to cry out for help and deliverance. That deliverance is fully supplied whenever a sinner surrenders his life to God;
that is, when by genuine God-given faith he welcomes into his heart and life
the Lord Jesus Christ, with the word of committal:

> Nothing in my hand I bring,
> Simply to thy cross I cling.

It is in this way that the Scriptures—hence also Paul and his
companions—*uphold the law* while teaching and insisting on the doctrine
about *faith*.

To every sincere believer the doctrine of justification by faith is a very
precious treasure. To realize for one's own soul what this glorious truth
means can be a very thrilling and unforgettable experience. We have already seen what the discovery of this marvelous theme meant for Paul (see
pp. 28, 29) and for Luther (pp. 61, 62). When John Bunyan read Rom. 3:24
it was as if he heard God saying to his deeply troubled, guilt-stricken soul,
"Sinner, thou thinkest that because of thy sins and infirmities I cannot save
thy soul, but behold my Son is by me, and upon him I look, and not upon
thee, and I will deal with thee according as I am pleased with him."

Is it possible that we have become so used to the expression "forgiveness
of sins" that it has lost most of its meaning for us? Do we reflect on the fact
that these sins are infinitely more heinous in God's sight than they are to
us? That he nevertheless blots them out once and for all, lovingly assuring
us, "I will forgive y o u r iniquity, and y o u r sin will I remember no
more"? Yes, he forgives even though, in order to do this, he, because of the
demand of his perfect righteousness, had to punish them in his Son, the
One whom he loved as God alone can love!

But justification implies more, much more, than forgiveness. The
heavenly Father, having canceled our debt, then as it were lovingly throws
his arms around us (cf. Luke 15:20), and tells each of his pardoned ones,
"You are *my* son, *my* daughter, my very own. And being my child, you are
also my heir" (Rom. 8:17).

Think of it, "Heirs of God" are we and "joint-heirs with Christ," united
with him by a bond of love that can never be severed!

So amazing and so abounding is God's love for us that never shall we be
able to measure it. Throughout all eternity the mysteries of that love,
infinite in number, will continue to be revealed to us. And we shall glorify
him:

> By the sea of crystal, saints in glory stand,
> Myriads in number, drawn from every land.
> Robed in white apparel, washed in Jesus' blood,
> They now reign forever with the Lamb of God.

Unto God Almighty, sitting on the throne,
And the Lamb victorious, be the praise alone.
God has wrought salvation, he did wondrous things;
Who shall not extol Thee, Holy King of Kings?

William Kuipers
(based on Rev. 15:1-4)

Practical Lessons Derived from Rom. 3:9-31

Verses 9, 10

"What then? Are we any better? Not at all. . . . There is no one righteous, not even one." When the new minister arrived, he was told, "Your work here will be easy, for we are all good people." So he preached on the text, "Reliable is the saying, and worthy of full acceptance, that Christ Jesus came into the world, sinners to save, foremost of whom am I" (I Tim. 1:15).

Verses 21, 22

"But now . . . a righteousness from God, attested by the law and the prophets, has been revealed, namely, a righteousness from God which, through faith in Jesus Christ, comes to *all* who exercise faith. . . ." Here something old is added to something new:

a. something old, for the righteousness here indicated, had been proclaimed long ago in the law and the prophets. Abraham, David, Habakkuk, etc., had borne testimony to it.

b. something new, for not until now—that is, very recently—Jesus Christ had entered this realm of sin and woe, had offered himself as a sacrifice for the sins of his people, had been raised from the dead, and ascended to heaven, having purchased salvation for all who place their trust in him.

The old and the new belong together: it was Jesus who, by means of his active and passive obedience, obtained for all who surrender themselves to him, "righteousness from God," hence salvation full and free.

So the old and the new are actually *one*. The idea that the Old Testament is for the Jews, the New Testament for the church, is in need of re-examination. To a considerable extent it should be discarded. He who thinks lightly of the Old Testament does not understand Paul, nor the Bible.

Verses 24, 25

". . . being justified freely by his grace through the redemption (accomplished) in Christ Jesus . . . the shedding of his blood." Those who think that they can be saved apart from "redemption through the blood of Christ" are committing a tragic error.

Verse 25

". . . a wrath-removing sacrifice." Then alone is it possible to do justice to the comforting truth of God's love (Jer. 31:3; John 3:16) when this love is seen in its relation to God's wrath.

Verse 27

"What room, then, is left for boasting? It is excluded."

Heaven will be filled with boasting . . . *in the Lord!* The redeemed "are casting their crowns before the throne, while they say, 'Thou art worthy, our Lord and God, to receive glory and honor and power. . . .'" (Rev. 4:10, 11).

In a sense this song already begins on earth, with the words:

> Thou art, O God, our boast, the glory of our power;
> Thy sovereign grace is e'er our fortress and our tower.
> We lift our heads aloft, for God our shield is o'er us;
> Through him, through him alone, whose presence goes before us,
> We'll wear the victor's crown, no more by foes assaulted,
> We'll triumph through our King, by Israel's God exalted.

Versification (of Ps. 89:17, 18)
by William Kuipers

Summary of Chapter 3:9–31

By means of a chain of Old Testament passages Paul adduces the evidence for the proposition that by nature everybody is under the power of sin, and that accordingly "there is no one righteous, no, not one." This being true, it follows that the attempt to gain salvation by performing works of obedience to God's law will fail. "Therefore by law-works no flesh [mortal being] will be justified in his sight, for through law comes consciousness of sin" (3:9–20).

However, when for the sinner things begin to look very dark, the light of the gospel suddenly breaks through the gloom and dispels it: "But now, apart from law, a righteousness attested by the law and the prophets has been revealed, namely, a righteousness from God." This righteousness, in order to be effective in the life of a person, must be appropriated by faith in Jesus Christ. This rule holds for everybody: Gentile and Jew alike, "for there is no distinction, since all have sinned and fall short of the glory of God" (verses 21–23).

The price paid by the Savior for the justification of those who place their trust in him, and through him in God Triune, was immeasurably heavy. It amounted to no less than the shedding of Christ's blood, that is, the offering up of himself. This meant that the full burden of wrath was transferred from his people to himself, so that he, Lord Jesus Christ, bore it in their stead. All this took place in harmony with God's design from eternity. What Jesus offered was therefore a voluntary wrath-removing sacrifice, made effective in the lives of God's children by means of their God-given faith. Not until a person welcomes Christ into his heart and life by genuine, humble trust and self-surrender, does God pronounce him to be just; that is, free from every speck of guilt and therefore also bound to receive all the other blessings that are included in the term *salvation.*

Although it is true that this heavy penalty was not paid by Christ immediately upon the entrance of sin, and that accordingly throughout the entire old dispensation God treated with indulgence the sins of his people, punishment could not be delayed indefinitely. Divine justice had to be satisfied. During Christ's entire life on earth and especially at Calvary the heavy price was paid: "God did not spare his own Son but gave him up for us all" (Rom. 8:31). God did this "to demonstrate his justice in the present time, that he might be just and the One who justifies the person who has faith in Jesus" (3:24-31).

Outline (continued)

Justification by Faith

B. *Scriptural.*
1. *The Example of Abraham.*
"What does the Scripture say? Abraham believed God,
and it was reckoned to him for righteousness."
4:1–12

2. *This example shows*
that God's promise is realized through faith, not works.
"Therefore what was promised came by faith, in order
that it might be a matter of grace."
4:13–25

CHAPTER 4

4 1 What then shall we say that Abraham, our forefather according to the flesh, has discovered? 2 For if Abraham was justified on the basis of works, he has something to boast about. But from God's point of view he has no reason to boast.[107] 3 For what does the Scripture say? "Abraham believed God, and it was reckoned to him for righteousness." 4 Now to the one who works, his wages are not reckoned as a favor but as a debt.[108] 5 On the other hand, to the person who does not work but rests his faith on him who justifies the ungodly, his faith is reckoned for righteousness; 6 just as David also pronounces a blessing upon the person to whom God reckons righteousness apart from works:
7 "Blessed (are) those
   whose transgressions are forgiven,
   whose sins are covered.
8 Blessed is the man
   whose sin the Lord will never reckon (against him)."
9 Is this blessing then [pronounced] only upon the circumcised, or also upon the uncircumcised? For we are saying, "To Abraham his faith was reckoned for righteousness." 10 Under what circumstances then was it so reckoned? Not after he had been circumcised, but while he was still uncircumcised.[109] 11 And he received the sign of circumcision as a seal of the righteousness by faith which he had while still uncircumcised, so that he might be the father of all who have faith but have not been circumcised, in order that righteousness might be reckoned to them; 12 and also the father of those circumcised people who not only are circumcised but also walk in the footsteps of the faith our father Abraham had (even) before he was circumcised.

B. *Scriptural.*
1. *The Example of Abraham.*
"What does the Scripture say? Abraham believed God,
and it was reckoned to him for righteousness."
4:1-12

1. What then shall we say that Abraham, our forefather according to the flesh, has discovered?[110]

In the preceding paragraph (3:21-31) Paul has been proclaiming a righteousness *from God,* and therefore valid before God and not dependent

---

107. Literally: but not before God.
108. Or: not as a gift but as an obligation.
109. Literally: While being in circumcision, or (while being) in uncircumcision? Not in circumcision but in uncircumcision. See footnote 119.
110. There are textual variants. Some MSS. omit the word εὑρηκέναι, which, however, does not seriously affect the central meaning of the passage. Others place this perf. act. infinitive

in any way on human merit. He has stated that the law and the prophets had already borne witness to this righteousness (3:21). It is this point which he is now going to develop.

It should be observed that, in doing so, the apostle does not try to make matters easy for himself. He attacks the proponents of the opposite view— salvation on the basis of human merit—at the very fortress in which they deem themselves to be the strongest, namely, the story of Abraham, that great patriarch who, according to the thinking of the Jews, had *earned* his way into God's good pleasure. Paul asks, "What then shall we say that Abraham, our forefather according to the flesh, has discovered?" He probably means, "What was it he discovered with respect to the manner in which a person enters into right relation with God?"

Note "Abraham, *our* forefather." Among authors who believe that the church of Rome consisted mainly of Jews there are some who appeal also to this passage. Their argument is that when Paul, being himself a Jew, calls Abraham "our forefather," he must mean that those whom he addressed were mainly Jews.[111] But by no means all who are of the opinion that the Jews predominated in that church use Rom. 4:1 in support of their contention, the reason being that such a "proof" (?) is very weak indeed; and this for the following reasons:

a. Abraham was the father not only of Jews but also of Ishmaelites and Edomites; hence even in the physical sense he was the father of Jews *and Gentiles.*

b. The very purpose of Paul in Rom. 4 was to show that in a sense Abraham was the father not only of Jews but also of Gentiles. See 4:11, 12.

c. In I Cor. 10:1 the apostle states, "*Our* ancestors were all under the cloud and all passed through the sea," but he could not have meant that the Corinthians he was addressing were mostly Jews. See I Cor. 12:2, ". . . when y o u were *pagans. . . .*"

d. As any unabridged *dictionary of the English language* indicates, the word *our* is not always used in the strictly literal sense "belonging to us." It can also mean "of interest to us," or "pertaining to the subject we are

after ἡμῶν. See Hodge, *op. cit.,* pp. 162, 163. The meaning would then be, "What did Abraham attain κατὰ σάρκα; that is, in a fleshly or carnal manner?" One might say, "in his own power." But not only is the textual support for this variant weak—see textual apparatus Grk.N.T. (A-B-M-W)—but this thought is also out of line with the context. The apostle is not discussing the subject of Abraham's "discovery" or even "attainment" *after the flesh.*

There is also the variant πατέρα instead of προπάτορα. But it is natural to assume that the rareness of the word προπάτορα (acc. s. of προπάτωρ) occurring only once in the New Testament, as contrasted with the frequency of the shorter one, which covers several pages in Moulton and Geden's *Concordance,* caused someone to start the process of substituting the latter for the former. Moreover, does not the fact that the longer word occurs only once point to its authenticity at this place?

The best procedure would seem to be to leave the Greek text exactly as given in the Greek New Testament to which reference has just been made.

111. The question, "To whom did Paul address Romans?" has been discussed earlier. See pp. 20-23.

discussing," etc. In the present context Paul, in referring to "Abraham, our forefather," may well have been thinking of him as "that distant ancestor of interest to all of us."[112]

What, then, had this forefather discovered with respect to the subject in question?

The apostle feels that he has a right to bring up this example of Abraham.

2a. For[113] if Abraham was justified on the basis of works, he has something to boast about.

A few lines earlier (3:27) Paul has drawn the conclusion that since justification—hence also salvation in general—is by faith alone, and faith is God's gift, every reason for human boasting is excluded. However, having been thoroughly drilled in Pharisaic doctrine, he knows that his *opponents* will immediately cite the example of Abraham as proof positive that the factor of *works,* and therefore *human merit,* cannot be entirely excluded when the question is asked, "How do people obtain acceptance with God?" Moreover, if there is really such a thing as human *merit,* then is there not also a basis for human *boasting?*—What follows therefore in chapter 4 is Paul's powerful defense of the proposition, expressed earlier (3:20, 27, 28), that justification is *by faith,* not by works.

By the Jewish teachers and their followers Abraham was considered the only righteous man of his generation. Moreover, they held that it was for that very reason that he had been chosen to be the ancestor of the holy nation. He was considered the first of seven men who, by their *merits,* brought back the Shekinah (cloud of light, cf. Exod. 24:15, 16), so that it could take up its abode in the tabernacle. We are told, moreover, that Abraham began to serve God at the age of three, and that his righteousness was made complete by his circumcision and his anticipatory fulfilment of the law.

Note also the following words from *The Prayer of Manasseh* 8, "Therefore thou, O Lord, God of the righteous, hast not appointed repentance for the righteous, for Abraham, Isaac, and Jacob, who did not sin against thee, but thou hast appointed repentance for me, who am a sinner."

The Book of Jubilees, probably dating from the second century B.C., minimizes the weaknesses of the patriarchs, and contains the statement, "Abraham was perfect in all his deeds with the Lord, and well-pleasing in righteousness all the days of his life (23:10).

Special note should be taken of the fact that the rabbis were not at all

---

112. The possibility must also be granted that the apostle meant, "the forefather of myself and my fellow-Jews." Even if he meant that, this would not prove that the members of the Roman church were mostly Jews.

113. γάρ can best be regarded as explaining the relevance of the question of verse 1 with respect to Abraham. This is another case of abbreviated expression. See N.T.C. on John, Vol. I, p. 206. More fully expressed, the meaning is probably, "I refer to Abraham *for* what is said about him proves that justification is by faith, not by works."

afraid of referring to Gen. 15:6 in defense of their doctrine of justification and salvation on the basis of human works and merit; witness this statement:

"Our father Abraham became the heir of this and of the coming world simply by the merit of the faith with which he believed in the Lord; as it is written, 'He believed in the Lord, who counted it to him as righteousness.' "[114]

It is clear therefore that *by appealing to Gen. 15:6 in defense of the doctrine of justification and salvation purely by faith the apostle was making use of the very passage which by the rabbis was regarded as supporting the opposite view.*

Paul's rejection of this doctrine of *merit* is clear-cut. He writes: **2b-5. But from God's point of view he [Abraham] has no reason to boast. For what does the Scripture say? "Abraham believed God, and it was reckoned to him for righteousness." Now to the one who works, his wages are not reckoned as a favor but as a debt. On the other hand, to the person who does not work but rests his faith on him who justifies the ungodly, his faith is reckoned for righteousness . . .**

What Paul is saying amounts to this:

Our opponents appeal to Gen. 15:6 in support of their doctrine of justification by works, by human merit. As they see it, Abraham was justified by works. But where, in Gen. 15:6 is even *one* word said about work or merit? According to Gen. 15:6 God bestowed righteousness on Abraham as a free gift. Abraham rested his faith on the gracious Giver, who "reckoned" the patriarch's faith for righteousness. More fully expressed this means that God counted for righteousness *that which Abraham appropriated by faith,* namely, the *righteousness* of Christ. That the apostle had this in mind he makes clear in this very chapter—see verses 6, 11 and 25—and in the next (5:6-21). See also II Cor. 5:21.

The Lord "reckoned" or "considered" or "counted" this "ungodly individual," yes this sinner, namely, Abraham, to be that which in and by himself he was not, namely *just.* The Lord was able to do this, without in any way becoming unjust, because of the certainty that the Coming Messiah would by means of his voluntary sacrifice secure this great blessing for Abraham and for all those who share Abraham's faith. In this connection read Isa. 53, especially verses 4-6, 8, 12 (material with which Paul was thoroughly acquainted; see Rom. 4:25; 5:19; I Cor. 15:3). On the question whether Abraham himself "saw Christ's day" see N.T.C. on John 8:56 (John, Vol. II, pp. 64-66).

I favor this interpretation, with its emphasis on Abraham's *faith,* for the following reasons:

a. In Gen. 15:6 the emphasis is entirely on Abraham's *faith.* No mention is made at all of his work or merit.

---

114. See S.BK. III, p. 186 ff.; 199 ff.; Mekilta on Exod. 14:31; Sanday and Headlam, *op. cit.,* pp. 100, 101, 330-332; Lekkerkerker, *op. cit.,* Vol. I, p. 164.

b. In Rom. 4:2–5 two forms of the verb *to exercise faith, to believe,* occur; so does the cognate noun *faith* (once).

c. To sharpen this emphasis on faith the passage (in verses 4, 5) even implies that Abraham belonged to the class of people who do not work (to obtain their salvation), and who accordingly earn no wages. God owes them nothing!

d. The Hebrew verb, a form of חָשַׁב (Gen. 15:6), in Rom. 4:3 rendered ἐλογίσθη, "was reckoned," is frequently used to indicate what a person, *considered by himself,* is not, or does not have, but is reckoned, held, or regarded to be, or to have. Examples: Gen. 38:15; I Sam. 1:13; Job 13:24. So also here (Gen. 15:6; Rom. 4:3) to Abraham is ascribed or imputed that which he does not himself possess. It is *graciously reckoned* to him because of the righteousness of Another. It is conferred on those who *trust* in God for their justification and salvation.[115]

e. In the parallel passage (Gal. 3:6–9) the emphasis on *faith* (in the sense already explained) is very strong:

"(It is) even as recorded: 'Abraham *believed* [rested his *faith* in] God, and it was reckoned to him for righteousness.' Know then that those who are of *faith*, it is they who are sons of Abraham. Now Scripture, seeing that it was by *faith* that God would justify the Gentiles, preached the gospel beforehand to Abraham, (saying): 'In you all the nations shall be blessed.' Therefore those that are of *faith* are blessed with Abraham, the man of *faith*."

From start to finish, *therefore, right standing with God* is God's gift. It is appropriated by *God-given faith* (Eph. 2:8; see N.T.C. on Ephesians, pp. 120–123). To God therefore belongs all the glory. For human boasting there is no room whatever.

Between verses 1–5 and verses 6–8 there is a close connection. The earlier passage made reference to Abraham, upon whom God graciously conferred the blessing of *right standing* with the Almighty, *justification.* The immediately following lines describe the blessedness of those whose transgressions are forgiven. Now forgiveness is a very important part of justification. Also note how often a form of the verb *to reckon* occurs in verses 1–5. There is an echo of this in verse 8.

6–8. ... just as David also pronounces a blessing upon the person to whom God reckons righteousness apart from works:

"Blessed (are) those
   whose transgressions are forgiven,
   whose sins are covered.
Blessed is the man
   whose sin the Lord will never reckon (against him)."

There are those who believe that, influenced by his earlier training under Gamaliel (Acts 22:3), Paul, in combining a reference to Abraham

---

115. See also H. W. Heidland on λογίζομαι, Th.D.N.T., Vol. IV, pp. 284–292.

(Gen. 15:6) with a reference to David (Ps. 32:1, 2a), is making use of one of the seven rules of interpretation formulated by Hillel, namely, the rule called *Analogy,* which allows one passage to be joined to another if the same word occurs in both (here the word "reckoned"), the purpose being that the meaning of the word in the first passage will then apply also to its use in the second. However that may be, in the present case this carryover in meaning is certainly legitimate, since the universe of discourse, namely, gracious imputation of righteousness, has not changed.

Note the following:

a. The words of Ps. 32:1, 2a are quoted here. David is jubilant. Why? Because he knows that *his* transgressions[116] have been forgiven,[117] *his* sins covered.[118] See Ps. 32:1-5; especially verse 5b.

If the sins to which this Psalm refers are those in connection with Bathsheba, which may well be the case, the historical background of Ps. 32 would be the same as that of the words quoted in Rom. 3:4. See on that passage.

However, David is thinking not only of the pardon he himself received. The very words, "Blessed (are) *those* whose transgressions are forgiven, whose sins are covered. Blessed is *the man,*" etc. indicate that he includes in his beatitude all those who have received a similar blessing.

b. The main point here stressed is that the forgiveness, granted and experienced, was the result not of human work but of divine grace. In this respect Abraham and David have something in common. Both are the recipients of God's sovereign, unearned favor.

c. In verse 5 of the immediately preceding section (verses 1-5) Paul used the expression "faith is reckoned for righteousness," meaning, "God counted for righteousness that which Abraham (or anyone who similarly places his trust in God) appropriated by faith, namely, the righteousness of Christ." This explanation is confirmed in the present section (verses 6-8); note the words, "the person to whom God reckons righteousness apart from works" (verse 6). In both cases, therefore, it is in the final analysis not faith considered by itself but the righteousness of Christ which is imputed to the sinner who, in genuine faith, has fled to God for refuge.

d. It has been shown that Abraham was declared righteous, justified, though he had not earned this blessing by the performance of any good work. Here, in verses 6-8, David pronounces a blessing upon contrite, conscience-stricken sinners, penitent wrongdoers. In both cases human

---

116. Literally: acts of lawlessness, law-violations, and in that sense *transgressions.*

117. Greek ἀφέθησαν, third per. pl. aor. pass. indicat. of ἀφίημι. This is the only passage in which Paul uses the verb ἀφίημι in the sense of to *forgive.* He does, however, use the noun ἄφεσις, forgiveness (Eph. 1:7; Col. 1:14). For the wide range of meaning which the verb has in the New Testament see N.T.C. on Luke, pp. 271, 364 (respectively on Luke 4:39 and 6:42).

118. ἐπεκαλύφθησαν, from ἐπικαλύπτω, *to cover,* same construction as the preceding verb. In the favorable sense, as here, of "blotting out" sin, the Hebrew original on which this Greek verb is based is found also in Ps. 85:2. There is, however, also an unfavorable sense in which sin can be covered (or concealed). See Job 31:33; Prov. 28:13.

works do not enter into the picture; only God's work of grace does. Far from pronouncing "blessed" those who have performed good deeds, David pronounces a blessing upon those whose transgressions were not laid to their account.

e. Justification transcends forgiveness. It includes but also goes beyond pardoning, as the very exclamation "Blessed" ("O the blessedness of") hints. The truly "blessed" person is not only conscious of having been pardoned. He rejoices with "joy unspeakable and full of glory" because he is able to say, "God has accepted me as his son, his daughter. He loves me." For evidence see this same Ps. 32:10. Cf. Ps. 103:11-13; Rom. 8:1, 16, 17.

f. In verse 7 David, by inspiration, is represented as pronouncing a blessing upon *those* whose transgressions have been forgiven, *on them all.* In verse 8 he individualizes this pronouncement. This time the singular is used, "Blessed is *the man*—that is, *the person*—whose sin the Lord will never reckon (against him)."

To speak about blessings granted to many is fine and necessary. Nevertheless, for any particular person these favors become real only then when he is able to say, "O God, thou art *my God*" (Ps. 63:1).

9-12. Is this blessing then (pronounced) only upon the circumcised, or also upon the uncircumcised? For we are saying, "To Abraham his faith was reckoned for righteousness." Under what circumstances then was it so reckoned? After he had been circumcised, or while he was still uncircumcised? Not after he had been circumcised, but while he was still uncircumcised. And he received the sign of circumcision as a seal of the righteousness by faith which he had while still uncircumcised, so that he might be the father of all who have faith but have not been circumcised, in order that righteousness might be reckoned to them; and also the father of those circumcised people who not only are circumcised but also follow in the footsteps of the faith our father Abraham had (even) before he was circumcised.

Paul now returns to Gen. 15:6. In light of his interpretation of Ps. 32:1, 2a his further remarks about the Genesis passage take on added significance. It now becomes clear that when, in the sense already explained, Abraham's faith was reckoned for righteousness, this was indeed an inestimable blessing, a blessing all the more significant because the patriarch could not have earned it. Moreover, as the reference to Ps. 32:1, 2a has shown, the blessing was not only for Abraham but also for David, and . . . for any others? For the circumcised and also for the uncircumcised? For the Jews and also for the Gentiles?[119]

---

119. The words περιτομή and ἀκροβυστία, both of which occur several times in Rom. 4:9-12, have a wide range of meanings. They can refer to a state or condition (respectively that of circumcision and uncircumcision) but can also indicate an individual or even a people. Besides, these words and their Hebrew equivalents can be used in a figurative or spiritual sense (Deut. 10:16; 30:6; Jer. 4:4; Rom. 2:29; Phil. 3:3; Col. 2:11). In any given case the correct English equivalent is determined by the context.

Standard Jewish doctrine answered, "Only for the circumcised."[120] Even
in the early church Jewish converts to Christianity found it difficult to
shake off their nationalistic prejudices: "Some men came down from Judea
to Antioch and were teaching the brothers, 'Unless y o u are circumcised
according to the custom taught by Moses, y o u cannot be saved.'" (Acts
15:1). If any further proof is needed see Rom. 2:25-27; Gal. 5:2, 6, 12;
6:12-15; Phil. 3:2, 3. Paul's question, "Is this blessing then (pronounced)
only upon the circumcised or also on the uncircumcised?" is therefore
understandable.

Paul's response is masterful. It should constantly be borne in mind that
he is writing by inspiration. He proves that *Abraham's faith*—meaning "the
righteousness of Christ appropriated by faith"—*was reckoned or imputed to
Abraham for righteousness* not after he had been circumcised but *while he was
still uncircumcised!* It was then already that Abraham was declared righteous
in God's sight.

This very significant chronological observation becomes clear from a
study of the following references:

a. Abraham was ninety-nine years of age when he was circumcised (Gen.
17:24).

b. On that same day Ishmael was also circumcised (Gen. 17:25).

c. Ishmael was then thirteen years of age (Gen. 17:25).

d. When God made his covenant with Abraham (Gen. 15:18), and "Abraham believed the Lord, and it was reckoned to him for righteousness"
(Gen. 15:6), Ishmael had not yet been conceived (Gen. 15:2, 3; 16:4).

Conclusion: between the moment when the blessing of Gen. 15:6 was
pronounced upon Abraham and the day he was circumcised there must
have been an interval of at least about fourteen years. An even longer
interval is possible. According to Jewish chronology the gap was one of
twenty-nine years (S.BK. III, p. 203). A considerably shorter period than
fourteen years is impossible.

*Accordingly, it was upon the still uncircumcised Abraham, who in that respect
resembled a Gentile, that the promise was given, the blessing pronounced. This proves
that circumcision has nothing to do with being declared righteous.*

If any unbelieving Jews heard these words, they must have been shocked.
Even some Christians from among the Jews must have been startled.

We are told that Abraham received "the sign of circumcision," meaning:
the sign, namely, circumcision.[121] Being a "sign," it signifies or indicates a
fact. *Sign* and *thing signified* are generally closely related. Thus in the present case the *cutting away* of the foreskin suggests and symbolizes the *excision* of the guilt and pollution of sin; hence, justification and, closely connected with it, sanctification.

Circumcision was also a *seal*. To Abraham it was a guarantee of the

---

120. See S.BK., p. 203.

121. περιτομῆς must be interpreted as a gen. of apposition.

trustworthiness of God's promise. It meant that this patriarch could depend upon it that in the way of faith, and the obedience resulting from faith, the righteousness of Christ was reckoned or imputed to him.

Signs and seals are very valuable. To be sure, it is possible to overestimate their significance. In and by themselves these signs—in the old dispensation the bloody ones of circumcision and Passover; in the new, the unbloody ones of baptism and the Lord's Supper—do not bring about justification or, in general, salvation. However, they do indeed signify and seal it in the manner already indicated. And is not that a source of comfort? The rainbow does not save mankind from being swallowed up by a flood, but it does signify and seal that God will never again drown the human race. The wedding ring does not bring married bliss, but what married person, who loves his (her) marriage partner, would ever think of doing away with the ring that means so much to him (her)? Indeed, signs and seals must not be underestimated. See Exod. 4:24-26; Josh. 5:1-12; II Kings 23:21-23; Acts 2:38, 39; I Cor. 11:23f. They have great educational and psychological value. *But neither should they be overrated!*

Paul clings to his subject. Therefore, what he really emphasizes is this, namely, that Abraham received *the sign of circumcision as a seal of the righteousness by faith which he had while still uncircumcised!*

These words "while still uncircumcised," with slight variations, are found in three succeeding verses: 10, 11, 12. It is as if Paul wanted to din into the ears of the uncircumcised Gentiles this enormous truth: "Believe in the Lord Jesus Christ. Don't hold back. Don't hesitate to place y o u r undivided trust in this marvelous Savior, the Revealer of God Triune. The fact that y o u have not been circumcised cannot prevent y o u from being saved. God is calling y o u. He is calling y o u *now.* It was while Abraham was still uncircumcised that God made his covenant with him. He stands ready to do the same for y o u."

It is clear, therefore, that Abraham, to whom the righteousness of Christ was reckoned or imputed before he had been circumcised, and to whom, once he had been circumcised, God repeated his gracious promise again and again, is the spiritual father, the head of the procession, of two *sub*-groups: (a) all who have faith but have not been circumcised; and (b) all who not only have been circumcised but also have and exercise faith, showing this to be true by following "in the footsteps of the faith Abraham had (even) before he was circumcised." These two *sub*-groups constitute *one large group of believers,* Abraham being the father of them all (verse 16).

This also indicates that circumcision is not essential to salvation.

It is maintained at times that neither is it a deterrent or excluding factor.[112] If this means, as it probably does, that the fact that a person has been circumcised does not *necessarily* prevent him from being saved, I fully agree, for this is what Rom. 4:12 clearly teaches.

---

122. Murray, *op. cit.,* p. 139.

What the apostle stresses again and again in his epistles is that, as far as being saved is concerned, circumcision makes no difference, amounts to nothing (I Cor. 7:19; Gal. 5:6; 6:15; Col. 3:11). But does this not also imply that if too much is made of circumcision—or today, of baptism—as if in some sense salvation were dependent upon it, it might in certain cases indeed become an excluding factor? Note what Paul says in Gal. 5:2:

"Now I, Paul, say to y o u that if y o u let yourselves be circumcised, Christ will be of no value to y o u at all." I feel sure that the author of the fine commentary to which I just now referred would have agreed with me.

This subject has practical significance for every age, including the present. Previously the importance of signs and seals has been established. See p. 151. (It should not be lost sight of, however, that the bloody signs and seals have been replaced by the unbloody ones.) Just now the danger of overestimating their value has been signalized. The reason for stressing the fact that both extremes should be avoided is that even today the Church administers sacraments: baptism and the Lord's Supper. With respect to these, too, extremes should be avoided. Rushing in to drop some water on a dying child's forehead, fearing that otherwise it might not enter heaven at death, makes no sense. On the other hand, the custom of some, needlessly to postpone baptism, is also not to be recommended. Both extremes are unbiblical.

Signs and seals do not save automatically. In this connection note how careful the apostle is. Here in Rom. 4:12 he first tells believers from the Gentiles (the uncircumcised) that, according to God's plan, Abraham became "the father of all who have faith but have not been circumcised." Then he adds, with respect to believers from the Jews, who, even after their conversion to Christ were prone to attach too great a value to the sign (Acts 15:1), "and also the father of those circumcised people who not only are circumcised *but also follow in the footsteps of the faith our father Abraham had (even) before he was circumcised.*" It is life—cf. "living for Jesus"—that is emphasized.

It would be difficult to overestimate the significance of Rom. 4:9-12. The passage means that with one stroke of the pen the entire huge wall of separation between Jew and Gentile was razed to the ground. Moreover, the promise made to Abraham, when God established his covenant with him (Gen. 15:6, 18; 17:7; 22:15-18), is still in effect,[123] and has significance for all believers and their families.[124]

---

123. For more on this see my booklet *The Covenant of Grace,* Grand Rapids, 1978, especially pp. 21-25.

124. Attention should be focused on a few points of grammar in verses 11, 12:

First of all note εἰς τὸ εἶναι αὐτόν . . . εἰς τὸ λογισθῆναι αὐτοῖς: there is no reason to subtract anything from the full telic sense. But purpose does not exclude (but here certainly includes) result.

δι' = διά expresses attendant circumstance, as in 2:27.

Τοῖς before στοιχοῦσιν. We translate, ". . . those who not only are circumcised *but also follow* in the footsteps . . ." It is difficult to explain this τοῖς. Many say nothing about it. Others are sure

13 For it was not through (the) law that Abraham or his seed received the promise that he would be heir of the world, but through righteousness resulting from faith. 14 For if those who live by law are heirs, faith is deprived of its value and the promise is rendered worthless; 15 for the law produces wrath, but where there is no law there is also no transgression.

16 For this reason what was promised came by faith, namely, in order that it might be a matter of grace, and in order that the promise might be certain of fulfilment[125] for all the seed, not for those who only live by the law, but for those who also live by the faith of Abraham (who is the father of us all, 17 as it is written, "Father of many nations have I made you"), in the presence of God on whom he rested his faith, the God who imparts life to the dead, and calls things that are not as though they were.

18 Against all hope, Abraham in hope believed, so that he became the father of many nations, in agreement with what had been told him, "So shall your seed be." 19 And without weakening in faith he took note of the fact that his own body was as good as dead—since he was about a hundred years old—and that Sarah's womb was also dead.[126] 20 Yet he did not waver in unbelief with respect to God's promise, but was strengthened in faith, giving glory to God, 21 being fully persuaded that what God had promised he would be able to perform. 22 That is why it was reckoned to him for righteousness.

23 Now the words, "It was reckoned to him," were written not for him alone, 24 but also for us to whom it is to be reckoned, to us who rest our faith on him who raised Jesus our Lord from the dead, 25 who was delivered up for our trespasses and was raised for our justification.[127]

---

2. This example shows
that God's promise is realized through faith, not works.
"Therefore what was promised came by faith, in order
that it might be a matter of grace."
4:13-25

Paul continues his demonstration of the fact that the doctrine of justification by faith, not through the works of the law, is indeed not a novelty but has its foundation in the Scriptures; that is, in what today we call the Old Testament.

In the preceding paragraph (4:1-12) he has already shown that *according to Scripture*, attaining the status of *righteousness in the eyes of God* is a matter not of works and merit but of faith and therefore of grace. Also, that it has nothing to do with circumcision. In fact, Abraham was pronounced righteous long before he was circumcised. Therefore Abraham should be regarded as the father or spiritual leader of all true believers, circumcised or not.

---

that someone made a mistake. The possibility that a very early copyist erred must be granted. The text is well attested, however, so that on that score there is no solution. What then? As I see it, Ridderbos, though not completely solving this puzzle, provides what may well be the best answer. See his comments, *op. cit.*, pp. 95, 96, 98, 99. He points to the fact that in verse 16 we find a similar construction (τῷ before ἐκ πίστεως) "which raises the question whether for Paul this kind of connection was as unusual as for his commentators."

125. Or sure, firmly grounded, unshakable.

126. Or: he considered his own body . . . and the deadness of Sarah's womb.

127. Instead of *for . . . for*, one may substitute *on account of . . . on account of*.

In the present paragraph (verses 13-25) this idea that divine grace, not human effort, is the basis upon which rests the building of salvation full and free is made to stand out even more clearly by the emphasis that is placed on *the divine promise.* That word *promise*—at times indicating the divine declaration itself, then again its effectuation or realization (the promised blessing)—occurs here for the first time in Paul's epistle to the Romans. The idea that the God of the covenant is the God of the promise is repeated several times (verses 13, 14, 16, 20, 21). This promise, moreover, is of *world-embracing* significance. It affects not only *all* true believers, Jew and Gentile alike, but also causes its influence to be felt in every age, past, present, and future. For this world-embracing application of the divine promise verses 11, 12 have already prepared us.

13-15. For it was not through (the) law that Abraham or his seed received the promise that he would be heir of the world, but through righteousness resulting from faith. For if those who live by law are heirs, faith is deprived of its value and the promise is rendered worthless; for the law produces wrath, but where there is no law there is also no transgression.

As the Jews saw it, the promise made to Abraham was to be realized through obedience to the Mosaic law. The rabbis even maintained that long before the law was promulgated from Sinai, Abraham already had a thorough knowledge of it and obeyed it in all its details.[128]

Over against this the apostle states that the promise was given to Abraham considered as a man of faith in his God, and that it was a result of this faith that righteousness had been reckoned or credited to him. Works or merit had nothing to do with the promise or its fulfilment. Obedience to the law was not in the picture, for the promise was made to Abraham many years before the law had been promulgated. Cf. Gal. 3:16-18.

Note the words, ". . . Abraham or his seed received the promise that he would be "heir of the world," that is, that, as a *gift* from God he would *obtain* "the world."[129] But what does that mean?

In answer to this question it may be well, first of all, to point out that God's promise to Abraham contained the following items:

a. title to the land of Canaan (Gen. 12:7; 13:14, 15, 17; 15:7; 17:8). This item is spelled out in some detail in 15:18-21.

b. the assurance that in number his seed would be as the dust of the earth (13:16; 15:5; cf. 18:18).

The book of Exodus shows us that the promise of an abundant posterity was realized. The book of Joshua shows us that also the land of Canaan became the possession of Abraham's descendants.

Before we proceed to item c. it should be pointed out that the conclusion drawn by many, namely, that *today,* because of item a., the entire land of

---

128. S.BK. III, pp. 186 ff.; 199-201; 204 ff.
129. On the meaning of the word χληρονόμος see W. Foerster, Th.D.N.T., Vol. III, pp. 781-785.

Canaan, in its widest dimensions, really belongs to the Jews, is unwarranted. Every fairminded person regrets the persecutions the Jews have endured, wants them to enjoy the full measure of security to which they are entitled, and is relentlessly opposed to every manifestation of anti-Semitism. But all this is no excuse for ignoring the fact expressed so clearly in Jer. 18:9, 10.

This brings us now to the next item:

c. the guarantee that in Abraham's seed all the *families of the earth* will be blessed. Gal. 3:16 states that it is in Christ, the real *Seed*, that all those who embrace him will be blessed. Gal. 3:29 adds, "And if y o u are Christ's, then y o u are Abraham's seed, heirs according to promise."

It is in light of such passages as these that we will have to interpret the passage that Abraham or his seed received the promise that he would be *heir of the world* (Rom. 4:13), "father of many nations" (verses 17, 18). And is it not also true that Abraham and all who by sovereign grace constitute his seed do actually in a sense own the universe? Do not all things work together for good for those who love God and are called according to his purpose (Rom. 8:28), so that Paul can say, "All things are y o u r s" (I Cor. 3:21)? Rightly interpreted, therefore, Abraham, to whom the righteousness of Christ was imputed, was "heir of the world." The same was and is true, of course, with respect to all those who have a share in Abraham's faith. If the Lord is *their* God, which is the very essence of the covenant of grace (Gen. 17:7), all is well.

It is understandable that if, instead, those people who believe that strenuous efforts to obey the law in all its details will save them, were right, then faith—reliance for salvation not on self but on God—would have lost its value. Also, on that basis no one would ever be saved, for the law demands perfection, which no sinner is able to render. Therefore the promise would be rendered worthless, for under those circumstances it could never be fulfilled.

Paul had tried very hard to be saved by the law. He had failed miserably (Acts 22:3, 4; Gal. 1:13; Phil. 3:4-7). Having been "snatched as a brand from the fire," he now understood that "the law produces wrath." It *condemns* the sinner, pronounces a curse on all those who do not comply perfectly with its demands (Deut. 28:58f.). Rom. 8:3 impresses this lesson upon us in very touching manner. The law cannot enable a person to fulfil its demands; hence cannot save anyone: "For what the law could not do, God did by sending his own Son."

When God had come to Abraham with his covenant promise, the law had not yet been promulgated, as mentioned in the preceding. Therefore conscious transgression of that law was also, in a sense, impossible: "Where there is no law there is no transgression." As a result God had provided ample room for *the promise* to function.

16, 17. For this reason what was promised came by faith, namely, in order that it might be a matter of grace, and in order that the promise

ROMANS

might be certain of fulfilment for all the seed, not for those who only live by the law, but for those who also live by the faith of Abraham (who is the father of us all, as it is written, "Father of many nations have I made you"), in the presence of God on whom he rested his faith, the God who imparts life to the dead, and calls things that are not as though they were.

In line with what the apostle has just now been saying about the manner in which God carries out his plan of salvation, namely, by not insisting that in order to be saved the sinner must earn his own entrance into the kingdom of heaven, but by providing a solution in which grace would triumph, he now states that the reason the promised salvation came *by faith* was that it might be *a matter of grace*.[130] This also implies that the promise, "I will be their—or y o u r—God," hence the promise of salvation full and free, would be certain of fulfilment, sure, firmly grounded, and unshakable. If the fulfilment of the promise had been dependent on human effort, so that salvation would have been the product of perfect obedience to the demands of God's law, this fulfilment would never have been attained. But now that it is a matter of grace, hence a matter of God's eternal and effective plan, its realization in the lives of all God's people is assured.

And what a source of comfort this is! That is why, it is with such gusto that the congregation, gathered for worship, professes its faith by breaking out into the words of Ps. 89:

> I sing of mercies that endure,
> Forever builded firm and sure,
> Of faithfulness that never dies,
> Established changeless in the skies.[131]
>
> Anonymous

The immediately following words (16b) present a problem. After "to the end the promise might be sure to all the seed," the A.V. has: "not to that only which is of the law, but to that also which is of the faith of Abraham, who is the father of us all." Almost all modern translations agree in affirming that the apostle has in mind two groups of people to whom the promise is made sure. According to Hodge (*op. cit.*, p. 192) these two are, respectively, believing Jews and believing Gentiles.

Now one objection to this construction is that in the immediate

---

130. In view of the almost immediately following ἵνα, it is best to interpret διὰ τοῦτο as pointing forward; hence, "For this reason ... namely, in order that."
131. Or, with no less enthusiasm, in the Dutch services one will hear:
Gij toch, Gij zijt hun roem, de kracht van hunne kracht;
Uw vrije gunst alleen wordt d'ere toegebracht;
Wij steken 'thoofd omhoog, en zullen d'eerkroon dragen,
Door U, door U alleen, om 'teeuwig welbehagen;
Want God is ons ten schild in 'tstrijdperk van dit leven,
En onze Koning is van Isrels God gegeven.

context—see verses 11, 12—Paul has indicated that he regards Abraham as the father of *all* believers, both Gentiles and Jews. It is therefore hard to see how the words "that which is of the faith of Abraham" (or "those who live by the faith of Abraham") could refer to Gentiles only; all the more so in the light of the appended clause "who is the father of us all."

Besides, the place which the little word "only" (Greek μόνον) occupies in the sentence would seem to indicate that Paul is not thinking of two groups for which the promise has validity, but of one group only. He is saying, "that the promise might be certain of fulfilment *for all the seed, not for that by the law only but also by the faith of Abraham,* thus literally; meaning: *not for those who live by the law only but for those who also live by the faith of Abraham;* or "not for those who only live by the law but for those who also live by the faith of Abraham," etc.[132]

The promise, then, is certain of fulfilment for one group only, namely, for that true seed, those people who, while honoring God's law (cf. 3:31), rest their faith on God, as did Abraham. All of them, whether Gentiles or Jews, "are blessed with Abraham, the man of faith" (Gal. 3:9). See also Gal. 3:29, "And if y o u belong to Christ, then y o u are Abraham's seed, heirs according to promise." What the apostle says here in 4:16 resembles what he has stated in 4:11, 12.

Abraham is here called "the father of us all." In verse 11 he is called "the father of all who believe." The apostle is evidently determined to see to it that the readers or hearers will understand that God does not recognize two separate groups on whom his special favor rests, but only one group, consisting of all genuine believers, whether they be Gentiles or Jews. In verse 17 he even adds evidence from the Old Testament, "Father of many nations have I made you" (Gen. 17:5).

Now it must be admitted that in the Genesis passage the words "many nations" apply to Abraham's natural posterity. In the physical sense this patriarch was indeed the father of many nations or peoples: of the Ishmaelites (Gen. 17:20) as well as of Isaac and his descendants (Gen. 21:1–3); and through Isaac, of the Edomites as well as of the Israelites (Gen. 25:21–25; ch. 36); in fact even of the seed of Keturah (25:1 f.).

Shall we say, then, that *the apostle,* in speaking about Abraham's *spiritual* fatherhood, and in this context directing our attention to Gen. 17:5, is committing an error? But who would dare to take the position that the Holy Spirit lacks the right to take an Old Testament passage and give it an application different from that which it had in its original setting? However, in the present instance we do not have to make use of this argument, for even in the Genesis passages a reference to spiritual fatherhood is not

---

132. On this construction see also Greijdanus, *op. cit.,* Vol. I, p. 238; and Ridderbos, *op. cit.,* pp. 98, 99.

altogether wanting. Note that in Gen. 12:3 Abraham is told that in and through him all the families of the earh *will be blessed.*[133]

Beautiful is the expression "the faith of Abraham ... in the presence of[134] God on whom he rested his faith." It describes the great patriarch as one who was the recipient of vivid experiences of the divine Presence. The father of all believers was filled with profound reverence; yet also with filial trust.

Paul further describes the object of Abraham's faith as "the God who imparts life to the dead." The reference is to the One who revived Abraham's power to beget, and Sarah's ability to bear. See verses 18, 19.[135] Paul may also have been thinking about the resurrection of Jesus, for when he describes God as the One who imparts life to the dead, he is by means of that statement professing also his own faith. Moreover, see 4:24, 25.

What is the meaning of "and calls things that are not as though they were"? Of these words there are several interpretations. The worst one is probably that volunteered by the leader of a certain sect. According to a newspaper report, when this person was caught in the act of telling an untruth, his excuse was, "What of it? Does not Scripture state that even God calls things that are not as though they were?"

The most reasonable explanation may well be that which refers this expression to the activity of the Almighty during the week of creation, when, according to Isa. 48:13, he *called into being* or *summoned* that which beforehand did not exist, namely, "the foundations of the earth" and "the heavens," probably representing the entire work of creation.

The main thrust of Paul's argument is this, that it was by *faith* in the Almighty and All Faithful God, and not by works, that Abraham received the fulfilment of the promise.

18-22. Against all hope, Abraham in hope believed, so that he became the father of many nations, in agreement with what had been told him, "So shall your seed be." And without weakening in faith he took note of the fact that his own body was as good as dead—since he was about a hundred years old—and that Sarah's womb was also dead. Yet he did not waver in unbelief with respect to God's promise, but was strengthened in faith, giving glory to God, being fully persuaded that what God had promised he would be able to perform. That is why it was reckoned to him for righteousness.

The character of Abraham's faith is set forth in a very striking manner.

---

133. For this passage (Gen. 12:3) a spiritual overtone or implication is also recognized by G. Ch. Aalders, *Korte Verklaring, Genesis,* Kampen, 1949, Vol. II, p. 63.

134. κατέναντι, closely related to ἔναντι, is the LXX equivalent of the Hebrew לִפְנֵי. See my dissertation, *The Meaning of the Preposition ἀντί in the New Testament,* pp. 68-70.

135. There are those who, in this connection, also mention the sparing of Isaac's life (Gen. 22). Heb. 11:17-19 may offer some support for this idea. However, Rom. 4:19 makes no reference to this incident. Its relevance at this point is therefore rather uncertain.

Note the following:

a. "Against all hope, Abraham in hope believed."

Basically *hope* means the expectation of something desirable. In the present case the object of hope was the fulfilment of God's promise that Abraham would have a son, in whose line the precious promise of God—"I will be your God . . . in your *seed* all the nations of the earth will be blessed . . . So shall your seed be"—would attain fulfilment.

A time arrived when *humanly speaking* this hope seemed impossible of realization. Nevertheless, "against all hope," that is, in spite of the fact that the birth of the child of promise appeared to be impossible, Abraham "in hope"—here the persuasion that God would be faithful to his promise—continued to trust in God. Result: the hope was fulfilled so that, through his son Isaac, Abraham became "the father of many nations" (see on verse 17).

b. "He did not waver . . . but was strengthened in faith. . . ."

Years passed, and still the promise had not been fulfilled. Bravely the patriarch faced the fact that he was now about a hundred years of age, that "his own body"—here with special reference to his reproductive capacity—was as good as dead,[136] and that Sarah was barren. Nevertheless, he not only continued to exercise faith in God and his promise but was even strengthened in his faith. That this is what actually happened is evident from the fact that when God repeated the promise to him in his very advanced age—"Sarah your wife will indeed bear you a son" (Gen. 17:19)—and ordered all the male membes of his household to be circumcised (Gen. 17:9-14), Abraham immediately glorified God by obeying this command (Gen. 17:23-26). And because of the fact that he thus glorified God he was strengthened in his faith. And since this faith expected everything from God, completely relying on him, it could be, and actually was, "reckoned to him for righteousness."

When a pastor presents to his congregation this account of Abraham's marvelous unwavering faith, it may well be that some people will become discouraged, thinking, "If God requires such faith as this, namely, that a man way past the age of begetting children, with a wife whose womb is *dead,* must believe God's promise that he is going to have a child, that this child will be a boy, and that this very wife, and not some other woman, will give birth to him, then there is no hope for me. When it comes to simple, steadfast faith, the kind of trust that takes hold of God *under any and every circumstance of life,* what a struggle I often experience!"

Close study of Scripture, however, should convince such a person that though, in a sense, Abraham's faith did not waver and was even

---

136. The reading ἤδη νενεκρωμένον, with retention of ἤδη, is subject to a considerable degree of doubt. It would seem to have a slight edge over the reading without ἤδη. The verbal form is the acc. s. neut. perf. pass. participle of νεκρόω, to put to death; in pass., as here, to be impotent, as good as dead.

strengthened, this cannot mean that he did not experience a struggle. He did! That is clearly implied in Gen. 17:18 (and perhaps even in 17:17, though with respect to that verse interpreters are divided). But God immediately reassured him (Gen. 17:19), and it was in that sense that Abraham's faith did not waver and was even strengthened. Every pastor should therefore point his congregation to the Savior who, in answer to the prayer of the struggling soul, and in co-operation with the teaching of the Word, will strengthen and reassure. An excellent hymn in this connection is:

> When I fear my faith will fail, Christ will hold me fast.
>
> A. R. Habershon

That these precious passages of Scripture were meant for every age is shown in the verses which conclude this chapter of Romans:

23-25. Now the words, "It was reckoned to him," were written not for him alone, but also for us to whom it is to be reckoned, to us who rest our faith on him who raised Jesus our Lord from the dead, who was delivered up for our trespasses and was raised for our justification.

" . . . not for him alone but also for us." That the words of Scripture were written not solely for the contemporaries of the respective authors but also for later generations is taught in both testaments (Ps. 78:1-7; Rom. 15:4; I Cor. 9:10; 10:11; and in a sense II Tim. 3:16). So also the experiences of God's children were to be related to later generations (Gen. 18:19). Today, an age in which for many the study of history has become a lost art, this reminder should serve a good purpose. What Paul is saying is that we too are vitally concerned with this story about Abraham, and with the manner in which the righteousness of Christ was imputed to him. Is it not true that we too are the ones to whom it is to be reckoned? Are not we included in the family of those who rest our faith on him who raised Jesus our Lord from the dead?

Note that Paul's attitude toward Jesus Christ is one not only of profound reverence ("Lord"), but also of deep gratitude, heart-warming love ("Our"). When the apostle wrote the words "Jesus our Lord" he was not just rattling off a few titles. No, this is the Paul of Gal. 2:20, the one who said, "the Son of God loved me and gave himself up for me."

Reflecting, then, on God's omnipotence and love employed in the interest of his people, Paul includes his addressees and himself in the circle of those who rest their faith on the One *who raised Jesus our Lord from the dead.*

The long list of references which indicate that The Twelve (often represented by Peter) and Paul were convinced not only of the fact that Jesus had risen from the dead but also that *God* had raised him—see Acts 2:24, 32; 3:15, 26; 4:10; 5:30; 10:40; 13:30, 33, 34, 37; 17:31; I Cor. 6:14; 15:15; II Cor. 4:14; Gal. 1:1; Eph. 1:20; Col. 2:12; I Thess. 1:10 (cf. Heb. 13:20; I Peter 1:21)—is significant. Does it not seem as if these passages are calling attention to the fact that God the Father must have been satisfied with the atoning sacrifice Jesus had offered?

Paul continues with words that have been, and continue to be, the occasion of much controversy, a controversy that centers in a little Greek word of three letters (διά), which can be translated "for" or "because of," or "on account of."

The controversial passage concerns "Jesus our Lord," and the dispute is focused on the clause "who was delivered up *for* our trespasses and was raised *for* our justification."

Some maintain that because these two clauses—(a) delivered up for our trespasses, (b) raised for our justification—are parallel, therefore if the first *looks back* (is retrospective), the second must do the same. Or if the first *looks forward* (is prospective), the second does likewise. See Murray, *op. cit.*, p. 154 f. That author chose the second of these alternatives: Jesus was delivered up in order to atone for our sins and was raised in order that we might be justified. A somewhat similar view can be found in Denney's commentary, *op. cit.*, p. 622. To be fair to these authors, both of whom have written commentaries that are worthy of serious study, their books should be consulted on this question.

It is interesting to notice that A. Schlatter, who also proceeds from the idea that διά must have the same meaning in both clauses, reaches the opposite conclusion. As he sees it, both are retrospective: because we fell, Jesus was condemned; because we had been justified, he arose.[137]

Is it true, indeed, that we are compelled to choose between these two alternatives? Probably not. There is a third possibility, namely, that while basically the little word may have the same meaning in both clauses, namely, may indicate causality, this causality could still look backward in the first clause, forward in the second. In fact, even in the almost immediately preceding line (verses 23, 24) it is clear that the first διά (the one in verse 23: "*for* him") looks backward, to Abraham; the second (in verse 24, "*for* us") looks forward. So also here "He was delivered up *for*, or *on account of*, our trespasses" *looks backward* and means that our trespasses made it necessary for him to be delivered up, while "(he) was raised *for*, or *on account of*, our justification" *looks forward* and indicates that he was raised in order to assure us that in the sight of God we are indeed without sin. In other words Christ's resurrection had as its *purpose* to bring to light the fact that all those who acknowledge Jesus as their Lord and Savior have entered into a state of righteousness in the eyes of God.[138] The Father, by raising Jesus from the dead, assures us that the atoning sacrifice has been accepted; hence, our sins are forgiven.

Before we leave this precious passage (Rom. 4:25) we must point out that here again the close connection between the Old and the New Testament is revealed. The words "who was delivered up [or: over to death] for our

---

137. A. Schlatter, *Gottes Gerechtigkeit, Ein Kommentar zum Römerbrief*, Stuttgart, 1952, p. 173.
138. On this debate with respect to the meaning of διά I have not been able to find anything better than that which is offered by S. Greijdanus, *op. cit.*, pp. 251, 252; and by Ridderbos, *op. cit.*, p. 104. Both of these are excellent.

trespasses" are a strong reminder of what is found in Isa. 53, where in verses 4, 5, 6, 8, 11, and 12, in one way or another, Messiah's *vicarious suffering* is described and predicted.[139]

That the truth with respect to the believers' justification, solely of grace and by faith, is a treasure so precious that nothing—no, nothing!—can top it, Paul confesses when, in jubilation of spirit, he exclaims:

"Nevertheless the things that once were gains to me these have I counted loss for Christ. Yes, what is more, I certainly count all things to be sheer loss because of the all-surpassing excellence of knowing Christ Jesus my Lord, for whom I suffered the loss of all things, and I am still counting them refuse, in order that I may gain Christ, and be found in him, *not having a righteousness of my own, legal righteousness,* but that (which is) through faith in Christ, the righteousness (which is) from God and is by faith . . ." (Phil. 3:7-9).

Among the many precious truths held before us in this fourth chapter of Romans is certainly also this outstanding one, namely, that the comforting doctrine of justification not by works but by faith is firmly rooted in Scripture (the Old Testament), as the example of Abraham proves.

Practical Lessons Derived from Romans 4

Verse 1

"What then shall we say that Abraham has discovered?" See also verses 3, 9, and 10. A hint for speakers: keep alive the interest of your audience by asking questions . . . but do not overdo this.

Verse 6

"Blessed are those whose transgressions are forgiven . . . whose sins are covered." The reference to David is certainly apt, for if ever a man received righteous standing with God without having *earned* it, it was David. But because of the sovereign grace of his God his sins were forgiven, blotted out. Moreover, as Ps. 32 proves, that same blessing is bestowed upon every truly penitent sinner.

Verse 11

"And he received the *sign* of circumcision as a *seal* of the righteousness by faith. . . ."

Because God is love (I John 4:8) and takes delight in saving sinners (see Isa. 1:18; Ezek. 18:23, 32; 33:11; Hos. 11:8; Matt. 11:28-30; John 7:37; Rev. 22:17), he strengthens his promises by means of signs and seals.

---

139. In fact, in the LXX version of Isa. 53 the very expression "deliver" in the sense of "deliver up to death" occurs twice (verses 6 and 12). Translated into English, verse 6 in the LXX reads, "And the Lord delivered him up for our sins." Verse 12 reads, "And on account of their sins he was delivered up." But in that verse the Hebrew reads differently, "And he made intercession for the transgressors."

Verses 16–18

"Abraham . . . the father of us all; the father of many nations." In God's kingdom there is no room for racial prejudice. All believers constitute one family, *Abraham's Family*; in an even deeper sense, *"God's Family"* (Eph. 3:14, 15).

Verse 18

"Against all hope, Abraham in hope believed." There is a kind of hope that has no real foundation, no anchor. Abraham's hope was firmly anchored, namely, in God's unfailing promise. See Heb. 6:19, 20; 11:1; and sing "We Have an Anchor" by Priscilla Owens.

Verse 21

". . . being fully persuaded that what God had promised he would be able to perform."

Points of Contrast Between the Divine Promise and Human Promises

a. God's promise is always right. Human promises are sometimes wrong.

b. God's promise is substantial; in fact, priceless. Human promises are often trivial.

c. God never forgets his promise. People frequently forget.

d. God—hence also Jesus—fulfils his promise. In this respect, too, people often fail. But as to the Lord, is it not true that what he grants is often even more than what he promised? Cf. Matt. 28:7 (or Mark 16:7) with Luke 24:34, 36.

Summary of Chapter 4

Having set forth the truth that the state of righteousness in God's sight cannot be achieved by means of human works but is God's gift, the apostle now, in harmony with 4:21, elaborates on the fact that this representation is not a novelty but is thoroughly scriptural.

In this connection he fixes the attention of the hearer and/or reader on the manner in which Abraham obtained this great blessing: "Abraham believed God, and it was reckoned to him for righteousness" (Gen. 15:6). He comments, "Now to the one who works, his wages are not reckoned as a favor but as a debt. On the other hand, to the person who does not work but rests his faith on him who justifies the ungodly, his faith is reckoned for righteousness." God counted for righteousness that which Abraham appropriated by faith, namely, the righteousness of Another, that is, of Jesus Christ, which was imputed to Abraham. Cf. Rom. 4:6, 11, 25; 5:6–21; cf. Isa. 53:4–6, 8, 12.

By means of a quotation from Ps. 32 the apostle proves that what was true with respect to Abraham holds for *all* believers: "Blessed (are) those whose transgressions are forgiven, whose sins are covered."

Returning to Gen. 15:6, Paul asks, "Is this blessing then pronounced only upon the circumcised or also upon the uncircumcised?" He shows that it was long before Abraham was circumcised that his faith was reckoned for righteousness. As a result Abraham became "the father of *all* believers";

that is, of those uncircumcised as well as of those circumcised; in other words, of Gentile as well as of Jewish believers (verses 1-12).

In close connection with the immediately preceding, Paul now emphasizes the importance of God's *promise* and its fulfilment. It was not through the law that Abraham received the promise. Human works or merit had nothing to do with it. It was *faith* in the *promise* that mattered. Cf. Gal. 3:9, 29. God *promised* Abraham that he would be "the father of many nations," therefore "heir of the world" (Gen. 17:5). Abraham did not waver in unbelief but was strengthened in faith. He rested his faith on him "who imparts life to the dead, and calls things that are not as though they were." In view of the fact that Abraham was almost a hundred years old and Sarah was barren, this faith of Abraham was indeed remarkable. The patriarch believed that whatever God promised he would also do. Moreover, the words "It was reckoned to him for righteousness" were meant not only for him but for all who rest their faith on God, the One who "raised Jesus our Lord from the dead."

The Savior "was delivered up for our trespasses and was raised for our justification." This probably means that our trespasses made it necessary for Jesus to be delivered over to death, and that he was raised to life in order to assure us that his vicarious sacrifice had been accepted. As a result believers are, in the very sight of God, without sin and therefore righteous (verses 13-25).

By means of corroborative evidence from the Old Testament Paul has made clear that the comforting doctrine of justification—hence salvation—by faith, on the basis of God's sovereign grace, is indeed thoroughly scriptural.

Outline (continued)

Justification by Faith

C. *Effective.*

1a. *It produces the fruit of* **peace** *and its concomitants:*
freedom of access, exultation, firmly anchored hope: assurance
of complete salvation.
"Therefore, having been justified by faith, we have peace
with God through our Lord Jesus Christ."
5:1–11

1b. *The certainty and copiousness of salvation confirmed by the parallel*
Adam—Christ
Correspondence and Contrast
"But where sin increased, grace increased all the more."
5:12–21

CHAPTER 5

5 1 Therefore, having been justified by faith, we have peace with God through our Lord Jesus Christ, 2 through whom we have also gained access by faith into this grace in which we stand, and we exult in the hope of the glory of God. 3 And not only this, but we even exult in our sufferings, because we know that suffering brings about perseverance; 4 perseverance, proven character; proven character, hope. 5 And this hope does not disappoint, because God's love has been poured out into our hearts by the Holy Spirit who was given to us.

6 For while we were still powerless, at the appointed time Christ died for the ungodly. 7 Now a man will scarcely die for a righteous person, though for a good person someone might possibly dare to die. 8 But God demonstrates his own love for us in this, that while we were still sinners Christ died for us.

9 Since, then, we have now been justified by his blood, we shall much more be saved through him from (God's) wrath. 10 For if, while we were enemies, we were reconciled to him through the death of his Son, much more, having been reconciled, shall we be saved through his life! 11 And not only this, but we also exult in God through our Lord Jesus Christ, through whom we have now already received our reconciliation.

C. *Effective.*

1a. *It produces the fruit of **peace** and its concomitants:*
freedom of access, exultation, firmly anchored hope: assurance
of complete salvation.
"Therefore, having been justified by faith, we have peace with God
through our Lord Jesus Christ."
5:1-11

Under the general heading *Justification by Faith, Exposition* (1:16-11:36) Paul has shown that this justification is *necessary and real* (1:16—3:31), as well as *scriptural* (chapter 4). In chapters 5-8 he demonstrates that it is also *effective, fruitful.*

It is clear that in Paul's thinking chapters 5, 6, 7, and 8 belong together. The fruits of justification are set forth in all of them. In addition, in its final verse each of these four chapters contains the phrase "through (or *in*) Jesus Christ (or Christ Jesus) our Lord."

The kind of fruit varies from chapter to chapter. Here, in 5:1-11, the attention of the hearer and/or reader is focused first of all on *peace*. In connection with it mention is also made of freedom of access, exultation, and hope, a hope that is firmly anchored and amounts to certainty with respect to salvation.

167

By means of the parallel Adam-Christ (verses 12-21) the *certainty* and especially the *copious character* of salvation receive further elucidation.

1, 2. Therefore, having been justified by faith, we have peace with God through our Lord Jesus Christ, through whom we have also gained access by faith into this grace in which we stand, and we exult in the hope of the glory of God.[140]

The apostle has reached a new phase in the discussion of *justification by faith*. He now simply assumes that he himself and those addressed have received and are enjoying this marvelous gift. It is from this fact, viewed as a startingpoint, that the discussion now moves forward.

The various units composing verses 1 and 2 may be grouped as follows:
a. "Therefore, having been justified by faith..."

The reasons implied in this "Therefore" are found in the first four chapters; especially in 3:21-4:25.

---

140. At the very beginning of this paragraph we encounter a difficulty. Did Paul say, and did Tertius (16:22) write, "*We have* peace," or "*Let us have* peace"? Among translators and commentators there is a sharp division of opinion with respect to this question. Fact is that the underlying Greek text is not uniform. Textual evidence in support of the subjunctive ἔχωμεν is strong. This form is supported by Sinaiticus and Vaticanus (original hand in both cases), and further by Alexandrinus, Ephraemi Rescriptus, Codex Bezae, etc., as well as by many cursives and patristic citations. Several ancient versions, too, as well as more recent translations, show that their authors accept this reading. Some writers express themselves very forcibly, as if the opposite view, favoring the indicative ἔχομεν, is entirely impossible. See, for example, Robertson, *Word Pictures,* Vol. IV, p. 355; and Lenski, *op. cit.,* pp. 333, 334. Among others who, in one sense or another, also favor the subjunctive ("Let us have peace," "Let us continue to have peace," "Let us live in peace," "Let us enjoy peace," or something similar) are Berkeley, Goodspeed, Moffatt, N.E.B.

But the indicative ἔχομεν, "we have," also has considerable support. In fact, the Wyman fragment, to which a very early date (latter part of the third century A.D.) has been ascribed, has the indicative ἔχομεν.

Among translations favoring the indicative are A.V., A.R.V., N.A.S., Beck, R.S.V., N.I.V. At times one possibility is recognized in the text, the other in a footnote or margin.

As to still another attempt to do justice to the original, namely, "Let us enjoy the peace we have," or something similar (see Murray, *op. cit.,* p. 159), I can see no justification for this compromise.

I accept the indicative. In addition to the evidence furnished by the third-century fragment mentioned above, two considerations have led me to adopt this reading:

a. At the time the New Testament was written the Greek letters o and ω were beginning to be pronounced alike and at times were used interchangeably. In this connection note also the variant διώκομεν for διώκωμεν in Rom. 14:19, where the spelling with the two omegas deserves the preference, a reverse application of the same pronunciation and writing peculiarity found in 5:1.

b. The logic of the context here in Rom. 5:1 strongly favors the indicative. Justified people *have* peace with God (Eph. 2:14-18). They do not say, "Let us have peace." The immediately following clause, "through whom we have also gained access by faith into this grace in which we stand" is a statement of *fact,* and, as shown by the word *also,* implies that the immediately preceding words similarly express a *fact.* "We have peace ... we have also gained access." Note the series of indicatives which follows: "... we exult ... we even exult ... we know, etc." Does not all this clearly indicate that in 5:1 the hortatory part of this section—see 6:1f., 6:15f., 7:7f., 8:31f.—has not yet begun?

b. "... we have peace with God ..."

For the meaning of the term *peace* see on 1:7; 2:10. As 5:10, 11 makes clear, in 5:1 the basic meaning of peace is *reconciliation* with God through the death of his Son. This implies the removal of divine wrath from the sinner, and the latter's restoration to divine favor.

The fact that *objective* peace is here in the foreground does not mean, however, that the *subjective* enjoyment of this great blessing is absent from Paul's mind. How could he even think about the cause without reflecting on the effect, namely, the condition of rest and contentment present in the hearts of those who know that the sins of the past have been forgiven, the evils of the present are being overruled for good, and future events cannot bring about separation from God's love? The mention of this "peace which passes all understanding" (Phil. 4:7) makes the transition to the next item very natural:

c. "... through our Lord Jesus Christ, through whom we have also gained access by faith into this grace in which we stand ..."

It was Christ's blood, representing his entire vicarious sacrifice, which brought reconciliation, and it was his Spirit which brought to the hearts of all true believers appreciation of that which redemption through blood had accomplished. So it was indeed through the person and work of the Savior, appropriated by faith, that access into this state of grace—that is, the state of justification—had been effected. Moreover, access to this state of grace implies confident access to the Father (Eph. 2:8; 3:12) and to his throne of grace (Heb. 4:16).

It is "our Lord (Owner, Master) Jesus (Savior) Christ (Anointed)" who, having paid his people's debt, introduces them to the Father. It is he who not only "makes intercession" for them (Rom. 8:34) but, even more meaningfully, "ever lives to make intercession" for them (Heb. 7:25). And if even his intercession for them while he was still on earth was filled with comfort (read John 17), can his pleading for them, now that he has returned to heaven, *clothed with the merits of his accomplished redemption,* be less precious and effective?

d. "... and we exult in the hope of the glory of God."

This "glory of God" indicates the marvelous salvation God has in store for those who place their trust in him. See such passages as the following: Rom. 2:7; 8:18, 30; I Cor. 15:43; II Cor. 4:17; Col. 1:27b; 3:4; II Tim. 2:10. For the meaning of the Greek word here rendered "exult" see on 2:17. Undoubtedly what Paul has in mind is, "We do not, like certain selfrighteous people, *brag* about our own accomplishments, but we place all our confidence in God. In him *we greatly rejoice.*"

> On Christ, the solid Rock I stand,
> All other ground is sinking sand.
>
> Refrain of "My Hope Is Built"
> by Edward Mote

Actually, however, the apostle does not say, "We exult in the glory of God," but "We exult in *the hope of* the glory of God." In light of Col. 1:27 the meaning is probably, "We rejoice greatly when we reflect on *the solid basis for the expectation* of future bliss." See N.T.C. on Col. 1:27. In principle we have this blessedness here and now; in perfection, at Christ's return.

Paul continues, **3, 4. And not only this, but we even exult in our sufferings, because we know that suffering brings about perseverance; perseverance, proven character; proven character, hope.**

Here "*in* our sufferings" means "*in the midst of and because of*" the tribulations we experience in carrying on the work of the Lord. Cf. Rom. 8:35–39; I Cor. 4:9–13; II Cor. 1:4–10; 11:23–30 (the long list); 12:7–10; Gal. 6:17; II Tim. 3:11, 12 (to the extent in which that passage reflects on earlier events).[141]

But how was it possible for the apostle to exult in sufferings? How can suffering—here probably especially tribulation for the sake of Christ and the gospel—be regarded as a blessing? For a somewhat detailed answer see N.T.C. on Philippians, pp. 90, 91. Be sure also to examine Heb. 12:5–11, and in the Old Testament Ps. 119:67, 71; Jer. 31:18.

To all this add II Cor. 12:7–10. Note especially verse 9, "My grace is sufficient for you, for my power is made perfect in weakness."

In this connection two facts should be borne in mind:

a. An afflicted believer's own *weakness*, by way of contrast, serves to magnify God's *power*.

b. It is exactly when the sufferer recognizes that he is weak but God is strong and ready to help that he will seek help from above. Since this help is sufficient, his faith will be strengthened. Thus *suffering brings about perseverance.*

Although it is true that perseverance (strength *to bear up under* plus the persistent application of this strength) is basically the result of the operation of the Holy Spirit in the hearts and lives of God's children, it implies human action. It is by no means a passive quality. The person who has it *perseveres.* He holds on to what he has (Rev. 2:25), is faithful even to the point of death (Rev. 2:10).[142]

Perseverance produces proven character, that is, character that has sustained *the test* to which it was subjected.[143]

---

141. Sometimes reference is also made to II Tim. 4:14–17. This is permissible if it be borne in mind that when Paul wrote Romans *he* could not have been thinking of suffering that was experienced at a later time.

142. For the word ὑπομονή, by Paul mentioned first in Rom. 2:7, next here in 5:3, 4, see also 8:25; 15:4, 5; II Cor. 1:6; 6:4; 12:12; Col. 1:11; I Thess. 1:3; II Thess. 1:4; 3:5; I Tim. 6:11; II Tim. 3:10; Titus 2:2; Heb. 10:36; 12:1; James 1:3, 4; II Peter 1:6; and see its various occurrences in Revelation, beginning with 1:9.

143. On δοκιμή and related words see W. Grundmann's article in Th.D.N.T., Vol. II, pp. 255-260.

With respect to this "test" see Zech. 13:9, "I will refine them like silver and test them like gold." Just as the refining fire of the goldsmith frees gold and silver from the impurities which in the natural state cling to them (cf. Isa. 1:25; Mal. 3:3), so also the patient endurance or perseverance of God's children purifies them, that is, by the operation of the Holy Spirit brings about "proven" character, a character that has successfully sustained the fiery test.

It is immediately clear that consciousness, on their part, of the fact that they have sustained the test, so that God's approval rests on them, will strengthen their *hope. Proven character brings about hope.* So, in this example of chain reasoning we are back to the *hope* mentioned in verse 2.

5. And this hope does not disappoint, because God's love has been poured out into our hearts by the Holy Spirit who was given to us.

Note the masterful transition from *faith* (verses 1, 2) to *hope* (verses 2, 4, 5), to *love* (verse 5). This is the sequence found also in I Cor. 13:13. (In I Thess. 1:3 the sequence is faith, love, hope.)

There are people without hope (Eph. 2:12; I Thess. 4:13). There are also those who cling to illusory or deceptive hope (Prov. 11:7; Acts 16:19). But those who have been justified by faith and have been reconciled with God cherish the kind of hope that does not disappoint (Ps. 22:5). Their hope is firmly anchored in God's redeeming love. Another way of expressing the same thought is this: their hope is moored to the throne of grace, that is, to that which is "within the veil," where Jesus is seated at God's right hand (Heb. 6:19, 20). He is living forevermore to intercede for his people (Heb. 7:25).

Moreover, God's love is not rationed out drop by drop. On the contrary, by the Holy Spirit it is "poured out" into the hearts of the redeemed; in other words, it is supplied freely, abundantly, copiously, lavishly, as is true with respect to God's gifts in general (Num. 20:8, 11; II Kings 4:1-7; Ps. 91:16; Isa. 1:18; 55:1; Ezek. 39:29; Joel 2:28, 29; Zech. 12:10; Matt. 11:27-30; 14:20; 15:37; Luke 6:38; John 1:16; 3:16; Acts 2:16-18; 10:45; 14:17; 17:25; Rom. 5:20; I Cor. 2:9, 10; II Cor. 4:17; Eph. 1:8; 2:7; James 1:5; Rev. 22:17). "He giveth and giveth and giveth again." See N.T.C. on John, Vol. I, pp. 88, 89 ("grace upon grace").

In fact, the Holy Spirit, who is the Dispenser of God's gifts, is also himself God's gift to the church (John 14:16; 15:7).

Over against the opinion of some it should be emphasized that the expression "the love of God" cannot mean "our love for God." How could such thoroughly inadequate love ever be the basis of hope that does not disappoint? The reference is clearly to God's own love, as verse 8 proves. See also Rom. 8:35; II Cor. 13:13.

Now all this sheds light on the glorious character of justification by faith. This divine deed whereby the sinner who flees to God for refuge is declared righteous is often compared to that which happens in a courtroom. It has accordingly been called a *forensic* action. It is indeed that, but, considered in its most comprehensive sense, it is far more than that. Note contrast:

The earthly judge	God as Judge
a. finding the accused "not guilty" acquits him; or finding him guilty sentences him.	a. finding the accused guilty—as is always the case—blots out his guilt, on the basis of the work accomplished by God's Son, the Guilt Bearer.
b. dismisses him from the courtroom and has no further dealings with him.	b. through his Spirit *pours his love into his heart* and adopts him as his own son or daughter.

But the comparison should be carried one step farther, for even human adoption is not an adequate illustration of divine adoption. In human adoption the parents would like to transmit something of their own character or spirit to that adopted child. Sometimes this succeeds to a degree; sometimes not at all. But when God adopts he also plants his own Spirit into the adoptee's heart, transforming him or her into God's own image (Rom. 8:15).

6–8. For while we were still powerless,[144] at the appointed time Christ died for the ungodly. Now a man will scarcely die for a righteous person, though for a good person someone might possibly dare to die. But God demonstrates his own love for us in this, that while we were still sinners Christ died for us.

In this passage Paul states the reason for saying that God poured his love into the hearts of sinners. He tells us that he was justified in making this assertion because "while we were still powerless," that is, helpless, totally unable to rescue ourselves from the effects of the fall, Christ, motivated by sovereign love and not by any human merit or accomplishment, died for us, the ungodly.

The unique character of this love becomes apparent when we consider the fact that while for a righteous person a man will scarcely die—though, by rare exception, it might after all happen that for such a good person someone would dare to die, God, on the other hand, demonstrates *his own* love in this remarkable way, namely, that while we were still in our helpless and sinful state Christ died for us.

In connection with this explanation note the following:

a. The "ungodly" people of verse 6 are the "sinners" of verse 8, namely, those sinners for whom Christ died, the "beloved of God, saints" of 1:7.

b. The distinction between "a righteous person" and "a good person" should not be pressed, as if the apostle were saying that for a person who is

---

144. Though Grk.N.T. (A-B-M-W) favors εἰ γε ... ἔτι textual support for ἔτι γὰρ ... ἔτι is not any weaker. Moreover, the double ἔτι would seem to link more logically with the preceding verse. Is it not possible that the other readings arose out of an attempt to get rid of the double ἔτι? The repetition of ἔτι may have resulted from the apostle's intention to place special stress on the all-surpassing eminence of God's love.

merely "righteous" it would be almost impossible to find someone who would die, but for a "good" person, or benefactor, it might under exceptional conditions be possible to find a substitute who would be willing to offer his life. This is over-interpretation. We should adhere to the one basic point Paul is making, and not obscure the thought by introducing unwarranted distinctions. Room should be left for stylistic variation.[145]

c. What Paul is saying is that God's love, as revealed in Jesus Christ, is both unprecedented and unparalleled. No merit from our side could have moved Christ to die for us, for he died for us "while we were still sinners." Moreover, he died for us "at the appointed time," that is, at the time appointed by *God* (cf. Mark 1:15; Gal. 4:4), not by *us*.

This death was unparalleled with respect to the marvel of the implied condescending and pardoning grace. Christ died for those who were bad, bad, bad! In them there was no goodness that could have attracted this love. In the death of Jesus for sinners God demonstrates "his own" sovereign love. See Isa. 1:18; 53:6; 57:15; Dan. 9:17–19; I John 4:10.

d. Note the word "demonstrates," *present* tense. Although it is true that for Paul, at the time he wrote this letter, as well as for us today, the death of Christ was an event that had occurred in the past, its lesson remains an ever *present* and glorious reality.[146]

e. Note "his own love for us."[147]

f. Though it is true that no less than four times in these three verses Paul uses a preposition (ὑπέρ) which has a very wide range of meaning, stretching all the way from *about* or *concerning* (cf. περί) to *in the place of* (cf. ἀντί), and which frequently means "for," "in behalf of," "for the sake of," "in the interest of," it would seem that here in Rom. 5:6–8 this little word, though not by itself meaning "in the place of" *implies* as much. Does not the context (see verses 9, 10) indicate that *by means of the shedding of his blood* Christ removed from us God's wrath? See also N.T.C. on Galatians, p. 130; on Philippians, pp. 82, 83; and on I and II Timothy and Titus, pp. 375, 376.

9, 10. Since, then, we have now been justified by his blood, we shall much more be saved through him from (God's) wrath. For if, while we were enemies, we were reconciled to him through the death of his Son, much more, having been reconciled, shall we be saved through his life!

---

145. The idea that δικαίου and ἀγαθοῦ (verse 7) are neuter and indicate things or qualities conflicts with the very personal context (see verses 6 and 8).

146. For the verb συνίστημι the following meanings are worthy of consideration:
   (1) intr.: to stand by or with (Luke 9:32); to hold together (Col. 1:17); to be composed of, to be formed out of (II Peter 3:5).
   (2) tr.: to confirm, bring out clearly, prove, demonstrate (Rom. 3:5; 5:8; II Cor. 7:11; Gal. 2:18).
   (3) to commend, in the favorable sense (Rom. 16:1; II Cor. 4:2; 6:4; 12:11); in the unfavorable sense (II Cor. 3:1; 5:12; 10:12). In II Cor. 10:18 the word *commend* is used first in the unfavorable, then in the favorable sense.

147. It is natural to construe εἰς ἡμᾶς (verse 8) with ἀγάπην. See Eph. 1:15 ("love for all the saints"); and cf. Col. 1:4; I Thess. 3:12; II Thess. 1:3.

The relation between verses 9, 10 and the immediately preceding context is as follows:

We will not be disappointed in our hope, for, in Christ, God loves us so deeply that the Savior *died* for us while we were still sinners. If, then, we were justified by that *death*—or that blood—of Christ, much more shall we be saved from any future outpouring of God's wrath.

Now the details:

a. Verses 9 and 10 run parallel. The first concerns our legal standing with God; the second, our personal relationship to him. Each of the two statements is in the form of an *a fortiori* argument: if God did the greater, will he not *even more readily* do the lesser?[148]

b. "justified by his blood."

The demands of God's justice must be satisfied. See Isa. 1:27; 53:5; Rom. 8:4. Here in Rom. 5:9, as in 3:24, the relation between justification and Christ's *death* is indicated: our justification required Christ's *eternal* (not in time but in quality) death (cf. Luke 24:26, 27). In 4:25, on the other hand, the relation described is that between justification and Christ's *resurrection*.

Blood points to *sacrifice, offering*. For more on Christ's death as an offering, a voluntary sacrifice, see such passages as Isa. 53:7, 10, 12; John 10:11, 15; I Peter 2:21-24.

c. "saved through him from God's wrath."

For this divine wrath see on Rom. 1:18. The deliverance from this wrath, by Christ's mediatorial work, and therefore by Christ himself, refers to our not having to endure the outpouring of the divine vengeance on the day of the final judgment. See I Thess. 1:10; 5:9; II Thess. 1:5-10.

d. "... if, while we were enemies ..."

The word *enemies* must be understood in the passive sense: so regarded by God, because as yet we had not been reconciled to him.

e. "... we were reconciled to him through the death of his Son."

Believers are those who, by God's grace, have attained a standing of righteousness in relation to God's holy law; in other words, they have been *justified*. God's law no longer condemns them. But not only is this true. What is now added is that God also *loves* them. His heart goes out to them. He has made friends of enemies.

It should be emphasized that reconciliation—as well as justification—is a divine act. It is God, not man, who brings about reconciliation, the change from enmity to friendship.

However, just as it is true that justification requires faith on man's part—God-imparted and God-sustained faith, to be sure, but human faith nevertheless—so also reconciliation requires obedience on man's part. Here too it is true that such obedience is God's gift. Nonetheless, it is man

---

148. For other instances of this kind of reasoning see in Romans the following verses: 5:15, 17; 8:32; 11:12, 24; and elsewhere: Matt. 6:30; 7:11; 10:25b; II Cor. 3:11; Heb. 12:9, 25.

who obeys the exhortation, "Be reconciled with God" (II Cor. 5:10). God's relation to man is not the same as that of a carpenter to the block of wood to which he is applying his skill, nor does it resemble the ventriloquist's relation to his dummy.

Preachers are in danger of becoming onesided, unbalanced. There are those who stress divine initiative and action at the expense of human responsibility and action. There are also those who do the very opposite. Scripture avoids both extremes. The right view is found in such passages as Phil. 2:12, 13; II Thess. 2:13. See also Luke 22:22; Acts 2:23.

f. ". . . saved through his life"

It is the resurrected, living, and exalted Son of God who, through his Spirit, carries to completion in our hearts and lives the work of salvation.

g. "much more . . . much more"

If God justifies and reconciles to himself enemies, he will *certainly* save friends.

11. And not only this, but we also exult in God through our Lord Jesus Christ, through whom we have now already received our reconciliation.

The structure of this sentence reminds one of verse 3 ("And not only this, but . . ."). In view of the context the meaning is probably, "Not only shall we be saved (verse 10b), but even now we exult." See 5:2, 3. Rejoicing in God because of blessings both present and future reminds one of the words, "In this y o u greatly rejoice . . . with joy inexpressible and full of glory" (I Peter 1:6, 8).[149]

Not all glorying or boasting can be recommended, however. As Rom. 2:17, 23 had indicated, Jews were boasting or bragging about the fact that they, in distinction from all other nations, possessed God's holy law. In the church at Corinth there were people who bragged about Christian leaders (I Cor. 3:21), and about special gifts or attainments (II Cor. 11:18). And in his letter to the Galatians Paul refers to men who bragged about the number of Gentiles they had "converted" (caused to be circumcised, Gal. 6:13). Does that sound up-to-date?

Over against all such sinful leaping for joy Paul informs the Romans, "We exult in God through our Lord Jesus Christ." And indeed, if, in speaking about the blessed results of Christian labor, one constantly keeps his attention focused on Jesus Christ, God's Chosen Servant, who was the very opposite of a boaster (Matt. 12:18-21; Phil. 2:5-8), and derives all his power from *him,* all will be well.

This is the One, says Paul, "through whom we have now already received our reconciliation." For those who, in faith and humility leap for joy when they consider the blessings they have already received there are even more glorious blessings in store in the hereafter.

No wonder that, in connection with blessings received through Jesus

---

149. For the various meanings of the verb καυχάομαι see on 2:17.

Christ, Paul is able to say, "Let him who boasts, boast in the Lord" (I Cor. 1:31; II Cor. 10:17).

---

12 Wherefore, just as through one man sin entered the world, and death through sin, and so death spread to all mankind, since all sinned— 13 for before the law (was given) sin was in the world. But sin is not taken into account when there is no law. 14 Nevertheless, death reigned from (the time of) Adam to (that of) Moses, even over those who did not sin by transgressing an express command, as did Adam,[150] who is a type of him who was to come. 15 But the free gift is not like the trespass. For if, by reason of the trespass of the one the many died, much more did God's grace and the gift that came by the grace of this one man, Jesus Christ, overflow to the many! 16 Again, the gift (of God) is not like (the result of) one man's sin. For the judgment followed one sin and brought condemnation, but the free gift followed many trespasses and brought justification. 17 For if by the trespass of the one, death reigned through that one, much more will those who receive the overflowing fulness of grace and of the gift of righteousness reign in life through the One, Jesus Christ.

18 Consequently, as one trespass resulted in condemnation for all men, so also one act of righteousness resulted for all men in justification issuing in life. 19 For just as through the disobedience of the one the many were made sinners, so also through the obedience of the One will the many be made righteous.

20 Moreover, the law came in besides, in order that the trespass might increase. But where sin increased, grace increased all the more, 21 in order that, as sin reigned in death, so also grace might reign through righteousness to bring everlasting life through Jesus Christ our Lord.

1b. *The certainty and copiousness of salvation confirmed by the parallel*
Adam—Christ
Correspondence and Contrast
"But where sin increased, grace increased all the more."
5:12-21

That there is a close connection between 5:1-11 and 5:12-21 is clear. In both of these sections the thought that is stressed is that salvation for time and eternity is through Jesus Christ. According to 5:1-11 it is through him that believers have been justified and have found peace, reconciliation with God. To this idea of certainty of salvation through Christ, Paul now, in verses 12-21, adds the thought that grace more than offsets sin. It not only nullifies the effects of sin, it also bestows everlasting life.

Paul's reasoning may at first seem somewhat difficult to follow. He starts a sentence but does not complete it. He begins by saying, **12. Wherefore, just as through one man sin entered the world, and death through sin, and so death spread to all mankind, since all sinned,** and then, instead of completing this statement, he first of all enlarges on one of its elements, namely the universality of sin. Not until he reaches verse 18 does he return to the sentence he started to write. He reproduces its thought in a modified form: "Consequently, as one trespass resulted in condemnation for all,"

---

150. Literally: "after the similitude of Adam's transgression" (A.V.).

and then he finally, in substance, completes the sentence as follows, ". . . so also one act of righteousness resulted for all men in justification issuing in life."[151]

Now it should be admitted that such a break in grammatical structure is in line with Paul's style and personality. See N.T.C. on Luke, p. 6. Yet it is not today, nor has it been in the past, an unusual style phenomenon.

For example, a minister, making an announcement to his congregation, regarding a picnic, might start out as follows:

"Since tomorrow we'll all be attending the church picnic. . . ."

He wishes to continue with, "We urge all to come early and to bring along food enough for your own family and, if possible, even something extra for poor people who may wish to join us."

But before he can even say this he notices that his words about a church picnic *tomorrow* are being greeted with skepticism. So, instead, he continues as follows:

"I notice that some of y o u are shaking y o u r heads, thinking that there can be no picnic tomorrow. Let me therefore assure y o u that the early morning prediction about a storm heading our way has been canceled. A new forecast was conveyed to me just minutes before I ascended the pulpit. According to it, the storm has changed its course and beautiful weather is expected for tomorrow. So we urge all to come early, etc."

With all this in mind, the various elements of verse 12, and also the verse viewed as a unit, may be interpreted as follows:

a. "*Wherefore*," that is, in view of the fact that, through his sacrificial death and resurrection life, Jesus Christ has brought righteousness, reconciliation (peace), and life, etc. See 5:1-11.

b. "just as through one man sin entered the world . . ."

The one man is obviously Adam. See verse 14. Cf. Gen. 2:16, 17; 3:1-6. In what sense is it to be understood that through Adam's fall sin entered the world? Only in this sense that gradually, over the course of the years and centuries, those who were born inherited their sinful nature from Adam, and therefore committed sins? Without denying that this indeed happened, we must nevertheless affirm that there was a far more direct way in which "through one man sin entered the world." On this same third

---

151. Not all agree with the idea that what we have here is an anacoluthon (change in grammatical construction). See, for example, Lenski, *op. cit.*, pp. 358, 359. He finds the "conclusion" of the sentence in the very first verse, which he translates, "even so the death went through to all men since all did sin." Objections:

a. His translation of καὶ οὕτως (verse 12b) is "even so," as if this marks the beginning of the conclusion of the sentence. But it is clear from three instances in this very chapter (18, 19, 21) that Paul would then have written οὕτως καί, not καὶ οὕτως. See also Rom. 6:4; 11:31; I Cor. 12:12, etc.

b. Logic, too, is entirely on the side of those who believe that not until verse 18b does the apostle write what may be regarded as the apodosis or conclusion of the sentence begun in verse 12. *The one man, Adam,* through whom sin entered the world, points to *the One, namely, Jesus Christ,* through whom many will be made righteous.

missionary journey, not very long before Paul composed Romans, he wrote letters to the Corinthians. In one of them (I Cor. 15:22) he says, "As in Adam all die, so in Christ shall all be made alive." In Rom. 5:15 he writes, "By reason of the trespass of the one the many died." He obviously means that *the entire human race was included in Adam,* so that when Adam sinned, all sinned; when the process of death began to ruin *him,* it immediately affected *the entire race.*

Scripture, in other words, in speaking about these matters, does not view people atomistically, as if each person were comparable to a grain of sand on the seashore. Especially in this present day and age, with its emphasis on the individual, it is well to be reminded of the truth expressed in the words which, in a former generation, were impressed even upon the minds of children:

> In Adam's Fall
> We Sinned All

Moreover, when we bear in mind that this very chapter (5) teaches not only the inclusion of all those who belong to *Adam*—that is, of the entire human race—in Adam's *guilt,* but also the inclusion of all who belong to *Christ,* in the *salvation* purchased by his blood (verses 18, 19; cf. II Cor. 5:19; Eph. 1:3-7; Phil. 3:9; Col. 3:1, 3), and that this salvation is God's free gift to all who by faith are willing to accept it, we shall have nothing to complain about.

c. "and death through sin, and so death spread to all mankind . . ."

Solidarity in guilt implies solidarity in death, here, as in I Cor. 15:22, with emphasis on *physical* death. Sin and death cannot be separated, as is clear from Gen. 2:17; 3:17-19; Rom. 1:32; I Cor. 15:22. In Adam all sinned; in Adam all died. The process of dying, and this not only for Adam but for the race, began the moment Adam sinned.

d. "since all sinned."[152]

In all probability this refers to sins all people have themselves committed after they were born. Such personal sinning has been going on throughout the centuries. Paul is, as it were, saying, "I know that *one* man, and in him all men, sinned, for if this were not true how can we account for all the sinning that has been going on afterward?"

This interpretation gives to the word *sinned* the meaning it has

---

152. ἐφ' ᾧ = ἐπὶ τούτῳ ὅτι, for this reason that; hence *because, since;* here probably to be interpreted inferentially ("I draw this inference because," or simply "since").

Among other meanings that have been assigned to this expression the following are, perhaps, the most important:

(1) the antecedent of ᾧ is θάνατος. This makes no sense.

(2) the antecedent of ᾧ is ἑνὸς ἀνθρώπου. The meaning would be that everybody sinned *in* the first man, Adam. Doctrinally this is sound, and, as was shown, is even taught in verses 12 and 15. Yet, unless there are very good reasons for doing so, we should not link ἐφ' ᾧ with an antecedent that is so far removed from it. Besides, it is not clear that ἐφ' = ἐπί should be interpreted to mean ἐν.

everywhere else in Paul's epistles. Why should "all sinned" mean one thing (actual, personal sins) in Rom. 3:23, but something else in 5:12? Besides if here in 5:12 we explain the words *all sinned* to refer to the fact that all sinned *in Adam,* would we not be making the apostle guilty of needless repetition, for the sinning of all "in Adam" is already implied in this same verse; note "through one man sin entered the world."[153]

To these two reasons for believing that this interpretation of the words "since all sinned" is the right one, a third can be added: it now becomes clear why Paul did not, at this point, complete the sentence beginning with "Wherefore," but went off on a tangent. The statement "since all sinned" could easily arouse disbelief, especially in the minds of those who attached great importance to the proclamation of the law at Sinai. The question might be asked, "If *to sin* means *to transgress the law,* how can Paul say that since the time of Adam *all* sinned? Until the giving of the law at Sinai there was no law, and therefore no transgression of the law, no sin." The apostle considers this possible objection to be of sufficient importance to justify the break in grammatical structure to which reference was made in the beginning of the explanation of verse 12 (see p. 176). Paul answers as follows:

13, 14. ... for before the law (was given) sin was in the world. But sin is not taken into account when there is no law. Nevertheless, death reigned from (the time of) Adam to (that of) Moses, even over those who did not sin by transgressing[154] an express command, as did Adam, who is a type of him who was to come.

In confirmation of the statement "all sinned," including even those people who lived on earth during the period Adam to Moses, Paul reasons as follows:

Sin was indeed in the world even before Sinai's law was given, as is shown by the fact that death, sin's punishment, ruled supreme during the period Adam to Moses. The apostle may have been thinking, among other things, about the deluge, which destroyed almost the entire population of the world. Yes, death reigned even over those who did not sin by transgressing an expressed command, as did Adam. See Gen. 2:16, 17. So, it is clear that even during the period Adam to Moses sin was indeed taken into account. Though *Sinai's* law, with its expressed commands, did not as yet exist, *there was law.* Here the apostle was undoubtedly thinking about what he had written earlier in this very epistle (2:14, 15). And this law, with death as punishment for wanton transgressors, was indeed applied (see Rom.

---

153. It is clear that on this point I am not in agreement with Murray, *op. cit.,* Vol. I, pp. 182-186. His position is that the clause cannot refer to actual, personal sins. As is clear, my own position resembles more closely that of E. F. Harrison, *op. cit.,* p. 62, according to which, while in verse 12, considered as a whole, the emphasis on original sin is primary, with reference to the clause in question personal sins are not entirely excluded.

One more point: I hope no one will conclude that because on this question I do not agree with Murray, I am a Pelagian!

154. For the noun παράβασις (here gen. s. -βάσεως) see footnote 157 on p. 180.

1:18-32). That there was law follows from the fact that there was sin. If there had been no law there would have been no sin.[155]

In introducing Adam, the transgressor of an expressed command, the apostle states, "who is a type of him who was to come."

Having said this, is Paul able now at last, to finish the sentence he began in verse 12? Not yet, for calling Adam a type of the One who was to come,[156] that is, of Christ, could easily lead to misunderstanding. Adam, whose fall resulted in incalculable misery for the human race, and Christ, the world's Savior (John 4:42; I John 4:14; cf. I Tim. 4:10), how is it possible to mention these two in one breath? How can Adam be a type of Christ? This Paul must first explain.

How can there be any *resemblance* between Adam and Christ? Nevertheless, there *is* resemblance; for just as it is true that Adam imparted to those who were his that which belonged to him, so also Christ bestows on his beloved ones that which is his. It is in this respect that Adam foreshadows Christ. For the rest, however, *the parallel is one of contrast,* a fact which the apostle sets forth as follows:

15-17. But the free gift is not like the trespass. For if, by reason of the trespass of the one the many died, much more did God's grace and the gift that came by the grace of this one man, Jesus Christ, overflow to the many! Again, the gift (of God) is not like (the result of) one man's sin. For the judgment followed one sin and brought condemnation, but the free gift followed many trespasses and brought justification. For if by the trespass of the one, death reigned through that one, much more will those who receive the overflowing fulness of grace and of the gift of righteousness reign in life through the One, Jesus Christ.

In these verses Paul shows that the parallel Adam-Christ is mainly one of *contrast,* in the sense that Christ's influence for good *far outweighs* Adam's effectiveness for evil: the free gift is "not like the trespass,"[157] that is, is far more effective than the trespass.

---

155. Paul's reasoning is so lucid, and the harmony between 5:13, 14 and his earlier statements (1:18-21; 2:14, 15), so clear, that I cannot understand the comments of John Knox (*The Interpreter's Bible,* Vol. 9, p. 464).

156. On Christ, "the Coming One" see N.T.C. on John, Vol. I, pp. 77-79; also J. Sickenberger, "Das in die Welt Kommende Licht," *ThG,* 33 (1941), pp. 129-134.

157. The noun παράπτωμα indicates a sin in the sense of a deviation from the path of truth and righteousness, a fault. The word occurs in Rom. 4:25; 6 times in chapter 5: verses 15 (twice), 16, 17, 18, 20; twice in chapter 11 (verses 11, 12); and further, once each in II Cor. 5:19; Gal. 6:1; Eph. 1:7; 2:1, 5; and twice in Col. 2:13. For the rest, in the New Testament it is found only in the clarification of the fifth petition of the Lord's Prayer, Matt. 6:14, 15 (twice), and in a similar passage in Mark (11:25, 26). For more on its meaning, in distinction from other words for sinning, see Trench, *op. cit.,* par. lxvi.

A παράπτωμα may be rather mild, so perhaps in Gal. 6:1, but may also be very serious. Thus, in Rom. 11:11 Israel's rejection of the gospel is called a παράπτωμα.

See also W. Michaelis, Th.D.N.T., Vol. VI, pp. 170-172. The παράβασις of Adam (Rom. 5:14) was a *transgression* of a distinct commandment. That same noun occurs also in Rom. 2:23; 4:15; Gal. 3:19; I Tim. 2:14; Heb. 2:2; 9:15.

By way of introduction to the further interpretation a few matters should be kept in mind:

a. The apostle uses the word *many* in a twofold sense. In its first use ("the many died") it indicates all of Adam's physical descendants. At the close of that same verse ("overflow to the many") it indicates all those who belong to Christ. This reminds one of Isa. 53:11, 12; Matt. 20:28; Mark 10:45.

b. Verse 12 has shown that Adam was responsible for bringing into the world two evils: sin and death. The apostle deals with both of these in turn: with Adam's sin or *trespass* (verses 15, 16), with *death* (verse 17). He conceives of them as being intimately related, and therefore at times mentions both in one breath.

It is understandable that Paul can say that by reason of *Adam's trespass* the many died. These *many* are those designated in 5:12 as "all mankind" (literally *all human beings, everybody*). Cf. I Cor. 15:22. But, in connection with the work of God in Christ, for God's children this evil has been *more than* canceled out. For them God's grace and his gift of salvation changed death into its very opposite. Death became a *gain* (Phil. 1:21)! Moreover, as to *sin,* when grace entered, it more than merely returned man to his former state of innocence. It bestowed on him *righteousness* (verse 17), and *life* (verse 18), that is, *everlasting life* (verse 21). For the glorious content of this term see above, on 2:7.

Again, in Adam's case a single sin was involved, a sin that resulted in condemnation. But Christ, by his work of redemption, made provision for the forgiveness not only of that one sin but also of all those that followed from it. His sacrifice *sufficed* for them all, and in fact *was efficacious* for all the sins committed by those who, by sovereign grace, were to place their trust in him. For them *condemnation was replaced by justification.* See on 1:17; 3:24; 5:1.

Paul now turns more especially to the subject of *death.* This time, after repeating that death resulted from the trespass of the one, Adam, he mentions *the reign* of death, the powerful and destructive sway it exercises over the affairs of human beings. In harmony with his thoughts on the supremacy of grace (the "much more" doctrine), the apostle now points out that in the case of believers the reign of *death* is not merely replaced by the reign of *life* but by a reign so inexpressibly glorious that those who participate in it will themselves be kings and queens. All this is the result of "the overflowing fulness[158] of grace[159] and of a righteousness that is God's gift to them through the One, Jesus Christ," that is, through his person and work.

---

158. Note περισσεία (here acc. s. -v) a περί-compound, probably basically indicating water that rises so high that "all around" it overflows its borders. See also II Cor. 8:2; 10:15; James 1:21.

159. Grace is God's love revealed to the undeserving. For a detailed word study of the word χάρις see N.T.C. on Luke, pp. 181, 182.

When the apostle has thus taken care of the difficulties that had to be cleared up before he was able to complete the thought begun in verse 12, he now, by means of somewhat varying phraseology, in verse 18a gives the gist of the earlier verse—so that essentially verse 18a amounts to verse 12, and then, in verse 18b brings this thought to a conclusion. In somewhat different wording the entire thought is repeated in verse 19.

18, 19. Consequently, as one[160] trespass[161] resulted in condemnation for all men, so also one act of righteousness resulted for all men in justification issuing in life. For just as through the disobedience of the one the many were made sinners, so also through the obedience of the One will the many be made righteous.

As the word "consequently" indicates, not only is Paul now returning to the thought expressed in verse 12; he is summing up the argument of the entire paragraph (verses 12-17). The present passage places over against each other *one* trespass, namely, that of Adam (Gen. 3:6, 9-12, 17), a trespass here called "the disobedience of the one," and *one* act or deed of righteousness, called "the obedience of the One," that One being Jesus Christ. Cf. Phil. 2:8. Since in the preceding context Paul has no less than three times mentioned Christ's death for his people (verses 6, 8, 10; cf. verses 7 and 9), it is certain that also here in verses 18, 19 the reference is to that supreme sacrifice. However, we should not interpret this concept too narrowly: Christ's voluntary death represents his entire sacrificial earthly ministry of which that death was the climax.

We can understand that one trespass resulted *for all men* in condemnation, but what does the apostle mean when he states that also *for all men* one act of righteousness resulted in life-imparting justification? If in the first case "all men" means absolutely everybody, does not logic demand that in the second instance of its use it has the same meaning? The answer is:

a. The apostle has made very clear in previous passages that salvation is for believers, for them alone (1:16, 17; 3:21-25, etc.).

b. He has emphasized this also in this very context: those alone who "receive the overflowing fulness of grace and of the gift of righteousness" will reign in life (verse 17).

c. In a passage which is similar to 5:18, and to which reference has been made earlier, the apostle himself explains what he means by "all" or "all men" who are going to be saved and participate in a glorious resurrection. That passage is:

"For as in Adam all die, so in Christ all will be made alive. But each in his own turn: Christ, the firstfruits; afterward those who are Christ's, at his

---

160. There are those who interpret ἑνός to refer to one *person*, namely, Adam. They translate "one man's misdeed." But in that case would not the apostle have used the article, as he did in verse 17? However, the difference in translation and interpretation is of little importance, since in any case Paul is speaking about the one act or deed of the one person over against the one act or deed of the other.

161. See footnote 157.

coming" (I Cor. 15:22, 23). Here it is clearly stated that the "all" who will be made alive are "those who are Christ's," that is, those who belong to him.

But though this answer proves that when Paul here uses the expression "all" or "all men" in connection with those who are or will be saved, this "all" or "all men" must not be interpreted in the absolute or unlimited sense, this still leaves another question unanswered, namely, "Why does Paul use this strong expresssion?" To answer this question one should carefully read the entire epistle. It will then become clear that, among other things, Paul is combating the ever-present tendency of Jews to regard themselves as being better than Gentiles. Over against that erroneous and sinful attitude he emphasizes that, as far as salvation is concerned, *there is no difference between Jew and Gentile*. The reader should carefully study the following passages in order to see this for himself: 1:16, 17; 2:7-11; 3:21-24, 28-30; 4:3-16; 9:8, 22-33; 10:11-13; 11:32; 15:7-12; 16:25-27. As concerns salvation, says Paul, "There is no distinction. God shows no partiality." *All men* are sinners before God. *All* are in need of salvation. For *all* the way to be saved is the same.

In a day and age in which, even in certain evangelical circles, the unbiblical distinction between Jew and Gentile is still being maintained and even emphasized, it is necessary that what God's Word says about this, particularly also in Paul's epistle to the Romans, be pointed out.

Note that in verse 18 we are told that the one trespass resulted in *condemnation* for all, but that the one act of righteousness resulted in justification issuing in *life*. This shows that justification not merely overturns the verdict of "guilty," setting aside the sentence of doom, but also opens the gate to life. For this concept of *life*—cf. verses 17 and 21—see above on 2:7.

Also in verse 19 Paul does not say, "Just as through the disobedience of the one the many were made sinners, so also through the obedience of the One will the many be made innocent or sinless," but ". . . will the many be made *righteous*." To be sure, this basically means "*to be declared* righteous." However, when God declares someone righteous, does that action ever stand all by itself? See the explanation of 5:5.

20. Moreover, the law came in besides. In order that the trespass might increase. But where sin increased, grace increased all the more . . .[162]

Paul has been speaking about Adam and Christ, type and antitype. Adam transgressed a specific command, as has been shown. That happened long before the pomulgation of Sinai's law. Now even before this there was law, as the explanation of 5:13 has shown. But at Sinai the Mosaic law came in besides "in order that the trespass might increase." That was the divine intention in giving this law.

This cannot mean that God became the cause of sin's increase. It means that it was God's will and purpose that in light of his demand of perfect love

---

162. Note ὑπερεπερίσσευσεν, 3rd per. s. aor. indicat. of ὑπερπερισσεύω, to superoverflow, abound all the more, increase all the more. The use of this verb points to Paul as the author. See N.T.C. on I and II Timothy and Titus, p. 75.

(cf. Matt. 22:37–40; Mark 12:29–31; Luke 10:27) man's consciousness of sin might become sharpened. A vague awareness of the fact that all is not well with him will not drive man to the Savior. So the law acts as a magnifying glass. Such an instrument does not actually increase the number of dirty spots on a garment. It makes them stand out more clearly and reveals *many more* of them than one can see with the naked eye. Similarly the law causes sin to stand out in all its heinousness and ramifications. In connection with this see also Rom. 3:20; 7:7, 13; Gal. 3:19.

Moreover, this increase in the knowledge of sin is very necessary. It will prevent a person from imagining that in his own power he can overcome sin. The more he, in light of God's law, begins to see his own sinfulness and weakness, the more also will he thank God for the manifestation of his grace in Jesus Christ. Result: where sin increases, grace increases also. Not as if these two forces, sin and grace, were equal. On the contrary, grace not only pardons; as verse 21 shows, it does far more: it brings "everlasting life through Jesus Christ our Lord!" Truly, where sin increases, grace increases *all the more!*

Among the many hymns that bring out this glorious truth there are these two: (a) Charles Wesley's "O For a Thousand Tongues," containing the line, "He breaks the power of canceled sin"; what an incisive combination of two mighty products of God's grace, namely, justification and sanctification; and (b) Julia H. Johnston's "Grace Greater Than Our Sin."

Since the apostle often makes mention of God's law, as also in the present passage, it may be useful to give a brief summary of the functions of this law, as indicated in Paul's epistles and elsewhere in Scripture. Undoubtedly one or more references can easily be added to each of the following:

a. to serve as a source of man's knowledge of sin and to sharpen his consciousness of sin (Rom. 3:20, etc., as has been indicated).

b. to fix the sinner's attention on the far greater power of God's grace in Jesus Christ, and to lead him to the Savior (Rom. 5:20; Gal. 3:24).

c. to serve as a guide for the expression of the believer's life of gratitude to God's honor (Ps. 19:7, 8; 119:105; Rom. 7:22).

d. to function as a bridle, restraining sin (I Tim. 1:9–11).

There is, of course, a very close connection between these various functions.

The purpose of "grace abounding" is expressed in the following unforgettable words: **21. ... in order that, as sin reigned in death, so also grace might reign through righteousness to bring everlasting life through Jesus Christ our Lord.**

What a strikingly beautiful close to this chapter! There are seven concepts, as follows:

a. *sin*

This is, first of all, *the sin of Adam*, here viewed as our representative, whose guilt, due to the solidarity of the human race, is imputed to us all, a fact to which all the *personal sins* of human beings bear witness. See especially verses 12, 15, 17.

b. *reigning*
When Adam fell, it seemed as if sin was about to triumph completely. However, according to God's plan, grace intervened, and in the case of all God's children, triumphed over sin. See verses 12–14 for the reign of sin; verses 15–19 for the triumph of grace.

c. *death*
Sin brought condemnation and death; first of all physical death, but also spiritual and eternal death. Sin and Death are personified: Sin being, as it were, the Sovereign; Death, his Viceroy. For the moment (think of Adam's fall) it seemed as if Sin would be able to claim the victory. See verses 12, 14. But note the next item:

d. *grace*
Grace meets sin head-on and defeats it. See verses 15–17, 20.

e. *righteousness.*
Not a righteousness provided by man but a righteousness imputed by God. It was through this righteousness that grace triumphed over sin. See 1:17; 3:21–24; 5:17.

f. *everlasting life*
When the sinner is clothed with the righteousness provided by God, he is on his way to everlasting life (verse 18), the glorious life in the new heaven and earth; a life which, in principle, is given to him even here and now. For this concept see on 2:7.

g. *Jesus Christ our Lord*
See verses 14, 15, 17, 19. It must not be forgotten that apart from the immeasurably marvelous sacrifice of "Jesus Christ our Lord," a sacrifice revealing a love which, in all its dimensions, surpasses all human understanding, grace would never have been able to conquer sin and death.

The unifying thought, as it were tying together all these seven concepts, is this, "Where sin increased, grace increased all the more," namely, the grace embodied in the supreme sacrifice of our Lord Jesus Christ, and revealed to us through him.

In reviewing this entire chapter what amazes us is Paul's limitless assurance, his radiant optimism. Here is a man who until rather recently has been subjected to all the afflictions mentioned in II Cor. 11. He is about to set out for Jerusalem, Rome, Spain. That was the plan. Whether he will ever be able to carry out that plan or any part of it he does not know, though he does know that perils confront him (Rom. 1:10, 13; 15:30–32). Also he knows that he has a story to tell. His heart is filled with a flame, the flame of love: God's love for him, his love for God. Others *must* hear the story! We feel like saying, "What a man, this apostle Paul!" But if we said that we would be doing what he does not want us to do. So, in the very spirit of Paul we sing, or/and turn to a musical instrument and play AMAZING GRACE!

ROMANS 5 IN POETRY

In order to put some spirit into the study of a chapter, more than one approach may help to make it part and parcel of a person's life. In addition to

a. *Careful exegesis,* which is basic to every sound approach,

b. *Practical lessons* may be added or interspersed,

c. The chapter, as a whole or in part, may be *acted out,* if it lends itself to this approach, or it may provide the topic for

d. A *debate.* Again, it may be illustrated with

e. *Pictures.* An even different approach would be the composition of

f. A *poem,* which *in an interpretive manner,* reproduces the contents of the chapter, verse by verse. I suggest the following for chapter 5:

Verses

1, 2 Therefore, since we've been justified
By *faith,* we've peace with God, and side
With him in Christ, through whom we gain
Access by faith, and we'll remain
In this same grace in which we stand.
With joy we *hope* to reach the land
Where God his glory will display
When darkness changes into day.

3-5 And sufferings, too, we greet with cheer
Because they make us persevere
And mold our character, and then
This character builds hope again,
A hope that disappoints us ne'er;
For through his Spirit, which is e'er
Our portion, did our gracious God
His *love* so richly spread abroad.

6-8 The time was ripe and we were weak
And even godless, when to seek
The lost, yes many, far and wide,
Christ Jesus came and for us died.
It rarely happens that a man
For someone who is righteous can
Be found to die. But though it's rare
Yet for a good man one might dare
To give his life. But God above
Showed his incomparable love
In that, while we were sinners still
Christ died for us. Such was his will.

9, 10   Hence, since we've now been justified,
And Jesus for our sins has died,
We know that we shall surely be
From future wrath forever free.
For if the greater deed God wrought
For those who then were in his thought
Still enemies, then will not he
The lesser do, and readily?
Will he who woos the enemy
Not bless a friend, whoe'er he be?
If through Christ's *death* we friends became
Of God, then all the more the name
Of Christ, the *Living* One, will save
And make us conquerors o'er the grave.

11   'Tis good these happenings to record
But better still is to the Lord
To render joyful songs of praise
For having made us friends through grace.

12   'Twas through one man that sin began
And also death through this one man.
In this one man did all men sin,
And through this sin did death begin.

13, 14   Now, long before God's law was given,
Sin filled the world and cried to heaven.
From Adam until Moses when
The writing of God's law began,
Death ruled supreme on every hand,
Though breaking God's express command,
As Adam did, that wicked deed
None could soon afterward repeat.
Now Adam, type of Christ was he,
Since each one mankind's Head would be.

15-17   Far stronger than man's sin is grace,
Far more effective in its place:
One fearful sin laid many low,
But grace made many overflow.
God's judgment condemnation brought;
Christ's blood justification bought.
One sin, and judgment came to stay,
But grace wiped all our sins away!
Now if the trespass of the one
Brought *death* to each and everyone,
Then *how much more* will they be blessed
On whom God's grace and righteousness
Has been bestowed! Through him, the Door,
They'll enter *life* forevermore.

18, 19   Just as a single sin plunged all
Of Adam's seed into the fall,
The condemnation, so one deed

187

Of righteousness fulfilled the need
Of the whole world. All who believe
Justification will receive.
As one man's disobedience caused
The many to be counted lost,
So, too, One Man's submissiveness
Will bring to many righteousness.

20, 21   The law came in besides. 'Twas so
The sense of sin might keener grow.
But when that consciousness increased,
Grace topped it, and this never ceased.
Result was this: O'er death reigned Sin,
But all the while Grace ruled within
The heart, as Conqueror in the strife,
Bringing, through Christ, eternal life!

Practical Lessons Derived from Romans 5

Verse 1

"Therefore, having been justified by faith, we have peace with God through our Lord Jesus Christ." This peace is:

a. the gift of God's love
b. the smile of God reflected in the heart of the believer
c. the heart's calm after Calvary's storm
d. the firm conviction that he who spared not his own Son will surely also, along with him, freely give us all things (Rom. 8:32)
e. the sentinel who mounts guard over the hearts and thoughts of God's children (Phil. 4:7).

Verses 1, 2

"Therefore, having been justified by faith, we have peace with God . . . access by faith . . . and we exult in the hope of the glory of God."

This implies that with respect to *believers: past* sins are forgiven, *present* access to the throne of grace is assured, and *future* glory is guaranteed. These are *priceless* values, obtained "without money and *without price* (cost)," as far as *they* are concerned.

For a cap and bells our lives we pay,
Bubbles we buy with a whole soul's tasking,
'Tis heaven alone that is given away,
'Tis only God may be had for the asking.

                             Lowell,
                     "Vision of Sir Launfal"

Verse 3

"We even exult in our sufferings." This cheerful statement becomes even more meaningful when we bear in mind that it was uttered by one who had already experienced a lengthy series of most bitter agonies for the sake of Christ. See I Cor.

188

4:11-13; 15:30-32a; II Cor. 11:24-32. Cf. Rom. 8:35. Such exultation in suffering is possible because of the truths expressed in Rom. 8:18, 28.

Verses 6-8

"... Christ died for the ungodly. Now a man will scarcely die for a righteous person ... But God demonstrates his own love for us in this, that while we were still sinners Christ died for us." Paul is amazed by his reflection on *such* love. It is as if he were saying, "Just think of it: God loves the unlovable! Why, even for a righteous person one would hardly want to die. But Christ died for the *un*righteous, the *un*godly!"

Verses 9, 15, 17, 20

"... much more ... much more ... much more ... all the more...." First of all study the picture of gloom drawn by Paul in Rom. 3:10-18. Does it prove that Paul was a pessimist? Now read 5:9, 15, 17, 20. Note how the very author who has given us the darkest picture of mankind, buried in sin, is, nevertheless, the most optimistic. It is as if he were saying, "Mankind's sinfulness is indeed frightening; but God's grace is far more powerful and wonderful than mankind's sinfulness is terrible.

The apostle was an optimist, and this was not because of what sinners are by nature but because of what God's grace is able to make of them. Should not every preacher—in fact, every true believer—imitate Paul in this respect?

Summary of Chapter 5

This chapter consists of two main sections: A and B. In A we are shown that the basic result of justification by faith is *peace* with God. Other blessings are associated with it. In B the main emphasis is on the generous character of the salvation provided by God.

A. (verses 1-11)

Paul has reached a new phase in the discussion of justification by faith. He begins to fix the attention of the hearers-readers on the favorable effects resulting from justification. First of all he mentions "peace with God through our Lord Jesus Christ." As 5:10 makes clear, this peace is basically "reconciliation with God through the death of his Son." Associated with this peace are such other blessings as access to God by *faith* and a joyful looking forward to the marvelous salvation God has in store for those who have placed their trust in him. Even present suffering for the sake of Christ and his kingdom cannot dim the luster of the glory that is to come and in principle is being experienced even now. In fact, such suffering is really a link in the chain of blessings: suffering, perseverance, proven character, firmly anchored *hope*. This hope is kept alive and strengthened by God's *love* "poured out into our hearts by the Holy Spirit" (verses 1-5).

Christ's timely death for the "ungodly" is a demonstration of God's love. By way of rare exception someone might be willing to sacrifice his life for a worthy person, but God demonstrated *his own* love by means of Christ's death for us while we were still *sinners* (verses 6-8).

Not only has our legal standing been changed from "guilty" to "righteous," i.e., from condemnation to justification, but our personal relation to God has also changed. Through Christ's death former enemies were changed into friends. It was God himself who brought about this *reconciliation*. Now if God has reconciled to himself *enemies*, he will certainly save *friends*. Believers need not become alarmed about any future divine wrath. With a view to all these blessings, present and future, even now "we exult in God through our Lord Jesus Christ" (verses 9-11).

B. (verses 12-21)

In a sentence beginning with verse 12, recaptured (as to essence) in verse 18a, and completed in verse 18b, the apostle states, "Just as through one man sin entered the world, and death through sin, and so death spread to all mankind, since all sinned; that is, as one trespass resulted in condemnation for all men, so also one act of righteousness resulted for all men in justification issuing in life."

"In Adam's fall we sinned all." Adam, by means of his transgression of an express divine command, involved all mankind in his sin and guilt. The entire human race is viewed as being already "in" Adam. Moreover, being involved in *sin* implies being involved in *death*. The reality of sin did not depend on the establishment of the Mosaic law. Even during the period Adam-Moses sin was taken into account, for God's law had been written in man's heart (cf. 2:14, 15). This explains why it is right to state that death reigned from Adam to Moses, even over those who did not sin by transgressing an express command, as did Adam (see Gen. 2:16, 17; 3:1-6). In this connection Paul calls Adam "a type of him who was to come," Adam being considered the head of fallen humanity; Christ, the head of redeemed humanity (verses 12-14).

In the remainder of the chapter the apostle shows that as all men were included in Adam, so also "all men," that is, all those who belong to Christ, whether they be Jews or Gentiles by race, are included in Christ. The parallel Adam-Christ is, however, mainly one of contrast, as now becomes very clear. Paul says, "For if, by reason of the trespass of the one the many died, much more did God's grace, and the gift that comes by the grace of this one man, Jesus Christ, overflow to the many." Adam's transgression brought condemnation. Christ's voluntary sacrifice of himself for his people brought justification issuing in life. Moreover, grace is ever far more effective than sin. "Where sin increased, grace increased all the more." Did grace merely offset sin and death, so that mankind returned to the state of innocence, that of Adam before the fall? On the contrary, grace changed death into a gain, substituted righteousness for sin, and everlasting life for death. All this "through Jesus Christ our Lord" (verses 15-21).

Outline (continued)

Justification by Faith

2a. *It produces the fruit of* **holiness.**
"We who died to sin, how can we any longer live in it?"
6:1-14

2b. *Who Is Y o u r Master? Sin or God?*
"But now, freed from sin and made servants of God, the benefit y o u reap
leads to holiness, and the outcome is life everlasting. For the wages of sin is
death, but the free gift of God is life everlasting in Christ Jesus our Lord."
6:15-23

CHAPTER 6

6 1 What shall we say then? Shall we go on sinning in order that grace may increase?
2 By no means! We who died to sin, how can we any longer live in it? 3 Or don't
y o u know that all of us who were baptized into Christ Jesus were baptized into his
death? 4 So then we were buried with him through baptism into death, in order
that, just as Christ was raised from the dead through the glory of the Father, so we too might
walk in newness of life.

5 For if we have become united with him in a death like his, we shall certainly also be united
with him in a resurrection like his.[163] 6 For we know that our old self was crucified with him,
so that the body of sin might be destroyed, that we should no longer be slaves of sin—
7 because the one who died is freed from sin. 8 Now if we have died with Christ, we believe
we shall also live with him; 9 since we know that Christ, having been raised from the dead, no
longer dies. Death no longer exercises lordship over him. 10 For the death he died, he died
to sin once for all; but the life he lives, he lives to God. 11 So then y o u yourselves should also
consider yourselves dead to sin but alive to God in Christ Jesus.

12 Accordingly, do not let sin reign in y o u r mortal bodies, to make y o u obey their
passions. 13 And do not offer the parts of y o u r bodies to sin, as weapons of wickedness, but
instead offer yourselves to God, as those who were brought from death to life, and offer
y o u r bodily parts to him, as weapons of righteousness. 14 For sin shall no longer be lord
over y o u, because y o u are not under law but under grace.

2a. *It produces the fruit of holiness.*
"We who died to sin, how can we any longer live in it?"
6:1-14

Chapter 6 introduces a new subject. Not that there is a sudden break. But
there is a difference, a transition from one fruit of justification, namely,
peace with God, to another, *holiness.*

Sin, mentioned frequently in chapter 5, is mentioned even more often in
chapter 6. And in this connection the emphasis turns away from the believer's legal *status* to his spiritual-moral *condition.* The new line of thought
centers about such concepts as holiness, living a new life, dying to sin, living
to God.

Nevertheless, chapters 5 and 6 are closely related, just as closely as are
justification and sanctification. The God who declares the sinner just at the
same time, and in close connection with it, pours the sanctifying Spirit into
his heart, producing holiness.

---

163. Literally: in the likeness of his death . . . (in the likeness) of his resurrection.

A very practical consideration contributed to the writing of chapter 6. With warm enthusiasm Paul had been proclaiming the riches of God's grace. To many people, especially Jews and those former pagans who had embraced Judaism, his emphasis on divine grace as the one and only source of salvation was something new. It seemed to some of them as if this preacher-missionary-writer was minimizing the value of works. They reasoned, "If works mean so little, why perform them at all? Besides, if grace is everything, why not sin flagrantly, lustfully, in order to give grace the opportunity to operate (to use a colloquial expression, 'to do its thing')?" Chapter 6 is Paul's pointed and animated reply to this fantastic distortion of his divinely inspired presentation of the doctrine of sin and grace.

As was true with respect to chapters 4 and 5, so also chapter 6 readily divides itself into two parts. In verses 1-14 Paul points out that it would be impossible for believers to continue to *live in* sin: those who have died to sin are alive to God in Christ Jesus. In verses 15-23 the apostle, by implication, asks the question, "Who is y o u r Master? Is it Sin or God"

1. What shall we say then? Shall we go on sinning in order that grace may increase?

It will be recalled that already in 3:8 Paul briefly combats this distortion of the doctrine of grace. Here, in chapter 6, his refutation is more detailed.

It should be emphasized that we are not dealing here with a merely theoretical objection to the doctrine of grace. In fact, though some of those who asked this question may indeed have intended it to be interpreted as an objection to Paul's teaching, others were not *objecting* at all. They were rather pleased with Paul's doctrine (as they interpreted it), and were saying, "Let us go on sinning that grace may increase."

When *Peter* states that some of Paul's teachings were being distorted (II Peter 3:16), he may well have been thinking of this particular attempt to twist the meaning of the words used by his "dear brother," the apostle to the Gentiles. We know, at least, that what made *Jude* change his mind about the contents of a letter he had planned to write was the fact that "certain individuals had turned (the doctrine of) the grace of God into a license for immoral living" (Jude 4).

Every age has produced its quota of such deceivers. An example that occurs to the mind immediately is that of the Russian monk Rasputin. For a while he was a very influential favorite of Emperor Nicholas II. His doctrine seems to have been, "The more a person sins, the more grace he will receive. So sin with gusto."

Another and far more recent example from life: this man was an ardent evangelist. One of his favorite passages was taken from this very chapter of Romans, "Y o u are not under law but under grace" (verse 14). He spoke persuasively, drawing large crowds. However, his immediate neighbor never went to hear him. When someone asked that neighbor, "How is it that we never see you in his audience?" the answer was, "Because I happen to know that his back yard is filled with stolen property."

Paul's response to the question, "Shall we go on sinning that grace may increase?" is, **2. By no means! We who died to sin, how can we any longer live in it?**

The very suggestion that the end justifies the means, that grace may be produced by living in sin, is so thoroughly obnoxious to Paul that he answers it by making use of one of his characteristic, blunt rejection formulas, "By no means." See on 3:4, p. 111. For a Christian, continuing to *live in* sin is not only impermissible, it is impossible! To be sure, Paul knows that even a believer commits acts of sin until the day of his release from this earthly existence. See 7:14f. But in the apostle's theology this circumstance does not provide a valid reason for easy living. See on 6:15. Moreover, the notion that a child of God should voluntarily give sin an opportunity to operate, that he should actually encourage it, produces a revulsion in Paul's heart. He is disgusted with the very suggestion!

He reminds his readers that something decisive has taken place in his and in their lives. By the grace of God *they had died to sin;* that is, they had renounced allegiance to their sinful selves and to all the allurements and enticements of this sinful world. Cf. Col. 3:3, "For y o u died, and y o u r life is hid with Christ in God." All this had happened when they had been converted, had professed their faith, and had been baptized. So Paul continues:

3, 4. Or don't y o u know that all of us who were baptized into Christ Jesus were baptized into his death? So then we were buried with him through baptism into death, in order that, just as Christ was raised from the dead through the glory of the Father, so we too might walk in newness of life.

When Paul asks, "Don't y o u know that," etc.? he reminds us of the style of the Master. See especially John 3:10; 19:10; but compare also such passages as Matt. 12:3, 5; 19:4; 21:16, 42; 22:31; Luke 6:3, to mention only a few. The question shows too that although Paul had not himself established the church of Rome, he takes for granted that the practical significance of Christ's death for Christian living is a matter on which his readers could be expected to be thoroughly informed. See also on 7:1, p. 214.

The apostle assumes that those (including himself) who had listened to the public preaching of the gospel or who by any other means had been converted, had publicly confessed their faith and had been baptized. See Matt. 28:19; Acts 2:37, 38; 9:18. He now asks, "Don't y o u know that all of us who were baptized into Christ Jesus were baptized into his death?"

To be baptized "into Christ Jesus" implies to be brought into personal relation to the Savior. For similar expressions see Matt. 28:19 ("baptizing into the name of the Father and of the Son and of the Holy Spirit"); I Cor. 1:13 ("baptized into the name of Paul"); and 10:2 ("baptized into Moses"). Paul, accordingly, points out that baptizing people into Christ Jesus implies baptizing them into—i.e., in connection with the sacrament of baptism bringing them into personal relationship with—Christ's *death*, so that this death becomes meaningful to them, teaching them that by it the *guilt* of their sins had been removed, and that they had received power to fight and overcome sin's *pollution.*

On the surface the statement, "*We were buried with him* through baptism *into his death*" may seem confusing, as if burial precedes death. Besides, how is it possible for any person to be *buried* into another's *death?* However, when we bear in mind the context, the difficulty disappears, as will be shown:

The dangerous doctrine of the antinomians was leading people astray. This sinister heresy caused Paul to emphasize the necessity of making a complete break with the sinful life of the past. So he says, "We were buried into his—i.e., Christ's—death; that is, by the power of the Holy Spirit we were made to delve down deeply into the meaning of that marvelous death. In fact, so deeply did we, with heart and mind, bury ourselves into it that we began to see its glorious meaning for our lives. Therefore we reject and loathe the terrible wicked slogan, *Let us continue to live in sin in order that grace may increase.*"

Through baptism and reflection on its meaning these early converts, including Paul, had been brought into a very close personal relationship with their Lord and Savior and with the significance of his self-sacrificing death. The meaning of that death had been blessed to their hearts by the Holy Spirit.

Paul now also reminds his readers that Christ was raised from the dead through "the glory"—here meaning "the majestic power" (see on 1:23, p. 74) —of the Father.

Since the Savior's beloved ones are "in him," the relationship being very close and inseparable (John 10:28; 17:24; Rom. 8:35-39; Col. 3:3), it follows that included in the purpose of his resurrection was this goal: "that we might walk in newness of life,"[164] a life dedicated no longer to sin but to the glory of God Triune.

It must be understood that *Christ's resurrection* from the dead must be given its full meaning, as that great event which led to his saving activity in heaven (Rom. 8:34; Eph. 1:20-23; Heb. 7:25).

For *walking,* in the sense of *conducting oneself* or *living,* see such passages as the following: Gen. 17:1; Exod. 16:4; Ps. 56:13; 101:2; 119:1; Rom. 4:12; 8:1, 4; 13:13; 14:5; I Cor. 3:3; II Cor. 5:17; Gal. 5:16, 25; Eph. 2:10; 3:6-19.[165]

---

164. Note ὥσπερ ... οὕτως, "just as ... so we too." The parallel is, however, one of analogy, not identity. Christ's resurrection was physical; the believer's resurrection here indicated is spiritual. It concerns newness of life. Also, the first is the cause of the second.

Note also καινότητι. In this case the full, distinctive meaning must probably be assigned to the implied καινός (not here νέος). The emphasis is on quality, not time.

165. There are those who believe that the expression "buried with him through baptism into death . . . raised from the dead" shows that baptism should be by immersion. For a defense of this view see A. T. Robertson's article on *Baptism,* I.S.B.E., Vol. I, pp. 385-388. For the

5. For if we have become united with him in a death like his, we shall certainly also be united with him in a resurrection like his.

The close connection between verses 3, 4 and verse 5 is indicated by the word *For.* Hence, the idea of some, that verse 5 refers to the future bodily resurrection of believers must be rejected.[166] Verse 5 repeats the thought of the immediately preceding context, namely, the believers' union with Christ in (a) his death and (b) his resurrection, considered respectively as the source of (a) their death to sin, and (b) their resurrection to newness of life. But it also *adds* something to the thought expressed in the preceding. Note the word *certainly.*

The meaning of verse 5, then, is as follows, "For if we have become united with Christ in a death like his, so that his death brought about our death to constantly living in sin, we shall *certainly* also be united with him in a resurrection like his; that is, then surely his (bodily) resurrection (understood in its most comprehensive sense, as explained above, see p. 196) will bring about our spiritual resurrection; that is, our walking in newness of life." The *emphasis* Paul placed on this fact must be ascribed to the ominous character of the antinomian heresy.[167]

6, 7. For we know that our old self was crucified with him, so that the body of sin might be destroyed, that we should no longer be slaves of sin—because the one who died is freed from sin.

The wicked error of the antinomians, a subject which has been on the apostle's mind from the very beginning of this chapter, and to which he also alluded previously, helps to explain verses 6, 7. What Paul is saying is this: instead of wallowing in sin in order that grace may increase, we should bear in mind that such a course would defeat the very purpose of our lives as believers.

Paul says, "For we know," thereby appealing to that which could be assumed as common knowledge among believers, including the addressees. The important fact with which they were assumed to be familiar was this: that our old self (lit. "our old man") was crucified with Christ. This old self is the person we once were, our human nature considered apart from grace. When the apostle now states that this old self was crucified with Jesus, it is clear that he again proceeds upon the basis of the believers'

---

opposite view see John Murray, *Christian Baptism*, Philadelphia, 1952, especially pp. 29-33. On two points there should be agreement:

a. Immersion is indeed an entirely proper and beautifully symbolic mode of adult baptism.

b. In Rom. 6:3, 4 (cf. Col. 2:11, 12) Paul's chief topic is not *the proper mode of baptism* but the effects of, and responsibility arising from, union with Christ.

166. Use of the future ἐσόμεθα cannot save that erroneous theory. Is it not natural to think of *newness* of life in future terms?

167. Whether σύμφυτοι is derived from συμφύω, which seems probable, and therefore basically means *grown together;* or from συμφυτεύω, hence *planted together,* makes little difference. What matters most is not the derivation of the word but its resultant connotation *in the present context,* namely, *united.* On this see also Cranfield, *op. cit.,* Vol. I, pp. 306, 307.

solidarity with Christ. Just as he considers all human beings as present "in Adam" (cf. 5:12, 17, 19), so he views all believers as being present "in Christ." Therefore, in a sense, when Christ died on the cross, his true followers all died there with him. We are reminded of Gal. 2:20:

"I have been crucified with Christ, and it is no longer I who lives, but Christ who lives in me; and that (life) which I now live in flesh I live in faith, (the faith) which is in the Son of God, who loved me and gave himself up for me." The passing of time has nothing to do with this. Since Scripture regards us as already present in Adam, it can also view us as ever being present in Christ.

The purpose and result of our solidarity with Christ in his crucifixion is "so that the body of sin might be destroyed," that is, that, by means of Christ's crucifixion and our crucifixion with him, this destruction might take place. With the expression "body of sin" (verse 6, cf. "old self," also verse 6; and see also "I," 7:14) is probably meant the person in his entirety, viewed as controlled by sin. It is clear that the reference is to human nature apart from regenerating grace.

Does Paul mean then that in this present life the believer can reach such a degree of holiness that he does not commit any sin? He does not, neither is that fallacy taught anywhere else in Scripture. See Matt. 6:12; Rom. 7:14–25; James 3:2; I John 1:8. But there is a vast difference between (a) committing a sin and (b) constantly living and delighting in sin. By the power and grace of the Holy Spirit a person can indeed reach the point where he no longer desires to be a slave of sin. For a synonym of this phrase "slaves of sin" see II Peter 2:19, and note the words of Jesus as reported in John 8:34. See N.T.C. on John, Vol. II, p. 53.

To all this, Paul now adds, ". . . because the one who died is freed from sin." In light of the context the meaning would certainly seem to be, "The person who has by God's sovereign grace been regenerated and converted, so that he no longer delights in sin but rather fights it, can be assured of the fact that God has, on the basis of Christ's atonement, forgiven his sins, with the result that he is now truly *free, justified* in God's sight."

However, several commentators, in their attempt to explain this passage, immediately point to the familiar rabbinical (and more general) rule according to which "death pays all debts."[168] An appeal is frequently made to the fact that Paul had been trained under the famous Jewish teacher Gamaliel (Acts 22:3) and was therefore well acquainted with rabbinical lore.

Now it need not be denied that in a formal manner the apostle may indeed here and there reveal the results of this earlier training. According to Scripture by no means all of the teaching of the rabbis was bad. Study the following passages: Matt. 23:1–3; Mark 12:28–34; Acts 5:34–39; 23:8, 9.

Does this mean, then, that when Paul states his views with respect to such

---

168. See S.BK., Vol. III, p. 232.

subjects as speaking in tongues, qualifications for ecclesiastical office, the position of women in the church, etc., we are justified immediately to dismiss that with which we do not happen to agree, basing our negative attitude on the supposition that Paul's views on such matters were influenced by the rabbis?

But such reasoning is hardly fair. A thorough examination of Paul's epistles reveals that on ever so many important subjects he had by the study of Scripture and the illumination of the Holy Spirit arrived at a position that differed substantially from that of the rabbis. See, for example, the following passages: Rom. 2:9, 14, 15, 17-29; 3:9, 20, 21f.; chapters 4, 5; 7:6; 9:8, 11; 10:3; 11:7; 14:17; 15:9-12; I Cor. 1:22-24; 3:16; 7:19; 9:20; 10:25; 15:1f.; II Cor. 3:14; 5:20, 21; 11:22f.; Gal. 1:6f.; 2:19-21; 3:1f., 24; 5:2-4; 6:12-16; Eph. 2:8-10, 11-22; Phil. 3:2f.; Col. 1:24f.; 2:11, 12, 16f.; 3:11; I Tim. 1:3, 4; 4:1f.; 6:13-16; II Tim. 2:8; Titus 3:4f.; and see especially I Thess. 2:14-16. Besides, one cannot very well endorse a low estimate of Paul's statements and still cling to the view that Paul wrote by inspiration.

In the present instance the appeal to the quoted rabbinical rule helps little if at all in the interpretation. The apostle refers, of course, to "death to sin," the determination (followed by action) by God's grace and power no longer to live in sin. When a person no longer feels at home in sin he can be sure of the fact that he has been freed from the guilt of sin and that even the power which sin has been wielding over him is on the way out.[169]

It was the desire to live this kind of *new* life that caused people to come forward in order to be baptized. The *water* of baptism, by whatever method it is applied (immersion, pouring, sprinkling) symbolizes and seals the *cleansing* power of the Spirit (Ezek. 36:25; I Cor. 6:11; Eph. 5:26; Heb. 10:22). It symbolizes and seals what *God* has done and is doing, and, as a result, incorporation of the person into the fellowship of God and of his church. On the error of underestimating the significance of the sacraments see above, p. 152; of overestimation, p. 151.

8, 9. Now if we have died with Christ, we believe we shall also live with him; since we know that Christ, having been raised from the dead, no longer dies.

If we died with Christ, that is, if, as a result of Christ's death for us, we died to sin, we shall also *spiritually live* in fellowship with him, and this not only in the hereafter but here and now. Cf. verses 3 and 5. We know that such living *with him* is possible because he, having died, was raised from the dead, never again to die. Death could not hold him (Acts 2:24), for it no longer exercises lordship over him.

Those who, during Christ's pre-Golgotha ministry, were by him raised from the dead, died again. According to heathen mythology certain deities

---

169. I agree, accordingly, with Cranfield, *op. cit.*, Vol. I, p. 311, that the rabbinic rule to which reference was made is singularly inappropriate as a confirmation of Rom. 6:7.

are constantly dying and rising. Not so Jesus. **Death no longer exercises lordship over him.** Having been raised, he lives forevermore (Rev. 1:18), and we with him. This *we believe:* we know it to be true!

10. For the death he died, he died to sin once for all; but the life he lives, he lives to God.

Without the assurance that Christ's death was a once-for-all death, believers would lack the comfort they need for this and the future life. Does not that comfort consist exactly in this that they can sing, "We serve a *living* Savior"?

It was through his death that Jesus conquered death. Having done so, he was able to say to John, an exile on the island of Patmos, "I was dead, but behold I am alive forevermore, and I hold the keys of Death and Hades" (Rev. 1:18).

Very significant is the expression, "He died to sin once for all." This surely implies that the blood and body of Christ cannot be offered again. Jesus offered himself "once for all for the sins of his people" (Heb. 7:27; see also 9:12; 10:10). No second offering is necessary or even possible! For this once-for-all self-sacrifice see also I Peter 3:18.

Christ's life on earth before his death was conditioned by sin, sin not his own but his people's. Read Isa. 53. Cf. Matt. 20:28; Mark 10:45.

Therefore, once sin had been atoned for, he now lives to God. Of course, his entire life, also that which preceded Golgotha, had been devoted to the glory of his heavenly Father. In his high-priestly prayer he was able to say, "I glorified thee on earth, having accomplished the work thou gavest me to do" (John 17:4). But once this task had been accomplished, he was able to live to God *in an unhampered manner,* that is, without having to carry the burden of his people's sin. It is in that sense that Paul is able to say, "But the life he lives, he lives to God."

In a sense—but only *in a sense*—one might say, "After his resurrection and ascension Jesus returned to the life with the Father as it had been before he left the riches and the glories of heaven to suffer for man's sin." See John 17:5. Scripture does not tell us much about that life. Here are a few glimpses:

> When he established the heavens, I was there;
>   When he set a circle upon the face of the deep.
> When he made firm the skies above,
>   When the fountains of the deep became strong,
> When he gave to the deep its boundary,
>   That the waters should not transgress his commandment,
> When he marked out the foundations of the earth;
>   Then I was at his side as a master craftsman;
> And I was daily his delight,
>   Rejoicing always in his presence.

Prov. 8:27-30

If this refers to Christ, "the Wisdom of God," the reference is indirect.

In the beginning was the Word, and the Word was face to face with
God, and the Word was God. He himself was in the beginning face to
face with God.   *John 1:1, 2*

... he was rich. ...   *II Cor. 8:9*

We should bear in mind, however, that there was at least this difference
between *then* (the time before Christ's humiliation) and *now* (after his
humiliation): he returned to heaven carrying with him the merits of his
fully accomplished redemption! Thus it is that the life he now lives he lives
to God; not, however, forgetting his people; note Heb. 7:25.

**11. So then y o u yourselves should also consider yourselves dead to
sin but alive to God in Christ Jesus.**

At this point doctrine makes way for exhortation. What has been established, namely, that believers are in principle dead to sin and alive to Christ,
must become the abiding conviction of their hearts and minds, the take-off
point for all their thinking, planning, rejoicing, speaking, doing. They
must constantly bear in mind that they are no longer what they used to be.
Their lives from day to day must show that they have not forgotten this.
They are "in Christ": chosen "in him" (Eph. 1:4), redeemed "in him" (Eph.
1:7), living "in him" (Gal. 2:20; Phil. 1:21; II Tim. 3:12). Christ's righteousness has been imputed to them. *His Spirit has been poured out into their
hearts.* In a sense it is true that when Christ died, they died with him. When
he arose, they arose with him. Cf. II Cor. 5:14, 15.

What may well be the best commentary on Rom. 6:11 is Paul's own: "If
then y o u were raised with Christ, seek the things that are above, where
Christ is, seated at the right hand of God. On the things that are above set
y o u r minds, not on the things that are upon the earth. For y o u died, and
y o u r life is hid with Christ in God. When Christ (who is) our life is
manifested, y o u also will be manifested with him in glory" (Col. 3:1-4).

**12. Accordingly, do not let sin reign in y o u r mortal bodies, to make
y o u obey their passions.**

Although it is true that believers are no longer constantly living in sin,
this does not mean that sin has ceased to be an opposing force in their lives,
a reality to be taken into account. See 7:14f.

No one acquainted with the story of David would deny that he was
indeed a child of God; in fact, "a man after God's own heart" (I Sam.
13:14). In ever so many ways Scripture proves this point.[170] Nevertheless,
at times he allowed sin to bear sway in his mortal body.[171] And David is no
exception. It is therefore understandable that the apostle urges believers
constantly to be on guard against this great danger of surrendering to evil

---

170. See my *Survey of the Bible*, pp. 98-101.
171. On this point, therefore, I share Cranfield's criticism of Murray's exegesis; see Murray,
op. cit., pp. 226, 227; Cranfield, *op. cit.*, pp. 316, 317.

passions, passions which, as also in the case of David, are often associated with the body and its functions, a body which, in man's fallen state, tends toward sin and death (hence "*mortal*" bodies).[172]

Paul becomes more specific as he continues, **13. And do not offer the parts of y o u r bodies to sin, as weapons of wickedness, but instead offer yourselves to God, as those who were brought from death to life, and offer y o u r bodily parts to him; as weapons of righteousness.**

What Paul means by "parts of y o u r bodies" is made clear by such passages as 12:4, 5, where these "parts" are clearly bodily *members;* while I Cor. 12:12–24 makes specific mention of such bodily "parts" as foot, hand, ear, eye, nose (actually "sense of smell"), head, unpresentable parts and presentable parts of a person's body. The expression "parts of y o u r bodies" therefore refers to bodily limbs, members, and organs.

What Paul is saying then is this, "Do not continue to put y o u r bodily parts at the disposal of sin, as weapons of wickedness. Stop doing this; and instead, right now, completely and decisively, put yourselves at God's disposal. Offer yourselves to him!"[173]

Note also the distinction between (a) "Do not offer *the parts of y o u r bodies*" and (b) "offer *yourselves,*" instead of (b) "offer those bodily parts." Devotion and consecration to God must be personal, wholehearted. Was it not God who, in his great love and kindness, had brought these people out of death into life?

Instead of *weapons* many prefer *instruments* or *tools* or *implements.*[174] Though something can be said in favor of that rendering, the arguments in support of the rendering *weapons* are probably stronger:

a. In *all* the other instances of the use of this word in the New Testament ὅπλα means *weapons, armor.* See John 18:3; Rom. 13:12; II Cor. 6:7; 10:4.

---

172. Almost all translations have retained the word *body* (or pl. *bodies* because the apostle is addressing more than one person; so also R.S.V., Phillips, Williams, Beck, etc.) here in verse 12. Calvin (*op. cit.,* p. 230) thinks the reference is to *man's degenerate state;* Cranfield translates *mortal selves* (*op. cit.,* pp. 296, 316, 317). Hodge (*op. cit.,* p. 319) would retain "body" as the organ in which sin manifests itself; so would Lange (*op. cit.,* p. 209).

The choice is difficult, perhaps due to the almost infinitely close relationship between soul and body. In Rom. 12:1; Phil. 1:20 the word σῶμα seems to refer to the entire personality. But, as Murray reminds us (*op. cit.,* p. 227) it is possible that "body" here in 6:12 is viewed in contrast with "spirit," as it is in Rom. 8:10, 11, and if that be true the rendering *body* (or *bodies*) also here in 6:12 would be correct. To this I would add that the rendering "bodies" also harmonizes better with "parts of bodies" in verse 13.

173. By means of this explanation I have tried to bring out the distinction between the continuative present imperative παριστάνετε and the aorist imperative παραστήσατε, forms, respectively, of παριστάνω (late form) and παρίστημι (original form of the same verb).

174. Nearly all modern, and even many of the older *translators* favor "instruments" or a close synonym as the equivalent of the original ὅπλα. *Commentators* (both English and other), on the other hand, prefer a more distinctly military term; for example, *weapons.* So Barth, Brunner, Denney, Lange, Lekkerkerker, Lightfoot, Meyer, Ridderbos, Sanday and Headlam, Schlatter, Van Leeuwen and Jacobs, Wilson. Among English *translations* in support of *weapons* are: Phillips, Montgomvery (*The New Testament in Modern English*). In support of *weapons* are also the following translations: Dutch (both old and new), German, Swedish, Frisian.

b. Here in Rom. 6:13 the context also points in that direction. Sin (personified) is pictured here as the dictator who demands military service, exacts soldierly obedience, and provides soldier's rations. See verses 12, 14, and 23.[175]

c. The description of a believer's life under the symbolism of a soldier is typically Pauline. See such passages as the following: I Cor. 9:7; II Cor. 6:7; Eph. 6:10–20; I Thess. 5:8; II Tim. 2:3; etc.

The whole includes the parts. When individuals offer themselves to God, their "bodily parts" constitute a portion of this offering. Result: weapons of righteousness replace weapons of wickedness. This *righteousness* indicates uprightness of conduct, the very opposite of wickedness. Cf. Eph. 6:13.

The reason Paul gives for this exhortation is: **14. For sin shall no longer be lord over y o u, because y o u are not under law but under grace.**

Law is able to do many things: it commands, demands, rebukes, condemns, restrains, even points away from itself to Another. There is, however, one thing law can never do. *It cannot save.* "By law-works will no flesh be justified" (Gal. 2:16). Does this mean then that the exhortations directed to believers in verses 12 and 13 are useless? Does it mean that everyone has to perish in his sins? The answer is found in Rom. 8:3, and it is an encouraging answer indeed, in complete accord with the passage we are now considering. Note how despair is replaced by hope, darkness by light: "For what the law was powerless to do ... God did by sending his own Son ... in order that the righteous requirements of the law might be fulfilled in us ..." That sending of the Son is the very essence of God's grace. And this grace not only pardons but also cleanses. *Grace dethrones sin. It destroys sin's lordship and enables the believer to offer himself, and whatever pertains to him, in loving service to God!* The child of God is able to do this because he is *not under law but under grace*, since in his infinitely condescending love and mercy Christ has redeemed him from the curse of the law, having become a curse for him (Gal. 3:10–14). Truly, "there is now no condemnation for those who are in Christ Jesus" (8:1). The context (note "sin shall no longer be lord over y o u") may well imply an even closer connection with the thought of 7:1–6. See on that passage, and note especially "in order that we might bear fruit for God ... so that we serve in newness of (the) Spirit." Cf. 8:5, 6.

---

15 What then? Shall we sin because we are not under law but under grace? By no means! 16 Don't y o u know that when y o u offer yourselves to someone to obey him as slaves, y o u are slaves of the one y o u obey; whether of sin, leading to death, or of obedience, leading to righteousness? 17 But thanks be to God: y o u were slaves of sin, but y o u wholeheartedly obeyed the pattern of teaching to which y o u were delivered; 18 and having been set free from sin, y o u have entered the service of righteousness.

19 I am speaking in human terms because of the weakness of y o u r flesh. For just as

---

175. Whether the word "wages" in verse 23 has this military connotation is not entirely certain. See on that verse.

formerly y o u enlisted y o u r bodily parts in the service of impurity and lawlessness for the promotion of lawlessness, so now enlist them in the service of righteousness for the promotion of holiness. 20 For when y o u were slaves of sin, y o u were free from the control of righteousness. 21 What benefit did y o u then obtain? Things of which y o u are now ashamed, for their outcome is death! 22 But now, freed from sin and made servants of God, the benefit y o u reap leads to holiness, and the outcome is life everlasting. 23 For the wages of sin is death, but the free gift of God is life everlasting in Christ Jesus our Lord.

2b. *Who Is Y o u r Master? Sin or God?*

"But now, freed from sin and made servants of God, the benefit y o u reap leads to holiness, and the outcome is life everlasting. For the wages of sin is death, but the free gift of God is life everlasting in Christ Jesus our Lord."

6:15–23

15a. What then? Shall we sin because we are not under law but under grace?

In verse 14 Paul had assured believers that they are not under law. (For explanation of this statement see on 7:1; pp. 214, 215.) Does that mean then that they are at liberty to sin? When the law, erroneously viewed as means of salvation, ceases to exist, does this imply that the law as standard of perfection, that is, as the expression of God's will for our lives, also ceases to exist and/or to operate, so that, as a result it is permissible to commit a sin here and a sin there?[176]

Not for a moment is Paul willing to grant even this concession to the antinomians. His answer is: **15b, 16. By no means! Don't y o u know that when y o u offer yourselves to someone to obey him as slaves, y o u are slaves of the one y o u obey; whether of sin, leading to death, or of obedience, leading to righteousness?**

At this point the curt and decisive "By no means" of verse 2 returns. Sin has a tendency to enslave the sinner. The first time he lies, he may be horrified; the second time, only somewhat shaken; the third time lying seems far more natural and easy. At last the sin of telling untruths has him in its grasp. For other sins the story is similar. At last this person is living in sin, has become enslaved by it. See N.T.C. on John 8:34 (Vol. II, p. 53). The result of this process, when continued to the end, is death. Cf. verse 23, and see also 5:12; 8:13. Paul does not specify whether he means physical, spiritual, or everlasting death. Is it reasonable to leave out any of these?

The opposite of sin is obedience, namely, to God. This leads to righteousness, both of state and condition. Cf. I Sam. 15:22; Rom. 4:3; James 2:20–24.

What the apostle is saying, then, is this: no man is free, in the sense of being absolutely independent, "his own boss." He has a Master. That Master is either Sin or God.

17, 18. But thanks be to God: y o u were slaves of sin, but y o u

---

176. Note difference between ἐπιμένωμεν, 1st per. pl. pres. (continuative) subj. of ἐπιμένω in verse 1; and ἁμαρτήσωμεν, aor. subj. of ἁμαρτάνω here in verse 15.

wholeheartedly obeyed the pattern of teaching to which y o u were delivered; and having been set free from sin, y o u have entered the service of righteousness.[177]

Note the following:

a. "Thanks be to *God!*" Paul does not praise the Roman church for having turned to God; he *thanks God* for having brought them where they are today. See also 7:25; and cf. I Cor. 15:57; II Cor. 2:14; 8:16; 9:15; I Peter 2:9. Nevertheless, he also generously acknowledges that these people "wholeheartedly," that is, not merely formally but with zeal, had obeyed "the pattern of teaching," that is, the gospel or sound doctrine, as it was being proclaimed everywhere in the Christian community, both now and later (I Tim. 1:10; II Tim. 1:13; 4:3; Titus 1:9; 2:1).[178]

b. "(the pattern) to which y o u were delivered."

There are those who consider "But y o u . . . delivered" to be a *gloss* (unauthentic insertion), and that Paul simply dictated the words, "Y o u were slaves of sin, but y o u have been set free." But anyone who has devoted years to the study of Paul's epistles knows that if this reasoning were correct, one would have to find hundreds of glosses in these writings. The apostle's sentence structure is often rather involved.

Paul does not say, ". . . the pattern of teaching *which y o u accepted*," but (ascribing all the honor to *God*) "to which y o u were delivered."[179]

c. "and having been set free from sin, y o u have entered the service of righteousness."

---

177. Though many interpreters admit that the term δοῦλος and its verbal cognates (see verses 16-22) can be rendered *servant* and *to render service*, as well as *slave* and *to be enslaved*, there is no unanimity with respect to the translation of these words in the verses indicated. Some throughout prefer *servant* and *render service*.

It is true that something can be said in favor of *slave*. In a sense even deeper than that which pertains to ordinary slaves and their earthly masters, believers have been bought with a price and are therefore owned by their Master (I Cor. 3:23; 7:22), on whom they are completely dependent, and to whom they owe undivided allegiance. They are totally committed to him. If by thus defining the concept *doulos* its meaning were exhausted, and if our word *slave* conveyed nothing of a sinister nature, the translation *slave* throughout, for *doulos*, might be unobjectionable. But as Paul uses the term, a *doulos*, in the spiritual sense, is one who ministers to the Lord with gladness of heart, in newness of spirit, and in the enjoyment of perfect *freedom*, as verse 18 shows (cf. verse 22; 7:6), receiving from God a glorious reward (verses 22, 23). Love and good will toward God and man fill the heart of this *doulos*. See Gal. 5:13; Eph. 6:7.

However, with the English word *slave* we immediately associate the ideas of involuntary service, forced subjection, and (frequently) harsh treatment. It is probably for this reason that, in addition to those who here in Rom. 6:16-22 throughout prefer *servant*, etc. (A.V., A.R.V., Phillips, Berkeley) and those who consistently use *slave*, etc. (Goodspeed, R.S.V., N.A.S., N.I.V.), there are also those who, while not altogether avoiding *slave*, etc., render verse 18b, ". . . y o u have entered the service of righteousness," and verse 22 "and having entered the service of God" (thus, for example, Dutch Nieuwe Vertaling, ". . . zijt gij in dienst gekomen van de gerechtigheid . . . en in den dienst van God gekomen."). In the main, I have followed that same course. See also N.T.C. on Philippians, p. 110, footnote 92.

178. The word used in the original for "pattern" is τύπος (here acc. s. -v): visible impression, mark, image, pattern; cf. *type*.

179. The verb παραδίδωμι, of which παρεδόθητε is a form (2nd per. pl. aor. indic. pass.), has a wide range of meanings, for which see N.T.C. on Luke 22:4 (p. 967). In the present case it

For the believer freedom never means laziness. It always means opportunity for rendering service. Notice that slaves to sin enjoy (?) a liberty not worthy of the name (see verse 20). On the contrary, those who have entered the service of righteousness enjoy true liberty, namely, freedom from sin; not, however, in the sense that they never commit any sin, but in the sense that Sin is no longer their Master!

Having stated that those who had accepted the gospel had exchanged their state of *slavery to sin* to that of *service of righteousness,* Paul continues: **19. I am speaking in human terms because of the weakness of y o u r flesh, that is, y o u r human nature.**[180]

When Paul in verses 17, 18 spoke of those who had at one time been slaves of sin but had subsequently become servants of righteousness, he was, of course, using an illustration; namely, that of someone who had been transferred from one master to another. So now, in verse 19, he explains that the reason for the use of this illustration was their weakness to grasp these great spiritual truths.

The people whom Paul addresses had made remarkable progress, intellectual, moral, spiritual. For this see above, p. 25. But although this progress was encouraging, they were still far from having reached the goal of maturity. That is why Paul used this illustration, taken from familiar human relationships. Cf. Gal. 3:15. It frequently happened that a person enslaved to one master was transferred to another, whose slave or servant he would then become. What Paul desires, therefore, is that these Romans, having formerly been enslaved to their master Sin, will, with a commitment that is no less total, serve their new Master, namely, Righteousness, sin's opposite. Undoubtedly, reflecting on this apt illustration, would help them to do so.

Verse 19 continues as follows: **For just as formerly y o u enlisted y o u r bodily parts in the service of impurity and lawlessness for the promotion of lawlessness, so now enlist them in the service of righteousness for the promotion of holiness.**

The thought of verse 13 reappears here in a slightly different form. Note the condition "Just as formerly . . . ," followed by the conclusion, "so now . . ." But this parallel includes an antithesis: former impurity and lawlessness are contrasted with *the exhortation* that those who had formerly practiced these vices should now enlist their "bodily parts" (as in verse 13) in the service of righteousness, for the promotion of holiness.[181]

---

probably has nothing to do with the authoritative passing down of tradition from one generation (or one witness) to the next, but simply means that the members of the Roman church had by God been transferred from one master to another. So also Cranfield, *op. cit.,* Vol. I, p. 324. For the opposite view see Ridderbos, *op. cit.,* pp. 139, 140.

180. For the various meanings of the word σάρξ see footnote 187, on p. 217.

181. Though some regard ἁγιασμός (here acc. s. -v) to mean *sanctification,* which is probably the meaning in such passages as I Thess. 4:3, 4, 7; II Thess. 2:13; I Tim. 2:15, here in Rom. 6:19 the *qualities* or *conditions* of impurity and lawlessness are contrasted with those of righteousness and holiness. If the first pair does not indicate processes neither does the second.

Note the emphasis here, and in this entire chapter, on *holiness,* the attitude and manner of life that is opposed to sin and dedicated to the service of God. Moreover, as before, in verse 13, so also here, even the bodily parts participate in this active promotion of holiness.

The reason for the exhortation of verse 19b, showing why this command is so necessary and urgent, is given in verses **20, 21. For when y o u were slaves of sin, y o u were free from the control of righteousness. What benefit did y o u then obtain? Things of which y o u are now ashamed, for their outcome is death!**[182]

The meaning is clearly this: To be slaves of sin means to be enemies of righteousness; to be enemies of sin means to be friends of righteousness. To be devoted to both sin and righteousness at the same time is impossible. Compare the words of Jesus, "No one can serve two masters; for either he will hate the one and love the other, or he will be devoted to one and look down on the other" (Matt. 6:24).

As to the "fruit" or "benefit" those people formerly obtained from their slavery to sin, Paul says it consisted of things of which y o u are now ashamed. He was probably thinking of such things as evil thoughts leading to evil words, issuing in evil deeds, resulting in evil habits. Cf. 1:24 f. In light of the gospel and of the worship of the one true God, who reveals himself in Jesus Christ, they are now ashamed of their former walk of life. No wonder, for the outcome or final result of such a course of behavior is death. Cf. Gal. 5:22; Eph. 5:9.

What a contrast between the past and the present! From the contemplation of the disgraceful conduct of the past Paul now, with joy and gratitude, turns to the description of the present: **22. But now, freed from sin and made servants of God, the benefit y o u reap leads to holiness, and the outcome is life everlasting.**

What a contrast!

Formerly bondage	Now freedom
Formerly slaves of sin	Now servants of God

---

182. The proper punctuation of this verse is uncertain. If the first nine words (τίνα . . . . . . ἐπαισχύνεσθε) must be construed as one continued question, which could be rendered, "What fruit (or benefit) did y o u then obtain from the things of which y o u are now ashamed?" the closing five words, "for their outcome is death," do not follow naturally. By omitting γάϱ from the translation the entire passage may become somewhat easier to read and understand. However, this too is no solution. Verse 21 seems to parallel verse 22, in the following manner:

Verse 21
What *benefit?* Things of which y o u are now ashamed . . . their *outcome* death.
Verse 22
The *benefit* leads to holiness . . . . . . the *outcome* life everlasting.

The best punctuation would therefore seem to be the one which does justice to this parallel construction, and which at the same time results in an intelligible interpretation of the entire verse. It is for these reasons that I have adopted the punctuation that appears in my translation. On the parallel between verses 21 and 22 see also Ridderbos, *op. cit.,* p. 142; and on the resulting translation see Cranfield, *op. cit.,* pp. 321, 327, 328.

Formerly vice	Now holiness
Formerly shame	Now peace of mind
Formerly death	Now life, even life everlasting.

The chapter ends with the unforgettably glorious sentence: **23. For the wages of sin is death, but the free gift of God is life everlasting in Christ Jesus our Lord.**

With this climactic conclusion compare similarly triumphant endings of chapters 8, 9, 12, 13, and 16. Note also how the contrasts of verse 22 are here continued. Here, in verse 23, the contrast is that between:

| wages | and | free gift |
| death | and | life everlasting |

The phrase "wages of sin" means wages paid by sin. Similarly "free gift of God" means free gift bestowed by God.

Death in all its forms, physical, spiritual, everlasting, is what the sinner has earned by his sin. As to life everlasting, it is a gift, entirely free. O yes, it has been earned; not, however, *by* the sinner, but by Christ Jesus *for* the sinner.

Whether the word *wages,* as used here in 6:23, is a military term has been debated. It should be frankly admitted that at times the word is used in a non-military context. It is not surprising, therefore, that in view of the master-slave context (verse 16f.) it has been argued that here in verse 23 the apostle views sin as a slave-master, not as a general who provides soldier's rations.

This argument may, however, not be as strong as it may sound. Consider also these other facts:

a. As is generally admitted, the word used in the original[183] indicates ration, pay; especially soldier's pay. That is the more usual meaning of the word.

b. Even in the New Testament in two of its three other occurrences ("*Soldiers* too were asking," Luke 3:14; "What *soldier* ever serves at his own expense?" I Cor. 9:7) the military sense is clear. And even in the remaining passage where this word is used (II Cor. 11:8) Paul, who throughout his epistles frequently employs figures drawn from the life of the soldier, may very well be using "a bold military metaphor." (See P. E. Hughes, *The Second Epistle to the Corinthians (New International Commentary),* Grand Rapids, 1962, p. 385).

It would seem, therefore, that all in all the opinion that the word *wages* has here a military sense, so that Sin is viewed as the General who pays out these wages, has a slight edge.

---

183. ὀψώνιον (here nom. pl. -α), from ὄψον, cooked food, plus ὠνέομαι, to buy.

"But the free gift of God is life everlasting." What a marvelous climax! What a comforting truth! The sinner who has fled to God in Christ for refuge receives the most for the least: life everlasting for nothing!

Life everlasting; that is, fellowship with God in and through Christ Jesus (John 17:3); the light of the knowledge of the glory of God in the face of Christ Jesus (II Cor. 4:6); the love of God poured out into one's heart by the Holy Spirit; the peace of God that transcends all understanding (Phil. 4:7), all this and far more forever and ever! All this is experienced "in intimate union" with Christ Jesus. Beautifully Paul closes the chapter with the language of faith-appropriation: *our* Lord!

Practical Lessons Derived from Romans 6

Verse 1

"What shall we say then? Shall we go on sinning in order that grace may increase?"

We are saved not by works but by grace. That was Paul's doctrine. His opponents reacted as follows, "Since we are saved by grace, a grace that specializes in forgiving sin, let us sin all the more, in order that grace may abound." This misrepresentation was by no means innocent. It was an intentional, wicked distortion, a heartless mockery. Cf. Luke 23:36, 37. The distorters were guilty of lifting a few lines out of the totality of Paul's doctrine and basely twisting them. Unbiased study of the apostle's teaching shows that according to his inspired presentation justification by faith immediately implies living a life of gratitude, and therefore of holiness, to the glory of God Triune. In fact Paul places no less emphasis on consecrated living than on grace. See Rom. 1:21; 2:7, 10; 5:3-5; 6:12-14, 16, 19, 22; ch. 12; 13:10-14; I Cor. 13; Gal. 5:22-24; Eph. 2:8-10.

The later history of the church furnishes many other examples of willful distortion of a preacher's words. See Acts 17:1-7. How often has not Calvin's doctrine been misrepresented as if it were totally devoid of the milk of human kindness? Congregations should be warned against this evil.

Verse 4

"So then we were buried with him through baptism into death, in order that, just as Christ was raised from the dead through the glory of the Father, so we too might walk in newness of life."

Easter Sunday had arrived. As usual on that day, the church was crowded. But not a word was said about Christ's physical resurrection. Of course, in a "liberal" church what else could one expect? But even in conservative preaching, where the resurrection of the Savior is clearly proclaimed and is even presented as the basis for the hope and certainty of the believers' resurrection, is it always made clear to the congregation that a further and equally important purpose of our Lord's glorious triumph over death was "so we might walk in newness of life"?

Verse 12

"Accordingly, do not let sin reign in y o u r mortal bodies, to make y o u obey their passions." This passage shows that true theology is a matter not merely of doctrine but also of life. It does not confine itself to the revelation of that which God has done for us, though that is basic. It also stresses what we, by his grace and power, should do in return. It not only *teaches* but also *pleads* lovingly and earnestly.

Verse 17

"But thanks be to God: y o u were slaves of sin, but y o u ... have entered the service of righteousness." Note how in chapter 6 doctrinal *exposition* (verses 1–10), *exhortation* (verses 11–16 for the most part), and *encouragement* (verse 17) follow each other: an example for all of us.

Verse 23

"For the wages of sin is death, but the free gift of God is life everlasting in Christ Jesus our Lord."

The choice is between these two: death and life. Though, to be sure, Scripture recognizes degrees of punishment and of glory, there is no neutral territory between death and life. Moreover, for rational beings there is no opportunity to avoid making a choice. And the contrast between the two destinies is immeasurable. Therefore this passage is so very important. The right choice should be made. It should, moreover, by the grace of God, be renewed every day.

Summary of Chapter 6

Justification, the basic blessing for every sinner who places his trust in Christ, implies union with the Savior, a union with him not only in his death but also in his resurrection. "For if we have become united with him in a death like his, we shall certainly also be united with him in a resurrection like this." Now being partakers of Christ's resurrection implies *holiness*, for it was the risen and exalted Christ who poured out upon the church his Holy Spirit, the Spirit of sanctification.

This means, of course, that those people who tried to use the doctrine of justification by faith as an excuse for leading a sinful life were dangerous heretics. Their slogan, "Let us go on sinning in order that grace may increase," was an inexcusable and horrible distortion of the doctrine proclaimed by Paul. Therefore he exhorts the members of the Roman church as follows, "Do not allow sin to reign in y o u r mortal bodies ... but offer yourselves to God, as those who were brought from death to life, and offer y o u r bodily parts to him, as weapons of righteousness. For sin shall no longer be lord over y o u, because y o u are no longer under law but under grace" (verses 1–14).

The sinister character of the antinomian heresy fills the soul of the apostle with such horror that for the moment he does not stop to give a further explanation of the statement, "Y o u are no longer under sin but under grace." He will, however, return to that subject a little later. See 7:1 f.; 8:1 f. For the present he continues to combat the soul-destroying heresy to which reference was made. He now points out that not only the sinful *life* should be avoided but so should even yielding to individual sins, for they have a tendency to make slaves out of those who fail to combat them. If allowed to gain the mastery over a person, they will lead him on to death. Paul is happy to be able to state, however, that those whom he addresses have abandoned their slavery to sin. They have exchanged death for life everlasting. He closes this chapter by saying, "For the wages of sin is death, but the free gift of God is life everlasting in Christ Jesus our Lord" (verses 15-23).

Outline (continued)

Justification by Faith

3a. *It produces the fruit of* **liberty:**
freedom from the law.
"We have been released from the law."
7:1-6

3b. *The sinner's relation to God's Law, in the light of Paul's*
own experience and that of others like him.
"In the absence of law sin is dead. Once I was alive apart from law; but
when the commandment came, sin sprang to life and I died."
7:7-13

3c. *Paul's own experience and that of others like him*
(continued):
The wretched man's struggle and victory.
"Wretched man that I am! Who will rescue me from this body of death?
Thanks be to God through Jesus Christ our Lord."
7:14-25

CHAPTER 7

7 1 Or do y o u not know, brothers—for I am speaking to those who know law—that the law has authority over a person (only) as long as he lives? 2 For example, by law a married woman is bound to her husband as long as he is alive; but if her husband dies, she is released from the law in so far as it binds her to her husband. 3 So then, if, while her husband is still alive, she marries another man, she will be called an adulteress; but if her husband dies, she is free from the law, so that she is not an adulteress if she marries another man.

4 So, my brothers, y o u too were made dead to the law through the body of Christ, so that y o u might belong to another, even to him who was raised from the dead, in order that we might bear fruit for God. 5 For when we were in the flesh, the sinful passions stimulated by the law were active in our members, so that we bore fruit for death. 6 But now, having died to that by which we were held fast, we have been released from the law, so that we serve in newness of (the) Spirit, not in oldness of (the) letter.

3a. *It produces the fruit of* **liberty:**
freedom from the law.
"We have been released from the law."
7:1–6

It is clear that Paul continues his discussion of the fruits of justification. Among them he had already considered *peace* (chapter 5) and *holiness* (chapter 6). This time he adds *freedom,* namely, from bondage to law, the glorious *liberty* enjoyed by the children of God. Cf. Rom. 8:21; II Cor. 3:17.

Previously in this same epistle Paul had mentioned freedom from *sin.* He had linked it to freedom from *law.* He had written, "For sin shall no longer be lord over y o u, because y o u are not under law but under grace" (6:14). Then, without first explaining what he meant, he had asked and answered the question, "Shall we sin because we are not under law but under grace?" (6:15). As has been pointed out, there was a very practical reason why the answer to that question was urgent, and could not be postponed. Therefore the entire sixth chapter was devoted to it. Note its climax, "For the wages of sin is death, but the free gift of God is life everlasting in Christ Jesus our Lord." *The glorious doctrine of justification by faith must not be used as an excuse for the practice of sin!*

This shows why the apostle had not yet been able to answer such questions as, "In what sense is it true and how did it come about that we are not

213

under law but under grace?" "For what purpose were we released from
bondage to law?" It is to these questions that he now gives an answer.

**1. Or do y o u not know, brothers—for I am speaking to those who
know law—that the law has authority over a person (only) as long as he
lives?**

Surely a believer is not "free from the law" in every conceivable sense! He
loves God's law. Did not the author of Ps. 119—to mention only that one
psalm—grow ecstatic when he reflected on the wonders of God's law?
Among his many enthusiastic statements are the following:

"Open my eyes that I may behold wondrous things out of thy law" (verse
18).

"O how I love thy law. It is my meditation all the day" (verse 97).

"Rivers of water run down my eyes because they do not observe thy law"
(verse 136).

"Great peace have they who love thy law" (verse 165).

However, a distinction must be made. The author of Ps. 119 regards
God's law as the expression of his wise, good, and merciful will. As such,
for the believer the law is a rule of gratitude, answering the question of Ps.
116:12.

But the term "law" can also be used as indicating a code that must be
adhered to in order to obtain salvation, "a statute wielding authority and
demanding absolute obedience." It is in that sense that the apostle obviously here uses the term. Add to this the fact that the Jewish religious
leaders had buried the original law of God under a load of oral traditions:
minute, hair-splitting regulations touching just about every human activity
and sphere of life. This was the law about which Jesus had said, "Y o u have
made the word of God null and void for the sake of y o u r tradition" (Matt.
15:6). Since, according to the teaching of the rabbis, these oral traditions, as
to their basic contents, had by God been given to Moses and handed down
from generation to generation, it is understandable that ever so many
people, in learning about them, had become filled with fear. The *law* had
become an unbearable yoke (Acts 15:10).

Accordingly, what the apostle is now telling the membership of the
Roman church is that from this yoke—in fact, even from Sinai's unadulterated written law regarded as a means whereby, through obedience, one can
earn salvation—they have been released.

Note the tactful manner in which Paul conveys this cheering news. He
asks, "Do y o u not know . . . ?" In other words, "Y o u should know, should
y o u not?" Cf. I Cor. 6:2, 9, 16, 19. See also on Rom. 6:3, p. 195.

The next word—"brothers"—should not be passed by unnoticed. As
here used, it is an affectionate term of address. Previously Paul has used it
only in 1:13. Careful examination of all the instances of its occurrence in
this epistle shows that whenever the apostle employs this term *in addressing*
his readers, he is deeply moved. He is writing about a subject which emo-
tionally affects him. He, as it were, embraces those whom he addresses with

his arms of love. In this light examine also the use of this same word in 1:13; 8:12; 10:1; 11:25; 12:1; 15:30; 16:17. In each case the subject discussed is one filled with emotion. So also here, in connection with 1:1, 4, we can probably assume that Paul had heard that some of the members of the Roman church entertained doubts about the doctrine of salvation by grace alone. Therefore, by means of this term of endearment, he is, as it were, wooing them back, tenderly pleading with them to put aside their doubts.

When he adds, "I am speaking to those who know law," the word *law* can perhaps be given its broadest meaning; for according to *any* law, whether Hebrew, Greek, Roman, etc., death ends obligations and attachments, dissolves ties, releases bonds. But if Paul was actually thinking of any specific law system, it must have been the Mosaic, with which, of course, not only the Jews were well acquainted, but so were also those people who were Gentiles by race; in other words, all the members of the Roman Church. See above, p. 23. To them all the principle that the law has authority over a person (only) as long as he lives was well known and would win immediate consent.

What Paul is implying, then, is this: when a person is dead—in the present case dead *to the law*—he is free from its authority, released from its domination.

To fortify his argument the apostle now uses an illustration:

2, 3. For example, by law a married woman is bound to her husband as long as he is alive; but if her husband dies, she is released from the law in so far as it binds her to her husband. So then, if, while her husband is still alive, she marries another man, she will be called an adulteress; but if her husband dies; she is free from the law, so that she is not an adulteress if she marries another man.

Little need be said about the illustration as such. It speaks for itself. According to Scripture marriage is a very solemn bond. It is for life (Gen. 2:22-24; Mal. 2:13-16). This implies that if, while the husband is still living, the wife rejects him and marries another man, she will be called[184] an adulteress.[185]

But although marriage is for life, it does not extend beyond life, the (feigned?) position of the Sadducees notwithstanding. See Luke 20:33, 34. Therefore after the death of her husband no law would prevent this woman from remarrying.

So far the illustration. Matters become a little more difficult when we inquire into the point it wishes to bring out. For example, if we should say

---

184. Note χρηματίσει, third per. s. fut. indicat. intransit. of χρηματίζω. The word has a rich variety of meanings: act. to warn (Heb. 12:25); pass. to be warned (Matt. 2:12, 22; Heb. 8:5; 11:7); to be directed (Acts 10:22); to be revealed (see N.T.C. on Luke 2:26, pp. 175, 176); here (Rom. 7:3) and in Acts 11:26, to be called, styled, branded.

185. Here the still living husband's faithfulness is assumed. Otherwise the rule implied in Matt. 5:32 (see N.T.C. on Matthew, p. 305) would apply.

that in this illustration the husband consistently indicates the law, and the married woman consistently the believer, we would soon reach a blind alley. For in that case the law would have to die before the believer could be made free. But nowhere does Paul teach that the law dies or is put to death. Quite the opposite: it is *we* who are put to death. It is *we* who therefore die (Rom. 7:4; Gal. 2:19).

Accordingly, in our attempt to interpret these words we should concentrate on just *one* item, namely, *the third of comparison*. It is this: as it is a *death* that dissolves the marriage bond, so it is also a *death* that dissolves the legal bond; i.e., the bondage to law. The marriage bond is dissolved by the death of one of the marriage partners (in this case the husband); the legal bond is broken by the believers' involvement in Christ's death; in other words, by the believers' death. Yes, we, the believers, have indeed died with Christ, in the sense which has already been explained in connection with 6:8. See above, p. 199. Once this third of comparison is grasped, there is no further difficulty. Paul's own clarification, moreover, follows in verse.

4. So, my brothers, y o u too were made dead to the law through the body of Christ, so that y o u might belong to another, even to him who was raised from the dead, in order that we might bear fruit for God.

Several points stand out in this strikingly beautiful passage:

a. We have already commented on "my brothers." See above, pp. 214, 215.

b. "Y o u too were made dead" or "were put to death."[186]

It was *God* who not only planned salvation but also carried out this plan. It was *he* who so loved the world that he gave his only Son in order that everyone who believes in him should not perish but have life everlasting (John 3:16); *he* who did not spare his Son but delivered him up for us all (Rom. 8:32). See also Isa. 53:4, 10; II Cor. 5:21. It was *through the body of Christ Crucified* that our indebtedness to the law was completely paid off, so that, as a result, believers were made dead to the law, the latter's "bill" having been fully paid.

c. In Paul's illustration it was stated that when the husband died, the wife was released from the marriage bond, and given the right to marry someone else. That part of the figure may also have been in the apostle's mind when he wrote, ". . . that y o u might belong to another, even to him who was raised from the dead . . ." Since the relation of the Christian to the Christ is very close, release from the law must mean union with Christ, the Risen One. See Col. 3:3.

d. This union or marriage is not unfruitful. Note: "in order that we might bear fruit for God."

Our Exalted Lord, through the outpouring of his Spirit, enables believers to do this. In the Pauline epistles, and in Scripture as a whole, great emphasis is placed on fruitbearing. The reference is to the fruit of good

---

186. I can see no good reason for weakening the meaning of ἐθανατώθητε, 2nd per. pl. aor. indicat. passive of θανατόω, to put to death.

attitudes, aspirations, words, and works; to all of these directed to the glory of God Triune. Among Pauline passages mentioning or implying fruitbearing see Rom. 1:13; 6:21, 22; Gal. 5:22, 23; Eph. 2:10; 5:9; Phil. 4:8, 9, 17; Col. 1:6; Titus 3:1. For the rest of Scripture see Ps. 1:3; 92:14; Prov. 11:30; Jer. 17:8, 10; Matt. 7:17; John 15:1-8.

e. Note the shift from the second person to the first: "so that y o u might belong to another . . . in order that we might bear fruit for God." This same peculiarity appears also in such passages, among others, as the following: Rom. 6:14-16; 8:11-13; 13:11-14.

Explanation: Paul is himself deeply involved in the truths about which he writes. The doctrine of sovereign grace grips him, causes his heart to beat faster, his eyes to fill with tears of gratitude. So again and again he shifts from y o u to we. Is a sermon really good if it lacks this feature?

5, 6. For when we were in the flesh, the sinful passions stimulated by the law were active in our members, so that we bore fruit for death. But now, having died to that by which we were held fast, we have been released from the law, so that we serve in newness of (the) Spirit, not in oldness of (the) letter.

The expression "when we were in the flesh"[187] means "when basically we were governed by our sinful human nature." By "the sinful passions (cf. 6:6; Col. 2:11) . . . active in our members," are probably meant such emotions as lust, anger, hatred, ill will, jealousy, envy, unreasonable fear, etc. Although these and similar passions pertain to a person's heart and mind, they express themselves physically: the jealous eye, the clenched fist, the hateful gesture, etc. Cf. 6:12, 13. The unbridled gratification of passions, so that those who nourish them produce the fruit indicated in Gal. 5:19-21, results in death. Cf. 6:21. Contrast "fruit for God" (verse 4) with "fruit for death" (verse 5).

For the answer to the question, "How is it to be understood that these sinful passions are stimulated by the law?" see on verses 7-13.

But now, says Paul, a great change has occurred. By means of our death—a death with Christ; hence a death to sin, which held us in its grip—we were released or discharged from the law.

---

187. In Paul's epistles the word σάρξ (flesh) has the following meanings:
   a. the chief substance of the body, whether of men or of animals (I Cor. 15:39);
   b. the body itself, in distinction from the spirit, mind, heart (Col. 2:5);
   c. earthly existence (Gal. 2:20; Phil. 1:22, 24);
   d. a human being, viewed as a weak, earthly, perishable creature (I Cor. 1:29; Gal. 2:16). This usage depends heavily on the Hebrew. Cf. Isa. 40:6, "All flesh is grass," etc.
   e. physical descent or relationship (Rom. 9:8);
   f. the human nature, without any disparagement (Rom. 9:5);
   g. human worth and attainment, with emphasis on hereditary, ceremonial, legal, and moral advantages; the self apart from regenerating grace; anything apart from Christ on which one bases his hope for salvation (Phil. 3:3);
   h. sinful human nature: the human nature viewed as the seat and vehicle of sinful desire (Rom. 7:5, 25; 8:3-9, 12, 13; Gal. 5:16, 17, 19; 6:8).

What he means is that *basically* our lives are no longer governed by our sinful nature. And since Christ, by means of his vicarious death, paid the debt we owed to the law, we are now no longer under the law's domination and curse.

This does not remove the fact that sin still exercises considerable influence over us, as 7:14–25 will indicate, but *basically* there has been a tremendous change.

The result[188] of all this is that we now serve (God) in newness of the Spirit, no longer in oldness of the letter, that is, the legal code. There used to be a time when we thought that by strict obedience to the external code—the Mosaic *written law*, as interpreted by tradition—we could be saved. But now, having been set at *liberty*, we serve (see 6:15–23) in newness of the Spirit. According to Gal. 3:3; 4:6; 5:18; II Cor. 3:17 that Spirit is the Author of our liberty. Paul's thought seems to be that this Spirit guides believers in their effort to live lives of gratitude for salvation received as the product of God's sovereign grace. The Spirit guides and enables them to live such lives.

What the apostle is saying, then, is that the glorious prophecy of Jer. 31:31–34 is being realized in the lives of himself and those addressed.

When Paul closes this section by writing, "so that we serve in newness of (the) Spirit, not in oldness of (the) letter," he places the *new* over against the *old* (as he does also in II Cor. 5:17; Eph. 4:22–24; Col. 3:9, 10); and the *Spirit* over against the *letter* (as in Rom. 2:29; II Cor. 3:6). Hence, he is contrasting true liberty—the blessing bestowed on all those who have become "free from the law," in the sense explained—with the bondage of those still enslaved by the law. As always, so also at this point, his teaching is in line with that of the Master. See Matt. 9:14–17 (Mark 2:18–22; Luke 5:33–39); and compare II Cor. 3:17 with John 8:36.

---

7 What shall we say then? Is the law sin? Not at all! On the contrary, I would not have come to know sin, had it not been through the law. For I would not have known what it meant to covet if the law had not said, "You shall not covet."   8 But sin, grasping the opportunity afforded by the commandment, produced in me coveting of every variety. For in the absence of law sin (is) dead.   9 Once I was alive apart from law; but when the commandment came, sin sprang to life and I died.   10 And I found that the very commandment which was intended to bring life, in reality brought death.[189]   11 For sin, grasping the opportunity afforded by the commandment, deceived me, and through the commandment killed me.   12 So then, in itself the law is holy, and the commandment holy and righteous and good.

13 Did that which is good then become death to me? Not at all! But sin, in order that it might stand out as sin, produced death in me through that which is good, in order that through the commandment sin might become thoroughly sinful.

---

188. Note ὥστε expressing result.

189. Literally: And there was found for me the commandment, the one for life, this very one for death.

3b. *The sinner's relation to God's Law, in the light of Paul's
own experience and that of others like him.*

"In the absence of law sin is dead. Once I was alive apart from law; but
when the commandment came, sin sprang to life and I died."
7:7-13

**7, 8. What shall we say then? Is the law sin? Not at all! On the contrary,
I would not have come to know sin, had it not been through the law. For I
would not have known what it meant to covet if the law had not said, "You
shall not covet." But sin, grasping the opportunity afforded by the commandment, produced in me coveting of every variety. For in the absence
of law sin (is) dead.**

The apostle had made several statements which might lead thoughtless
people to believe that the law itself was a sinful thing. Had he not made
mention of "the sinful passions stimulated by the law"? (7:5). See also 5:20
and 6:14.

So in the present section (see especially verse 12) the writer makes very
clear the fact that, considered in and by itself, the law is not at all sinful. On
the contrary, it is exactly God's holy law—with special reference here to the
Ten Commandments—that reveals sin in all its gruesomeness. It does this
in order that people may earnestly wage war against sin.

This does not mean that without the written law sin is impossible. Even
those who are without that law do sin, as 1:18-20; 2:12, 14, 15; 5:12-14
prove. It means that apart from the written law the terrible, soul-destroying
character of sin would not have been known.

By nature people have only a dim awareness of their sinfulness. To be
sure, they are often deeply conscious of *the other person's* guilt. At times they
even reprimand the other person while at the same time committing the
very sin they condemn.

Examples from life:

a. The following words were spoken by a (very guilty) husband to his
wife, after several hours of pastoral counseling: "Well, I'll forgive you; but
I'll never forget what you did to me!"

b. Mother reprimanding her little son: "I have told you at least a million
times not to exaggerate!"

The very existence of the written law makes *sin*, that is, (in this case)
transgression of that law, possible. We should also bear in mind that the
only exclusively positive command of the Decalog is, "Honor your father
and your mother," etc. Do not all the other commands, namely, "You shall
not have any other gods before me," "You shall not kill," "You shall not
commit adultery," etc., suggest to *sinners* that they do the very thing that is
forbidden?

What strikes us in reading Rom. 7:7-13 is the fact that, in discussing this
subject of transgressing God's written law, Paul no less than ten times refers
to *himself.* There are those who believe that Paul is here using the first

person singular *in a general sense,* hence not in an autobiographical manner.[190]

Calvin did not share that view, and I believe Calvin was correct in taking that position. Paul—unlike Mark and the author of the epistle to the Hebrews—is not in the habit of hiding his identity. Again and again, throughout his epistles, definitely including Romans, he reveals himself, telling us how a certain matter has affected, or is affecting, him personally, what *he* is doing, intends to do, is experiencing, or has experienced: Rom. 1:8-16; 6:19; 7:1; 9:1-3; 11:11-13; 12:1-3; 15:14-32. Note how the pronouns "I," "my," and "me" are also liberally sprinkled throughout the Greetings section (16:1, 2, 3, 4, 7, 8, 9, 11, 13, 17, 19, 21, 23). It is therefore natural to believe that also here (7:7-13) the apostle is actually speaking about himself. He is recounting how the law "killed" him, that is, how it struck down this self-righteous Pharisee.

Not as if the events he records were in every respect peculiar to him. Undoubtedly, they must be viewed as being, *to a certain extent,* the experience of all those who from the notion of salvation by human merit are brought to the conviction of salvation by grace alone.

Now Paul informs us that he never would have come to know sin had it not been through the law; specifically that he would not have known what it meant *to covet* if the law had not said, "You shall not covet."

It is not surprising that it was especially this tenth commandment that stopped Paul in his tracks. The other commandments, superficially interpreted, forbid transgressions that are, or seem to be, of a more or less external character; especially those of the second table. In this connection read the story of "the rich young ruler" (Matt. 20:18-20, with parallels in Mark and Luke). But the tenth commandment strikes directly at the very root of sin, namely, man's sinful *heart,* his evil *desire.*

Perhaps the covetousness here forbidden is a hankering for things that are sinful in themselves. Or it may be an inordinate yearning for things which, *used with moderation,* would not be sinful but might even be useful (e.g., sports). Or it may be that which is specifically mentioned in the commandment, namely, a craving to deprive a neighbor of anything at all that belongs to him.

Now Paul mentions the fact that sin, grasping the opportunity[191] afforded by the commandment, produced in him coveting *of every variety.* As to the different ways in which sinful coveting may express itself, note the following: The parents of the human race coveted the forbidden fruit (Gen. 3:6); Joseph's brothers, the position of their father's favorite (Gen. 37:4); Achan, a beautiful Babylonian garment and other objects included

---

190. Cranfield, *op. cit.,* p. 351.

191. ἀφορμήν, acc. s. of ἀφορμή (=ἀπό, from, and ὁρμή, impulse, incentive), place from which one starts out, base of operations, springboard; and so: pretext (II Cor. 11:12); occasion (II Cor. 5:12; I Tim. 5:14); opportunity (Rom. 7:8, 11; Gal. 5:13).

in the spoils of Jericho (Josh. 7:21); Ahab, Naboth's vineyard (I Kings 21:1 f.); Amnon, Tamar (II Sam. 13:1); Absalom, the crown (II Sam. 15:1 f.); Ananias and Saphira, prestige (Acts 5:1 f.); Simon the Sorcerer, magical healing power (Acts 8:18 f.); Demas, "this present world" (II Tim. 4:10); and Diotrephes, ecclesiastical pre-eminence (III John 9).

Moreover, as is true of every commandment, so also this one must not be interpreted too narrowly. Jesus has made this clear in such passages as Matt. 5:21 f.; 5:27 f.; 5:31 f.; 5:33 f.

Along this line the Heidelberg Catechism (Lord's Day XLIV, Q. and A. 113) gives us a meaningful interpretation of the tenth commandment:

"Q. What does the tenth commandment require of us?

"A. That not even the slightest inclination or thought contrary to any of God's commandments shall ever rise in our hearts, but that at all times we shall hate all sin with our whole heart and delight in all righteousness."

It is not surprising, therefore, that Paul states, "Sin, grasping the opportunity afforded by the commandment, produced in me coveting of every variety." On the other hand, remove that tenth commandment, with its almost endless multitude of suggestions as to how it can be transgressed, and sin lies dormant.

9. Once I was alive apart from law; but when the commandment came, sin sprang to life[192] **and I died.**

Meaning: There was a time when I felt secure, under no conviction of sin. At that time the full implication of the law had not yet registered in my consciousness, had not yet become an unbearable burden upon my heart. I thought that morally and spiritually I was doing quite well.

But when the commandment came, that is, when it was brought home to me what the law really demanded (nothing less than that which is summarized in Mark 12:29–31), I realized what a great sinner I was. It was then that I died; that is, that was the end of me as a self-satisfied, self-secure person.

10–12. And I found that the very commandment which was intended to bring life, in reality brought death. For sin, grasping the opportunity afforded by the commandment, deceived me, and through the commandment killed me. So then, in itself the law is holy, and the commandment holy and righteous and good.

---

192. When the prefix ἀνά in the verb ἀναζάω retains its full force, as it does in a variant reading of Rom. 14:9, the meaning is *to live again, to return to life.* Here, in Rom. 7:9 the prefix has probably lost some of its force, as happens often in the case of prefixes, so that the meaning of the entire verb is simply *became alive, sprang to life.* See L.N.T. (A. and G., p. 53). With respect to the simple verb ζάω, the basic meaning is *to live.* As to Rev. 20:4 (ἔζησαν) translators are divided in their opinion: some (R.S.V., N.A.S., Phillips, N.I.V.) have adopted the rendering *they came to life* or even "These came to life again" (N.E.B.). Others (A.V., A.R.V., Beck, Williams, Berkeley) translate "They lived." It is a matter if interpretation, the result in some cases probably depending on the theology of the translator. In order to reach the right conclusion the subject of the sentence ("souls") should be taken into account. For the rest, see the author's *More Than Conquerors,* pp. 230, 231; and *The Bible on the Life Hereafter,* pp. 154–156.

The purpose of the commandment had indeed been to bring life; yes, life everlasting. It was true from the beginning and has always remained true that loving God with all of one's heart, soul, mind, and strength, and loving the neighbor as one loves himself brings life, salvation. Cf. Lev. 18:5, "Keep my decrees and laws, for the person who obeys them will live by them." See also Ezek. 20:11. That Paul has in mind the quoted passage seems probable, in view of Rom. 10:5.

And so, the self-righteous Jew, the one with little self-knowledge, imagined that by trying very hard, he would be able to earn everlasting life. There was a time when Paul too was of that opinion, as Phil. 3:6 implies. That was before he discovered that all his righteous deeds (lit. "righteousnesses") amounted to nothing better than filthy rags (Isa. 64:6). So for Paul too that very commandment, whose intention was to bring life, actually brought death.

How was it that while Paul expected life, he found death; and that while he expected happiness, he found gloom? The reason was not that something was wrong with the law. On the contrary, that law was, and always is, holy and righteous and good, since it not only strives to promote these very qualities, as becomes clear from the reading of each commandment, but also reflects the holiness and righteousness and goodness of God.

Is it not a merciful arrangement that, by means of the first and second commandments, God warns against the evil of idolatry, with all the corruption, filth, disappointment, and grief that attends it? That by means of the fourth commandment he sets aside a much needed day of rest and worship for man? That by means of the fifth commandment he places the child under the rule, care, and protection of those who love him most? That by means of the seventh commandment he guards the sacredness of marriage, and by means of the sixth and the eighth, protects human life and property?

So it is made very evident that it was not the law, as such, but it was sin—in the present case Paul's own sinfulness—that made it impossible for the law to make a person holy and happy. The commandment, operating by itself, never kills or even hurts anyone. It is sin that kills. It was sin that even deceived Paul, in his unconverted state, into thinking that he would be able to live in strict obedience to God's law. It deceived him, . . . until one day, in a very dramatic way, it was made clear to him that no matter how hard he tried, he would never, no never, be able *thus* to attain to the status of righteousness before God.

13. Did that which is good then become death to me? Not at all! But sin, in order that it might stand out as sin, produced death in me through that which is good, in order that through the commandment sin might become thoroughly sinful.

Paul had stated that the commandment brought death (verse 10). But how can something that is holy and righteous and good (verse 12) bring death? Paul answers, as it were, "It is not the commandment, operating by itself, that brings death. It is the transgression of the commandment that does this." In the final analysis, therefore, the real cause of death is *sin*. The serious character of sin becomes apparent in this very fact that, in order to expose the sinner, it makes use of something which in itself is perfect, namely, God's holy law. The very *whiteness*—that is, moral-spiritual purity—of God's commandment makes the *blackness* of sin stand out all the more sharply! In the background is the comforting thought, "How majestic, holy, wise, and loving is the God who has provided a way in which sin is removed for those who trust in him!"

As has become clear, Paul has allowed us to take a look into his own diary. He has given us a glimpse into his experience prior to, during, and shortly after his conversion. He has said, "Once I was alive apart from law, but when the commandment came, sin sprang to life and I died."

There are those who link this and similar expressions with Paul's experience when, as a lad of thirteen, he became a *bar mitzvah* (son of the law). It was then that, in accordance with Jewish custom, he assumed responsibility to keep the law.[193] However, such a statement as, "Sin sprang to life and I died" seems to point to a far more radical experience; namely, to that which is recorded in Acts 9:1–22; 22:3–21; 26:1–23; and especially to what Paul tells us in Gal. 1:13–18. While we should certainly leave room for earlier influences upon Paul's mind and heart, not excluding those exerted on his subliminal consciousness, it was in connection with (a) the dramatic experience on the way to Damascus, (b) the events that took place during the days immediately following, and (c) the happenings during the three years spent in Arabia, that "sin sprang to life and Paul—the old, Pharisaic Paul—died." It was then that the former persecutor had time to reflect on: the kind of man he had been, the witness of Stephen and other Christian martyrs, the way of salvation as summarized in such passages as Gen. 15:6; Ps. 32; Isa. 53; Hab. 2; etc., and the words spoken to him by Ananias and by Jesus himself.

Was Paul's conversion experience unique? In certain respects it surely was; in other respects not. There are traits of similarity between the path the apostle had to travel before he surrendered himself wholeheartedly to Christ, and the path others traveled, among them that wonderful child of God, namely, Robert M. McCheyne (1813–1843), as he describes so touchingly in his poem:

JEHOVAH TSIDKENU = JEHOVAH OUR RIGHTEOUSNESS
(Jer. 23:6)

I once was a stranger to grace and to God,
I knew not my danger, and felt not my load,
Though friends spoke in rapture of Christ on the tree,
Jehovah Tsidkenu was nothing to me.

193. For more on this see N.T.C. on Luke, p. 183.

I oft read with pleasure to soothe or engage,
Isaiah's wild measure and John's simple page;
But e'en when they pictured the blood-sprinkled tree,
Jehovah Tsidkenu seemed nothing to me.

Like tears from the daughters of Zion that roll,
I wept when the waters went over his soul,
Yet thought not that my sins had nailed to the tree
Jehovah Tsidkenu— 't was nothing to me.

When free grace awoke me by light from on high,
Then legal fear shook me; I trembled to die;
No refuge, no safety in self could I see,—
Jehovah Tsidkenu my Savior must be.

My terrors all vanished before the sweet name,
My guilty fear banished, with boldness I came
To drink at the Fountain, life-giving and free:
Jehovah Tsidkenu is all things to me.

Jehovah Tsidkenu! my treasure and boast;
Jehovah Tsidkenu! I ne'er can be lost:
In thee shall I conquer by flood and by field,
My cable, my anchor, my breastplate and shield!

Even treading the valley, the shadow of death!
This "watchword" shall rally my faltering breath;
For while from life's fever my God sets me free,
"Jehovah Tsidkenu!" my death-song shall be.

---

14 For we know that the law is spiritual, but I am carnal, sold as a slave to sin. 15 Indeed, that which I am accomplishing I do not approve of. For not what I want (to do), that do I practice, but what I loathe, that I do. 16 But if I do the very thing I do not want to do, I agree that the law is good. 17 But, this being so, then it is not I who accomplish it, but it is sin dwelling in me. 18 For I know that nothing good dwells in me, that is, in my flesh. For I have the desire to do what is good, but I cannot accomplish it.[194] 19 For what I do is not the good I want to do; no, it is the evil I do not want to do, this I practice. 20 But if I am doing the very thing I do not want to do, it is no longer I who am doing it, but it is sin dwelling in me.

21 So I discover this law[195]: When I want to do good, evil lies close at hand. 22 For according to my inner being I delight in God's law; 23 but I see in my (bodily) members a different law, waging war against the law of my mind and making me a prisoner of the law of sin which is in my members. 24 Wretched man that I am! Who will rescue me from this body of death? 25 Thanks be to God through Jesus Christ our Lord! So then, I myself with my mind serve the law of God, but with my flesh the law of sin.

---

194. Or: For to will is present with me, but to do that which is good is not.
195. Or: rule, principle. So also three times in verse 23.

3c. *Paul's own experience and that of others like him*
(continued):
The wretched man's struggle and victory.
"Wretched man that I am! Who will rescue me from this body of death?
Thanks be to God through Jesus Christ our Lord."
7:14-25

In connection with Rom. 7:14-25 the question that must be answered is:
Who is the person described here?
Is he:

a. *An unconverted person,* whether Paul himself before his conversion, or
any other unregenerate individual, perhaps a Jew who has not embraced
Christ?

b. *An immature believer?*

c. *Paul himself, the believer,* and by extension, *the believer generally*

An Unconverted Person?

From the days of the early church, throughout the middle ages, and also
today, there have been and are many who claim that what Paul says in
7:14-25 cannot refer to the believer but must have reference to the unbeliever. The older Greek fathers endorsed this view. For a while even the
great Augustine was of this opinion.

The one who in the twentieth century has perhaps done most to per-
petuate this theory was W. G. Kümmel. See his book, in which there is
much that is valuable, *Römer 7 und die Bekehrung des Paulus,* Leipzig, 1929.
H. R. Ridderbos, whose fine commentary on Romans (*Commentaar Op Het
Nieuwe Testament,* Kampen, 1959) deserves diligent study, also defends the
view that Rom. 7:14-25 portrays a man apart from Christ, a person engaged in a desperate struggle under the law (*op. cit.,* p. 165). Ridderbos
presents a series of arguments in defense of his view, and claims that his
position was not only favored in the early church but is also shared by most
present-day exegetes (p. 162). Those who are able to read Dutch should by
all means make a careful study of pp. 153 f.; 162-170. Not only is such a
study fair to the author but it is also advisable because in my commentary
there is no room to enter into all the details of the Dutch scholar's lengthy
reasonings. In part he argues as follows:

a. In verse 14 Paul says "For (γάρ) we know that the law is spiritual but I
am carnal . . ." How can the fact that "I am carnal," if that "I" indicates a
person redeemed by Christ and led by the Holy Spirit, prove the superior
power of sin mentioned in verse 13?

b. Between 8:1 and 7:14-25 there is a sharp contrast. The "now" of
Rom. 8:1 ("Therefore, there is *now* no condemnation") does not represent
the deplorable situation pictured in Rom. 7:14-25 but a situation which
arises afterward; that is, the reign of the Spirit cannot be identified with but
follows the reign of sin.

c. The view according to which 7:14-25 pictures the discord that remains in the life of the believer conflicts with the statements of Paul in chapter 6 and elsewhere regarding this new life. Thus, according to 6:2, 6, 7, 11, 12, 13, 17, 18, 22, for the Christian sin is the dethroned lord, the lord who has lost his ruling power. In fact, all of chapter 6 is a continuous refutation of the position according to which the "I" of Rom. 7:14-25 could represent the new man, redeemed by Christ.

Answer

As to a. This argument misinterprets the word *for* (γάρ) as here used. Here, as frequently, this word belongs not merely to a part of verse 13 but to the verse taken as a whole.[196] It has a continuative sense, and by some— e.g., N.I.V.—is not even translated. The apostle is saying that the fact that the law is spiritual but I am carnal is in harmony with the fact that the law is good but I am exceedingly sinful.

As to b. The situation pictured in 7:14-25 is not all dark. The contrast between 7:14-25 and 8:1f. must not be exaggerated. To be sure, the earlier passage dwells on sin, but it also dwells on the struggle against sin. *Victory* over sin is even recorded (verses 24, 25). The words, "Thanks be to God through Jesus Christ our Lord" (7:25) harmonize beautifully with, "So then there is now no condemnation for those who are in Christ Jesus," etc. (8:1).

Similarly, the situation pictured in 8:1f. is not as bright as some represent it to be. Even chapter 8 recognizes the paradox in the Christian's life between good and evil. This conflict is implied in verse 10 and clearly expressed in verse 13.

Elsewhere too Paul teaches that a spiritual struggle continues in the life of the believer until the day he enters glory. See I Cor. 9:27; Gal. 5:17; Phil. 3:12-14. The child of God receives the assurance that the One who has begun a good work in him will carry it on to completion until the day of Christ Jesus (Phil. 1:6).

As to c. Though these statements do indeed picture the Christian as walking in newness of life, having been brought from death to life, and in a sense having died to sin, nevertheless, nowhere does chapter 6 or any other Pauline chapter or passage either state or imply that the believer during his present life here on earth has been completely delivered from his struggle against sin. Do not the exhortations of 6:12, 13, 19 imply that this struggle must be continued?

With respect to the claim that many present-day exegetes favor Kümmel's view, as did also many earlier scholars, this must be granted. As could be expected, the view according to which the unbeliever is able to do whatever is mentioned in 7:14-25, including even the good things, is in favor with Pelagians and to a certain extent with Arminians. However, even some Reformed writers have endorsed the position of Kümmel. But, on the

---

196. So also Cranfield, *op. cit.*, p. 355.

whole, Reformed theologians reject this theory, and so do, and did, many others, as will be shown.

Since the arguments proving that the man pictured in 7:14-25 cannot be an unbeliever are the same as those establishing the fact that this person must be a believer, see below (p. 228) for the defense of the latter theory.

An Immature Believer?

The question can be asked, however, "Though it be granted that the man pictured by Paul in 7:14-25 cannot be an unbeliever, nevertheless, in view of the fact that he makes many unfavorable statements about himself—see 7:14, 15, 18, 19, 21, 23, 24—is it possible that he is a mere 'babe in Christ' (cf. I Cor. 3:1; Heb. 3:13)?"

According to this theory three stages of religious position and development are pictured by Paul: (a) that of a person still under the dominion of sin (7:5, 9a); (b) that of the struggling individual, one who hates sin but has not advanced very far on the road of sanctification (7:14-25); and (c) that of the mature and grateful believer, rejoicing in the fact that for him there is now no condemnation (8:1 f.).

But according to Scripture it is exactly the more advanced Christian, the mature believer, who is most deeply concerned about his sin. The more a person has made progress in sanctification, the more also will he abhor his sinfulness.

Thus, Scripture pictures *Job* as a paradigm of virtue (Job 1:1; Ezek. 14:14; James 5:11). Nevertheless, it was exactly Job who exclaimed, "I abhor myself and repent in dust and ashes" (Job 42:6). All will agree that Daniel, the hero of the book of *Daniel,* was an example of Godfearing life and conduct.[197] But listen to his humble plea, in which he confesses his own and his people's sin: "Alas, O Lord, we have sinned and done wrong... We are covered with shame because of our sins against thee" (Dan. 9:4, 5, 8). A king among the prophets, a most Godfearing person, was *Isaiah.* Yet, it was precisely Isaiah who cried out, "Woe is me, for I am ruined, because I am a man of unclean lips..." (Isa. 6:5).

This should indicate that the person whom the apostle has in mind in Rom. 7:14-25 need not be considered, and was not necessarily, an immature believer.

Paul Himself, and by Extension, Believers Generally, Including Even the Most Mature

In line with the humble and self-incriminating language of eminent believers is the fact that Paul too, in referring to himself elsewhere, uses language not far removed from "Wretched man that I am!" Note the following:

---

197. The question whether the "Daniel" mentioned in Ezek. 14:14 was the one of Dan. 1:6 or was someone else need not detain us.

"I am the least of the apostles, not fit to be called an apostle, because I persecuted the church of God!" (I Cor. 15:9).

"To me, the very least of all the saints, was this grace given, to preach to the Gentiles the unsearchable riches of Christ" (Eph. 3:8).

"Christ Jesus came into the world sinners to save, foremost of whom am I!" (I Tim. 1:15).

The person described in Rom. 7:14-25 hates sin (7:15), wishes to do what is good (verses 19, 21), in his inner being delights in God's law (verse 22), deeply regrets his sins (verses 15, 18-24), and thanks God for his deliverance (verse 25). Is it at all probable that such a person has not been regenerated by the Spirit of God? Contrast all this with the description of the unregenerate (7:5, 9a; 8:5a). Clearly, in Rom. 7:14-25 the apostle, in the words of John Calvin, "in his own person describes the weakness of believers and how great it is" (*Romans*, p. 264).

Important also is the change of tense between 7:5, 9a, on the one hand, and 7:14-25, on the other. Surely the most natural explanation is that there has been a radical change; that is, that the "I" of the second passage is no longer the unregenerate of 7:5, 9a but is spiritually reborn.[198]

But this regenerated individual is still experiencing a struggle. He has not yet reached heaven. Those who reject the existence of a kind of dualism within the rescued person Paul and, in general, within believers, find it very difficult to explain 7:24, 25:

"Wretched man that I am! Who will rescue me from this body of death? Thanks be to God through Jesus Christ our Lord! So then, I myself with my mind serve the law of God, but with my flesh the law of sin."

The reasons for believing that in 7:14-25 the regenerated individual, Paul, is describing his own condition and that of believers generally, have been given. It has been shown that *it cannot be the unbeliever who is here being pictured*. Something should now be said about the claim that the opposite view was held by many in the early church and is cherished by most present-day exegetes.

It has already been admitted that there was a time when Augustine, along with many others, supported the view according to which the person described in Rom. 7:14-25 is the unregenerate. Calvin points out what happened next, and, in doing so, also again reveals his own interpretation of the disputed passage:

"Augustine was for a time involved in the common error, but having more thoroughly examined the passage, not only retracted what he had

---

198. The point made by both Mitton and Robinson (for reference see footnote 199) that in verse 14 ("The law is spiritual, but I am carnal") the contrast is not between what I *am* and what I *was*, but between *the law* and *myself*, can be readily granted. But the real argument in favor of viewing verses 14-25 as a description of Paul the believer, is the contrast between, on the one hand, the *past* tense in such passages as 7:5, 9a, and the *present* tense, from *start to finish*, in 7:14-25.

falsely thought, but in his first book to Boniface proves, by many forceful arguments, that what is said cannot be applied to any but the regenerate" (Calvin on *Romans*, p. 264).

It has also been admitted that throughout the centuries many exegetes,[199] especially but by no means exclusively Pelagians, have endorsed the theory according to which Rom. 7:14-25 is a description of the unregenerate, and that today that view is being propagated, at times even by those confessing the Reformed faith.

However, it certainly merits serious reflection that in one way or another, and with varying opinions on details, the belief according to which Paul is here referring to himself and, in general, to believers, is endorsed by the following, among many others:

Batey, R. A., *The Letter of Paul to the Romans*, Austin, 1969, pp. 98-104.

Bavinck, H., *Gereformeerde Dogmatiek*, third edition, Vol. III, p. 65 f.; IV, pp. 282, 283.

Berkhof, L., *Systematic Theology*, Grand Rapids, 1949, p. 540.

Berkouwer, G. C., *Dogmatische Studiën, Geloof En Heiliging*, Kampen, 1949, p. 61, tr. *Faith and Sanctification*, pp. 59, 60.

Bruce, F. F., *The Epistle of Paul to the Romans*, (*Tyndale Bible Commentaries*), Grand Rapids, 1963, pp. 150-156.

Calvin, J., as has been shown.

Cranfield, C. E. B., *op. cit.*, Vol. I, pp. 344, 355-370.

Fraser, J., *A Treatise on Sanctification*, London, 1898, pp. 254-356.

Greijdanus, S., *op. cit.*, Vol. I, pp. 337-339.

Haldane, R., *The Epistle to the Romans*, London, 1966, p. 299.

Hamilton, F. E., *The Epistle to the Romans*, Grand Rapids, 1958, pp. 111-121.

Hodge, C., *op. cit.*, pp. 357, 386.

Knox, J., *op. cit.*, pp. 498-500.

Kuyper, A., *Het Werk van den Heiligen Geest*, Kampen, 1927, pp. 583, 612. Engl. tr., *The Work of the Holy Spirit*, Grand Rapids, 1941, pp. 636-640.

Lenski, R. C. H., *op. cit.*, pp. 473-492.

Luther, M., *Lectures on Romans*, p. 203.

Murray, J., *op. cit.*, Vol. I, pp. 256-273.

Nygren, A., *Commentary on Romans*, Philadelphia, 1949, pp. 284-296.

Pronk, C., "Who is the man of Romans 7:14-25?," article in *The Outlook*

---

199. For example, J. A. Bengel, R. Bultmann, J. Denney, C. H. Dodd, A. E. Garvie, F. Godet, C. Gore, K. E. Kirk, W. Sanday and A. C. Headlam, J. Weiss, to mention only a few, in addition to W. G. Kümmel and H. R. Ridderbos. For a kind of compromise position—*Rom. 7:14-25 is the description of the experience of any morally earnest man, whether he be a Christian or not*—see the interesting article by C. L. Mitton, "Romans vii Reconsidered," *ET* 65 (1953, 1954), pp. 78-81, 99-103, 132-135. Interesting and instructive, but to me not entirely convincing! For a view somewhat resembling that of Mitton see John A. T. Robinson, *Wrestling with Romans*, Philadelphia, 1979; see especially p. 82 f.

(Journal of Reformed Fellowship, published in Grand Rapids, Mich.), Nov. 1978, pp. 9-13.

Steele, D. N., and Thomas, C. C., *Romans, An Interpretive Outline,* Philadelphia, 1963, pp. 126-130.

Van Andel, J., *Paulus' Brief Aan De Romeinen,* Kampen, 1904, pp. 143-151.

Van Leeuwen and Jacobs, *op. cit.,* Vol. I, pp. 124-137.

Wilson, G. B., *op. cit.,* pp. 117-126.

This is also the stand taken by *Evangelical Creeds:*

The Westminster Confession of Faith, 1647. speaking about the believers' "best works" (Chapter XVI, par. VI), states, "they are defiled and mixed with so much weakness and imperfection that they cannot endure the severity of God's judgment." The annexed scriptural passages include Rom. 7:15, 18. See *Creeds of Christendom,* edited by Philip Schaff, Vol. III, p. 635.

The Belgic Confession, 1561, referring to those who have received Jesus Christ as their only Savior (Article XXIX), states, "But this is not to be understood as if there did not remain in them great infirmities; but they fight against them through the Spirit all the days of their life . . ." To the French text of the quoted words are appended the following references: Rom. 7:6, 17, etc.; Gal. 5:17. *Creeds of Christendom,* Vol. III, p. 420.

The Heidelberg Catechism, 1563, in Lord's Day XLIV, Q. & A. 114, asks, "But can those who are converted to God keep these commandments perfectly?" and answers, "No, but even the holiest men, while in this life, have only a small beginning of this obedience; yet so that with earnest purpose they begin to live not only according to some but according to all the commandments of God." The appended references include Rom. 7:22. See also Lord's Day LII, Q. & A. 127.

For *Lutheran* creedal support for this interpretation, see Lenski, *op. cit.,* pp. 473, 474.

14. For we know that the law is spiritual, but I am carnal, sold as a slave to sin.

As has been indicated, there is a close connection between verses 13 and 14 (see p. 226). Now here in verse 14, Paul starts out by making it very clear that he is not finding fault with God's holy law when it exposes him, even Paul, as being still a sinner. He says that the law is spiritual. He means, as he has already explained (see verse 12), that the law is holy, and the commandment holy and righteous and good; that it is the work of God, the product of the Holy Spirit. Cf. Mark 12:36; Acts 1:16; 4:24, 25; II Peter 1:20, 21.

The same absolute goodness and purity cannot be ascribed to the confessor, Paul. On the contrary, he is carnal.[200]

---

200. Though it is true that the best reading favors σάρκινος, basically meaning "composed of

Care should be exercised in defining this quality. The apostle does not say, "I am in the flesh," or "controlled by the flesh"—see 7:5; 8:8 (cf. 8:5), but " I am carnal," which is something else. To be "in the flesh" means to be basically controlled by one's sinful human nature. A person so described is not a believer. To be fleshly or carnal, on the other hand, means to be the opposite of what the law is. The law of God is spiritual, perfect, divine. In a sense Paul is unspiritual, imperfect. As I Cor. 3:1, 3 indicates, such a carnal person can still be a Christian.

Moreover, in verse 18 of the section now under discussion the apostle makes an important distinction. By saying, "I know that nothing good dwells in me, *that is, in my flesh*," is he not clearly implying that there is more to him than his flesh, his sinful human nature? Both verse 18 and verse 25—note contrast between "my mind" and "my flesh" in the latter verse— show that Paul is making a distinction between that which he is with respect to his sinful human nature and that which he is in his more basic inner self. Even a Christian can therefore say, "We know that the law is spiritual, but I am carnal."

The question occurs, however, "What about the second characterization, namely, 'sold as a slave to sin' "? On the surface this description would seem to exclude Paul from the company of the saved; or, if not, it might appear to indicate that when the apostle says "I" he is here not thinking of himself but of somebody else, an unbeliever. On closer inspection, and without in any way doing injustice to the deplorable situation here described, we will, however, have to conclude that it is the apostle Paul, the Christian, who is here speaking, and describing his own state, as well as that of all other believers still dwelling on earth.

In the present connection we should first of all take note of the fact that Paul is not saying that he had sold or abandoned himself to sin, as had been true with respect to King Ahab (I Kings 21:20, 25=LXX III Kings 20:20, 25; II Kings 17:17=LXX IV Kings 17:17). Paul has not sold himself. Someone else has sold him. He, Paul, deplores this situation. It is as if we hear him utter a sigh of agony when he complains, "I am . . . sold as a slave to sin!" Can one who so intensely laments his remaining sinfulness be anything but a true believer? When Paul confesses,

"I am carnal, sold as a slave to sin,"

does he not remind us of another contrite child of God, who sighed:

"Surely I have been a sinner from birth,

A sinner from the time my mother conceived me"? (Ps. 51:5).

Does this mean, then, that when David made this confession he was not a believer? See also Luke 18:13, 14.

When Rom. 7:14 is interpreted in light of verses 22-25, it becomes clear that the one who in verse 14 deplores his sinful condition is the same

---

flesh"—in II Cor. 3:3 note contrast between *stone* and *flesh*—, and not the more usual σαρ-κικός; yet, as used here in Rom. 7:14, σάρκινος must mean *carnal*, that is unspiritual, worldly. Proof: (a) "sold as a slave to sin"; (b) in I Cor. 3:1 σάρκινος is contrasted with πνευματικός; hence, *carnal* with *spiritual*.

person who in the chapter's closing verses expresses his delight in the law of God, looks forward with impassioned and irresistible longing to the day of his deliverance from his present momentous inner struggle, and is filled with the blessed assurance that Victory is bound to come; in fact, that "in principle" it is here already!

However, for the present, the Christian is living in an era in which two ages, the old and the new, overlap. There was a time when Paul was *exclusively a sinner*. There will be a time when he will be *exclusively a saint*. Right now, as he is dictating this letter, he is *a sinner-saint*. A "saint," to be sure; but also still a "sinner"; hence the tension, the inner conflict. It is a struggle which every true believer experiences, and about which the apostle continues to speak, as follows:

15. Indeed, that which I am accomplishing I do not approve of. For not what I want (to do), that do I practice, but what I loathe, that I do.[201]

In view of the fact that the speaker ("I") is serving "in newness of the Spirit" (verse 6) and heartily confesses God's law to be holy, and his commandment holy, righteous, and good (verse 12, and cf. verses 22-25, to which reference has just been made), it is again obvious that Paul, the sincere and humble child of God, is continuing to speak.

As a grateful, warm-hearted believer, his ethical standard is nothing short of moral-spiritual perfection. Cf. Phil. 3:12-14. But when—shall we say at the close of day—he reviews what he has accomplished, he is disgusted with himself: God has done so much for him. He (Paul) has done so little in return. Not only that, but the little he has accomplished is tainted with sin. His aim is so much higher than his reach.

It is indeed wonderful to say with Longfellow:

> Not enjoyment and not sorrow
> Is our destined end or way,
> But to live that each tomorrow
> Finds us farther than today.

---

201. κατεργάζομαι. As is clear from other instances of its use, the meaning of this verb is basically *to work out, to accomplish;* hence also: *to bring about, to produce.* The emphasis is generally on effective action. Thus Rom. 1:27 makes mention of persons who *perpetrate* indecent acts; and 2:9 castigates evil-*doers.* According to 4:15 the law *produces* wrath. According to 5:3 suffering *brings about* perseverance. See also 7:8, 13.

γινώσκω. For the use of this verb (basically: *to know*) in the sense of *to recognize, acknowledge* (perhaps Rom. 7:15) see Josephus, *Antiquities* V. 112 ("They acknowledge but one God"). A slight transition in meaning produces: *to approve of, acknowledge as one's own;* see Matt. 7:23; I Cor. 8:3; Gal. 4:9. *To approve of* is probably the meaning here in Rom. 7:15. See the explanation.

πράσσω. Basically this verb means *to do, to practice, to be occupied with.* It is therefore a synonym of ποιέω, in one of the latter's meanings. In the New Testament πράσσω is often used in an unfavorable sense (Luke 22:23; John 3:20; Acts 19:36; 25:11, 25; Rom. 1:32; 2:1-3; 13:4; II Cor. 12:21; Gal. 5:21). In Rom. 7:19 note the contrast: *do* good—*practice* evil.

However, there are exceptions. In Rom. 9:11 and II Cor. 5:10 the verb πράσσω is used with objects both good and bad; while the objects mentioned in Acts 26:20; Rom. 2:25; and Phil. 4:9 are wholly good.

But what if that ideal is not always realized? The merely *moral* man may be able to deceive himself into thinking that he is, after all, doing quite well. It is precisely *the Christian* who will say with Paul, "Indeed, that which I am accomplishing I do not approve of. For not what I want (to do) do I practice, but what I loathe, that I do."[202]

And is not this the very conflict also mentioned in Gal. 5:17, where the same apostle states, ". . . the flesh sets its desire against the Spirit, and the Spirit against the flesh: for these are opposed to each other, so that these very things y o u may wish to be doing, those y o u are not doing"?

There are those, however, who have objected that Gal. 5:17 and Rom. 7:14-25 cannot be referring to the same inner conflict, because while the former passage mentions the Spirit, the latter does not. But why would it have been necessary for Paul to repeat his mention of the Holy Spirit, as the Author of sanctification? Are not the references to the Spirit in Rom. 2:29; 7:6 sufficient? They are, unless they are interpreted as indicating a "spirit" other than the divine. But in view of such parallel passages as II Cor. 3:6, 17, this position would be difficult to defend.

I repeat, therefore, what I wrote in N.T.C. on Galatians, p. 215: "Paul, writing as a converted man (Rom. 7:14-25) and recording his *present state of grace* experiences . . . complains bitterly about the fact that he practices that in which his soul no longer takes delight; in fact, practices that which his regenerated self *hates.*"

16. But if I do the very thing I do not want to do, I agree that the law is good.

But is there not an easy way out of this painful conflict? Why not simply throw out the law? Why not call it bad and reject it?

Though, on the surface, this might seem to be an easy solution, in reality it is not a solution at all. The Holy Spirit is dwelling in Paul's heart (and in the hearts of all true believers). So very close is the relationship between that Spirit and Paul's own spirit that the apostle is able to say, "The law is good. It is excellent! I must not disobey it!" And though Paul does indeed disobey, and is therefore experiencing a bitter struggle, his own voice and that of the Holy Spirit are joined in a marvelous *symphony* when they eulogize the law.

17-20. But, this being so, then it is not I who accomplish it, but it is sin dwelling in me. For I know that nothing good dwells in me, that is, in my flesh. For I have the desire to do what is good, but I cannot accomplish it. For what I do is not the good I want to do; no, it is the evil I do not want to do, this I practice. But if I am doing the very thing I do not want to do, it is no longer I who am doing it, but it is sin dwelling in me.

The logical deduction—note the words "this being so"—derived from the

---

202. It is clear that in this statement the verb γινώσκω is in *a*pposition with θέλω, and in *o*pposition to μισῶ. Therefore, from among a series of possible meanings for the verb γινώσκω, the meaning *approve* (of) is probably the best.

situation as described in verse 16 is that, since Paul himself does not want to act contrary to God's will, the sins committed should be *basically* ascribed not to him but to sin. It is *sinful nature*, here and elsewhere called *the flesh*, which is the real culprit, the actual offender. It is that wicked squatter, dwelling with Paul in the latter's own house (his soul) who is at the bottom of all this inquity. It is that intruder who so often makes it impossible for Paul to do the good he wants to do.

It may seem as if Paul, by means of this line of reasoning, is disavowing responsibility for his own sins. That, however, is not actually the case. Two facts remain true: (a) even the squatter is not a total stranger but is Paul's own sinful nature; and (b) a wicked intruder, an illegal squatter, must not be allowed to remain!

The latter part of verse 18 and the entire verse 19 are similar in meaning to the thought expressed in verse 15. Verse 20 substantially repeats verses 16a, 17.

21. So I discover this law: When I want to do good, evil lies close at hand.

The word "So" shows that the apostle here summarizes the contents of the preceding verses (14-20). It is immediately clear that when he here uses the word "law," he is not thinking of the Ten Commandments. "Law," as here used, must mean something like *operating rule* or *governing principle*. For more on this see verse 23.

The inflexible "law" to which reference is here made, and which the author of this epistle—as well as every believer—is constantly discovering, is this: "When I want to do good, evil lies close at hand." In view of the fact that, according to verses 17, 20, sinful human nature has established its residence in Paul's own house (his soul), and has done this with a wicked purpose, the statement "evil lies close at hand," is indeed very logical. This "evil," here personified, may be lying down, but is certainly not sleeping. It is pictured as if it were watching the apostle to see whether he is about to carry out a good intention. Whenever such a noble thought or suggestion enters Paul's heart, evil immediately interrupts in order to turn the good deed into its opposite.

In complete harmony with verse 21 the author continues:

22, 23. For according to my inner being I delight in God's law; but I see in my (bodily) members a different law, waging war against the law of my mind and making me a prisoner of the law of sin which is in my members.[203]

---

203. συνήδομαι, not here "rejoice with" but "rejoice in." See M. M., p. 607; cf. Liddell & Scott, *Greek-English Lexicon*, Vol. II, p. 1715. For a different view see A. T. Robertson, *Word Pictures*, Vol. IV, p. 370; also L.N.T. (A. and G.), p. 797.

ἀντιστρατευόμενον, acc. s. masc. pres. participle of ἀντιστρατεύομαι, to wage war against. αἰχμαλωτίζοντα (same construction as the above), from αἰχμαλωτίζω (from αἰχμή, spear, and ἁλίσκομαι, to capture); hence, originally, to capture with the spear; then, as here, simply!

The word "*For*" shows that what is found in verses 22, 23 explains the contents of verse 21. The conflict between good and evil mentioned in the earlier verse is amplified and clarified in the present passage.

The apostle speaks of two opposing "laws." The first is "God's law." Though there is a wide difference in opinion with respect to the meaning of this expression, yet in view of the fact that Paul has been referring to God's law as being the revelation of his good and perfect will, and has even quoted a specific commandment of the Decalog (see verses 7, 8, 12), how can there be any good reason to doubt that also here in verse 22 the expression "God's law" indicates that very system of moral principles or rules that is summarized in the ten commandments and even more concisely in Matt. 22:37-40 (and parallels)?

It should be borne in mind, however, that for the believer that divine law is not a dead letter, and it certainly is not in any sense a means of salvation. On the contrary, for him it is *the ruling principle* for the expression of his gratitude.

Understood in this sense, it is not at all strange that he "delights" in God's law. Right-minded children delight in discovering a way in which they can show their parents, or other benefactors, how much they love them! For the manner in which God's children express this delight in God's law see above, p. 214.

Now the apostle states that he delights in God's law according to his "inner being." When he uses such phraseology he is not copying Plato or the Stoics. He is not expressing a contrast between man's rational nature and his lower appetites. With Paul the inner man is the one that is hidden from the public gaze. It indicates *the heart.* It is here that a new principle of life has been implanted by the Holy Spirit. By means of this implantation the sinner has become a *new* man, a person who is being daily transformed into the image of Christ. In this connection study such passages as II Cor. 4:16; Eph. 3:16; Col. 3:9, 10.

In his "bodily members" (more about that in a moment) Paul sees a different law, one that is constantly waging war against the law of his mind and is making him a prisoner of the law of sin.

If "God's law" should be interpreted as *a governing principle,* as has just now been shown, logic requires that also this "different law" must be thus explained. Clearly—as the apostle states in so many words—that "different law" is the law of sin. How it operates has been indicated in verse 21. That it

---

to capture, to carry off as a captive or prisoner. The verb also occurs in Luke 21:24; II Cor. 5:10; II Tim. 3:6. See N.T.C. on Luke, p. 947.

It is clear that Paul is here making use of military metaphors. For another possible example see on 6:13, pp. 202, 203. If the word ἀφορμή (7:8, 11) is rendered "base of operations," this would be still another such figure of speech. On military metaphors see also N.T.C. on Ephesians, pp. 271-280.

is making the apostle, and all true believers everywhere, prisoners is probably another way of expressing the thought of verse 14b.

Again and again "the law of sin" causes the author of this letter to do what he does not want to do, and again and again it prevents him from doing what he wants to do, facts about which he bitterly complains, and which he deeply and sincerely deplores.

Emphasis should be focused on the phrase "the law of sin which is *in my members*." Often this phrase is either passed by in silence or touched on very lightly. Nevertheless, it could be more important than is generally realized. That it must have been rather significant to the mind of the writer is clear from the fact that he makes frequent use of it. See 6:13 (twice); 6:19 (twice); 7:5; 7:23 (twice); all this in addition to the figurative (or at least largely figurative) use of this expression, for which see Rom. 12:5; I Cor. 6:15; 12:12, 27; Eph. 4:16, 25; 5:30.

In addition to the comments made previously with respect to these bodily *parts* or *members* (see on 6:13, 19; 7:5; pp. 202, 206, 207) note, therefore, also the following: Paul was an ardent missionary. His soul was wrapped up in his work. See Rom. 15:17–29; I Cor. 9:22; II Cor. 5:20, 21. To win people for Christ, to the glory of God, meant more to him than even his personal freedom (Phil. 1:12 f.). He desired intensely that others too would share this enthusiasm (Phil. 1:4, 18).

Now he was well aware of the fact that the way to reach his audiences was through his and their bodily organs. Very important were: the swiftness of his *feet*, the utterances of his *lips*, the look in his *eyes*, the movements of his *hands*, the attentiveness of their *ears*, etc., the more so because such communication devices as airplanes, eye-glasses, hearing-aids, etc., had not yet been invented.

Unsurprisingly, therefore, in both the Old Testament and the New, far greater emphasis is placed on bodily parts or members than in present-day literature. In many of the following passages would we today even make mention of the involved bodily members?[204]

mouth

Gen. 24:57; Job 3:1; Ps. 17:10　　　Matt. 5:2; 13:35; Luke 11:54

lips

Lev. 5:4; Num. 30:6; Deut. 23:23　　　Matt. 15:8; Heb. 13:15; I Peter 3:10

tongue

II Sam. 23:2; Job 6:30; Ps. 35:28　　　Acts 2:26; Phil. 2:11; I Peter 3:10

---

204. Those who are unable to read the original are advised to look up these references in the A.V., since in the more recent translations the names of these bodily parts are sometimes omitted.

	feet
II Sam. 22:37; I Kings 14:6, 12	Luke 1:79; Acts 5:2; Heb. 2:8
	hands
Gen. 3:22; 8:9; Josh. 2:24	Luke 21:12; Acts 7:41; Heb. 10:31
	eyes
Deut. 7:16; Job 7:7; Isa. 13:18	Luke 11:34; I Cor. 2:9; Rev. 1:7
	ears
Neh. 1:6; Job 4:12; 13:1	Matt. 10:27; Luke 12:3; I Cor. 2:9

A striking instance of this constant reference to bodily parts occurs in this very epistle to the Romans (3:13-18), where tongue, lips, mouth, feet, and eyes, are mentioned in one breath, in quotations from the Old Testament.

In *mentioning* the physical parts and qualities the *possibility* must not be ruled out that the spiritual part of man's being may have been included. So interpreted, what the writer is saying is this: "If I could only serve God in a thoroughly unhampered manner! If only *all* my faculties of body and soul could be made effective for him and his cause!" In any event the continuation is understandable:

24. Wretched man that I am! Who will rescue me from this body of death?

The writer genuinely deplores the fact that due to the law of sin still operating in him, he is unable to serve God as completely and wholeheartedly as he desires.

The poignant grief here expressed is definitely that of a believer. No unbeliever would ever be able to be so filled with sorrow because of his sins! The author of the outcry is Paul, speaking for every child of God.

The cry he utters is one of distress, but not of despair, as verse 25 proves. Paul suffers agony, to be sure, the wretchedness brought about by strenuous exertion; that is, by trying hard, but never satisfactorily succeeding, to live in complete harmony with God's will but failing again and again. He is looking forward eagerly to the time when this struggle will have ended.

With that in mind he yearns to be rescued from "this body of death," that is, from the body in its present condition, subject to the ravages of sin and death.[205] He knows that as long as he lives in this present "body of humilia-

---

205. The correct translation of the phrase τὸ σῶμα (here gen. τοῦ σώματος, after ἐκ) τοῦ θανάτου τούτου is probably not "the body of this death" but "this body of death." Reasons:

a. The immediately preceding verse clearly refers to members or parts of Paul's physical body.

b. Previously there has been a reference to "y o u r mortal body" (6:12).

c. In 8:23 the apostle is still speaking about a physical body.

For the opposite view see Murray, *op. cit.,* p. 268.

tion" (Phil. 3:21) the terrible struggle will be continued. But once the life in that body ceases, the state of sinless glory will commence; first for the soul, then also for the body.

So he answers his own question with a jubilant: **25. Thanks be to God through Jesus Christ our Lord!** He speaks with full assurance. He knows that when a believer dies, this death is gain. To be with Christ is better by far (Phil. 1:21, 23). Sin will have been left behind forever. The conflict will have ended, never to return. In the language of the apostle John, nothing that is impure will enter the Holy City (Rev. 21:27). Moreover, the time is coming when even the body will be redeemed (Rom. 8:23; cf. John 5:28, 29).

In his jubilant thanksgiving the apostle goes back to the Source of every blessing. He exclaims, "Thanks be to *God!*" See John 3:16; Rom. 8:32; II Cor. 9:15. He realizes too that it was through the One whom he mentions by his full name *Jesus* (Savior), *Christ* (Anointed One), *our Lord* (Sovereign Ruler, Owner), that salvation, full and free, was obtained. Obtained, moreover, not only for Paul but for all believers. And so he looks forward to the day of glory for them all (I Cor. 15:56, 57; II Tim. 4:8).

Summing up the entire argument, Paul concludes this chapter by writing, **So then, I myself with my mind serve the law of God, but with my flesh the law of sin.**

Note the sharp contrast:

a. the law of God *versus* the law of sin;

b. my mind *versus* my flesh.

Is the apostle saying, then, that his *mind* (verse 25b) or *inner being* (verse 22) serves *the law of God* (verses 14, 16, 22); but his *flesh* (verses 18, 25b) or *indwelling sin* (sinful human nature, verses 17, 20), serves *the law of sin* (verse 23)?

Here we should be very careful, for the writer does not consider such things as *mind* and *flesh* to be independent beings. On the contrary, as has been pointed out previously, both of these belong to Paul. It is he himself—that is, it is the believer himself—who remains fully responsible, as is clear from a careful reading of verses 15, 16, 19.

On the other hand, it is also clear that these two (mind, flesh; Paul the saint, Paul the sinner) are not strictly co-ordinate. No, it is with his inner being or mind that Paul wants to do the will of God (see verses 15, 16, 18, 20, 21, 22). The flesh is the intruder, who is being driven out and will certainly lose the battle. That is due not to Paul's goodness but to God's grace, as the apostle loudly and cheerfully proclaims by shouting, "Thanks be to God through Jesus Christ our Lord." Compare I Cor. 15:57, also written by the triumphant believer, Paul!

We see, therefore, that the passage (verse 25b), considered in both of its parts—(a) "I myself with my mind serve the law of God"; and (b) "but with my flesh the law of sin"—links beautifully with chapter 8, note verse 10 of that chapter; and also that verse 25a—"Thanks be to God through Jesus

Christ our Lord!"—is a very appropriate introduction to 8:1, "There is therefore now no condemnation for those who are in Christ Jesus."

For more on Rom. 7:14-25; see pp. 245, 246, 249, 250.

Practical Lessons Derived from Romans 7

Verses 4 and 6

"So, my brothers, y o u too were made dead to the law through the body of Christ, so that y o u might belong to another, even to him who was raised from the dead, in order that we might bear fruit for God . . . We have been released from the law, so that we serve in newness of (the) Spirit, not in oldness of (the) letter."

It is clear from this that the genuine Christian life is not that of bondage but that of freedom. It is not motivated by external regulations but by love for the One to whom believers belong, even Christ. It is not guided by selfish interests but by the Spirit. And it is not barren but fruitful.

Verse 7

"What shall we say then? Is the law sin? Not at all! On the contrary, I would not have come to know sin, had it not been through the law."

Often the statement is heard, "We have nothing to do with the law." Or "The law was for the Jews. It is not for us." That is not the language Paul uses. For him God's holy law was of value in more ways than one. See above, p. 184. But it cannot save. It can and does reveal our sinfulness, and because of its very impotency, it points to Another, namely, Christ, as our Savior. See Rom. 7:13; Gal. 3:24.

Verses 15 and 20

"For not what I want (to do), that do I practice, but what I loathe, that I do . . . But if I am doing the very thing I do not want to do, it is no longer I who am doing it, but it is sin dwelling in me."

A very frequent and practical question is, "Am I a child of God?" Would not the answer be, "Do you recognize yourself in the words quoted just now?" If you do, then will you not also be able to say, "Wretched man that I am! Who will rescue me from this body of death? *Thanks be to God through Jesus Christ our Lord!*"? Those who can say that are surely Christians.

A dear child of God told the author of this book, "whenever I read Rom. 7:14-25, I see myself." By sovereign grace this brother had within his heart the blessed assurance, "Jesus is mine."

Summary of Chapter 7

Just as a woman, by means of a death (that of her husband) is released from her marriage bond and allowed to marry another man, so also by a death (the believers' death with Christ) God's children are released from indebtedness to the law, the latter's "bill" having been fully paid by Christ's voluntary and vicarious sacrifice. Believers have, accordingly, obtained *lib-*

erty. This liberty is a freedom *from* and a freedom *for*. It is a freedom *from* the obligation to keep the law in order to be saved, and is therefore also a freedom *from* the curse which the law pronounces upon the disobedient. But it is at the same time a freedom *for* or *with a view to,* a freedom *in order* to render service to God "in newness of the Spirit, not in oldness of the letter" (verses 1–6).

Release from the law, in the sense indicated, does not imply that the law is sinful. On the contrary, the law is good and useful, for it lays bare our sinfulness. It puts to death our sinful pride and vaunted self-sufficiency. "I would not have come to know sin, had it not been through the law. For I would not have known what it meant to covet if the law had not said, 'You shall not covet.'" Therefore, "In itself the law is holy, and the commandment holy and righteous and good."

Paul has stated that the commandment slays us. But how can something that is good bring death? The apostle answers that it is not the commandment, operating by itself, that slays us; it is our transgression of the commandment that does this. Hence, the real cause of death is sin. It remains true, however, that the very whiteness (moral-spiritual purity) of God's commandment causes the blackness of our sin to stand out all the more sharply.

By saying such things as "*Once I was alive* apart from the law, but when the commandment came, sin sprang to life and *I died* . . . the commandment *killed me* . . .," Paul gives us a glimpse into his own experience prior to, during, and shortly after his conversion (verses 7–13).

In verses 14–25, which section follows logically upon verses 7–13, Paul, the believer, reflecting on his own situation and that of others like him, discusses *The Wretched Man's Struggle and Victory.* He does not find fault with God's holy law when it exposes him, even Paul, and others like him, as being still polluted with sin. He clearly and openly confesses, "We know that the law is spiritual, but I am carnal, sold as a slave to sin." He admits, therefore, that although absolute goodness can be ascribed to God's law, it cannot be predicated of himself, Paul. He knows that as long as he is on this sinful earth, he is *carnal,* that is, unspiritual, worldly, far from perfect. Being a true child of God, the apostle genuinely deplores the fact that he had been sold as a slave to sin. He confesses, "Indeed, that which I am accomplishing I do not approve of. For not what I want (to do), that do I practice, but what I loathe, that I do . . . For what I do is not the good I want to do; no, it is the evil I do not want to do, this I practice."

Is not this the very conflict which is also mentioned in Gal. 5:17, where the same apostle states, "The flesh sets its desire against the Spirit, and the Spirit against the flesh: for these are opposed to each other, so that those very things y o u may wish to be doing, those y o u are not doing"? And is not this realization of imperfection similar to that expressed in Phil. 3:12, 13, "Not that I have already gotten hold or have already been made perfect . . . I do not count myself yet to have laid hold"?

However, the very fact that in his inner being Paul does not really want to do what is contrary to God's will but loathes this situation, fills him with courage, so that he is able to exclaim,

"For according to my inner being I delight in God's law; but I see in my (bodily) members a different law, waging war against the law of my mind and making me a prisoner of the law of sin which is in my members. Wretched man that I am! Who will rescue me from this body of death? Thanks be to God through Jesus Christ our Lord!" The fact, frankly admitted by him in a summarizing statement, namely, "So then, I myself with my mind serve the law of God, but with my flesh the law of sin," does not cancel the essence of the assurance of victory expressed in those memorable words, "Thanks be to God through Jesus Christ our Lord!" (verses 14–25).

Outline (continued)

Justification by Faith

4a. *"No condemnation" for those in Christ Jesus. The indwelling Spirit imparts life to them, assures them of the realization of their hope of eagerly awaited glory, helps them in their infirmities, and intercedes for them, so that everything turns out for their welfare. The three groanings.*

"And we know that all things work together for good to those who love God, that is, to those who are called according to his purpose."

8:1–30

4b. *It produces the fruit of **super-invincibility**; i.e., of being more than conquerors.*

"No, in all these things we are more than conquerors
through him who loved us"

8:31–39

CHAPTER 8

8   1 There is therefore now no condemnation for those who are in Christ Jesus. 2 For through Christ Jesus the law of the Spirit of life has set me[206] free from the law of sin and of death. 3 For what the law could not do, because it was weak through the flesh, God did: by sending his own Son in the likeness of sinful flesh and for sin, he condemned sin in the flesh, 4 in order that the righteous requirement of the law might be fully met in us, who do not walk according to the flesh but according to the Spirit. 5 For those who live according to the flesh set their minds on the things of the flesh, but those who live according to the Spirit set their minds on the things of the Spirit. 6 Now the mind of the flesh is death, but the mind of the Spirit is life and peace; 7 because the mind of the flesh is hostility to God, for it does not submit to the law of God, nor can it do so. 8 And those who are in the flesh cannot please God.

9 Y o u, however, are not in the flesh but in the Spirit, seeing that God's Spirit dwells in y o u. (Anyone who does not possess Christ's Spirit does not belong to Christ.) 10 But if Christ is in y o u, though the body is dead because of sin, yet the Spirit is life because of (y o u r) justification. 11 And if the Spirit of him who raised Jesus from the dead dwells in y o u, he who raised Christ from the dead will also impart life to y o u r mortal bodies through his Spirit, who dwells in y o u.

12 Therefore, brothers, we have an obligation, but it is not to the flesh, to live according to its standard. 13 For if y o u live according to its standard y o u are doomed to die; but if, by the Spirit, y o u put to death the disgraceful deeds of the body, y o u will live. 14 For as many as are being led by the Spirit of God, these are sons of God. 15 For y o u have not received a spirit of slavery, to fill y o u once more with dread, but y o u have received the Spirit of adoption, who moves us to cry, "Abba!," that is, "Father!" 16 This Spirit himself bears witness with our spirit that we are children of God.

17 And if children, then heirs, heirs of God and fellow-heirs with Christ; since the fact that we are now sharing in his sufferings means that (hereafter) we shall share in his glory. 18 For I consider that the sufferings of this present time are not worthy to be compared with the glory that is to be revealed in us.

19 For the creation, with outstretched head, is eagerly looking forward to the revelation of the sons of God. 20 For it was not by its own choice that the creation was subjected to futility, but (it was) because of him who subjected it, in hope, 21 because the creation itself too will be set free from its bondage to decay, so as to share the glorious liberty of the children of God. 22 For we know that the whole creation, with one accord, has been, and still is, groaning as in the pain of childbirth.

23 Not only this, but also we ourselves, who possess the firstfruits of the Spirit, even we ourselves groan within ourselves, as we eagerly await our adoption, that is, the redemption of our bodies. 24 For it was in hope that we were saved; but when once something hoped for is seen it is no longer an object of hope, for who hopes for what he sees? 25 But since we hope for that which we do not see, we wait for it with patient endurance.

---

206. Or you.

26 And in the same way the Spirit too is helping us in our weakness, for we do not know what we ought to pray, but the Spirit himself intercedes for us with unspoken groanings. 27 And he who searches the hearts knows what is the Spirit's intention, that he is interceding for the saints in harmony with God's will.

28 And we know that to those who love God all things work together for good, that is, to those who are called according to (his) purpose. 29 For whom he foreknew, he also foreordained to be conformed to the image of his Son, so that he might be the firstborn among many brothers; 30 and whom he foreordained, these he also called; and whom he called, these he also justified; and whom he justified, these he also glorified.

4a. *"No condemnation" for those in Christ Jesus. The indwelling Spirit imparts life to them, assures them of the realization of their hope of eagerly awaited glory, helps them in their infirmities, and intercedes for them, so that everything turns out for their welfare. The three groanings.*

"And we know that all things work together for good to those who love God, that is, to those who are called according to his purpose."

8:1-30

As was true with respect to chapters 5, 6, and 7, so also chapter 8 points to a result of the believers' justification by faith. The fact that justification is indeed at the center of Paul's thinking is clear from the opening words, "There is now no condemnation," for condemnation is the opposite of justification.

Moreover, as has been stated previously, Paul himself seems to endorse the co-ordination of chapters 5, 6, and 7, causing each to close with the same (or a very similar) phrase. This holds too for chapter 8, ending with "in Christ Jesus our Lord."

The question as to the theme of this chapter is easily answered. It is not expressed immediately, though everything in verses 1-30, and again in verses 31-36, leads up to it; as, for example, verse 28, printed above the present section, indicates. The central thought, which is also the fourth main fruit of justification by faith, is found in the words, "No, in all these things we are more than conquerors through him who loved us" (verse 37). Note: not merely conquerors but *more than conquerors;* not merely invincible but *super-invincible.*

1. There is therefore now no condemnation for those who are in Christ Jesus.[207]

The statement, "There is therefore now no condemnation" is closely connected with the main thrust of Paul's previous reasoning, taken as a unit. See especially verses 1:16, 17; 3:21, 24; 5:1, 2, 6-8, 15-21; 7:6. In these passages the apostle has been setting forth the fact that, through Christ's debt-removing and sanctifying self-sacrifice, believers have been released from the curse of the law. Because of the entrance of sin (cf. 8:3) the law cannot now be regarded as a means of obtaining salvation, nor does

---

207. The continuation (as a whole or in part): "who walk not after the flesh but after the Spirit" lacks sufficient textual support, and is probably an interpolation from verse 4.

it have the power to condemn believers. Rather, the law is the means for the expression of their gratitude. As such it is the object of their delight, even though, as 7:14 f. has shown, in the present life complete obedience is impossible.

This does not mean that there is no connection between 8:1 f. and the immediately preceding context. As has been indicated—see pp. 238, 239— there is a close connection between "Thanks be to God through Christ Jesus our Lord" (7:25a) and "There is therefore now no condemnation, etc." (8:1). But even what Paul says in 7:25b—and more generally in 6:1-7:25—about the enslaving power of sin, is not absent from his mind in 8:1, as the sequel (8:1 f.) indicates. For Paul "no condemnation" means freedom not only from sin's *guilt* but also from its *enslaving power.*

To be sure, a distinction must be drawn between justification and sanctification. But this distinction must never become a separation. Calvin has made this clear by stating, "As Christ cannot be divided, so also these two blessings which we receive together in him are also inseparable" (*Institutes* III, xi, 6).

In line with this twofold reference of the words "no condemnation" is the phrase "in Christ Jesus." What Paul is saying is that for those who not only *forensically* are in Christ Jesus—the guilt of their sins having been removed by his death—but also *spiritually*—the sanctifying influences of his Spirit dominating their lives, there is *now* (=consequently) no condemnation. For them there is justification and therefore salvation full and free (see 8:29, 30). For more on the phrase "in Christ Jesus" see above on 3:24, p. 131, and on 6:3 f., p. 196. See also N.T.C. on Ephesians, pp. 70, 71.

Justification and sanctification always go together. The fact that the expression "no condemnation" implies both pardon and purification is also clear from verse

2. For through Christ Jesus the law of the Spirit of life has set me free from the law of sin and of death.[208]

Paul speaks about "the law of the Spirit of life." That the Holy Spirit is life in his very essence and also imparts life, both physical and spiritual, is

---

208. Technical questions that should be touched upon are the following:

a. What does "through Christ Jesus" modify: "the law of the Spirit of life"? Or "has set me free"? The contents of verses 3 and 4, showing that it was through the sending of God's Son that the law was fulfilled (so that sinners might be set free) favors the latter construction.

b. Does "of life" modify "the law" or does it go with "the Spirit"? I see no reason to depart from the rule that, unless there is cause to do otherwise, a modifier should be construed with the noun that is nearest to it. Besides, in ever so many passages Scripture associates the Holy Spirit with the impartation of life.

c. Should we read "has set *me* free" or "has set *you* free: με or σε? Textual evidence, though somewhat favoring σε (א B G), is not entirely conclusive. Since from 7:7 on the apostle has so very frequently been referring to himself, με seems more natural. On the other hand, a change of style from the more strictly personal to the far more general has already occurred (see 8:1). This may account for the fact that even the reading ἡμᾶς (us) has some support. The matter is not very important. We may rest assured that through Christ Jesus the law of the Spirit of life has set free *all* who place their trust in the Savior: you, me, us.

clear from ever so many passages of Scripture. The basis for this doctrine is probably found already in Gen. 1:1; Ps. 51:11; 104:30. For closer references see John 6:63; II Cor. 3:6; Gal. 6:8; and do not forget Rom. 8:11. *The law of the Spirit of life* is the forceful and effective operation of the Holy Spirit in the hearts and lives of God's children. It is the very opposite of "the law of sin and death," for which see on 7:23, 25. Just as the law of sin produces death, so also the law, or ruling factor, of the Spirit of life brings about life. Cf. Rom. 6:23. It does this "through Christ Jesus," that is, on the basis of the merits of his atonement, and by means of the vitalizing power of union with him.

The question arises, "If in Rom. 7:14–8:2 Paul throughout speaks about himself as a believer, how can he say not only, "I am carnal, sold as a slave to sin . . . a prisoner" (7:14, 23); but also, "Through Christ Jesus the law of the Spirit of life has set me free from the law of sin and death"? How can a slave and prisoner also be a free person? Does not this very contradiction show that we have erroneously interpreted Rom. 7:14, 23?

The answer is, "Not at all." On the contrary, when we read these passages—both 7:14, 23 and 8:1, 2, we say, "How wonderful is the Word of God! What a true picture it draws of the person I really am! On the one hand I am a slave, a prisoner, for sin has such control over me that I cannot lead a sinless life (Jer. 17:9; Matt. 6.12; I John 1:8, 10). Yet, on the other hand, I am a free person, for though Satan tries with all his might and trickery to keep me from doing what is right—such as trusting God for my salvation, invoking him in prayer, rejoicing in him, working for his causes, etc., he cannot throughout stop me from doing so. He cannot completely prevent me from experiencing the peace of God that transcends all understanding. The sense of victory, which I possess in principle even now and will possess in perfection in the future, sustains me in all my struggles. I rejoice in the freedom which Christ has earned for me!" (cf. Gal. 5:1).

When an interpreter of 7:21—8:2 limits Christian experience to what is found in 7:22, 25a, 8:1, 2, leaving out 7:21, 23, 24, 25b, does he not resemble the musician who tries to play an elaborate piece on an organ with a very restricted number of octaves, or on a harp with many broken strings?

3, 4. For what the law could not do, because it was weak through the flesh, God did: by sending his own Son in the likeness of sinful flesh and for sin, he condemned sin in the flesh, in order that the righteous requirement of the law might be fulfilled in us, who do not walk according to the flesh but according to the Spirit.

a. For what the law could not do, because it was weak through the flesh, God did.

The word "For" indicates that what, according to verses 3, 4, God accomplished by sending his Son into the world, is the basis of the believer's freedom (verse 2). The law was unable to provide this basis. That, however, was not the law's fault. Sinful human nature ("the flesh," see p. 217) was to blame. It was that which made perfect obedience impossible. Does this mean, then, that sinners are never going to be saved, and that God's plan, made before the founding of the world (Eph. 1:4), is not going to be carried out? It does not, for—O glorious divine love!—what the law was unable to accomplish God accomplished! It was he who, by sending into the world his own Son to die for sinners, satisfied the demands of justice, thereby setting sinners free and flooding their hearts with love for God and a desire to do his will out of gratitude.

b. by sending *his own* Son.

What depth of feeling, what compassion, what pathos is contained in this expression! Involuntarily our mind travels back to Gen. 22:2 (God addressing Abraham), "Take now your son, your only son, whom you love, Isaac . . . and offer him for a burnt offering. . . ." See also John 3:16, "For *so* loved God the world that his Son, the only-begotten he gave. . . ." Cf. Matt. 21:37.

Philosophers may argue that implied in the doctrine of God's immutability is the fact that the Divine Being cannot experience any emotions. The question may be asked whether that inference does full justice to such passages in this epistle as the present one and 8:32 ("God did not spare his own Son but gave him up"). In order to save us, God did not spare *his own*—yes, his very own, his dear and only—Son. He caused him to descend to hell for us, the hell climaxed at Calvary.[209]

c. in the likeness of sinful flesh.

In his incarnation the divine Son assumed the human nature, so that from that moment on he has two natures, the divine and the human, indissolubly united, yet each retaining its own properties. But he took on that human nature not as it came originally from the hand of the Creator ("and behold it was very good," Gen. 1:31), but *weakened by sin*, though remaining itself without any sin. Note: *not* "in sinful flesh" but "*in the likeness* of sinful flesh." He "emptied himself, assuming the form of a servant" (Phil. 2:7). "Though he was rich, yet for our sake he became poor" (II Cor. 8:9). See also N.T.C. on Philippians, pp. 102–113.

d. and for sin.

Probable meaning: and in order to deal with sin.[210]

e. He condemned sin in the flesh, in order that the righteous requirement[211] of the law might be fulfilled in us.

---

209. For more on this subject of divine emotion see pp. 251, 276, 277, 287.
210. Though it must be granted that περὶ ἁμαρτίας can mean "For a sin-offering" (cf. Lev. 9:2), that sense would seem to be somewhat foreign to the present context.
211. Though the basic notion of justice or rightness is never absent, the various shades of meaning the word δικαίωμα has in the New Testament can be summarized as follows:
   a. righteous demand, requirement (Luke 1:6; Rom. 2:26; 8:4)
   b. righteous deed or act (Rom. 5:18; Rev. 15:4; 19:8)
   c. judicial ordinance, decree, sentence (Rom. 1:32)
   d. justifying sentence, justification (Rom. 5:16)
   e. regulation (Heb. 9:1, 10).

That righteous requirement is clearly indicated in such passages as Lev. 19:18b; Deut. 6:5; Mic. 6:8; Matt. 22:35-40 (cf. Mark 12:28-34; Luke 10:25-28). See also Matt. 23:23; Luke 11:42; Rom. 13:9.

It was in Christ's "flesh," his human nature, that God condemned and punished[212] the sins of his people. It was in his people's place that Jesus bore God's wrath. See Isa. 53:4-6, 8, 11b; Matt. 20:28; Mark 10:45; John 1:29; 10:11, 15; Rom. 5:6-9, 18, 19; II Cor. 5:21; Gal. 3:13. The purpose and result of Christ's work of redemption was that his people, by means of the operation of the Holy Spirit in their hearts and lives, should strive, are striving, to fulfil the law's righteous requirement. Out of gratitude for, and in response to, the outpouring of God's love, they now love God and their neighbor.

f. **who do not walk according to the flesh but according to the Spirit.**

Such devout conduct, being the result of the Holy Spirit's active indwelling, reveals "the fruit of the Spirit." The opposite way of life, that which is "according to the flesh" stems from men's sinful nature and is characterized by the acts associated with that nature. For both see Gal. 5:16-25. Does not the present passage give a hint with respect to the *obligation* voiced in verses 12, 13?

5-8. For those who live according to the flesh set their minds on the things of the flesh, but those who live according to the Spirit set their minds on the things of the Spirit. Now the mind of the flesh is death, but the mind of the Spirit is life and peace; because the mind of the flesh is hostility to God, for it does not submit to the law of God, nor can it do so. And those who are in the flesh cannot please God.

As the word "For" indicates, verse 5 (in a sense verses 5-8 considered as a unit) gives a further description of the two classes of people to whom reference was made in verse 4b: (a) those who walk according to the flesh (their existence *implied* in verse 4b), and (b) those who walk according to the Spirit (their existence *mentioned* in verse 4b).

Those who live according to the flesh allow their lives to be basically determined by their sinful human nature. They set their minds on—are most deeply interested in, constantly talk about, engage and glory in—the things pertaining to the flesh, that is, to sinful human nature.

Those who live according to the Spirit, and therefore submit to the Spirit's direction, concentrate their attention on, and specialize in, whatever is dear to the Spirit. In the conflict between God and sinful human nature the first group *sides with*[213] human nature; the second sides with God.

Paul is reminding the members of the church in Rome that it is impossible to be on both sides at once; that is, the *basic*—this adjective should be

---

212. Here the verb κατακρίνω clearly has the double meaning: to condemn and to punish; to sentence and to carry out that sentence. So also in I Cor. 11:32; II Peter 2:6.

213. φρονοῦσιν, 3rd per. pl. indicat. of φρονέω, to be minded; cf. φρήν, mind. To the Greeks τὰ 'Ρωμαίων φρονεῖν meant: to join the party of the Romans, to be on their side.

stressed!—disposition or direction of our lives is either on God's side or on the side of sinful human nature. If a person persists in being worldly, he is on the side of the world and must expect the world's *doom*. On the other hand, if the things concerning God and his kingdom are his *chief* concern, he can expect *life*: sweet communion with God, God's love shed abroad in the heart, joy unspeakable and full of glory, all this and far more forever and ever. See on 2:7, pp. 92, 93.

He can expect *peace*: the inner assurance that past sins are forgiven, that present events, no matter how painful, are being overruled for good, and that nothing that might occur in the future will be able to separate him from the love of God in Christ. Such peace means basic freedom from fear and from restlessness. It implies contentment, sense of security, inner tranquility.

Among the many passages of Scripture where peace is mentioned are Ps. 4:8; 37:37; 119:165; Isa. 26:3; 48:22 (cf. 57:21); Luke 1:79; 2:14; John 14:27; Rom. 5:1; 14:17; 15:13, 33; Phil 4:7, 12. See also the Pauline and Petrine opening salutations. Often, especially in the Old Testament, the line of demarcation between *peace* and *prosperity* or *well-being* is almost imperceptible; cf. Ps. 122:7.

When Paul says, ". . . but the mind of the Spirit is life and peace," does he mean that the believer is *never* disturbed? Does he intend to say that the Christian's heart and mind are *always* filled with *perfect* peace, and therefore, that the exclamation, "Wretched man that I am!" (7:24) could not have been uttered by the child of God?

The answer must be, "Not at all." Though the *basic* disposition of the person whose life is controlled by the Holy Spirit is indeed life and peace, this does not mean that such an individual is no longer deeply sorry for his sin and ardently wishing to be rid of it. *In fact, the more thoroughly he is under the Spirit's control, the knowledge of which gives him life and peace, the more also he will regret and fight against his still remaining sinfulness!*

The idea that the believer is a person who is always staying on an even keel should be given up. A believer's life is not that simple. It is tremendously complex. Are we willing to say that Simon Peter, the man who made the great confession (Matt. 16:16), was not a believer? Read what Jesus said about him (16:17). Nevertheless, it was Peter who afterward denied his Lord, and this not once but thrice!

And the writer of Ps. 77, was he not a believer? Yet, what a struggle he endured!

> The thought of God brought me no peace,
> But rather made my fears increase;
> With sleepless eyes and speechless pain
> My fainting spirit grieved in vain.
> The blessedness of long ago
> Made deeper still my present woe.

> Recalling days when faith was bright,
> When songs of gladness filled my night,
> I pondered o'er my grievous woes
> And searching questioning arose:
> Will God cast off and nevermore
> His favor to my soul restore?

The Lord answers his plea, so that his response is:

> These doubts and fears that troubled me
> Were born of my infirmity.
> Though I am weak, God is most high,
> And on his goodness I rely;
> Of all his wonders I will tell,
> And on his deeds my thoughts shall dwell.

Does this mean, then, that the believer is "a split personality"? When this term is used to indicate a personality structure composed of two or more behavior patterns, each apparently operating independently of the other(s), it would, of course, be improper to use it in connection with the present subject. And since we cannot always know in what sense this term is used, might it not be best to avoid it altogether in the present context?

However, according to the plain language of Scripture, and the testimony of ever so many Christians, even the believer may experience a tremendous struggle between "the old man" and "the new man," between doubt and trust, unrest and peace. In addition to Ps. 77 see also Ps. 73; Gal. 5:17; Eph. 4:22f.; 6:10f.; Heb. 12:4. To be sure, the Christian is comforted by Isa. 26:3, "Thou wilt keep him in perfect peace whose mind is stayed on thee," but during his earthly life the believer's mind is not always stayed on God. It is not always steadfast.

As long as Peter's faith was fixed on Jesus he was able to walk on water, "But when he saw the wind he was afraid and . . . cried out, 'Lord, save me!'" (Matt. 14:29, 30).

It is clear, therefore, that the interpretation of Rom. 7:14-25 which this interpreter, in common with many others and with the Evangelical Confessions, holds, must stand.

Nevertheless, when one compares the mind of unbelievers with that of believers, as Paul does in 8:5-8, the contrast is striking, for *basically* the mind of believers, that is, the mind of the Spirit, is life and peace. The very opposite is true with respect to the mind of unbelievers, a mind that is hostile to God. And since this is true, it stands to reason that the fruit of this mind or disposition is death (verse 6).

Such a mind is self-centered, which explains the fact that it does not submit itself to God's law. In fact, as long as it continues to concentrate its attention upon itself, it is, of course, not even able to submit to God. Those people who are "in the flesh," that is, who in their affections, purposes, thoughts, words, and deeds, are basically controlled by their sinful nature, are unable to please God.

It is interesting and instructive to note how often Scripture, especially Paul, describes the purpose of human life to be that of *pleasing God* (Rom. 12:1, 2; 14:18; I Cor. 7:32; II Cor. 5:9; Eph. 5:10; Phil. 4:18; Col. 3:20; I Thess. 4:1). Paul even exhorts *children* to obey their parents in everything "for this pleases the Lord" (Col. 3:20); as if to say, "It fills God's heart with delight." God's heart is not an iceberg! In this connection see what was said previously (p. 247), with reference to God sending "his own Son."

Paul, either explicitly or by implication, expresses his disapproval upon those who please not God but themselves. Cf. Rom. 15:3; I Thess. 2:15.

Like Paul, the apostle John also regards doing what is pleasing to God as being the true goal of the believers' life. He points out how God regards this kind of life (I John 3:22). And the author of Hebrews directs the attention of the readers to the fact that without faith it is impossible to please God (11:6).

From those who are "in the flesh" and therefore "cannot please God" (verse 8) Paul's attention now turns more directly to the members of the church to which he is writing. With the warmth of heart that is characteristic of a true pastor he addresses them as follows:

9-11. Y o u, however, are not in the flesh but in the Spirit, seeing that God's Spirit dwells in y o u. (Anyone who does not possess Christ's Spirit does not belong to Christ.) But if Christ is in y o u, though the body is dead because of sin, yet the Spirit is life because of (y o u r) justification. And if the Spirit of him who raised Jesus from the dead dwells in y o u, he who raised Christ from the dead will also impart life to y o u r mortal bodies through the Spirit, who dwells in y o u.

The meaning of the entire passage, viewed in light of the immediately preceding context, can be summarized as follows:

Y o u, by contrast, are not basically under the control of sinful human nature but of the Spirit. Y o u are therefore not unable to please God, since God's Spirit is dwelling in y o u. (Now if there should be anyone who shows by his life and actions that he does not possess the Spirit of Christ, such a person does not belong to Christ. He is not a Christian at all.) But if Christ is living in y o u, then, though because of sin the body must die, nevertheless, because y o u have been justified, the Spirit, himself Life, is alive within y o u. And if that Spirit, namely, the Spirit of him who raised Jesus from the dead, is dwelling in y o u, then he who raised Christ from the dead will, on the day of the resurrection, impart life also to y o u r mortal bodies. He will do it through the agency of the Spirit who is dwelling within y o u.

Brief comment on words and phrases:

a. "Y o u, however, are not in the flesh but in the Spirit . . ."

Lovingly Paul assures the addressees that, as far as the basic direction of their life is concerned, they are under the control not of sinful human nature but of the Spirit. This implies that, speaking collectively, they do not belong to the category of those concerning whom the apostle just now (verse 8) has stated that they cannot please God.

b. "seeing that God's Spirit dwells in y o u."

The rendering "if the Spirit of God dwells in y o u," as if Paul was not sure about the collective indwelling of the Holy Spirit in the hearts of these people, is incorrect. In view of what the apostle says about them in 1:6, 8; 15:14, such a low estimate on his part must be rejected.[214]

c. "(Anyone who does not possess Christ's Spirit does not belong to Christ.)" More literally: "(If anyone does not have the Spirit of Christ, he is not of his)."

Though, speaking collectively, the apostle has assured the Roman congregation that he regards it as being under the control of, and indwelt by, the Spirit, this does not mean that a church member can take his salvation for granted, in the sense that self-examination would no longer be necessary. Besides, in the church of Rome by no means everything was perfect. See 11:17-25; 14:10-15, 19; 15:1f.

Paul states that if anyone's life marks him as lacking Christ's Spirit, he has no right to consider himself a Christian.

Note in this verse the interchange of the designations "God's Spirit" and "Christ's Spirit." This certainly indicates that in Paul's thinking Christ was fully divine.

d. "But if Christ is in y o u, though the body is dead because of sin, yet the Spirit is life because of y o u r justification."

Meaning: not only is it true that because of sin the body of each of y o u is bound to die, but it is also true that because y o u are justified y o u can be assured of the fact that the Spirit, who is Life and life's Author, is dwelling within y o u.

The word *Spirit*, occurring in verse 10, should not be spelled with a small "s," as if the reference were to any person's invisible entity, but with a capital "S," for the apostle is definitely thinking of the Holy Spirit. Proof:

(1) In all the preceding eight instances of its use (verses 1-9) the word *pneuma* (Greek word for the divine *S*pirit as well as for the human *s*pirit) refers to the Holy Spirit. In verse 11 the apostle refers twice to this Spirit ("the Spirit of him who raised Jesus from the dead," "his Spirit who dwells in y o u"). It would be rather strange, then, if the intervening *pneuma* (here in verse 10) would have a different meaning.

(2) The *pneuma* of verse 10 is taken up again in verse 11. Note resem-

---

214. Besides, the word εἴπερ (=Latin si quidem) refers to a fulfilled condition. It can be rendered "seeing that," or "since," or "since indeed," or "if . . . as is certainly true." See the use of the same word in Rom. 3:30; 8:17; I Cor. 15:15; and see N.T.C. on II Thess. 1:6, p. 157.

blance: verse 11 refers to the life-imparting Spirit, naturally the Holy Spirit. This corresponds to "the *pneuma* of life" of verse 10.

(3) Also in verse 2 of the present chapter the Holy Spirit is called "the Spirit of life." Similarly in John 14:6 Jesus calls himself "the life."

e. "And if the Spirit of him who raised Jesus from the dead dwells in y o u, he who raised Christ from the dead will also impart life to y o u r mortal bodies through his Spirit, who dwells in y o u."

It is clear from verses 9-11 that the designations "Spirit," "*God's* Spirit," "*Christ's* Spirit," "the Spirit of him who raised Jesus from the dead," and "his Spirit who dwells in y o u," all refer to the same Holy Spirit. The variety of titles is by no means meaningless. It indicates the glorious unity existing between *Father, Son,* and *Holy Spirit,* a unity not only of *essence* (ontological oneness) but also of *operation* in the interest of our salvation.

Similarly John 14:26 informs us that *the Father* was going to send *the Holy Spirit;* John 16:7, that *the Son* would send him. There is no contradiction but glorious harmony. Note John 14:16, "I will ask the Father, and he will give y o u . . . the Spirit of truth." Also 14:26, "the Holy Spirit, whom the Father will send in my name."

In verse 11 the subject "He who raised Jesus—or Christ—from the dead," refers, of course, to the Father. Does it not also follow from such passages as Rom. 6:4; Gal. 1:1; and Eph. 1:20 that in the activity of raising the Savior from the dead it was the Father who, as it were, took the lead?

But note how very closely the two other persons of the Holy Trinity are related to the Father, hence also to each other. That the Father acts through the Spirit is plainly stated in verse 11. That even Jesus himself did not remain entirely passive in his resurrection is implied in John 10:17, 18. It is he who claims the power not only to lay down his life but also to take it up again. Moreover, the very One who in Rom. 8:11 is described as the Spirit *of the Father* is in verse 9 called *Christ's* Spirit. In fact, as it were in the same breath, *God's* Spirit is in verse 9 called *Christ's* Spirit. The relationship between Father, Son, and Holy Spirit is so close, the union so intimate and indissoluble, that it is impossible to dishonor the Son without also dishonoring the Father and the Holy Spirit. Cf. John 5:23.

This truth is filled with practical significance. We are living in an age in which in some evangelistic circles a disproportionate interest is shown in Jesus, as if honor and glory should be ascribed to *the Son* alone. Others, again, filled with the wrong kind of ecumenical fervor, the kind that aims at uniting all religious bodies into one huge world-church, minimize the work of the Savior and emphasize that all men are brothers, God being *the Father* of them all. And a third party, of late becoming more vocal, magnifies charismatic gifts, and cannot stop talking about *the Spirit.*

As Rom. 8:9-11 shows, and as Scripture throughout proves, it is God Triune, that is, Father, Son, and Holy Spirit, the one and only true God, who should be the central object of our love and worship.

253

12, 13. Therefore, brothers, we have an obligation, but it is not to the flesh, to live according to its standard. For if y o u live according to its standard y o u are doomed to die; but if, by the Spirit, y o u put to death the disgraceful deeds of the body, y o u will live.

At this point there is a transition from exposition to exhortation; from concentration on blessings bestowed by the Giver, to focusing on the obligation incurred by the recipients, including Paul himself.

However, the recipients are by no means represented as being able to act independently. Salvation is not a 50-50 affair. It is God's gift from start to finish. It is *by the Spirit* that God's children must put to death the disgraceful deeds of the body (verse 13), that they are being led (verse 14), and are being moved to cry, "Abba!" (verse 15). It is *from the Spirit* that they receive the assurance that they are indeed children of God (verse 16). But all this does not take away the fact that the recipients of these favors must go into action. They have an obligation to perform; nevertheless, they cannot do this in their own power. How then? As already indicated, "by the Spirit," and see also Phil. 2:12, 13.

The apostle calls attention to this obligation by saying, "Therefore," that is, in view of all the blessings *we* have received, are receiving, and are going to receive, stretching from one eternity to another (see verses 29, 30), *we*—note how he includes himself, a hint for pastors, etc.—have an obligation.

We do not owe this obligation to the flesh (corrupt human nature), however, to live according to its standard. That we owe the flesh no favors is clear from the fact that it was because of that very flesh that the law was unable to save us (8:3). In fact, having the mind or disposition of the flesh spells death (verse 6), a thought which Paul, in somewhat different phraseology, repeats in verse 13, by saying, "If y o u live according to its standard y o u are doomed to die."[215] So, instead of catering to the flesh, this enemy should be put to death. Has not the apostle already clearly stated this in 6:1, 6, 11, 12-14?

A rich reward is promised to those who "by the Spirit"—for they have no power of their own—put to death the disgraceful deeds[216] of the body: they *will live,* and this, of course, in the most glorious sense; see above, pp. 92, 93 on 2:7.

With Paul all this is not a piece of abstract theology, dry as dust. On the contrary, his heart is in his epistle. He loves these Romans, and desires most intensely to keep them from going astray. In fact, he also wants them to keep others from making the wrong choice. That his soul is, indeed, deeply

---

215. Note μέλλετε ἀποθνῄσκειν. The periphrastic future stresses the inevitability of their doom.

216. πράξεις, acc. pl. of πρᾶξις, here used in an unfavorable sense (cf. Luke 23:51; Acts 19:18), as is often the case with respect to the cognate verb πράσσω, see p. 232 on 7:15.

moved is clear from the fact that here again he makes use of the affectionate term of address "brothers" (verse 12). See what has been said about this word previously (pp. 214, 215).

Note the sharp contrast: those who are living according to the standard of the flesh are doomed to die. Those who by the Spirit are putting to death the disgraceful deeds of the body will live.

Scripture is full of illustrations of

The
Inescapable Alternative
Behold, I am setting before y o u today

a blessing	a curse (Deut. 11:26 f.)
life and prosperity	death and destruction (Deut. 30:15 f.)
building one's house on rock	building it on sand (Matt. 7:24-27)

Many other examples could easily be added. Among them would be those to which reference is made in such passages as Ps. 1; Matt. 25: 31–46; II Cor. 2:16; Gal. 5:19-22; I John 4:2, 3; Rev. 22:14, 15.

The fact to be emphasized is that the right choice must be made, for where a person will spend eternity is at stake. Even more important: whether a person's life will reach what should be its goal depends, in a sense, upon his decision (I Cor. 10:31; cf. I Cor. 7:32; Phil. 1:20, 21; I Thess. 4:1). "Choose for yourselves this day whom y o u will serve, whether the gods y o u r forefathers served beyond the River . . . but as for me and my household, we will serve the Lord" (Josh. 24:15).

Those, and those alone, who by the Spirit, put to death the disgraceful deeds of the body, are able to rejoice in the fact that they are being led by the Spirit, and therefore will truly live.

14. For as many as are being led by the Spirit of God, these are sons of God.

The connection between verse 13b and verse 14 is clear; note the word "For." In other words, the people who are putting to death the disgraceful deeds of the body are able to do so because they, being sons of God, are being constantly led by the Spirit of God.

Being Led by the Spirit

1. *Its Beneficiaries*
An illustration may be helpful. Whether the incident about to be related actually happened is not the point. One may have his own opinion about that. Suffice it to say that those who told the story were convinced of its historicity:

It was the year 1834 or shortly afterward. Religious persecution raged in The Netherlands. On one of these days, in the late afternoon, the faithful minister of village X was informed that a certain member of his congregation, a devout widow, was seriously ill and would welcome a pastoral call.

The minister decided not to wait until the next morning but to start out at once on foot. The path from the parsonage to the widow's home, a distance of about two miles, led through heavily wooded territory, where men intending to commit murder could easily conceal themselves. But the minister arrived safely at the widow's home. His call was deeply appreciated and greatly strengthened the sick lady.

On the way back to the parsonage ... nothing happened. Apparently there had been no ambush.

A few years passed by. Then one day two men, who through the faithful efforts of this very minister, had recently been brought from darkness to light, spoke to him as follows:

"Do you recall that a few years ago—it was on a Friday afternoon—you went to visit the widow living in the house on the other side of these woods?" When the minister answered affirmatively, they continued, "Who were those two men, in shining armor, walking on either side of you, guarding you?" The astonished minister replied, "I was alone, my friends; I was all by myself; either going or returning no one accompanied me." The two continued, "This is very strange, for we distinctly saw them. It made us afraid. So we hurried away. And now, having been brought to the knowledge of Christ through your ministry, how happy we are that we were prevented from carrying out our sinister plot."

Those who told the story were sure that this minister must have been one of the few very special "saints" of God who, being led by the Spirit, were the objects of exceptional divine protection.

However, this view, which in certain religious circles used to be rather popular—whether this is still the case I do not know—is certainly not what Paul had in mind when he wrote Rom. 8:14. The spiritual leading of which he speaks is definitely not the Spirit's gift to the select few. It concerns every Christian. Every child of God is being led by the Spirit. Everyone who is being led by the Spirit is a child of God.[217]

Those who are being led by the Spirit are the people who are described as being in Christ Jesus (8:1), walking according to the Spirit (verse 4), being Spirit-indwelt (verses 9, 11), and putting to death the disgraceful deeds of the body (verse 13).

2. *Its Nature*

What, then, does *the leading of the Spirit*—to change from the passive to the active voice—actually mean? It means sanctification. It is the constant, effective, and beneficent influence which the Holy Spirit exercises within

---

217. An excellent chapter on "The Holy Spirit and Guidance," written in a very interesting style, is found in E. H. Palmer's book *The Holy Spirit*, Grand Rapids, 1958, pp. 101–117.

the hearts and lives of God's children, enabling them more and more to crush the power of indwelling sin and to walk in the way of God's commandments freely and cheerfully.

The influence which the Holy Spirit exercises is:

a. Not sporadic but constant.

It is not being injected into the lives of God's children now and then, in moments of great need or danger. On the contrary, it is steady, constant, as even the tense here in Rom. 8:14 implies. Believers *are being led*[218] by the Spirit.

b. It is not (at least not primarily) protective but corrective.

In the entire context nothing is said about guarding God's children from receiving physical harm, nothing about keeping them out of danger when traveling. On the other hand, the immediately preceding context refers to putting to death the disgraceful deeds of the body, doing this "by the Spirit."[219]

c. It not merely directs but controls.

To be *led* by the Spirit means more than to be *guided* by him, though, to be sure, the Spirit is also our Guide (John 16:13). Cf. Matt. 15:14; Luke 6:39; Acts 8:31. But the leadership provided by the Spirit amounts to more than merely pointing out the right way. It reminds us not so much of the Indian guide who pointed out to the white explorers the pass through the Rockies, as of the people who led the blind man (of Jericho) to Jesus (Luke 18:40). Merely pointing out the way to him would not have helped him. When the Holy Spirit leads believers he becomes the controlling influence in their lives, bringing them at last to glory.

d. On the other hand, it does not stifle or repress but helps and encourages.

When the Holy Spirit leads God's child, the latter's responsibility and activity are not canceled or repressed. The blind man of Jericho *was not carried* to Jesus. He did his own walking. It is exactly as Warfield has pointed out: "Though it is indeed the Holy Spirit who keeps us in the path and brings us at last to the goal, it is we who tread every step of the way; our limbs that grow weary with the labor; our hearts that faint . . . our faith that revives our sinking strength, our hope that instills new courage into our souls, as we toil over the steep ascent."[220]

3. *Its Fruits*

These are so numerous that it would be impossible to mention them all. Accordingly, no attempt will be made to list them all, for this would be just as impossible as to

---

218. ἄγονται, third per. pres. (continuative) indicat. of ἄγω, here, as often, to lead.

219. By all means ask God to give you traveling mercy and guidance. But that is not the theme here in Rom. 8:14. *However, see on 15:30-33.*

220. *op. cit.,* p. 555.

> Count your many blessings
> Name them one by one.

It is for this very reason that in Gal. 5:22, 23 Paul, after stating, "Now the fruit of the Spirit is love, joy, peace, long-suffering, kindness, goodness, faithfulness, meekness, self-control," continues, "against *such* there is no law." He means, "The list I have given is incomplete; therefore I say, 'against *such*,' meaning: against *these and other* fruits." Another *summarizing* description of these fruits is certainly this one, "He who sows to . . . the Spirit will from the Spirit reap *life everlasting*" (Gal. 6:8), for who has ever been able to give a definition of life everlasting from which nothing is lacking? An orchard may contain a rich variety of fruit trees: orange, mango, tangelo, lemon, grapefruit, etc. However, each tree bears only one kind of fruit. The tree of grace, watered by the Spirit of life, bears *every* variety of spiritual fruit, and apart from that Spirit no spiritual fruit has ever been produced.

The fruit on which Paul's epistle to the Romans now rivets our attention is that of assurance of salvation, more precisely, that of *assurance of adoption as children of God:*

15, 16. For y o u have not received a spirit of slavery, to fill y o u once more with dread, but y o u have received the Spirit of adoption, who moves us to cry, "Abba!" that is "Father!" This Spirit himself bears witness with our spirit that we are children of God.

Blessed Assurance

One might summarize the meaning of this passage as follows: Y o u who are being led by the Spirit are not slaves but children. Having been adopted as *children,* y o u, of course, are no longer filled with the spirit of slaves, that of dread. No longer are y o u oppressed with fear as y o u were when y o u were still living in paganism or in Judaism, with their emphasis on all the rules one has to keep in order to be saved. On the contrary, y o u have received the Holy Spirit, who transforms slaves into children. That Spirit would not even think of filling y o u once more with dread. No, that Spirit fills us with the sense of freedom and confidence, so that, in approaching God, we utter the cry of joyful recognition, sweet response, overwhelming gratitude, and filial trust, "Abba!" (Father). In fact, that Spirit confirms that to which our own regenerated souls already bear witness, namely, that we, believers, are God's own children, having been adopted by him.

Among the various matters with respect to which opinions differ there are especially these three:

1. When the apostle mentions *adoption* did he have, in the background of his mind, (a) Greek-Roman or (b) Jewish adoption practices?

Those who favor the first alternative point out that "adoption," as a legal institution, did not even exist among the Hebrews, and that in the entire Old Testament the word never occurs. In the Roman world, on the other hand, the custom was rather common. Thus in his will Julius Caesar named Octavian (later called Emperor Augustus) his "son and heir." See N.T.C. on Luke, p. 137. On inscriptions the word "adopted son" occurs with great frequency.

It should be borne in mind, however, that (a) the *purpose* of this adoption practice was generally not philanthropic but egocentric: the perpetuation of property ownership and political and/or social privilege in the line of one's descendants, (b) its *beneficiaries* were males—legal adoption did not extend to females.

How completely different is the nature of adoption as pictured in the Old Testament. Instances of *essential*, though *not formal* or *technical, adoption* are indeed recorded in that sacred document. Did not Pharoah's daughter "adopt" Moses (Exod. 2:10), even though he was only a "humanly speaking" helpless child? Did not Mordecai bring up his cousin, *a girl* named Esther (Esther 2:7)? A *New Testament* passage which in a summarizing manner reproduces the teaching of the *Old Testament* regarding adoption—that is, *divine* adoption—is certainly II Cor. 6:17, 18:

> Come out from among them
> and be separate, says the Lord,
> And touch no unclean thing;
> And I will receive y o u,
> And I will be to y o u a Father,
> And y o u will be to me sons and daughters.

Note how beautifully this New Testament passage reflects the sense of the following passages: II Sam. 7:8, 14; Ps. 27:10; Isa. 43:6; and Hos. 1:10. Note especially that Isa. 43:6 as well as II Cor. 6:17, 18 mention both "sons *and daughters*" as the objects of God's adopting love.

It is clear, therefore, that when in Rom. 8:15 and Gal. 4:5 Paul uses the term "adoption" the *word* and the *legal standing* were borrowed from Roman practice, but the *essence* from the divine revelation in the Old Testament.

2. Is the outcry "Abba!" to be interpreted as the exclamation of the individual believer in addressing his God, or as the collective (perhaps congregational or liturgical) utterance of the church, gathered for worship?

A form of the word *Abba*, meaning "father," was originally used by small children. Later on its use became far more general. It was the very word uttered also by Jesus when, in deep agony, he, in the garden of Gethsemane, unburdened his soul to his Father in heaven (Mark 14:36). In this word filial tenderness, trust, and love find their combined expression.

It was, of course, a very personal word, that is, a word by means of which the intimate spiritual relationship between the believer and his God expresses itself. As such it reminds one of a line in a popular hymn,

> And the joy we share as we tarry there
> none other has ever known.

From *In the Garden*
by C. A. Miles

There are those who have criticized this hymn, and particularly this line. I believe, however, that this criticism is unfair. Is it not true that between each individual Christian and his God there exists a very personal relationship; or, expressing it differently, that God, in addition to loving and caring for his redeemed collectively, also enters into a uniquely personal fellowship with each of them, so that, prompted by the Holy Spirit (Gal. 4:6) the individual, in pouring out his heart, cries, "Father"?

Of course, the very personal use of this word in individual prayer, including *The Lord's Prayer* (in the original the first word; see Matt. 6:9), by no means excludes the possibility that it was also uttered collectively by the congregation, gathered for worship; just as even today we use The Lord's Prayer both collectively and individually.

Being a Hebrew of Hebrews (Phil. 3:5) Paul must have been fond of the language spoken by the Jews as they returned from the lands of their captivity, namely Aramaic, akin to Hebrew (cf. Acts 21:40). Aramaic, in fact, was a very important language in those days, spoken not only by the Jews, but by others besides, even by many people living far away from the borders of Palestine. Jesus too spoke Aramaic, and it is probable that in his frequent teaching about the Father he had often used the term *Abba*. His disciples therefore relished the use of this word. Thus it entered into the vocabulary of the primitive church. Naturally in writing to a church or to churches consisting of people who for the greater part were non-Jews, the word *Abba* had to be translated into the Greek word ὁ πατήρ (Father). Understandably Mark, addressing a Greek-speaking audience, wrote "Abba!" and quickly added the Greek word for "Father"; and so, probably for a similar reason did Paul.[221]

3. Does Rom. 8:16 mention one witness or two witnesses?

There are those who say that in reality Paul mentions only one witness or testifier, and that accordingly the correct rendering of verse 16 is, "The Spirit himself assures our spirit that we are children of God." Thus, or along this line, the Vulgate, Beck, Cranfield. The reasoning that lies at the root of this interpretation is that the verb used in the original, and generally rendered *to bear witness with*,[222] or *to testify in support of* (someone), can also mean *to assure*, and that our spirit in and by itself has no right to testify

---

221. Here (Rom. 8:15; cf. Mark 14:36; John 20:28) the articular nominat. form indicates the vocative. See Gram.N.T., p. 261.

222. συμμαρτυρεῖ, third per. s. pres. indicat. of συμμαρτυρέω.

to our being sons of God. However, in fairness to those who so argue, one should read what Cranfield himself says on pp. 402, 403 of his excellent commentary.

Fact is, however, that in each of the other instances in which Paul uses this verb there are two that bear witness: one testifies along with the other. Thus in Rom. 2:15 what is written on a man's heart is one witness; the other is the voice of his conscience. Similarly, in Rom. 9:1 Paul himself testifies that Israel's unbelief is for him a heavy burden. His conscience confirms this, and in so doing proves to be the second witness. I see no good reason, therefore, to depart from the rendering of Rom. 8:16 that has been adopted, with slight variations, by most translators, namely, "This Spirit himself bears witness with our spirit that we are children of God."

Just how the Spirit does this, Paul does not indicate. According to some, the Spirit testifies along with our regenerated consciousness by exerting a *direct* influence on heart and mind. See Gal. 4:6. Others insist that he works *by applying the Word* to the heart and mind of individual believers and also of the church viewed as a unit. See John 8:47; 16:13. Could not both positions be true?

In the midst of these debates and differences of opinion we are in danger of forgetting "the wonder of it all." Just think of it:

a. At the cost of the death—and what a death!—of his own Son, God decided to save *us*. (Did y o u notice how in 8:15 Paul makes the change, as he does often, from *y o u* to *we*?). See p. 217.

b. As if this were not enough, God even adopts us, so that we become his sons and daughters, his dear children (8:15).

c. His infinite and tender love extends even beyond this, for not only does he save us and make us his children but he also wants us to know that these great blessings have been bestowed upon us. By means of two witnesses he imparts to us this "blessed assurance" (8:16). *He saves, adopts, assures!*

"Behold what love the Father has lavished on us, that we should be called children of God! And that is what we are!" (I John 3:1).

And the glory of *sonship* expands very logically into that of *heirship,* as Paul now continues:

17. And if children, then heirs, heirs of God and fellow-heirs with Christ; since the fact that we are now sharing in his sufferings means that (hereafter) we shall share in his glory.

If Children, Then Heirs

The state of being a child implies that of being an heir, which, in turn, implies that there is an inheritance in store for us. That this inheritance is reserved for the future, Paul makes clear when he states, ". . . we shall share in his glory." In verses 11 and 13 the apostle had already kindled the hope of those whom he addresses. He had pointed to glories to come for both body and soul. He now enlarges on that theme. He tells us something about the Testator, the Inheritance, and the Heirs.

A. *The Testator*

If there is to be an inheritance there must be someone who bequeaths it. Our passage does not leave us in doubt with respect to the identity of this Testator. It reads "heirs of God," meaning, of course, that God is that Testator. Also, Christ is clearly the main Heir, and "we," says Paul, are fellow-heirs with Christ, destined, accordingly, to share in his glory.[223]

In looking forward to receive an inheritance, very much depends on the character of the testator. So we commonly ask, "What kind of person was the testator? When did he die? Was he rich or poor? Just or unjust?"

In the present case the answers are most encouraging. Earthly testators die. This means that a purely earthly inheritance is limited. When it is used up, no goods can be added. But the Testator whom Paul has in mind is "from everlasting to everlasting." Therefore our inheritance will not give out; in fact, will never even diminish.

Moreover, this Testator is rich. Not only is it true that all the silver and gold is his (Hag. 2:8), and that he owns every animal of the forest, and the cattle on a thousand hills (Ps. 50:10), but it is also a fact that his riches cannot even be measured. Also, so generous is he that whatever he demands of us he is eager to give us. For example, he demands that we repose our trust in him (John 3:16). This very trust or faith is also his gift to us. See N.T.C. on Ephesians, pp. 120-123 (on Eph. 2:8).

A very common item of human experience is dissatisfaction over the stipulations of a will. However, so just and fair is the Testator whom Paul has in mind that on that future day when God's children will take possession of their inheritance, they will be saying, "The boundary lines have fallen in pleasant places for me; indeed, a delightful inheritance is mine" (Ps. 16:6).

B. *The Inheritance*

Two facts with respect to this inheritance have already been made clear: (a) that it pertains to the future, and (b) that it consists of riches which we shall posssess "in connection with Christ."

That in full measure "the inheritance of the saints in the light" (Col. 1:12) is indeed a blessing that pertains to the future follows also from the fact that Rom. 8:18 speaks of a glory that "is to be revealed in us." It will, moreover, be a glory to which the whole creation looks forward (verse 19).

According to the book of Revelation *together with Christ* we shall inherit a new name (3:12) and a crown of gold (4:4; cf. 14:14). With him we shall reign (20:4). In fact, we shall even sit beside Christ on his throne (3:21). To be sure, all this is symbolic language. But do not these passages indicate that

---

223. Confusion arises when, since God is, in a sense, the believers' possession (Ps. 73:25, 26; Lam. 3:24), the idea that the apostle is viewing God as the believers' inheritance is injected into the interpretation of Rom. 8:17. As I indicate, *the context* points in a different direction. The inheritance here described pertains not to something or Someone we possess even now, but distinctly to the future.

the blessing of communion with Christ, which is our portion even now in principle, will be ours in a far higher degree then?

Moreover, this future bliss will not be confined to the soul. It definitely will pertain also to the body. We shall bear the image of the heavenly (I Cor. 15:49). For more on this see below, on verse 23.

Along with this transformation of soul and body we can look forward to the transformation of the universe. Creation itself will be set free from the bondage of corruption. See on verses 19–22.

What will make all this even more wonderful is the fact that, in close fellowship with the Savior, each of the redeemed will inherit these riches *together with all the others* (Eph. 3:18; II Tim. 4:8), and with the purpose of glorifying God Triune forever and ever.

Moreover, it should be emphasized that this future glory for soul and body, though indeed a gift of God's sovereign grace, is also *more than a gift.* It is *an inheritance,* which, in the present connection can imply no less than (a) that it will be the possession of God's children *by right,* that right having been established by Christ's self-sacrifice; and (b) that it is inalienable (I Peter 1:4; cf. I Kings 21:3, 4).

C. *The Heirs*

Paul says, "If *children,* then heirs."

If children, not "*if enemies.*" Even among those who wish to be regarded as believers there are those who actually are "enemies of the cross of Christ" (Phil. 3:18). As long as they remain enemies the inheritance is not for them.

If children, not "*if slaves.*" There are those who serve Christ outwardly, not inwardly, not motivated by love and trust, not wholeheartedly. Think of the Galatians (Gal. 3:1 f.), of Ananias and Sapphira (Acts 5:1), of Demas (II Tim. 4:10), and of Diotrephes (III John 9).

If "*children*" then heirs; otherwise not. This is also entirely in line with Christ's teaching (Luke 18:17).

But how do I know that I am a child? In light of the present passage the answer is, "I know that I am a child if I am willing, when necessity demands, to endure suffering for the sake of Christ." (See Matt. 5:11, 12; 10:22, 39; 24:9; Mark 8:35, 13:13; I Peter 4:16).

When we suffer *as Christians,* then Christ's afflictions overflow toward us, as the following passages clearly indicate: Matt. 10:25; John 15:18-21; Acts 9:4, 5; II Cor. 1:5, 10; Gal. 6:17; Phil. 3:10; I Peter 4:13. We can add nothing to Christ's redemptive suffering for us, but by means of our willingness to suffer for his sake we are drawn closer to the Savior's heart.

Paul assumes that *the church* he is addressing is indeed willing to suffer for Christ, just as the apostle himself is also constantly enduring such affliction. That is why he states, ". . . since the fact that we are now sharing in his suffering means that hereafter we shall share in his glory."[224] But let every *individual member* answer for himself the question, "Am I willing to suffer *as a Christian?*" Could it be that the reason why some boldly affirm, "I have

---

224. Note here again εἴπερ, as in verse 9. See footnote 214 on p. 252.

never suffered for Christ," is that they are such poor Christians . . . if Christians at all?

Suffering as a Christian takes many forms. It does not mean that our experience has to be that of a Polycarp or a John Huss. Today a believer may lose his job because he refuses to perform unnecessary work on the Lord's Day. Or because he says No when he is being tempted to participate in a crooked business deal, or makes up his mind not to marry an unbeliever, or insists on honoring the Word of God in the classroom. How many have not been expelled from positions in school, church, or government because of their stand for the truth?

It is comforting to know that all who share in Christ's suffering will at last hear from his lips the welcoming words, "Well done, good and faithful servants. Enter into my rest."

18. For I consider that the sufferings of this present time are not worthy to be compared with the glory that is to be revealed in us.

SUFFERING AND GLORY
A COMPARISON

The conjunction "For" indicates that what follows is a further explication and amplification of the *glory* to which reference was made in the preceding verse.

A. *The Two Elements Compared*

"I consider (or reckon)," says Paul, making use of an understatement,[225] for what he actually means is, "I am firmly convinced."

Of what is he firmly convinced? Of the fact that the sufferings of this present time are not worthy to be compared with the glory that is to be revealed in us. It is clear that the apostle is, as it were, holding in his hand a scale or balance. As always, it has two scalepans. In the one pan he places "the sufferings of this present time"; in the other "the glory that is to be revealed in us."

The first (sufferings) is a result of sin. Had there been no sin, human beings would not have had to suffer (Gen. 3:16–19). The second (glory) is the result of grace. As far as God's children are concerned, the first is temporal, the second never-ending.

What kind of sufferings does Paul have in mind? Those experienced as a result of our relation to Christ? Such sufferings are certainly included. Otherwise there would be no connection between verses 17 and 18. Nevertheless, it is not advisable to limit the word "sufferings" as here employed,

---

225. The verb is λογίζομαι, cf. λόγος in the sense of *account;* hence, to take into account (Love does not take into account a suffered wrong, I Cor. 13:5); and so: to reckon, consider, regard, etc. Sometimes even: to impute a quality to a person which in and by himself he does not possess; see above, p. 147, on Rom. 4:3.

to such afflictions. As verses 19-23, 28, 38, 39 clearly indicate, other afflictions are also included. The apostle is thinking of sufferings in general; therefore also including pain (physical as well as mental), sickness, disappointment, unemployment, poverty, frustration, etc. This follows too from the fact that he uses the very broad expression "the sufferings of this present time," that is, "of this present age," the "time" or "age" which extends to, and ends with, Christ's second coming.[226]

And what about the glory of which Paul speaks? Is he referring to the blessings of the intermediate state; that is, the beatific joys which the souls of the redeemed begin to experience the very moment they breathe their last? That this intermediate state is real, and that at this very moment the departed dear ones who died "in the Lord" are participating in its activities I have tried to prove in my book *The Bible on the Life Hereafter,* Grand Rapids, 1959. See especially pp. 53-57. However, that cannot be what Paul has in mind here in Rom. 8:18. Verses 19 and 23 make very clear that he is referring to what will transpire at the time of "the revelation of the sons of God," and of "the redemption (glorious resurrection) of our bodies"; in other words, at the time of Christ's Return.

Significant is also the fact that the apostle, in dictating this letter, did not say "the glory that is to be revealed *to* us," but "the glory that is to be revealed *in* us." In other words, this glory will, as it were, come to us, enter us, and then, having filled us and enveloped us, will be revealed in us. We ourselves will be part of that glory: the redeemed will see it in each other. The angels will behold it in us, and will be filled with thanksgiving and praise to God.

B. *The Result of This Comparison*

"I consider that the sufferings of the present time are not worthy to be compared with the glory that will be revealed in us," says Paul; that is, the pan in which the glory has been deposited outweighs the other one by so much that the heavier pan drops to the bottom immediately. Our present sufferings, be they ever so many and severe, fade into insignificance when compared with our future glory.

C. *The Reason for This Comparison*

The very strategically situated church of Rome, surrounded by dangers and enemies (16:3, 4, 17-20), was in need of encouragement. The present passage richly supplies it.

In reflecting on the glory to be revealed *in* us, as well, of course, as *to* us,

---

226. Mark 10:30 makes clear that the terms *time* (καιρός) and *age* (αἰών) are synonyms: the *now* or *present* time = the *now* or *present* age; and the *coming* time = the *coming* age. One might call these expressions "technical terms." See also Matt. 12:32; Luke 16:8; 20:34, 35; Rom. 12:2; Gal. 1:4; Eph. 1:21.

we realize that the reality will by far surpass our *fondest* expectations. Mrs. Elizabeth Mills was surely correct when she wrote:

> We speak of the land of the blest,
> A country so bright and so fair,
> And oft are its glories confest,
> But what must it be to be there?

Especially to be there, in redeemed soul and body, at Christ's glorious Second Coming and forever afterward!

19-22. For the creation, with outstretched head, is eagerly looking forward to the revelation of the sons of God. For it was not by its own choice that the creation was subjected to futility, but (it was) because of him who subjected it, in hope, because the creation itself too will be set free from its bondage to decay, so as to share the glorious liberty of the children of God. For we know that the whole creation, with one accord, has been, and still is, groaning as in the pain of childbirth.

THE THREE GROANINGS

The word "For" is understandable: the glory to be revealed (verse 18) is so marvelous that the (whole) creation is eagerly looking forward to it (verses 19-22), we ourselves are ardently awaiting it (verses 23-25), the Spirit too joining us (verses 26, 27). All three (creation, we, the Spirit) groan as in childbirth, hopefully looking forward to the birth of the promised glory. We might say, therefore, that "For" introduces *The Three Groanings*. It continues the discussion of the subject (future glory) that had already been mentioned, a very common use of "For."

A. *Creation's Groaning*

What is here three times called "the creation" is finally (in verse 22) called "the whole creation." How much does it include? It cannot include the good angels, since they were never subjected to futility (verse 20) and never succumbed to corruption or decay (verse 21). Satan and his demons are also ruled out, for they will never be set free (II Peter 2:4; Jude 6). This holds also for all those people who will never be saved, the non-elect (II Thess. 1:8, 9). And the elect are not included *here,* for they are here treated as a separate group. We are told that the creation is looking forward to the revelation of the sons of God, implying that creation's deliverance from the bondage of corruption will take place at the time when the revelation of God's children will occur. Besides, what the elect are doing and what is going to happen to them is described in verses 23-25.

With the exclusion of all these four groups, what is left is the animate and inanimate irrational creation. One might call it the sub-human creation or simply Nature.

We are told, therefore, that this remaining "whole creation" is, with outstretched head,[227] eagerly looking and watching for the revelation of the sons of God. It is, as it were, craning its neck to see this.

When the question is asked, "But how is it possible for birds and plants to show such intense interest in what will happen to God's children, the answer might well be, "If, according to Scripture, trees can rejoice (Ps. 96:12), floods can clap their hands (Ps. 98:8), the wilderness can be glad (Isa. 35:1), and mountains and hills can burst into song (Isa. 55:12), why should not birds and plants be able to look forward with longing? As is clearly evident, we are dealing here with *personification*.

However, that answer is incomplete. More must be added: (a) that the restoration of the animate and inanimate irrational creation is intimately related to "the revelation of the sons of God." The two are linked together, so that restoration and glory for "the sons of God" implies the same for "the whole creation." And (b) that it will most certainly take place.

Beautiful and very meaningful is the phrase "the revelation of the sons of God.[228] It indicates that not until the day of Christ's Return will it become a matter of public knowledge how much God loves them and how richly he rewards them. "Then, in the kingdom of their Father, the righteous will shine as the sun" (Matt. 13:43), "as the brightness of the firmament and as the stars forever and ever" (Dan. 12:3). They will be on exhibition, so that all will be able to see what God has wrought for and *in* them.

The whole creation is looking forward eagerly for the revelation of the sons of God because that event will also mean glory for the whole creation. We must bear in mind that "it was not by its own choice"—hence, was not its own fault—that the creation was made subject to futility. It was not the irrational creation that sinned. It was man. And the One who subjected the creation to futility was God. It was he who, because of man's sin, pronounced a curse on . . . what or on whom? Well, in a sense on creation, but in an even deeper sense upon man:

> Cursed is the ground because of you;
> In toil you will eat of it
> All the days of your life.
> Thorns and thistles it will produce for you,
> And you will eat the plants of the field.
> By the sweat of your brow
> you will eat your food

---

227. Note ἀποκαραδοκία = ἀπό, away from κάρα, head; δοκία, cf. δοκέω, meaning (in Ionian) *to watch.r*

228. That in all such cases the word υἱός, son, has nothing to do with sex (male or female), and amounts to τέχνον, child, is clear from a comparison of passages: those who, in one passage, are called *sons* are, in another passage, called *children*. Cf. our present passage with verse 16. *If* there is any shade of difference at all in such cases, it would be that *sons* emphasizes legal standing; *children*, (spiritual) offspring.

until you return to the ground,
because from it you were taken;
For dust you are,
and to dust you will return.

Gen. 3:17-19

So, since creation's humiliation was not its fault, as the passage specifically states, it will certainly participate in man's restoration. Nature's destiny is intimately linked up with that of "the sons of God." That is why the whole creation is represented as craning its neck to behold the revelation of the sons of God.

Note the expression, "The creation was subjected to futility." A.V. reads "to vanity." However, when this word is interpreted as meaning *inflated pride*, it has nothing to do with the present passage. The word used in the original does not refer to ambitious display. It indicates that since man's fall Nature's potentialities are cribbed, cabined, and confined. The creation is subject to arrested development and constant decay. Though it aspires, it is not able fully to achieve. Though it blossoms, it does not reach the point of adequately bearing fruit. It may be compared to a very powerful world-champion boxer or wrestler, who is chained in such a manner that he cannot make use of his tremendous physical prowess. The curse of plant disease decimates the crops. The loss is estimated at many millions of dollars for each separate disease. Plant pathologists direct their efforts toward developing methods of disease *prevention* or at least *reduction* or *control*. And, in a modified sense, what is true with respect to the world of plants holds too for the animal sphere.

What a glorious day that will be when all the restraints due to man's sin will have been removed, and we shall see this wonderful creation reaching self-realization, finally coming into its own, sharing in "the glorious liberty of the children of God!"

That this hope is not unrealistic is shown by the words, "in hope, because[229] the creation itself too will be set free . . ."

Paul compares the earnest yearning and eager forward looking of creation to the groaning of a woman who is in the process of giving birth to a child.[230] To be sure, such groaning indicates suffering, but it also implies hope. As Calvin reminds us, these groans are birth-pangs, not death-pangs. The addition "with one accord" or "together" indicates that every division of this "whole creation" participate in these birth-pangs.

---

229. Is the true text ὅτι (A B C etc.) or διότι (D* F G)? If the latter, the meaning is probably *because*, though even διότι can mean *that*. If the true reading is ὅτι, the choice between *because* and *that* is about even. In the present case making the right decision is not important since either reading introduces a clause that is true to fact and harmonizes with the context.

230. The two third per. s. pres. indicatives he uses are συστενάζει and συνωδίνει. They rhyme, as do groaning and moaning. Meaning: "is groaning and travailing"; but the two form a unit: hence, "has been, and still is (note ἄχρι τοῦ νῦν) groaning as in the pain of childbirth."

Does the rest of Scripture furnish any further information about the meaning of Nature's future deliverance from bondage and participation in the glorious liberty of God's children?

Indeed, it does! It informs us that the universe is going to be purged by *a great conflagration* (II Peter 3:7, 11, 12).

Closely linked with this conflagration there is going to be a *rejuvenation*. The fire will not destroy the universe. It will still be the same heavens and earth, but gloriously renewed, and in that sense *a new heaven and earth* (II Peter 3:13; Rev. 21:1–5). Accordingly, not only will we be going to heaven, but heaven will, as it were, come down to us; that is, the conditions of perfection obtaining in heaven will be found throughout God's gloriously rejuvenated universe.

We can also view this wonderful transformation as a *self-realization*, as has been explained. See above, p. 268.

Finally, this transformation will include *harmonization*. At present Nature can be described as being "raw in tooth and claw." Peace and harmony are lacking. Various organisms seem to be working at cross purposes: they choke each other to death. But then there will be concord and harmony everywhere. There will be variation, to be sure, but a most delightful blending of sight and sound, of life and purpose, so that the total effect will be unity and harmony. The prophecy of Isa. 11:6–9 will reach ultimate fulfilment:

> The wolf will dwell with the lamb,
> And the leopard will lie down with the goat,
> And the calf and the young lion and the yearling together,
> And a little child will lead them.
> The cow and the bear will graze,
> The young will lie down together,
> And the lion will eat straw like the ox.
> And the nursing child will play near the hole of the cobra,
> And the weaned child will put his hand into the viper's nest.
> They will not hurt or destroy in all my holy mountain,
> For the earth will be full of the knowledge of the Lord
> As the waters cover the sea.

23–25. Not only this, but also we ourselves, who possess the firstfruits of the Spirit, even we ourselves groan within ourselves, as we eagerly await our adoption, that is, the redemption of our bodies. For it was in hope that we were saved; but when once something hoped for is seen it is no longer an object of hope, for who hopes for what he sees? But since we hope for that which we do not see, we wait for it with patient endurance.

B. *Our Own Groaning*

Not only does the whole subhuman creation groan, but so do also "we ourselves," says Paul, thus including himself, as well as those whom he

269

addresses, in the sphere of those who groan. When he adds "who possess the first fruits of the Spirit" does he mean, "We groan *even though* we possess," etc. or "*because* we possess," etc.? Either would make excellent sense. He may have meant, "Even though we are already so rich, we are reaching out for riches even more precious." Or he may have intended to convey the thought, "Since we already have the Spirit, we are convinced that more, much more, is still in store for us. We are therefore eagerly yearning to receive it." In view of the fact that we are not sure which of these alternatives was uppermost in the apostle's mind, it may well be best, *in our translation,* to leave the participle exactly as it is, namely, *having* or *possessing.* Personally I, along with many other commentators, rather favor the concessive interpretation, since it seems to harmonize best with the idea of *great surprise* implied in the emphatic introduction, "also we ourselves . . . even we ourselves,"[231] as if to say, "Though we have already received so much, we are still groaning within ourselves for more."

Paul says, "we ourselves, who possess the firstfruits of the Spirit." What does he mean?

From Exod. 23:19; Deut. 18:4, and other passages, we learn that the Israelites were told to offer to God the firstfruits of the soil (grain, wine, oil), and even of the wool from the shearing of the sheep. But the reverse is also a fact. God too gives firstfruits. He gives the firstfruits of the Spirit, so that Paul could state that he himself and those whom he addresses are now in possession of this blessing.[232]

Was the apostle referring to a certain supply of the Spirit that had been poured out so far, with more of the Spirit to follow later? See L.N.T. (A. and G.), p. 81, an opinion that is rather popular, especially among people who frequently refer to "the second blessing." It is, however, erroneous.

There is no reason to doubt that the apostle, here in Rom. 8:23, is referring to *the Holy Spirit himself.* That Spirit is himself the firstfruits or pledge of subsequent salvation in all its fulness, in store for God's children at Christ's Return. There is no reason to believe that Paul refers to one thing in Eph. 1:13, 14, and to something else here in Rom. 8:23.[233]

"Also we ourselves . . . even we ourselves groan within ourselves, as we eagerly await our adoption, that is, the redemption of our bodies." How is it to be understood that even Christians groan? Is it not reasonable to assume that the groaning of God's children resembles that of Nature (verse 22)? If then the groaning of the whole creation consisted of two elements, namely,

---

231. This surprise element is lost in the rendering, favored by some, which, rather arbitrarily, it would seem to me, abbreviates the original into the mere "Not only so, but we ourselves."

232. In addition to "the firstfruits of the Spirit" (Rom. 8:23) the New Testament mentions: the firstfruits of dough (Rom. 11:16); firstfruits = first convert (Rom. 16:5; I Cor. 16:15); Christ as firstfruits of those who fell asleep (I Cor. 15:20, 23); firstfruits of creatures (James 1:18); and the 144,000, offered as firstfruits to God (Rev. 14:4). See also N.T.C. on I and II Thessalonians, pp. 187, 188, on II Thess. 2:13.

233. So also Ridderbos, *op. cit.,* p. 188; and J. Behm (on ἀρραβών, Th.D.N.T., Vol. I, p. 475).

(a) experiencing pain and (b) looking forward in hope, we may conclude that the same holds also for those who possess the firstfruits of the Spirit, God's dear children.

Is Paul thinking of the fact that Christians realize that they are still very imperfect? So sinful that at times they cry out, "Wretched man that I am, Who will rescue me from this body of death?" (Rom. 7:24)? That they are indeed imperfect is clear from Scripture throughout. Nevertheless, the present context—think especially of the combination *pain* and *hope*—points also in a different direction. The very fact that God's children even now possess—that is, are indwelt by—the Holy Spirit, arouses within them a painful sense of lack. What they already have makes them hungry for more; that is, for salvation in all its fulness. It is in this sense that pain and hope are here combined.

Even now believers have been adopted as God's sons (8:15, 16). But, in another sense, they are still waiting for their adoption. They are waiting for the public display of their standing as children of God. As of right now their bodies are still subject to death. But one day their souls will have been completely delivered from sin, and their bodies will have become transformed, so that they will resemble the glorious body of the Lord Jesus Christ himself. To that great day they now look forward *in hope* (Rom. 8:11; I Cor. 15:50-55; II Cor. 5:2, 3; Phil. 3:21; I John 3:2).

Verse 24 takes up this subject of the Christian's hope. The translation of this verse in the A.V. is, however, not the best (to put it mildly). It is as follows:

"For we are saved by hope; but hope that is seen is not hope: for what a man seeth, why doth he yet hope for?"

We naturally ask, "Has Paul changed his theology? Did he not always tell us that we were saved *by faith* (Rom. 1:16, 17; 3:22, 26, 28, 31; 4:5, 11, 12, 16, 20, 24; 5:1, 2), and is he not going to confirm this same truth later on (Eph. 2:8)? Yet here I read that we are saved *by hope!* Besides, what does the apostle mean when he mentions "hope that is seen"? How can a person see hope?

In order to understand Rom. 8:24 we should start out by affirming that the rendering "We are saved by hope" is wrong. Paul wrote "in hope." What he meant was that when, sometime in the past (probably at different dates for each person) we *were* saved, that salvation was not delivered to us complete in one package. It did not arrive "cut and dried." On the contrary, it came to us "with a promise of more to follow." Such elements included in salvation, as election, calling, regeneration, basic conversion, faith, justification, and even, in part, sanctification, had already occurred. Still to come were further progress in sanctification, and finally, at death, and even more fully at Christ's Return, glorification. It is clear, therefore, that Paul could write, "We were saved *in hope.*"

Christian hope, however, must be distinguished from the "hope" we speak about in daily life. Such hope often amounts to no more than a desire that something nice may happen to us, plus a belief that it might just take place. In fact, such hope can frequently be defined as "that which precedes disappointment." Its picture is at times that of a drowning man grasping at a straw. But Christian hope is "an anchor for the soul, safe and sure, entering into the inner sanctuary, behind the curtain, where Jesus has gone as a forerunner on our behalf." (Heb. 6:19, 20).

As to the rest of the verse (24), everything becomes clear when we realize that the word *hope* can have three different meanings. It can indicate (a) *a feeling* or even *a conviction* that what is desired will take place; (b) *the person* who is considered able to make it take place, as in "Our Hope for years to come," and (c) *the thing* hoped for. It would seem that in Greek this last meaning is more common than in English. So we translate the remainder of verse 24 as follows:

"But when once something hoped for is seen, it is no longer an object of hope, for who hopes for what he sees?"[234]

The truth here expressed is obvious: when that for which a person was hoping has arrived, and is now standing or lying in front of him, so that he sees it (implying: and can take hold of it), it ceases to be an object of hope.

Paul is emphasizing the necessity of making use of the anchor of hope. He is, as it were, saying, "Just as *faith* is necessary to appropriate the salvation which Christ merited for y o u in the past, so *hope* is necessary to take to yourselves future blessings. Those bounties are reserved for all who humbly confess their shortcomings and rely wholly on God, the Merciful Giver. Remember, y o u were saved 'in hope.'"

The present-day practical application is clear. There are those who seem to think that they have already arrived. They believe that the petition "Forgive us our debts, as we also have forgiven our debtors" (Matt. 6:12) was not meant for them. Perhaps they also believe that they have received "the second blessing" and are therefore superior Christians. There are even those who make propaganda for the error that also the body is already perfect, sickness being a figment of the imagination. Any future "redemption of the body" (8:23) has little significance for them. To them all Paul is, as it were, saying, "Y o u have done away with the biblical doctrine of salvation *in hope*, for how can one hope for what he already has ... or thinks he has?"

The objection might be raised, "But the apostle was not living in our day. Was there any reason why he felt it to be necessary *in this epistle* to stress the importance of hope, in the life of the believer? Are we able to prove that there were people in the Roman church who considered themselves *strong*, and able, accordingly, to dispense, at least to some extent, with *hope*, since they had already arrived?"

The answer is in the affirmative. By and large the Roman church ranked

---

234. The reading of P[46]B* is followed here, being the shorter.

high in Paul's estimation. See 1:8; 15:14. But there were exceptions, as the following passages indicate:

"Do not think too highly of yourself" (12:3).

"You, then, why do you judge your brother?" (14:10).

"Therefore let us stop passing judgment on one another" (14:13).

"We who are strong ought to bear with the failings of the weak, and not to please ourselves" (15:1).

The conclusion is truly beautiful: "But since we hope for that which we do not see, we wait for it with patient endurance."[235]

This reminds us of a similar Pauline passage, namely, "We fix our eyes not on the things that are seen, but on the things that are not seen; for the things that are seen are temporal, but the things that are not seen are eternal" (II Cor. 4:18). In the meantime:

> Ye fearful saints, fresh courage take;
> The clouds ye so much dread
> Are big with mercy and shall break
> In blessings on your head.
>
> His purposes will ripen fast,
> Unfolding every hour,
> The bud may have a bitter taste,
> But sweet will be the flower.
>
> William Cowper, 1772

26, 27. And in the same way the Spirit too is helping us in our weakness, for we do not know what we ought to pray, but the Spirit himself intercedes for us with unspoken groanings. And he who searches the hearts knows what is the Spirit's intention, that he is interceding for the saints in harmony with God's will.

C. *The Spirit's Groanings*

Having discussed the groaning of the creation (verses 19–22) and of God's children (verses 23–25), Paul now introduces the groanings of the Spirit (verses 26, 27). He tells us something about their (a) necessity, (b) Author and character, and (c) effectiveness.

1. *Their Necessity*

The apostle points to "our weakness," human limitation due to sinfulness. That weakness consists, at least in part, in this, that "we do not know

---

235. δι' ὑπομονῆς (gen. of attendant circumstance). For the noun see also 2:7; 5:3, 4; 15:4, 5; cf. footnote 142 on p. 170. In view of the context (see especially verse 23), "patient endurance" is probably the best translation. The apostle was thinking of *the power to bear up persistently under stress.* This patient endurance is accompanied by *ardent longing;* for note also ἀπεκδεχόμεθα, first per. pl. pres. indicat. of ἀπεκδέχομαι, which, by means of its double prefix, emphasizes the ardent character of the believers' waiting. This recalls to our minds a form of the same verb in verse 19, but there with the addition of "with outstretched head."

what we ought to pray." We are not sure about the prayer content that is in harmony with God's will (see verse 27). By saying "we" the apostle is including himself.

It may seem strange for a man of Paul's stature to make this admission. How was it possible for this marvelous missionary, ardent lover of souls, divinely inspired author, to make such a statement? With the exception of the prayers of Jesus Christ, is there anything in the line of prayer more thought-filled, fervent, and sublime than the apostle's prayer recorded in Eph. 3:14-19?

The solution is probably along this line: Paul certainly knew what the general content of prayer should be. He knew that one should pray for the forgiving spirit, for peace among the members of the church, increase in knowledge of spiritual things, readiness to bear witness for Christ, courage amid affliction and persecution, helpfulness toward all who are in need, gratitude toward God; in fact, all the fruits of the Spirit (see Gal. 5:22, 23). But what to pray for *in any particular difficulty* or *situation* was not always clear.

A good illustration is the incident recorded in II Cor. 12:7, with reference to "the thorn in the flesh." Exactly what that thorn may have been no one knows. What we do know is that the apostle found it to be very bothersome. So he prayed, "Lord, please remove that thorn." Three times he uttered this prayer. He seems to have been of the opinion that the removal of the thorn would make him *a more powerful* witness for Christ. But God's answer was, "My grace is sufficient for you, for *my power* is perfected *in weakness.*" And see also Phil. 1:22-24.

Another illustration taken from life runs as follows: A pastor, loved by his people, became grievously ill. The congregation prayed, "Lord, please restore him to health." But he died. At the funeral a minister who had been a lifelong friend of the departed made this remark to the assembled mourners, "Perhaps some of you are in danger of arriving at the conclusion that the heavenly Father does not hear prayer. He does indeed hear prayer, however. But in this particular case two prayers were probably opposing each other. Y o u were praying, 'O God, spare his life, for we need him so badly.' *The Spirit's* unspoken prayer was , 'Take him away, for the congregation is leaning altogether too heavily upon *him*, not upon *thee.*' And the Father heard that prayer."

If the objection should be raised, "Then why not permit the Holy Spirit to do all the praying? Why should *we* pray at all?," the answer would be: (a) a child of God needs to, and wants to, pour out his heart to God in prayer and thanksgiving; (b) the Holy Spirit prays only in the hearts of those who pray; (c) God has commanded his people to pray and has promised to grant all such requests as are in harmony with his will; and (d) there must be many prayers which do not need to be counteracted by the Holy Spirit.

The words, "the Spirit is helping us in our weakness" must not be interpreted too narrowly, as if the meaning would be that the Spirit only helps us *to pray.* He helps us "in our weakness," of whatever nature that weakness may be, including our weakness in prayer.

2. *Their Author and Character*[236]

How does the Spirit help us? The answer is, "The Spirit himself intercedes for us with unspoken groanings." What do these words mean?

The most obvious interpretation, the one which the person unaquainted with doctrinal presuppositions would be most likely to adopt is certainly this, that *these unspoken words are those of the Spirit.*

Not all interpreters agree with this conclusion, however. In order to prove their contention that these groanings are those of the saints, not those of the Holy Spirit, an appeal is made to Gal. 4:6, where the same apostle states, "And because y o u are sons, God sent forth the Spirit of his Son into our hearts, crying, 'Abba! Father!'" The further reasoning is as follows, "Even though Paul seems to be saying that *the Spirit* is crying 'Abba! Father!' he cannot mean this, for God cannot be the Father of the Holy Spirit. Therefore, it must be true that the cry is uttered not by the Spirit but *by God's children,* although through the Spirit. The same must be true here in Rom. 8:26b: the groanings, though ascribed to the Spirit, who may well be their Author, are actually those of God's children. It is they who groan."

With due respect for those who so reason, I must, nevertheless, disagree. The appeal to Gal. 4:6 is not conclusive. Note the following meaningful differences, which at the same time are reasons for believing that the groanings are those of the Spirit:

1. Here in Rom. 8:26b Paul does *not* say, "the Spirit intercedes for us." He says, "The Spirit *himself*[237] intercedes for us with groanings," etc. There is therefore a real difference between Gal. 4:6 and Rom. 8:26b.

2. In order to make his meaning even more unambiguous, the apostle continues in verse 27 by saying, "And he who searches the hearts knows

---

236. The following Greek words are in need of some comment: ὡσαύτως, in the same way; similarly (Matt. 20:5; 21:30, 36; 25:17; Mark 12:21; 14:31; Luke 13:5; 20:31; 22:20). Paul uses it also in I Cor. 11:25, and 6 times in the Pastorals, beginning with I Tim. 2:9

συναντιλαμβάνεται, third per. s. pres. middle indicat. of συναντιλαμβάνομαι, to take hold of along with someone, to help. See N.T.C. on Luke 10:40, p. 603.

προσευξώμεθα, first per. pl. aor. middle deliberative subjunctive (after an indirect question) of προσεύχομαι, to pray.

ὑπερεντυγχάνει, third per. s. pres. indicat. of ὑπερεντυγχάνω basically: *to come upon* (or meet) and speak or act *in behalf* of (ὑπέρ); to intercede.

στεναγμοῖς, dat. pl. of στεναγμός, groaning, sighing. Cf. German *stönen;* Dutch *steunen* (also *stenen*).

ἀλαλήτοις, masc. dat. pl. of ἀλάλητος. Some interpret this to mean unutterable, inexpressible, (groans and sighs) "too deep for words" (Ridderbos, Lenski, etc.); others translate unuttered, unspoken, wordless. We cannot be sure, although verse 27 seems to favor the latter interpretation. The Spirit's groanings do not need to be translated into actual words because the Father is able to discern the Spirit's meaning even though no words were spoken. But interpreted either way, the main thought of verses 26, 27 remains about the same.

237. αὐτὸ τὸ πνεῦμα.

what is *the Spirit's* intention." Not: the intention of believers, but that of *the Spirit*. Exegetically, therefore, I am forced to agree with those who say that the groanings to which reference is made here in verse 26 are those of the Spirit.

Is not the real reason why certain eminent interpreters refuse to ascribe these groanings to the Spirit *theological* rather than exegetical? They do not wish to ascribe to any of the three persons of the Holy Trinity qualities that would seem to be unworthy of him. At times this reason is stated in so many words.[238] And even though I cannot agree with their exegesis of Rom. 8:26, particularly with their unwillingness to ascribe *to the Spirit* these groanings, I honor them for their desire to remain doctrinally sound, especially in a day and age when by many such soundness is ridiculed. But exegetical accuracy is as important as doctrinal purity. Both are needed.

To the reasons given for believing that the groanings of verse 26 are those of the Spirit, the following should be added:

3. Since in verse 23 Paul has already discussed the groanings of the saints, it is hard to believe that he would return to this subject in verse 26. Moreover, the words introducing verse 26, namely, "And in the same way" imply a comparison; most likely between, on the one hand, the groanings of the creation and of believers (respectively verses 19–22; verses 23, 24); and, on the other, the groanings of the Spirit (verses 26, 27).

4. In verse 26 these groanings are linked inseparably with the Spirit's intercession. This intercession is mentioned again in verse 27. In verse 34 the verb which in verse 27 describes *the Spirit's* intercession, is used in connection with *the Son's* intercession. If, then, verse 34 refers to *Christ's own* intercessory prayer, why should not verse 27 describe *the Spirit's own* intercession, accompanied by groanings?[239]

Exactly what this groaning of the Holy Spirit implies would be difficult to define. Are we in error when we state that it means at least the following: the Spirit loves the saints so exceedingly that he yearns for that great day when, delivered from every speck of sin, they will glorify God forever and ever in the perfection of holiness and joy? Although it would be difficult to prove that the words, "That Spirit which he made to dwell in us yearns for us even unto jealous envy" (James 4:5) are the best translation of the original, yet, they may shed light on the meaning of the Spirit's groaning. And do we not meet with similar highly emotional expressions by means of which we are given a glimpse into the very heart of God? See, for example, the following:

> How can I give you up, O Ephraim?
> How can I cast you off, O Israel?
> How can I treat you like Admah?

---

238. See, for example, Lenski, *op. cit.*, p. 547.

239. It must have become clear that my interpretation of verse 26 (and also of verse 27) agrees with that of A. Kuyper, *Het Werk van den Heiligen Geest*, pp. 787, 788; Engl. tr., p. 636.

How can I make you like Zeboiim?
My heart is turned over within me,
All my compassions are kindled.

Hos. 11:8

If one wishes he may call the statement, "The Spirit himself intercedes for us with unspoken groanings," "highly anthropomorphic." Still, it expresses a truth we can ill afford to neglect. If human knowledge points back to divine omniscience; and human power, to divine omnipotence, it is hard to believe that human emotion reflects nothing at all in God. According to Scripture God is not Buddha, and heaven is not Nirvana!

Romans 8 teaches that believers have two intercessors: the Holy Spirit and Christ. Christ performs his intercessory task in heaven (Rom. 8:34; Heb. 7:25; I John 2:1); the Holy Spirit, on earth. Christ's intercession takes place outside of us, the Holy Spirit's within us; that is, in our very hearts (John 14:16, 17). Christ prays that the merits of his redemptive work may be fully applied to those who trust in him. The Holy Spirit prays that the deeply hidden needs of our hearts, needs which we ourselves sometimes do not even recognize, may be met. Christ's intercession may be compared with that of a father, the head of the family, for all the family members. The Holy Spirit's intercession reminds us rather of a mother kneeling at the bedside of her ailing child, and in her prayer presenting that child's needs to the heavenly Father.[240]

3. *Their Effectiveness*

The Spirit's intercession, accompanied by groanings, is not fruitless. Would not he who is constantly searching human hearts be able to read the intention of his own Spirit, who dwells in these hearts? Would he not know the meaning of that Spirit's unspoken groanings?

Again and again Scripture bears testimony to the truth of God's omniscience. See, for example, the following passages:

"Man looks at the outward appearance, but the Lord looks at the heart" (I Sam. 16:7).

"Thou alone knowest the hearts of all the sons of men" (I Kings 8:39).

"The Lord searches every heart and understands every motive" (I Chron. 28:9).

"O Lord, thou hast searched me and known me. Thou knowest when I sit down and when I rise up . . ." (Ps. 139:1, 2). The entire Psalm bears testimony to God's omnipresence and omniscience.

"Sheol and Abaddon lie open before the Lord" (Prov. 15:11).

"The heart is deceitful above all things. It is exceedingly corrupt: who can know it? I, the Lord, search the mind. I try the heart" (Jer. 17:9, 10).

---

240. For a similar representation see A. Kuyper (for reference see above, footnote 238, p. 276); and R. C. Harder, in *De Heilige Geest*, edited by J. H. Bavinck, P. Prins, and G. Brillenburg Wurth, Kampen, 1949, p. 396.

"Lord, thou knowest everyone's heart" (Acts 1:24).

"The Lord will bring to light what is hidden in darkness and will expose the motives of men's hearts" (I Cor. 4:5).

"There is no creature hidden from God's sight. All things are open and laid bare before the eyes of him to whom we must give account" (Heb. 4:13).

But not only does God *know* everything. What is emphasized is that he knows that the Spirit is interceding *in harmony with his (God's) own will*. Are not Father, Son, and Holy Spirit the *One* true God? Any clash between them is therefore impossible.

Note too that the Holy Spirit is described as constantly interceding "for the saints," that is, for those people who have been set apart in order to live lives to the glory of the Triune God as revealed in Christ Jesus. See on 1:7.

And since there is perfect harmony between the persons of the Holy Trinity, so that the Spirit's intercession, accompanied by groanings, coincides completely with the Father's will, the result must be that this intercession is always effective. It never fails. None of the saints is ever lost. All reach heaven at last. Better still: see verse 28.[241]

28. And we know that to those who love God all things work together for good; that is, to those who are called according to (his) purpose.

The present passage is a kind of summary of 8:1-27. It prepares for, and to some extent is similar to, the grand climax found in verses 37-39. It cannot be fully understood except in the light of verses 1-27. It draws a conclusion; in fact, a very comforting conclusion.

Paul has shown that for those who are in Christ Jesus there is now no condemnation (verses 1-8). They are indwelt by that Spirit who will even raise their bodies gloriously (verses 9-11). They receive the assurance that they are God's children, and as such, his heirs (verses 14-16). Their present suffering for Christ and for his cause means that one day they will share his glory, a glory so marvelous that in comparison with it hardships fade away into nothingness (verse 18). They will dwell in that new heaven and earth to which all creation with groaning is looking forward (verses 19-22). They themselves also groan as they eagerly await their adoption (verses 23-25). In all their weaknesses the Holy Spirit helps them. That Spirit always intercedes for them in harmony with God's will, so that this intercession, accompanied by wordless groanings, will certainly be effective (verses 26, 27).

So Paul says, "*And we know*—see also 3:19; 7:14; 8:22; I Cor. 8:1, 4; 13:9; II Cor. 5:1; I Tim. 1:8—that to those who love God all things work together for good . . ." On what else does he base this knowledge? Probably on two

---

241. In verse 27 note ἐραυνῶν, pres. participle of ἐραυνάω, to search; in the New Testament occurring only here and in John 5:39; 7:52; I Cor. 2:10; I Peter 1:11; and Rev. 2:23: "I am he who searches hearts and minds."
Because of the context ὅτι in verse 27 should be rendered *that*, not "because."

additional grounds: (a) *Experience;* that is, the effect on him of knowing how God had dealt with him and with others in the past. See such passages as Gen. 46:30; 48:3, 4; Deut. 5; Josh. 24:1-15; I Sam. 7:1-12; II Sam. 23:1-5; I Kings 8:22-24; Isa. 63:9; Acts 26:1-23; Gal. 2:19, 20. And (b) Acquaintance with *specific biblical passages* which teach that in God's providence all things result in blessing for God's children, evil being overruled for good (Gen. 45:5, 7, 8; 50:20).

Some find it difficult to accept the statement, "All things work together for good." They seem to think that such an expression ascribes to mere "things" qualities—such as wisdom and intelligence—which these things do not possess. In order to overcome this difficulty these interpreters suggest that the statement should read, "In all things [or: in everything] *God* works for good," or "*God* causes all things to work for good." Somehow the word *God* must be included in this clause. Otherwise, as some see it, it would result in heresy: a materialistic, perhaps evolutionistic, philosophy of life and history. Even if we must disagree, should we not love and honor these people for their motive? And if we answer them by stating "Y o u have no right to insert the word *God* where the original does not have it," they quickly answer that they have found a reading that supports their view.[242]

The answer to this is as follows:

Though no one knows how this variant originated, its acceptance results in a sentence that would make Paul a rather clumsy stylist.[243] Besides, if Paul really dictated, and Tertius really wrote, "In all things *God* works for good," or "*God* causes all things to work for good," it is very hard, indeed, to believe that this second mention of the word *God*—the first was in the clause "who love God"—would ever have been dropped from the text.

Others, rightly dissatisfied with making the word *God* the subject of the clause, borrow a subject from the preceding context. They go back to "*The Spirit* is helping us in our weakness . . . intercedes for us," etc., and then continue the sentence as follows: "and in everything, as we know, he [that is, the Spirit] co-operates for good with those who love God."[244]

But this rendering, if adhered to all the way, runs into difficulty when it reaches verse 29, for that verse would then read as follows, "For whom he [the Spirit, *if* N.E.B.'s translation of verse 28 is correct] foreknew, he also foreordained to be conformed to the image of his [the Spirit's] Son." This,

---

242. P⁴⁶ A B Origen, by Grk. N.T. (A-B-M-W) included in the apparatus, while the adopted text (without ὁ θεός) is given a C rating.

243. Note the doubling of the word θεός in what Paul then supposedly wrote: τοῖς ἀγαπῶσιν τὸν θεὸν πάντα συνεργεῖ ὁ θεός εἰς ἀγαθόν. Is it not reasonable to assume that it was a very early burdened soul who inserted the second θεός? Besides, unless there are sound reasons to do otherwise, should not the shorter reading—in this case the one without the second θεός—prevail? Also "causes to work" is not a faithful rendering of συνεργεῖ.

244. See N.E.B.'s translation in its *text.* To the credit of N.E.B. it should be stated that in a footnote it recognizes what I would call the correct reading and translation, the one that makes "all things" the subject of the clause.

of course, is impossible, for nowhere in Scripture is Jesus Christ called the Son of the Holy Spirit! So at this point N.E.B. inserts the word *God:* "For God knew his own . . ." But here the word *God* is not in the original Greek text.

As I see it, every attempt to avoid making "all things" the subject of the clause has failed.[245] The old—yes, *very old!*—rendering, namely, ". . . all things work together for good"[246] should stand. It is only fair to add that whether one translates one way or the other—that is, whether one (a) erroneously accepts the word "God" or "he" [the Spirit] as the subject of the clause; or (b) correctly views "all things" as being the real subject—hence, "all things work together for good"—the result remains about the same, namely, that in God's all-embracing providence all things work together for good to those who love God.

What is more important and necessary is that we accept the following three facts:

a. *"All things,"—no less!—cooperate for good.*

Not only prosperity is included but so also is adversity; not only joy and happiness but also suffering and sadness (Rom. 8:18, 35-37). Evil designs are by God overruled for good (Gen. 50:20; Neh. 4:15). Not only what the saints themselves experience is included but also whatever lies outside the sphere of their personal experience. Specifically, the following entities are among those that are divinely ordered and directed so that they work together for good to those who love God: the good angels (Heb. 1:14) and Satan together with his hosts (Rom. 16:20; Eph. 6:10-16); the nations of the world and their rulers (Ps. 2:2-9; 48:4-8; 149:9; Acts 9:15); rain and thunder (I Sam. 12:18-20); streams, mountains, and clouds (Ps. 46:4; 72:3; Matt. 24:30; Rev. 1:7); and even the stars in their courses (Judg. 5:20).

b. *It is only to those who love God that all things work together for good.*

In the original—as also in A.R.V. and in my rendering—the words "And we know that to those who love God all things work together for good" stand *at the very beginning* of the sentence. The meaning is this: they, and they alone, have a right to be comforted by this fact. Only in the case of those who love God is it true that all things work together for good. This is clear from such passages as the following: Exod. 20:6; Deut. 7:9; Neh. 1:5; Ps. 37:17, 20, 37-40; 97:10, 116:1 f.; Isa. 56:6, 7; I Cor. 2:9; 8:3; James 1:12; 2:5. All these references emphasize the importance of loving God and/or delighting in him.

c. *They love God because he first loved them.*

That surely is the meaning of the words, ". . . to those who love God all

---

245. For a more complete list of these attempts see the excellent summary and discussion by Cranfield, *op. cit.,* pp. 425-428.

246. Some prefer "co-operate for good"; others "prove advantageous for (their true) good." But these variations do not touch the main issue and, I believe, require no further discussion.

things work together for good; that is, to those who are called according to *(his) purpose.*" Though it is true that the word "his"—that is, God's—does not occur in the original, nevertheless, the only other passage in the entire book of Romans where this word *purpose* is found, namely 9:11 ("in order that God's purpose in election might stand"), proves that Paul was thinking about *God's* purpose, not man's.

The people who were called according to God's purpose are, therefore, those who were effectively called. They are those whose hearts and minds were so thoroughly influenced by the Holy Spirit that they became aware of their sinfulness, began to understand their need of Christ, and embraced him as their Lord and Savior. See above, on Rom. 1:7, p. 47. See also Rom. 8:30; 9:24; I Cor. 1:2, 24; 7:17f.

Paul felt that it was necessary to add the words, "to those who are called according to his [God's] purpose," in order that the Romans and all who would read this letter or hear it read to them would realize that no one can ever truly love God unless first of all he is effectively called. In other words, the apostle to the Gentiles is here expressing substantially the same thought as did the apostle John when he wrote, "We love God because he first loved us" (I John 4:19).

What Paul is really saying then, here in Rom. 8:28, is this, "We know that to those who love God and do so because of God's work in them, as determined by his sovereign, elective purpose, all things work together for good." In this manner human responsibility is fully maintained, but God Triune receives all the honor. Cf. Phil. 2:12, 13; II Thess. 2:13.

29, 30. For whom he foreknew, he also foreordained to be conformed to the image of his Son, so that he might be the firstborn among many brothers; and whom he foreordained, these he also called; and whom he called, these he also justified; and whom he justified, these he also glorified.

THE SALVATION CHAIN

When Paul states that to those who love God and are called according to his purpose all things work together for good, he is not thinking only of those things that can be seen round about us *now,* or those events that are taking place *now;* no, he includes even time and eternity. The chain of salvation he is discussing reaches back to that which, considered from a human standpoint, could be called the dim past, "the quiet recess of eternity," and forward into the boundless future.

One very important fact must be mentioned: every link in this chain of salvation represents a divine action. To be sure, human responsibility and action is not thereby ruled out, but here (Rom. 8:29, 30) it is never specifically mentioned.

There are five links in this chain. Note that the predicate of the first clause becomes the subject of the next one, a construction called *sorites*.[247]

A. *Foreknowledge*

". . . whom he foreknew."

Is it possible to interpret Paul's words in this sense: Before the world was created God foresaw who were going to believe in him and who would not. So, on the basis of that foreseen faith, he decided to elect to salvation those good people who were going to exercise it?

Answer: such a construction is entirely impossible, for according to Scripture even faith is God's gift. See N.T.C. on Ephesians, pp. 120-123 (on Eph. 2:8). See also John 6:44, 65; I Cor. 4:7; Phil. 1:29. In fact, even the good works performed by believers are prepared beforehand by God! (Eph. 2:10).

On the contrary, the foreknowledge mentioned in Rom. 8:29 refers to *divine active delight*. It indicates that, in his own sovereign good pleasure, God set his love on certain individuals, many still to be born, gladly acknowledging them as his own, electing them to everlasting life and glory. Note the following:

"For I have known him [Abraham] so that he may direct his children and his household after him" (Gen. 18:19).

"Before I formed you in the womb I knew you, Before you were born I set you apart" (Jer. 1:5).

"I am the good shepherd, and I know my own" (John 10:14). Cf. 10:28.

"The Lord knows who are his" (II Tim. 2:19).

Add the following: Ps. 1:6; Amos 3:2; Hos. 13:5; Matt. 7:23; I Cor. 8:3; Gal. 4:9; I John 3:1; and see also on Rom. 11:2.

"The term *prognosis* [foreknowledge] reveals the fact that in his purpose according to election the persons are not the objects of God's 'bare foreknowledge' but of his 'active delight.'"[248]

B. *Foreordination with a View to Conformation*

". . . he also foreordained to be conformed to the image of his Son, so that he might be the firstborn among many brothers."

In reality "foreknowledge" already imples "foreordination." Nevertheless, there is a difference of emphasis. Whereas the first term directs our attention to the persons whom God elected and only in a general way to their final destiny (everlasting life, glory), the term *foreordination* fixes our thought more definitely on the purpose for which they were elected and on

---

247. F. F. Bruce, *op. cit.*, p. 176.
248. H. Bavinck, *The Doctrine of God*, Grand Rapids, 1951, Vol. II, p. 343; my published translation of Bavinck's *Gereformeerde Dogmatiek;* see above, footnote 16.

the means of attaining it. That goal is not just "to enter heaven at last" but "to be conformed to the image of God's Son."

Man was created *as*—this is probably better than *in*[249]—God's image. That image was distorted by sin, but was restored in Christ, who was and is the image of God (II Cor. 4:4; Col. 1:15).

The question has been asked, "When Paul describes the purpose of foreordination to be that those whom God foreknew should be conformed to the image of his Son, does he have in mind (a) *only* the *final* conformation; that is, only that part of transformation into Christ's image that will take place at his Return; or is he referring to (b) the entire process of transformation, beginning already when the sinner is brought out of the darkness into the light?" On this point there is a difference of opinion among commentators.

Position (a) *Only Final*	Position (b) *Also Present*
Greijdanus, Vol. I, p. 390	Calvin, p. 318
Lenski, p. 561	Cranfield, Vol. I, p. 432
Murray, Vol. I, p. 319	Lekkerkerker, Vol. I, p. 354
Ridderbos, p. 196	Robertson, W. P., IV, p. 377
	Van Leeuwen-Jacobs, p. 160
	Zahn, p. 417[250]

Those who accept Position (a) point out that the context favors this position: verses 11 and 23 refer to the glorious resurrection of the body, and verse 21 to a gloriously renewed universe. These renewals will not take place until the day of Christ's Return. From this they draw the conclusion that also the conformation to the image of Christ must be interpreted as a great eschatological event that will occur on the day of The Great Consummation.

Now if the conformation to the image of God's Son is limited to the refashioning of our lowly body so that it will have a form like Christ's glorious body (Phil. 3:21, to which reference is often made in this connection), then the question is immediately settled in favor of Position (a), for that conformation will certainly not take place until then.

However, in a context which deals with such matters as calling, justification, and glorification not many interpreters would accept this narrow interpretation of the words "to be conformed to the image of his Son." It is the *spiritual* conformation or transformation Paul has in mind here.

Once this is granted, the weight of the evidence, I believe, turns sharply in the direction of Position (b), and this for the following reasons:

1. In arriving at the meaning of "He also foreordained to be conformed

---

249. So also G. Ch. Aalders, *Het Boek Genesis (Korte Verklaring)*, Kampen, 1949, Vol. I, p. 96.
250. The references are to the *Commentaries*—not to any other works—written by these authors.

to the image of his Son" the chief determining factor is not 8:11, 21, 23, but the much closer "For whom he foreknew" of verse 29a. That word carries us back to the "eternity" which, humanly speaking, preceded the foundation of the earth (Eph. 1:4). Is it not logical, therefore, to view the conformation "to the image of his Son" to pertain not only to what will happen on the day of Christ's Return but also to what happens in the lengthy period before that Return? If we do not do this, are we not then creating a gap of very lengthy duration about which nothing is said?

2. Other passages—such as Rom. 12:1; Eph. 4:32—5:2; Phil. 3:10; Col. 3:10—regarding spiritual renewal cannot be interpreted as being connected with the day of Christ's Return.

3. *Basically* the required transformation is not man's work but God's. Is not that also the thought expressed in II Cor. 3:18—which even contains the words "we are being transformed into the same image"? Here, again, the renewal described is happening *now*, not solely at Christ's Return.

4. If gradual renewal into the image of Christ is not what Paul had in mind, are we not forced to conclude that one very important link in the chain of salvation, namely the link of *sanctification*, is missing? The answer given by some that justification includes sanctification does not satisfy. There is indeed a very close relation between these two but never are they identified.

On the basis of the given reasons I believe that the conformation to the image of his Son, of which the apostle speaks here in 8:29, refers to sanctification. This, too, is basically *God's* work (II Thess. 2:13).

Very significant are the words "*so that he might be the firstborn* among many brothers."

Two ideas are emphasized here. They form a contrast, yet also harmony. The *first* is that of *Christ's pre-eminence*. Decorating a wall of a certain home in Florida—and no doubt many other walls elsewhere—is a plaque that reads:

THAT in All Things
HE Might Have
THE PRE-EMINENCE

Col. 1:18

This makes sense; for, if the duty as well as the destiny of believers is to be conformed to the image of God's Son, then *he* must indeed be pre-eminent. Besides, what a worthwhile reminder this plaque is in the interest of day-to-day Christian life and practice!

The *second* idea conveyed by this passage is that of *Christ's humility and marvelous love* for those whom he, by means of his redemptive sacrifice, has made his own. Note "that he might be the firstborn *among many brothers!*" In other words, the Exalted Savior does not consider himself complete apart from those whom he came to save! See Heb. 2:11, noting also its reference to *sanctification*.

For the idea of Christ as firstborn see also Col. 1:15; Heb. 1:6; and Rev. 1:5.

C. *Calling*

". . . and whom he foreordained, these he also called."

From that which pertains to *eternity*, namely, foreknowing and foreordaining—though their effects are being historically realized, Paul now, by a very logical transition, enters into the realm of *time*. The apostle refers, of course, to the effective call. What this call means has been explained in connection with Rom. 1:7 (see p. 46) and 8:28 (see p. 281). By means of Spirit-wrought conversion and faith man responds to this call.

D. *Justification*

". . . and whom he called, these he also justified."

As has been explained earlier, in a sense "Justification by Faith" is the theme of Romans. Its meaning has been set forth on pp. 61-66, 128-131.

E. *Glorification*

". . . and whom he justified, these he also glorified."

Believers will share in Christ's glory (Rom. 8:17). Nothing can be greater glory than that which is bestowed upon Christ's followers because of their intimate union with Christ (Col. 1:27).[251]

Not only will God's children receive gloriously transformed bodies (Rom. 8:11, 23; I Cor. 15:43-53; Phil. 3:21; I John 3:2), but on and after the day of the resurrection they will shine forth in all their glory in both soul and body, these having now become reunited.

So certain is the believers' future glory that, even though it can be considered an object of hope (Rom. 5:2), and therefore a matter pertaining to the future, here in Rom. 8:30 it is described as if it had already become a reality: "he also glorified."[252] And is it not true that in a sense believers "were raised with Christ" (Col. 3:1), and were in his train when he ascended to heaven (Eph. 4:8)? Are they not even now being transformed from glory to glory (II Cor. 3:18)?

This past tense (cf. Jude 14; also most of Isa. 53) indicates the certainty that a future event will take place and, perhaps, in the present connection, also the fact that the glory promised for the future has already begun to be realized.

All this reminds us of a stanza from Wordsworth's *See the Conqueror Mounts in Triumph:*

---

251. For the meaning of δόξα (glory) see footnote 38 on p. 74.
252. ἐδόξασε, third per. s. aor. indicat. of δοξάζω, to glorify.

285

Thou hast raised our human nature
On the clouds to God's right hand;
There we sit in heavenly places,
There with thee in glory stand.
Jesus reigns, adored by angels,
Man with God is on the throne,
Mighty Lord in thine ascension
We by faith behold our own.

---

31 What, then, shall we say in response to these things? If God is for us, who is against us? 32 He who did not spare even his own Son, but gave him up for us all, how will he not also with him graciously give us all things? 33 Who will bring any charge against God's elect? It is God who justifies. 34 Who is he that condemns? (It is) Christ Jesus who died, what is more, who was raised from the dead, who is at the right hand of God, who is also interceding for us.

35 Who will separate us from the love of Christ? Affliction or distress or persecution or famine or nakedness or peril or sword? 36 As it is written:
"For thy sake we are being put to death all the day long;
We are considered as sheep to be slaughtered."
37 No, in all these things we are more than conquerors through him who loved us. 38 For I am convinced that neither death nor life nor angels nor principalities nor things present nor things to come nor powers 39 nor height nor depth nor any other created thing will be able to separate us from the love of God which is in Christ Jesus our Lord.

4b. *It produces the fruit of **super-invincibility;** i.e., of being more than conquerors.*
"No, in all these things we are more than conquerors
through him who loved us."
8:31-39

31. What, then, shall we say in response to these things? If God is for us, who is against us?

What Paul means is, "To what conclusion do these things lead us?" The expression "these things" probably refers not only to the matters mentioned in verses 28-30, or even 18-30, but to everything the apostle has so far written in this epistle. What, then, is the summary of that which Paul has been saying in this letter?

He has pointed out that the one thing a sinner needs above all else is right standing with God, and that this right standing is not obtainable by human exertion or merit. That inestimable blessing is God's free gift, and there is only one way to obtain it, namely, by faith. See 1:17; 3:24, 28, 30; 4:1, 2, 7, 8; 5:1, 8, 9; 7:24, 25; 8:1. The blessing of salvation has been earned for everyone, whether Jew or Gentile, who will, by God's power and grace, repose his trust in the Savior. It was *he* who earned salvation for his people by the shedding of his blood. They are saved by *his* substitutionary death, *his* resurrection, and *his* intercession (1:4, 5; 3:21-26; 4:25; 5:1, 2, 8-21; 6:23; 7:24; 8:1-4; and see also 8:34).

If, then, God is on our side, as he clearly proved by what he did and does for us, who is against us? Not as if all the enemies have already been swept away, but what is any enemy able to achieve *against* us, God being *for* us?

286

When Paul says, "*If* God is for us," he is not calling in doubt God's protecting care, love, and promises. On the contrary, *this* "if" means, "If . . . as he certainly is!"

In light of all this the opening question, "What, then, shall we say in response to these things?" will have to be answered with a very strong, "We have nothing to fear. Victory is certainly on our side."

But the apostle himself gives a far more complete answer in verses 32–39. The beginning of this answer is found in the next verse:

32. He who did not spare even his own Son, but gave him up for us all, how will he not also with him graciously give us all things?

"He . . . did not spare even his own Son, but gave him up." The depth of feeling implied in the words of verse 3—"sending his own Son"—is expressed even more vividly here in verse 32.[253] If this does not mean that, in a sense, giving up his only-begotten and fathomlessly beloved Son was for the Father a genuine sacrifice, words no longer have meaning.

It is possible to think of a judge who does not spare a vicious criminal but pronounces on him the severe sentence he deserves. It is not inconceivable that such a judge might afterward enjoy a good night's sleep.

But what we have here in Rom. 8:32 is something else. The following facts should be kept in mind:

God, the Judge, has a Son, an only Son, very precious to him. That Son never committed any sin. In all he did he was ever pleasing his Father (John 8:29).

On the other hand:

> *We* all like sheep have gone astray,
> Each of *us* has turned to his own way.
>
> Isa. 53:6.

Yet, on this precious and beloved Son God now pronounces the sentence *we* deserved. It is a sentence immeasurable in its severity, and is carried out in every detail. *God did not spare* his Son, did not mitigate the severity of the sentence in any way whatever, the Son himself agreeing with the Father and the Spirit in all this. He, the Son, fully bore that horrendous curse. He drank the cup of unspeakable agony to the very last drop. "That bitter cup, Love drank it up. It's empty now for me." See Isa. 53; Rom. 5:6–8; 8; 3, 4; II Cor. 5:21; Gal. 3:13. It would have been unthinkable for God to reject the demands of his justice. "Will not the Judge of all the earth do right?" (Gen. 18:25).

We ask, "But why was the curse lifted from our shoulders and transferred to the Son of God?" The answer is: So deeply, intensely, and marvelously did God love the world that his Son, the only-begotten, he gave, in order that everyone who believes in him should not perish but have life everlasting. Is not that the meaning of John 3:16?

---

253. Note presence of γε in the clause ὅς γε τοῦ ἰδίου υἱοῦ οὐκ ἐφείσατο.

There is, of course, a resemblance between:
"You [Abraham] have not withheld your son, your only son" (Gen. 22:12, 16)

and

"He [God] did not spare even his own Son . . ." (Rom. 8:32).

Yet, it is not the similarity which arrests our attention most of all. It is the contrast. Abraham was rescued in the nick of time, and so was his son Isaac. But Christ bore the wrath fully, willingly.

" . . . for us all." In accordance with the immediately preceding context, the apostle must have been thinking of all those who love God (verse 28), who were foreknown and foreordained (verse 29), were (or were going to be) called, justified, and glorified (verse 30). To this can be added the similar expressions contained in the statements which follow; namely, the elect (verse 33), those for whom Christ makes intercession (verse 34), those who are "more than conquerors" (verse 37). It was to these people, to them all, to them alone, that the merits of Christ's death had been, were being, or were going to be savingly applied.

Here again, as in connection with 5:18—see above, pp. 182, 183, it is not at all improbable that when Paul says, "He [God] gave him [his own Son] up for *us all*," he included in his thought this idea: "God gave up his Son *for Jew and Gentile alike*," for all his dear children regardless of race, sex, nationality, social standing, etc. See also Rom. 3:22, 23, 29; 10:11–13.

"How will he not also with him graciously give us all things?"

The argument is from the greater to the lesser, as in 5:9, 10, 15, 17; 11:12, 24. Nothing could ever be a greater gift than the gift of Christ to the church. That gift is clearly implied in the statement, "God did not spare his own Son but gave him up for us all." Moreover, even though giving this Son was an unfathomable sacrifice as plainly implied in "God did not spare," nevertheless, it is never a solitary gift: how will he not also *together with him* graciously—that is ungrudgingly, freely, gladly, generously—give us *all things?*

I can see no good reason to limit the expression "all things" to spiritual blessings, as some do. Paul was a very practical man. He knew that the people he was addressing were men of flesh and blood, who were vexed at times with worries over matters mundane. The expression "all things" should therefore be interpreted in an unqualified sense: material as well as spiritual things; cf. 8:28, where it has the same broad meaning.[254]

It is not only about matters in general, both physical and spiritual, that anxieties arise. Underneath everything else, there is that basic worry, "What is my standing with God?" Paul answers as follows:

33, 34. Who will bring any charge against God's elect? It is God who justifies. Who is he that condemns? (It is) Christ Jesus who died, what is

---

254. F. F. Bruce, *op. cit.*, p. 179, correctly refers to Matt. 6:33. Note context: "What are we going to eat, drink, wear?" See also Denney, *op. cit.*, p. 653.

more, who was raised from the dead, who is at the right hand of God, who is also interceding for us.

Verse 33 is probably an intentional echo of words found in Isa. 50:8, 9a:

"He is near who justifies [or vindicates] me. Who is my accuser? . . . Behold, the Lord Jehovah will help me. Who is he that will condemn me?"[255]

The rhetorical questions—"Who will bring any charge . . .?" "Who is he that condemns?"—amount to a vigorous denial of the suggestion that there could be any valid charge or condemnation.

Are these people not God's elect? Is that not what is implied in 8:29: "foreknown . . . foreordained"? Surely, when, in the dispute between Joshua the highpriest and Satan, God defended Joshua and rebuked Satan, the latter was immediately silenced (Zech. 3:1-5). When God justifies a person, all accusations at once lose their validity.

The logical nature of this answer is brought out even more clearly by the words that follow, namely, "It is Christ Jesus who died . . . was raised from the dead . . is at the right hand of God . . . is also interceding for us."

Here note especially the phrase "what is more" inserted between the reference to Christ's death and his resurrection. It probably expresses the climactic relationship not only between the first two items but between all the items in the series. To be sure, by means of Christ's death the sins of his people were blotted out. But this fact was established beyond possibility of successful contradiction by the resurrection from the dead. See on Rom. 4:25, p. 161. And the exaltation of God's Son to the right hand of God— Matt. 26:64; Mark 14:62; Luke 22:69; Acts 2:33; 3:13; 5:31; 7:55, 56; Eph. 1:20; Col. 3:1; Heb. 1:3; 2:9; 8:1; 10:12; 12:2; I Peter 1:21; 3:22; Rev. 5:12, symbolizing the honor, power, and authority given to him as a reward for his fully accomplished mediatorial work, strengthens this conclusion even more.

The *climax* of assurance is reached in the clause, "who is also interceding for us"—Isa. 53:12;[256] Luke 23:34; John 14:16; I John 2:1; Heb. 7:25, for how would it even be conceivable that the Father should deny the intercessory prayers of the Son, who so fully, marvelously, and gloriously accomplished the task assigned to him (John 17:4)? Did not the Son himself say to the Father, "I knew that thou dost always hear me"? (John 11:42a).

35. Who will separate us from the love of Christ? Affliction or distress or persecution or famine or nakedness or peril or sword?

Another rhetorical question, meaning, "No one will ever be able to separate us from the love Christ has for us." Not our love for Christ is meant but Christ's love for us, as verse 37 clearly indicates: "through him who loved us."

To give an adequate description or definition of that love of Christ is

---

255. When this close relation between Rom. 8:33, 34 and Isa. 50:8, 9a is accepted, this will solve the problem of the punctuation of the Pauline passage.
256. See what was said in footnote 139, p. 162, about Isa. 53:12 in Hebrew.

impossible. Cf. Eph. 3:19. All we can do is stammer. We might say, for example, that it is the outgoing disposition of Christ's compassionate heart which revealed itself in the most marvelous and self-sacrificing action that was ever taken. See John 15:13; Rom. 5:8; I John 4:10. God is Love (I John 4:8), and since Christ is God, Christ too is Love.

Charles Wesley, in his hymn *Love Divine*, probably came about as close to describing Christ's love as anyone can get apart from quoting the words of Scripture:

> Jesus, thou art all compassion,
> Pure, unbounded love thou art.

Paul enumerates seven circumstances that might be brought up for consideration in answering the question whether anything can separate us from Christ's love:

a. b. *affliction, distress.* Not only is "affliction" a good translation of the first of the seven Greek words but it is even etymologically related to it. While this word occurs more than forty times in the New Testament, the apostle uses it only four times (besides here in Rom. 8:35, also in Rom. 2:9; II Cor. 6:4; 12:10). In the first three instances both words *affliction* and *distress* occur. The fact that Paul uses both words indicates that in his mind there was a distinction between them. The suggestion of several commentators that the two words used in the original[257] refer respectively to *outward affliction* and *inward distress* is probably correct. In the New Testament Paul is the only writer who uses the word *distress,* and even in his epistles it is found only four times (in addition to Rom. 8:35 also in 2:9; II Cor. 6:4; 12:10).

c. *persecution.* In the New Testament this word occurs for the first time in Matt. 13:21, "When affliction or persecution arises on account of the message he immediately falls away." Paul uses the word *persecution* five times (here and also in II Cor. 12:10; II Thess. 1:4; twice in II Tim. 3:11).

d. *famine.* The word used in the original means hunger, famine. Its first occurrence is in Matt. 24:7, "There shall be famines and earthquakes in various places." See also Luke 15:14, "When he had spent everything a severe famine arose. . . ." Though the word is used a dozen times in the New Testament, Paul has it only here and in II Cor. 11:27 (hunger).

e. *nakedness.* In the New Testament this noun is found only three times: here, in II Cor. 11:27; and in Rev. 3:18, but the related adjective (naked) occurs several times; for example, in Matt. 25:36, "I was naked, and y o u clothed me." Often the meaning is somewhat more general than *naked* might suggest; hence, *in need of clothes* is at times a better rendering.

f. *peril.* This noun occurs here and eight times (!) in II Cor. 11:26.

g. *sword,* a word of frequent occurrence in the New Testament, begin-

---

257. θλῖψις and στενοχωρία (basically *narrow place*).

ning with Matt. 10:34, "I did not come to bring peace but a sword." Paul uses it only here and in Rom. 13:4; Eph. 6:17.

We should not forget that when Paul spoke about these adverse circumstances which Satan and the other enemies of the cross used in order to bring about separation between believers and their Lord, he was not speaking as an armchair theologian or philosopher. On the contrary, as II Cor. 11:23-29 indicates, he had already suffered the first six of these seven hardships before writing this epistle to the Romans. Moreover, by means of the seventh, i.e., the sword, he was going to be put to death. The apostle was speaking not only by inspiration but also from experience, therefore, when he stated that none of these things can bring about separation between believers and their Lord. He knew what he was saying!

Moreover, by implying, "Nothing will separate us from Christ's love" was he not also saying, "On the contrary, suffering for Christ's sake will bring us closer to him and to his love"? Cf. Phil. 1:29, "For to y o u it has been granted in behalf of Christ not only to believe in him but also to suffer in his behalf." On the theme *Suffering for Christ a Blessing* see N.T.C. on Philippians, pp. 90, 91.

36. As it is written:
"For thy sake we are being put to death all the day long;
We are considered as sheep to be slaughtered."
By quoting Ps. 44:22 (Heb. 44:23; LXX 43:23) Paul shows that there is nothing strange or unexpected about present-day suffering for the Lord's sake. The Psalmist trusted in God. Otherwise how could he have exclaimed, "Thou art my King, O God." And how could he have said, "In God do we boast all the day long"?

Yet, *he* did not derive the comfort from this suffering that *Paul* derived from his painful experiences. Otherwise he would not have said, "Awake, O Lord! Why sleepest thou? Rouse thyself! Do not reject us forever."

The apostle, on the other hand, understood that suffering for the sake of Christ meant entering into closer communion with him. Such suffering was gain, not loss.

Where did Paul learn this lesson? Is it possible that he had learned it not only from experience and by direct inspiration but also from tradition, early believers having transmitted to him the words of Jesus? It was Jesus who had said:
"Blessed those persecuted for righteousness sake, for theirs is the kingdom of heaven. Blessed are y o u whenever people heap insults upon y o u and persecute y o u, and, while telling falsehoods, say all kinds of evil against y o u for my sake. Rejoice, yes, be filled with unrestrained gladness, for y o u r reward is great in heaven, for in the same way did they persecute the prophets who lived before y o u r time" (Matt. 5:10-12).

37-39. No, in all these things we are more than conquerors through him who loved us. For I am convinced that neither death nor life nor angels nor principalities nor things present nor things to come nor pow-

ers nor height nor depth nor any other created thing will be able to separate us from the love of God which is in Christ Jesus our Lord.

Paul has been speaking about affliction, distress, persecution, famine, nakedness, peril, and sword. For the moment it almost seemed as if he was unable to think of anything but suffering and hardship. Nevertheless, his real intention was the very opposite: he wanted to emphasize that in the midst of all these unpleasant experiences, in fact even by means of them and with their help, we are more than conquerors. Not just: we shall conquer in the end; no, even now we *are* super-conquerors. And this *not*—let it be added immediately—by reason of our marvelous character and unflinching courage.

Mrs. Merrill E. Gates, 1886, was surely right when she wrote:

> Thy love to me, O Christ,
>   Thy love to me,
> Not mine to thee, I plead,
>   Not mine to thee.
> This is my comfort strong,
> This is my joyful song,
>   Thy love to me,
>   Thy love to me.

Just what does the apostle mean when he calls believers "super-conquerors"? Did he mean, "We are winning a sweeping, overwhelming victory"? To be sure, that is what he meant. But is that all he wanted to say? Words, after all, should be interpreted in light of their context. The apostle says, "in all these things." The reference is, of course, to the things enumerated in verse 35. Other "things" and "beings" will be added in a moment, those mentioned in verses 38, 39: death, life, angels, etc. The structure of the sentence (note the conjunction *for*) indicates that these too should be added. Finally, note the very close connection between verse 28 and verse 31 f. ("for" verse 29; "what then" verse 31); and also the parallel "all things" (verse 28) and "in all these things" (verse 37).[258]

The similarity will become apparent when the two lines are placed under each other:

Verse 28
"And we know that to *those who love God all things* work together for good."

Verse 37
"No, in *all these things* we are more than conquerors through *him who loved us.*"

Since our love for God results from his love for us, a sequence that never fails, for by nature we do not love God, the two statements resemble each other also in that respect. They are not the same, but they are certainly similar.

---

258. In the original: πάντα. . . . ἐν τούτοις πᾶσιν.

Once this close connection is grasped, we begin to understand that what Paul is saying is that not only do these various hardships and forces which he mentions not hurt us, but they help us: they all work together for *good*. It is for this reason that he states that in connection with them we are *more than conquerors*. A conqueror is a person who defeats the enemy. One who is more than a conqueror causes the enemy to become a helper.

If anyone knew the meaning of "more than conquerors" it must have been Paul. Was it not exactly this apostle who had been "more than conquered" by God? From a bitter persecutor he had been changed into an enthusiastic supporter! No wonder he could say, "I am convinced." *He* would be!

A few words should be added with reference to the "things" and "beings" enumerated in verses 38, 39. There are four pairs of objects plus two separately mentioned ones.

THE PAIRS

1. neither death nor life (can separate us from God's love in Christ Jesus our Lord).

Having just now made mention of *death* (verse 36), it is not surprising that Paul makes this word the first of the series. The questions of psalmists regarding the possibility of fellowship between God and man even after death—see Ps. 6:5; 30:9; 88:10-12—are answered here (Rom. 8:38, 39) with a definite "Yes," a confession already anticipated in the Old Testament (Ps. 49:5; 73:24, 25; Job 19:26, 27). The fact that even death would bring about no separation between God and the believer was firmly entrenched in the heart and mind of Paul (II Cor. 5:8; Phil. 1:21-23). For further confirmation see Luke 23:43; John 14:2; 17:24; Heb. 12:18-24.

As to *life*, in spite of all its distractions, especially for the unbeliever (Luke 8:14), the believer's life is one in communion with God. That is the teaching of both Testaments (Ps. 23:42; 63:1-8; 73:23; 116:1, 2; Rom. 14:8, 9; Col. 3:1-3).

2. nor angels nor principalities.

Angels are mentioned with great frequency in both Testaments (Gen. 24:7, 40; 31:11; Ps. 68:17; Matt. 1:20, 24; 2:13, 19; 28:2, 5; Luke 1:11; Col. 2:18; II Thess. 1:7; etc.) For a Chart summarizing Scriptural doctrine regarding the angels see N.T.C. on Matthew, p. 694.

In Jewish literature *principalities* are angels. In Eph. 3:10 the reference may well be to a category of good angels. See N.T.C. on Ephesians, pp. 158, 159. See also I Cor. 15:24; Eph. 1:21; 6:12; Col. 1:16; 2:10, 15. The Dead Sea Scrolls too contain many references to angels, especially *evil* angels. Other references are found in the pseudepigraphic Book of Enoch. The names of angels, the various categories into which they were to be classified, the worship due to them, were some of the topics on which especially heretics would concentrate their attention.

293

What Paul is saying in the present context (Rom. 8:38) is simply this, that even angels, whether *good or bad*, real or unreal (the latter referring to classes of supermundane spirits that exist only in people's imagination) can do nothing to separate us from the love of God in Christ.

3. nor things present nor things to come.

This grouping is along a horizontal time line.

Time, whether *present* or *future*—the present with its problems, the future with its forebodings—can do nothing to separate us from the great and deep love with which God in Christ smiles down upon us, and which from moment to moment he bestows on us, forgiving, helping, and encouraging us on our way through life.

4. nor height nor depth.

This classification is along a vertical line.

Does danger coming from above seem to threaten? Does hell seem to open its jaws? God's child is safe. If time cannot separate him from God's love, neither can space: nor *height* nor *depth*.

THE SINGLE ITEMS:

1. nor powers.

In the New Testament *powers* are included in the angel groupings. See Eph. 1:21; 3:10; 6:12; Col. 1:16; 2:15; I Peter 3:22). That is where they belong.[259]

Just why it was that Paul placed "nor powers" between "nor things present nor things to come" and "nor height nor depth" is unknown.

2. nor any other created thing.

The apostle adds this comprehensively inclusive item in order to emphasize that *nothing whatever* will be able to separate believers from "the love of God which is in Christ Jesus our Lord."

And so this lengthy subdivision of Paul's epistle to the Romans, namely chapters 5-8 (see pp. 30, 167) ends as it began: note in both cases (5:1 and 8:39) the reference to "our Lord Jesus Christ" (or "Christ Jesus our Lord"). Everything mentioned must serve to strengthen the saints' experience of the love of God which is in his Son. To God be all the glory!

Romans 8 In Poetry

Verses

1-4   For those who in Jesus their refuge have found
            There's no condemnation. Their blessings abound.
            For through what Christ Jesus has done within me
            The Spirit from sin and from death set me free.

---

259. I can see no merit in the suggestion that δυνάμεις, as used *here* might refer to "mighty works" or "miracles." The context (angels . . . principalities) does not favor this interpretation.

For that which the law, by our nature laid low,
Could never achieve and much less could bestow,
God wrought, when, in order to save us from sin,
He sent his own Son our salvation to win.

God did this in order that Law's just demand
In us might be met, and we righteous might stand,
And show by our conduct from day unto day,
That, shunning the flesh, we his Spirit obey.

5–8   For those who have chosen the flesh as their Guide,
In things of the flesh, not the Spirit, take pride.
But those who have chosen the Spirit as Guide
In things of the Spirit, not flesh, do take pride.

Now those who take pride in the flesh sure should know
That flesh and its fruit, death, together will go.
So, too, those who honor the Spirit will see
That life and deep peace their requital will be.

For fav'ring the flesh will mean hating the Lord,
Since keeping God's statutes it cannot afford.
And it should be obvious to those in the flesh
That pleasing both God and one's sin do not mesh.

9–11   But not in the flesh, my dear brothers, are y o u.
The Spirit who's in y o u proves this to be true.
If one lacks the Spirit, it sure would be wrong
To say that *this* man could to Jesus belong.

But if Christ is in y o u, then though, due to sin,
The body may die, yet the Spirit within
Is life and brings life, so that y o u before God
Stand sinless and pure through the ransom Christ brought.

And if y o u're indwelt by the Spirit of God
Who raised Christ from death, then that Father who brought
To life the dead Jesus will also restore
Y o u r bodies from death. They'll be living once more.

12–16   Therefore, my dear brothers, our duty is clear:
To live by the standard of flesh while y o u're here
Will lead but to death. It's y o u r duty to give
The deathblow to sin's shameful ways. Then y o u'll live.

It is by the strength of the Spirit alone
That this is successful and this can be done.
For all God's true children, with him as their Head,
Are by the blest Spirit of God being led.

Y o u're children indeed, for y o u've not received
The spirit of slavery when y o u believed.
No longer does sickening dread y o u oppress,
With joy y o u y o u r God as y o u r *Father* address.

The Spirit bears witness, and not from afar,
But from close within us, that children we are,
Confirming the voice of our own heart and mind,
And leaving uncertainty far, far behind.

17, 18   And if we are children, then, too, we are heirs
Of God and with Christ, for the person who shares
With Christ in his sufferings must certainly know
That on him indeed God will glory bestow.

For this I consider; of this I am sure!
That sufferings and hardships which now we endure
Are nothing compared with the glory which then
Will shine from within us, ne'er leave us again.

19-22   And this is established that Nature entire
For the revelation of saints does aspire,
For not by its own choice did Nature grow dim.
'tWas man who transgressed, and the Lord punished him

By rendering Nature unable to cope
With enemies many; yet not without hope
That Nature itself, though now bound to despair
One day will the freedom of God's children share.

Now *all of creation,* all Nature, 'tis known,
In anguish of childbirth does *suffer and groan.*
23-25   Not only is this true but we must confess:
We also do groan, who the Spirit possess.

Yes, we also groan, even though we are free,
Enriched by the Spirit, as firm guarantee
That also our bodies the Lord will display
As dear to himself on that glorious day.

In hope we were saved, for its object, though near,
Is hidden from view and does not yet appear.
But when we no longer of it are deprived,
It stops to be object of hope; 't has arrived!

But since for the present we hope for still more,
For fulness of bliss which for us is in store,
We long for these blessings, so rich and so great,
And therefore with patient endurance we wait.

26, 27   The Spirit, too, knows that we sinners are weak,
And often unable to find what we seek,
Not knowing at certain times just how to pray:
The words will not come; we don't know what to say.

The Spirit then helps us, for he knows our need.
With unspoken groanings he does intercede.
The Searcher of hearts knows the Spirit's intent;
He'll ever agree, and the Spirit's plea grant.

28-30 Therefore we conclude that to those who love God
All things, in a sense not restricted but broad,
Co-operate fully, in line with God's plan
Established and ordered before time began.

In line with this program or purpose of old
The lovers of God were effectively called.
For whom he foreknew he did also elect
The image of Jesus, his Son, to reflect.

In this way it was that God did foreordain
That Christ should become and forever remain
Close linked to his people, *firstborn* among all,
Yet humble, and willing them *brothers* to call.

Resulting is therefore salvation's firm chain:
Those whom God foreknew he did, too, foreordain,
And those foreordained he did afterward call,
And justify later and glorify all.

31-34 How then shall we answer? How shall we reply?
If he who is for us is God from on high?
Who, now, of all creatures against us can be
When he who is for us is certainly he?

His love is so matchless, so tender his care
That even his own Son he never did spare.
For us, wretched sinners, he gave him to die.
How will he not with him our own needs supply?

Who dares to bring charges against God's elect?
Whom God declares pure, and will ever protect?
Who's really so bold that he dares to condemn
The children of God when he justifies them?

It's Jesus who died, and what's more, who was raised
From death to God's right hand. Let heaven be praised!
Christ Jesus this place of trust occupies thus.
It's he who is now interceding for us.

35, 36 Who then can he be who will tear us apart
From Christ and his love, which was ours from the start?
Distress, persecution, pain due to the Word?
Or famine or nakedness, peril or sword?

It is as the Psalmist declared long ago:
"Each day we face death and are being brought low.
As sheep that are led to the slaughter are we,
For doing thy will and for honoring thee."

37-39 And yet it's a fact that by these very things
Which might seem to harm us God victory brings
To us whom he loves, so that conquerors we,
No, rather far better than this, we should be.

For this I know well, and on this I can count
That nothing at all can forever be found
That causes the Savior his own to forsake,
Twixt him and his dear ones division can make.

Not death and not life and not angels above
Can ever exclude us from God's lasting love.
Nor present nor future can ever avail
To cause that great love for his dear ones to fail.

Not demons or powers, not depth and not height
Can weaken its glow or diminish its might
No creature can part us, whatever the sort,
From God's love that is in Christ Jesus our Lord.

Practical Lessons Derived from Romans 8

A most comforting chapter is Romans 8. It answers some of the most soul-stirring questions often asked by believers and/or by serious enquirers.

1. It is a fact of common knowledge that during the last few decades the science and art of healing has made great progress. Smallpox has been wiped out, if the reports are true. Antibiotics have saved many lives which, humanly speaking, otherwise would have been lost. Cancer research is having many favorable results, and so one could continue. *Is there, however, also a remedy for those who are standing at death's portal; worried, perhaps, about entrance into the halls of glory?* For God's children there is this comforting answer:
Verse 1 "There is therefore now no condemnation for those who are in Christ Jesus." Add also verses 33, 34 and 38, 39.

2. *How can I know whether I am a Christian?* Answer:
Verse 5 "For those who live according to the flesh set their minds on the things of the flesh, but those who live according to the Spirit set their minds on the things of the Spirit." In other words, "What is your—my—*one absorbing interest?* Is it the world or is it God's kingdom?" If the latter, then I am indeed a child of God.

3. *I know that I love God. But how do I know that he loves me?* Answer:
Verse 28 "And we know that to those who love God all things work together for good; that is, to those who are called according to his purpose." Cf. I John 4:19, "We love God because he first loved us."

4. *I know that God loves me, but will he continue to do so?* Answer:
Verses 38, 39 "I am convinced that neither death nor life nor angels nor principalities nor things present nor things to come . . . nor any other created thing will be able to separate us from the love of God which is in Christ Jesus our Lord."

5. *How do we know that prayer is effective?* Answer:
Verses 26, 27 "And in the same way the Spirit too is helping us in our weakness, for we do not know what we ought to pray, but the Spirit himself intercedes for us

with unspoken groanings. And he who searches the hearts knows what is the Spirit's intention, that he is interceding for the saints in harmony with God's will."

6. *How rich are we going to be in the life hereafter?* Answer:
Verses 17, 18 "And if children, then heirs, heirs of God and fellow-heirs with Christ; since the fact that we are now sharing in his sufferings means that (hereafter) we shall share in his glory. For I consider that the sufferings of this present time are not worthy to be compared with the glory that is to be revealed in us."

7. *What, according to Romans 8, etc., is the Christian's chief duty?* Answer:
To conduct oneself according to the Spirit's direction.
Verse 14 "For as many as are being led by the Spirit of God, these are sons of God." They walk (verse 4) "not according to the flesh but according to the Spirit." They exhibit in their lives "the fruits of the Spirit," for which see Gal. 5:22, 23.

8. *Has the Christian the right to be an optimist?* Answer:
The Christian alone, of all people, has that right. See verses 15-18, beginning with, "For y o u have not received a spirit of slavery, to fill y o u once more with dread, but y o u have received the spirit of adoption . . ." Also verses 35-39, beginning with "Who will separate us from the love of Christ?"

Summary of Chapter 8

A. *For God's children all things work together for good* (verses 1-30).

In close connection with the immediately preceding paragraph—note "Thanks be to God through Jesus Christ our Lord" (7:25)—, as well as with the entire preceding contents of this epistle, this chapter opens with the triumphant exclamation, "There is therefore now no condemnation for those who are in Christ Jesus." Christ's substitutionary atonement has removed the guilt of their sins. As to sin's polluting power, the effective operation of the Holy Spirit, who dwells within their hearts and is the controlling influence in their lives, has "set them free from the law of sin and death."

God did for them what the law, operating by itself, could never have accomplished. Because of sin the law was unable to save. But God, by means of his Son's vicarious death, brought about salvation. He did this without in any way sacrificing the demand of divine righteousness according to which sin must not be allowed to go unpunished. Only those people whose aim is to live in accordance with the demands of the Spirit can derive comfort from this great truth. On the other hand, those who are "in the flesh," that is, who allow their lives to be basically governed by their sinful human nature, do not have this comfort. They "cannot please God" (verses 1-8).

Directly addressing his Roman audience, Paul continues, "Y o u, by contrast, are not basically under the control of sinful human nature; on the contrary, y o u are being governed by the Spirit," implying, "Therefore y o u are, indeed, able to please God, and y o u do, in fact, please him. (Of course, not necessarily every one of y o u: if any individual reveals by his words, actions, and attitudes that he does not wish to be controlled by the Spirit, that person does not belong to Christ)."

It should be our aim, therefore, to live in harmony with the Spirit's direction for our lives. Those who do so will truly live. Those who do not are doomed to die. All those, and only those, whose lives prove that they are being led by the Spirit are truly sons of God.

Those people are not slaves but *children.* The Spirit adds his own testimony to the voice of their regenerated consciousness, thus providing them with a double assurance that they are God's children. And if they are *children,* they are also *heirs.* Their Testator is God. It is he who will bestow on them a glorious inheritance, an inheritance which they will share with Christ, who, being God's Son by nature, is Chief Heir. They are co-heirs, that is, heirs along with him. Those who here and now share Christ's suffering will afterward share his glory (verses 9-18).

To the day of this future glory for God's children the entire sub-human creation is eagerly looking forward. As the groaning of a woman who is in labor indicates both pain and hope, so does also Nature's groaning. The entire sub-human creation is, as it were, craning its neck in order to behold "the revelation of the sons of God," because that event will also mean glory for the entire creation.

But this is not the only groaning that is taking place. "Not only this, but we ourselves, who possess the firstfruits of the Spirit, even we ourselves groan within ourselves, as we eagerly await our adoption, that is, the redemption of our bodies."

Not only does Nature groan and do we groan, but "the Spirit too is helping us in our weakness, for we do not know what we ought to pray, but the Spirit himself intercedes for us with unspoken groanings."

Such groaning is not ineffective. God discerns and grants the ardent desire of the Spirit, so that full salvation for both soul and body will come to us (verses 19-27).

This is true not because of the saints' love for God, but because of his love for them, as is shown by the words, " . . . to those who love God all things work together for good; *that is, to those who are called according to his purpose.*"

Moreover, this cooperation of all things for good is happening not only now but *has always been the case*—"For whom he foreknew, he also foreordained to be conformed to the image of his Son, so that he might be the firstborn among many brothers; and whom he foreordained, these he also called; and whom he called, these he also justified"—*and will continue thus:* "and whom he justified, these he also glorified," that is, "these he will most certainly also glorify." So certain is this fact that the past tense is used, as if it had already happened! (verses 28-30).

B. *Therefore More Than Conquerors Are They* (verses 31-39).

"If God is for us, who is against us?"

It is God who gives. In fact, he did not spare even his own Son, but gave him up for us all. "How will he not also with him graciously give us all things?"

It is God who forgives. He blots out our sins so completely that no sustainable charge can be brought against God's elect. "It is God who justifies. Who is he that condemns?" The assurance that our sins have been blotted out is, however, not based solely on the fact that Christ died for us, but also on the fact that in addition the Father raised him from the dead, thereby proving that this death had been accepted as a fully adequate atonement for our sins. To make assurance even more sure we are comforted by the Savior's session at God's right hand. Here he is interceding for us, without ceasing taking care that the merits of his sacrifice are fully applied to us (verses 31-34).

It is clear therefore that Christ loves us with a love from which no one and nothing can ever separate us. And for this very reason we are "more than conquerors." Not merely conquerors, so that the forces that oppose us are neutralized, rendered ineffective, but *more than* conquerors, so that death, life, angels, principalities, things present, things to come, heights and depths, yes every created thing that has anything to do with us, works in our favor, for in all of them, and in the manner in which they affect us, there is revealed to us the love of God which is in Christ, a love from which no one and nothing will ever be able to separate us (verses 35-39).

Select Bibliography On Romans 1—8

Calvin, J., *Commentaries on The Epistle of Paul The Apostle, To The Romans,* translated and edited by J. Owen, Grand Rapids, 1947.

Cranfield, C. E. B., *A Critical and Exegetical Commentary on The Epistle To The Romans (The International Critical Commentary),* Volume I (on Romans 1-8), Edinburgh, 1975.

Murray, J., *The Epistle To The Romans (The New International Commentary on The New Testament),* Volume I (on Romans 1-8), Grand Rapids, 1959.

A *General Bibliography* is planned for Vol. II; also a *Select Bibliography* for chapters 9-16.

New Testament Commentary

Romans

New Testament Commentary

Romans

VOLUME 2: CHAPTERS 9-16

William Hendriksen

THE BANNER OF TRUTH TRUST

THE BANNER OF TRUTH TRUST
3 Murrayfield Road, Edinburgh EH12 6EL

*

© 1980 William Hendrikson
First Banner of Truth edition 1980
ISBN 0 85151 324 7
Library of congress Catalog Card Number 80:1869
Reprinted as combined volume with volume 1 1982
ISBN 0 85151 365 4

*

*

Printed and bound in Great Britain at
The Camelot Press Ltd, Southampton

TABLE OF CONTENTS

EXPOSITION (continued)

PRACTICAL APPLICATION

LIST OF ABBREVIATIONS

A. Book Abbreviations

A.R.V.	American Standard Revised Version
A.V.	Authorized Version (King James)
Gram. N.T.	A. T. Robertson, *Grammar of the Greek New Testament in the Light of Historical Research*
Gram. N.T. (Bl.-Debr.)	F. Blass and A. DeBrunner, *A Greek Grammar of the New Testament and Other Early Christian Literature*
Grk. N.T. (A-B-M-W)	*The Greek New Testament*, edited by Kurt Aland, Matthew Black, Bruce M. Metzger, and Allen Wikgren
I.S.B.E.	*International Standard Bible Encyclopedia*
L.N.T. (Th.)	Thayer's *Greek-English Lexicon of the New Testament*
L.N.T. (A. and G.)	W. F. Arndt and F. W. Gingrich, *A Greek-English Lexicon of the New Testament and Other Early Christian Literature*
M.M.	*The Vocabulary of the Greek New Testament Illustrated from the Papyri and Other Non-Literary sources,* by James Hope Moulton and George Milligan
N.A.S. (N.T.)	New American Standard Bible (New Testament)
N.E.B.	New English Bible
N.I.V.	New International Version
N.T.C.	W. Hendriksen, *New Testament Commentary*
R.S.V.	Revised Standard Version
S.BK.	Strack and Billerbeck, *Kommentar zum Neuen Testament aus Talmud und Midrasch*
S.H.E.R.K.	*The New Schaff-Herzog Encyclopedia of Religious Knowledge*
Th.D.N.T.	*Theological Dictionary of the New Testament*, edited by G. Kittel and G. Friedrich, and translated from the German by G. W. Bromiley

LIST OF ABBREVIATIONS

B. *Periodical Abbreviations*

EQ	*Evangelical Quarterly*
ET	*Expository Times*
GTT	*Gereformeerd theologisch tijdschrift*
JBL	*Journal of Biblical Literature*
ThG	*Theologie und Glaube*
ThZ	*Theologische Zeitschrift*

Please Note

In order to differentiate between the second person plural (see Rom. 1:11: "I am yearning to see y o u") and the second person singular (see Rom. 2:1: "Therefore you have no excuse"), the letters in "y o u pl." are spaced, those in "you sing." are not.

Summary of Chapters 1—8 and
Preview of Chapters 9—11

After a prologue (1:1-15) Paul has shown that *Justification by Faith is* both *Real*, having been provided not by man but by God (1:16, 17), *and Necessary*; and this both for Gentile (1:18-32) and Jew (2:1—3:8); in fact for everybody (3:9-20), without any distinction between Jew and Gentile (3:21, 22). "All have sinned and fall short of the glory of God, being justified freely by his grace through the redemption (accomplished) in Christ Jesus; whom God designed to be, by the shedding of his blood, a wrath-removing sacrifice (effective) *through faith* . . ." (3:23-25a). As a result, there is no room whatever for boasting (3:27). Does this mean, then, that we invalidate the law through our insistence on faith? "On the contrary," says Paul, "we uphold the law" (verse 31).

In chapter 4 the apostle has shown that this way to be saved, the one and only way, is also definitely *Scriptural* (examples: Abraham and David). And it is *Effective*. Among many other blessings which flow forth from God-given faith, according to the divine *system* or *philosophy* of redemption, the following are probably the most pronounced. Note the first four consonants of the word   p h i l o s o p h y.

```
      e o    i    u
      a l    b    p
      c i    e    e
      e n    r    r
        e    t    i
        s    y    n
        s         v
                  i
                  n
                  c
                  i
                  b
                  i
                  l
                  i
                  t
                  y
```

These fruits are described, respectively, in chapters 5, 6, 7, and 8.

In chapters 9—11 Paul will show that this divinely provided method of obtaining salvation is also *Historical. In the course of history God's most precious promises were intended not for the unbelieving nation but for the believing remnants. Thus, it was, is now, and will always be,* until Christ returns. *The nation* was rejected because of its unbelief (9:27, 31,32; 10:21). Cf. Matt. 8:11, 12; 21:41;

22:8, 9; Luke 20:16; I Thess. 2:14b-16. *All Israel* will be saved. See Rom. 9:6; 11:1-6, 26.

The Gentiles too are saved in no other way than by faith. *This rule holds for everyone, without ethnic distinctions.* (Rom. 9:24-26; 10:4-13; 11:20, 23, 25).

Paul shows how the disobedience of the Jews opens the door of salvation to the Gentiles, and how, in turn, the latter's salvation causes the Jews—in both cases the elect remnant, of course—to become filled with a jealousy that leads to salvation (11:11, 30, 31). This constantly recurring turn of events results in the rapturous doxology of 11:33-36. But, as has been shown, for both Jew and Gentile the way of salvation is ever the same, namely, that of justification by faith, the product not of human works or merit but of divine sovereign grace.

We notice, therefore, that when Paul reaches chapter 9 he has by no means forgotten his main theme.

It is true, nevertheless, that, as in the first eight chapters, so also here, in chapters 9-11, the apostle touches on a variety of subjects, some of them closely related to the main theme, others not so closely. Thus "the special advantages enjoyed by the Jews," in 9:3-5 enumerated in somewhat expanded form, reflect 2:17, 18; 3:1, 2; and "what it means to be a true Israelite" (9:6) echoes 2:28, 29. Compare also the following:

9:5—1:25	9:26—8:14	11:15—5:11
9:19—3:7	9:33—5:5	11:28—5:10
9:23—8:30	10:9—4:24	11:32—3:9; 5:19
9:24—3:29	10:12—3:22, 29, 30	

Even the doctrine of divine predestination, for which one generally turns immediately to Rom. 9:10-24; 11:5-8, 29, is foreshadowed in 8:29, 30.

The question may be asked, "Why was it necessary for Paul to place such emphasis on *Justification by faith, apart from the works of the law?* In light of what the writer himself states in 9:6 f., the answer must be, "Because the Jews, by and large, misconstrued God's most precious promise, believing that it was intended for Abraham's natural posterity, and that its fulfillment was conditioned, at least to some extent, on human merit." Besides, is it not true that the human heart, whether that of a Jew or of a Gentile, is ever proud and by nature unwilling to be "saved by grace"? Finally, not only was it necessary for the Roman church itself to be pure in doctrine but its membership must also be able to defend its convictions when these are attacked by outsiders; that is, by unbelieving Jews and/or Gentiles.

One additional factor, a very important one, must not be left unmentioned in any introduction to chapters 9—11: The apostle was not only a man with a keen intellect and iron will, but, as has been pointed out previously (see p. 13), also with a loving heart. Is it surprising, then, that, as he reflects on the treasures of salvation, about which he writes so touchingly in chapter 8 and also earlier, he, as it were, heaves a sigh of deep sympathy and poignant grief when he considers the fact that many of his own countrymen failed to share in these glorious blessings?

All these factors must be taken into consideration. They shed necessary light on the meaning and purpose of chapters 9—11. Paul is going to show that God's well-meant invitation is still being extended to the Jews. The Lord is by no means "through with the Jews." Until the day of Christ's return, that is, throughout the present era or dispensation of grace, their rejection is *never complete* (chapter 9; see especially verses 6 and 27), *never arbitrary* (chapter 10; see verse 21); and *never absolute and unqualified* (chapter 11; see verses 14 and 26). In his anger God does not withhold compassion. Neither does Paul.

The writer of this commentary is well aware of the fact that in the opinion of many able scholars, both past and present, one of the purposes of chapters 9-11 is to show that when the finishing line of human history is reached, or is about to be reached, the Jews then living on earth will be saved. As they see it, this will happen to (a) the nation Israel as a whole, (b) the mass [of the Jews], (c) the whole nation. It will be (d) a comprehensive eschatological recovering of the unbelieving Jews.[260] Whether this is actually what Paul has in mind will be among the subjects to be discussed in the following pages.

260. a. S. Greijdanus, *Kommentaar op het Nieuwe Testament, Romeinen*, Vol. II, pp. 515, 516; C.E.B. Cranfield, *op. cit.*, Vol. II, pp. 576, 577.

b. J. Murray, *op. cit.*, Vol. II, p. 98; cf. p. xiv.

c. C. Hodge, *op. cit.*, p. 589.

d. G. Vos, *The Pauline Eschatology*, Princeton, 1930, p. 89.

Outline (continued)

Justification by Faith

D. *Historical*
1. *Paul's Sorrow*
"I have great sorrow and unceasing anguish in my heart . . . for the sake
of my brothers, my fellow-countrymen"
9:1-5

2. *Divine Election and Rejection*
"Not all who are of Israel are Israel . . . Jacob I loved, but Esau I hated"
9:6-18

3. *God's Wrath and Mercy*
"Does not the potter have the right to make, out of the same lump of clay
one vessel for honor and another for dishonor?"
9:19-29

4. *Conclusion*
"He who puts his faith in him will not be put to shame"
9:30-33

CHAPTER 9

9 1 I am speaking the truth in Christ—I am not lying; my conscience bears witness along with me in the Holy Spirit—(when I declare) 2 that I have great sorrow and unceasing anguish in my heart. 3 For I could wish that I myself would be accursed (and cut off) from Christ for the sake of my brothers, my fellow-countrymen according to the flesh, 4 since they are Israelites, and theirs is the adoption and the glory and the covenants and the legislation and the worship and the promises; 5 and theirs are the fathers, and from them, as far as his human nature is concerned,[261] is Christ, who is over all God blest forever. Amen.

D. *Historical*
1. *Paul's Sorrow*
"I have great sorrow and unceasing anguish in my heart . . . for the sake of my brothers, my fellow-countrymen"
9:1-5

1, 2. I am speaking the truth in Christ—I am not lying; my conscience bears witness along with me in the Holy Spirit—(when I declare) that I have great sorrow and unceasing anguish in my heart.

With the words, "I am speaking the truth . . . I am not lying" compare II Cor. 11:31; 12:6; Gal. 1:20; I Tim. 2:7.

It is clear that Paul is deeply moved when he dictates these words. The sorrow of his heart is *great* in its intensity, *deep* in its nature, amounting to nothing less than anguish, and *unceasing* in its duration.

Why does Paul say that he is indeed speaking the truth when he thus describes the inner state of his mind and heart?

To discover the answer we should bear in mind that he has already expressed his opinion about the Jews in language that was anything but complimentary (See 2:5, 17-24; also I Thess. 2:14b-16), and he is going to do so again (Rom. 9:31, 32; 10:2, 3, 16, 21; 11:7-10). His kinsmen might easily draw the conclusion, "Paul hates us." Cf. Acts 21:28 f.; 24:5 f. But nothing could be farther from the truth. This explains why Paul considered it necessary to declare that Israel's unbelief and consequent rejection was for him indeed a heavy burden. Truly and deeply Paul loves his kinsmen. But he loves Christ even more. He is speaking the truth "in Christ." To an extent,

---

261. Literally, as concerning the flesh.

at least, his sadness results from love for him whom the Jews have repudiated. His conscience confirms what he is saying; and, as the expression "in the Holy Spirit" shows, that *conscience* belongs to a man who is constantly being indwelt and led (see 8:9, 14, 16) by the Holy Spirit. Contrast 2:15 which refers to the conscience of those who are still living in darkness.

3. For I could wish that I myself would be accursed (and cut off) from Christ for the sake of my brothers, my fellow-countrymen according to the flesh . . .[262]

As the word "For" indicates, Paul is here beginning to give the reason for the strong statement found in verses 1, 2. So deep is his grief resulting from the unbelief of the Jews and from the divine displeasure with them, that he states, "I could wish myself to be accursed (and cut off) from Christ for the sake of my brothers, my fellow-countrymen according to the flesh." He means every word of it. This expression "I could wish . . . to be cut off from Christ" is all the more striking because it issued from the heart and lips of the very man for whom the impossibility of being separated from Christ meant so much, as 8:38, 39 has shown! He is, as it were, saying, "I could wish to be separated from Christ for the sake of others *if this were possible*, but I realize that this is impossible, which in a sense adds to my woe!"

This is clearly the language of *a Christian*. The person who is unconcerned about those who are perishing may well wonder whether he is a Christian.

Paul's sentiment reminds us of Judah, who, as Surety for his brother Benjamin, said, "Please permit your servant to remain here as my lord's slave in the place of the lad" (Gen. 44:33). It recalls to us the thrilling words of Moses, as he interceded for his people, "Yet now, if thou wilt forgive their sin—; but if not, blot me, I pray thee, out of the book which thou hast written" (Exod. 32:32). It brings back to our memory David's agonizing cry, "O my son Absalom! My son, my son Absalom! If only I had died instead of you; O Absalom, my son, my son!" (II Sam 18:33). But most of all, it fixes our attention on *him who really became* his people's Substitute (cf. Rom. 3:24, 25; 8:32; II Cor. 5:21; Gal. 3:13; I Tim. 2:6; and see also Isa. 53:5, 6, 8; Matt. 20:28; Mark 10:45).

---

262. The verb ηὐχόμην, first per. s. imperf. of εὔχομαι, here probably in the sense *to wish* (other meaning: *to pray*). The Attic form would have been ἐβουλόμην ἄν, I could wish. See H. Greeven, Th.D.N.T., Vol. II, p. 778; Ridderbos, *op. cit.*, p. 206. ἀνάθεμα εἶναι . . . ἀπὸ τοῦ Χριστοῦ, an abbreviated expression (see N.T.C. on John, Vol. i, p. 206) meaning "to be accursed (of God) and separated (or banished) from Christ."

According to S.BK., Vol. III, p. 260, in the terminology of the Septuagint the word ἀνάθεμα indicates anything which by God or in God's name has been devoted to destruction and ruin. The rabbinical *"ḥerem"* is a broader concept, inasmuch as it comprises *whatever* is devoted to God, not only that which is devoted to him for destruction. The same distinction is carried over into the New Testament, where the noun ἀνάθημα (in Luke 21:5, according to the best reading) means "that which has been devoted to God as a votive offering," naturally with no curse implications; while ἀνάθεμα (here in Rom. 9:3 and also in Acts 23:14; I Cor. 12:3; 16:22; Gal. 1:8, 9) refers to that which is devoted to God without hope of being redeemed; hence, that which, or he who, is doomed to destruction, accursed.

In this passage Paul certainly proves what a wonderful missionary he is, how passionately he yearns to save the lost. Cf. Rom. 11:14; I Cor. 9:22.

The dismal character of Israel's tragedy and therefore also the heart-rending nature of Paul's anguish become clear when the advantages which caused this nation to stand out above all others (Ps. 147:19, 20) are listed in greater detail than had been done previously (Rom. 2:17, 18; 3:1, 2):

4, 5. since they[263] are Israelites, and theirs is the adoption and the glory and the covenants and the legislation and the worship and the promises; and theirs are the fathers, and from them, as far as his human nature is concerned, is Christ, who is over all God blest forever. Amen.

The list of advantages contains nine items; as follows:

a. *They are Israelites*

Meaning: they are descendants of Jacob, who, until God blessed him, would not let him go, and whose name was changed to Israel ("he struggles with God"). See Gen. 32:22-28. Accordingly, when used in its most favorable sense, the appellatives *Israel, Israelites* were titles of honor, as is clear from such passages as John 1:31, 47, 49; 3:10; 12:13. The honor attaching to the name *Israel* is also reflected in speeches by Peter and Paul recorded in the book of Acts (2:22; 3:12; 13:16). *Historically* was not Israel a nation which by God had been separated from the nations of the world? See Num. 23:9.

However, it should be constantly borne in mind that an advantage is not necessarily a virtue, and a privilege is not a merit. In fact, when, in spite of the many unique advantages conferred upon Israel, that nation turns its back upon the Lord, these very advantages result in increasing Israel's punishment. See 9:30-32; and also what has been said in connection with 3:3, 4 (pp. 110, 111).

b. *and theirs is the adoption*

They had been accorded the high privilege of having been adopted as *God's firstborn* (Exod. 4:22), his *own possession* (Exod. 19:5), his *son* (Hos. 11:1), his *people*, his *chosen* (Isa. 43:20).

The calling and adoption of Israel, its separation from all the nations of the world to be God's very own, was certainly a high honor. When Paul dictated these words, was he not really saying, "Consider the Rock from which y o u were hewn"? See Isa. 51:1.

c. *and the glory*

Another blessing that could not be omitted from the list![264] A detailed study of this concept is indeed very instructive. As the word is here used it indicates *the divine radiance*, generally described as a body of light or fire, often pictured as being surrounded by a cloud. Sometimes the emphasis is

263. In addition to the sense *who, whoever*, the relative pronoun ὅστις (here nom. pl. masc. οἵτινες) at times has a causal meaning. So probably also here; and cf. 1:25.
264. For the various uses of the word δόξα in Scripture see on Rom. 1:23, footnote 38, p. 74. See also G. Kittel, Th. D.N.T., Vol. II, p. 237; and G. von Rad, same volume, pp. 238-242.

on the fire, sometimes on the cloud. It has been called "the visible manifestation of the invisible God."

When the building of the tabernacle had been completed, this "glory of the Lord" came and filled it (Exod. 40:34). It took its stand above the mercy-seat in the holy of holies (Lev. 16:2). During the wilderness journeys when it rested, the Israelites did not travel. When it was taken up, they marched (Exod. 40:36, 37). It was a cloud by day and a pillar of light by night (Exod. 14:20). It is pictured as a devouring fire on top of the mount where Moses spoke with God face to face (Exod. 24:17). When Solomon finished his very impressive prayer at the dedication of the temple, this glory filled the temple (II Chron. 7:1, 2). It indicated the presence of the Lord with his people. However, at times it is associated with the presence of God for the purpose of rendering judgment and inflicting punishment (Num. 14:10; 16:19, 42; 20:6; cf. vss. 12, 13).

By means of this "glory," too, the people of Israel had been separated from all other nations.

d. *and the covenants*

There is a degree of doubt whether one should read the plural "covenants," or—with an important papyrus, with Vaticanus, and with several other witnesses—the singular "covenant." At any rate the word seems to point to the various affirmations and re-affirmations of God's covenant with his people and/or with their leaders. Even though there is only one covenant of grace, in essence identical in both dispensations, it was revealed more and more fully in course of time. See, for example, Gen. 15:1 f.; 17:7; 22:15 f.; 26:1 f.; 28:10 f.; Exod. 2:24; 6:4, 5; Deut. 5:1 f.; 8:18; Josh. 24:1 f.; Luke 1:72, 73; Acts 2:38, 39; 3:25; Gal. 3:9, 28, 29.[265]

Godfearing people in Israel rejoiced in this covenant: David did (II Sam. 23:5); so did Mary, the mother of Jesus (Luke 1:54, 55); and so did Zechariah, the father of John the Baptist (Luke 1:72, 73).

e. *and the legislation*

It was indeed an inestimable privilege that at Sinai Israel had received the law, as it were, out of the very hands of God. Even though by the law no one is justified in God's sight, nevertheless the law is good and serves useful purposes. See on 5:20, p. 184.

f. *and the worship*

Opportunity for worship, first in connection with the tabernacle (cf. Heb. 9:6), later in connection with the temple (Luke 18:9-14), was another high privilege. Nevertheless, the word used in the original is broad enough also to include worship in the synagogue. In fact, does not the occurrence of the same word for "worship" or "service" in John 16:2—"The hour is coming when whoever kills y o u will think that he is offering *service* to God"—point

---

265. See my book, *The Covenant of Grace*, Grand Rapids, revised edition 1978, pp. 21-25.

in the direction of a broader connotation than *cultic* service?[266] Moreover, even family worship was, to a certain extent, regulated by law (Exod. 13:14-16). It would appear, therefore, that Paul here in Rom. 9:4 is referring to far more than temple worship or even public worship in general. He was probably thinking of the *true* worship or service of the one and only God wherever and in whatever manner such homage is rendered. Though things were changing, for a long time both the object and the character of properly tendering religious devotion had been revealed only to the Jews (John 4:21-23). What an inestimable privilege!

g. *and the promises*
The reference is to those made to Abraham, Isaac, Jacob, and to the Jewish people as a whole. To Abraham God had promised, "I will be your God and the God of your seed after you" (Gen. 17:7). In various forms essentially that same promise had been repeated to Isaac, Jacob, and Israel as a nation. In view of its comprehensive character it included many other promises, certainly also the one mentioned in Gen. 18:10, 14 and Rom. 9:9.

It is understandable that the fulfilment of that one basic promise (Gen. 17:7) and therefore also of all subsidiary promises was dependent on the certainty of the coming and mediatorial work of the Redeemer. It is through Christ that all the promises are capable of being realized (II Cor. 1:20; Gal. 3:16). And what an abundance of promises is revealed to us in the pages of Holy Writ, all of them centering in Christ!

In the following list each Old Testament reference in the left column is paralleled by *one* new Testament reference, indicating the fulfilment of the indicated promise. With a little effort it will be easy for the reader to add other references to both lists. By no means all of the Old Testament passages here indicated are in the *form* of promises, but every one at least *implies* a promise.

Old Testament Predictions and Promises	*Fulfilment as recorded in the New Testament*
Gen. 3:15	Rom. 16:20
Gen. 12:3	Gal. 3:8, 9
Gen. 17:7	Acts 2:38, 39
Gen. 18:10, 14	Rom. 9:9
Gen. 22:15-18	Heb. 6:13, 14
Gen. 29:35	Rom. 2:28, 29
Exod. 12:13; Lev. 17:11	Heb. 9:22
Num. 21:8	John 3:14, 15
Num. 24:17a	Rev. 22:16

266. Both Jesus (in John 16:2) and Paul (here in Rom. 9:4) use the term λατρεία. See also the apocryphal writing Ecclesiasticus 4:14: λατρεύοντες αὐτῇ λειτουργήσουσιν Ἁγίῳ: "Those who *serve* her [Wisdom] *will minister* to the Holy one." This too proves that λατρεία and its cognate verb λατρεύω have a wider meaning than λειτουργία and λειτουργέω.

Deut. 18:15, 18	Acts 3:22
II Sam. 7:12, 13	Luke 1:31-33
Ps. 2:7, 8	Eph. 1:22
Ps. 8:4 f.	Heb. 2:6-8
Ps. 16:10	Acts 13:35
Ps. 22:1	Matt. 27:46
Ps. 68:18	Eph. 4:8
Ps. 69:20, 21	Matt. 27:34
Ps. 110:1	Matt. 22:44
Ps. 118:22, 23	Acts 4:11; Matt. 21:42 and see N.T.C. on Luke, p. 876
Isa. 7:14	Matt. 1:23 and see N.T.C. on Matthew, pp. 133-144
Isa. 9:1, 2	Matt. 4:12-16
Isa. 9:6	Luke 2:11
Isa. 10:22	Rom. 9:27
Isa. 28:16	Rom. 9:33; 10:11; I Peter 2:6, 8
Isa. 53	Matt. 8:17 and see N.T.C. on Luke, p. 977, and on Philippians, pp. 82, 83
Isa. 59:20, 21	Rom. 11:26, 27
Isa. 61:1 f.	Luke 4:18, 19
Jer. 23:5	Luke 1:32, 33
Jer. 31:31-34	Heb. 8:8-12
Dan. 2:34, 35, 44	Matt. 28:18
Dan. 7:13, 14	Matt. 26:64
Dan. 9:24-27	Rom. 3:21, 22
Joel 2:28, 29	Acts 2:17 f.
Amos 9:11-15	Acts 15:16-18
Mic. 5:2	Matt. 2:6
Hag. 2:6-9	Heb. 12:26
Zech. 3:8, 9	Heb. 10:12-14
Zech. 6:12, 13	Heb. 6:20-7:3
Zech. 9:9	John 12:15
Zech. 11:12	Matt. 26:15
Zech. 12:10	John 19:37
Mal. 3:1 f.	Matt. 11:10

What a blessing, all these promises, withheld from others but given to Israel.

h. *and theirs are the fathers*

It has been said, "If one wishes to be successful, he should choose his ancestors!" Paul may have been thinking especially of Abraham (4:1-3, 16-23; 9:7; 11:1); Isaac (9:7, 9, 10); and Jacob (9:13; 11:26). In many respects parents, in training their children, were able to point with pride to these three patriarchs. See also Rom. 11:28 and 15:8. Besides, we should never lose sight of the fact that these three ancestors were living on earth before the proclamation of God's holy law from Sinai. For a considerable period of time, therefore, they were *the bearers of tradition, the transmitters of the divine predictions and promises.*

But Paul also makes mention of David (1:3; 4:6-8; 11:9, 10; and see also 3:4). In fact, when the apostle refers to "the fathers," he was probably thinking of all the devout ancestors who played an important role in the history of redemption. Although it is true that none of these forefathers had been perfect in their earthly life and conduct, by and large they could be exhibited as examples to follow. All in all how supremely privileged were the people who were able to claim such ancestors!

i. *and from them, as far as his human nature is concerned, is Christ, who is over all God blest forever. Amen.*

This item serves as a fitting climax. From *them*, that is, from *the Israelites* (see verse 4) Christ derived his human nature. He was and is a Jew. What a source of intense satisfaction and rejoicing this *should be* for Jews!

The apostle hastens to add that although Jesus is indeed a Jew, he is also much more than a Jew. Though he has a human nature, he also has a divine nature. He is God!

It should be clear that when Paul says, "Christ, who is over all God blest forever," he confesses Christ's deity. He does, unless one is willing to adopt the kind of rendering favored by some, namely, "May God, supreme above all, be blessed forever!" (N.E.B.) or "God who is over all be blessed forever" (R.S.V.).

The reasons for rejecting these and similar translations, and adopting one that ascribes deity to Christ are as follows:

(1) The fact that in the preceding clause Paul has commented on Christ's *human* nature makes it reasonable to believe that he would now say something about his *divine* nature.

(2) A word-for-word translation of the original would be: ". . . and from [or *of*] whom (is) Christ according to (the) flesh, the one being above all God blessed forever . . ." It is clear that the words "the one being" or "who is" refer to Christ. They cannot refer to anyone else.

(3) The rendering, "Let God be blessed forever" would be a doxology in honor of *God*. It is Paul's custom, in such doxologies, to include in a preceding line or clause a reference to God; for example,

". . . since they had indeed exchanged God, (who is) the truth, for a lie, and worshiped and served the creature rather than the Creator, who is blessed forever. Amen" (Rom. 1:25).

". . . according to the will of our God and Father, to whom be the glory forever and ever. Amen." (Gal. 1:4, 5. See also II Cor. 11:31; II Tim. 4:18. The present passage, interpreted as a doxology, would therefore clash with Paul's style.

315

(4) Those who, in line with N.E.B. and R.S.V., translate the Greek words in question as if they were an *independent* doxology should bear in mind that in both Old and New Testament the word *Blessed* in such doxologies is found at the beginning of the sentence; as, for example, "Blessed (be) the Lord, the God of Israel" (Luke 1:68). See also II Cor. 1:3; Eph. 1:3. That is not the case here in Rom. 9:5.

(5) It is not unusual for the writers of New Testament books, including Paul, to ascribe deity, or the qualities pertaining to deity, to Christ. See, for example, Matt. 28:18; Mark 1:1; John 1:1-4; 8:58; 10:30, 33; 20:28; Phil. 2:6; Col. 2:9; Titus 2:13; Heb. 1:8; II Peter 1:1.

(6) A doxology to God would sound very strange in a paragraph in which Paul expresses "great sorrow and unceasing anguish" because of Israel's unbelief! Today it is unlikely that a missionary, reporting back to his board, would say, "Even though the people among whom I carry on my evangelistic activity have been blessed with many advantages—such as prosperity, good health, intelligence, etc.—there have been very few conversions. *Praise the Lord!*"

For the solemn addition "Amen" see on 1:25, p. 77.

What Paul has been saying, then, may be summed up as follows, "It grieves me deeply that in spite of all the remarkable advantages which God has showered on Israel, it has failed to reciprocate."

How can this negative reaction be explained? Also, does this mean that God has *totally* rejected Israel? The answers are given in the verses that follow; in fact, in a sense, in the entire argument beginning at 9:6 and ending at 11:36.

---

6 But it is not as though the word of God had failed. For not all who are of Israel are Israel; 7 nor, because they are Abraham's seed, are they all (his) children; but

"It is through Isaac that your seed will be reckoned."

8 This means that it is not the natural children who are children of God, but it is the children of the promise who are reckoned as seed. 9 For the language of promise is this:

"At the appointed time I will return, and Sarah will have a son."

10 But not only this; (there is) also Rebecca, who conceived (her two sons) at one time by one and the same husband, namely, our father Isaac. 11 For, before the twins were born or had done anything either good or bad, in order that God's purpose according to election might stand, 12 (a purpose) based not on (human) works but on him who calls, she was told,

"The elder shall serve the younger";

13 as it is written,

"Jacob I loved, but Esau I hated."

14 What then shall we say? There is no injustice on God's part, is there? Not at all! 15 For to Moses he says,

"I will have mercy on whom I have mercy; and I will
have compassion on whom I have compassion."

16 So then, it does not depend on (man's) will or exertion but on God's mercy. 17 For the Scripture says to Pharaoh,

"For this very purpose have I raised you up, that I might display my power in you, and that my name might be proclaimed in all the earth."

18 So then, on whom he wills he has mercy, and whom he wills he hardens.

2. *Divine Election and Rejection*
"Not all who are of Israel are Israel . . . Jacob I loved, but Esau I hated"
9:6-18

6-8 But it is not as though the word of God had failed. For not all who are of Israel are Israel; nor, because they are Abraham's seed, are they all (his) children; but

"It is through Isaac that your seed will be reckoned." This means that it is not the natural children who are children of God, but it is the children of the promise who are reckoned as seed.

Paul was apparently afraid that the statement with respect to his great sorrow and unceasing anguish might be interpreted as if he meant that God's *word*—his promise regarding Israel—had failed, his purpose frustrated.[267] So the apostle explains that although a marvelous promise had indeed been made to Israel (as has been indicated; see p. 313), that promise was never meant to be realized in the entire nation but only in the true Israel.

The thought expressed here is essentially the same as that found in Rom. 2:28, 29. Not in all the descendants of Abraham or of Israel was the covenant promise destined to be fulfilled but only in the hearts and lives of those who by God's grace would repose their trust in him and strive to obey his will out of gratitude. See Gen. 15:6; 17:1, 2, 9; Deut. 30:2, 3, 9, 10; I Kings 8:47-50; Jer. 18:5-10.

Moreover, in harmony with all this, the line of the covenant would run through Isaac. It was he who would be counted as Abraham's *seed*, in whom the covenant promise would be fulfilled. The true seed was *Isaac*, not Ishmael. Similarly, it was *Jacob*, not Esau (9:13). Cf. Gal. 3:9, 29.[268]

---

267. Note at beginning of verse 6: οὐχ οἷον . . . ὅτι, a combination of οὐχ οἷον and οὐχ ὅτι. The meaning is: it is not as though; it is not so that. Cf. Gram.N.T. (Bl. Debr.), par. 480. κληθήσεται (lit. "will be named or called") is a Hebraism. To be named after someone means to be counted as his offspring. Cf. Gen. 48:6.

268. In connection with verse 8 the question arises, "When Paul says, 'This means that it is not the children *of the flesh* (thus literally) who are the children of God, but it is the children of the promise who are reckoned as seed,' what does this expression 'children of the flesh' mean?" On this point commentators are divided. Some, appealing to the contrast pictured in Gal. 4:23, 29 between flesh-born Israel and Spirit-born Isaac, are of the opinion that the term "children of the flesh" as used here in Rom. 9:8 refers to the Jews who rejected Christ, while the term "children of the promise" points to those people who were reposing their trust in him. We have no quarrel with the latter part of this equation. But as to the former, which would pour the full meaning of Gal. 4:21-31 into Rom. 9:8, with this it is hard to agree.

The expression "children of the flesh" as used here in Rom. 9:8, should be explained in light of its own context. It then becomes clear that the terms "all who are of Israel" (verse 6), "Abraham's seed," here meaning *descendants* (verse 7), and "children of the flesh" (verse 8) are parallel, in the sense that they all indicate *natural* or *physical* offspring. Correct are, therefore, those translations and interpretations which, for verse 8a, have adopted the rendering, "It is not the natural [or physical] children who are children of God," etc.

Thus N.I.V., Phillips, N.E.B., Williams, and Berkely must all be considered correct. Of course, those who retain the more literal rendering—"It is not the children of the flesh"— are also correct. That one of these "children of the flesh," who was not a child of promise, was indeed Ishmael, is, of course, admitted.

It is important to point out that although the statement "For not all who are of Israel are Israel" is cast in a negative mold, the positive implication is, *"There is, indeed, a true Israel. God's rejection of Israel is not total or complete."* His word has not failed and never will fail. The remnant will be saved (verse 27). He who puts his faith in Christ will not be put to shame (verse 33).

God's people are here called "the children of the promise," a strikingly beautiful designation! Their spiritual birth was due not to anything residing in them but entirely to God's covenant promise. It was the promise that gave them birth! They "were born not of blood nor of the will of the flesh nor of the will of man, but of God" (John 1:13), a fact exemplified clearly in the story of the birth of Isaac, to which reference is made in verse

9. For the language of promise is this:
"At the appointed time I will return, and Sarah will have a son."

As the conjunction "For" shows, what follows proves that not Abraham's natural children are necessarily God's children, and that only those can claim that distinction who are products of God's promise, his sovereign grace.

Note emphatic position of ". . . the language of promise is this." This is followed by the astounding statement that at the appointed time—that is *next year* (see Gen. 18:10, 14)—Sarah, the very wife, who according to Gen. 11:30 was *barren*, according to Gen. 18:11 was *past the age of childbearing*, and according to Gen. 17:17 was *ninety years old*, would give birth to a child. Not only this, but the child would be *a son!*

That this would happen seemed to be so impossible that when the Lord had told Abraham that he would have a child by Sarah, he had answered, "Will a son be born to a man a hundred years old? And will Sarah, at the age of ninety, bear a child?" (Gen. 17:17). And though Abraham probably quickly conquered his earlier misgiving,[269] even later Sarah had greeted the promise of a child with the laughter of unbelief (Gen. 18:10-12).

Nevertheless, the promise was fulfilled, proving that Isaac was indeed the child of promise, the product solely of divine, sovereign power and grace. God had *returned;* that is, his promise had been fulfilled in every detail.

Paul has made clear, therefore, that the ability to trace one's line of descent to Abraham does not entitle a person to believe that he will inherit that which was promised to Abraham. What matters is whether he belongs to that seed of Abraham which originates in the sovereign grace, will, and disposal of God Almighty.

Not to any extent is it a matter of human merit. The very history of Abraham and Sarah makes this clear. If from what has been said so far about Sarah the conclusion should be drawn that, judged by spiritual standards, she ranked far below Abraham, it should be pointed out that, all in all, Scripture's estimate of her is high. See Isa. 51:2; Heb. 11:11; I Peter 3:6. Abraham certainly must have loved her. Note what efforts he put forth in

---

269. That this patriarch had been briefly afflicted with misgiving is also the opinion of G. Ch. Aalders, *Genesis II (Korte Verklaring)*, p. 66.

order to secure for her an honorable burial (Gen. 23). And observe how Isaac needed to be comforted because of her death (Gen. 24:67).

And, on the other hand, measured by these same standards, Abraham does not fare as well as we had probably expected. In spite of whatever extenuating circumstances may be mentioned in his defense, what he did, as reported in Gen. 12:10 f. and again (!) in Gen. 20:1 f., was shocking.

Isaac too, though certainly a child of God (Gen. 25:21; 26:23-25; 28:1-4) was by no means perfect (Gen. 26:7; 27:1-4).

The only conclusion we can reach is that in the case of Abraham, Sarah, and their son Isaac, salvation, appropriated by faith, was definitely a matter of divine, sovereign grace. Human merit had nothing to do with it. Cf. Gen. 15:6; Rom. 4:3; Gal. 3:6.

Moreover, that salvation and preferential standing in the line of the covenant are indeed matters of grace, gifts proceeding from God's sovereign will and power, is even more strikingly illustrated in the story of Rebecca:

10-13. But not only this; (there is) also Rebecca, who conceived (her two sons) at one time by one and the same husband, namely, our father Isaac. For, before the twins were born or had done anything either good or bad, in order that God's purpose according to election might stand, (a purpose) based not on (human) works but on him who calls, she was told,

> **"The elder shall serve the younger";**

as it is written,

> **"Jacob I loved, but Esau I hated."[270]**

In defense of his reasoning Paul states, "But not only this"; that is, "Consider not only the case of Isaac and Ishmael." In their case one might be tempted to argue that the reason why the line of the covenant ran through Isaac, not through Ishmael, was that Isaac's mother was Sarah, but Ishmael's mother was Sarah's Egyptian slave-handmaid Hagar. Jacob and Esau, however, not only had the same father but also had the same mother, and were conceived at the same moment. They were twins, though Esau was born just before Jacob and was, accordingly, "the elder."

Note also the following: in the case of Abraham's children it was possible to point to the contrast in the cause of their birth. Ishmael was, in a sense, the product of his parents' sinful scheming (Gen. 16:14), but Isaac was the realization of God's promise.

Nothing resembling this was true in the case of Jacob and Esau. Both were born in answer to prayer (Gen. 25:21).

---

270. The compressed style of verse 10 leads to certain difficulties in translation. Also, the word κοίτη has more than one meaning, although the various senses in which it is used are closely related. In Luke 11:7 it means *bed*; cf. κεῖμαι, to lie down. In Heb. 13:4 the reference is to the *marriage-bed*; in Lev. 15:24, to *sexual intercourse*; and in Lev. 15:16, to the *emission of semen*. Here, in Rom. 9:10, what Paul probably means is that Rebecca, having one husband, namely, Isaac, conceived (her twins) at one time; that is, from one seminal emission.—In Rom. 13:13 κοίτη = indecency, sexual excess.

Nevertheless, in spite of their remarkable similarities, before these twins were even born, or had done anything either good or bad, their mother was already told, "The elder shall serve the younger" (quoted from Gen. 25:23). And this is also what actually happened, for not only did Esau forfeit, and Jacob receive, the birthright (Gen. 25:29-34), but the latter also obtained the blessing which father Isaac wrongfully had intended to pronounce upon Esau (Gen. 27:1-29).

The contrast was, however, even sharper, for, quoting from Mal. 1:2, 3, the apostle adds, "as it is written, 'Jacob I loved, but Esau I hated.' " The divine *purpose*, springing from election and executing its design, determines who are saved. Everything depends on God who *calls* (effectively draws) some, not others. Cf. 8:28.

What Paul is saying, then, in verses 6-13, is this: In the final analysis the reason why some people are accepted and others rejected is that God so willed it. The divine, sovereign will is the source of both election and reprobation. Human *responsibility* is not canceled, but there is no such thing as human *merit*. God's eternal purpose is not ultimately based on human works.

Additional Reflections on Election and Reprobation

As is well-known, this passage (Rom. 9:13) is considered a prooftext for the doctrine of predestination: election and reprobation. *Predestination* is God's eternal purpose whereby he has foreordained whatever comes to pass (Eph. 1:11). *Election* may be defined as God's eternal purpose to cause certain specific individuals to be *in Christ* the recipients of special grace, in order that they may live to God's glory and may obtain everlasting salvation (Luke 10:20; Acts 13:48; Rom. 11:5; Eph. 1:4; II Thess. 2:13). *Reprobation* is God's eternal purpose to pass by certain specific individuals in the bestowment of special grace, ordaining them to everlasting punishment for their sins (Rom. 9:13, 17, 18, 21, 22; I Peter 2:8).[271]

Although both of these decrees are equally ultimate, it would be wrong to say that they are co-ordinate in every respect. For example, although sin is indeed the meriting cause of the punishment mentioned in the definition of the decree of reprobation, faith is not the meriting cause of the salvation to which the definition of the decree of election refers. Also—to quote from my published translation of Dr. H. Bavinck's *Doctrine of God*[272]—"In a certain sense, the fall, sin, and eternal punishment are included in God's decree and willed by him. But this is true *in a certain sense* only, and not in the same sense as grace and salvation. These are the objects of his delight, but God does not delight in sin, neither has he pleasure in punishment."

The question is often asked, "How was it possible for a Loving God to ordain certain individuals to everlasting punishment?" A more logical ques-

---

271. Also often mentioned as a prooftext for the doctrine of reprobation is Jude 4, but the translation of this passage is disputed. Also Rom. 11:7 does not prove reprobation. See the context: 11:11f.
272. Grand Rapids, 1979, p. 390.

tion would be, "How was it possible for a God whose righteousness demands that sin be punished, to ordain some individuals to everlasting life and glory?" Surely "the wonder of it all" is the substitutionary death of Christ!

The Westminster Confession of the year 1647 has this to say about Election and Reprobation:

> God from all eternity did, by the most wise and holy counsel of his own will, freely and unchangeably ordain whatsoever comes to pass; yet so as thereby neither is God the author of sin, nor is violence offered to the will of the creatures, nor is the liberty or contingency of second causes taken away, but rather established—Ch. iii, I

> Those of mankind that are predestinated unto life, God, before the foundation of the world was laid, according to his eternal and immutable purpose, and the secret counsel and good pleasure of his will, hath chosen in Christ, unto everlasting glory, out of his mere free grace and love, without any foresight of faith or good works, or perseverance in either of them, or any other thing in the creature, as conditions, or causes moving him thereunto, and all to the praise of his glorious grace.—Ch. iii, V

> The rest of mankind God was pleased, according to the unsearchable counsel of his own will, whereby he extendeth or withholdeth mercy as he pleaseth, for the glory of his sovereign power over his creatures, to pass by, and to ordain them to dishonor and wrath for their sin, to the praise of his glorious justice—Ch. iii, VII

Essentially the same truths are expressed in Canons of Dort, First Head of Doctrine, articles 7 and 15, and in the Belgic Confession, article XVI. The Heidelberg Catechism contains very little on this subject. See Answers 52 and 54.

In addition the Canons (in its Fifth Head of Doctrine, Rejection of Errors, Conclusion) warn against those who teach that the doctrine of the Reformed Churches "makes God the author of sin," and that he

> . . . by a mere arbitrary act of his will, without the least respect or view to any sin, has predestined the greatest part of the world to eternal damnation, and has created them for this very purpose; that in the same manner in which election is the foundation and cause of faith and good works, reprobation is the cause of unbelief and impiety; that many children of the faithful are torn, guiltless, from their mothers' breasts, and tyrannically plunged into hell . . . and many things of the same kind which the Reformed Churches not only do not acknowledge but even detest with their whole soul.

A couple additional matters should not be omitted:

a. "The reprobate receive many blessings, which do not result from the decree of reprobation, but from the goodness and grace of God. They receive many natural gifts: life, health, strength, food, happiness, etc. (Matt. 5:45; Acts 14:17; 17:28; Rom. 1:19; James 1:17, etc.). Also with respect to the reprobate, God does not leave himself without witness. He endures them with much longsuffering (Rom. 9:22). He causes the gospel of his grace to be proclaimed to them, and has no pleasure in their death (Ezek. 18:23;

33:11; Matt. 23:37; Luke 19:41; 24:47; John 3:16; Acts 17:30; Rom. 11:32; I Thess. 5:9; I Tim. 2:4; II Peter 3:9)."[273]

Cain was a reprobate. Of this there can be no doubt (I John 3:12; Jude 11). Yet, how tenderly God addressed him! (Gen. 4:6, 7).

b. There is a problem that must be faced. Our Creeds, as has been shown, proceed from the infralapsarian position, according to which those people who were destined for glory were chosen out of the state of sin and destruction into which they had plunged themselves; and those destined for perdition were, by God's decree, left in that state. The question, however, arises, "Why did God at all allow the fall to take place?"

To that question there is no answer, except it be that of Deut. 29:29, "The secret things belong to the Lord our God, but the things revealed belong to us and to our children forever . . ." And that of Job 11:7, 8,

> Can you by searching fathom God?
> Can you probe the limits of the Almighty?
> They are higher than the heavens—what can you do?
> Deeper than Sheol—what can you know?

Permit me to quote once more from my translation of Bavinck's *Doctrine of God*, this time p. 396:

> Round about us we observe so many facts which seem to be unreasonable, so much undeserved suffering, so many unaccountable calamities, such an uneven and inexplicable distribution of destiny, and such an enormous contrast between the extremes of joy and sorrow, that anyone reflecting on these things, is forced to choose between viewing this universe as if it were governed by the blind will of an unbenign deity as is done by pessimism; or, upon the basis of Scripture and by faith, to rest in the absolute and sovereign, yet—however incomprehensible—wise and holy will of him who will one day cause the full light of heaven to dawn upon these mysteries of life.

Among the many objections that have been raised against the doctrine of election and reprobation, and particularly against the view that Rom. 9:13 supports this doctrine, are the following:

Objection a. Election, yes; reprobation, no! Neither Rom. 9:13 nor any other biblical passage teaches reprobation.

Comment. That Scripture does indeed teach both election and reprobation has been shown. See above, p. 320. Besides, election and reprobation stand and fall together. Those whom the Lord does not elect he rejects. God's counsel is all-comprehensive (Prov. 16:4; Eph. 1:11).

Moreover, when God elects a person, he not merely decides to cause him to enter heaven at last, but guides him all the way from conception to glorification. David proclaims this truth in Ps. 139:16, which, in rhyme, is as follows:

---

273. This quotation is taken from my translation of Bavinck's material on this subject. See *Doctrine of God*, p. 400.

Ere into being I was brought,
Thine eye did see, and in thy thought,
My life in all its perfect plan
Was ordered ere my days began.

Now the believer does not live in a vacuum, and between his life and that of the unbeliever there is no Chinese Wall. The life of the elect and that of the non-elect are so thoroughly intertwined—at play, in school, in the place of business, in factory, in government, etc.—that any divine plan that affects the elect must also affect the non-elect, without canceling human account-ability in either case. A half plan is no plan at all. Many a battle has been lost because this or that small (?) item had been excluded.

> For the want of a nail the shoe was lost,
> For the want of a shoe the horse was lost,
> For the want of a horse the rider was lost,
> For the want of a rider the battle was lost,
> For the want of a battle the kingdom was lost
> And all for the want of a horseshoe nail.
>
> —Franklin, Poor Richard Almanac

Objection b. The divine oracle (Mal. 1:2, 3), quoted by Paul in Rom. 9:13, really means, "Jacob have I loved intensely, but Esau have I loved less."

Comment. The verb used in the original for *to hate* can indeed have the meaning *to love less.* See N.T.C. on Luke, pp. 734, 735. The question is, "Does it have that meaning *here* (Rom. 9:13)?" Clearly, it does not! The context of Mal. 1:2, 3 is one of judgment, punishment, indignation: ". . . Esau have I hated, and made his mountains a desolation . . . They will build, but I will throw down." Also, when Esau receives his father's "blessing," that blessing amounts to what might almost be called a curse. Correctly trans-lated, it begins as follows,

"Away from the fatness of the earth will be your dwelling, and away from the dew of heaven from above" (Gen. 27:39). In fact, the "blessing" was of such a negative nature, and the deception by Jacob so painful, that Esau hated Jacob because of what had happened, and threatened to kill him. Conclusion: "loved less" will not do for Mal. 1:3 or for Rom. 9:13. These passages refer to reprobation, nothing less.

Objection c. Gen. 25:22, 23 and Mal. 1:2, 3 do not refer to individuals, Jacob and Esau, but to nations, Israel and Edom.

Comment. Though it is true that in Gen. 25:22, 23 the text turns quickly from babes to nations, nevertheless the starting-point has to do with persons, not nations. The words, "Two nations are in your womb" can, of course, not be taken literally. The meaning is, "The two babes within your womb will become rival nations."

The Malachi context is similar. Here too the starting-point is certainly personal: "Was not Esau Jacob's brother . . . yet I loved Jacob but Esau I hated." Paul had every right, therefore, to apply these passages to persons, as he did.

Objection d. The doctrine of a twofold predestination—election and reprobation—is wrong because Jacob is always Esau also, and Esau is also Jacob; or, again, in each of us there is a Jacob and an Esau, etc.

Comment. Can anyone really believe that this is actually what Scripture is saying in these passages?

Having examined the objections, the result is that the doctrine of divine election and reprobation, based, among other passages, on Rom. 9:13, stands. The arguments against it are shallow and fallacious. See also the excellent "Paper" by F. H. Klooster, "Predestination: A Calvinistic Note," in *Perspectives on Evangelical Theology*, Grand Rapids, 1979, pp. 81-94.

14, 15. What then shall we say? There is no injustice on God's part, is there? Not at all. For to Moses he says,

"I will have mercy on whom I have mercy; and I will have compassion on whom I have compassion."

For "What [or What then] shall we say?" see also 3:5; 4:1; 6:1; 7:7; 8:31; 9:14, 30. The apostle anticipates an objection, whether from the side of an opponent or from that of those addressed; in fact, perhaps even a possible objection that might arise in *anybody's* mind. For the rest, two interpretations have been advanced.

According to the first, the meaning of verses 14, 15 is as follows: The question arises, "When God chose Isaac instead of Ishmael, and when he elected Jacob instead of Esau, making known his decision to their mother before the twins had even been born and had done either good or bad, that was not possibly unjust, was it?" According to this interpretation Paul answers, in substance, "Not at all, for that is God's way of acting, as is clear from what he said to Moses (verse 15) and to Pharaoh" (verse 17).

So interpreted, however, the answer would make little sense. It would amount to saying, "God is not unjust, for that is the way he is used to doing things!"

According to the second, the meaning is this: "Paul, by reasoning as you did [in Rom. 9:6-13] about God's sovereignty, you are not, perhaps, doing injustice to God, drawing inferences from the passages (about Abraham's seed and Rebecca's twins) that you have no right to draw?" The answer then is, *"Not at all* (see on 3:4), for, in speaking to Moses, God has definitely declared that he has the right to show his mercy and compassion to whomsoever he wishes." Cf. Matt. 20:15. What the apostle declares, therefore, is that when he underscores the doctrine of God's sovereignty he is simply saying what God himself also said.[274] I accept this explanation.

Continued: **16. So then, it does not depend on (man's) will or exertion but on God's mercy.**

Literally what Paul says is, "So then (it is) not of a person's willing nor of a person's running, but of God's showing mercy."

---

274. For this interpretation see S. Greijdanus, *Kommentaar Romeinen* II, pp. 422, 423; and Ridderbos, *op. cit.*, pp. 14, 15.

To the question, "What is the subject of the sentence?"—for in the original there is no subject—the answers differ. Some say it is "Mercy." They point to the immediate context (verse 15). Others go back a little farther, to verses 6-15, and answer, "It is being a child of God" (see 9:8), or "salvation," "life everlasting." But do not all these answers basically agree? Hymn writers have caught the idea; see on 1:17, pp. 60, 61, and on 3:24, 25, p. 133. Neither man's volition nor his exertion brings about salvation. *God* does. Election, and therefore also salvation, is a matter of God's sovereign will. Equally ultimate is reprobation.

Therefore, parallel with verse 15 is verse **17. For the Scripture says to Pharaoh, "For this very purpose have I raised you up, that I might display my power in you, and that my name might be proclaimed in all the earth."**

Since this passage is presented as being a direct quotation, the Lord's own message to Pharaoh, a message conveyed to that king by Moses, and recorded in Scripture—note "the Scripture says"—it is advisable to study the text (Exod. 9:16) in which it is first recorded.

Its context shows us that there had been six plagues on Egypt: water turned into blood, frogs, lice, flies, murrain of cattle, boils on man and beast. There were going to be four more: hail, locusts, three days of intense darkness, all the firstborn of Egypt slain. Between the sixth and the seventh plague God ordered Moses to say to Pharaoh, "By now I could have stretched out my hand and struck you and your people with a plague that would have wiped you off the earth. But for this reason did I cause you to stand [or survive], to show you my power, and that my name might be proclaimed in all the earth" (Exod. 9:15, 16).

It is clear, therefore, that in Exod. 9:16 the expression "made you to stand" or "survive" means "spared you." There is accordingly no reason to interpret Rom. 9:17 differently. To be sure, the Greek verb has other meanings also, but these meanings do not fit the Exodus account.[275]

I agree, therefore, with the interpretation of Rom. 9:17 found also in the following commentaries: E. F. Harrison, *op. cit.*, p. 106; Ridderbos, *op. cit.*, pp. 216, 217. God spared Pharaoh so that he might display his power in him, by punishing him and his people. Cf. Rom. 9:22.[276]

That God did indeed fulfil his purpose of displaying his power in Pharaoh, so that his (God's) name might be proclaimed in all the earth, is clear from Deut. 6:22; 7:18, 19; 11:3; 34:11; I Sam. 4:8; Ps. 135:9; Acts 7:36. These passages prove that what God did in Egypt with Pharaoh and his people

---

275. The Hebrew verb used in Exod. 9:16 is the Hiph. pret. first per. s., with sec. per. s. suffix, of the verb עָמַד, to stand. This verb at times has the meaning: to spare, keep alive. See W. H. Gispen, *Exodus (Korte Verklaring)*, Kampen, 1932, p. 102. Also in harmony with this interpretation is the LXX rendering διετηρήθης, you have been spared.

276. For a different interpretation of the verb ἐξεγείρω, used in Rom. 9:17, see L.N.T. (A. and G.), p. 273, and several commentaries, including Cranfield, Greijdanus, Murray. Popular is the interpretation: to cause to be born, to cause to appear on the stage of history.

made a very deep impression on the minds and hearts of later generations. Even today when, in the home, in Sunday School, Christian School, or church, the story of the ten plagues is told, or when that story is read, is not God's name and greatness being proclaimed?

It is clear that when God hardens the heart of a person who has hardened himself against his Maker, God cannot be accused of being unjust. Whether God will actually do this, or whether, instead, he will show mercy, is not for that person or for us to decide. It is a matter pertaining to God's own will, power, and eternal decree. It is exactly as stated in verse

18. So then, on whom he wills he has mercy, and whom he wills he hardens. Cf. verse 15. A striking expression of *God's sovereignty!*

There is no reason to doubt that the hardening of which Pharaoh was the object was final. It was a link in the chain: reprobation—wicked life—hardening—everlasting punishment. This does not mean, however, that divine hardening is always final. See on 11:7b, 11.

---

19 You will say to me then, "Why does he still find fault, for who is resisting his will?" 20 But who are you, O man, to talk back to God? Will what is molded say to its molder, "Why did you make me thus?" 21 Does not the potter have the right to make, out of the same lump of clay, one vessel for honor and another for dishonor?[277] 22 And what if God, choosing to show his wrath and to make known his power, bore with great patience vessels of wrath, prepared for destruction, 23 (doing this) in order to make known the riches of his glory (lavished) upon vessels of mercy, which he prepared beforehand for glory, 24 even us, whom he also called, not only from the Jews but also from the Gentiles? 25 Just as he says in Hosea:

"'Not my people' I will call 'My people,'
and
'Not my loved one' (I will call) 'My loved one.' "

26 And it will happen that in the very place where it was said to them, "You are not my people," they will be called "sons of the living God."

27 But Isaiah cries out concerning Israel:

"Though the number of the children of Israel be as the sand of the sea, (only) the remnant will be saved. 28 For the Lord will carry out his sentence on earth completely and quickly."

29 And as Isaiah predicted:

"If the Lord of hosts had not left us a seed, we would have fared like Sodom, and have been made like Gomorrah."

---

3. *God's Wrath and Mercy*
"Does not the potter have the right to make, out of the same lump of clay, one vessel for honor and another for dishonor?"
9:19-29

A plausible objection is now presented: **19. You will say to me then, "Why does he still find fault, for who is resisting his will?"**

The objection arises from failure to distinguish between God's secret (decretive) and his revealed (preceptive) will. Man can, of course, do nothing

---

277. Or: one for ornamental ... one for everyday use.

about the former. But he certainly and rightly is held responsible for what he does about the latter. This two-fold fact is clearly set forth in two easy-to-remember passages: Deut. 29:29 and Luke 22:22.

It is, therefore, not surprising that the apostle continues as follows:

20, 21. But who are you, O man, to talk back to God? Will what is molded say to its molder, "Why did you make me thus?" Does not the potter have the right to make, out of the same lump of clay, one vessel for honor and another for dishonor?

The answer rebukes the questioner for his impudence and for his imbecility; for his shamelessness and for his senselessness. The objector calls in question God's justice, and is therefore impudent, arrogant. He forgets that if that which is molded has no right to say to its molder, "Why did you make me thus?," then *all the more*, human beings have no right thus to address their Sovereign Maker. The objector is stupid.

This passage about the potter and his lump of clay brings back to the memory several biblical passages; such as Job 10:9; Isa. 64:8; II Tim. 2:20; and especially Isa. 29:16; 45:9. See also the apocryphal book Wisdom of Solomon 15:7-17.

Note: "out of the same lump of clay, one vessel for honor and another for dishonor?" Several translators and commentators agree with this or a very similar rendering.[278] Others prefer "ornamental . . . everyday; or noble . . . common." The difference is minor. In favor of the first alternative is the fact that the context, here in Rom. 9:20, 21 (see 9:13 f.) is replete with sharp contrasts; such as, love, hatred; Moses, Pharaoh; mercy, hardening; vessels of wrath, vessels of mercy.[279]

The main idea Paul is putting across is this: If even a potter has the right out of the same lump or mass of clay to make one vessel for honor, and another for dishonor, then certainly God, our Maker, has the right, out of the same mass of human beings who by their own guilt have plunged themselves into the pit of misery, to elect some to everlasting life, and to allow others to remain in the abyss of wretchedness.

22-24. And what if God, choosing to show his wrath and to make known his power, bore with great patience vessels of wrath, prepared for destruction, (doing this) in order to make known the riches of his glory (lavished) upon vessels of mercy, which he prepared beforehand for glory, even us, whom he also called, not only from the Jews but also from the Gentiles?[280]

---

278. For example, A.V., A.R.V., Berkeley, Williams, Phillips, Greijdanus, Lekkerkerker.

279. See also the meaning of the word ἀτιμία in Rom. 1:26; I Cor. 11:14; 15:43; II Cor. 6:8; 11:21; namely, shame, disgrace, dishonor. And study N.T.C. on II Tim. 2:20, p. 270.

280. In the original this sentence, beginning with verse 22, and extending at least through verse 24, has no subject. Its anacoluthic character reminds us of 5:12 f. Nevertheless, the unexpressed but assumed subject can be conjectured on the basis of the context. See especially verses 19, 20, which indicate the unreasonableness of questioning God's justice or fairness. The subject—or subject clause—is therefore probably, "*Who* would dare to find fault with

Note the following:

a. *God . . . bore with great patience*

The patience of God, his reluctance to punish sinners, is stressed in several passages; among them being Rom. 2:4—see p. 90; Gen. 6:3b; 18:26-32; Exod. 34:6; I Kings 21:29; Neh. 9:17b; Ps. 86:15; 10:8-14; 145:8, 9; Isa. 5:1-4; Ezek. 18:23, 32; 33:11; Luke 13:6-9; Rev. 2:21.

b. *vessels of wrath*

Who are these vessels of wrath? Some identify them with the prospective believers of Eph. 2:3. But is it not more natural, in the present context, to think of men like Pharaoh, the impenitent; in other words, of reprobates? It is comforting to know that, as remarked previously—see p.321—God shows patience even with those who are ultimately lost! This explanation also harmonizes with the next point:

c. *prepared*[281] *for destruction*

Paul does not state who it was that prepared these people or made them ripe for destruction. From 9:18 some have drawn the conclusion that it was God. But here in verse 22 we are not told that it was God. And even if it was God, then must we not assume that his action of hardening their hearts, and thus preparing them for destruction, followed, and was a punishment for their own action of hardening themselves? But it is not at all impossible that the apostle wishes to present a contrast between the present passage and verse 23, where the active agent is mentioned, in order to show that here, in verse 22, *the people themselves*—in co-operation with Satan!—were the active agents; as, for example, also in I Thess. 2:14b, 15, 16; whereas in Rom. 9:23 *God* is said to be the One who prepares, and there in a favorable sense; see below.

d. *choosing to show his wrath and to make known his power*

It is exactly to hardened sinners, men like Esau (9:13), Pharaoh (9:17, 18), and Judas the traitor (Luke 22:22; John 13:18; 17:12; Acts 1:15-20, 25), impenitents all; that is, to those people who to the very end refuse to respond favorably to God's patient appeals, that God shows his wrath and makes known his power.

e. *(doing this)*, that is, bearing with great patience vessels of wrath, *to make known the riches of his glory (lavished) upon vessels of mercy*.

God" (continued: "if he, etc."). In English such a sentence would generally begin with "What if," etc.

After the introductory words the main clause is "[he] bore with great patience vessels of wrath, prepared for destruction." This is modified as follows:

a. choosing—that is, because he chose; cf. verse 17—to show his wrath.

and

b. . . . . to make known his power

c. in order to make known the riches of his glory (lavished) upon vessels of mercy, which he prepared beforehand for glory, even us, whom he also called, not only from the Jews but also from the Gentiles.

281. κατηρτισμένα, having been prepared; hence ripe, acc. pl. neut. perf. pass. participle of καταρτίζω, here: to prepare.

This reason is co-ordinate with that mentioned above under d. Both modify the main clause (a. God bore with great patience).

It was exactly God's *great patience* with Pharaoh and his people, his delay in pouring out upon them the full measure of the punishment they had deserved, that provided the opportunity to make known the riches of God's glory lavished on the Israel of that early day. If Pharaoh had been immediately destroyed, who would have become aware of God's *mercy* toward Israel? But as the ten plagues followed each other, one by one, that *mercy* became increasingly evident. Note the following:

In connection with the

fifth plague: "But the Lord will make a distinction between the livestock of Israel and the livestock of Egypt, so that no animal belonging to the Israelites will die . . . All the livestock of the Egyptians died, but of the animals belonging to the Israelites died not one" (Exod. 9:4, 6).

seventh plague: "Only in the land of Goshen, where the children of Israel lived, was there no hail" (Exod. 9:26).

ninth plague: "No one could see anyone else or leave his place for three days; but all the children of Israel had light in their dwellings" (Exod. 10:23).

tenth plague: "There will be loud wailing throughout all the land of Egypt . . . but among the Israelites not a dog will bark at any man or animal, that y o u may know that the Lord makes a distinction between the Egyptians and Israel . . . The blood will be a sign for y o u on the houses where y o u are; and when I see the blood, I will pass over y o u" (Exod. 11:6, 7; 12:13).

The same principle is always operating. God is ever bearing with great patience vessels of wrath, to make known the riches of his glory lavished on vessels of mercy.

f. *the riches of his glory*

This phrase refers to the glorious sum-total of all God's attributes. See their meaningful enumeration in such passages as Ps. 85:10; 145:8, 9; Rom. 11:33; Eph. 1:6-8; 2:4, 5, 7; 3:8.

g. (vessels—or objects—of mercy) *which he prepared beforehand*[282] *for glory*

For contrast see above, under c. The expression "which he prepared beforehand for glory" reminds us of Eph. 2:10, "For his handiwork are we, created in Christ Jesus for good works, which God prepared beforehand, that we should walk in them." The thought of Rom. 8:28-30 returns here.

h. *even us, whom he also called*

The calling to which this passage refers is that operation of the Holy Spirit whereby he so applies the gospel to the minds and hearts of sinners that they become aware of their guilt, begin to understand their need of Christ, and embrace him as their Lord and Savior. It is the *effective* call, the invitation savingly applied to heart and life. See on 1:7 and 8:28.

---

282. προητοίμασεν, third per. s. aor. indicat. of προετοιμάζω, to prepare in advance or beforehand.

i. *not only from the Jews but also from the Gentiles*

As far as the Jews are concerned, *historically* only the true Israel is effectively called and saved; as, in many different ways, the apostle impresses upon us again and again (Rom. 2:28, 29; 9:6, 27, 28; 11:5, 7, 26). There is indeed such a remnant. *Israel's rejection is never total or complete.*

But not only Jews, also Gentiles are saved. In fact, Paul, throughout this epistle, and also elsewhere, emphasizes the thought that there is no distinction between Jews and Gentiles. All God's children constitute *one* people, the church universal: Rom. 1:5, 13-16; 2:10, 11; 3:22-24, 30; 4:11, 12; 8:32 ("us all"); 10:4, 9 (cf. John 3:16); 10:12; 11:32; 16:26. Cf. Gal. 3:9, 29; Eph. 2:14-18.

25, 26. **Just as he says in Hosea:**
> *"Not my people"* **I will call** *"My people,"*
> **and**
> *"Not my loved one"* **(I will call)** *"My loved one."*

And it will happen that in the very place where it was said to them, Y o u are not my people, they will be called sons of the living God.

Hosea was a prophet to Israel, the kingdom of the ten tribes. See Hos. 7:1. He prophesied during the eighth century before Christ; that is, during what may be called the Glamor Age and the Growth of Assyria Period. Great victories were being won by Israel—hastening Israel's doom! The nation resembled a polished piece of furniture, inside of which the termites were at work. On the inside Israel was being devoured by moral and spiritual decay. From the outside Assyria, capturing nation upon nation, was approaching and threatening Israel's very existence. The *prosperity*, of which the Israelites boasted, was, accordingly, illusive.[283]

At God's command Hosea married a woman named Gomer. She was not true to her husband. She became a woman of whoredom and conceived children of whoredom (Hos. 2:4): Jezreel, Lo-ruḥamah, and Lo-ammi (son, daughter, son). We are concerned here only with the last two. Their names are symbolical of Israel's condition as seen by the Lord. Lo-ruḥamah means "Not my loved one"; and Lo-ammi, "Not my people."

Hosea, instead of rejecting his wife, slips away to the haunt of shame, buys her back, and mercifully restores her to her former position of honor, so that "Not my loved one" becomes "My loved one," and "Not my people" becomes "My people."

In Rom. 9:25 Paul quotes this passage from Hos. 2:23, reversing the lines, so that what Hosea had said about "Not my loved one" becomes Paul's second line, and what the Old Testament prophet predicted with reference to "Not my people" is placed first by the apostle. The sense is, however, unchanged.

---

283. For more on the Israel of that day and on Hosea see Leon J. Wood, *The Prophets of Israel*, Grand Rapids, 1979, pp. 275-283; and W. Hendriksen, *Survey of the Bible*, pp. 235-238.

Paul's next line ("And it will happen that in the very place where it was said to them, 'Y o u are not my people,' they will be called 'sons of the living God' ") is quoted from what in our Bibles is Hos. 1:10b.[284]

It is clear, therefore, that what Hosea describes is Gomer's sin, punishment, and restoration: a symbol of Israel's sin, punishment, and restoration to divine favor.

Hosea clearly was speaking of *restoration* (to God's favor) *of Israelites*. However, when Paul makes use of this passage, he makes no such limitation. He speaks about "us, whom he also called not only from the Jews but also from the Gentiles." And Peter (I Peter 2:10), addressing congregations of predominantly Gentile origin (see I Peter 1:14, 18; 2:9, 10; 4:6), applies the Hosean passage directly to converts from the Gentile world. The question may be asked, therefore, How is it possible for Paul and Peter to take a passage which predicts restoration for *Israelites* and apply it to audiences in which *Gentiles* predominated?

The answer is simple: the same principle operates throughout. Whether it be restoration to divine favor of Israelites, or conversion of Gentiles, or even both, the cause or source of restoration and salvation in each case is the same. That which brings about the restoration or conversion is ever the active, powerful, and sovereign grace of God Almighty! The rule is always, " 'Not my people' *I* will call 'My people,' and 'Not my loved one' (*I* will call) 'My loved one.' " When that principle goes into operation, then in the very place—that is, in *every* place—where it was said to sinners, "Y o u are not my people," they will be called—and will actually be—sons of the living God. What is stressed in these quotations is the sovereign and pitying grace of God shown to those who—whether Jews or Gentiles—lack the right to consider themselves God's people.[285]

The next quotation has reference especially to Israel. After reading or hearing Rom. 9:25, 26, the question might very well occur, "Does Paul have in mind a *total* restoration of Israel?" The answer is clear:

27, 28. But Isaiah cries concerning Israel:

"Though the number of the children of Israel be as the sand of the sea, (only) the remnant will be saved. For the Lord will carry out his sentence on earth completely and quickly."

The quotation is from Isa. 10:22, 23. The prophet predicts that, due to the Assyrian invasion, Israel will be greatly reduced in number. The nation which at one time was as numerous as the sand by the sea (cf. Gen. 22:17) would be reduced to a remnant. Yes, only a remnant would return.

---

284. Our Rom. 9:25 is a "free" quotation of what in the Hebrew Bible and the LXX is found in Hos. 2:25, and in our Bibles in Hos. 2:23. Our Rom. 9:26 is quoted from what in the Hebrew Bible is found in Hos. 2:1b. So also in the LXX, of which Rom. 9:26 is an exact transcription.

285. Thus also Ridderbos, *op. cit.*, p. 223.

At this point we should guard ourselves against committing an error in our interpretation. It is a rather common practice to say that Paul now begins to spiritualize, by stating that only the remnant *will be saved*. However, a close look at Isaiah's own prophecy shows that he by no means restricts his prophecy to a prediction of a physical *return* from captivity, but states that the remnant will return "to the mighty God" (Isa. 10:21). They will *lean on Jehovah*, will rely on the Lord (verse 20). Paul is therefore exactly reproducing Isaiah's thought when he says that of the total number of Israelites only the remnant *will be saved*. The apostle adds that the Lord will carry out his sentence "completely and quickly" or "with vigor and dispatch."[286] In the days of Isaiah's prophecy the rigors of warfare, deportation, living in a strange country under distressing conditions, being cut down by the sword and/or seeing one's friends and relatives being thus cut down, must have been included. When *Paul*, guided by the Holy Spirit, makes use of this language, it is hard to believe that the Fall of Jerusalem in the year A.D. 70 was not at least part of the picture. But see also 9:13b, 18b. 22b.

29. And as Isaiah predicted: "If the Lord of hosts had not left us a seed, we would have fared like Sodom, and have been made like Gomorrah."

The quotation is from Isa. 1:9. The Hebrew original may be rendered as follows:

"Unless the Lord of hosts had left us a remnant ever so small, like Sodom should we have been, to Gomorrah should we have been compared."

The LXX is essentially the same, except that for "remnant ever so small" it uses the word "seed." It is this LXX text which is exactly reproduced by Paul here in Rom. 9:29. Of course, "seed" and "small remnant" are alike in meaning. If there is any difference at all, it might be that "seed" points directly to the Sower, namely, God, and has hopeful implications for the future.

What Isaiah, and after him Paul, are saying, then, is this: It is due exclusively to God's sparing love and providential care that the people—the authors include themselves and those addressed; note "we"—have not become like Sodom and Gomorrah. Stronger rejection of any personal merits or

---

286. This is the R.S.V. rendering. See below in this footnote. Note the word κράζει, third per. s. pres. indicat. of κράζω, to cry. According to Calvin (*Romans*, p. 373) Paul describes Isaiah as *exclaiming*, not speaking, "in order that he might excite more attention." Now although it is certainly true that even today the biblical truth that of Israel *only the remnant* (never the whole nation) is saved, needs to be exclaimed and emphasized, because so many persist in denying it, it is, nevertheless, also a fact that, according to S.BK. Vol. III, p. 275, the verb used in the original was probably no more than a then current indication of prophetic speech.

The expression λόγον συντελεῖν καὶ συντέμνειν is not easy to interpret, and has therefore been explained in various ways. The general idea is clear enough from the context: God will take definite and vigorous action. He will carry out his sentence completely and quickly. Punishment will not be postponed and will be severe. In the present context this also implies that Israel will be "cut down to size." Only a remnant will be saved.

pretensions was certainly impossible, for these cities were considered the very culmination of wickedness. See Gen. 13:13; 18:20, 21, 32 (cf. 19:29); Isa. 3:9; Jer. 23:14; Matt. 10:15; 11:23, 24; II Peter 2:6; Jude 7.

When a person reviews the ground covered in this chapter, he is surprised about the great number of scriptural quotations (verses 7, 9, 11-13, 15, 17, 20, 21, 25-29, and, still coming, 33). It is as if Paul purposely somewhat holds his own judgments in abeyance, so that the readers and listeners may be able to see for themselves what God had been saying in the past. And if even Paul, who, after all, was divinely inspired, made this use of Scripture, should not we today? Is not a sermon all the more powerful and effective if the preacher can prove to his audience, "Thus saith the Lord"?

Also here, as often previously, the lesson is: There is, indeed, a seed, a remnant, by God's sovereign grace. *Israel's rejection is not total.* Election is still having its effect.

---

30 What then shall we say? That Gentiles, who were not pursuing righteousness, have obtained righteousness, but the righteousness that is by faith. 31 Israel, however, though ever in pursuit of (the) law of righteousness, has not attained to (that) law. 32 Why? Because (they pursued it) not by faith but by relying on (their) works. They stumbled over[287] The Stumbling Stone; 33 as it is written:

"Behold, I lay in Zion A Stone of Stumbling
And A Rock of Offense.
But he who puts his trust in him
will not be put to shame."

---

4. *Conclusion*
"He who puts his faith in him will not be put to shame"
9:30-33

30, 31. What then shall we say? That Gentiles, who were not pursuing righteousness, have obtained righteousness, but the righteousness that is by faith. Israel, however, though ever in pursuit of (the) law of righteousness, has not attained to (that) law.

Though the words "What then shall we say?" are the same as those in verse 14, their import is not the same. In verse 14 Paul was anticipating an objection, which he then obliterates. Here, in 9:30, 31, he states the conclusion to which he has arrived on the basis of his previous reasoning.

That conclusion amounts to this: Gentiles—that is, those Gentiles who have embraced Christ—have obtained righteous standing before God. Yet, beforetime they had not been seeking to obtain righteousness where alone it could be found. At that time they had been living in moral and spiritual darkness. See Rom. 1:18-32; and cf. Acts 14:16; 17:30; Eph. 2:1-3. But when they heard the gospel, many of those Gentiles had, by God's grace, accepted it, and had thus obtained righteousness. Cf. Rom. 9:25, 26. However, it was

---

287. Or *against.*

not a righteousness based on their own goodness in the sight of God. It was *God's* righteousness, appropriated by God-given faith. It was a righteousness purchased by Christ's redeeming blood.

On the contrary, Israel, though ever in pursuit of the law of righteousness, zealously seeking to overtake it—so far, so good!—had failed to attain to it, to reach it. It ever eluded Israel. The reason is stated in verse

32a. Why? Because (they pursued it) not by faith but by relying on (their) works.

There was, of course, nothing wrong with seeking to attain to a state of righteousness in God's sight. The trouble with Israel was that these people proceeded from the false presupposition that by trying very, very hard they would be able, some day, to observe God's entire law, so that they would be able to shout, "Success! We made it!" Paul preaches an entirely different gospel. See Rom. 3:27, 28; Gal. 1:8, 9; 3:10; 5:6. The law, with its uncompromising demand of perfect love and obedience, should have driven each Israelite to God with the fervent prayer, "Oh, God, be thou merciful to me, the sinner." Instead, Israel took for granted that men would be able, by their own power, and on the basis of their own resources, to fulfil the law's demands.

Result: though ever pursuing, Israel never achieved. The law ever remained miles ahead of Israel. It could not be reached.[288]

32b, 33. They stumbled over The Stumbling Stone; as it is written:
> **"Behold, I lay in Zion A Stone of Stumbling**
> **and A Rock of Offense.**
> **But he who puts his trust in him**
> **will not be put to shame."**

Paul now goes to the very root of Israel's failure to attain to righteousness. They stumbled over—or against—the Stumblingblock. They failed to recognize Christ as their Savior. Of course, as long as Israel relied on works it could not embrace Christ. It was either the one or the other. It could not be both.

For Jews Christ was a stumblingblock (I Cor. 1:23). To be sure, for many a Gentile too he was foolishness. But on the whole Jews were far more adamant in their belief that they had found the solution of the problem of achieving the status of righteousness in God's sight. And their failure humbly to flee to Christ and to embrace him by faith proved their undoing, spelled their doom.

The words quoted by Paul here in verse 33 are a combination of two biblical passages: Isa. 28:16 and 8:14:

"Behold, I lay in Zion a tested stone, a precious cornerstone for a solid foundation. The one who trusts will never be dismayed" (Isa. 28:16).

"For both houses of Israel he will be a stone that causes people to stumble, and a rock that makes them fall" (Isa. 8:14).

---

288. Note οὐκ ἔφθασεν, third per. s. aor. act. indicat. of φθάνω, here probably in the sense of *to attain to, reach, come up to, overtake*. Also see N.T.C. on Luke, p. 634.

Skillfully Paul combines the essence of both in his quotation. Even though in Isa. 8:14 it is the Lord of hosts who is described as being a stone of stumbling, the apostle does not hesitate to apply this passage to Jesus. Cf. Matt. 21:42; Mark 12:10; Luke 20:17; Acts 4:11; I Peter 2:6-8. Solution: Christ is God!

Israel's pursuit of the law, as if a person could be saved by keeping the law, amounted to unwillingness to accept the righteousness offered by God on the basis of the redemptive work of Christ. Gentiles, on the other hand, in great numbers, had accepted Christ by faith. As noted earlier, the church in Rome too consisted for the most part of converts from the Gentile world. Paul asserts that by putting their trust in Christ *they will not be dismayed or put to shame.* This reading of the passage (Isa. 28:16), seems to have been the basis of the LXX translation and also of Paul's quotation here in Rom. 9:33.[289]

By far the main point to be emphasized is this, that the truth here expressed holds for Jew and Gentile alike. Is it not a statement in prophetic, and now also in Pauline, language, of the precious truth embodied in John 3:16?

Practical Lessons Derived from Romans 9

Verse 1

"I am speaking the truth in Christ—I am not lying; my conscience bears witness along with me in the Holy Spirit. . . ." The apostle knew that his statements were going to be challenged, and, what is more important, shows that he is deeply conscious of writing in the very presence of God and under the constant direction of the Holy Spirit. See also 1:25; 6:17; 7:25; 8:35-39; 11:33-36; 15:13, 32; 16:25-27; Gal. 1:20; Eph. 1:3 ff.; 1:15 ff.; 3:14-21; I Tim. 2:7. Does not this fact make Paul's epistles even more precious to us?

Verses 1 and 3

"I am speaking the truth in Christ . . . I could wish that I myself would be accursed . . . for the sake of my brothers, my fellow-countrymen . . ." Here is *a great theologian . . .* who is at the same time *a very warm-hearted lover of souls!* To be sure, books are very important. Every minister should have access to a fine theological library. But what is even more important: he should love people, and be deeply concerned about their everlasting welfare. The same spirit should mark *every* believer!

---

289. It is, therefore probably incorrect to say that Paul's wording "varies from the Hebrew." (Murray, *op. cit.*, p. 45). The real question is, "Was the LXX rendering of Isa. 28:16 based on the masoretic text, and was that the text Paul, too, had in mind?" If not, then the difficulty disappears entirely, and one no longer has to say, "The Hebrew really means 'will not make haste,' but the apostle is following the LXX text."

Verse 5

"Christ, who is over all God blest forever. Amen." This reminds us of "But we see Jesus . . . crowned with glory and honor" (Heb. 2:9). It is the consciousness, in all circumstances of life, of the reality and closeness of the ever-living and ever-active Christ that imparts courage to stand firm, knowing that *he* is in complete control!

Verse 6 and Verse 27

"Not all who are of Israel are Israel." "Though the number of the children of Israel be as the sand of the sea, (only) the remnant will be saved."

Is it not high time that, in the preaching of the Word, the doctrine of *the remnant* be revived? See such passages as the following: I Kings 19:18; Isa. 1:9; 10:20-22; 11:11; 46:3; Jer. 23:3-6; Ezek. 6:8-10; Joel 2:32; Amos 5:15; Micah 2:12; 4:5-7; 7:18; Zeph. 3:12, 13; Matt. 7:14; 9:37; 22:14; Luke 12:32; 13:23, 24; Rom. 9:27-29; 11:4, 5; Rev. 12:17.

Verse 16

"So then, it does not depend on (man's) will or exertion but on God's mercy."

This passage shows how deeply conscious was Paul of the need of God, every step of the way. What do we find today, often even in church-going families? The children are brought up in schools were evolution is taught, and where creation, if it is ever mentioned, is frowned upon. The speaker who has been invited to address the graduates tells them "Y o u will undoubtedly be very successful if only y o u do y o u r darndest" (an example taken from life). What can be done to correct this evil?

When the youth looks for a wife or husband, he (she) demands that his (her) marriage partner possesses all kinds of qualities . . . without ever asking the most important question of all, "Is he (she) a Christian?" And so life continues. Religion— if present at all—is a side issue. To be sure, by no means all young people are like that. Many show in their lives that they love the Lord and figure with him and his will as revealed in his Word! But is it not true that many too are in the opposite camp? As verse 16 shows, Paul was ever fully conscious of the fact that his welfare for time and eternity was subject to God's good pleasure!

Verse 22

"And what if God . . . bore with great patience vessels of wrath, prepared for destruction?"

If God bore with *great* patience those whom he knew would never be saved, should not we have at least *a little* patience with people who, though now unconverted, may still, by God's grace, experience a fundamental change, a genuine conversion?

Summary of Chapter 9

Paul opens this chapter by solemnly declaring that Israel's unbelief and consequent rejection is for him a heavy burden. So genuine, profound, and

336

heart-rending is his anguish that he states, "I could wish myself to be accursed (and cut off) from Christ for the sake of my brothers, my natural kinsmen." In saying this he reminds us of Judah (the son of Jacob and brother of Joseph), of Moses, of David, and, in fact, of Jesus Christ. See Gen. 44:33; Exod. 32:32; II Sam. 18:33; Isa. 53:5-8, 12b.

The depth of Israel's tragedy and of Paul's grief becomes especially clear when the advantages that enabled this nation to place all others in its shade are listed. Greatest of them all is surely this: ". . . from them, as far as his human nature is concerned, is Christ, who is over all God blest forever. Amen." (verses 1-5).

No one should imagine, however, that Israel's rejection meant that God's Word—his promise to Israel—had failed. Fact is that this promise was never meant to be realized in the nation as a whole. It was meant for the true Israel, the body of God's elect from Israel: "Not all who are of Israel are Israel" (verse 6). This true Israel includes Jacob but not Esau. It includes all those, and only those, who are born of the Spirit. In the final analysis who these true Israelites are is determined by God's eternal decree. "Jacob I loved, but Esau I hated" (verses 6-13).

"So then," says Paul, "it [probably our *salvation*] does not depend on man's will or exertion but on God's mercy." After the first six plagues God had spared wicked Pharaoh's life in order, by means of the remaining plagues, now more than ever to display his power in connection with the outpouring of his wrath on Egypt's king and people, so that God's name might be proclaimed in all the earth. It is clear that God should not be accused of being unjust when he hardens the heart of a person who has hardened himself against his Maker. Whether God will show mercy to such a person or will harden him is up to God (verses 14-18).

Paul continues, "You will say to me, then, 'Why does he [God] still find fault, for who is resisting his will?' " The objector forgets that God certainly has a right to find fault with the man who disobeys God's revealed will (Deut. 29:29; Luke 22:22). Besides, "Who are you, O man, to talk back to God? Will what is molded say to its molder, 'Why did you make me thus?' "

Two facts stand out in God's dealings with people:

a. He bears with great patience the objects of his wrath.

b. While doing this, he is not forgetting his elect, the objects of his mercy. In fact, "God . . . bore with great patience objects ["vessels"] of wrath . . . in order to make known the riches of his glory (lavished) upon objects ["vessels"] of mercy, which he prepared beforehand for glory, even us, whom he also called [effectively drew to himself], not only from the Jews but also from the Gentiles" (verses 19-24).

With quotations from the prophecies of Hosea (first from 2:23 and then from 1:10b) the apostle now shows that just as for the Israelites of the old dispensation there was a promise of restoration, so also now that promise of restoration to divine favor still holds. However, with a quotation from Isa. 10:22, 23 Paul emphasizes (cf. Rom. 9:6) that he is not speaking about a

337

national but about a *remnant* restoration. He states, "Though the number of the children of Israel be as the sand of the sea, (only) *the remnant* will be saved." Also, quoting Isa. 1:9, the apostle adds, "If the Lord of hosts had not left us *a seed*, we would have fared like Sodom, and have been made like Gomorrah" (verses 25-29).

Paul's conclusion is that, although Gentiles had formerly not been seeking to become righteous in the eyes of God, they had, nevertheless, obtained righteousness; that is, they had by faith accepted the Christ of the gospel.

On the contrary, Israel, though ever pursuing (seeking to fulfil) the law of righteousness, had failed to reach the status of righteousness in the eyes of God. Why? Because they relied on their own vaunted works and imagined merits, instead of placing their trust in Christ. He, *The Precious Cornerstone*, had become for them *A Stone of Stumbling and Rock of Offense*.

Paul closes this chapter with a quotation from Isa. 28:16, "But he who puts his trust in him will not be put to shame." The apostle, as is clear, has not forgotten his theme. Cf. Rom. 1:16, 17; 3:21-24, 28-30; 4:3-8, 22-24; 5:1, 2, 9, 18, 19; 8:1 (verses 30-33).

Outline (continued)

Justification by Faith

5. *Self-righteousness versus the Righteousness*
that Comes from God and Is Appropriated by Faith
"For it is with the heart that a person exercises faith leading to
righteousness, and with the lips that he makes confession issuing in
salvation."
10:1-13

6. *Israel Is Responsible for Its Own Rejection.*
That Rejection Is Not Arbitrary.
"All day long I have stretched out my hands to
a disobedient and defiant people"
10:14-21

10 1 Brothers, my heart's desire and prayer to God for them is that they may be saved. 2 For I can testify about them that they have a zeal for God, but it is not based on knowledge. 3 For, failing to acknowledge the righteousness that comes from God, and seeking to establish their own, they did not submit to God's righteousness. 4 For Christ is the goal[290] of the law, so that there is righteousness for everyone who puts his trust (in him). 5 For Moses describes in this way the righteousness that is by the law: "The one who does these things shall live by them." 6 But the righteousness that is by faith says, "Do not say in your heart, 'Who will ascend into heaven?'" that is, to bring Christ down; 7 "or, 'Who will descend into the abyss?'" that is, to bring Christ up from the dead. 8 But what does it say? "The word is close to you; (it is) on your lips[291] and in your heart;" that is, the word of faith we are proclaiming. 9 Because, if on your lips is the confession, "Jesus is Lord," and in your heart the faith that God raised him from the dead, you will be saved. 10 For it is with the heart that a person exercises faith leading to righteousness, and with the lips[292] that he makes confession issuing in salvation. 11 For the Scripture says, "No one who puts his trust in him will ever be put to shame." 12 For there is no distinction between Jew and Greek. For the same Lord (is Lord) of all and richly blesses all who call on him. 13 For everyone who calls on the name of the Lord will be saved.

---

*5. Self-righteousness versus the Righteousness
that Comes from God and Is Appropriated by Faith*
"For it is with the heart that a person exercises faith leading to
righteousness, and with the lips that he makes confession issuing in
salvation."
10:1-13

1. Brothers, my heart's desire and prayer to God for them is that they may be saved.

For the use of the emotion-filled word of affection "brothers" see on 1:13 and 7:1. Especially now that Paul is about to enlarge on the subject of Israel's guilt, showing that *their rejection was not arbitrary but deserved*, he wisely first of all reaffirms (cf. 9:1 f.) his deep attachment to, and affection for, his kinsmen. By stating that his heart's desire and prayer to God is that they may be saved, is he not implying that he loves them intensely? The apostle knew that in Israel there was always a remnant that would be saved (9:23, 27). But even aside from this, is it not the believer's duty and joy to love *everyone*? See Matt. 5:43-48. Then certainly also one's kith and kin! Very properly the

---

290. Or: meaning and substance.
291. Literally: *in your mouth*, both here and in verse 9.
292. Literally: with the mouth.

apostle desires and earnestly prays for their salvation. He enlarges on this
theme by adding:

**2. For I can testify about them that they have a zeal for God, but it is
not based on knowledge.**

Zeal or enthusiasm can be a very good thing. See Ps. 69:9; John 2:17. The
apostle admits that his fellow-countrymen wear themselves out to assure
themselves of God's favor. Was not this already implied in 9:31? Is it not
definitely confirmed by such passages as Acts 21:20; 22:3; Gal. 1:14?

So far, so good! The fly in the ointment, however, was this: this zeal for
God, this enthusiasm about him, this strong and deep-seated urge to live in
accordance with God's will, was not based on proper understanding! It was
not in harmony with God's revelation concerning the way of salvation. Paul
explains this in verse

**3. For, failing to acknowledge the righteousness that comes from God,
and seeking to establish their own, they did not submit to God's
righteousness.**

In words so clear that explanation is hardly necessary, Paul points out that
Israel's basic fault consisted in this:

a. It failed *to acknowledge*, that is, to accept and welcome, the righteousness
that has God as its Author (3:21-24; 8:1; 9:30), is based on Christ's substitutionary atonement (3:24; 5:8, 17, 18; 8:3, 4, 32; cf. Isa. 53:4-8; Matt. 20:28;
Mark 10:45; II Cor. 5:21; Gal. 3:13; I Tim. 2:5, 6), and is appropriated by
faith (some of these same passages and also Rom. 1:17; 4:3-5, 16, 23-25;
5:1; cf. Hab. 2:4; Gal. 3:11).

b. It substituted its own work-righteousness for God's grace-righteousness.
For the sad results, as pointed out by Paul, see Rom. 2:17 f.; 3:20; 9:31, 32.

That God did indeed provide righteousness is clear from that which, by
an easy transition, follows in verse

**4. For Christ is the goal of the law, so that there is righteousness for
everyone who puts his trust (in him).**

Does one wish to understand the goal, the meaning and substance, of the
Old Testament law? Then study Christ. Is not the very purpose of the law
the establishment of *love*? See Deut. 6:5; Lev. 19:18 (in *that* order); cf. Matt.
22:37-39. Is not Christ the very embodiment of that love, both in his life
and in his death? And is it not true that because of this love which caused
him to suffer and die in his people's stead, there now is right standing with
God for everyone who reposes his trust in the Savior? Is not this the very
theme of Romans?[293]

---

293. Instead of "For Christ is the *goal* of the law," many prefer, "For Christ is the *end* of the
law." As a *translation* this can stand. The further question is, "What is meant by the Greek
word τέλος and the English word *end*? In addition to other meanings, both of these words
can mean: (a) termination, finish; or (b) goal, intention, purpose, meaning and substance.
However, meaning (a) does not apply in the present case, for the notion that because of the
work of Christ the Old Testament law has in every respect lost its usefulness, and is therefore
"finished," is contrary to Paul's teaching, as is clear from Rom. 3:31; 7:7. See especially on
5:20, Vol. I, p. 184. Accordingly, to avoid ambiguity and misunderstanding, it is probably
better, even in the translation, to substitute the term *goal* for *end*.

Since verse 4 refers to Christ, as the law's goal, in the sense explained, it would seem to be logical, in the present case, to refer to Christ also in the next verse.

5. For Moses describes in this way the righteousness that is by the law: "The one who does these things shall live by them."

The reference is to Lev. 18:5 (quoted also in Gal. 3:12; cf. Luke 10:28). It was Christ, *he alone*, who by his life and death completely fulfilled the demands of the law, and thereby secured *for himself* the Father's approval and the place at the latter's right hand (Heb. 12:2); and *for his followers* everlasting life (Heb. 5:8, 9). Accordingly, for all those who place their trust in Christ the path that leads to salvation has, in a sense, become incredibly easy. That which was infinitely difficult, hard, and painful, in fact for sinners *impossible*, has been accomplished by Christ. No mere sinner should now try to do what for him is both impossible and unnecessary.

Now listen to what "the righteousness that is *by faith*" says:

6, 7. But the righteousness that is by faith says, "Do not say in your heart, 'Who will ascend into heaven?' " that is, to bring Christ down; "or, 'Who will descend into the abyss?' " that is, to bring Christ up from the dead.

Note the word "But." It marks a sharp contrast between (a) the state of righteousness *earned* by Christ (verses 4, 5), and (b) that same state which, on the basis of Christ's righteousness, is *freely obtained* by all those who believe in him.

This latter "righteousness," the one that is "by faith," is here personified and presented as speaking. It delivers a New Testament message in Old Testament terms. It is able to do this because in both testaments the way of salvation is the same, as Paul has already established (1:17; 3:21, 22; 4:1f.).

The words that are quoted carry us back to the time when Moses was giving instructions to the people of Israel with respect to their entrance into the land of Canaan. He sets forth the curses that would be poured out upon the disobedient (Deut. 27:9-26), as well as the blessings that would be bestowed upon the obedient (Deut. 28:8-14). He then addresses each Israelite as follows:

"Now what I am commanding you today is not too difficult for you, nor is it beyond your reach. It is not up in heaven, so that you have to ask, 'Who will ascend to heaven for us and bring it down to make us obey it?' Nor is it beyond the sea, so that you have to ask, 'Who will cross the sea for us and bring it to us to make us obey it?' " (Deut. 30:11-*13*).

The point Moses emphasizes is that the law has been given to Israel in the context of grace, and that Canaan, which the people are about to enter, is *God's gift* to them. It is in no sense whatever the product of their own righteousness or strenuous effort. See also Deut. 8:17, 18; 9:4-6.

That there is a striking analogy between entrance into earthly Canaan and obtaining salvation was clear not only to the writer of the epistle to the

Hebrews (see Heb. 4:6-10) but also to Paul; or, in the present context, to "the righteousness that is by faith."

Here too the truth to be emphasized is that *the really difficult task is not for us to undertake. It has been accomplished for us by Christ.* It is he who came down from heaven, dwelt among us as in a tent (John 1:14), suffered the agonies of hell for us, died, was buried, rose again, ascended to heaven. *The hard work was accomplished by him!* Therefore, any attempt on *our* part to ascend to heaven to bring Christ down would amount to a most ungracious denial of the reality and value of Christ's incarnation. Similarly, any attempt to descend into the realm of the dead in order to bring Christ up from the dead would be a disavowal of the genuine character and meaning of Christ's glorious resurrection from the dead and triumph over the grave. (See Ps. 16:10; Acts 2:27; Rom. 4:25; I Cor. 15:20, 55-57; Rev. 1:17, 18).[294]

When we study this reassuring teaching of the apostle Paul, it reminds us of Christ's own unforgettable words:

"Come to me all who are weary and burdened, and I will give y o u rest. Take my yoke upon y o u, and learn from me, for I am meek and lowly in heart, and y o u shall find rest for y o u r souls. *For my yoke is kindly, and my burden is light*" (Matt. 11:28-30).

8. But what does it say? "The word is close to you; (it is) on your lips and in your heart;" that is, the word of faith we are proclaiming.

The apostle continues to "quote" *the righteousness that is by faith.* The quotation found in Rom. 10:6, 7 ended with words from Deut. 30:*13.* So here in Rom. 10:8 the words of Deut. 30:*14* are quoted: "The word is close to you; it is on your lips and in your heart." By means of his very gracious assurances, promises, and admonitions—present in abundance in Deuteronomy; study, for example, such precious gems as Deut. 5:6; 6:4-9; 7:7-9; 10:12, 13; 11:13-15, 22-25; 18:15-18; 26:16-19; 28:1-14—the Lord had, as it were, drawn his people very close to his heart. Let them now answer with the response of love.

The more one takes time to study Deuteronomy, the more also he will agree with Paul's statement that this is indeed "the word of faith we are proclaiming." It *must* be, for the heart and center of this book and of the entire Old Testament, is Christ, exactly as the apostle has affirmed (see Rom. 10:4).

There is only one way, however, in which this can be appreciated. That is the way of faith; for God's word, as revealed both in the Old Testament and in the New, is "*the word of faith*"; that is, it is the word which, in order to exert its saving effect, must elicit the response of faith!

Paul now shows that the statement, "The word is close to you; (it is) on your lips and in your heart" is true:

---

294. Although "the abyss" can indicate the depth of the sea (cf. Ps. 107:26=LXX 106:26), in the present passage death and the grave are indicated. See Acts 2:27.

9, 10. Because, if on your lips is the confession, "Jesus is Lord," and in your heart the faith that God raised him from the dead, you will be saved. For it is with the heart that a person exercises faith leading to righteousness, and with the lips that he makes confession issuing in salvation.

Note the following:

a. "Because" (rather than "That") is natural here, the sense being that the statement that the word is close to you (verse 8) is true is shown by the fact that, instead of requiring superhuman exertion, salvation is obtained simply by confessing with the lips and having faith in the heart.

b. In verse 9 the confession on the lips precedes the faith in the heart; in verse 10 the opposite sequence prevails. Probable reason: first Paul is thinking of Deut. 30:14 where "on your lips" precedes "in your heart." Next, he follows the natural order, according to which a person confesses with his lips that which is already present in the heart.

c. Not the Roman emperor but Jesus was to receive all honor and glory. Moreover, it is clear from I Cor. 16:22 (māránā thā, "Our Lord, come!") that the exaltation of Jesus as Lord was customary even in the early, Aramaic-speaking, church. That the title *Lord* is here (in Rom. 10:9) used in the most exalted sense, indicating Jesus' equality with God, is clear not only from the fact that the apostle frequently, without any hesitancy, ascribes to Jesus qualities which in the Old Testament are predicated of God, but also from the circumstance that already in 9:5 he has called Jesus "over all God blest forever."

d. Note "heart" and "lips" (literally "mouth"). The *heart* is not merely the seat of affection or emotion. According to biblical usage, it is the hub of the wheel of human existence and life (intellectual, emotional, and volitional). See Prov. 4:23.

First of all there must be faith in the heart. Without such faith a confession with the lips would be mockery (Matt. 7:22, 23). But also, even if there is faith in the heart, confession with the lips is not only required (Ps. 107:2) but altogether natural if the faith is genuine (Acts 4:20). Faith and confession should be combined (Luke 12:8; John 12:42; I Tim. 6:12; I John 4:15).

e. By means of the resurrection from the dead the Lordship of Jesus had been made abundantly clear. See Rom. 6:9; I Cor. 15:20; Eph. 1:20-23; Phil. 2:9-11; Col. 3:1-4; Heb. 2:9; Rev. 1:17, 18.

f. When in verse 10 *faith* is said to issue in *righteousness*, and *confession* in *salvation* (lit . . . is unto righteousness—is unto salvation), the two concepts, righteousness and salvation, are conceived of as synonyms. This is also clear from verse 9, where salvation is described as being the product both of confession and faith.

g. Note "you will be saved" (verse 9), and "issuing in salvation" (verse 10). For the meaning of *salvation* and *to save* in Paul's epistles see p. 60 on 1:16.

The fact that faith does indeed lead to justification, hence to salvation is confirmed by verse

11. For the Scripture says, "No one who puts his trust in him will ever be put to shame." Or, if one prefers, **"Everyone who puts his trust in him will never be put to shame."** Again, as in 9:33 Paul quotes Isa. 28:16; this time, however, in somewhat strengthened form, "he who . . . will never" being changed to "No one . . . will ever" (or to "Everyone . . . will never"). But is not Paul's version here in Rom. 10:11 already implied in Isa. 28:16? For the meaning see, accordingly, on Rom. 9:33.

That the truth which the apostle has just now reaffirmed cannot be successfully denied is demonstrated in the three sentences which follow in verses 12, 13. Each of the three supports the one that precedes it:

12, 13. For there is no distinction between Jew and Greek. For the same Lord (is Lord) of all and richly blesses all who call on him. For everyone who calls on the name of the Lord will be saved.

Note the following:

a. "For there is no distinction between Jew and Greek."

The word "for" shows that what immediately follows proves the preceding line which states that *no one* who puts his trust in him will ever be put to shame.

Though the fact that, as concerns the way of salvation, *there is no distinction between Jew and Greek*, is emphasized by Paul again and again, it must have been very difficult for Jews to believe this. What? Did Paul really mean to say that *they*, the highly privileged descendants of Abraham, were in God's eyes not any better than Greeks or Gentiles?

Even today are there not many church members who endorse the theory that the Jews, as a people, are still the objects of God's *special* delight and that a glorious future is in store for them? Note how, in many books written by authors who cling to this opinion, the truth expressed here in 10:12 is touched on very lightly, is passed over very quickly. Nevertheless, so thoroughly convinced was Paul of its importance that he dwelt on it, at least mentioned it, again and again. Let the reader see this for himself by carefully examining the following passages: Rom. 1:16; 2:11; 3:10-18, 22-24; 3:29, 30; 4:9-12; 5:18, 19; 9:24; 10:12; 11:32; and elsewhere in Paul's epistles: I Cor. 7:19; Gal. 3:9, 29; 5:6; 6:15; Eph. 2:14-18; Col. 3:11.

That there is indeed no distinction between Jew and Greek is clear from the fact which the apostle states in the following words:

b. "For the same Lord (is Lord) of all and richly blesses all who call on him." Not only is it true that one and the same *God* is God of the Gentiles as well as of the Jews (cf. Rom. 3:29), but also, as the apostle states here in 10:12, that the same *Lord* (=Jesus) is Lord of all.

God is rich! In fact, his wealth is incalculable. If there is anything at all which, for the moment, he does not possess, all he has to do is assert his sovereign will, and there it is! See Gen. 1:3, 6, 9, 11, 14, 20, 24, 26. All the gold and silver belongs to God (Hag. 2:8). Every beast of the forest is his, and so are the cattle on a thousand hills (Ps. 50:10-12).

And if *God* is rich, then so is *Christ*, for Christ is God. Eph. 3:8 mentions *the unsearchable riches of Christ.* Rev. 5:12 shows that the Savior is indeed *worthy to receive* all this wealth.

But not only is God infinitely rich, he is also intensely desirous to bestow his riches on his creatures. He is rich in revealing to them his kindness, patience, glory, and mercy (Rom. 2:4; 9:23; Eph. 2:7). He is, in fact, generous beyond the capacity of human words to express. See such a precious passage as John 1:16, according to which one manifestation of divine grace or favor is hardly gone when another one arrives, like the waves of the ocean which follow one another in close succession as they dash against the shore. Truly "He giveth and giveth and giveth again."

Especially when one lives in a state that borders on the ocean (or makes a visit to such a state)—for example, Florida—it is rewarding, when watching the constantly approaching billows, to reflect on John 1:16. See N.T.C. on John, Vol. I, pp. 88, 89. It hardly needs to be added that here too what is said with reference to God applies also to Christ, who, "though he was rich, yet for our sake became poor, that we through his poverty might become rich" (cf. II Cor. 8:9).

Note also that, according to Paul's inspired teaching, not only a few people, or a certain group of people, whether Jews or Gentiles, are the beneficiaries of this enormous wealth, but that, on the contrary *all* who call on God in Christ receive a rich blessing. The Lord richly blesses—literally, is rich toward—them all.

Of course, this calling on God—or specifically on Jesus—must be done in the spirit of the centurion (Matt. 8:8) and of the publican (Luke 18:13).

Proof of this universality (in a sense) of divine generosity is offered by Paul in his third sentence:

c. "For everyone who calls on the name of the Lord will be saved."

See Acts 7:59; I Cor. 1:2. That which here in Rom. 10:13 follows the word "For" is an exact reproduction of what in our Bibles is found in Joel 2:32 but in the Hebrew Bible and the LXX in Joel 3:5. In fact, in the present case even the word *everyone* was already in the original of the Old Testament passage. Contrast this with Rom. 10:11 where, in quoting Isa. 28:16, Paul himself inserted this word.

For "will be saved" see the explanation of 10:9.

---

14 How, then, can they call on one in whom they have no faith? And how can they have faith in one whom they have not heard? And how can they hear without a preacher?   15 And how can people preach unless they have been commissioned? As it is written, "How beautiful are the feet of those who bring good news!"

16 But not all accepted the good news. For Isaiah says, "Lord, who has believed our message?"   17 Consequently, faith (comes) from hearing the message, and the message is heard through the word of Christ.

18 But I ask, "Can it be that they never heard (it)?" Of course they did:
"Into all the earth there went out their sound,
And to the ends of the inhabited world their words."

19 But I ask, "Can it be that Israel did not understand?" First, Moses says,

"I will make y o u envious of a non-nation,
And with a nation (that is) senseless will I make y o u angry."
20 And Isaiah is so bold as to say,
"I was found by those who did not seek me;
I revealed myself to those who did not ask for me."
21 But concerning Israel he says,
"All day long I have stretched out my hands to a disobedient and obstinate people."

---

6. Israel Is Responsible for Its Own Rejection.
That Rejection Is Not Arbitrary.
"All day long I have stretched out my hands to
a disobedient and defiant people"
10:14-21

Rom. 10:13 stated, "For everyone who calls on the name of the Lord will be saved." The connection between the line and the beginning of the subsection, verses 14-21, is clear, for in 10:14 the subject of *calling on the Lord* is continued by means of the question, "How, then, can they call on one in whom they have no faith?" The spirit of this question, especially in light of what follows in verses 16 and 21, indicates that the apostle is leveling a charge against Israel. He is saying that because of Israel's lack of faith it is fully responsible for its rejection by God. In other words, that rejection, to the extent in which it was real, was not arbitrary but deserved.

14, 15a. How, then, can they call on one in whom they have no faith? And how can they have faith in one whom they have not heard? And how can they hear without a preacher? And how can people preach unless they have been commissioned?[295]

A few points should be noted:

---

295. ἐπικαλέσωνται verse 14), third per. pl. aor. middle subjunct. (deliberat.) of ἐπικαλέω, here in the sense of: to call on God in prayer. Cf. II Tim. 2:22. For calling on "the name" of the Lord see the preceding verse (10:13), in which the third per. s. aor. subjunct. middle of the same verb occurs.

ἐπίστευσαν (verse 14), third per. pl. aor. indicat. of πιστεύω. For the εἰς ὅν ... ἐπίστευσαν construction see also Gal. 2:16 and Phil. 1:29. In both cases the faith to which reference is made is *in Christ*. In the Gospel and First Epistle of John this construction ("in him" or "in his name"), with reference to faith in Christ, occurs frequently. See John 3:16.

In verse 14 note πιστεύσωσιν and ἀκούσωσιν; and in verse 15 κηρύξωσιν. All are third per. pl. aor. act. subjunctives (deliberative). The meaning (after πῶς in each case, and add Πῶς ... ἐπικαλέσωνται at the beginning of verse 14, already discussed), is "How can they ... ?" In other words, "They cannot ..." οὖ οὐκ ἤκουσαν (verse 14) = whom they have not heard; not "of whom they have not heard." In that case would not περὶ οὖ have been more natural? See Gram.N.T., p. 506. Compare Luke 9:35 "Hear him," not "Hear of or about him." Note also the difference in the construction and meaning of (a) οὖ οὐκ ἤκουσαν, where, after the gen., this verb means *to hear*; and (b) οὐκ ἤκουσαν (verse 18), where, without the gen., the same verb indicates *to understand*.

κηρύσσοντος (verse 14), gen. s. masc. pres. act. participle of κηρύσσω, to announce, make public proclamation, preach. Cf. κῆρυξ, herald; also κηρύξωσιν ("How can they preach?") in verse 15.

ἀποσταλῶσιν (verse 15), third per. pl. aor. pass. subjunct. of ἀποστέλλω, to send out, especially on a divine mission, to commission.

a. In this series of questions what is the subject? To whom is Paul referring? The apostle writes: they . . . they . . . they . . . they . . . they . . . they . . . they; though, for the sake of variation and clarity, one of these they's can be changed to *the people* (or something similar).

To whom, then, is Paul referring? The usual answer is: to Israel. Some translations even insert the word "Israel" in places where the original does not have it. Now it must be admitted that to a considerable extent this answer is correct. See, first of all, what has been said in the introduction to this section (p. 348). Examine also the following passages: 9:3-5, 27, 31-33; 10:1-3, 19, 21; 11:1 f. On the basis of all this the conclusion "the reference is to Israel" cannot be escaped.

But is this a *complete* answer? Not every commentator is of that opinion.[296] And rightly so. Does not the fact that in this section (10:14-21) Paul does not even mention Israel until he reaches the very close (verses 19-21) prove that he wants *every hearer or reader* to wrestle with these questions in his own heart and conscience?

b. We have here a series of questions. The Old Testament also contains groups of questions (Job 38:2-39:27; 41:1-7; Isa. 40:12-14, 21). However, the present series is different. It is a kind of chain in which each link bears a close relationship to its immediate neighbor(s).

Is this chain similar, then, to the one found in Rom. 5:3b-5, and to the one described in 8:29, 30? No, the difference is that in the latter two instances the chain is *progressive*: its links follow one another in historical, cause and effect, manner. The sequence may be compared to the series 1, 2, 3, etc. Here, in Rom. 10:14, 15a, and also in 10:17, the chain is *regressive*. It proceeds from effect to cause, and is comparable to the series 5, 4, 3, 2, 1. Calling upon Christ in prayer is mentioned first though in reality, of course, it follows having faith in him, which, however, is the second link in this chain. Having faith in Christ results from hearing him, the third link as here arranged. This hearing implies that there must have been a preacher, the fourth link, who addressed the people. He did this because even earlier someone, the fifth link, had authorized him to bring the message.

c. What may have been the reason for Paul's decision to arrange these links in this regressive order?

To answer this question we should bear in mind that the apostle was not only a fully inspired, very learned, deep-thinking theologian; he was also a very practical, warm-hearted Christian friend. As such he may well have had a twofold purpose in mind for writing as he did.

First of all, he is thinking of the audience, the one in Rome, to be sure, but, along the line of the centuries to follow, any audience, including also today's. For the audience, then, and for every person in that audience, the apostle has so arranged the series that the reference to God—or, if one

---

296. See, for example, Ridderbos, *op. cit.*, p. 240.

prefers, to Jesus Christ—who commissioned the preacher, would be mentioned last of all, in order that all the emphasis might fall upon him! Every person in the audience must be made aware of the fact that when he rejects the preacher who, as a faithful minister of the word, with insight and enthusiasm presents the glad and glorious tidings of salvation in Christ, *then he is rejecting Jesus Christ himself*! In addressing the seventy (or seventy-two) missionaries Jesus said, "He who listens to y o u listens to me, but he who rejects y o u rejects me; and he who rejects me rejects him who sent me" (Luke 10:16).

Secondly, Paul is thinking of the preacher. The climactic reference to the duly commissioned preacher contains a lesson for him also. Any preacher better be sure that he has actually been called of God to do this kind of work. To arrive at a true answer to this question he should turn to Jer. 23:21, 22. If this preacher is earnestly and prayerfully trying to do that which is mentioned in the twenty-second verse, he will find it much easier to arrive at a positive and encouraging answer to the question with reference to the genuine character of his ordination.

For the preacher Rom. 10:14, 15a contains still another lesson. Just what is meant by *preaching*? As the footnote (p. 348) shows, preaching is actually *heralding, proclaiming*. Genuine preaching, therefore, means that the sermon is lively, not dry; timely, not stale. It is the earnest proclamation of the great news initiated by God. It must never be allowed to deteriorate into an abstract speculation on views merely excogitated by man!

That there could be no doubt about the fact that the people—here especially Israel, as has been shown—have actually heard the gospel, and that it has been proclaimed to them by divinely authorized ambassadors, is indicated in verse

15b. As it is written, "How beautiful are the feet of those who bring good news!"

This passage is quoted from Isa. 52:7[297] where the prophet describes the exuberance with which the exiles welcome the news of their imminent release from captivity. This news was regarded by them as being very wonderful not just because they could now return to their homeland but also, and probably especially, because for them it meant that God's favor was still resting on them, and that not this or that earthly power but God—their own God— was still reigning. See the Isaiah context, and add Ps. 93:1; Rev. 19:6. Moreover, can there be anything more spiritually exhilarating and invigorating than the message of God's ambassadors, as reported, for example in II Cor. 5:20, 21?

How beautiful[298] are those feet! As over the mountains those messengers approached with their electrifying news, how dust-covered and dirty these

---

297. Here, rather than in the LXX, correctly translated from the Hebrew.
298. ὡραῖοι, nom. pl. masc. of ὡραῖος, timely, seasonable, blooming, beautiful; cf. ὥρα, season, time, *hour*.

feet must have been! Yet also, how beautiful . . . for they were the feet of those who brought the long-awaited marvelous news!

16. But not all accepted the good news. For Isaiah says, "Lord, who has believed our message?"

There was nothing wrong with the good news. It should have been accepted with joy and gratitude by all. "But," says Paul, "Not all" accepted the good news, the wonderful gospel. Note "not all." What an understatement! A merciful meiosis indeed; for we already know that by far the most of the Israelites did not accept the gospel. See Rom. 9:27. Cf. Isa. 53:1; Rom. 10:21; I Cor. 10:5.

We learn, therefore, that although items 4 and 5 (of 10:14, 15a) had been fulfilled—there had been preachers, and they had been duly commissioned—yet, as far as most of the people were concerned, items 1 and 2—*calling on Christ* in prayer because of the presence of *faith* in him—had not.

That this was true, indeed, with respect to *most* of the people follows also from the words of Isa. 53:1 quoted by Paul: "Lord, who has believed our message?" This basically means, "Lord, who has believed that which was heard by us?"[299]

17. Consequently, faith (comes) from hearing the message, and the message is heard through the word of Christ.

Of the many interpretations of this passage, some very involved, the best is probably the one which views it as a summarizing conclusion. Does not the opening word "Consequently" point in this direction? What Paul is saying, then, is that faith in Christ presupposes having heard the word that proceeds from and concerns Christ. Here a word, in the original, that has just (verse 16) been used in a passive sense—"that which was heard"—is now also used in the active sense: *hearing* the message.[300]

The great importance Paul attached to *hearing* immediately reminds one of Jesus. In all Christ's teaching, both on earth and from heaven, it would be difficult to discover any exhortation which he repeated more often, in one form or another, than the one about hearing; better still: listening (Matt. 11:15; 13:9, 43; Mark 4:9, 23; Luke 8:8; 14:35; Rev. 2:7, 11, 17, 29; 3:6, 13, 22; 13:9). Add 8:18 in both Mark and Luke.

18. But I ask, "Can it be that they never heard (it)?" Of course they did:

"Into all the earth there went out their sound,

---

299. ἀκοῇ, dat. s. of ἀκοή. As is true with respect to many words, the meaning of this word, in any given case, depends on the context in which it is used, and, at times, as here, from which it is quoted. The Greek noun can mean: faculty of hearing, act of hearing, that which is heard, account, report, message.

In the Hebrew passage (Isa. 53:1) from which Rom. 10:16 is quoted, the noun is שְׁמוּעָה from שָׁמַע, to hear; and the word including suffix is שְׁמֻעָתֵנוּ, our report; literally: *that which was heard* by us, and was revealed to us. It is in that sense that it becomes: our report, message. We convey to others what was previously revealed to us.

300. The reference is to the Greek word ἀκοή; here in the combination ἐξ ἀκοῆς: from hearing.

And to the ends of the inhabited world their words."

This passage found in Ps. 19:4 is here quoted literally according to the LXX text (there Ps. 18:5). We should not misinterpret what Paul is saying. He is not trying to tell us that the Old Testament Psalm was describing the universal spread of the gospel. What he means is that what in Ps. 19 applies to the language of the heavenly bodies is also applicable to the spread of the gospel.

But perhaps the comparison is more than superficial. Should we not rather say that God's revelation in the realm of creation and in that of redemption is such that in both cases it forces itself on our attention?

That in the days of Christ and the apostles the gospel was indeed spreading fast is clear from such passages as Rom. 15:22-24; Phil. 1:12, 13; Col. 1:6; cf. John 12:19; Acts 2:41, 47; 4:4; 17:6.

The rapid progress of the gospel in the early days has ever been the amazement of the historian. Justin Martyr, about the middle of the second century, wrote, "There is no people, Greek or barbarian, or of any other race, by whatever appellation or manners they may be distinguished, however, ignorant of arts or agriculture, whether they dwell in tents or wander about in covered wagons, among whom prayers and thanksgivings are not offered in the name of the crucified Jesus to the Father and Creator of all things." Half a century later Tertullian adds, "We are but of yesterday, and yet we already fill y o u r cities, islands, camps, y o u r palace, senate, and forum. We have left y o u only your temples." R. H. Glover (*The Progress of World-Wide Missions*, New York, 1925, p. 39) states, "On the basis of all the data available it has been estimated that by the close of the Apostolic Period the total number of Christian disciples had reached half a million."

19. But I ask, "Can it be that Israel did not understand?" First, Moses says,

"I will make y o u envious of a non-nation,

And with a nation (that is) senseless will I make y o u angry."

"But I ask" matches the opening of verse 18. The question regarding *hearing* (verse 18) is followed by one regarding *understanding*. Note that now Israel, already implied in the earlier verses, is definitely mentioned.

The purport of the question is whether Israel, even though it has indeed heard the gospel, has nevertheless not been able to understand it sufficiently so that it could be held responsible for its unbelief. What is found in verses 19b-21, though not a direct answer to this question, implies the answer. It shows that not ignorance but unwillingness was the cause of Israel's lack of faith. The quotation is from Deut. 32:21b.

A non-nation is a mere mass of people. It is a vast multitude which had not received the many privileges that had been bestowed on Israel, "the people for God's own possession." That non-nation was going to receive those blessings which earlier had been granted to Israel. It was going to take Israel's place.

This very fact, of course, implies Israel's guilt, since it also implies that Israel had received sufficient understanding of the way of salvation to be held fully accountable for its unbelief.

Does not this passage immediately remind us of Luke 20:15, 16 (cf. Matt. 21:41; Mark 12:9): "What, then, will the owner of the vineyard do to them? He will come and kill those sharecroppers and give the vineyard to others." The privileged position, once granted to Israel, was going to be transferred to those very people who had been despised by Israel. Cf. Acts 13:46.

The envy and anger to which our passage refers is illustrated in Mark 12:12. But envy can also have a positive result. For this see Rom. 11:11.

20. And Isaiah is so bold as to say,
"I was found by those who did not seek me;
I revealed myself to those who did not ask for me."

These lines from Isa. 65:1 (quoted here in reverse order) are even more incisive. If among those who first heard them there were any self-righteous Jews, they must have been shocked by this statement, especially in its present context. It is in the form of a paradox. By reminding the hearers that God was found by those who did not seek him, and was revealed to those who did not ask for him, it emphasizes God's sovereign right to bestow salvation on whomsoever he wills. In no sense is it true that man, by means of any merit he may dare to claim, brings about God's saving attention. The Gentiles, their minds and hearts darkened by sin, and therefore not even asking for God's help, receive it. Israel is passed by because of its obstinacy, as is clear from verse

21. But concerning Israel he says,
"All day long I have stretched out my hands to a disobedient and obstinate people."

Sound exegesis demands that this passage—a quotation from Isa. 65:2— be interpreted in light of the immediate context (see verses 19, 20; and in Isa. 65 see verses 3-7). The passage indicates that Israel was fully responsible for the divine judgment that was pronounced upon it. The fact that the nation day after day, week after week, year upon year, continued *to be disobedient* and *to contradict God, even in spite of God's outstretched hands of patience and invitation*, made matters worse for Israel. The predominant impression Rom. 10:21 leaves upon a person is therefore one of gloom, not one of cheer. It is darkness rather than light upon which the emphasis falls here.[301] When God pronounces a judgment on Israel he is not acting arbitrarily. Israel has earned that judgment. We cannot help thinking of these words of Jesus:

"Jerusalem, Jerusalem, who kills the prophets and stones those that are sent to her! how often would I have gathered your children together as a

---

301. It is for this reason that I do not agree with Cranfield's explanation of this passage, *op. cit.*, Vol. II, pp. 541, 542.

hen gathers her brood under its wings, but y o u would not. Behold, y o u r house is left to y o u a deserted place" (Matt. 23:37, 38).

This does not mean that the light has been completely replaced by darkness, that God's hands have ceased to be outstretched in loving patience and appeal, and that God is, accordingly, "through with the Jews."

We are not forgetting such passages as the following—and more could be added—which show that even now mission work among the Jews is not fruitless: 1:16; 3:3, 30; 4:12; 5:18, 19; 7:4; 9:6, 23, 27, 29; 10:1, 11-13, 16. There is a remnant of Israel that is destined for grace and glory. God has not thrust *his people* away from himself (11:1). There is a sense in which "all Israel" will be saved (11:26).

Besides, once the hardening process has begun in the life of this or that Israelite, no one has a right to say that it will continue until that man dies and perishes everlastingly. God's grace is sufficiently powerful to reach even the temporarily hardened sinner. See further on 11:28-31.

Practical Lessons Derived from Romans 10

Verse 1

"Brothers, my heart's desire and prayer to God for them is that they may be saved." The Jewish opponents were constantly persecuting Paul. Again and again they tried to kill him. Nevertheless, Paul continued to pray that they might be saved. He was putting into practice the rule laid down by Jesus (Luke 6:27-31). A lesson for us all.

Same passage. How was it possible for Paul to pray for the salvation of the Jews when he knew that, to a considerable extent, God had rejected them? See Matt. 8:10-12; Mark 12:9; Luke 20:15, 16; Rom. 9:27; I Thess. 2:14-16.

Answer: The identity of reprobates is known to God alone. Therefore it was right for the apostle to pray for individual Jews and for Jews in general.

Verse 2

"For I can testify about them that they have a zeal for God ..." Being filled with zeal and being sincere may be excellent, but not if the zeal is without understanding. As to sincerity: it is possible for a person to be sincerely ... wrong!

Verse 8

"The word is close to you; (it is) on your lips and in your heart ..." Is it not strange that, by nature, man wants to go to heaven the hard way? Yet, Rom. 10:8-10 is clear as daylight. See also Matt. 11:28-30 and John 3:16.

Verse 9

"Because, if on your lips is the confession, 'Jesus is Lord,' and in your heart the faith that God raised him from the dead, you will be saved." The original says: your ... your ... you; not y o u r ... y o u r ... y o u. It is fine to recite the

Apostles' Creed in unison during public worship. More than this is necessary, however; namely, the personal, individual profession of heart and lips.

Same passage. This confession, with specific mention of two supernatural facts—Christ's lordship and his bodily resurrection—deals the deathblow to all liberalism, showing that liberalism and Christianity cannot live together harmoniously under the same roof.

Same passage once more. Even though the two truths that are here mentioned may well be regarded as implying all the central doctrines of the Christian religion, does Paul not also imply that believers do not need to think alike on every minor point of theology? Room must be left for differences of opinion. See Luke 9:49, 50.

Verse 12

"For there is no distinction between Jew and Greek." God's love in Christ overarches distinctions with respect to race, nationality, sex, age, social and/or financial standing, degree of accomplishment, etc. With respect to any and all of these matters God is impartial. Rom. 10:12 is very clear on this point. So is John 3:16.

Verse 21

"All day long I have stretched out my hands to a disobedient and defiant people." How marvelous is God's patience. However, this does not mean that it has no limits. See Prov. 29:1; Luke 13:8, 9; 17:26-29. The only "safe" procedure, therefore, is the one described in Ps. 95:7, 8; Heb. 3:7, 8.

Summary of Chapter 10

This chapter consists of two main parts: verses 1-13; verses 14-21.

As at the beginning of chapter 9 so also here Paul reveals his tender affection for his kinsmen. He states that his prayer to God is that they may be saved. He testifies that they have a zeal for God, but deplores the fact that this zeal is not based on proper insight into God's revelation concerning the way of salvation (verses 1, 2).

Israel's tragic error consisted in this, that they sought to establish their own righteousness and refused to accept the righteousness provided by God in Christ. It is Christ, he alone, in whom the law attained its goal, so that, as a result, there now is righteousness for everyone who exercises saving faith (verses 3, 4).

It was Christ who came from heaven and who, in his people's stead, suffered the agonies of hell. The hard work was done by him, and should therefore not be attempted by us. Moses (Deut. 30:11-14) already made clear that Canaan was God's free gift, not the product of human exertion. As it was with Canaan so it is with salvation in general. It is given to those who trust in the Lord Jesus Christ. Therefore, "if on your lips is the confession, 'Jesus is Lord,' and in your heart the faith that God raised him from the dead, you will be saved . . . For the Scripture says, 'No one who puts his trust in him will ever be put to shame' " (verses 5-11).

Ethnic considerations play no part in the bestowment of salvation: "there is no distinction between Jew and Greek. For the same Lord (is Lord) of all and richly blesses all who call on him. For everyone who calls on the name of the Lord will be saved" (verses 12, 13).

In the second part of this chapter Paul, by means of a series of questions, arranged in effect-to-cause order, stresses the supreme importance of taking to heart the message of the duly authorized preacher. He who accepts his message accepts Christ. He who rejects it rejects Christ. It is understood, of course, that this is true only when the preacher truly represents Christ and actually conveys Christ's message.

To those who in the proper frame of mind listen to the gospel, blessings abound. To them the feet of those who bring good news are indeed beautiful (verses 14, 15).

There are many, however, who refuse to accept the gospel, as Isaiah proves by saying, "Lord, who has believed our message?" Everyone should therefore examine himself to see whether he really belongs to the company of those who heed whatever it is that God, through the proclamation of the word, is saying.

Excuses will not avail. The gospel is being circulated far and wide, re-minding us of the heavens which all around are declaring God's glory (verses 16-18).

Israel too not only heard God's message, but understood it well enough to be responsible for its lack of faith. Rejection and replacement are God's penalties imposed on the rejecters. Moses declared, "I will make y o u envious of a non-nation. And with a nation (that is) senseless will I make y o u angry" (Deut. 32:21b). And Isaiah was so bold as to say, "I was found by those who did not seek me; I revealed myself to those who did not ask for me" (Isa. 65:1). Concerning Israel he said, (65:2) "All day long I have stretched out my hands to a disobedient and obstinate—literally *contradicting*—people" (verses 19-21).

Outline (continued)

Justification by Faith

The Election of Israel's Minority (or Remnant)
versus
The Hardening of its Majority
"The elect have obtained it. The others were hardened"
11:1-10

Ingrafted Branches
"But they, if they do not persist in their unbelief, will be grafted in, for
God has the power to graft them in again"
11:11-24

God's Mercy on "the Fulness of the Gentiles" and on "All Israel"
"For God has locked up all in the prison of disobedience
in order that he may have mercy on all"
11:25-32

Doxology
"For from him and through him and to him are all things.
To him be the glory forever. Amen."
11:33-36

358

CHAPTER 11

11 1 I ask then, "Did God reject his people?" Of course not! Why, I myself am an Israelite, of the seed of Abraham, of the tribe of Benjamin. 2 God did not reject his people whom he foreknew. Or do y o u not know what the Scripture says in (the section about) Elijah, how he complains to God about Israel,
3 "Lord, thy prophets they have killed,
thine altars they have demolished,
and I am the only one left,
and they are seeking my life"?
4 But what is God's reply to him? "I have left for myself seven thousand men who have not bowed the knee to Baal." 5 So, too, at the present time a remnant has come into being, chosen by grace. 6 And if by grace, (then it is) no longer by works; since (if it were) grace would no longer be grace.
7 What then? What Israel is seeking so earnestly it has not obtained, but the elect have obtained it. The others were hardened, 8 as it is written:
"God gave them a spirit of stupor,
eyes not to see,
and ears not to hear,
to this very day."
9 And David says,
"Let their table become a snare and a trap,
a stumbling block and a retribution for them.
10 Let their eyes be darkened so as not to see,
and their back do thou bow down forever."

The Election of Israel's Minority (or Remnant)
versus
The Hardening of its Majority
"The elect have obtained it. The others were hardened"
11:1-10

The description (in 10:21) of Israel as "disobedient and obstinate" naturally introduces the question whether God has perhaps rejected his people (11:1).

This theme, divine rejection, is not new. The apostle has already shown that divine rejection, though in a sense real, is *not complete* (chapter 9) and not *arbitrary* (chapter 10). Here in chapter 11 he will point out that it is also *not absolute* or *unqualified*. It is not the whole story. Running side by side with rejection there is also election. Divine saving activity parallels divine hard ening. See 11:7, 25, 26. In a sense some of the ideas of chapter 9—see especially verses 6-13; 23-27—recur in chapter 11. But chapter 11 goes farther. It shows that between hardening and saving, between breaking off and grafting in, there is a kind of cause and effect relationship: the disobedience of the Jews brings about the obedience of the Gentiles (verses 11, 12, 15, 30); the mercy shown to the Gentiles is a blessing for the Jews (verse 31b); so that, in the end, not only *the fulness of the Gentiles* but also *the salvation of "all Israel"* is secured.

Of course, this double *interaction* (German *Wechselwirkung*) does not come about automatically. It is God who produces this favorable result: "For God has locked up all in the prison of disobedience in order that he may have mercy on all" (verse 32). It is not surprising therefore that the chapter is climaxed by an enthusiastic doxology (verses 33-36).

1a. I ask then, "Did God reject his people?"

Were not the Jews God's "peculiar treasure," his very own? See Exod. 4:22; 19:6; Deut. 14:2; 26:18; Ps. 135:4; Isa. 43:20; Hos. 11:1. Nevertheless, in complete harmony with previous statements (2:17-25; 9:30-32; 10:3, 16) Paul has just now stated that the Jews are disobedient and obstinate (10:21), a people deserving to be condemned. Does the apostle mean, then, that God has totally rejected, has thrust away from himself, *his people*?

Paul wants the addressees to become concerned about this question. He, accordingly, to arouse their interest, asks *them* to answer it. He says, "I ask then,[302] Did God reject his people?"

Paul now answers his own question:

1b, 2a. Of course not! Why, I myself am an Israelite, of the seed of Abraham, of the tribe of Benjamin. God did not reject his people whom he foreknew.

Note the terse, almost indignant, negative answer, "Of course not!"[303] Or "Perish the thought!" See on 3:4. Does not I Sam. 12:22 state, "For the sake of his great name the Lord will not reject his people," and is not this assurance repeated in Ps. 94:14, which adds, "He will never forsake his inheritance"?

The words, "Why, I myself am an Israelite . . . of the tribe of Benjamin," remind us of a similar statement in Phil. 3:5. See N.T.C. on Philippians, pp. 154-159. Paul was a direct descendant not only of Abraham but of Abraham, Isaac, and Jacob; in fact, of Jacob's son Benjamin! That son was the youngest child of Jacob's most beloved wife, Rachel. Benjamin was the only son of Jacob born in the land of promise.

Being able to claim such ancestry, the apostle was therefore "a Hebrew of Hebrews," a Hebrew if there ever was one, unquestionably an *Israelite*.

---

302. The verb λέγω does at times have this meaning. See Matt. 18:1; Mark 5:30 f.; and here in Rom. 10:18, 19; 11:11.

303. This negative answer is already implied in the very wording of *the question* as found in the original. Added stress appears in *the answer*. In both cases note μή.

Moreover, even though this was true, Paul had been a fierce persecutor of God's dear children. Nevertheless, the former enemy had become a friend, a true believer and even an enthusiastic apostle and proclaimer of the gospel. All this because divine sovereign love rested upon him, and this not only during his lifetime but from all eternity.

Indeed, God did not reject his people, including Paul, *whom he foreknew*; that is, on whom, from before the foundation of the world, he had set his love. He had made them the object of his special delight, a delight beginning in eternity, continuing in connection with their conception and birth, and never leaving them. For more on divine foreknowledge see on 8:29. Also see John 8:27, 28.

So here in verses 1b, 2a Paul is, as it were, saying, "Does anyone need proof that God fulfils his promise and has not rejected Israel? Well, then look at me. God did not reject me, and I am an Israelite!"

2b-4. Or do y o u not know what the Scripture says in (the section about) Elijah, how he complains to God about Israel,
"Lord, thy prophets they have killed,
thine altars they have demolished,
and I am the only one left,
and they are seeking my life"?
But what is God's reply to him? "I have left for myself seven thousand men who have not bowed the knee to Baal."[304]

Further proof of the fact that God is still concerned about Israel and has not completely rejected it is drawn from the story recorded in I Kings 19:1-18; see especially verses 9, 10, 14, and 18. According to this narrative, when disconsolate Elijah had entered a cave of Mt. Horeb, the Lord came and asked him, "What are you doing here, Elijah?" He replied, "I have been very zealous for Jehovah, the God of hosts; for the children of Israel have forsaken thy covenant, thrown down thine altars, and slain thy prophets with the sword; and I, only I, am left, and they are seeking my life, to take it away." The Lord's answer had included these words, "Yet I reserve for myself seven thousand in Israel—all whose knees have not bowed down to Baal and whose mouths have not kissed him."

The appropriate character of Paul's reference to this Old Testament account is immediately evident. In a sense the times of Elijah had returned.

---

304. ἐν Ἡλίᾳ, in the section about Elijah; cf. Mark 12:26. ἐντυγχάνει τῷ θεῷ κατὰ τοῦ Ἰσραήλ, appeals to God against Israel; i.e., complains to God about Israel.
κατέσκαψαν, third per. pl. aor. act. indicat. of κατασκάπτω, to tear down, demolish. Cf. Acts 15:16.
ζητοῦσιν τὴν ψυχήν μου, they are seeking my life; that is, they are trying to kill me.
χρηματισμός (in the New Testament only here), a divine *statement* or (as here) *reply*; cf. χρησμός, oracle. For the cognate verb see N.T.C. on Luke, pp. 175, 176 (on Luke 2:26).
τῇ Βάαλ. Note the fem. article. Yet the Baals or Baalim were generally regarded as masculine, in distinction from the feminine Ashtaroth and Asherim. Explanation: when Scripture was read aloud, the name of the god was not pronounced. Instead, the reader would say *shame*; Grk. αἰσχύνη; Heb. בֹּשֶׁת, both fem.

Unbelief was again rampant. In Elijah's day Jehovah's prophets had been slain, and recently the Jews had killed (Matt. 27:25; I Thess. 2:14, 15) the greatest Prophet of all (Deut. 18:15, 18; Acts 7:37). Nevertheless, as was true in the days of Elijah so also now, not all was dark: there were true believers. The words, "Or do y o u not know," (cf. 6:3, 16; 7:1; I Cor. 3:16; 5:6; 6:2, 3, 9, 15, 16), arousing interest and telling the addressed that they *should* have known, remind us of the same and similar words ("Have y o u not read?") spoken by Jesus (Matt. 12:3, 5; 19:4; 21:16, 42; 22:31; John 3:10).

There are those who attach significance to the fact that for the words "altars . . . prophets," in the Old Testament account, Paul substitutes "prophets . . . altars." One explanation is that the apostle wanted to point out that not only had wicked Jezebel seen to it that *the prophets* had been slain, but, in order to make it impossible immediately to substitute new prophets for the old, she had even ordered *the altars*, frequently used by the prophets, and here mentioned last for the sake of emphasis, to be demolished. Other interpreters explain the transposition as evidence of poor memory on Paul's part. Fact is that Paul correctly reproduces the substance of the original; i.e., as much of it as he needs for his purpose. In this particular instance the exact order of these two words was probably of no significance.

"I am the only one left, and they are seeking my life," Elijah had said. The Lord, on the other hand, had assured him that no less than seven thousand faithful men were left. Seven thousand *men*,[305] probably to be understood in the sense "in addition to the women and children," for it would be hard to imagine a situation in which only the men had remained faithful to God. Cf. Mark 6:44 with Matt. 14:21. To be sure, these seven thousand constituted only a remnant of Israel's population, but it was a *significant* remnant. In accordance with the symbolical meaning which Scripture attaches to the number seven and its multiples, we can say that this seven thousand amounted to *the full number* of Elijah's contemporary kinsmen chosen from eternity to inherit life everlasting. There must have been at least seven thousand.

Note especially "*I have left for myself*." The fact that seven thousand had remained loyal to God must not be ascribed to Elijah's energetic activity— he evidently did not even know anything about these seven thousand—or to the innate goodness of these faithful people, but to the sovereign will of God, to his delight in preserving for himself a remnant.

5. So, too, at the present time a remnant has come into being, chosen by grace.

As it was *then*, says Paul, so it is *now*. God did not then, does not now, and never will completely reject Israel. He is not "through with the Jews." Was it not he himself who had caused them to be an ore-bearing vein? Was it not he too, who, by means of his sovereign grace, had seen to it that also at the

---

305. Grk. ἄνδρας.

present time a remnant of Israel had come into being, a remnant "chosen by grace"? Cf. 9:11; 11:28.

The doctrine of *the salvation of the remnant* is taught throughout Scripture: At the time of *Noah* the many perished, the few were saved (Gen. 6:1-8; Luke 17:26, 27; I Peter 3:20).

The same thing happened in the days of *Lot* (Gen. 19:29; Luke 17:28, 29).

Elijah too, as we have just now been told, was acquainted with the idea of the saved remnant, though he did not realize that it amounted to no less than seven thousand.

Previously (Rom. 9:27; cf. Isa. 10:22 f.) the apostle has reminded us of the remnant in the days of *Isaiah*.

It does not surprise us therefore that also "at the present time," that is, in the apostle's own day, there was a saved remnant, and that *Paul* belonged to it. In Romans the remnant doctrine is either taught or implied also in the following passages: 9:6 f.; 9:18a; 10:4, 11, 16; 11:14, 24, 25.

Further substantiation of the doctrine that salvation is for the elect remnant can be found in such Old Testament passages as Isa. 1:9 (=Rom. 9:29); 11:11, 16; 46:3; 53:1; Jer. 23:3; 31:7; Joel 2:32; Amos 5:15; Mic. 2:12; 4:5-7; 7:18; Zeph. 3:13, to mention but a few. Was not a son of Isaiah named Shear Jashub, meaning *A remnant shall return?*

As to the New Testament, it may or may not be significant that in the parable of The Sower (or The Four Kinds of Soil)—see Matt. 13:1-9, 18-23; Mark 4:1-9, 13-20; Luke 8:4-15—it is *only the final kind of soil* that yields a good crop. But even if no conclusion can be drawn from this parable as to the proportion of saved to unsaved among those who hear the gospel, we have the Master's clear statement,

"For many are called, but few chosen" (Matt. 22:14). Cf. Luke 12:32.

The view of some—and among them those whose writings we regard highly—that a day is coming when this rule will no longer apply, in fact that the very principle of the remnant implies that one day the nation of Israel as a whole will be saved, seems rather strange. Are those who favor this opinion guilty of reading the words of Rom. 11:26 ("And so all Israel shall be saved"), *as they interpret it*, into 11:5?

6. And if by grace, (then it is) no longer by works; since (if it were) grace would no longer be grace.

Paul feels the need of adding this, probably because *salvation by works*, and therefore by human merit, was the very cornerstone of the Jewish (rabbinical) religion. Not only did Christians constantly have to defend themselves and their beliefs against this false doctrine, but, as is clear from such passages as Gal. 1:6-9; 3:1-5, they themselves were in danger of slipping back into the heresy which they, upon becoming Christians, were supposed to have left behind.

It is as if Paul were saying, "If salvation is by grace, it is no longer by works or by *merit*. Why not? Because the very essence of grace is *unmerited divine favor*." Cf. 4:4.

7-10. What then? What Israel is seeking so earnestly it has not obtained, but the elect have obtained it. The others were hardened, as it is written:

"God gave them a spirit of stupor,
eyes not to see,
and ears not to hear,
to this very day."

And David says,

"Let their table become a snare and a trap,
a stumbling block and a retribution for them.
Let their eyes be darkened so as not to see,
and their back do thou bow down forever."

"What then?" Paul means, "What follows?" When he continues, "What Israel is seeking so earnestly it has not obtained," he is repeating the thought of 9:30, 31. See especially 9:31: "Israel, however, though ever in pursuit of (the) law of righteousness, has not attained to (that) law." See the explanation of that passage. However, here (in 11:7) the apostle adds, "but the elect have obtained it. The others were hardened." By comparing our present passage with 9:30, 31 it becomes clear that *historically* the thing which Israel as a nation was constantly seeking but was not obtaining was *right standing with God*, righteousness.

One rather important difference between the former passage (9:30, 31) and this one (11:7) is that in the earlier one we were told that the Gentiles had obtained that which Israel as a nation had not obtained; but now, in 11:7, Paul, without in any way denying what he had said previously about the Gentiles, limits himself to Israel. He now states that "the elect"—that is, the elect[306] among the Jews—had obtained it." Cf. 9:6.

After saying, "The others were hardened," Paul immediately describes this hardening as an act of *God*. He quotes two Old Testament passages. In the first Moses is the speaker; in the second David.

The first quotation (verse 8) is from Deut. 29:4, which, as found there, reads as follows, "But to this day the Lord has not given y o u a mind that understands or eyes that see or ears that hear." With this passage may be compared Isa. 6:9. The spirit of stupor, mentioned in Rom. 11:8, is that of mental and moral dulness or apathy. The giving of this spirit describes the divine hardening process. The stupor resembles a deep sleep in which a person is insensitive to the impressions that come to him from the outside; hence, no seeing and hearing. Cf. Isa. 29:10.

Moses tells the Israelites that this condition has prevailed "to this very day." Paul was able to say the same with respect to the "day" when he was writing Romans: the Jews who had rejected Christ and the righteousness of God in

---

306. Literally "the election." This is simply an idiom for "the elect," as "the circumcision" is for "the circumcised." See footnote 119 on 4:9, p. 149.

and through the Savior, were continuing to attempt to establish their own righteousness.

The second passage (verses 9, 10) reflects Ps. 69:22, 23. However, Paul, in quoting these words, is for the most part following the LXX translation (there Ps. 68:23, 24), which is as follows:

> *English from Greek Translation (LXX)*
> "Let their table become a snare before them,
> a retribution and a stumbling block. /
> Let their eyes be darkened so as not to see;
> and their back do thou bow down forever."

A superficial glance at Ps. 69:22, 23, quoted by Paul here in Rom. 11:9, 10, might lead to the conclusion that its moral tone is not very high. The Psalmist seems to be pronouncing curses upon his enemies because, without good cause, they hate, reproach, and persecute him. However, a closer look at the psalm reveals that the reason—at least part of the reason—why his enemies hate him so implacably is the closeness of the fellowship existing between him and his God (see verses 7, 9). It is therefore not surprising that Ps. 69 is a Messianic Psalm (see especially verses 20, 21). Note also its stirring climax (verses 29-36).

It remains true, nevertheless, that in this psalm the author (David) is flinging an imprecation at his foes. He invokes a curse upon them. The meaning of the four lines (after "And David says") can be reproduced as follows:

Let their wasteful lifestyle prove to be their undoing.

Let it become the disaster they deserve.

Fill them with moral and spiritual blindness

And cause them to be bent down with continuous grief.

The concept to be emphasized in this connection is *retribution*: the disaster they deserve.

Verses 7-10 establish the following facts:

a. The elect have obtained salvation.

b. God hardens those who have hardened themselves.

c. They get what is coming to them.

Even for the hardened ones there is hope; that is, if they repent. It will then become clear that they too belong to the elect. In a marvelous manner (see the interpretation of 11:25, pp. 377, 378) God gathers to himself a remnant even from the hardened majority.

Accordingly, to include Rom. 11:7 (or 11:7-10) in a list of passages proving reprobation is an error. Scripture teaches reprobation as well as election, as has been shown; and see Rom. 9:13, 17, 18, 21, 22; I Peter 2:8, but Rom. 11:7f. does not prove this. It can be included in the list of proof passages only if the context (11:11f.) is ignored. On this point I agree with Ridderbos, *op. cit.*, p. 249 and with Cranfield, *op. cit.*, p. 549.

---

11 I ask then, "Did they stumble so as to fall?" Of course not! Rather, because of their trespass salvation (has come) to the Gentiles to make Israel envious. 12 Now if their trespass

(means) riches for the world, and their defeat (means) riches for the Gentiles, how much more (does) their fulness (mean)? 13 It is to y o u, Gentiles, that I am speaking. Inasmuch as I am an apostle to (the) Gentiles, I take pride in my ministry, 14 in the hope that I may somehow arouse my own people to envy and save some of them. 15 For if their rejection (means the) reconciliation of the world, what (is) their acceptance but life from the dead? 16 And if the cake that is offered as firstfruits (is) holy, so (is) the entire batch; and if the root (is) holy, so (are) the branches.

17 Moreover, if some of the branches have been lopped off, and you, being a wild olive shoot, have been grafted in among them, and have come to share the nourishing sap[307] from the olive root, 18 do not gloat over this at the expense of those branches. But if you do gloat, (then remember that) it is not you who support the root, but the root that supports you. 19 You will say then, "Branches were lopped off so that *I* might be grafted in." 20 True! But it was for lack of faith that they were lopped off, and it is by faith that you stand. Don't be arrogant but fear! 21 For if God has not spared the natural branches, neither will he spare you.

22 Consider then the kindness and the severity of God: toward those who have fallen there is severity, but toward you God's kindness, if you remain in his kindness. Otherwise you also will be cut off. 23 But they, if they do not persist in their unbelief, will be grafted in, for God has the power to graft them in again. 24 For if you were cut out of an olive tree that was wild by nature, and, contrary to nature, were grafted into a cultivated olive tree, how much more readily will these, the natural olive branches, be grafted (back) into their own olive tree?

Ingrafted Branches

"But they, if they do not persist in their unbelief, will be grafted in, for God has the power to graft them in again"

11:11-24

11, 12. I ask then, "Did they stumble so as to fall?" Of course not! Rather, because of their trespass salvation (has come) to the Gentiles to make Israel envious. Now if their trespass (means) riches for the world, and their defeat (means) riches for the Gentiles, how much more (does) their fulness (mean)?

Paul now informs us about God's purpose in hardening those who had hardened themselves. That purpose is ultimately one of grace, and this for the benefit of both Gentile and Jews.

In quoting from Ps. 69 (LXX Ps. 68) Paul had said, "Let their table become a stumbling block" (see also Rom. 9:33). He now asks, "Did they stumble so as to fall?"[308] In other words, "Was their final and irrevocable doom what God had in mind? With another and very comforting "Of course not!" or "Far from it!" the apostle buries that idea and emphatically proclaims the opposite, namely, that blessings were in store for both Gentile and Jew; all of this because of God's marvelous providential guidance and love, able to cause something good, yes very good, to come forth out of evil.

First of all, then, because of Israel's trespass (see footnote 157 on 5:15)—clearly, their rejection of the gospel—salvation has come to *the Gentiles*. That

---

307. Or fatness.
308. In the original the construction of this part of the sentence is the same as in 11:1, "I ask then, Did God reject his people?" So footnote 302 applies here also.

this was what had actually happened and was occurring right along is clear from such passages as Acts 13:44-48; 18:6; 28:23-28.[309] But indirectly *the Jews* themselves were also being blessed. Paul says, "salvation has come to the Gentiles *to make Israel envious.*" In the present context *envy* has a positive effect. Such an effect is, however, not universal, as 10:19 has already shown. To reconcile these two passages (Rom. 10:19 and 11:11b) we must assume that 11:11b has reference to the true Israel (9:6). In his marvelous kindness God causes their envy to be the means of their salvation. These people take note of the peace that passes understanding present in the hearts and lives of the Gentiles who, by God's sovereign grace, have embraced Christ as their Lord and Savior. The elect Jews then become envious, yearning to participate in this peace of God and in all the other blessings God is bestowing on the converted Gentiles. Result: the Holy Spirit uses envy to save these Jews.

The apostle draws this conclusion: If *their trespass*—the sin of the Jews in rejecting the gospel—means riches for the world, and *their defeat* riches for the Gentiles, for by this rejection the door to the evangelization of the Gentiles had been opened, then how much does *their fulness*[310] mean?

In the manner already explained, Israel's *defeat* had brought riches to the Gentiles. Then surely the salvation of the full number of Israelites who had been predestined to be saved (cf. 9:6)—hence, not just the salvation of a remnant at any *one* particular time (see 11:5)—would progressively bring an abundance of blessings to the entire world. Think of such blessings as spiritual unity and fellowship (Eph. 2:14, 18), co-operation in providing aid to the sick and needy, and presenting a strong, united evangelical testimony to the world. Just imagine that on history's final day one could look back on all those blessings!

The interpretation according to which Rom. 11:12 is limited to the conversion and restoration of the people of Israel at *history's close* is vulnerable on two counts:

---

309. In view of the clear language in these passages of the book of Acts, in which Paul is himself the speaker (or, as in one case, one of the speakers, the other being Barnabas), the explanation offered by K. Barth, namely, that the reference would be to the action of the Jews in nailing Jesus to the cross and thereby activating the reconciliation of the world, must be rejected. See K. Barth, *Kirchliche Dogmatik* II, p. 307; *Church Dogmatics* II, p. 279.

310. For the term πλήρωμα (pleroma) see N.T.C. on Colossians, p. 79, footn. 56. It lends itself to a variety of interpretations. By examining (a) the article on this word found in L.N.T. (A. and G.), p. 678, where for the present passage two meanings are discussed; (b) the various commentaries, containing many different opinions; and (c) G. Delling's article on this word in Th.D.N.T., Vol. VI, p. 305, one becomes aware of the existing confusion. As I see it, the best results will probably be obtained if:

a. the same English equivalent is assigned to the word in verse 12 as in verse 25.

b. in the *explanation* of the term, as used here in verse 12, the contrast Paul undoubtedly had in mind, between ἥττημα and πλήρωμα is recognized.

The result is that I have adopted *fulness* as the English equivalent in both instances. In my explanation of the term, as used here in verse 12, I suggest that the contrast is that between *defeat*, on the one hand, and *arrival at full strength* (implying full number), on the other.

a. As 11:5, 14, 30, 31 indicate, Paul is referring to events that include those which are taking place "at the present time," during Paul's current ministry, "now."

b. His words "their fulness" pertain to the salvation not of a physical unit, "the people of Israel"; but of the sum of all Israel's remnants. See 11:1-7, 26.[311]

At this point Paul begins to address specifically the Gentile portion of the Roman church:

13, 14. It is to y o u, Gentiles, that I am speaking. Inasmuch as I am an apostle to (the) Gentiles, I take pride in my ministry, in the hope that I may somehow arouse my own people to envy and save some of them.

Note the following:

a. As some see it, when Paul says, "It is to y o u, Gentiles that I am speaking," he is addressing the congregation as a whole, calling its members *Gentiles* because most of them were Gentile converts. However, this view is hard to accept since in the same verse the word *Gentiles* occurs again ". . . Inasmuch as I am an apostle to (the) Gentiles" in a context where it must mean *Gentiles in distinction from Jews*. Also in verse 17 the designation "a wild olive shoot" is best explained as referring to a Gentile.

It would seem, accordingly, that, beginning at verse 13 and continuing through verse 24, Paul is addressing especially the Gentile portion of the church at Rome. In fact, starting with verse 17, he is speaking to *a*—that is "any"—representative member of that part of the congregation.

b. "Inasmuch as[312] I am an apostle to (the) Gentiles . . ."

Although the sphere of Paul's apostolic labors and authority included Jews as well as Gentiles (Acts 9:15; 26:15-20), in a preeminent sense he had been appointed to be, and actually became, "apostle to the Gentiles" (Acts 18:6; 22:21; Rom. 1:5; 15:15, 16; Gal. 2:2, 8; Eph. 3:1, 8; I Tim. 2:7; II Tim. 4:17).

c. "I take pride in my ministry," etc.

The apostle is enthusiastic about, and adds prestige to, his ministry to the Gentiles, one reason being that he hopes to be a means in God's hand for the realization of God's purpose mentioned in verse 11, namely, to promote salvation for the Gentiles in order thus to make Israel envious with a view to salvation. Note similarity between verses 11b and 13b, 14.

Not as if conversion of Israelites is the one and only goal of Paul's Gentile mission activity. For the apostle missionary endeavor among the Gentiles to the glory of God is also an end in itself. See I Cor. 9:22. However, in the present context Paul indicates that his ministry to the Gentiles is not in conflict with, but in the interest of, the salvation of his kinsmen.

d. ". . . and save some of them."

---

311. For the opposite interpretation see J. Murray, *op. cit.*, Vol. II, p. 79.

312. ἐφ' ὅσον, basic meaning: to the extent that, inasfar as; and so: inasmuch as. See also Matt. 25:40, 45.

Paul's hope that some Jews might be saved through his current ministry, a hope strengthened by his affection for his own people (9:1-5; 10:1), was not without solid foundation. It was based on God's promise concerning the salvation of Israel's *remnant*.

Continuing in the style of verse 12 Paul writes:

15, 16. For if their rejection (means the) reconciliation of the world, what (is) their acceptance but life from the dead? And if the cake that is offered as firstfruits (is) holy, so (is) the entire batch; and if the root (is) holy, so (are) the branches.

It will be recalled that all but a remnant of the Jews had hardened themselves against the gospel (verse 7) and in turn had become hardened. Now God, in his beneficent and overruling providence, brings about a twofold result:

a. The gospel was now being proclaimed to the nations of the world. Those Gentiles who accept it by faith become reconciled to God; that is, the bond of fellowship between God and themselves is restored. Cf. 5:11; II Cor. 5:18-20.

b. Sin-hardened Israelites, taking note of the peace and joy experienced by these Gentiles, become filled with envy, but, in a marvelous manner that envy is by God changed into living faith in the Lord Jesus Christ.

Imagine for a moment the radical change here implied for these Israelites. They now love what they formerly hated. They hate what they formerly loved. Above all, they know that no longer are they God's enemies. They have now been accepted by the very God against whom earlier they had hardened themselves and by whom they had been further hardened. The change was simply astounding, as especially Paul, the former persecutor, knew by his own experience! It was a turnabout to life from the dead, a truly spiritual resurrection. Cf. Luke 15:32; Eph. 2:1-10. It reminds one of the hymn, "Out of My Bondage, Sorrow, and Night" by William T. Sleeper. Think especially of the stanza beginning with the line:

"Out of the fear and dread of the tomb, Jesus I come, Jesus I come."

A Jew who used to hate every Christian experienced a dramatic conversion. Afterward he was heard to say, "The change from darkness to day is great, but the change brought about in me is greater by far."

This change implies the consciousness that one has been *set apart* to devote one's life to God. See I Peter 2:9.

This is in line with the illustration Paul uses: if the cake that is offered as firstfruits is holy, that is, *set apart for sacred use*, then surely the entire batch is holy. If the root is holy, so are the branches that are upheld by that root and receive their nourishment from it.

This illustration owes its origin to the offering to the Lord of a cake prepared from the firstfruits of grain worked into dough (Num. 15:17-21). When the Israelites brought this offering they thereby consecrated to the Lord the entire grain harvest. All of it was now regarded as *set apart* to the

Lord, so that whatever was subsequently used by the people was regarded as a gift out of his hand. Similarly, if the root of a tree *is consecrated* to the Lord, so are all its branches. The cake and the root probably symbolize Abraham; better still: Abraham, Isaac, and Jacob. See Rom. 11:28. The branches are the descendants of these forefathers. They are the people of Israel, highly privileged (Rom. 9:4 f.). They—cf. "the entire batch"—had been *set apart* by the Lord, to live for him (Exod. 19:5, 6; Deut. 14:2; cf. I Peter 2:9).

When the apostle mentions "their rejection" and "their acceptance" he is not referring to what is going to happen in connection with The Great Consummation. We should not forget the context. The *immediately preceding* context is: "I take pride in my ministry, in the hope that I may somehow arouse my own people to envy and save some of them." The *immediately following* context is: "Moreover, if some of the branches have been lopped off, and you, though being a wild olive shoot, have been grafted in among them and have come to share the nourishing sap from the olive root, do not gloat over this at the expense of those branches." It will not do, therefore, to interpret the intervening reference to "their acceptance . . . life from the dead," as being a reference to what by some is expected to happen at the close of the world's history. Those interpreters who, nevertheless, have adopted that theory will at times inform their readers that the "life from the dead" change means that in the last days the radical turnabout or conversion of the people of Israel will result in unexampled blessings for mankind, worldwide quickening, with Israel advancing from one missionary triumph among the Gentiles to another. Are they forgetting that, according to the interpretation of Rom. 11:25, 26, favored by them and/or by their friends, there will be no more Gentiles left to become candidates for conversion, since, as these exegetes see it, it is only *after* the totality of Gentile believers has been gathered into God's fold that Israel will finally be saved?

17-21. Moreover, if some of the branches have been lopped off, and you, being a wild olive shoot, have been grafted in among them, and have come to share the nourishing sap from the olive root, do not gloat over this at the expense of those branches. But if you do gloat, (then remember that) it is not you who support the root, but the root that supports you. You will say then, "Branches were lopped off so that *I* might be grafted in." True! But it was for lack of faith that they were lopped off, and it is by faith that you stand. Don't be arrogant but fear! For if God has not spared the natural branches, neither will he spare you.[313]

---

313. ἐξεκλάσθησαν, in verses 17, 19, and 20, third per. pl. aor. pass. indicat. of ἐκκλάω, to break off; and, in connection with a tree, to lop off.
ἀγριέλαιος = ἄγρος, field, plus ἐλαία, here olive shoot; hence, *field* = *wild* olive shoot. In verse 17 ἀγριέλαιος is probably an adjective; in verse 24 a noun. Cf. the English word *oak* which can also be a noun or an adj. (oaken).
συγκοινωνὸς τῆς ῥίζης τῆς πιότητος τῆς ἐλαίας "(having come) to share the root of fatness

Continuing to address the Gentiles (see on verse 13), Paul feels the need of issuing a warning to them with respect to their attitude toward his kinsmen, the Jews. The contents of the present passage (verses 17-21) will be discussed under the following three captions: Why was this warning necessary? In what form is it presented? What is its content? Discussion of the third question will also cover verses 22-24.

> *Paul Warns the Gentile Members of the Roman Church*
> *To Shun Sinful Pride*

A. *Why was this warning necessary?*

As has been indicated, p. 25, the spiritual condition of the Roman church was, on the whole, very favorable. This does not mean, however, that perfection had been attained. In connection with the discussion of 8:23-25 it has already been shown that there seems to have been some people in this church who were lacking in the basic Christian virtue of humility. Similarly, from the present passage it appears that there were Gentile Christians who, filled with sinful pride, were tempted to look down with a degree of contempt on their Jewish fellow-members. At first the real clash may well have been between these Gentiles and the unbelieving Jews, those outside the church. It would seem, however, that little by little the Gentile church members caused their feeling of superiority to be manifested also within the church. See verses 17, 18. It is not ruled out, of course, that not only Gentiles but even Jews may have become infected with this evil. Paul does not always differentiate between the two, but most of all it was a Gentile blemish. For evidences of the presence of a boastful frame of mind among those addressed see the following passages: 12:3; 14:1, 3, 4, 10, 13; 15:1, 2, 5, 7, 15, 16, in addition to the present passage (11:17-21; in a sense 11:17-24).[314]

For the present, then, we are dealing with the spirit of arrogance as it manifested itself in a typical *Gentile* member of the Roman church, as is clear from the fact that the apostle describes this representative member as "a *wild* olive shoot." Contrast verse 17b where the root of a *cultivated* olive tree is presupposed; and see also verse 24.

B. *In what form is it presented?*

The answer is: in the form of a metaphor, an implied comparison, in the present case *reminding one* of the practice of arboreal grafting, in which, for

---

(= the fat root) of the olive"; or else: "(having come) to share the root of the olive, that is, its fatness." For "fatness" one can substitute "nourishing sap."

ἐνεχεντρίσθης, sec. per. s. aor. pass. indicat. of ἐγκεντρίζω, to ingraft. In verse 19 the first per. s. aor. pass. subjunct. (ἐγκεντρισθῶ) of the same verb occurs.

ἐν αὐτοῖς, among them.

κατακαυχῶ, sec. per. s. pres. imperat., and κατακαυχᾶσαι, sec. per. s. pres. indicat. of κατακαυχάομαι, to glory over, gloat over.

ἐφείσατο, third per. s. aor. act. indicat., and φείσεται, third per. s. fut. indicat. of φείδομαι, to spare.

314. See S. K. Williams, "The 'Righteousness of God' in Romans," *JBL*, No. 99 (June 1980), pp. 241-290. Note especially pp. 245-255.

any one of several reasons, a shoot ("scion") of one tree is inserted into the stem ("stock") of another. The transition between verses 16 and 17 is, however, not abrupt. The apostle has just now been speaking about "branches," meaning people, and here in verse 17 he continues to do so. In verse 16 he described these branches as being *holy*, in the sense of "set apart for sacred use or duty." This cannot mean, however, that all the people so described were also marked by inner holiness, sanctity of heart, life and conduct. The apostle makes clear that some of "the branches" revealed the opposite character, and had to be lopped off. Clearly such branches symbolize unfaithful covenant members. They were descendants of the patriarchs but had abandoned the faith of the fathers.

Note that the *y o u* of verses 2 and 13 changes into the *you* of verses 17-24, the reference now being to a—that is, any—Gentile member of the Roman church. Let each take the lesson to heart! Paul says that this typical member, "being a wild olive shoot" *was grafted in among* the branches of the cultivated olive tree.

For this "application of the practice of grafting" Paul has been severely criticized. It has been remarked that it is customary to graft a slip of a cultivated olive tree into a wild olive tree, but not the reverse. To reestablish Paul's reputation some have answered that it is exactly in Palestine that a wild olive shoot is at times grafted into an old cultivated olive tree in order to reinvigorate it.[315] Others, however, in their effort to rescue the apostle, employ the very opposite method of reasoning. They argue as follows: Granted that Paul refers to a kind of grafting that is contrary to customary practice, he admits it, does he not? He calls grafting anything from a wild olive tree into a cultivated olive tree 'contrary to nature" (verse 24). So at least he knows what he is saying. Some authors even use both of these arguments in order to help Paul out of his (imagined) difficulty, though it is hard to see how the apostle can receive help from those who on the one hand insist that the type of grafting he presupposes was in harmony with customary practice, be it only in Palestine, but who, on the other hand, point to Paul's admission that the grafting to which he refers was "contrary to nature." When two lines of argumentation clash, they cannot both be right. But even if the problem of grafting a wild shoot into a cultivated tree can be solved, how can we justify Paul's language when he speaks about grafting lopped off branches (back) into their own tree (verses 17, 19, 23, 24)?

The true solution is probably wholly different. To begin with, it is not true that in verse 24 Paul, in calling something "contrary to nature," is even indirectly referring to a method of horticultural grafting. See on that verse. And secondly, with respect to the first attempt to rescue Paul, those who endorse it seem to forget that Paul, in writing about grafting and regrafting

---

315. William M. Ramsay, *Pauline and Other Studies*, London, 1906, pp. 223, 224.

is under no obligation whatever to adhere to the rules and practices of Nature grafting. He is talking about grafting *in the spiritual realm*. How often did not Jesus, in his parables, draw pictures that departed strikingly from daily life customs and practices? Think especially of his parable of The Laborers in the Vineyard (Matt. 20:1-16).

What the apostle is saying, then, is clear. He is telling the typical Gentile member of the Roman church, who was tending to become somewhat arrogant, that he, that member, should never forget who he really is. He had come in from the outside and *had been spiritually grafted in among the Jews*. Only in this manner had he come to share "the nourishing sap from the olive root." To the proud Gentile member Paul is saying, "Consider how much you owe to the Jews!"

Was not Peter, whose possible connection with the founding of the church at Rome has been discussed earlier—see pp. 18, 19—a Jew? Was not Paul, who even before writing his present epistle seems to have been in contact with many prominent members of the Roman church (16:3-16), a Jew? Is it not true that the very gospel of *justification by faith* was based on the Jewish Scriptures? See 1:1, 2, 17; ch. 4. And, according to his human nature, was not even "the Author and Perfecter of faith" a Jew? Is it not true, therefore, that "salvation is from the Jews" (John 4:22)?

Must we not thank the Lord for the fact that the Holy Spirit so inspired Paul that, in addition to employing precious, unembellished theoretical arguments, he also made use of many vivid illustrations, the present grafting symbolism being one of them?

C. *What is its content?*

Paul warns the Gentile that he should not gloat over the fact that, while some of the natural branches—unbelieving Jews—have been lopped off, he, this Gentile, has been grafted in among the remaining (Jewish) branches, with all this implies with reference to partaking of "the nourishing sap from the olive root," the blessings promised to the patriarchs and realized in their lives and in the lives of their God-fearing children.

The Gentile, inclined to look down with a degree of contempt on his fellow-members, the Jews, is warned not to deem himself better than they. Let him bear in mind that it is not he, this boastful Gentile, who supports the root. How would it even have been possible for him to contribute anything to the blessings flowing forth from God's eternal decree, and from the promises, and imparted to the patriarchs, the all-inclusive promise being, "I will be your (or y o u r) God"? No, it was not the Gentile who supported the root, but the root that supported the Gentile.

The possible counter-remark made by the typical Gentile was, "Branches were lopped off so that *I*—with tremendous emphasis on this pronoun[316]—

---

316. Note how in the original this *I* is not merely included in the verb, as often, but is spelled out in full! It is ἐγώ.

might be grafted in" (verse 19). Paul answers, "True." Historically speaking as verse 11 has shown, that was indeed true. But there was another, even more important side to the answer. It was this: "it was for lack of faith that they were lopped off, and it is by faith that you stand." This *faith*, by virtue of its very essence, excludes all boasting, all arrogance or self-esteem. It includes godly *fear*, the kind of fear that is wholesome. See Prov. 3:7; Phil. 2:12, 13; Heb. 4:1; I Peter 1:17. Such fear leans wholly on God and his sovereign grace, and claims no merit of its own. The conclusion follows very naturally, "For if God has not spared the natural branches—the Jews to whom the promise was first made but who in large numbers had turned away from God—neither will he spare you."

22-24. Consider then the kindness and the severity of God: toward those who have fallen there is severity, but toward you God's kindness, if you remain in his kindness. Otherwise you also will be cut off. But they, if they do not persist in their unbelief, will be grafted in, for God has the power to graft them in again. For if you were cut out of an olive tree that was wild by nature, and, contrary to nature, were grafted into a cultivated olive tree, how much more readily will these, the natural olive branches, be grafted (back) into their own olive tree?

In preceding passages Paul has been speaking about the disobedience and rejection of many of the Jews (9:27, 31; 10:21; 11:7-10, 15), the "lopping off of branches" (11:17, 19, 20, 21). He has also commented on the salvation, riches, and grafting in of Gentiles (11:11, 12, 17, 19). It is God who rejects. It is also God who saves. Accordingly, Paul now rivets the attention of those addressed on the *kindness and the severity of God*. Not just on *one* of these qualities, namely, kindness, as is the habit of some preachers, who over-emphasize the love of God at the expense of his wrath, but on both. For those who have fallen—in the present context the Jews—there is severity, the rigor of the divine judgment. See 1:18, where God's *wrath* is directed especially against the unbelieving world of the Gentiles; but turn from there imme-diately to 3:19 where "the entire world is exposed to the judgment of God." That includes the Jews. So also here, in 11:22, God's severity of sternness[317] is directed against "those who have fallen," namely, the Jews, as the context clearly indicates.

"But toward you God's kindness." Note that the object of this kindness is still being described as the typical or representative Gentile Christian. Paul, who is himself "the apostle to the Gentiles," delights in calling attention to the salvation and riches God is imparting to the Gentiles (11:11, 12). On the concept of divine kindness see also 2:4; Eph. 2:7; Titus 3:4.

---

317. ἀποτομία, from ἀποτέμνω, to cut off; hence abruptness, rigor, severity, sternness. In the New Testament this noun is found only here. The adverb ἀποτόμως, sharply, harshly, occurs in II Cor. 13:10 and in Titus 1:13.

The manifestation of this kindness is, however, not unconditional. It requires genuine faith on man's part. Says Paul, "toward you God's kindness, if you remain in his kindness. Otherwise you also will be cut off."

This must not be understood in the sense that God will supply the kindness, man the faith. Salvation is ever God's gift. It is never a 50-50 affair. From start to finish it is the work of God. But this does not remove human responsibility. God does not exercise faith for man or in his place. It is and remains man who reposes his trust in God, but it is God who both imparts this faith to him and enables him to use it. For the interrelation between God's activity and man's, see Phil. 2:12, 13; II Thess. 2:13.

There is a sound, biblical sense, therefore, in which we can speak about salvation as being *conditional*. Its reception is conditioned on the life of trust in the Triune God who has revealed himself in Jesus Christ unto salvation and ultimately unto his own glory. This "if" character of salvation is very important. It is expressed beautifully in Felix Mendelssohn's *Elijah*. Note the words, "If with all y o u r hearts ye truly seek me, ye will ever surely find me" (based on Deut. 4:29). Note a similar "if" in such passages as Deut. 30:10; I Kings 8:47-50; Jer. 18:5-10; Col. 1:21-23; Heb. 3:6, 14. And is not a similar "if" *implied* in many other passages, including Matt. 11:28-30; John 3:16; Rev. 22:17? Absolute, unconditional promises, guaranteeing salvation to either Gentiles or Jews, *no matter how they live* exist only in people's imaginations, not in Scripture. Even if the condition is not always mentioned, for every responsible, thinking, individual it is always implied.

What happens when the condition remains unfulfilled? Ultimate rejection follows; and this, as Paul says in so many words, not only with respect to the Jew but also with respect to the Gentile.

Let not the Gentile believer imagine that God is through with the Jews; that, under no circumstances is salvation in store for them. The apostle states, "But they, if—there is that *if* again—they do not persist in their unbelief, will be grafted in, for God has the power to graft them in again." That the door of opportunity for the entrance of Jews—even for initially hardened Jews—is standing open, Paul is now going to demonstrate.

He starts out by saying, "For if you were cut out of an olive tree that was wild by nature, and, contrary to nature, were grafted into a cultivated olive tree . . ." In this part of the sentence what does Paul mean by "contrary to nature"? Does he mean "contrary to customary horticultural practice"? Would not such a statement, if at all deemed necessary, have been made much earlier; for example, in connection with verse 17? Is it not far more in harmony with the present context to interpret Paul's words as follows: "You, being a Gentile, belong by nature to the realm of unbelief. You are, as it were, part of a wild olive tree. Nevertheless, you were grafted into a cultivated olive tree, meaning: you were brought into the domain of grace, promise, and faith, the realm of Abraham, Isaac, and Jacob (cf. Gal. 3:9). For you this was an enormous change. It was contrary to nature, for not only did you have to be delivered from the pit of paganism, with all its vices (cf. 1:24-32); but, in addition, you had to be transplanted into the sphere of God's covenant, the realm of sovereign grace, holiness, light, and love. Accordingly, if, contrary to nature, *you* were grafted into a cultivated olive tree, how much more readily, then, will *the natural branches*, the children of the covenant, who were never immersed in paganism, and who, in addition, were in possession of all the remarkable privileges mentioned in 9:4, 5, be grafted back into their own olive tree; that is, be restored to their native stock"?

Note that the apostle does not say or imply that one day all unbelieving Jews are going to be grafted back into their own olive tree, are going to be saved. He carefully avoids saying anything of the kind. He states that the regrafting will take place "*if* they do not persist in their unbelief." Undoubtedly what he means is, "Some will persist; others will not." This interpretation is in line with previous statements about the hardened majority and the saved minority or remnant. See especially on 9:27 and on 11:5 (pp. 321, 322 and 362, 363).

In reading what Paul says about the olive tree there is one very important point that must not be overlooked. The apostle recognizes *only one (cultivated) olive tree*! In other words, the church is *one* living organism. For Jew and Gentile salvation is the same. It is obtained on the basis of Christ's atonement, by grace, through faith. The notion according to which God recognizes two objects on which he bestows his everlasting, saving love, namely, the Jews and the church, is contrary to Scripture. Here in Romans Paul has expressed himself on this subject again and again (3:29, 30; 4:11, 16; 5:18, 19; 9:22 f., 10:12, 13). *One olive tree* represents *all* the saved, regardless of their origin. And, as the result of the operation of God's saving grace, all the reborn are headed for the same everlasting home. Remember: *ONE OLIVE TREE*.

---

25 For I do not want y o u to be unaware of this mystery, brothers, so that y o u may not be conceited, that a hardening has come upon part of Israel (and will last) until the fulness of the Gentiles has come in.　26 And so all Israel will be saved, as it is written:

"Out of Zion will come the Deliverer;
he will turn godlessness away from Jacob.
27 And this is my covenant with them
whenever I shall take away their sins."

28 As far as the gospel is concerned, they are enemies for y o u r sake; but as far as election is concerned, they are beloved for the sake of the fathers,　29 for irrevocable are God's gracious gifts and his calling.　30 For just as at one time y o u were disobedient to God but now have received mercy as a result of their disobedience,　31 so they too have now become disobedient in order that, as a result of the mercy shown to y o u, they too may now[318] receive mercy.　32 For God has locked up all in the prison of disobedience in order that he may have mercy on them all.

---

318. Some MSS. omit this "now," but support for it is by no means weak.

God's Mercy on "the Fulness of the Gentiles" and on "All Israel"
"For God has locked up all in the prison of disobedience
in order that he may have mercy on all"
11:25-32

25. For I do not want y o u to be unaware of this mystery, brothers, so that y o u may not be conceited, that a hardening has come upon part of Israel (and will last) until the fulness of the Gentiles has come in.
Resuming use of the plural,[319] Paul directly addresses the entire congregation. Nevertheless, it is clear that even now he is thinking especially of those Gentile believers who stood in need of being warned against anti-Semitism. In no uncertain terms he has just told them that for the Jews, even for those who had become delinquent, and initially hardened, the door of opportunity to be saved was standing open at least as widely as it did for the Gentiles (verse 24). It is in connection with this thought that he now continues by using the explanatory conjunction *For*.

The words, "I do not want y o u to be unaware" signify, "I want y o u to take to heart." Note also here the word of tender affection "brothers." On both of these points (a. not unaware, and b. brothers) see 1:13.

". . . of this mystery." In referring to a mystery Paul is not using this term in the pagan sense of an esoteric doctrine for the initiated, but as indicating *a truth which would not have been known if God had not revealed it.*[320]

As appears from the very wording of verse 25—note "that a hardening has come upon part of Israel" (literally, "that a hardening in part has come on Israel"), this petrifaction is not absolute and unqualified; there is always a saved remnant, called into being in a marvelous manner:

a. Carnal Israel stumbles and is rejected because of its unbelief. Result:

b. The gospel is proclaimed to the Gentiles. The elect Gentiles are saved. Result:

c. God uses this salvation of Gentiles in order to arouse the envy of the Jews. Result:

d. The Jewish remnant accepts Christ, in accordance with God's eternal plan. In connection with each item it is God himself who brings about these results. But let us quote Paul's own words (verses 11, 12, 31):

a. "Because of their trespass

b. salvation (has come) to the Gentiles

---

319. Note change from σύ in verse 24 to ὑμᾶς in verse 25.

320. The word μυστήριον occurs also in Rom. 16:25 and six times in I Cor., six times also in Ephesians, four times in Colossians, once in II Thessalonians, and twice in I Timothy.
It is also found in the book of Revelation (1:20; 10:7; 17:5, 7). As there used it is perhaps best explained as "the symbolical meaning" of that which required explanation. In the LXX of Dan. 2, where the word occurs no less than 8 times (as a singular in verses 18, 19, 27, 30, and 47b; as a plural in verses 28, 29, and 47a) it refers to a "secret" that must be revealed, a riddle that needs to be interpreted. The meaning "divinely revealed truth" fits very well into the context of Luke 8:10 and its parallels (Matt. 13:11; Mark 4:11), the only Gospel instances of its use.

c. to make Israel envious, so that,

d. as a result of the mercy shown to y o u [Gentiles], they [Israel] too may now receive mercy."

Now is not that just too wonderful for words? Moreover, the blessed interaction Paul has in mind must not be given too limited a scope. It even reaches beyond that which is enclosed in these four items. For example, we may be sure that saved Gentiles (item b.) do not sit still, but, in turn, become witnesses for Christ; and so do saved Jews (item d.). This interdependence between the salvation of the Gentiles and that of Israel is the substance of the divine "mystery."[321]

In harmony, then, with the substance of this mystery, here in verse 25 the apostle states that the hardening has come *upon part of Israel*. That was true in the past, is true now, will still be a fact in the future. Is not this the same as to state that a remnant of Israel, *in every age*, is saved (see 9:27; 11:1-5)?

Israel's rejection is not absolute and unqualified, nor necessarily final. It is partial. Paul feels the need of stressing this fact because certain Gentiles seemed to have harbored contrary thoughts, as was pointed out in connection with verses 17-24. So he tells them, "I do not want y o u to be unaware of this mystery, brothers, *so that y o u may not be conceited*."

Not only is it true, however, that the divine hardening (in punishment for human hardening) affects part of the people in any period of history, but it is also a fact, as the apostle states here in verse 25, that a definite time-span has been assigned to this hardening. For the people as a whole it will last "until the fulness of the Gentiles has come in." In connection with verse 12, where the same word *fulness* (pleroma) occurs, it has been shown that by "fulness" the apostle means "full number." What Paul is saying, then, here in verse 25, is that Israel's partial hardening—the hardening of part of the people of Israel—will last until the full number of elect Gentiles has been gathered into God's fold.

And when will that full number have been brought to salvation in Christ? Scripture is very clear on this point. It will be on the day of Christ's glorious Return. Once he has returned, there is no longer any opportunity for accepting the gospel call. See Luke 17:26-37; II Peter 3:3-9. Cf. Belgic Confession, Article XXXVII:

"Finally we believe, according to the Word of God, when the time appointed by the Lord (which is unknown to all creatures) is come *and the number of the elect complete* (italics added), that our Lord Jesus Christ will come from heaven, corporally and visibly, as he ascended, with great glory and majesty to declare himself Judge of the living and the dead, burning this old world with fire and flame to cleanse it."

It has become clear, therefore, that the hardening of part of Israel and the gathering of Gentiles occur side by side. With respect to Israel this partial

---

321. So also Ridderbos, *op. cit.*, p. 263.

hardening began already during the days of the old dispensation (Rom. 9:27; 10:16, 21; 11:3), was taking place in Paul's own day, and will continue until the close of the new dispensation. Side by side with this hardening process, the gospel is being proclaimed to the Gentiles. Some reject it; some, by God's sovereign grace, accept it.

Returning now to Israel, it is obvious that if, in every age, some Israelites are hardened, it must also be true that in every age some are saved. Paul expresses this thought in words that have given rise to much controversy, namely, **26a. And so all Israel will be saved.**

THREE INTERPRETATIONS

A. *The Most Popular Theory*

"All Israel" indicates the mass of Jews living on earth in the end-time. The full number of elect Gentiles will be gathered in. After that the mass of the Jews—Israel on a large scale—will be saved. This will happen just previous to, or at the very moment of, Christ's Return.

For the names of some of the advocates of this theory see p. 307.

Evaluation

a. The Greek word οὕτως does not mean *then* or *after that*. The rendering "*Then* all Israel will be saved" is wrong. In none of the other occurrences of this word in Romans, or anywhere else in the New Testament, does this word have that meaning. It means *so, in this manner, thus.*

b. This theory also fails to do justice to the word *all* in "all Israel." Does not "all Israel" sound very strange as a description of the (comparatively) tiny fraction of Jews who will still be living on earth just before, or at the moment of, Christ's Return?

c. The context clearly indicates that in writing about the salvation of Israelites and Gentiles Paul is not limiting his thoughts to what will take place in the future. He very definitely includes what is happening *now*. See especially verses 30, 31.

d. Would it not be strange for God to single out for a very special favor— nothing less than salvation full and free—exactly that generation of Jews which will have hardened its heart against the testimony of the longest train of Christian witnesses, a train extending all the way from the days of Christ's sojourn on earth—in fact, in a sense, all the way from Abraham—to the close of the new dispensation?

e. The reader has not been prepared for the idea of a mass conversion of Israelites. All along Paul stresses the very opposite, namely, the salvation, in any age (past, present, future) of *a remnant*. See the passages listed under 11:5, p. 363. If Rom. 11:26 actually teaches a mass conversion of Jews, would it not seem as if Paul is saying, "Forget what I told y o u previously"?

f. If Paul is here predicting such a future mass conversion of Jews, is he not contradicting, if not the letter, at least the spirit, of his earlier statement found in I Thess. 2:14b-16:

". . . the Jews, who killed the Lord Jesus and the prophets, and drove us out, and do not please God, and are hostile to all men, in that they try to prevent us from speaking to the Gentiles that they may be saved, so as always to fill up the measure of their sins. But upon them the wrath [of God] has come to the uttermost"[322]?

g. The immediately following context (11:26b, 27) refers to a coming of "the Deliverer" who will turn away godlessness and remove sin from Jacob. Was not that the purpose of Christ's *first* coming? But the popular interpretation of Rom. 11:26 predicts a mass conversion of Jews in connection with Christ's *second* coming. That theory is, accordingly, not in harmony with the context.

For these several reasons Interpretation A. should be rejected.

B. *John Calvin's Theory*

"All Israel" refers to the total number of the elect throughout history, all those who are ultimately saved, both Jews and Gentiles. In his Commentary on this passage Calvin expresses himself as follows:

"I extend the word *Israel* to all the people of God, according to this meaning: when the Gentiles shall come in, the Jews also will return from their defection to the obedience of faith, and thus will be completed the salvation of the whole Israel of God, which must be gathered from both . . ."

The same view is defended by J. A. C. Van Leeuwen and D. Jacobs, *op. cit.*, p. 227; and, in a sense, by Karl Barth, *Der Römerbrief*, Zürich, 1954, p. 401; English tr., p. 416.

Evaluation.

Inasfar as Calvin interprets the term *Israel* spiritually—"Israel" refers to the elect—his theory must be considered correct. Cf. Rom. 9:6. Also his claim that the section, verses 25-32 (considered as a unit), describes *the one people of God* cannot be successfully refuted. On the other hand, Calvin's application of the term "Israel," in verse 26, to all the people of God, both Jews and Gentiles, is wrong. In the preceding context the words *Israel, Israelite(s)* occur no less than eleven times: 9:4; 9:6 (twice); 9:27; 9:31; 10:19; 10:21; 11:1; 11:2; 11:7; and 11:25. In each case the reference is clearly to Jews, never to Gentiles. What compelling reason can there be, therefore, to adopt a different meaning for the term *Israel* as used here in 11:26? To be sure, at the close of verse 25 the apostle makes mention of the Gentiles, but only in order to indicate that the partial hardening of the Jews will not cease until every elect Gentile will have been brought into the kingdom. Accordingly, Paul is still talking about the Jews. He does so also in verse 26b. Even verse 28 contains a clear reference to Jews. Not until verses 30-32 are reached does the apostle cause the entire body of the elect, both Jews and Gentiles, to pass in review together.

322. Or: at last; or, to the end.

Therefore, while appreciating the good elements in Calvin's explanation, we cannot agree with him in interpreting the term "all Israel" in 11:26 as referring to all the elect, both Jews and Gentiles. A passage should be interpreted in light of its context. In the present case the context points to Jews, not to Gentiles, nor in verses 26-29 to a combination of Jews and Gentiles.

C. A Third Theory

The term "All Israel" means *the total number of elect Jews, the sum of all Israel's* "*remnants.*" "All Israel" parallels "the fulness of the Gentiles." Verses 25, 26 make it very clear that God is dealing with both groups, has been saving them, is saving them, and is going to save them. And if "All Israel" indicates, as it does, that not a single elect Israelite will be lacking "when the roll is called up yonder," then "the fulness of the Gentiles" similarly shows that when the attendance is checked every elect Gentile will answer "Present."

For the meaning of "will be saved" see on 1:16, p. 60. For Jew and Gentile the way of salvation is the same. In fact, their paths run side by side. Opportunity to be saved will have ended for both when Christ returns. As indicated previously, the two—"the fulness of the Gentiles" and "All Israel"—constitute *one* organism, symbolized by a single olive tree. It should be clear that if, in the present connection, *fulness* must be interpreted in its unlimited sense, the same holds for *all* in "All Israel."

The words "And so" are explained by Paul himself. They indicate, "In such a marvelous manner," a manner no one could have guessed. If God had not revealed this "mystery" to Paul, he would not have known it. It was, in fact, astonishing. The very rejection of the majority of Israelites, throughout history recurring again and again, was, is, and will be, a link in the effectuation of Israel's salvation. For details, see above, p. 366, 367, 377, 378 (Rom. 11:11, 12, 25).

Although, to be sure, this interpretation is not nearly as popular as is theory A, among its defenders are men of recognized scholarship (as holds also, of course, for theories A and B). Let me mention but a few.

One of the propositions successfully defended by S. Volbeda, when he received his summa cum laude doctor of theology degree from the Free University of Amsterdam was: "The term 'all Israel' in Rom. 11:26a must be understood as indicating the collective elect out of Israel."[323]

H. Bavinck, author of the four-volume work *Gereformeerde Dogmatiek* [Reformed Dogmatics], states, " 'All Israel' in 11:26, is not the people of Israel, destined to be converted collectively, neither is it the church consisting of united Jews and Gentiles; but it is the full number which during the course of the centuries is gathered out of Israel."[324] Cf. H. Hoeksema, *God's Eternal Good Pleasure*, Grand Rapids, 1950, p. 465.

---

323. Quoted from *De Intuitieve Philosophie Van James McCosh*, Grand Rapids, n.d., p. 415.
324. Vol. IV, p. 744. This is my translation from the Dutch. So also for the quotation from Volbeda.

And L. Berkhof states, " 'All Israel' is to be understood as a designation not of the whole nation but of the whole number of the elect out of the ancient covenant people . . . and the adverb οὕτως cannot mean 'after that,' but only 'in this manner.' "[325]

For a similar interpretation see H. Ridderbos, *op. cit.*, p. 263.

Not only scholars of *Reformed persuasion and Dutch nationality or lineage* have adopted this interpretation, but so have many others, as is clear from a glance at Lenski's commentary on Romans, pp. 714, 726, 727. See also O. Palmer Robertson, "Is There a Distinctive Future for Ethnic Israel in Romans 11?," in *Perspectives on Evangelical Theology*, Grand Rapids, 1979, pp. 81-94. These interpreters are convinced that this is the only interpretation that suits the text and context.

Objections Stated and Refuted
Objection No. 1. This interpretation destroys the contrast between the *remnant* mentioned in 11:5, on the one hand, and *the mass of Israel*, on the other.

Answer. Our interpretation does not destroy a contrast but defines it more accurately. The real contrast is that between single remnants (see, for example, 11:5), on the one hand, and "all Israel," that is, the sum of all the remnants throughout history (verse 26), on the other.

Objection No. 2. According to this interpretation the "mystery" mentioned by Paul amounts to no more than that all Israel's elect will be saved. But that is a truth so obvious that it fails to do justice to the implications of the term "mystery."

Answer. Not so! The mystery of which Paul speaks has reference to the marvelous chain of events that results in Israel's salvation. It points to seemingly contradictory factors which in God's loving and overruling providence are so directed that ultimate salvation for "all Israel" is effected. See above, pp. 377, 378.

* * * *

26b, 27. . . . as it is written:
　　"Out of Zion will come the Deliverer;
　　he will turn godlessness away from Jacob.
　　And this is my covenant with them
　　whenever I shall take away their sins."
Note the following:

a. It is logical to connect "And so all Israel will be saved" with "Out of Zion will come the Deliverer," and to interpret this divine deliverance as *rescue from sin* and *bestowment of salvation*, which blessings Jehovah brought about through the person and work of the Mediator, Jesus Christ.

b. As the words "as it is written" indicate, what immediately follows upon "And so all Israel will be saved" is material quoted from the Old Testament.

---

325. *Systematic Theology*, pp. 699, 670.

It does not consist, however, in a quotation of this or that single passage, but rather in a skillful symposium of several passages; such as, Isa. 59:20; 27:9; 59:21, in *that* order, with reminders of Micah 5:2 (or a similar verse) and probably Jer. 31:31 f. In addition, it should be borne in mind that Paul is conversant with the LXX (Greek) translation of the Old Testament as well as with the original Hebrew text. What is to be admired is that he is able to weave these various strands into one beautiful, consistent pattern.

c. The words "Out of Zion will come the Deliverer" are quoted from LXX Isa. 59:20, except for the fact that LXX has "for the sake of Zion," the original Hebrew "to Zion," and Paul "out of Zion." This presents no real difficulty, for all three are true. Did not the Deliverer come "for the sake of Zion," that is, to rescue Zion? And did he not also come "to Zion"? How else could he have saved it? And is it not also true that according to his human nature he came "out of Zion"? Think of Mic. 5:2.[326] In connection with "out of," "from" or "from among," see also Deut. 18:15, 18; Ps. 14:7; 53:6; and Isa. 2:3.

d. The task which, according to prophecy, the Deliverer was to perform, consisted, according to the LXX of Isa. 27:9, in this: to turn away godlessness or lawlessness from Jacob, that is, from Israel. Naturally it would be turned away only from the elect of Israel. We now understand why Paul has a right to quote these very passages to prove that "all Israel" would be saved; for, in order to save Israel it must be delivered not from this or that earthly foe but from godlessness, from sin.

e. Returning again to Isa. 59, this time to verse 21, the apostle continues (quoting the Lord as saying), "As for me, this is my covenant with them." He then quickly turns his attention to another precious passage in which *that divine covenant* is mentioned in connection with *the removal of sins*, namely, Jer. 31:31 f. There we read, "This is the covenant that I will make with the house of Israel and with the house of Judah . . . I will forgive their iniquity, and their sin will I remember no more." So he writes, ". . . whenever I shall take away their sins."

f. It is clear that in this entire passage (11:26b, 27) *Paul is not thinking of what Jesus will do at his second coming, when he will come not "out of Zion," but "from heaven" (I Thess. 4:16), and when forgiveness of sin will no longer be possible.* Paul is thinking of Christ's first coming when, by means of his vicarious death, he established the basis for the forgiveness of sins, and therefore also for the salvation of "the fulness of the Gentiles" and of "all Israel."

g. Paul is not deviating from his central theme. Is not the removal of sin one of the main ingredients of *justification by faith*? See Rom. 4:25; 5:8, 9, 19; 8:1-3. The promise of the covenant goes into effect "whenever" in the life of any Israelite sin is removed. Romans 9-11 shows that this doctrine is

---

326. As here used *Zion* in all probability represents Israel, viewed as "the people of God." See G. Fohrer's article on this subject in Th.D.N.T., Vol. VII, p. 309.

historical, indicating what happens again and again during history's course. **28-31.** **As far as the gospel is concerned, they are enemies for y o u r sake; but as far as election is concerned, they are beloved for the sake of the fathers, for irrevocable are God's gracious gifts and his calling. For just as at one time y o u were disobedient to God but now have received mercy as a result of their disobedience, so they too have now become disobedient in order that, as a result of the mercy shown to y o u, they too may now receive mercy.**

In harmony with verses 25, 26, which speak first of a hardening of part of Israel and then about "all Israel" which will be saved, so here too the apostle first reminds us of those Israelites who, as far as the gospel is concerned, are enemies, and then of those who, as far as election is concerned, are beloved for the sake of the fathers. In reading on (see verses 30, 31), however, we soon become aware of the fact that these "enemies" and these "beloved ones" are the same people, namely, the elect. At first they were hostile to the gospel, but later on, because of the wonderful manifestation of God's mercy (see verse 25 f.) they become friends.

Note the following:

a. "As far as the gospel is concerned . . . enemies for y o u r sake." Note "for y o u r sake."

The explanation is found in verse 11: "Because of their trespass salvation (has come) to the Gentiles."

b. ". . . as far as election is concerned, they are beloved."

The same Jews who at one time had been enemies of the gospel had become friends, beloved of God and fellow-believers. This great change had been brought about because of the fact that these former enemies had been designed by God, in his eternal decree, to become friends.

c. "for the sake of the fathers."

Not because of any innate goodness or merit pertaining to Abraham, Isaac, and Jacob, but because of God's promise to the fathers, "I will . . . be y o u r God and the God of y o u r seed after y o u." See Gen. 17:7; cf. 26:23, 24; 28:12-15.

d. "for irrevocable are God's gracious gifts and his calling."

There are those who interpret this entire passage (verses 28-31) as a description of God's love for the people of Israel in general. The present clause shows that this interpretation is incorrect, for it refers to *God's irrevocable calling, a call that is not subject to change and is never withdrawn.* This is certainly the inner or effectual call, one that pertains only to the elect.[327]

e. This also proves that "God's gracious gifts" must not be identified, as often happens, with the special privileges granted to the Jews as a people (9:4, 5), but must refer to such products of God's special grace as faith, hope, love, peace that surpasses all understanding, life everlasting, etc., all of them being gifts bestowed on God's elect, *on them alone.*

---

327. So also L. Berkhof, *Systematic Theology*, p. 469, on Rom. 11:29.

f. The explanation of the words, "For just as at one time y o u were disobedient to God but now have received mercy as a result of their disobedience, so they too . . . may now receive mercy," is found in verse 11; note especially "to make Israel envious," and see the explanation of that verse on p. 367.

g. It is clear that the entire passage (verses 28-31), correctly explained, harmonizes with 11:26a, "And so all Israel will be saved." In both cases Paul is speaking about the true Israel. *They* are enemies (at first). *They* are beloved . . . have become disobedient in order that *they* too may now receive mercy. The apostle is telling the Romans, especially the Gentiles among them, who in all probability constituted the majority of the congregation, that, as a result of the mercy shown to them—that is, to this predominantly Gentile church—the Jews, stirred to envy, now receive God's *mercy*, his love to those in need.

h. The repetition of the word *now*, occurring either twice or three times in verses 30, 31, shows that all the while Paul is thinking not of something that will happen at, or just previous to, Christ's Return, but of events that are occurring right now, in fulfilment of God's plan from before the founding of the universe.

32. For God has locked up all in the prison of disobedience in order that he may have mercy on them all.

As the conjunction "For" shows, there is a close connection between verse 32 and the preceding passage. Therefore, although when verse 32 is lifted out of its context and applied to the whole human race, an intelligible meaning results (cf. 3:9-18), it is probably better to regard this verse as applying to "the fulness [=full number] of the Gentiles" and "all Israel."

What Paul is saying, then, is that God *has locked up* all these Israelites and the total number of these Gentiles. He has shut them all up as in a prison, "the prison of disobedience," for by nature all are disobedient to God's holy law. Cf. Gal. 3:22, 23.

Their situation is desperate: sin disturbs, the law condemns, conscience frightens, the final judgment threatens, and God has not accepted them. *By nature* such is their situation.

Suddenly the darkness is dispelled. It is God himself who opens the prison door and is letting the light shine in. The prisoners—every one of them without exception—walk out into freedom. God did it "in order that he may have mercy on them all."

The best commentary on these triumphant words is certainly Paul's own, "being justified freely by his grace through the redemption (accomplished) by Christ Jesus, whom God designed to be, by the shedding of his blood, a wrath-removing sacrifice (effective) through faith" (3:24). Hallelujah!

33 O the depth of the riches both of the wisdom and knowledge of God!
   How unsearchable his judgments,
   and untraceable his ways!

34 For who has known the mind of the Lord
　Or who has been his counselor?
35 Or who has ever given (something) to God,
　that God should repay him?
36 For from him and through him and to him are all things.
　To him be the glory forever! Amen.

Doxology
"For from him and through him and to him are all things.
To him be the glory forever. Amen."
11:33-36

Reflecting on (a) what he has just now written (verse 32), on (b) "the
mystery" introduced in verse 25 (the interdependence between the salvation
of "the fulness of the Gentiles" and "all Israel," see pp. 377, 378, 381), and
probably also on (c) all he has written so far on the glorious theme of *justification by faith*, it is not at all surprising that exuberant Paul, himself a marvelous product of God's sovereign grace, breaks out into a doxology.

All the more striking is this doxology when it is contrasted with the "great
sorrow" which Paul expresses at the beginning of this large Section (see
9:1 f.).

**33. O the depth of the riches both of the wisdom and knowledge of
God!**
How unsearchable his judgments,
and untraceable his ways!

When Paul reflects on the matters mentioned in connection with (a), (b),
and (c) above—perhaps especially on (b)—his soul, filled with admiration,
adoration, and awe, expresses itself in an exclamation, which can even be
called a *song*, of praise to God. He has become aware of ocean-depths (cf.
I Cor. 2:10) of riches (cf. Rom. 2:4; 9:23; 10:12) that cannot be plummeted,
riches of God's wisdom and knowledge.

God's *wisdom* is his ability to select the best means for the attainment of
the highest goal. One might call it the divine efficiency evident in all his
works. The term *knowledge*, as applied to God, in the present connection
(linked with wisdom), must not be understood in the sense of his eternal
delight, a meaning which the word has at times, but rather as his insight into
the very essence of things, people, ideas, etc., his omniscience.

The apostle adds, "How unsearchable are his *judgments*"; that is, God's
sovereign decisions, decrees, disposals. In the present context the reference
is especially to those judgments that are revealed in the divine plan of salvation and in the effectuation of that plan. The addition "and untraceable

his ways," probably indicates, "and how impossible it is to trace or track down the means God uses to put his decisions into effect."[328]

**34, 35. For who has known the mind of the Lord
Or who has been his counselor?
Or who has ever given (something) to God,
that God should repay him?**

Still lifting up his heart in praise to God, Paul asks three questions. The first one is, "For who has known the mind of the Lord?" This question is quoted, almost unchanged, from the LXX version of Isa. 40:13. It is quoted also in I Cor. 2:16. It immediately reminds us of Isa. 55:8, "For my thoughts are not y o u r thoughts, neither are y o u r ways my ways." Of late more and more is becoming known about the mysteries of the human brain. The *real* men of science, pondering these new discoveries, are beginning to say, "How great is God!" But surely, if God is marvelous and incomprehensible in the work of creation, is he not at least equally astounding in his work of redemption? Who, indeed, has ever been able, even to a small extent, actually to probe God's mind?

The second question is, "Or who has been his counselor?" This question too is quoted from Isa. 40:13.

We have all met people whom we correctly consider wise and knowledgeable, but they have not always been wise. There was a time when they lacked both wisdom and knowledge. How, then, did they obtain these qualities? To a certain extent, at least, by making good use of the counsel and information they received from parents, teachers, and friends.

But God never had any counselor to whom he could go for help!

The third question is, "Or who has ever given (something) to God, that God should repay him?" In other words, "Who has ever put God in debt to him?" As to its essence this question is quoted from Job 41:11 (Hebrew original).

What? God in debt to us? Impossible. In fact, our indebtedness to him is so great that our hearts are thrilled whenever we reflect on what he has done, is doing, and will do for us. An *adequate* response to God is simply impossible. So, we begin to respond in prayers of thanksgiving or of joyful exclamation. We copy Paul's words as recorded here in Rom. 11:35, or in II Cor. 8:9, or in II Cor. 9:15. Or, thrilled to the very depths of our soul, we sing Charles Wesley's song, ending with the words,

> Amazing love! how can it be
> That thou, my God, shouldst die for me?
>
> —Lines taken from
> "And Can It Be That I Should Gain?"

---

328. ἀνεξεραύνητα, note double prefix; hence the meaning of the compound is: *in*capable of being searched *out*; unsearchable, nom. pl. n. of ἀνεξεραύνητος. Originally the simple verb was ἐρευνάω, later changed to ἐραυνάω, to search (John 5:39; 7:52; Rom. 8:27; I Cor. 2:10; I Peter 1:11; Rev. 2:23). In the New Testament the *compound* is found only here.

ἀνεξιχνίαστοι, nom. pl. f. of ἀνεξιχνίαστος, also in Eph. 3:8; from ἀν plus ἐξιχνιάζω, to trace or track out. Cf. ἴχνος, footstep, track (Rom. 4:12; II Cor. 12:18; I Peter 2:21). The meaning of the compound is, therefore: incapable of being traced or explored, untraceable.

Or, with an equal thrill of amazement, we turn to the old, familiar *Amazing Grace* by John Newton.

36. For from him and through him and to him are all things. To him be the glory forever! Amen.

Interpreters have tried to discover the source of these words. Could Paul have borrowed them, perhaps, from this or that Greek poet or philosopher? Now although it is true that the apostle was acquainted with Epicurean and Stoic poetry and philosophy (Acts 17:18, 28), and therefore perhaps also with the saying, "All things come from thee [Nature], subsist in thee, and return to thee," he was by no means a pantheist. His song of praise is dedicated not to Nature or to the Universe but to God Triune who revealed himself in Jesus Christ unto salvation. The source of the apostle's saying, therefore, is Scripture, its teachings applied to his heart by the Holy Spirit.

What is the meaning of "all things"? Does this expression refer to all things in creation? Cf. John 1:3; I Cor. 8:6. Probably not. The immediate context (verse 25 f.) has to do with the gospel, and therefore with the realm of salvation.

Does the saying refer, then, to the Holy Trinity, so that the meaning would be: "The Father thought it; the Son bought it; the Holy Spirit wrought it"? Although there are those who favor an explanation of this kind, it should be immediately rejected. To assign the three separate elements (from him, through him, to him) respectively to the three persons is about as unreasonable as anything can be.

What then? In the immediately preceding quotations the reference was to Jehovah; that is, to God. So here too "from him" must mean "from the Triune God," and this holds also for the other two little phrases.

The correct interpretation, as I see it, is therefore this: God is the source of our salvation; it is through his grace and power that salvation becomes a reality in our lives; and to him, accordingly, all the glory is due. *He is the source, accomplisher, and goal of our salvation.*

It is certainly very logical that the apostle, nearing the conclusion of his doxology, writes, "To him be the glory forever." Since it was he who not only planned our salvation but who also caused it to become a reality, it follows that he—he *alone*—should receive all the glory.

Paul concludes this little paean of praise and thanksgiving, and therefore also chapters 9-11, and, in fact, the entire predominantly doctrinal Section of his book (chapters 1-11), by adding the word of solemn affirmation and enthusiastic personal approval, *Amen.*

Practical Lessons Derived from Romans 11

Verses 3, 4

"I have left for myself seven thousand men who have not bowed the knee to Baal."

388

Christian leaders—whether pastors or teachers, evangelists or missionaries—are prone to forget that the Christian work they are doing is in many cases receiving the constant but unheralded support of ever so many others who are not in their group. Every congregation has its devout members who by their prayers are supporting the work these leaders are doing. And let us not forget even the children. When a certain pastor's wife was seriously ill with a sickness that led to her death, he was being wonderfully supported by children who would come to him and say, "We are praying for you and your family." What a help this proved to be!

Verse 11

". . . because of their trespass salvation (has come) to the Gentiles to make Israel envious."

What an astounding statement! So wonderful is God that he is even able to use human trespasses in order to bring about salvation for Gentiles and Jews!

Verse 13

"I take pride in my ministry."

Humanly speaking, one important reason for Paul's success as a missionary was his joy in performing his task, the enthusiasm he was ever revealing. Study, for example, such passages as:

"Woe to me if I do not preach the gospel" (I Cor. 9:16)!

"I have become all things to all men in order that by any and all means I may save some" (I Cor. 9:22).

"Thanks be to God for his indescribably precious gift" (II Cor. 9:15)!

Such enthusiasm is catching. So is also the opposite frame of mind. A grumpy preacher—or any other person connected with religious work—who with a woe-begone appearance and a hangdog disposition goes about his task, resembles a salesman who begs his customers not to buy his goods!

Verse 14

". . . in the hope that I may somehow arouse my own people to envy and save some of them."

In this connection see also Dan. 12:3, Rom. 10:1; I Cor. 9:22. In order to bring Jews to Christ, Paul was willing, if need be, even to make use of "envy," in the sense of a yearning, on the part of unbelieving Jews, to obtain the same precious blessings as those possessed by believing Gentiles.

We too should concentrate our attention on this great objective of being instruments in God's hand for the conversion of the Jews. To present a correct interpretation of Rom. 11:26 is important, but to be instrumental, even in some small way, in bringing a Jew to a saving knowledge of Christ is even far more important. We rejoice, of course, in the "Jews for Jesus movement" in the United States, and in the fact that through this and similar means a considerable number of the ancient covenant people have already been won for the Savior. It gladdens our heart to read the statement of Moishe Rosen, leader of the Jews for Jesus Mission, that "This past decade has seen more Jewish people making decisions for Jesus Christ than any other similar period of time since Apostolic Days." But we should remember that by far the most people who belong to this ethnic group have not been won over. Instead of confusing these people by telling them that they will all be saved if they can just remain healthy long enough to reach the day of Christ's Return, we should preach Christ to them, as their only Hope, and as the fulfilment of their need of *an atonement by blood*. Some Jews are keenly aware of this lack in their religion as now practiced.

None of this evangelistic work among the Jews will avail, however, unless it be accompanied by fervent prayer, and the power of Christ's resurrection be shown in our own lives. We should constantly bear in mind that for every Jew who reads *the New Testament* there are a hundred or more who read us!

The attempt to inspire the Jews with false hope, as if somehow, in spite of their rejection of Christ, they are still God's special favorites, is inexcusable. Our Lord wants the Jews to come to *him*. To be sure, everything that can possibly be done should be done in the present dispute between Jews and Arabs, in order, if possible, to reach a conclusion by means of which the needs of both parties are satisfied. But even if such a political solution should ever be reached, it would not, in and by itself, solve the deep-seated spiritual problem of the Jews. Salvation, to the glory of God Triune, is what the Jews stand in need of most of all, as is true with respect to us all. "For there is no distinction between Jew and Greek. For the same Lord (is Lord) of all and richly blesses all who call on him. For everyone who calls on the name of the Lord will be saved" (Rom. 10:12, 13).

Verse 18

"It is not you who support the root, but the root that supports you."

"We pay ... thousand dollars annually in support of kingdom causes," said the boaster. He forgot to mention how much effort and pain these same kingdom institutions were expending to contribute to the spiritual welfare of himself and his family. It would have been a sum that cannot be expressed in monetary phraseology.

When through the mouth of Nathan the Lord told David, "I will establish a house for you. When your days are over ... I will raise up your offspring ... He is the one who will build a house for my name, and I will establish the throne of his kingdom forever," David, seeing from afar the dawn of the bright morning of glory which would culminate in the birth of Christ, poured out his heart in language of humble thanksgiving:

"Who am I, O Sovereign Lord, and what is my family, that thou has brought me this far?" He realized that it was basically not he who was supporting the root, but the root that was supporting him.

Religion without humility and gratitude does not deserve the name religion.

Verse 23

"But they, if they do not persist in their unbelief, will be grafted in, for God has the power to graft them in again."

But is not the idea of the regrafting of lopped off branches (the reincorporation into Christ's body of those who have become untrue to the faith) in conflict with the teaching of Heb. 6:4-6? A possible solution has been suggested by F. F. Bruce in his fine commentary on Hebrews (*The New International Commentary on the New Testament*, Grand Rapids, 1964, pp. 118, 119), namely, that as a matter of human experience the reclamation of such people is practically impossible; but also, that nothing of this sort is ultimately impossible for the grace of God.

Well, in the present passage (Rom. 11:23) we are told that "God has the power to graft them in again," that is, by his Spirit to regenerate them and reincorporate them into the organism of his church.

Summary of Chapter 11

Since chapter 10 closed with a description of Israel as disobedient and obstinate, it is not surprising that chapter 11 starts with the question, "Did God reject his people?" Did he in his wrath completely and irrevocably thrust Israel away from himself?

Paul answers, "God did not reject his people whom he foreknew," that is, on whom, from before the founding of the universe, he had set his love. "Look at me," says Paul, as it were. "I am an Israelite, and God did not reject me." He implies: there is always a remnant chosen by God. In fact, does not verse 5 suggest this thought?

This was true in the days of Elijah, as related in I Kings 19:1-18. When the disconsolate prophet complained that he alone had remained faithful and that his life too was in jeopardy, the Lord told him, "I have left for myself seven thousand men who have not bowed the knee to Baal."

As to those Israelites who did not respond favorably to God's gracious invitations but hardened their hearts against the gospel, God "gave them a spirit of stupor, eyes not to see, and ears not to hear, to this very day." Cf. Deut. 29:4; Isa. 6:9. To such people the words of David (see Ps. 69:22, 23) apply, "Let their table become a snare before them, a retribution and a stumbling block," etc.

All this is summarized in the words of Rom. 11:7, "What Israel is seeking so earnestly it has not obtained, but the elect have obtained it. The others were hardened" (verses 1-10).

Does this mean then that for these hardened ones, who as yet have not displayed any signs of having been elected from eternity, there is no hope? It does not.

We now learn that God gathers to himself a remnant even from this sin-hardened majority. Paul asks, "Did they stumble so as to fall?" He answers, "Of course not! Rather, because of their trespass salvation (has come) to the Gentiles to make Israel envious." This shows that it was not final, irrevocable doom God had in mind when he initially hardened the hearts of those who had hardened themselves. On the contrary, God was using even Israel's trespass in order to serve as a link in the chain of salvation, so as to save both Gentile and Jew.

"Because of their trespass salvation (has come) to the Gentiles." When the apostle wrote these words he must have vividly recalled how previously he and Barnabas had told the Jews in Pisidian Antioch, "Since y o u reject the word of God . . . we now turn to the Gentiles." Subsequently similar words were spoken and actions taken.

ROMANS

But that was not the end of the story. The salvation which thus came to the Gentiles filled some of the hardened Jews with envy. They began to yearn for the peace and joy that had come to the Gentiles who had yielded their hearts and lives to the Savior. Result: some of these Jews were now also gathered into the fold, thereby proving that they too had been elected from eternity. Now if even Israel's spiritual defeat had brought riches to the Gentiles, as had actually occurred, was occurring, and was going to occur, then surely Israel's arrival at full strength—the salvation, during the course of the centuries of the full number of Israelites destined for life everlasting—would progressively result in an abundance of blessings for the entire world.

That Paul, in saying these things, is not thinking of what will take place at history's close, but of what has been happening and is occurring right along, is clear from verses 13, 14, "Inasmuch as I am an apostle to (the) Gentiles, I take pride in my ministry, in the hope that I may somehow arouse my own people to envy and save some of them."

For the Israelites who had previously experienced God's punishment the consciousness that they are now accepted by God and are a blessing to mankind amounted to nothing less than "life from the dead."

They knew that they had been set apart to render service to God. In fact, of old the entire nation of Israel had been thus consecrated to God. Were they not all descendants of Abraham, Isaac, and Jacob with whom and with whose descendants God had established his covenant? Surely, if the cake offered as firstfruits is holy, then the whole batch is holy; if the root is holy, so are the branches. If the patriarchs had been set apart to render service to God, as was true, this held also with respect to their offspring.

But this did not mean that every Israelite was marked by inner holiness. Some of the "branches," that is, people, revealed the opposite character. They were branches that had to be, and were, lopped off the olive tree.

Such unfaithfulness seemed to give this or that rather arrogant Gentile church-member the excuse to say, "Branches were lopped off that *I* myself might be grafted in." Paul answers, "True! But it was for lack of faith that they were lopped off, and it is by faith that you stand. Don't be arrogant but fear! ... For if you were cut out of an olive tree that was wild by nature, and, contrary to nature, were grafted into a cultivated olive tree, how much more readily will these, the natural olive branches, be grafted (back) into their own olive tree?" (verses 11-24).

Paul continues, "For I do not want y o u to be unaware of this mystery, brothers, so that y o u may not be conceited, that a hardening has come upon part of Israel (and will last) until the fulness of the Gentiles has come in." He means: throughout the ages a portion of the Jews is hardened, the others are saved. Reflecting on the marvelous manner in which God gathers the various remnants that constitute the collective body of those saved Israelites, he calls this chain of salvation, with its various links, "the mystery." It was indeed a mystery, for Paul could never have discovered it if God had not revealed it to him. For more on this mystery see Rom. 11:11, 12, 31, and pp. 366, 367, 377, 378, 384, 385. Paul adds, "*And so*—that is, in this manner—*all Israel*, the entire body of elect Jews, *will be saved.*"

By referring to Old Testament passages—Isa. 59:20; 27:9; 59:21, in that order, and probably also Mic. 5:2; Jer. 31:31 f.—the apostle proves that the truth he is proclaiming is not a novelty but rests upon the solid foundation of Scripture. The coming and work of the Deliverer had assured sin's removal. Those who previously had been enemies of the gospel had, accordingly, become friends, beloved ones. This had been brought about through the effectuation of the divine decree of election and the fulfillment of the promises made to the forefathers. Moreover, the state of being saved, once a reality, would never be lost; for "irrevocable are God's gracious gifts and his calling."

In verses 30, 31 Paul summarizes the mysterious ways of God, issuing in the salvation of the full number of Gentiles and of "all Israel." In verse 32 he adds, "For God has locked up all in the prison of disobedience in order that he may have mercy on them all" (verses 25-32).

Contemplation of God's wonderful plan of redemption causes the apostle to conclude this chapter with a meaningful doxology. It may be conveniently divided into three parts: (a) verse 33; (b) verses 34, 35; and (c) verse 36.

Verse 33 is an exclamation in praise of God's wisdom and knowledge. Paul is probably reflecting especially on these divine qualities as revealed in the plan of redemption and in the manner in which that plan is carried out. He is sure of the fact that the way of salvation decreed by God and the manner in which this salvation is realized in human lives surpasses anything mere human beings could ever have devised.

In verses 34 and 35 the author praises the divine self-sufficiency or independence. Who can compare with God? Who has ever imparted any wisdom or knowledge to him or helped him in any way in originating and/or carrying out the plan of salvation? No one, of course. Therefore the glory belongs to him alone.

Accordingly in verse 36 Paul ascribes glory to him who is the source, accomplisher, and goal of man's salvation.

To this sincere and thrilling doxology the writer attaches his very personal and enthusiastic word of solemn affirmation and approval: AMEN (verses 33-36).

393

Chapters 12—16

Practical Application

Outline of Chapters 12—16

Paul, having brought to completion his Exposition of the doctrine of Justification By Faith, now proceeds to its Practical Application. To be sure, there has been application right along, but every careful reader of this epistle will have to grant that whereas doctrine predominates in chapters 1—11, practical application to life in general and to concrete life situations holds sway in the remaining five chapters. Besides, as we shall see in a moment, the fact that the apostle himself so regards the connection between what he has said in chapters 1—11 and what he is about to say in chapters 12—16 is clear from 12:1.

PRACTICAL APPLICATION
Chapters 12—16
Outline
I. *Main Body of This Part of the Letter*

What Should Be the Attitude of the Justified Believer Toward:

Chapter

12:1, 2	A. God "Offer yourselves as living sacrifices, holy and well-pleasing to God . . ."
12:3-13	B. Fellow-Christians
3-8	"We, who are many, are one body in Christ."
9-13	"Be devoted to one another in brotherly love."
12:14-21	C. Outsiders, including Enemies "Bless those who persecute y o u."
13:1-7	D. The Authorities "Let every person be subject to the governing authorities."
13:8-10	E. Everybody "Do not keep on owing anyone anything except to love one another."
13:11-14	F. The Lord Jesus Christ "The night is far advanced; the day is drawing near . . . Clothe yourselves with the Lord Jesus Christ, and make no provision for (the fulfillment of) the lusts of the flesh."
14:1-15:13	G. The Weak and the Strong
14:1-23	"Him who is weak in faith accept."
15:1-13	"We who are strong ought to bear the failings of the weak and not to please ourselves."

397

II. *Conclusion*

15:14-16 H. Closing Commendation and Explanation of Boldness in Writing

"I myself am convinced . . . that y o u yourselves are rich in goodness . . . I have written to y o u rather boldly . . . because of the charge God gave me to be a minister of Christ Jesus to the Gentiles . . ."

15:17-22 I. Review of the Past

"From Jerusalem all the way around to Illyricum, I have fully proclaimed the gospel of Christ."

15:23-29 J. Plan for the Future

"Now I am on my way to Jerusalem in the service of the saints . . . When I have completed this task . . . I will go to y o u on my way to Spain."

15:30-33 K. Prayer Request

"I exhort y o u, brothers, by our Lord Jesus Christ and by the love of the Spirit, to join me in my struggle by praying to God for me."

16:1-16 L. Commendation of Phoebe. Paul's Own Greetings and those of all the churches

"Greet Priscilla and Aquila, my fellow-workers in Christ Jesus."

16:17-20 M. Final Warning

"I exhort y o u, brothers, to watch out for those who cause divisions."

16:21-23 N. Greetings of Friends

"Timothy, my fellow-worker, greets y o u."

16:25-27 O. Doxology

"Now to him who is able to establish y o u in accordance with my gospel and the proclamation of Jesus Christ . . . be glory forever through Jesus Christ! Amen."

In most cases the paragraph heading covers the entire contents of the paragraph. In others it covers most, but not all, of the contents.

The Outline is intended as a useful tool to indicate, from the very beginning, what, on the whole, chapters 12 through 16 are all about.

Outline (continued)

Practical Application

A. *What Should Be the Attitude of the Justified Believer Toward God*
"Offer yourselves as sacrifices, living, holy,
and well-pleasing to God"
12:1, 2

B. *What Should Be the Attitude of the Justified Believer Toward Fellow-Christians*
"We who are many, are one body in Christ"
12:3-8
"Be devoted to one another in brotherly love"
12:9-13

C. *What Should Be the Attitude of the Justified Believer Toward Outsiders, Including Enemies*
"Bless those who persecute y o u"
12:14-21

CHAPTER 12

12 1 I exhort y o u, therefore, brothers, in view of God's great mercy, to offer your-selves[329] as sacrifices, living, holy, and well-pleasing to God, (which is) y o u r spir-itual worship. 2 And stop allowing yourselves to be fashioned after the pattern of this (evil) age, but continue to let yourselves be transformed by the renewing of y o u r mind, so that y o u may prove what is the will of God, namely, that which is good and well-pleasing and perfect.

A. *What Should Be the Attitude of the Justified*
Believer Toward God
"Offer yourselves as sacrifices, living, holy,
and well-pleasing to God"
12:1, 2

1. I exhort y o u, therefore, brothers, in view of God's great mercy, to offer yourselves as sacrifices, living, holy, and well-pleasing to God, (which is) y o u r spiritual worship.

The very first expression, namely, "I exhort" (in the original *one word*) indicates the character not only of the opening paragraph but of the five final chapters of this epistle. Exhortation is not completely absent from the earlier chapters, but by and large it is *exposition* that is found in Rom. 1-11, while *exhortation* dominates Rom. 12-16.

It is as "a called apostle" (1:1), "a minister of Christ Jesus" (15:16), clothed with authority, that Paul, in the spirit of love and concern, exhorts his dearly beloved brothers in the church of Rome. On this word "brothers" see what has been said earlier (pp. 52, 214, 215). Literally Paul exhorts those ad-dressed to offer their *bodies* as sacrifices[330] to God. However, that in such a context the word *body* refers to the entire personality is clear from 6:11-14; see also Phil. 1:20. Calvin states, "By *bodies* he means not only our skin and bones but the totality of which we are composed. He adopted this word that he might more fully designate all that we are, for the members of the body are the instruments by which we carry out our purposes."

---

329. Literally: y o u r bodies.
330. The apostle uses the sing. *sacrifice* where we would probably use the pl.

Paul states that these sacrifices must have the following characteristics: they must be "living," that is, must proceed from the new life within the believer; "holy," the product of the sanctifying influence of the Holy Spirit; and, accordingly, "well-pleasing" to God, not only accepted by, but most heartily welcome to, the One to whom believers dedicate themselves. The apostle adds, "which is y o u r . . . worship."[331] What has been said earlier (see on 9:4, pp. 312, 313) about this word *worship* applies here also.

Paul is thinking about the action of worshiping, the wholehearted consecration of heart, mind, will, words, and deeds, in fact of all one is, has, and does, to God. Nothing less!

Rendering such devotion will amount to y o u r logikēn worship, says Paul. The debate about *logikēn* (acc. sing. f. of *logikos*) is continuing. The word reminds us of *logical*. But the meaning of a word is not determined first of all by its etymology but by its use in given contexts. Nevertheless, in the present case *logical*, in the sense of *reasonable*, deserves consideration. Several translators have accepted "reasonable" or "rational."[332] As I am writing this, I am looking at the two volumes by W. à Brakel, a Dutch work on Dogmatics, to which he gave the title, based on Rom. 12:1, *Redelijke Godsdienst* (Leiden, 1893), that is, *Reasonable Religion* (or *Reasonable Worship of God*). What, according to this interpretation, Paul is saying is that rendering wholehearted devotion is the only logical or reasonable worship of God.

But though this interpretation of the Greek adjective makes sense, it is not the only possible one, perhaps not even the best. In the only other New Testament passage in which the adjective occurs, namely, I Peter 2:2, it means *spiritual*, as the context makes clear. Peter cannot have been referring to *logical* or *reasonable* milk! Moreover, in the context he mentions "a spiritual house" and "spiritual sacrifices."

It is not surprising, therefore, that also for Rom. 12:1 several English translators have accepted the rendering "spiritual worship."[333]

But even though "spiritual" may well be the best rendering of the adjective Paul uses, the meaning of 12:1, *considered as a unit*, is certainly this, that it is right and proper—hence logical, reasonable—that those who have been highly favored should offer themselves to God wholeheartedly, as sacrifices, living, holy, and well-pleasing to him. In fact, the emphasis in 12:1 is on the word "Therefore."

331. τὴν λογικὴν λατρείαν ὑμῶν is probably in apposition to παραστῆσαι . . . τῷ θεῷ.

332. A.V., Williams, Conybeare, Broadus, N.T. in Modern English. Similarly N.T. in Basic English points out that this is the worship "which it ℟ right for you to give," and in a footnote N.E.B. offers a similar suggestion. At times—by no means always—Greek philosophers used the word in this sense. See Liddell and Scott's *Greek-English Lexicon*, Vol. I, p. 1056.

333. See, for example, A.R.V., R.S.V., N.I.V. See also G. Kittel, Th.D.N.T., Vol. IV, p. 142. The Amplified New Testament combines the two ideas: "reasonable and spiritual worship." The Berkeley Version, however, favors "worship with understanding," and Cranfield, similarly, "understanding worship."

What the apostle is saying is that in view of God's *mercy*,[334] a voluntary and enthusiastic response of gratitude is required. Accordingly, when in this connection he mentions "God's great mercy," he must be referring to the marvelous goodness of God described in the first eleven chapters of this letter: his *kindness* (2:4), *patience* (9:22; 11:22), *love* (5:5; 8:35, 39), and *grace* (1:7; 3:24; 4:16; 5:2, 15, 20, 21; 6:1, 14, 15, 17; 11:5, 6). Particularly, he must be reflecting on his great theme, namely, Justification by Faith, a justification based solely on the substitutionary self-sacrifice of Christ (3:24, 25). What he is saying, then, is that this sovereign divine mercy calls for *a life* of complete dedication and wholehearted commitment. *Animal* sacrifices will not do! Nothing less than thorough self-surrender out of gratitude is required.

What the apostle is teaching, therefore, is that Christian ethics is based on Christian doctrine. Accordingly, I Cor. 15:1-57 is followed by 15:58 f.; II Cor. 1:3, 4a, by 1:4b f.; 5:1-8 by 5:9 f.; Eph. 2 and 3 by Eph. 4; 4:32b by 5:1; Phil. 3:20, 21 by 4:1; Col. 2 by chapter 3; *and Rom. 1-11 by 12-16.*

Returning once more to the opening chapters of Paul's epistle to the Romans and from there quickly reviewing the remainder of this precious writing, one cannot help becoming aware of the fact that in 1:1—3:20 man's *sin and misery* are described; in 3:21—11:36 the way of *deliverance* is opened to him; and in 12:1—16:27 the rescued believer is shown how, by a life of *gratitude* to God and helpfulness toward God's children and, in fact, toward everybody, man should respond.

This reminds us of several passages in the Psalter, especially of Ps. 50:15, "Call upon me in the day of trouble, and I will deliver you, and you will glorify me"; and of Ps. 116:

MISERY
The cords of death had compassed me,
and the anguish of Sheol had overtaken me;
I was overcome by distress and sorrow.

DELIVERANCE
Then I called on the name of the Lord: O Lord, save me!
When I was in great misery he saved me.

GRATITUDE
I will lift up the cup of salvation and call on the name of the Lord.
I will fulfil my vows to the Lord in the presence of all his people.

This shows too how very appropriate is Q. and A. 2 of the Heidelberg Catechism:

Q. How many things are necessary for you to know, that you in this comfort may live and die happily?

---

334. The apostle uses the pl.: διὰ τῶν οἰκτιρμῶν, based upon the Hebrew pl. רַחֲמִים. See II Sam. 24:14; I Chron. 21:13; Ps. 25:6; 40:11 (Hebrew 40:12); cf. Phil. 2:1. This is an intensive pl., correctly rendered by the English sing. However, the intensive character of such a noun can be retained in the translation by prefixing an adjective; in the present case such as *tender, great, manifold.*

403

A. Three; the first, how great my sins and miseries are; the second, how I am delivered from all my sins and misery; the third, how I am to be thankful to God for such deliverance.

The division into these three parts is, however, not rigid or mechanical. Even in Ps. 116:1, 2 deliverance is clearly indicated, as is true also in Rom. 1:16, 17; and as to the Heidelberg Catechism, even its famous very first Q. and A. already implies all the "three things" that are necessary.

2. And stop allowing yourselves to be fashioned after the pattern of this (evil) age, but continue to let yourselves be transformed by the renewing of y o u r mind, so that y o u may prove what is the will of God, namely, that which is good and well-pleasing and perfect.

It is one thing to point out a goal to a person and to encourage him to try to reach it. Paul has done this in verse 1. It is a different matter to show him what he should do to reach that goal. The apostle does not fail us at this point. Here in verse 2 he shows the hearers and readers what *should be shunned* and what *should be done* in order to reach the goal.

First, what should be *shunned*!

The members of the Roman church were "saints," to be sure. But they had not as yet reached the pinnacle of sinlessness. They were saints but also still sinners, for on this side of heaven no mere human being ever attains to the condition of moral-spiritual perfection.

There is one more fact that should be added: the members of that church were imitators. Aren't we all to a certain extent? Or does this rule apply only to *children*? In a sense does it not apply to everybody? It holds especially in the realm of sin and evil. Did not even Juvenal say, "We are all easily taught to imitate what is base and depraved"?[335] "Bad company corrupts good character" (I Cor. 15:33), and in this present world it is well-nigh impossible completely to avoid "bad company" or even to steer clear of the bad habits which are still clinging to what, on the whole, can be called "good company." Therefore, unless we are on our guard, we are in great danger of falling prey to "the pattern of this evil age."

When Paul says, "And stop allowing yourselves to be fashioned after the pattern of *this (evil) age*"[336] (I Cor. 2:6, 8; Gal. 1:4), he is warning the membership then and now against yielding to the various manifestations of worldliness by which they are being constantly surrounded; such as the use of dirty or offensive language, the singing of scurrilous songs, the reading of filthy books, the wearing of tempting attire, engaging in questionable pastimes, associating, on intimate terms, with worldly companions, etc. There is hardly any end to the list.

Take the matter of amusements. It is possible to be guilty in this respect even though there is nothing wrong with the recreation of one's choice; for

---

335. *Satires* XIV.40.
336. τῷ αἰῶνι τούτῳ, associative instrumental case of ὁ αἰών οὗτος. See p. 265, footnote 226.

example, if a person sets his heart on it, becomes absorbed in it, depriving him of time and energy for involvement in necessary and noble causes (family, Christian education, church, charity, missions, etc.).

The main reason Paul warns against allowing oneself to be fashioned after the pattern of this (evil) age is that man's chief aim should never be to live only for himself. He should do everything to the glory of God (I Cor. 10:31). A second reason is this: constant yielding to the temptation of becoming fashioned after the pattern of "this (evil) age" (I Cor. 2:6, 8; Gal. 1:4) ends in bitter disappointment; for, "The fashion[337] of this world is passing away" (I Cor. 7:31).

The experience of those who permit their lives to be frittered away in this manner resembles that of travelers in the desert. They are completely exhausted. Their lips are parched with thirst. Suddenly they see in the distance a sparkling spring surrounded by shady trees. With hope revived they hasten to this place . . . only to discover that they had been deceived by a mirage. "The world and its desires are passing away, but the person who does the will of God lives forever" (I John 2:17).

Secondly, what should be *done!*

"Let yourselves be transformed by the renewing of y o u r mind." Note the contrast: *not fashioned . . . but transformed.*[338]

---

337. Note similarity between συσχηματίζεσθε (Rom. 12:2) and τὸ σχῆμα (I Cor. 7:31).

338. Although this significant difference or contrast is admitted by most commentators, the admission is not unanimous. The reason for maintaining that in Rom. 12:2 a contrast is indeed pictured between (a) "Stop allowing yourselves to be *fashioned* (or conformed)" . . . and (b) "But continue to let yourselves be *transformed,*" may be formulated as follows:

When elsewhere in the New Testament the verbs συσχηματίζω (in Phil. 3:21, μετασχηματίζω) and μεταμορφόω, or their respective cognates σχῆμα and μορφή (in Phil. 3:21, σύμμορφος), occur side by side, there is a significant distinction in meaning between the two.

Thus, in the Kenosis passage (Phil. 2:5-8) there is a distinction in meaning between μορφή and σχῆμα. See N.T.C. on Philippians, pp. 103-105.

So also in Phil. 3:21 Paul uses both a σχῆμα and a μορφή compound. We are told that, in connection with his glorious Return, Christ will refashion our lowly body so that it will have a form like his own glorious body. The new outward *fashion* or appearance will truly reflect the new and lasting inward *form.* The distinction in meaning is again clear.

Similarly we have every right to believe that when the two verbs συσχηματίζω and μεταμορφόω are used side by side here in Rom. 12:2 a significant difference in meaning is implied. In the present case, because of the context, that difference even amounts to a contrast. Note the strongly adversative particle ἀλλά.

There are those who deny this significant difference in meaning. In support of their view they point to the fact that the verb μεταμορφόω is used in the account of Christ's transfiguration (Matt. 17:2; Mark 9:2) even though there was no transformation of Christ's inner being.

In answering this argument I wish to point out two things: (a) the possibility must be allowed that the change in Christ's outward appearance was brought about by the glory from *within* irradiating his whole being; and (b) the transfiguration account in no way contradicts the *rule* mentioned above, for only *one* of the two verbs is used in that account.

The difference in meaning, here in Rom. 12:2, between the two verbs should accordingly be recognized. See also R. C. Trench, *Synonyms of the New Testament,* par. lxx.

This is my answer to the reasoning of Cranfield, *op. cit.,* second volume, pp. 605-607. He rejects the view which I share with most commentators. For the sake of fairness I urge the reader to read and study the indicated pages in Cranfield's excellent commentary.

Paul does not say, "Substitute one outward fashion for another." That would be no solution, for the trouble with those who allow themselves to be fashioned after the pattern of this present (evil) age is deep-seated. What is needed is *transformation*, inner change, the renewing of the mind, that is, not only of the organ of thinking and reasoning but of the inner disposition; better still, of the heart, the inner being. Cf. 1:28; 7:22-25.

It is important to pay close attention to the exact manner in which the apostle expresses himself in this exhortation. Note the following details.

a. He uses *the present tense*: "Continue to let yourselves be transformed." Accordingly, this transformation must not be a matter of impulse: on again, off again. It must be continuous.

b. The verb used is in *the passive voice*. Paul does not say, "Transform yourselves," but "Let yourselves be transformed." Transformation is basically the work of the Holy Spirit. It amounts to progressive sanctification. "And we all, with unveiled faces, reflecting the glory of the Lord, are being changed into his likeness from one degree of glory to another, which comes from the Lord, who is the Spirit" (II Cor. 3:18).

c. Nevertheless, the verb is in *the imperative mood*. Believers are not completely passive. Their responsibility is not canceled. They must allow the Spirit to do his work within their hearts and lives. Their duty is to co-operate to the full. See Phil. 2:12, 13; II Thess. 2:13.

Finally, the apostle describes the glorious result of this continuous transformation: "so that y o u may prove what is the will of God . . ." This is a very significant statement. It shows that in order to discern the will of God for their lives believers cannot just depend on their conscience. Conscience is indeed very important, but it must constantly be sent back to the school of Scripture to receive instruction from the Holy Spirit. It is in this manner that believers become and remain aware of God's will. Which will? Decretive or Preceptive? The latter, of course. See Deut. 29:29. In this way the will of God will become an increasingly well-established or proven component of the consciousness and lives of God's children. The more they live in accordance with that will and approve of it, the more also, through this experience, will they learn to know that will, and rejoice in that knowledge. They will exclaim, "Thy will is our delight."

And what is the contents of that preceptive will? In other words, what is it that God wants us to be and to do? The answer is: "that which is good and well-pleasing and perfect."[339]

Paul probably knew that adding these words was very necessary. He is as it were telling the Romans that what avails before God is not how *important* they are or deem themselves to be (cf. the immediate context, verse 3; see also 11:17-21), or how *charismatic* (verses 4-8), or how *strong* (cf. 15:1); but

---

339. The rendering "his good and well-pleasing and perfect will" is incorrect. The words τὸ ἀγαθὸν καὶ εὐάρεστον καὶ τέλειον indicate that what God wants his children to be and to do is to be and do what, *in his sight*, is good, well-pleasing, perfect.

rather how grateful, loving, outgoing they are. What matters is how obedient they are to the commandment, addressed to each one individually, "You shall love the Lord your God with all your heart and with all your soul and with all your mind. This is the great commandment. And a second like it is this: You shall love your neighbor as yourself." See Deut. 6:5; Lev. 19:18; Matt. 22:37, 39; Mark 12:30, 31; Luke 10:27; Rom. 13:8-10. In God's sight such a life is good and well-pleasing. The aim of such a life is nothing short of perfection. See Matt. 5:48 and add Phil. 3:7-11.

---

3 For, through the grace given me, I bid every one among y o u not to think of himself more highly than he ought to think, but so to think (of himself) as to think soberly, each person according to the measure of faith God has apportioned to him. 4 For, just as we have many members in one body, and these members do not all have the same function, 5 so we, who are many, are one body in Christ, and severally members of one another. 6 Moreover, having different gifts, according to the grace given us, if (a person's gift is) prophesying, (then let him exercise it) in accordance with the standard of faith; 7 or if (it is rendering) practical service, then let him use it in (rendering) such practical service; or if one is a teacher, (let him exercise his gift) in teaching; 8 or, if one is an exhorter (let him use his gift) in exhorting. Let him who contributes to the needs of others (do so) without ulterior motive. Let him who exercises leadership (do so) with diligence. Let him who shows mercy (do so) with cheerfulness.

B. *What Should Be the Attitude of the Justified Believer*
Toward Fellow-Christians
"We, who are many, are one body in Christ"
12:3-8

In immediate thought-connection with verse 2 Paul continues:

3. For, through the grace given me, I bid every one among y o u not to think of himself more highly than he ought to think, but so to think (of himself) as to think soberly, each person according to the measure of faith God has apportioned to him.

Because of certain conditions existing in the Roman church, as we have seen, and perhaps also because of recent experiences in connection with the church at Corinth (I Cor. 12:14-31), Paul warns against the sin of exaggerated self-esteem. He issues a specific command ("I bid"; cf. Matt. 5:22, 28, 32, 34, 39, 44), appeals to his authority as an apostle ("according to the grace given me"; see on 1:5, pp. 44, 45), and addresses himself to everyone without exception ("everyone among y o u"). By means of a play on words, difficult to reproduce in English—something like "not to overestimate (himself) beyond a true estimate"—he urges everyone to be sober-minded, level-headed, sensible. To each member of the Roman church he says, as it were, "Don't fancy yourself to be Mr. BIG! The other person also has gifts. Each individual should evaluate himself not by measuring himself with his own yardstick but by the measure of faith God has apportioned to him."

The term *faith* is here used in the more usual sense of the trust in God by means of which an individual lays hold on God's promises. In the present context, however, the apostle is not thinking in quantitative terms (a large or a small amount of faith). He is thinking rather of the various ways in which each distinct individual is able to be a blessing to others and to the church in general by using the particular gift with which, *in association with faith*, God has endowed him or her. He is admonishing each of those addressed to recognize the diversity of gifts amid the unity of faith, and to ask himself, "How can I make the best use of my gift so as to benefit each and all?"

4, 5. For, just as we have many members in one body, and these members do not all have the same function, so we, who are many, are one body in Christ, and severally members of one another.

The comparison of the church and its members to the human body and its parts is a familiar one in the letters of Paul. *A little earlier* Paul had made use of this illustration in writing to the Corinthians. He had referred to this symbol in order to counteract sinful divisions (I Cor. 3:3, 4). He had written, "We who are many are one body" (I Cor. 10:17); and "Now y o u are the body of Christ, and each one of y o u is part of it" (12:27). *Later*—that is, after writing Romans—the apostle, in composing Colossians, with its theme, *Christ, the Pre-eminent One, the Only and All-Sufficient Savior*, was going to call the church "Christ's body" (1:24). He was going to describe Christ as "the Head, from whom the entire body, supported and held together by joints and ligaments, grows with a growth (that is) from God" (2:19). He was going to include the solemn and beautiful admonition, "And let the peace of Christ, for which y o u were called in one body, rule in y o u r hearts" (3:15). In his epistle to the Ephesians, also written during that first Roman imprisonment, with its theme, *The Unity of All Believers in Christ*, the description of the church as being one body in Christ, a body of which all believers are members, would occur again and again (1:23; 4:4, 12, 15, 16, 25).

Here, in Romans 12:4, 5, Paul emphasizes (a) *the organic unity of the body* ("many members in one body"), (b) *the purposeful diversity of the members and of their functions* ("and these members do not all have the same function"), and (c) *the mutual needs and benefits of these several members who are united in Christ* (". . . so we, who are many, are one body in Christ, and severally members of one another").

6-8. Moreover, having different gifts, according to the grace given us, if (a person's gift is) prophesying, (then let him exercise it) in accordance with the standard of faith; or if (it is rendering) practical service, then let him use it in (rendering) such practical service; or if one is a teacher, (let him exercise his gift) in teaching; or, if one is an exhorter (let him use his gift) in exhorting. Let him who contributes to the needs of others (do so) without ulterior motive. Let him who exercises leadership (do so) with diligence. Let him who shows mercy (do so) with cheerfulness.

Notes on This Summary of Gifts and Functions

1. It is marked by abbreviated style. The words implied but not expressed are numerous. See N.T.C. on John, Vol. I, p. 206, on Abbreviated Expression.

2. Paul is describing seven "gifts," distributed among individuals or groups of individuals who, making use of these gifts, exercise the corresponding functions.
3. The seven functions are:
   a. prophesying
   b. rendering practical service
   c. teaching
   d. exhorting
   e. contributing to the needs of people
   f. exercising leadership
   g. showing mercy.
4. Among commentators there is considerable difference of opinion with respect to the meaning of some of these functions.
5. Somewhat similar lists are found in I Cor. 12:8-10, where nine functions are mentioned; in I Cor. 12:28, 29 which mentions eight; and in Eph. 4:11 which lists four (as some see it five, but see N.T.C. on Ephesians, p. 197).
6. It is clear that Paul believes that not only ministers, elders, and deacons have gifts, but every believer has one or more divinely bestowed gifts or endowments. The apostle shows how these *charismata* should be used to benefit the church and, in fact, men in general.

Note "according to the grace given us." No one has the right to boast about his gift. Each member should bear in mind that his ability to serve others is a product of God's grace, his love for the undeserving.

a. *Prophesying*

So very important did Paul consider the gift and function of prophesying that both in I Cor. 12:28 and in Eph. 4:11 he mentions it immediately after that of the apostolate.

The question has been asked, "How is it that here in Romans 12, where Paul is describing how persons endowed with various gifts should conduct themselves in the performance of their respective duties, there is no mention at all of the function of *an apostle*?" Some answer: "This proves that no apostle had anything whatsoever to do with the founding of that church or with its early history." But such an argument is surely basing too much on too little. See also above, p. 19. Even the statement, "Paul is silent on the matter of telling another apostle how to conduct himself because it would have been very improper for one apostle to lay down the law for another apostle," is not absolutely true, as Gal. 2:11 f. proves, though in normal circumstances it is probably correct. What is true is that Paul had already alluded to his own apostolic office (in 12:3), and also that at this particular time there was no apostle in Rome. If there had been one, would his name not have been included in the list of greetings found in chapter 16?

Returning to the subject of the importance Paul attaches to the gift of prophecy, it is to be noted that in I Cor. 14:1 those addressed are told, ". . . eagerly desire spiritual gifts, especially the gift of prophecy." In verse 39 of that same chapter the writer adds, "Therefore, my brothers, be eager to prophesy."

One important reason for attaching such a high value to prophesying must have been that the message of the true prophet was the product not of his own intuition or even of his own study and research but of special revelation. The prophet received his message directly from the Holy Spirit (Acts 11:27, 28; note, "and through the Spirit predicted"). So also in Acts 21:11 Agabus, one of these prophets—there were others, both men and women (Acts 13:1; 21:9)—is quoted as follows, "*The Holy Spirit* says, In this way the Jews of Jerusalem will bind the owner of this belt . . ." (21:11).

Another reason why on Paul's list of spiritual gifts prophesying ranked so high was its comprehensive content. It was by no means restricted to the utterance of a prediction now and then. It included edification, exhortation, consolation, and instruction (I Cor. 14:3, 31).

However, not everyone who presented himself as a prophet was necessarily a genuine prophet. Not everything a "prophet" said was necessarily true. So in addition to supplying the church with prophets, God also saw to it that there were people who were able to distinguish between the true prophet and the false (I Cor. 12:10; 14:29) and between truth and falsehood. In line with this, here in Rom. 12:6 Paul writes, "If (a person's gift is) prophesying, (then let him exercise it) *in accordance with the standard of faith.*" Here some interpreters interpret the word "faith" in the objective sense, as if the apostle was referring to God's revealed truth, the gospel. Others, however, accept the subjective sense, and view the word "faith" as indicating *trust* in God and in his promises.

Since just a moment ago (in verse 3) Paul has used this word in the latter sense, which, in the present connection, yields an excellent meaning, we need look no farther. The prophet must say nothing that is in conflict with his faith in Christ. For example, he might be tempted, for selfish reasons, to make startling statements which he himself did not believe. He is warned not to do so. He must be and remain God's mouth to the people.

b. *Rendering Practical Service*

The apostle uses the word *diakonia*, that is, practical service, ministry. Cf. I Cor. 12:5; Eph. 4:12. This service or ministry can be of various kinds. In the story concerning Martha and Mary (Luke 10:40) it amounted to whatever work was necessary in preparing a meal. "The diakonia" of *the word* is mentioned in Acts 6:4; that of *reconciliation* in II Cor. 5:18. Since in the present connection Paul is enumerating various functions pertaining to church life, it is natural here to connect the term with that particular type of work which we too ascribe to the *diaconate*, that is, to the office performed by the deacons. Accordingly, Paul is encouraging those who are qualified for this type of work to accept the opportunity to do so.

It may well be rather difficult for us to estimate the importance the apostle attached to the work of the deacon, the Church's ministry of mercy. We should bear in mind, however, that in the days of the apostle many believers were anything but wealthy. Some were slaves or freedmen. In fact, in this very epistle to the Romans (15:25) the apostle states the reason why he cannot travel straight to Rome but must first visit the saints in Jerusalem. Elsewhere he says, "I came to Jerusalem to bring my people gifts for the poor" (Acts 24:17). See also I Cor. 1:26 f., 16:1 f., II Cor. 8:1 f. It is worthy of special attention that the very man who insisted on purity in doctrine was at least equally interested in the cause of showing generosity in aiding the poor. In II Cor. 8:7, 8 he most strikingly connects the "grace" of giving to supply the needs of the poor with a central doctrine of the Christian religion, namely, that of Christ's voluntary humiliation in the interest of sinners. He says:

"But just as y o u excel in everything . . . see that y o u also excel in this grace (of giving) . . . For y o u know the grace of our Lord Jesus Christ, that though he was rich, yet for y o u r sake he became poor, that y o u through his poverty might become rich."

So also today the diaconate is no less important than the eldership. The cause of Christ is served equally by each. In each the love of Christ is reflected.

c. *Teaching*

The prophet received his message by direct revelation. The teacher derived his knowledge from the study of the Old Testament and of the teaching of Jesus, in whatever form this was accessible to him. Since *direct* revelations do not always occur, and besides, since the deposit of divine revelation found in Scripture—which, in Paul's day meant in the Old Testament—is of abiding and very important significance, it is clear that also for the teacher there is a very definite and important place in the life of the church. So, "if one is a teacher (let him exercise his gift) in teaching."

d. *Exhorting*

Acts 13:15 shows that in the synagogue, after a portion of the law and of the Prophets had been read, the rulers of the synagogue invited Paul and Barnabas to speak a word of exhortation. Such was the custom in those days. Here, in Rom. 12, those who have been blessed with the talent of exhorting are urged to make use of it for the benefit of all. Today *the minister* of the gospel is—at least should be—adequately equipped to take care of both teaching and exhorting. He not only teaches doctrine but also shows how doctrine should be applied to life so that all may be edified and encouraged. Among the laity, too, there may be excellent teachers and/or exhorters.

e. *Contributing to the Needs of People*

Paul writes, "Let him who contributes to the needs of others (do so) without ulterior motive."

The reasons why Paul devoted so much attention to pointing out the importance of the ministry of mercy (namely, great need and example of

Christ) have been given. See above, under b. So here, at first glance, we seem to detect a repetition of point b. Nevertheless, there is a difference. The *diaconate* has to do with the cause of *church benevolence*. By means of the deacons the entire church, functioning as a unit, engages in this important work. More, however, is needed. In addition to *collective* there must also be *private benevolence*. Let those who are able to function in this capacity by all means do so! Since the Lord has blessed them so abundantly let them, in turn, be a blessing to others.

But in so doing they must be sure to contribute "without ulterior motive."[340] Here the giving with ulterior motive, denounced by Malachi (1:13, 14), immediately occurs to the mind, and so does that of Ananias and Sapphira (Acts 5:1 f.). True givers are those who give wholeheartedly, all the while remembering what they themselves have received from their Lord and Savior Jesus Christ.

f. *Exercising Leadership*

There are those who believe that by placing f. between e. and g., both of which are, in a sense, concerned with benevolence, Paul, in f., must be referring to people who are in charge of church benevolence. However, e. does not seem to have anything to do with the diaconate, and g. does not necessarily refer to what is commonly meant by benevolence.

Besides, in other passages where the same word for leadership occurs as the one used here in Rom. 12:8 the reference is to overseers, elders (I Thess. 5:12; I Tim. 3:4; 5:17).[341] And even when one makes due allowance for the fact that it is not the apostle's intention to list every spiritual gift and function of church members, would it not seem strange if he were to include in his summary the ministry of the deacons, as he does (see point b.), but completely to omit from it that of the presbyters? With respect to their age and dignity these men were called presbyters or elders; with respect to the nature of their task they were called overseers or superintendents. Because a heavy burden rested on the shoulders of these men, and the temptation to shirk their responsibility was great, they are admonished to exercise their leadership "with diligence."

g. *Showing Mercy*

The sick, dying, and bereaved are in need of visits by someone who knows how to impart genuine Christian sympathy and understanding, someone who shows mercy *with cheerfulness*. "For as nothing gives more solace to the sick

---

340. Greek: ἐν ἁπλότητι. Basically the meaning of ἁπλοῦς, -ῆ, -οῦν is uncomplicated, uncompounded, simple; and, accordingly, ἐν ἁπλότητι would mean "in simplicity," and therefore: with a single goal in mind. This, by a very easy transition, becomes "without ulterior motive," though "without reserve," hence "generously" also deserves consideration. Cf. II Cor. 8:2; 9:11, 13. See also Eph. 6:5; Col. 3:22: with undivided mind, with singleness of heart.
341. Note prominence of the word προΐστημι, in participial form, in all these cases. Also, in I Tim. 3:1 the synonym "overseer" is used, and in 5:17 the synonym "presbyters" (elders).

or to anyone otherwise distressed, than to see those cheerful and prompt in assisting them, so to observe sadness in the countenance of those by whom assistance is given makes them feel themselves despised" (John Calvin on this passage). I would only add to this that a brief, cheering visit by a wise and sympathetic fellow-member, who is willing to help in every possible way, is certainly of far more benefit than the almost endless recital of all the horrendous details of the operation recently performed on the caller, namely, Mr. Sad. Truly, "A cheerful heart is good medicine, but a crushed spirit dries up the bones" (Prov. 17:22). This holds both for the patient and the visitor.

9 Love must be genuine. Abhor what is evil; cling to what is good. 10 Be devoted to one another in brotherly love. Prefer one another in honor. 11 Never come on behind in showing enthusiasm. Be aglow with the Spirit, serving the Lord. 12 Be joyful in hope, enduring in affliction, persistent in prayer. 13 Help to relieve the needs of the saints. Eagerly practice hospitality.

B. *What Should Be the Attitude of the Justified Believer Toward Fellow-Christians*
(continued)
"Be devoted to one another in brotherly love"
12:9-13

The connection between verses 8 and 9 is close: cheerfully showing mercy presupposes a love that is sincere. So Paul says:

9. Love must be genuine. Abhor what is evil; cling to what is good.

It is reasonable to believe that the "love" of which Paul speaks here is more wide-embracing than the "brotherly love" mentioned in verse 10. The apostle mentions the more inclusive concept first, then the more restricted one. What he emphasizes first of all is that love, taken in any sense—whether its object is God or fellow-believers or neighbors or even "enemies"—must be "unhypocritical," that is, unfeigned, sincere, genuine. It must not be faked, must not consist in empty words. Remember the saying, "Your deeds speak so loudly that I cannot hear your words."

In line with this is the exhortation, "Abhor what is evil." This does not refer only to insincerity in love, a mere show, which must be avoided. On the contrary, what Paul is saying amounts to this: "Avoid *whatever* is evil; cling to *whatever* is good." It should be clear that Paul's emphasis is on *agapē*, that is, love.[342]

342. According to Ridderbos, *op. cit.*, p. 281, the word ἀγάπη, when used by Paul, nearly always refers to the love of believers for one another.
    As the Concordance shows, the apostle employs that term about 80 times. It is indeed true that in *very many* of these cases it refers to the believers' mutual love. However, when, in order to reach the number of times this agapē indicates the believers' love for each other, one subtracts the references to (a) agapē for the neighbor, (b) agapē with reference to God, and (c) agapē in general, without mention of subject or object, the resulting figure, though still *high*, is not so high that "nearly always mutual love among believers" is a justifiable characterization. In its 9 occurrences in Romans only 2 refer to the love of the saints for each other

10. Be devoted[343] to one another in brotherly love.
Whenever Paul thinks of believers he conceives of them as constituting (in the Lord) one family (Eph. 3:15). All have one Father (cf. Rom. 8:15; Gal. 4:5). This thought is entirely in line with the teaching of Jesus (Matt. 12:46-50 and parallels).

According to this teaching the bond that unites the members of this spiritual family are far more secure and lasting than those which bind together the members of a purely physical family (Luke 14:26). What the apostle is saying, therefore, is that the members of this spiritual family should do all in their power to be and remain devoted to each other in tender affection.

There is a sense in which believers should love everybody, including even those who hate and persecute them (see verse 14; add Luke 6:35). But tender, brotherly affection, implying intimacy, understanding, spiritual unity, is reserved for the inner circle. Believers have the right and the duty to discriminate between those who hate God and those who love him. As the apostle says elsewhere, "Let us do good to everybody, especially to those who are of the household of faith" (Gal. 6:10).

Paul adds: **Prefer one another in honor.**
What does this mean and how is this possible? Of the many interpretations offered note the following three:

a. The other person is the one in whom Christ is mysteriously present for me. Therefore I should honor him above myself.[344]

Evaluation. Must I assume, then, that Christ is not present in every believer, including even myself?

b. Do not wait for others to praise you but be the first to bestow praise whenever this can be done in harmony with the truth.

Evaluation. Though this is excellent advice, is it really what the passage means? Probably not. It seems to require that I regard my fellow-believer to be worthy of greater honor than I am, and that I, therefore, esteem him higher than myself.

(12:9; 14:15); 2 to love in inter-human relations (both in 13:10); the other 5 pertain to love proceeding from God (5:5; 5:8), from Christ (8:35), from God and described as "the love of God which is in Christ Jesus our Lord" (8:39), and from the Spirit (15:30). In II Thess. agapē refers to mutual love among believers only once (1:3). In the other 2 instances of its use one refers to love of the truth (2:10), the other to love of—i.e., proceeding from—God (3:5). Elsewhere in Paul's epistles, however, the love of the saints for each other is mentioned frequently: Gal. 5:13; Eph. 1:15; 4:2, 15, 16; etc.

The conclusion we arrive at is that in the New Testament the situation with respect to φιλία and ἀγάπη is somewhat similar to that between φιλέω and ἀγαπάω. Only once does φιλία occur in the New Testament (in the sense of friendship, James 4:4). There is, however, also φιλαδελφία (Rom. 12:10; I Thess. 4:9; Heb. 13:1; I Peter 1:22; and II Peter 1:7 twice). As to the cognate *verbs* see N.T.C. on John, Vol. II, pp. 494-501, footnote 306.

343. φιλόστοργοι = nom. pl. masc. of φιλόστοργος, devoted, tenderly affectionate. In the New Testament the word occurs only here.

344. Thus Cranfield, *op. cit.*, Vol. II, p. 633.

c. The exhortation does not demand of me that I deem every fellow-member to be in every respect wiser and abler than I am myself. But it asks that in humble-mindedness I count my fellow-member to be better than I am myself. See Phil. 2:3.

A Christian knows that his own motives are not always pure and holy (I Cor. 11:28, 31). This is a kind of knowledge which at times causes him to utter the prayer, "O Lord, forgive my good deeds." On the other hand, the Christian has no right to regard as evil the motives of his brothers and sisters in the Lord. Unless a consistently evil pattern is clearly evident in the lives of fellow-members, their outwardly good deeds must be ascribed to good, never to evil, motives. It follows that the child of God who has learned to know himself sufficiently so that at times he feels inclined to utter the cry of the publican (Luke 18:13) or of Paul (Rom. 7:24) will indeed regard others to be better than himself.

11. Never come on behind in showing enthusiasm. Be aglow with the Spirit, serving the Lord.

However, sinful human nature being what it is—and even saints are still sinners—it is not reasonable to expect that those whom Paul is addressing will, with enthusiasm, go about the business of preferring one another in honor. On the other hand, religion without enthusiasm hardly deserves the name *religion*.

Of course, the source of enthusiasm is not in man. If a person is going to be "set on fire," it is the Holy Spirit who must do this. So Paul says, "Never come on behind in showing enthusiasm." And he immediately adds, "Be aglow *with the Spirit*." Not only should the saints take care that they do not quench the Spirit, that they do not resist the Spirit, and even that they do not grieve the Spirit; they should earnestly ask the Holy Spirit to fill them with zeal, the enthusiasm needed for properly carrying out their Christian duties and attaining their goal. Only then will the command, "Be aglow with the Spirit" be fulfilled when, from the heart, they are able to sing:

> Teach me to love thee as thine angels love,
> One holy passion filling all my frame—
> The baptism of the heaven-descended Dove;
> My heart an altar, and thy love the flame.
> —Lines from "Spirit of God, Dwell Thou
> Within My Heart" by George Croly, 1854.

Then they will not be passive, but with joy and enthusiasm will address themselves to the task of actually and wholeheartedly *serving the Lord*. Observe that when the believer is really aglow with the Spirit, he does not show this by resorting to manifestations of religious (?) excitement, but by humbly carrying out his mandate of serving the Lord.

12. Be joyful in hope, enduring in affliction, persistent in prayer.

The hope of future salvation (cf. 5:2, 4, 5; 8:24, 25; 15:4, 13) stimulates present joy; in fact, to such an extent that God's children are even able patiently *to endure*[345] in the midst of affliction. This endurance indicates *strength to bear up under stress, plus the persistent application of this strength.* It is not the product of human wisdom or skill but of God's grace. Therefore Paul immediately adds "(Be) persistent in prayer."

Without constant prayer such joy and endurance would be impossible. The opposition coming from the side of the world and the doubts from within would prove too strong. In fact, without steadfastness in prayer obedience to none of the exhortations of chapter 12 or of other passages can be expected.

Paul continues:

13. Help to relieve the needs of the saints. Eagerly practice hospitality.

The urgent need for "relief" has already been explained. See verses 6-8, under the heading *Practical Service*, pp. 410, 411. Here, in verse 13, the apostle rivets our attention especially upon those saints who are in need of *lodging*. Finding a good and safe place to stay for the night, or perhaps even for several days, was by no means easy at that time. Besides, the apostle, himself a great traveler, understood this need. He wants those whom he addressed to become thoroughly involved in the business of supplying good lodging places. He wants them to practice hospitality gladly, not grudgingly, as seems to have happened at times (I Peter 4:9). Not only must the *overseer* be a hospitable person (I Tim. 3:2; Titus 1:8), but *every believer* should be. What should at all times be clearly taken to heart is that whatever is done for the person in need of hospitality is done for him who on the great Judgment Day is going to say, "I was a stranger, and y o u welcomed *me*" (Matt. 25:35). What the apostle is urging, therefore, is that believers will not only show hospitality when they are asked to do so, but will go out of their way to offer it. They should practice this grace . . . eagerly! See also Gen. 18:1-8; Heb. 6:10; 13:2.

---

14 Bless those who persecute y o u. Bless and do not curse.　15 Rejoice with those who rejoice; weep with those who weep.　16 Live in harmony with one another. Do not be snobbish, but readily associate with humble folk. Do not be conceited.　17 Do not return evil for evil to anyone. Always see to it that (y o u r affairs are) right in the sight of everybody.　18 If it is possible, as far as it depends on y o u, live at peace with everyone.　19 Do not take revenge, beloved, but leave room for the wrath (of God); for it is written, "Vengeance belongs to me; I will repay," says the Lord.　20 On the contrary:

"If your enemy is hungry, feed him;

if he is thirsty, give him something to drink;

for, by doing this, you will heap coals of fire on his head."

21 Do not be overcome by evil, but overcome evil by good.

C. *What Should Be the Attitude of the Justified Believer*
Toward Outsiders, Including Enemies
"Bless those who persecute y o u"
12:14-21

---

345. See p. 273, footnote 235.

14. Bless those who persecute y o u.

The relation between the preceding paragraph (on brotherly love) and this one (on being persecuted) is not as remote as it may seem to be. In fact, there may be a twofold connection:

a. *material.*

Offering hospitality (verse 13) amounts to being engaged in a good work. According to I Peter 3:17 f. the anti-Christian world persecutes believers even for doing good!

b. *verbal.*

In the original the same verb,[346] used in verse 13, recurs in verse 14. The contextual meaning of the two forms used—one in verse 13, one in verse 14—though closely related, is not exactly the same. In English one obtains the identical result by rendering the two exhortations as follows:

Pursue hospitality (verse 13).

Bless those who *pursue* y o u (verse 14).

In the first instance *pursue* means *practice*. In the second it means *persecute*.

What we have in verse 14 is clearly an echo of the words of Jesus, "Love y o u r enemies and pray for those that persecute y o u (Matt. 5:44; cf. Luke 6:27 f.; I Cor. 4:12)." To bless, in this connection, means "to invoke God's blessing upon." See also Luke 2:34; Heb. 11:20.

Paul even adds: **Bless and do not curse.**

In other words, not the slightest desire for the outpouring of divine vengeance on our persecutors must be intermixed with our prayer that the Lord may bless them.

That this exhortation runs contrary to our sinful human nature is pointed out strikingly by Calvin who, in his comment on it, reveals keen psychological insight:

"I have said that this is more difficult than to let go revenge when anyone is injured; for though some restrain their hands and are not led away by the passion of doing harm, they yet wish that some calamity or loss would in some way happen to their enemies; and even when they are so pacified that they wish no evil, there is yet hardly one in a hundred who wishes well to him from whom he has received an injury; nay, most men daringly burst forth into imprecations. But God by his word not only restrains our hands from doing evil, but also subdues the bitter feelings within; and not only so, but he would have us be solicitous for the wellbeing of those who unjustly trouble us and seek our destruction."

A beginning of obedience to this command is possible for those who stop allowing themselves to be fashioned after the pattern of this (evil) age and continue to let themselves be transformed by the renewing of their mind (12:2).

15. Rejoice with those who rejoice; weep with those who weep.

---

346. διώκω, in verse 13 *nom.* pl. pres. participle; in verse 14 the same except *acc.*

One way of proving to ourselves that our hearts are in the right place is to identify with other persons, so that we not only weep with those who weep but even rejoice with those who rejoice; and this not only with fellow-believers but with all those with whom we enter into a relationship of relative closeness, be they believers or unbelievers. If we truly love our neighbor as we love ourselves (Luke 10:27), this should be possible. But never will it be possible for us truly to identify with the other person, whether believer or unbeliever, unless by God's sovereign grace the truth of Christ's taking upon himself our guilt and misery is by the Holy Spirit deeply impressed upon our heart and mind. The result will certainly be the advancement of the glory of God (Matt. 5:16), the entrance into our heart of the peace of God that surpasses all understanding (Phil. 4:7), and perhaps even the winning of the neighbor for Christ (I Peter 3:1).

The opposite of *rejoicing* is being filled with *envy* (Titus 3:3); and over against *weeping* stands *gloating* (over). Note sad result (Prov. 17:5).

16. Live in harmony with one another. Do not be snobbish, but readily associate with humble folk. Do not be conceited.

Believers are exhorted to agree among themselves, doubtlessly in order to exert a wholesome influence upon those who are still outside the kingdom (see context).

Now in order to live in harmony it is necessary that every manifestation of sinful pride be banished. So Paul says, "Do not lift up y o u r eyes to what is high," that is, "Do not be haughty" (cf. 11:20), or something on that order. That this is, indeed, the general sense of the passage follows also from the added exhortation, "Do not be conceited."

The A.V., however, reads, "Mind not high things but condescend to men of low estate." Today this rendering, especially because of the pejorative meaning attached to the word "condescend" (graciously descend to the level of inferiors!), will not do. Besides, it is hard to believe that Paul would be drawing a contrast between *things* and *people*. The A.R.V. rendering, "Set not your mind on high things but condescend to things that are lowly," is also unsatisfactory, especially because elsewhere the word used in the original refers not to things but to people who, in a sense, are lowly.[347] What Paul

---

347. The following translations of ταπεινός deserve consideration:
a. humble; (person or, if pl. people) of low degree (Luke 1:52; James 1:9; 4:6; I Peter 5:5).
b. lowly (Matt. 11:29).
c. downcast (II Cor. 7:6).
d. timid; according to some: ineffectual, inferior (II Cor. 10:1).
Here (Rom. 12:16) the meaning (*if n.*) could be "small and insignificant services"; (*if masc.*) humble people, humble folk.
Since the first part of the verse means, "Do not lift up y o u r eyes to what is high"; that is (something on the order of), "Do not be proud (or haughty)," and accordingly condemns an undesirable personal quality, and since the word ταπεινός elsewhere in the New Testament always expresses a personal trait, it is natural that also here in Rom. 12:16 it be so interpreted. The best translation of the words intervening between, "Live in harmony with one another," and "Do not be conceited," is probably, "Do not be snobbish (cf. Phillips, "Don't become snobbish"), but readily associate with humble folk." Although "haughty" will do, "snobbish"

is saying is, "Do not be snobbish, but readily associate with humble folk." See also Luke 14:13.

Was he thinking, perhaps, of the beautiful words recorded in Prov. 3:6, 7? Here they are:

> In all your ways acknowledge him,
> And he will make your paths straight.
> Do not be wise in your own eyes.

In verse 14 Paul had issued the positive command, "Bless those who persecute y o u." After repeating the word "Bless" he had added the prohibition, "and do not curse." He now elaborates on this prohibition by saying:
17. Do not return evil for evil to anyone.
Two closely related wrongs are here combated:

a. *vindictiveness, the desire to get even with someone for a suffered wrong.* In this connection we are reminded of such earlier Pauline passages as:

See to it that no one renders to anyone evil for evil. I Thess. 5:15.

When we are cursed we bless; when we are persecuted we endure it; when we are slandered we answer kindly. I Cor. 4:12, 13

Why not rather be wronged? Why not rather be cheated? I Cor. 6:7

Compare the words of another apostle:

"Do not repay evil with evil or insult with insult, but blessing with blessing" (I Peter 3:9).

The condemnation of vindictiveness is basic.

b. *assuming that private individuals have the right to take upon themselves the function of the civil magistrate in punishing crime.*

Even in the Old Testament the commandment "eye for eye . . . stripe for stripe" (Exod. 21:24, 25; cf. Lev. 24:20; Deut. 19:21) refers to the *public* administration of criminal law (see Lev. 24:14), and was issued in order that the practice of seeking *personal* revenge might be discouraged.

What (here in Rom. 12:17) Paul forbids—the yearning to retaliate—was the very sin against which Jesus warned (Matt. 5:38-42; cf. Luke 6:29, 35). And this teaching of our Lord can be considered a further development of such Old Testament instruction as is found in Lev. 19:18; Deut. 32:35; Prov. 20:22. See also S.BK. I, pp. 368-370; II, p. 299.

The manifestation of a vindictive spirit destroys Christian distinctiveness, the absolute prerequisite for success in winning people for Christ. It is this lack that causes outsiders to say, "Those Christians are no different than we are." Paul, the great missionary, wants believers to conduct themselves in such a manner that unbelievers will take note. It is for this reason that he continues as follows:

---

is perhaps even more precise because it refers to the character of those who look down on people whom they consider to be inferior. In the present context ("but readily associate with humble folk") that would seem to be the meaning the apostle intends to convey.
Cf. W. Grundmann, on ταπεινός, Th.D.N.T., Vol. VIII, pp. 1-26, especially pp. 19, 20.

17. Always see to it that (y o u r affairs are) right in the sight of everybody.

This reminds us of Prov. 3:3, 4:

> Let love and faithfulness never leave you;
>   bind them around your neck,
>   write them on the tablet of your heart.
> Then you will win favor and a good name
>   in the sight of God and man.

Paul wants the addressed to live such lives of thorough consecration to God and genuine love for all, including even the persecutors, that outsiders will not be given a legitimate opportunity to complain or accuse (cf. I Tim. 5:14), and that slanderers will be put to shame (I Peter 3:16). He does not want the addressed to be a hindrance or stumblingblock, preventing the unconverted from accepting the gospel (I Cor. 10:32). Instead, he wants them so to conduct their affairs that the public conscience (cf. Rom. 2:15) will approve. His noble aim, as a lover of God, is that the devout lives of believers may be a means in God's hand for the conversion of sinners, to the glory of God (Matt. 5:16; I Peter 2:12).

Calvin has summarized the meaning of verse 17 as follows: "What is meant is that we ought diligently to labor, in order that all may be edified by our honest dealings ... that they may, in a word, perceive the good and the sweet odor of our life, by which they may be allured to the love of God."

Proceeding along the same line Paul continues as follows:

18. If it is possible, as far as it depends on y o u, live at peace with everyone.

This exhortation to live at peace with everyone is in line with such other passages as, "Let there be no quarreling between you and me, or between your herdsmen and mine, for we are brothers" (Gen. 13:8); "Make every effort to live in peace with everybody" (Heb. 12:14); and "The wisdom that is from above is first pure, then peace-loving" (James 3:17). Jesus said, "Blessed (are) the peace-makers, for they shall be called sons of God" (Matt. 5:9).

In a world of peace-breaking this beatitude shows what a thoroughly relevant, vital, and dynamic force Christianity is. True peace-makers are all those whose Leader is the God of peace (I Cor. 14:33; Eph. 6:15; I Thess. 5:23), who aspire after peace with everyone (as here in Rom. 12:18), who proclaim the gospel of peace (Eph. 6:15), and pattern their lives after the Prince of Peace (Luke 19:10; John 3:12-15; cf. Matt. 10:8).

Nevertheless, the charge to live at peace with everyone is not presented in an unqualified form. There are two qualifications:

a. "If it is possible." There are circumstances under which the establishment or maintenance of peace is impossible. Heb. 12:14 not only advocates peace but also sanctification. The latter must not be sacrificed in order to maintain the former, for a peace without sanctification (or holiness) is not worthy of the name. If the maintenance of peace means the sacrifice of truth and/or honor, then peace must be abandoned. Cf. Matt. 10:34-36; Luke 12:51-53.

    b. ". . . as far as it depends on y o u." There are situations that require the sacrifice of peace. But we must be sure that it is not we who are to blame for such exigencies. We have done everything in our power to establish and maintain peace. The other person (or persons) was (were) not willing to have peace except on conditions we, as Christians, were unable to accept. In such cases God does not hold us accountable for the lack of peace.

    19. Do not take revenge, beloved, but leave room for the wrath (of God); for it is written, "Vengeance belongs to me; I will repay," says the Lord.

    The tender appeal—note the word "beloved" here in verse 19—reminds us of the similarly affectionate appellative "brothers" in verse 1. In this connection see also 1:7; 16:5, 9, 12; I Cor. 4:14, 17; 10:14; 15:58; II Cor. 7:1; 12:19; Eph. 5:1; 6:21; Phil. 2:12; 4:1; Col. 1:7; 4:7, 9, 14; I Thess. 2:8; II Tim. 1:2; and Philem. 1 and 16.

    Striking is the repetition of basically the same exhortation, namely, in slightly varying forms, "Do not take revenge." See verses 14, 17, 19, and 21. There must have been a reason for this, although exactly what it was has not been revealed. A suggestion would be that it resulted from (a) the fact that the members of the Roman church, or at least some of them, were greatly in need of this admonition; and (b) that the composer of this letter had been blessed, especially since his conversion, with an exceptionally sensitive and loving disposition. He was a man whose entire soul entered into the business of sympathizing and forgiving, in view of the pardon he had himself received from God.

    After "Do not take revenge, beloved," Paul continues, "but leave room for the wrath . . ." The words, "of God" are not in the original. Accordingly, some commentators have suggested that what the apostle meant was, "Leave room for the adversaries' wrath." Others would fill in the lacuna with the phrase "y o u r wrath," and still others with "the civil magistrate's wrath."

    However, it is not necessary to deal separately with each of these guesses, and to show why it cannot be correct. One solid reason will do for all three, namely, in the other cases where, in the New Testament, the word "wrath" occurs without a modifier showing whose wrath is being referred to, we are dealing with *God's* wrath. Moreover, it makes no difference whether the article ("the") is used (hence "the wrath") or is omitted (hence simply "wrath").[348] So it is altogether reasonable to believe, with most commentators, that also here, in Rom. 12:19, it is the wrath *of God* to which Paul refers.

---

348. *With* the article: Rom. 3:5; 5:9; 9:22; 13:5 (yes, also Rom. 13:3, though some deny this; see on that passage); *without* the article: Rom. 2:5, 8; Eph. 2:3; I Thess. 5:9).

When Paul says that those addressed—and ultimately all of us—must "leave room" for the wrath of God, he, in harmony with the entire context, is again emphasizing that we ourselves should not "play God," should abstain from attempting to usurp the divine prerogative of pouring out wrath, of wreaking vengeance.

In substantiation of this charge the apostle, as so often previously, appeals to the Old Testament, this time to Deut. 32:35; really to that passage in light of its context; see especially verses 20, 34, 36-43.

Did not Jesus himself, though he was the object of deeper and far more agonizing suffering, *unjustly* laid upon him by sinners—from *their* side it was certainly unjust!—instead of taking vengeance, commit himself to the One who judges righteously? See I Peter 2:23. Cf. the similarly beautiful words of Ps. 37:1-17.

In view of the fact that our Lord Jesus Christ, by his vicarious suffering, removed God's wrath from us, should we not be happy to refrain from taking revenge? What, then, is our duty when we are being unjustly treated? Is it, perhaps, to ask God to pour out his wrath upon those terrible people who have been so cruel to us? Is that what Paul means when he says, "Leave room for the wrath (of God)"? Is it not rather that we ask God to grant to the persecutors the grace of true repentance and faith? Should we not leave any notion of retributive righteousness entirely to the all-wise and sovereign God? And will not every true child of God, who has experienced the love of God in his own life, respond in this manner?

Instead of wreaking vengeance it is the Christian's duty and joy to return good for evil. The day of divine retribution has not yet arrived. Moreover, as indicated previously, the injured person has no right to assume the functions of an official magistrate.

The one who has suffered wrong should treat the one who hates him (not with concealed resentment or with a feeling of wrath but) *with kindness*.

So, after saying, "Do not take revenge . . . ," Paul continues:

20. On the contrary:

"If your enemy is hungry, feed him;

if he is thirsty, give him something to drink;

for, by doing this, you will heap coals of fire on his head."

The quotation is taken from Prov. 25:21, 22. If the enemy is hungry, the injured person should give him something to eat.[349] He should give him something to drink if he is thirsty. In other words, he should treat the enemy as did Elisha (II Kings 6:20-23).

In words that have given rise to many different interpretations, the apos-

---

349. ψώμιζε, 2nd per. s. pres. imperat. of ψωμίζω, to feed, to give something to eat. A ψωμίον is a small piece of bread. See John 13:26, 27, 30.

tle, still quoting from Proverbs, continues, "for by doing this, you will heap[350]
coals of fire on his head."

Four different views. Heaping coals of fire on his head symbolizes
a. a form of self-inflicted torment,
b. a deed of benevolence (giving live coals to those in need),
c. a gesture of sorrow for sin,
d. a way of making the enemy ashamed of himself.

Explanation a. contradicts the present context, according to which one
should treat an enemy with kindness. Both a. and c. describe the enemy's
sorrow for sin rather than what the one whom he injured should do to him.
The most widely accepted interpretation is d. The coals of fire in that view
symbolize the burning pangs of shame and contrition resulting from the
unexpected kindness received. The wronged person's magnanimous behavior, returning good for evil, has this effect.

As to meaning b.—an interpretation mentioned by Ridderbos, and in an
interesting article revived (without definite endorsement) by E. J. Masselink—when the phrase "to those in need" is interpreted to mean, "*even though
they are enemies*," resulting in the sense, "Overpower the enemy with your
kindness" (E. J. Masselink), would not the effect be the same as that indicated
in d.?

In stating a preference for d., therefore, I am not rejecting b.

Reasons for accepting this view (that of d. and possibly b.):

1. The words, "overcome evil by good" (verse 21) point in this direction.
2. So does I Peter 2:15, "For it is God's will that by doing good you should
silence the ignorant talk of foolish people."

In the spirit of verse 20 Paul's concluding exhortation is:

21. Do not be overcome by evil, but overcome evil by good.

To be overcome by evil means (a) to allow the enemy to get you down, and
(b) to plan and return evil for evil.

To overcome evil by good means (a) to continue living a life of faith in, and
love for, God and for everyone, not excluding the person who has injured
you, the kind of life marked by transformation into the image of Christ
(verse 2), and therefore by humility (verses 3 and 16), helpfulness (verses
6-8), and peace (verse 16); and (b) to go out of your way, by word and deed,
to show kindness to the one who has injured you.

---

350. σωρεύσεις, 2nd per. s. fut. act. indicat. of σωρεύω, to heap, pile up. In the New Testament
this word occurs only here and in II Tim. 3:6.
For the different ways in which this saying is interpreted I have received help from the
following sources:
C. E. B. Cranfield, *op. cit.*, Vol. II, pp. 648-650.
W. H. Gispen, *De Spreuken van Salomo (Korte Verklaring)*, Kampen, 1954, Vol. II, p. 234 f.
F. Lang, on πῦρ, Th.D.N.T., Vol. VI, p. 945.
E. J. Masselink, article in *Christian Cynosure*, Winter 1979, p. 21.
H. Ridderbos, *op. cit.*, p. 286.

This is the victorious life. But the victory cannot be obtained by human effort or exertion but only by faith. It is given to all those, and only to those, who, having been justified by faith, on the basis of Christ's vicarious sacrifice, derive all their power from the indwelling Holy Spirit.

Practical Lessons Derived from Romans 12

Verse 2

". . . Continue to let yourselves be transformed . . ." Certain suggestions showing how progress can be made toward this goal:

a. *Study the Word.* If possible not only on Sunday but even during the week, by means of the midweek Bible class, young people's group, or similar get-together.

b. Become involved in God-glorifying causes by contributing financially to them, and/or becoming a volunteer worker.

c. With the help of the minister or the church librarian post a list of the best literature, arranging the titles in various categories, to suit age-groups. For adults and adolescents be sure to include the books by Francis A. Schaeffer and C. Everett Koop (*How Should We Then Live?* and *Whatever Happened to the Human Race?*).

d. All of this—and much more—in conjunction with constant prayer for God's blessing.

Verses 3 and 16

". . . I bid every one among y o u not to think of himself more highly than he ought to think . . ." "Do not be conceited." Was it not the wish to be like God that caused the fall of Satan and his demonic followers? See Isa. 14:13, 14. And was it not a similar sinful desire that brought about man's fall? See Gen. 3:1-6.

Therefore, though it is true that "the love of money is *a* root of all kinds evil" (I Tim. 6:10), sinful pride is THE root of all evil. See also I Cor. 8:1-3.

Verses 4, 5

"For, just as we have many members in one body, and these members do not all have the same function, so we, who are many, are one body in Christ, and severally members of one another."

Diversity without unity spells confusion. Unity without diversity means monotony. As it is in the human body, so also in the church: both unity and diversity are needed and have been provided.

Imagine, for a moment, a marriage characterized by undiversified unity. In selecting garments to wear the bridegroom prefers blue. So does the bride for herself. In going out to eat, she gives the waiter her order. He says, "Make mine the same." The two even use the same dental cream, wear the same kind of glasses, talk with the same accent, etc., etc. How stale and monotonous such a marriage! Happy is the Christian marriage in which there is unity with respect to basic religious and moral beliefs and practices, but variety in tastes and talents. As long as this variety is made a servant of unity, and this unity a friend of diversity, all will be well. And this holds too for the human body and for the church, of which it is a symbol.

Verse 8

". . . without ulterior motive." This is indeed a very important restriction, for the person who contributes to the needs of others, but does this "with an ulterior motive," for example, merely to win public approval, is a hypocrite. He is "making as if . . ." On no class of people did Jesus pronounce such severe judgments as on the hypocrites of his day. See Matt. 23. The person who gives "with an ulterior motive" is leading a double life. He is generous only on the outside.

Therefore our prayer should always be, "Unite my heart to fear thy name," or, as this passage may also be rendered, "Give me an undivided heart, so that I may fear thy name" (Ps. 86:11).

Psalm 19 is ascribed to David. In rhyme its closing words, very appropriate in the present connection, are:

> When thou dost search my life,
> May all my thoughts within
> And all the words I speak
> Thy full approval win.
> O Lord, thou art a rock to me,
> And my Redeemer thou shalt be.

Verses 14, 17, 19, 21

"Bless those who persecute y o u . . . Do not return evil for evil . . . Do not take revenge, beloved . . . overcome evil with good."

Why does Paul, with but slight variation, repeat this exhortation again and again? Answer: (a) Because he himself, as a pastor was Kindness Personified (see I Thess. 2:7-10); (b) because he knew that returning good for evil was something against which sinful human nature violently rebels; and (c) because he knew that, nevertheless, if anything would succeed in filling the heart of an opponent with shame and penitence, *this* method would do it.

There are those who, on reading these verses, have made the comment, "Paul's advice will not work." They have even added that the apostle's recommended method of winning the opponent shows how little he knew about human nature. They are wrong. Paul does not say that the method he urges upon the Romans will always have the desired effect, but he knows that it is, nevertheless, the most effective method, and above all, that it is the only *right* method. See Luke 23:34; Acts 7:60; I Cor. 13.

Example from life. It was "under a cloud" that the former pastor had left. With part of the congregation he was, however, still popular. So, when his successor arrived, one of the members told the latter, "I do not recognize you as my pastor." The person to whom these words were addressed received grace to remain calm. Afterward he took special pains to perform his pastoral duties when sickness entered the home of the disgruntled church member. Result: the day came when that man told the minister, "I now fully and gladly recognize you as *my pastor*."

Summary of Chapter 12

When we arrive at chapter 12 we have reached the beginning of this letter's Practical Application, covering chapters 12-16. Chapter 12 consists of three well-defined sections, the second of which readily divides itself into two parts.

In the first of the three sections the apostle lovingly—note the word "brothers"—exhorts those whom he addresses to offer themselves to God as sacrifices which, in his sight, are living, holy, and well-pleasing. This first section, accordingly describes what should be the attitude of believers *to God*. They should render the wholehearted *spiritual worship* that is due him in view of "the great mercy" he has bestowed on them. As chapters 1-11 have shown, solely on the basis of divine grace, that is, the unmerited divine favor manifested in Christ's substitutionary self-sacrifice, believers have been declared righteous before God.

In keeping with this need of responsive wholehearted devotion, to be rendered by those who had been so abundantly blessed, is the exhortation that the addressed—which includes us all—in their life-style must no longer allow themselves to be outwardly conformed or fashioned after the pattern of this (evil) age, but instead must permit themselves to undergo a progressive and positive inner change, so as to become more and more Christlike. The goal and result of this inner transformation will be that they will *prove*— that is, will perceive, experience, and delight in—that which in the sight of God is good, well-pleasing, and perfect; that is, that which is in accordance with his will (verses 1 and 2).

In the first part of the second section—the section in which Paul describes what should be the attitude of believers *to fellow-believers*—it is made clear that progressive transformation will be impossible for those who, in their arrogance, imagine that they have already arrived. "Be and remain humble," is the essence of the exhortation. The saints must realize that the church resembles the human body, in which each part has a distinct function and none is self-sufficient. Similar is the situation in the church: each member needs the others. Each member should use his divinely imparted gift or gifts for the advantage of all the others. A list of seven gifts-functions follows, namely, that of prophesying, rendering practical service (probably in the capacity of deacon), teaching, exhorting, contributing to those in need (private benevolence), exercising leadership (probably as an elder), and showing mercy (as a visitor to the sick, etc.).

These tasks should be performed in accordance with the standard of faith (mentioned in connection with prophesying), without ulterior motive (in contributing to the needs of others), with diligence (in this manner exercising leadership), and (in connection with showing mercy) with cheerfulness (verses 3-8).

In the second part of this same section Paul emphasizes the supreme importance of love, here especially "brotherly love." Believers should prefer one another in honor. For further light on this see Phil. 2:3. The exercise of this virtue is possible only when believers have learned to know themselves.

This exhortation is followed by a miscellaneous group of admonitions, urging the exercise of Spirit-imparted virtues; such as enthusiasm, joy, hope, endurance, and prayer. The necessity of helping to relieve the needs of the saints is again stressed (see what has been said on this subject in connection with verses 7 and 8). In view of the fact that Paul will soon be starting out on his journey to Jerusalem with gifts (collected from several churches) for the poor saints in that city (Rom. 15:25; Acts 24:17), this emphasis is not surprising. Moreover, when Paul thinks about traveling—not just his own but that of many gospel witnesses—the exhortation, "Eagerly practice hospitality," fits in very well at this point (verses 9-13).

The final section (verses 14-21) shows what should be the believers' attitude *to outsiders*, including even *enemies*. In the midst of his own people, and even of people in general, the Christian should rejoice with those who rejoice, weep with those who weep, remain humble, showing this by readily associating with humble folk, and, as far as consonant with Christian principles, should live in peace with everybody. He should see to it that his affairs are right, so that nobody can accuse him of wrong-doing, and all will be impressed by his lofty moral-spiritual idealism.

In this connection there is one virtue Paul praises above all else, and, in varying phraseology, mentions again and again (verses 14, 17, 19-21). It is *the virtue of never returning evil for evil but always good for evil*. One should invoke God's blessing on persecutors, and by means of kindness strive to "heap coals of fire upon the heads" of those who had made the saints the objects of their cruelty. Yes, one should try to make these bitter opponents ashamed of themselves, so that, as a result they, in sorrow, flee to God for refuge. In this connection study the example of Joseph (Gen. 45:1-15; 50:15-21); Elisha (II Kings 6:20-23); Stephen (Acts 7:59, 60), and, above all, Jesus (Luke 23:34).

Outline (continued)

Practical Application

D. *What Should Be the Attitude of the Justified Believer*
Toward the Authorities
"Let every person be in subjection to the governing authorities"
13:1-7

E. *What Should Be the Attitude of the Justified Believer*
Toward Everybody
"Do not keep on owing anyone anything except to love one another"
13:8-10

F. *What Should Be the Attitude of the Justified Believer*
Toward the Lord Jesus Christ
"The night is far advanced; the day is drawing near . . . Clothe yourselves
with the Lord Jesus Christ, and make no provision for (the fulfilment of)
the lusts of the flesh"
13:11-14

CHAPTER 13

ROMANS

13 1 Let every person be in subjection to the governing authorities. For there is no authority except from God, and those that exist have been ordained by God. 2 Consequently, he who opposes the authority is resisting the ordinance of God, and those who do that will bring judgment on themselves. 3 For rulers are not a terror to good conduct but to bad. Do you want to be free from fear of the one in authority? Then do what is right, and you will receive his approval. 4 For he is God's servant to do you good. But if you do wrong, be afraid, for he does not bear the sword in vain. He is God's servant, an avenger to bring (God's) wrath upon the one who practices evil. 5 That is why it is necessary to be in subjection, not only to avoid (God's) wrath, but also for the sake of conscience. 6 This is also why y o u pay taxes, for when (the authorities) faithfully devote themselves to this end, they are God's ministers. 7 Pay to all whatever y o u owe (them): tax to whom tax (is due), custom to whom custom, respect to whom respect, honor to whom honor.

D. *What Should Be the Attitude of the Justified Believer*
Toward the Authorities
"Let every person be in subjection to the governing authorities"
13:1-7

When one reaches 13:1-7 a problem arises, that of apparent discontinuity. As many see it, there is no connection between 13:1-7 and either the preceding or the following context. *Love*, so very prominent in 12:9-21 and again in 13:8 f., is absent from 13:1-7. What is present is "the sword" (13:4).[351]

Besides, the theme of the fear-inspiring civil authority, "an avenger" who brings (God's) wrath upon the evil-doer (13:4), is completely absent from the preceding context of 13:1-7, as well as from the succeeding one (13:8 f.). As some see it, the distinctly spiritual flavor which marks the rest of this epistle is absent from 13:1-7.

It is for this reason that, as some see it, no Christian motif is to be heard in 13:1-7.[352] In fact there are those who regard this section as an alien body in Paul's exhortation.[353] But the mere statement of such a negative position does not constitute proof.

Still different is the method of treating 13:1-7 favored by those who say

---

351. There is, however, a close connection between the preceding context (12:9-21) and the following (13:8 f.), as is clear from the fact that μηδενί occurs in both 12:17 and 13:8, and in both cases in a context manifesting the spirit of love.
352. See O. Michel, *Der Brief an die Römer*, Göttingen, 1966, p. 2ఁɔ
353. E. Käsemann, *Commentary on Romans* (tr. of *An Die Römer*), Grand Rapids, 1980, p. 352.

that when Paul mentions "governing authorities" (13:1) he is referring not only to civil authorities but also to a group of angels. That this "solution" should be rejected is shown in the footnote.[354]

On the positive side—i.e., the side of those who maintain that 13:1-7 is not only a part of the word of God, and was composed by Paul, but that it also suits the present context—note the following:

a. The section is not nearly as foreign to the context—whether preceding or following—as some seem to think. As to *the preceding context*, in 12:1, 2 Paul has urged the addressees to sacrifice their lives to God. Grateful and complete self-surrender is the only proper answer to the marvelous mercy God has shown. This means, of course, that the new life must reveal itself in every sphere of Christian enterprise and endeavor. Consistent with this starting point the apostle has indicated what should be the relation of believers *to God* (12:1, 2), to *one another* (verses 3-14), and *to outsiders*, even including *enemies* (12:14-21). Is it, then, so strange that he now also comments on the proper attitude of believers to *the civil authorities*, and this all the more so because he, being himself a Roman citizen by birth, and one who has received many favors from the Roman government, is writing to a church located in the very capital of the Roman Empire, the heart and center of government?

b. The exhortation to obey those in authority begins to look even more reasonable when one considers the following facts: a considerable proportion—though probably not the majority—of the membership of the Roman church consisted of Jews. That many of the Jews of that day and age were looking for an opportunity to shake off the yoke of subjection to Rome, and

---

354. Oscar Cullmann, in his book *Christ and Time* (tr. of *Christus und die Zeit*, Zürich, 1948), London, 1962 (see especially pp. 192-196), proceeds from the supposition that the late Jewish teaching concerning angels belongs to the content of New Testament doctrine. According to him evil angels, having been overcome by Christ, lost their sinister character, and were recommissioned to render favorable service for Christ.

Further, he argues that since the term used in Rom. 13:1, namely, ἐξουσίαι (here dat. pl. -αις) occurs also in Eph. 1:21; 6:12, where it refers to angels, it must indicate angels too in Rom. 13:1. But, as the context shows, in Rom. 13:1 it also signifies civil authorities. Accordingly, as Cullmann sees it, the word has a double meaning, referring both to the civil authorities and to the angels who, as it were, stand behind them. Cullmann finds that double sense also in I Cor. 2:8, "None of the rulers of this age understood it, for if they had, they would not have crucified the Lord of glory"; and in I Cor. 6:3, "Do y o u not know that we will judge angels?" Here, as he sees it, the civil authorities are viewed as the executive agents of the angelic powers.

Criticism.

1. The belief that in one and the same context a term or a statement can have two different meanings, in the present instance referring both to human beings and angels, reminds us of the double rule of interpretation adopted by some of the religious leaders of the sub-apostolic age. As they saw it, all Scripture passages must be interpreted *literally and allegorically*. In course of time this principle developed into the fourfold rule of exegesis: historical, aetiological, analogical, and allegorical. If one sets out on that road, where will he land? See L. Berkhof, *Principles of Biblical Interpretation*, Grand Rapids, 1950, p. 22. It is only fair to state, however, that Cullmann's theory is far more limited in its application.

2. Nowhere does Scripture teach that certain angels lost their evil character and were recommissioned to render service for Christ.

3. As to I Cor. 2:8, nowhere does Scripture ascribe the crucifixion of the Lord of glory to angels, whether good or bad.

were eager to become politically independent once more, with a king of their own, is clear from Scripture (John 6:14; 8:33; Acts 5:36, 37), from the writings of Josephus, and from other sources. Even in the capital there had been disturbances, with the result that Emperor Claudius had expelled all the Jews from that city (Acts 18:2, and see above, p. 18). When this edict was no longer in force many exiles had returned to Rome. But in view of the fact that the basic attitude of some of these people had probably not undergone a complete change, it is understandable that the apostle would issue this warning.

c. This all the more because he does not want Rome to think that the gospel of salvation through Jesus Christ is in any sense antagonistic to a properly functioning Roman government. In this connection it must be borne in mind that the epistle to the Romans was written several years before the terrible days of A.D. 64 (see N.T.C. on Luke, p. 32).

d. The connection between 13:1-7 and the preceding context may well be even closer than indicated so far. In 12:14-21 Paul had emphasized the principle of non-retaliation. Is it not possible that a believer might respond by saying, "With the help of God I will indeed return love for hatred. I will continue, by his grace, to do so even if my opponent remains hostile. I will invoke God's blessing on him and I will continue to be kind to him.—However, does this mean, then, that cruel, hardened criminals must be allowed to triumph? Is that in the best interest of the people as a whole, and would that really serve the cause of the gospel?" If his thinking was along this line,

4. With respect to I Cor. 6:3, how this passage can be interpreted to mean that people will be the executive agents of angelic powers is difficult to fathom. The real meaning of the passage is: If we are going to judge angels, how much more should we be able to settle disputes pertaining to the present life?

5. Here in Rom. 13:1-7 everything points to an earthly ruler, not to an angel or to angels. Note such items as the following: the ruler does not bear the sword "in vain." He punished the wrong-doer and commends the well-doer.

6. Reference to the necessity of paying taxes (13:6) also proves that the passage has nothing to do with angels or with the celestial realm.

7. A parallel to Rom. 13:1-7 is I Peter 2:13-17. But Peter describes the rule of the king and of governors as being "a human institution," probably indicating an institution established among human beings but deriving its authority from God. There is no hint here of any connection with angels. In fact, according to apostolic teaching, Satan and his underlings are never described as standing behind and supporting the good work carried on by civil authorities. On the contrary, the influence exerted by evil spirits is and remains evil, and their authors are doomed. See Rom. 16:20; II Cor. 4:4; Eph. 6:10-12; I Peter 5:8; II Peter 2:4.

Cullmann was by no means the only defender of the double meaning theory, as applied to Rom. 13:1-7. See for example, also M. Dibelius, *Die Geisterwelt im Glauben des Paulus*, Göttingen, 1909. Others who, for a while at least, defended it in one form or another, were K. L. Schmidt, K. Barth, G. Dehn, etc. Even Cranfield for a while felt attracted to it. It is only fair to state, however, that among those who upon further study abandoned this theory, were Dibelius, Barth, and Cranfield. See the latter's admission, *op. cit.*, p. 659.

Lekkerkerker, in his very interesting summary (*op. cit.*, Vol. II, pp. 129-136) traces the essence of this theory back to some second century A.D. gnostics, and shows how it gave rise to the persuasion, among many, that governments were able to yield themselves to demonic powers; example, Germany during Hitler's reign. In other words, people began to see a close link between Rom. 13:1-7 and Rev. 13, as interpreted by them.

It is probably fair to state that by now the double-meaning theory has lost much of its earlier fascination.

the apostle supplies the answer in 13:1-7: *the ruler does not bear the sword in vain!*

e. To all this should be added the fact that what Paul is saying here in 13:1-7 corresponds with the very teaching of Jesus Christ himself (Mark 12:13-17), unless, with some, we adopt the position of certain redactionists, namely, that Mark's report is nothing but a fabrication. With such a position one cannot argue. The debate ends, and believer and non-believer each goes his way.

Paul does not, within the compass of these few verses, give us a complete treatise on the respective rights of church and state. He does not give us *explicit* answers to such questions as, "If the government orders me to do one thing, and God, through his Word, tells me to do the opposite, what must I do?" and "Does the moment ever arrive when, because of continued governmental oppression and corruption, the citizens have the right, and perhaps even the duty, to overthrow such a government and to establish another in its place?" Though the answers may well be *implied* in the statement that "the one in authority . . . is *God's servant to do you good*," and though the answer to the first question has been clearly stated by Peter (Acts 5:29), inquiries into such matters lie beyond the sphere of Paul's immediate interest. See, however, also under verse 2.

Being, except for Jesus Christ himself, the greatest missionary who ever walked the earth, Paul is interested in the preservation of good order so that the cause of gospel proclamation to the glory of God may go forward.

With respect to the connection between 13:1-7 and *the immediately following context*, this can be indicated in a few words, for it is very clear. Verse 7 reads, "Pay to all whatever y o u *owe* them . . ." And verse 8 (the first verse of the new section) begins with, "Do not *keep on owing* anyone anything except to love one another."

1. Let every person be in subjection to the governing authorities.
Literally Paul says, "Let every *soul* . . . ," but the word "soul," as here used, means person, human being.[355] The apostle, writing by inspiration, wants

---

355. In the New Testament as a whole ψυχή occurs about 100 times, πνεῦμα more than 370 times. It is entirely impossible to draw a sharp distinction—as is often done—between these two words, as if in the New Testament ψυχή always has one meaning, πνεῦμα another. It is true that when *the apostle Paul* was thinking of man's invisible being in its relation to God, he generally used the word πνεῦμα. However, in the New Testament as a whole there is considerable overlapping of meanings. One should never say, "In the New Testament ψυχή is man's invisible part considered as that which animates his body; πνεῦμα is that same immaterial entity viewed in its relation to God." The subject is far more complicated than this generalization indicates. For example, the Greek equivalent for *breath* can be either ψυχή (Acts 20:10) or πνεῦμα (II Thess. 2:8). Similarly, the concept *life*, with emphasis on the physical, can be expressed either by πνεῦμα (Luke 8:55) or by ψυχή (Matt. 2:20). Not only is it possible for the πνεῦμα to be provoked (Acts 17:16), the ψυχή too can be stirred up (Acts 14:2). The πνεῦμα rejoices in God, to be sure (Luke 1:47), but the ψυχή too is said to magnify the Lord (Luke 1:46). An incorporeal being may be a πνεῦμα (Heb. 12:23), but may also be a ψυχή (Rev. 6:9). On the other hand, when the reference is to the Holy Spirit the word used is always πνεῦμα, with or without modifier (Mark 1:8-12; 3:29; 12:36; 13:11; Luke 1:15, etc.). An *unclean spirit* is πνεῦμα ἀκάθαρτον (Mark 1:23, 26, etc.). At times a synonym is used (Mark 9:17, 25). The word πνεῦμα can even indicate a disposition (I Cor. 4:21, "a spirit of gentle-

432

everyone to subject himself voluntarily to the then existing governing authorities.[356] In the divine providence the Roman government of Paul's day was such that within its boundaries compliance with the will of God and wholehearted consecration to him were possible. As Paul puts it: **For there is no authority except from God, and those that exist have been ordained by God.**

The civil magistrates to whom Paul refers, from the emperor down to the rulers of the lowest rank, in the final analysis owed their appointment and right to govern to God. It was by his will and in his providence that they had been appointed to maintain order, encourage well-doing, and punish wrong-doing.

2. Consequently, he who opposes the authority is resisting the ordinance of God . . .

Does this mean, then, that the apostle was urging unlimited compliance, a subjection so absolute that even when the command of the magistrate should be in direct conflict with God's revealed will, it must nevertheless be obeyed? Of course not!

We should not forget that Paul was a Jew, well-versed in the Old Testament, as he proves again and again in his epistles. Therefore he also knew about, and heartily approved of, the courage shown by Daniel and/or his three friends when they disobeyed royal edicts and ordinances that were manifestly contrary to God's will as revealed in his law. See chapters 1, 3, and 6 of the book of Daniel. These chapters show that God rewards those who, in extremely difficult circumstances, remain faithful to himself, and who therefore deliberately disobey their earthly ruler.

---

ness"). On the other hand, when the reference is to the entire *self* or *person*, so that in a parallel passage a personal pronoun is used, or so that such a pronoun might have been substituted, this *self* is always ψυχή (Mark 10:45; cf. I Tim. 2:6). Here belong also Rom. 2:9, where the expression "for every soul of man" means "for every person (or human being)," and Rom. 11:3 where "my soul" or "my life" means "me." The word ψυχή also indicates the personal pronoun in Matt. 12:18; Luke 12:19; Acts 2:27, 41, 43; 3:23; 7:14; Heb. 10:38, 39; James 1:21; 5:20; I Peter 1:9; 3:20; Rev. 16:2. And so also here in Rom. 13:1 "every soul" amounts to "every person." This meaning of ψυχή is probably influenced by Hebrew usage.

Since there are these distinctions but also many areas of overlapping, it is impossible to lay down rigid rules. One can perhaps say that in general πνεῦμα stresses mental activity, ψυχή emotional. It is the πνεῦμα that perceives (Mark 2:8), plans (Acts 19:21), and knows (I Cor. 2:11). It is the ψυχή that is sorrowful (Matt. 26:38). The πνεῦμα prays (I Cor. 14:14), the ψυχή loves (Mark 12:30). Also ψυχή is often broader in scope, indicating the sum-total of life that rises above the physical; while πνεῦμα is more restricted. In Paul's epistles), *but by no means always*, πνεῦμα indicates the human spirit in its relation to God, man's self-consciousness or personality viewed as the subject in acts of worship or in acts related to worship, such as praying, bearing witness, etc. But again, no hard and fast rule can be laid down. Every occurrence of either word will have to be interpreted in the light of the origin of the particular passage in which it occurs, and in the light of its specific context and of parallel passages.

356. Note the word ὑπερεχούσαις, dat. pl. f. pres. participle of ὑπερέχω, to hold (power) over. The sense "being" or "holding" over, being supreme, being better (than), shines through in every instance of the word's use in the New Testament: counting the other person *better* than himself (Phil. 2:3); all-*surpassing* excellence (Phil. 3:8); the peace of God *surpassing* all understanding (Phil. 4:7); *supreme* authority (I Peter 2:13).

It is clear, then, that, in writing as he does here in Rom. 13:2, the apostle is thinking of the ruler who is performing his duty of preserving order, approving good behavior, and punishing evil. In *that* case he who opposes the authority is, indeed, resisting the divine ordinance. Paul adds:

... and those who do that will bring judgment [not necessarily *damnation*, A.V.] **on themselves.**

The apostle is not establishing a universally valid principle that opposing the authority and disobeying a command issued by a civil magistrate is always wrong. In reading Paul's letters, filled with instructions and exhortations, one must be sure to make allowance for restrictions or qualifications, whether expressed or implied. See, for example, I Cor. 5:9, 10, where the apostle is, as it were, saying, "Please do not interpret this exhortation as if there were no limits to its application."

That the apostle was referring to normal, and not to outrageous or mistaken, governmental functioning is clear from verse

3. For rulers are not a terror to good conduct but to bad.

In these verses Paul refutes the exclusively negative attitude toward civil authorities, as if they were always intent on doing evil, and as if one should be afraid of them. To be sure, the magistrates punish, but under normal circumstances those who receive punishment have only themselves to blame. "Rulers," says Paul, "are not a terror to good conduct but to bad." It is clear that in saying this he is personifying these two kinds of conduct. He means, of course, that rulers are not a terror to those who conduct themselves properly but to those who conduct themselves badly. It is the latter who have reason to fear.

It has been said that it is strange that Paul would speak so favorably about rulers. Had he not himself been treated cruelly by the civil authorities? See Acts 16:19-24. Cf. II Cor. 11:25: "thrice was I beaten with rods." And was it not the Roman "governor" Pontius Pilate who had unjustly condemned Jesus to death?

The answer generally given is, "These were the exceptions that prove the rule." Though there may well be some merit in this answer, is it not possible to add something to it, which will bring out even more clearly that the apostle was right when he said what he did here in Rom. 13:3?

In the case of Paul's experience at Philippi the authorities had been led astray by the mob, so that *they thought* that they were actually punishing wrongdoers. Subsequently, when they became aware of their mistake, they tried to make up (Acts 16:38, 39).

And as to Pilate, again and again he refused to condemn Jesus to death (Luke 23:4, 13-16, 20, 22). Finally, for selfish reasons, he succumbed to the demands of the Jews (23:24). In this connection note also the significant words, "Y o u handed him over to be killed, and y o u disowned him before Pilate, though *he* had decided to release him" (Acts 3:13).

Paul's statement that, in the normal run of events, rulers are not a terror to good conduct but to bad, stands therefore.

Turning now to the individual believer—note change from plural (those who) to singular (*you* instead of *y o u*)—the apostle continues:

Do you want to be free from fear of the one in authority? Then do what is right, and you will receive his approval.

This does not necessarily mean that the person who does what is right is going to receive a merit badge, ribbon, medal of honor, or—speaking in terms of Paul's own day—that a monument will be erected for him. It does mean, however, that the one in authority will form a favorable opinion of that well-behaved person, and will, whether only in his heart or even by means of an openly expressed commendation, approve of him. Cf. Rom. 2:29; I Peter 2:14.

4. For he is God's servant to do you good.

The civil magistrate is indeed God's servant, for, as verses 1 and 2 have shown, he was, in the final analysis, appointed by God and received his authority from God. Under normal conditions and circumstances the ruler, in the sphere of civil government, represents the divine will with respect to the people's conduct as citizens.

Moreover, the basic aim of the one in authority is not to hurt but to help, "to do you good." As the result of the work and watchfulness of these governmental representatives the believer is able to lead "a tranquil and quiet life in all gravity and godliness" (I Tim. 2:2).

But if you do wrong, be afraid, for he does not bear the sword in vain.

The *wrong-doer* better be afraid. First of all, he should have been afraid to do wrong. Having done wrong, he better be afraid, for punishment will not stay away. He should realize that the magistrate does not bear the sword "in vain," that is, "to no purpose," "for nothing," or, in colloquial language, "just for fun." The ruler bears that sword in order to instill fear of doing wrong; and, in order to inflict punishment when wrong has been done. The opinion according to which Paul simply means that the emperor and those who represent him wield military power merely to enable them to quell the forces of rebellion, hardly does justice to the present context, which refers to wrong-doers in general, not only to rebels. By means of the sword wrongdoing is punished. In fact, the vicious, dangerous criminal may even be put to death.

The fact that in the New Testament the use of the sword is often connected with the idea of putting to death is clear from such passages as Luke 21:24; Acts 12:2; 16:27; Rev. 13:10. See also Heb. 11:34, where "escaped the edge of the sword" means "escaped death." It should be clear, therefore, that the argument in favor of executing dangerous criminals, who have committed horrible crimes, is based not only on Gen. 9:6 but also on Rom. 13:4.

He—that is, the one in authority—**is God's servant, an avenger to bring (God's) wrath upon the one who practices evil.**

The fact that the authority is "*God's servant*" is repeated here. See verses 1, 2 and the beginning of verse 4. The apostle adds, ". . . an avenger to bring (God's) wrath," etc. The question has been asked, "Whose wrath? His own or God's?" The answer, however, is clear, for the sentence begins with the words, "He is *God's* servant to bring wrath," *God's* wrath, therefore. For further proof see on 12:19, p. 421.

In his infinite kindness God, through Paul, caused this message to be delivered to the Roman church, in order that its members—and further all, throughout the ages, who would read this letter or to whom it would be read and/or explained—might be kept from practicing evil, and might, by the grace of God and the power of the Holy Spirit, turn to God for pardon and for strength to live orderly and sanctified lives.

5. That is why it is necessary to be in subjection, not only to avoid (God's) wrath, but also for the sake of conscience.

Now a Christian's political conduct must not be motivated or regulated *only* by fear of incurring God's wrath. On the contrary, subjecting oneself to the divinely authorized civil authority has something to do with the believer's relation to *God*. The Christian knows that it is God's will that he subject himself to the authorities which God, in his providence, has placed over him for his (the subject's) good. Accordingly, failure to subject himself results in the accusing voice of conscience. Therefore, for both of these reasons, namely, to avoid God's wrath and to satisfy his conscience, one should voluntarily subject himself to the ruling authority.

This matter of conscience must not be passed over lightly. It should be borne in mind that a Christian's enlightened conscience is his sense of obligation *to God*. Note the words, "Submit yourselves *for the Lord's sake* to every authority instituted among men" (I Peter 2:13).

On *conscience* see also pp. 97, 98 (on Rom. 2:15), p. 310 (on 9:1); further: Acts 23:1; 24:16; I Cor. 8:7, 10, 12; 10:25-29; II Cor. 1:12; 4:2; 5:11; I Tim. 1:5, 19; 3:9; 4:2; II Tim. 1:3; Titus 1:15.

6. This is also why y o u[357] pay taxes, for when (the authorities) faithfully devote themselves to this end, they are God's ministers.

The nearest antecedent to the word "this" is "for the sake of conscience." It was because their conscience told them that it was right to pay taxes that they paid them. It was right, since it was in harmony with God's purpose for their lives. The collection of taxes must not be considered a disgraceful, tyrannical imposition. No, it is necessary for the maintenance of conditions that make normal living possible. Therefore those who faithfully discharge their duty of collecting taxes are doing so in their capacity as God's *ministers*.

For the word "ministers" Paul here uses a word (pl. of *leitourgos*; cf. *liturgy*) which generally has religious implications. Thus angels are God's *ministers* (Heb. 1:7) and *ministering* spirits (Heb. 1:14). Very properly the word is used with reference to *priests*, and in Heb. 8:2 Christ, in his capacity as highpriest, is called "a minister *(leitourgos)* of the sanctuary, the true tabernacle . . ." Also very properly Paul calls himself "a minister *(leitourgos)* of Christ Jesus to the

---

357. Note return to plural.

Gentiles" (Rom. 15:16). Nevertheless, here in Rom. 13:6 Paul, instead of using the more common word (pl. of *diakonos*, cf. deacon), as a designation of these *servants* who collect taxes, calls them *leitourgoi*; i.e., *ministers*; in fact, "*God's* ministers."

Is not the implication this, that, in the final analysis, the governing authorities owe their authority not to people but to God to whom they are responsible for all their actions; and that the citizens should so regard them; and, when these officials faithfully carry out their duty, even that of collecting taxes, should so honor them?[358]

Of course, this very principle has implications also for the officials, as Calvin correctly observes when he states, "It behooves them to remember that whatever they receive from the people is, as it were, public property, and not to be spent in gratification of private indulgence."

In close connection with the immediately preceding passage ("This is also why y o u pay taxes," etc.), Paul continues:

7. Pay to all whatever y o u owe (them): tax to whom tax (is due), custom to whom custom, respect to whom respect, honor to whom honor.

In connection with monetary obligations owed to the government the addressed—which includes us all—are exhorted that whatever is due should be paid to the proper persons: "tax," levied on persons and property (Luke 20:22-25), should be paid to whom tax is due; "custom," levied on imported and exported goods, similarly, to whom custom is due.

On the next expression ("respect to whom respect") opinions differ widely. The word here rendered "respect"[359] at times indicates "terror" (see verse 3 above), or "fear" (for example, "of the Jews," John 7:13; 19:38; 20:19), or "reverence" with God as object (Phil. 2:12). The same word can, however, also mean "respect" (of a slave for his master, I Peter 2:18; and cf. Eph. 5:33, where the cognate verb is used to indicate the *respect* a wife owes her husband). Since Paul is here (in Rom. 13:7) exhorting the Romans to render to *the officials* their due, the rendering "respect" would appear to be best.[360]

What Paul probably means is something on this order: "Simply paying y o u r taxes is not enough. Telling the officials, 'Here's the money, and now get out,' will never do. Y o u should *respect* these men for the sake of their

---

358. Considered ideally, that is, as God sees them and as they should be regarded, the spiritual and the political spheres are not nearly as widely separated as we generally view them. Note how in the New Testament the same terminology is applied to both spheres:

		Spiritual Sphere	Political Sphere
ὑποτάσσω	to be subject to	Rom. 8:7	Rom. 13:1
ἐξουσία	authority	Rev. 22:14	Rom. 13:1
διάκονος	servant	Col. 1:7	Rom. 13:4
λειτουργός	minister	Rom. 15:16	Rom. 13:6

359. φόβος (here acc. s. - ν).

360. The arguments of Cranfield in defense of the theory that the apostle is referring to the debt, namely fear, owed to *God* have not convinced me. Reference to Mark 12:17, where the word does not even occur, does not rescue this theory. But for the sake of fairness by all means read Cranfield's lengthy argument in substantiation of his view, *op. cit.*, pp. 670-673.

office, and *honor* them in view of their faithful devotion to their task (see verse 6). Remember: they are *God's ministers!* And by means of what is done with this money not only the people in general, including y o u yourselves, are benefited, but so is the cause of the gospel."

---

8 Do not keep on owing anyone anything except to love one another, for he who loves his neighbor has fulfilled the law. 9 For this, "You shall not commit adultery, you shall not murder, you shall not steal, you shall not covet," and whatever other commandment there may be, is summed up in the saying, "You shall love your neighbor as yourself." 10 Love does no harm to the neighbor. Therefore the fulfilment of (the) law is love.

E. *What Should Be the Attitude of the Justified Believer*
Toward Everybody
"Do not keep on owing anyone anything except to love one another"
13:8-10

8. Do not keep on owing anyone anything except to love one another . . .

Other translations:

a. "Y o u owe no man anything . . ."[361] Although grammatically this translation is indeed possible, it would be out of line with the context, for Paul has just now been telling those addressed that they should pay to all whatever they owed them; hence, all their debts (verse 7). So not the indicative but the imperative mood must be meant here in verse 8.

b. "Owe no man anything . . ." This rendering would create the impression that Paul calls all borrowing wrong, a position that is clearly contrary to Scripture. See Exod. 22:25; Ps. 37:26; Matt. 5:42; Luke 6:35.

c. "Owe no man anything; only do love one another." This is perhaps even worse. It changes the one beautiful thought of the original into two separate ideas: not only are the readers-hearers told never to owe anything to anybody, but in addition they are exhorted to love one another! The original clause of eight words cannot be made to convey all this.[362]

d. "Let no debt remain outstanding, except the continuing debt to love one another . . . ," N.I.V., and somewhat similar: N.E.B., Weymouth. I can find no fault whatever with this excellent rendering. It is completely true to the original. On the other hand, if one wishes to show most clearly the close connection between verses 7 and 8, where the original uses words based on the same stem,[363] the rendering "Pay to all whatever y o u owe . . ." (verse 7), followed by "*Do not keep on owing* anyone anything except to love one another . . ." (verse 8) would seem to be required.

---

361. The word used in the original can be interpreted either as a second per. pl. present indicative or imperative. The original would use the same form for either: ὀφείλετε.
362. I cannot agree, therefore, with Murray's interpretation, *op. cit.*, pp. 158, 159; instead I am in accord with Cranfield's reasoning on this point, *op. cit.*, p. 674.
363. ὀφειλάς . . . ὀφείλετε.

Three thoughts are clearly implied here:

First of all, this is a condemnation of the practice of some, who are ever ready to borrow but very slow to repay the borrowed sum. In this connection see Ps. 37:21, "The wicked person borrows but does not repay . . ."

Secondly, this is clearly a eulogy of love, composed by an author who, somewhat earlier, had written I Cor. 13. He is saying that among all the debts a person may have incurred there is one that can never be repaid in full, namely, the debt of love. Moreover, in the present connection Paul is thinking not, first of all, of the debt we owe to God, but, *as the context indicates*, of the debt we owe to our fellowmen. So,

Thirdly, it is a love "for one another." But this "one another," does not, in this instance, merely mean "for all fellow-believers." These, to be sure, are included. One can even say, they are included *in a special way* (see 12:10, 13; Gal. 6:10), but by adding **"for he who loves his neighbor has fulfilled the law"** it is made clear that all those with whom the believer comes into contact—and of course particularly those with special needs—are included. In fact, in a sense no one is excluded from this all-embracing love.

God's holy law, to be sure, does not save anyone. See Rom. 8:3. Nevertheless, once a person has been justified by faith, he, out of gratitude, motivated and enabled by the Holy Spirit, desires to do what God wants him to do. And this is found in the law of the Ten Commandments, as summarized in Lev. 19:18, and later in the words of Jesus as recorded in Matt. 22:39; Mark 12:31; Luke 10:27b.

9. For this, "You shall not commit adultery, you shall not murder, you shall not steal, you shall not covet," and whatever other commandment there may be, is summed up in the saying, "You shall love your neighbor as yourself."

The very fact that Paul mentions these commandments in the order Nos. 7, 6, 8, 10 (cf. Exod. 20:1-17), not even mentioning the fifth and the ninth, but covering these with the summarizing expression "and whatever other commandment there may be," shows that it is not his main intention to enter into the substance of each separate "Thou shalt not." Rather he wishes to emphasize the one great truth, namely, that all these commandments touching the believer's attitude toward his fellowmen "are brought together under one head" in the one, great summarizing rule, "You shall love your neighbor as yourself."

This proves that every negative command ("You shall not") is at bottom a positive command. The meaning, therefore is: "You shall love, and therefore not commit adultery but preserve the sacredness of the marriage-bond. You shall love, and therefore not murder but help your neighbor keep alive and well. You shall love, and accordingly not steal anything that belongs to your neighbor but rather protect his possessions. You shall love, and as a result not covet what belongs to your neighbor but rejoice in the fact that it is his."

The expression, "You shall love your neighbor *as yourself"* merits a word of explanation. What Paul—and before him Jesus—actually means must at least include this thought: it is a certain thing that a person will love himself, and it is also certain that he will do so in spite of the fact that the self he loves has many faults. So, then, also he should most certainly love his neighbor. He may not *like* him, but he should *love* him, and should do so regardless of that neighbor's faults.

10. Love does no harm to the neighbor. Therefore the fulfilment of (the) law is love.

In the words, "Love does no harm to the neighbor," we have an example of a figure of speech called *litotes*. This means that a negative expression of this type implies a strong affirmative. So, "He's no fool" may mean, "He is very shrewd." And similarly "Love does no harm to the neighbor" means "Love greatly benefits the neighbor." ". . . does no harm" is an understatement for "greatly benefits." The reason that this truth is here expressed negatively may well have been to make it coincide with the law's prohibitions.

Notice how beautiful is the style of verse 10: the verse begins and ends with the word *love*. The apostle is indeed very consistent, for if *the fulfilment* of the law does no harm to the neighbor but benefits him, and if love—and only love—does exactly that, then the fulfilment of the law must be love.

It is exactly Spirit-wrought love, this alone, that is sufficiently powerful to cause a person to remove all obstacles and to love his neighbor even though that neighbor is perhaps not a pleasant person! It is *love* that "is not easily angered, keeps no record of wrongs, always protects and always hopes" (I Cor. 13:5, 7). Such human love has its origin in God, for "God is love" (I John 4:8). It was Jesus who, a few hours before his crucifixion told his disciples, "A new precept I give y o u, that y o u keep on loving one another; just as I have loved y o u, that y o u also keep on loving one another" (John 13:34).

11 And (do this) especially because y o u know how critical the time is. The hour has arrived for y o u to wake up from (y o u r) slumber, for our salvation is nearer now than when we (first) believed.   12 The night is far advanced; the day is drawing near. So let us put aside the deeds of darkness and put on the armor of light.   13 Let us walk honorably, as in the daytime, not in orgies and drinking bouts, not in sexual excesses and debaucheries, not in dissension and jealousy.   14 Rather, clothe yourselves with the Lord Jesus Christ, and make no provision for (the fulfilment of) the lusts of the flesh.

F. *What Should Be the Attitude of the Justified Believer*
Toward the Lord Jesus Christ
"The night is far advanced; the day is drawing near . . . clothe yourselves
with the Lord Jesus Christ, and make no provision for (the fulfilment of)
the lusts of the flesh"
13:11-14

The discussion of this section will follow this outline:
  a. Exegesis of verses 11, 12a; of verses 12b, 13; and of verse 14.

b. Statement of the problem that arises in connection with this section (verses 11-14).

c. Discussion of proposed solutions.

That there is a close connection between verses 11, 12a and that which precedes is evident from the very opening words:

11, 12a. And (do this) especially because y o u know how critical the time is. The hour has arrived for y o u to wake up from (y o u r) slumber, for our salvation is nearer now than when we (first) believed. The night is far advanced; the day is drawing near.³⁶⁴

When Paul says, "And (do this)," he is referring at least to what is found in the immediately preceding verses. Therefore, he is now saying, " 'Love your neighbor as yourself,' but do it not only because the law demands this, but *especially also* because y o u know how very critical is the time in which we are now living." It is possible, however, that in saying "And (do this)" he is referring to the broader context, extending all the way back to 12:1 f.

By saying, "especially because y o u know how critical the time is," and immediately adding, "The hour has arrived for y o u to wake up from y o u r slumber, for our salvation is nearer now than when we first believed," he is exhorting the membership of the Roman church—and us all—to lay aside their (our) sinful practices and, with the help of the Holy Spirit, to advance in sanctification. "Our salvation is nearer now than when we (first) believed" means "The culmination of our salvation is closer to us in time now than it was at the moment when we first confessed our faith in the Lord Jesus Christ and were baptized."

It is clear that the apostle is making an appeal to eschatology; that is, to the doctrine of the Lord's Return. He is using this as an incentive to holy living. One finds a similar exhortation and argument in Phil. 4:4-7; I Thess. 5:1-11, 23; Heb. 10:24 f.; James 5:7-11; I Peter 4:7-11; and, of course, also already in the teaching of Jesus (Matt. 25:31-46; Mark 13:33-37 etc.).

Such an appeal is especially understandable when we consider that the Lord is coming "to reward his servants." Cf. the parable of *The Watchful Servants* (Luke 12:35-48); that of *The Five Foolish and The Five Sensible Girls* (Matt. 25:1-13); and, in fact, also the rest of Matt. 25. Add Rom. 14:10; II Cor. 5:10; II Tim. 4:1; James 5:9; I Peter 4:5; cf. Eccl. 12:14.

---

364. καὶ τοῦτο, and at that; or and that too; and especially. See I Cor. 6:6, 8.

εἰδότες, 2nd perf. masc. act. nom. pl. participle of οἶδα, with sense of present.

The principal verb has to be supplied, perhaps ποιήσατε, 2nd per. pl. aor. act. imperat. of ποιέω, to do.

καιρόν, acc. s. of καιρός, here probably the critical time, decisive moment, moment of destiny. In 5:6 and 9:9 the word means appointed time; in 8:18 and 11:5 present time. The word καιρός should be distinguished from χρόνος, which indicates time as progression from past into present into future, progression of moments.

ὕπνου, gen. s. of ὕπνος, sleep, slumber. Cf. *hypnotism*.

ἐγερθῆναι, aor. mid. and pass. infin. of ἐγείρω, to awaken; in mid. to rouse oneself; hence, to wake up; here used symbolically, to a life of greater sanctification.

προέκοψεν, 3rd per. s. aor. indicat. of προκόπτω, to go forward; here: to be (far) advanced.

ἤγγικεν, 3rd per. s. perf. indicat. of ἐγγίζω, to approach, draw near.

The words, "The night is far advanced; the day is drawing near" indicate that for God's people the present era of darkness, sin, and sadness is rapidly coming to an end; and the never-ending age of light, holiness, and gladness is near. Paul, as it were, hears the cry of the night watchman, "Wake up, for the morning is dawning."

Here we must be careful, however. Paul cannot have meant, "Christ will return tomorrow. He will come back immediately." Such teaching would have amounted to a refutation of his own earlier statement, namely, that the Return would be preceded by the coming of the apostasy and the arrival of "the man of lawlessness, the son of perdition" (II Thess. 2:1-5). Compare with this the similar teaching of Jesus himself (Matt. 24:21, 29; 25:5). What the apostle is saying, therefore, is this, "*The day* will be here very soon."

12b, 13. So let us put aside the deeds of darkness and put on the armor of light. Let us walk honorably, as in the daytime, not in orgies and drinking bouts, not in sexual excesses and debaucheries, not in dissension and jealousy.[365]

Because of the critical time in which Paul and his contemporaries were living, and because of the tremendous issues at stake—nothing less than to glorify God forever in heaven or to suffer forever with Satan and all the lost in hell—Paul urges all—including even himself (note "Let us")—to put aside the deeds of darkness and to put on the armor of light.

He summarizes the deeds of darkness in verse 13. Though the six vices mentioned do not constitute a complete list, they are sufficiently representative to indicate what the apostle has in mind. Besides, we are permitted,

---

365. ἀποθώμεθα, let us put aside; and ἐνδυσώμεθα, let us put on, are 1st per. pl. aor. middle subjunctives; respectively, of ἀποτίθημι and ἐνδύω. Of the latter verb the 2nd per. aor. imperat. mid. occurs in verse 14 ("Put on," or "Clothe yourselves with").
τὰ ὅπλα, weapons, armor; see also on Rom. 6:13, p. 202, including footnote 174.
ὡς, as, meaning: as actually the case.
εὐσχημόνως, lit. in good form; hence, in a becoming manner, gracefully, honorably. Cf. I Cor. 14:40; I Thess. 4:12.
The following six nouns (three pairs of two each) are all in the dative. In the original the first four nouns are in the pl., the last two in the sing.
κῶμος (see also Gal. 5:21; I Peter 4:3), boisterous merrymaking, carousing, orgy.
μέθη (Luke 21:34; Gal. 5:21), drinking bout.
For the meaning of κοίτη see above, on Rom. 9:10, p. 319. Here (in Rom. 13:13) indecency, sexual excess.
ἀσέλγεια, debauchery, licentiousness; so also in Mark 7:22; II Cor. 12:21; Gal. 5:19; Eph. 4:19; I Peter 4:3; II Peter 2:2; Jude 4.
ἔρις (Rom. 1:29; see p. 81), strife, dissension. Besides its occurrence in Rom. 1:29 and 13:13 it is also found in I Cor. 1:11; 3:3; II Cor. 12:20; Gal. 5:20; Phil. 1:15; I Tim. 6:4; and Titus 3:9.
ζῆλος, depending on the context, can mean zeal, enthusiasm, ardor (Rom. 10:2; II Cor. 9:2; Phil. 3:6; but can also mean jealousy, as here in Rom. 13:13 and in I Cor. 3:3; II Cor. 11:2; 12:20; Gal. 5:20. In II Cor. 7:7, 11 it seems to refer to *ardent concern*. The πυρὸς ζῆλος of Heb. 10:27 is a raging, devouring fire; and the ζῆλος of James 3:14, 16 spells *envy*. The word also occurs in John 2:17 in the sense of *zeal*, and twice in the book of Acts (5:17; 13:45) in that of *jealousy*.

of course, to add "and the like" to the list, as in a similar but lengthier list found in Gal. 5:19-21.

These vices comprise the deeds of darkness, often even performed in the dark, but certainly always encouraged by "the prince of darkness."

Though it is not necessary to suppose that either Jews or Gentiles were exempt from these evil deeds and dispositions, some of those that are mentioned remind us especially of the sins pertaining to the world of the Gentiles (cf. Rom. 1:28 f.). As has been shown—see pp. 20-23—most of the members of the Roman church had probably been gathered out of the world of the Gentiles. For more information on the individual vices here mentioned see footnote 365.

Living as we do, in an age in which all the emphasis is on the positive, so that we are constantly being warned never to say "Don't" but always "Do," we note that Paul is not afraid to say, "Do not . . . not . . . not."

However, he also knows that the only way to overcome evil is by means of goodness. So, between two negatives—"let us put aside" and "not in orgies," etc., he places, "Let us put on the armor of light." Now if *darkness* indicates (spiritual) dullness, depravity, and despair, *light* certainly spells (spiritual) learning, love, and laughter (the joy inexpressible and full of glory mentioned in I Peter 1:8), though in the present context the emphasis is on *love* (13:8-10).

Note that here again Paul uses military language ("armor of light,") as he does often (Rom. 6:13; 13:2; I Cor. 9:7; II Cor. 6:7; 10:4; Eph. 6:10-20; I Thess 5:8; II Tim. 2:3). There must be a reason for this. A good soldier does not lie down on the job, exerts himself to the full, has a definite goal in mind, uses effective armor, obeys rules. Does not all this apply also to soldiers for Christ?

14. Rather, clothe yourselves with the Lord Jesus Christ, and make no provision for (the fulfilment of) the lusts of the flesh.[366]

This closing admonition is a most apt and beautiful summary of what the apostle has been saying in 12:1-13:13. It touches on both justification and sanctification. It means that, having accepted Christ and having been baptized, believers should now not rest on their laurels, but should continue to do in practice what they have already done in principle (Gal. 3:27). Paul is, as it were, saying, "Having laid aside the garment of sin, now deck yourselves more and more with the robe of Christ's righteousness, so that whenever

---

366. For ἐνδύσασθε see above, footnote 365.

σαρκός, "for the flesh" (objective gen.). Literally the final clause reads: "and for the flesh do not make (or: stop making) provision for lusts." Another instance of abbreviated expression. On the meaning of σάρξ see footnote 187, p. 217. Meaning h. (sinful human nature) applies here.

πρόνοια, in the New Testament only here (in the sense of *provision*) and in Acts 24:2 (*foresight*).

ἐπιθυμίας, acc. pl. of ἐπιθυμία, here meaning lust, sinful desire. For a more detailed study of this word see N.T.C. on II Tim. 2:22, footnote 147, pp. 271, 272.

Satan reminds y o u of y o u r sinfulness, y o u immediately remind him and yourselves of y o u r new standing with God.

"*Become more and more spiritually united with Christ*, so that he will be the Light of y o u r light, the Life of y o u r life, the Joy of y o u r joy, and the Strength of y o u r strength." The person who, by virtue of the enabling power of the Holy Spirit, does this is able to sing

Jesus is all the world to me. . . .

—Will L. Thompson

Such a person must make no provision for the satisfaction of the urges of his sinful human nature. To be sure, there will be these temptations, for the believer remains a sinner even when he becomes a saint (Rom. 7:14 f.). But if he is truly a child of God he must and will learn more and more to control and subdue these enticements in the realm of *Pleasure* (inordinate craving for the satisfaction of physical appetites), *Power* (lust to shine and be dominant), and *Possessions* (uncontrolled yearning for material possessions and for the prestige that accompanies them). With Christ as his Sovereign Lord, the victory is assured!

*   *   *   *   *

It was toward the end of the summer of the year A.D. 386. In the garden of a villa near Milan, Northern Italy, sat Augustine, born Nov. 13 of the year 354. Beside him, on a bench, there was lying a copy of Paul's epistles. But he seemed not to be particularly interested in it. He was experiencing an intense spiritual struggle, a violent agitation of heart and mind. Getting up from the bench he flung himself down on the grass beneath a fig tree.

As he is lying there he hears the voice of a child, boy or girl he could not tell. That voice was repeating again and again, "Tolle, lege; tolle, lege" ("Take up and read; take up and read").

He gets up, returns to the bench, and, having picked up the copy of Paul's epistles, reads the first passage on which his eye lights, a Latin version of Rom. 13:13b, 14, "Not in orgies and drinking bouts, not in sexual excesses and debaucheries, not in dissension and jealousy. Rather, clothe yourselves with the Lord Jesus Christ, and make no provision for the (fulfilment of) the lusts of the flesh."

It was this passage plus the love and constant prayers of devout mother Monica that led to the conversion of Augustine, who became one of the greatest leaders of the church. See *Conf.* VIII,xii.28,29.

*   *   *   *   *

The Problem

Paul wrote, "Our salvation is nearer now than when we (first) believed. The night is far advanced; the day is drawing near" (13:11, 12). But more than nineteen centuries have gone by since the apostle wrote this. Did he commit an error?

By no means all commentators attempt to solve this problem. Several do not even mention it. By those who tackle it the following solutions have been proposed:

Proposed Solutions

I

Paul is not necessarily thinking—or is not thinking only—of the day of Christ's Return. He may have been thinking of, or at least including, the moment when a person dies. It is then that for the child of God darkness turns into day.[367]

This solution will not do, for when Paul, in the present connection, refers to future salvation, he must have been thinking about salvation's culmination for body and soul. This great blessing will be bestowed not on individual believers, one by one, but on all God's children simultaneously, at Christ's Return. Moreover, the "day" to which he refers in verse 12 is best interpreted as is the same term in I Cor. 3:13; I Thess. 5:4; Heb. 10:25; and II Peter 1:19. In all these cases the reference is to the day of Christ's Return and the final judgment.

II

The words "Our salvation is nearer now than when we (first) believed. The night is far advanced; the day is drawing near" mean that in the unfolding of God's redemptive plan there is *only one great event* that must still take place, namely, Christ's Return to judge the living and the dead.[368]

This suggestion is very helpful. We might summarize the course of redemptive history as follows:

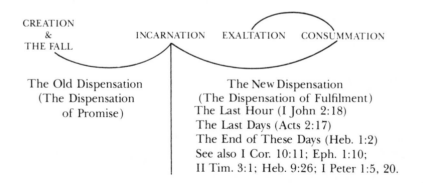

| CREATION & THE FALL | INCARNATION | EXALTATION | CONSUMMATION |

The Old Dispensation
(The Dispensation
of Promise)

The New Dispensation
(The Dispensation of Fulfilment)
The Last Hour (I John 2:18)
The Last Days (Acts 2:17)
The End of These Days (Heb. 1:2)
See also I Cor. 10:11; Eph. 1:10;
II Tim. 3:1; Heb. 9:26; I Peter 1:5, 20.

---

367. Thus Sanday and Headlam, *op. cit.*, p. 378; Greijdanus, *Kommentaar*, Vol. II, pp. 578, 579; A. T. Robertson, *Word Pictures* IV, p. 410; Cranfield, *op. cit.*, p. 682.
368. Murray, *op. cit.*, Vol. II, p. 168; and several others.

In this diagram INCARNATION implies crucifixion (II Cor. 8:9). We are now living in the very last part of the period that extends from INCARNATION to CONSUMMATION; that is, in the part extending from EXALTATION (resurrection, ascension, coronation, outpouring of the Holy Spirit) to CONSUMMATION (Second Coming, resurrection of the dead, final judgment).

This answer, accordingly, goes a long way in explaining the language Paul uses here in Rom. 13:11, 12. But it may not go quite far enough. It hardly explains what the apostle meant when he said, "for our salvation is nearer now than when we (first) believed," for the objection might still be raised, "If the time intervening between the composition of Romans and the arrival (at Christ's Return) of full salvation is still not less than nineteen centuries, then what difference does the interval between (a) first believing and (b) 'now' (the date of the composition of Romans), make?" In view of the very lengthy time period of more than nineteen centuries it is hard to understand why Paul would say, "for our salvation is nearer now than when we (first) believed." We feel like saying, "Yes, nearer, Paul, but by a very, very small fraction, indeed!"

Besides, we still experience some difficulty with the expression "the day *is drawing near*," when more than nineteen centuries have gone by, and the prediction remains unfulfilled.

III

Perhaps we should refer, first of all, to II Peter 3:8. Thorough interpretation of that passage belongs to commentaries on II Peter. One observation can be made, however. The unbelievers and scoffers of Peter's day were told that *their time calculation was faulty*.

For a different reason, the time calculation adopted by those who have difficulty with Rom. 13:11, 12 is probably also wrong. The error is committed not by Paul but by us *when we apply earth's chronology to heaven's mode of life*. We really have no right to say that the saints to whom Paul was addressing this letter had to wait at least another nineteen centuries before the night of darkness would for them be changed into the daylight of full salvation.

What happens when a person dies and his soul goes to heaven? Does that soul then become timeless? Does it adopt one of God's incommunicable (!) attributes, that of *eternity*, ex-temporal existence? Of course not. Not then, nor ever. The oft-quoted passage (Rev. 10:6) proves nothing of the kind. Neither do some of our popular hymns that are based upon the wrong translation of Rev. 10:6. "No more time" should be "no more delay."

What is true, however, is that the computation of time will be different on the other side of the grave. Sorrow spells slow time, but joy inexpressible and full of glory indicates fast-flying time. Rev. 6:11 tells us that for the redeemed souls "under the altar" the period between their martyrdom and the final judgment would amount to "a little while." We will, as it were, be geared to a different kind of time-scale.[369]

So, we arrive at the conclusion that what Paul wrote here in Rom. 13:13, namely, "Our salvation is nearer now than when we (first) believed" makes sense, after all. And so does, "The night is far advanced; the day is drawing near."

We should not forget, however, that the main lesson taught in Rom. 13:11-14 is, "let us put aside the deeds of darkness and put on the garment of light." In other words, "Clothe yourselves with the Lord Jesus Christ."

Practical Lessons Derived from Romans 13

Verse 1

"Let every person be in subjection to the governing authorities." A presidential election year has arrived. In a newspaper someone wrote an article which could be summarized as follows: "The minister, in his preaching, should not discuss the implications of the gospel for the exercise of Christian citizenship, for Church and State must remain separate." Right or Wrong?

Verses 2, 3, 4

". . . he who opposes the authority is resisting the ordinance of God . . . rulers are not a terror to good conduct but to bad . . . he [the magistrate] is God's servant to do you good."

If the church wishes to exert an influence for good upon the State, it should not take recourse to separation but should try spiritual infiltration. It is not surprising that some time later Paul was able to write, ". . . it has become clear throughout the whole praetorian guard and to all the rest that my bonds are for Christ" (Phil. 1:13); and "All the saints greet y o u, especially those of Caesar's household" (4:22).

Verse 6

"This is also why y o u pay taxes, for when (the authorities) faithfully devote themselves to this end, they are God's ministers." Does not this thought make paying taxes somewhat less burdensome?

Verse 8

"Do not keep on owing anyone anything except to love one another . . ."

The attempt to pay a continuing debt may seem to be a very disappointing task. Yet, in the present case this is not really true, for during the process of paying this debt one receives at least the following blessings: (a) the satisfaction of knowing that we are helping the neighbor; (b) assurance of salvation (I John 3:18, 19); and (c) the conviction that we are doing what God wants us to do; that is, that out of gratitude we, with the help of the Holy Spirit, are fulfilling his law.

---

369. For a more complete discussion of TIME in HEAVEN see W. Hendriksen, *The Bible on the Life Hereafter*, pp. 70-74.

Verse 12

"The night is far advanced; the day is drawing near."
Said the minister from the pulpit, "About the day and the hour of Christ's Return
we know nothing (Matt. 24:36). In fact, about the life hereafter the Bible tells us
almost nothing. So, let those who wish to indulge in wild speculations do so. I shall
concentrate my attention on more important subjects." Is that the right approach?

Summary of Chapter 13

Having commented on the believers' proper attitude to God, to fellow-
believers, and to outsiders (including enemies), Paul now describes how
God's children should relate to *governing authorities*. He states that these
rulers have been ordained by God, so that those who oppose them are
resisting God's ordinance. Moreover, the addressed should bear in mind that
magistrates have by God been appointed to promote the interests of the
people over whom they were placed in charge. Therefore, in order to avoid
God's wrath and also for the sake of conscience those for whom Paul's letter
was written—believers in every age—should submit themselves to the civil
authorities. Those who follow the opposite course better remember that they
are opposing God himself; also, that the magistrate does not bear his sword
in vain.

Taxes too, of whatever kind, should be paid, and those who judiciously
and faithfully collect them should be respected. This section closes with the
words, "Pay to all whatever y o u owe (them): tax to whom tax (is due),
custom to whom custom, respect to whom respect, honor to whom honor"
(verses 1-7).

Having just a moment ago stated, "Pay to all whatever y o u owe (them),"
Paul now adds, "Do not keep on owing anyone anything except to love one
another." Thus he condemns the practice of those who are ever ready to
borrow and ever slow to repay; emphasizes that the debt of love we owe to
others can never be repaid in full; and makes clear that in our loving embrace
we should not only include fellow-believers but *anyone at all* whom God has
placed in our path for help and protection of any kind. He says, "For this,
'You shall not commit adultery, you shall not murder, you shall not steal, you
shall not covet,' and whatever other commandment there may be, is summed
up in the saying, 'You shall love your neighbor as yourself.' " Paul closes this
section with the striking understatement, "Love does no harm to the neighbor. Therefore the fulfilment of (the) law is love" (verses 8-10).

It is clear, therefore, that we should love our neighbor as we love ourselves
because that is what God's holy law demands. The apostle now adds another
reason why we should do this, and probably also why we should strive to
live in accordance with all the exhortations found in 12:1 f. (thorough devotion to God, etc.). He writes, "And (do this) especially because y o u know
how critical the time is. The hour has arrived for y o u to wake up from

(y o u r) slumber, for our salvation is nearer now than when we (first) believed. The night is far advanced; the day is drawing near." He was undoubtedly referring to the day of Christ's Return in glory. That what he stated with reference to the imminent character of this great event and of full salvation for both body and soul, to be imparted to all who walk in the light, is true, has been indicated on pp. 445-447. Paul, accordingly, exhorts the addressed to abandon the kind of deeds associated with darkness (orgies, drinking bouts . . . dissension, jealousy), and, instead, to put on "the armor of light." In closing this section he states, "Clothe yourselves with the *Lord Jesus Christ* [i.e., strive to attain to full spiritual union with him], and make no provision for (the fulfilment of) the lusts of the flesh" (verses 11-14).

Outline (continued)

Practical Application

G. *What Should Be the Attitude of the Justified Believer*
Toward the Weak and the Strong
"Him who is weak in faith accept"
14:1-23
"We who are strong ought to bear the failings of the weak
and not to please ourselves"
15:1-13

CHAPTER
14:1—15:13

ROMANS

14 1 Him who is weak in faith accept, but not with the idea of passing judgment on (his) opinions. 2 One person believes he may eat anything, but another, being weak, eats (only) vegetables. 3 Let not him who eats look down on him who does not, and let not him who does not eat judge him who does, for God has accepted him. 4 Who are you that you dare pass judgment on someone else's servant? To his own master he stands or falls. And he will stand, for the Lord is able to make him stand.

5 One person regards one day as being better than another; another regards every day as being good. Let each one be fully convinced in his own mind. 6 He who regards one day as being special, does so in honor of the Lord; and he who eats does so in honor of the Lord, since he gives thanks to God. And he who abstains does so in honor of the Lord and gives thanks to God. 7 For none of us lives to himself alone, and none of us dies to himself alone. 8 If we live, we live to the Lord; and if we die, we die to the Lord. So then, whether we live or whether we die, we are the Lord's. 9 For to this end Christ died and lived, that he might be Lord of both the dead and the living.

10 But you, why do you pass judgment on your brother? Or why do you look down on your brother? For we shall all stand before the judgment seat of God. ¹ 11 For it is written,
" 'As surely as I live,' says the Lord,
'Before me will every knee bow down,
And every tongue will acclaim God.'"
12 So then each of us will give an account of himself to God.

13 Therefore let us stop passing judgment on one another; but rather, let this be y o u r judgment, namely, that y o u should not put any stumbling block or obstacle in y o u r brother's way. 14 I know and am convinced in the Lord Jesus that nothing is unclean in itself; but if anyone considers something to be unclean, then for him it is unclean. 15 For if your brother is seriously upset because of what you eat, you are no longer walking in love. Do not by your eating destroy your brother for whom Christ died. 16 Therefore do not allow that which for you is a good thing to become an occasion for slanderous talk. 17 For the kingdom of God is not eating and drinking but righteousness and peace and joy in the Holy Spirit; 18 for anyone who serves Christ in this way is pleasing to God and respected among men.

19 Let us then pursue the things that lead to peace and to mutual edification. 20 Do not tear down the work of God for the sake of food. Everything, indeed, is clean, but it is wrong for a person to eat anything that causes (someone else) to stumble. 21 It is better not to eat meat or drink wine or to do anything else that will cause your brother to stumble.

22 Whatever you believe (about these things) keep between yourself and God.³⁷⁰ Blessed is the person who does not need to condemn himself over what he approves. 23 But the

---

370. Literally: The faith which you have, have it to yourself before God.

one who has misgivings[371] when he eats is condemned, because (his eating does) not (spring) from faith; and everything (that does) not (spring) from faith is sin.

G. *What Should Be the Attitude of the Justified Believer Toward the Weak and the Strong*
"Him who is weak in faith accept"
14:1-23

As Paul is approaching the end of this epistle he is aware that there is one important problem on which he has not yet touched, namely, that of the relation between *the weak* and *the strong*. The strong were those who were able to grasp the significance of Christ's death for daily living; that is, for eating and drinking, etc., the weak were not.

1. *Origin of the problem*

God had laid down certain rules with respect to clean versus unclean animals. Only the clean were permitted to be used as food. See Lev. 11:1-45; Deut. 14:3-21. Cf. Dan. 1:8 f.; Tobit 1:10-12; I Macc. 1:62; II Macc. 7: Josephus, *Antiq.* IV.vi.8.

In connection with his teaching that whatever enters a person from the outside is undefiling, Jesus had pronounced all foods clean (Mark 7:15-19). But if even Peter was slow in taking to heart the full implications of this dominical pronouncement, as Acts 10:9-16; 11:1-18; Gal. 2:11-21 indicate, it is understandable that for other Jewish converts to Christianity the situation became even more difficult.

It has been suggested that in the church of Rome the clash between meateaters and abstainers became more explosive when Jews who had been expelled from the capital by Claudius (see p. 18) returned. During their absence the Roman church experienced no difficulty, but with their return to Rome a somewhat strained relation began to develop between the two ethnic groups. Whether this theory is correct cannot now be determined, but it may well be. The view according to which "the strong" consisted of the Gentile portion of the congregation, the majority (see pp. 21-23), while "the weak" consisted of the Jewish portion, seems to be confirmed by 15:7 f. (See on that passage). However, this does not mean that only Gentiles belonged to the strong portion, and only Jews to the weak. A Hebrew of Hebrews was Paul; nevertheless, he included himself among the strong (15:1).

But had not Christ, by his death on the cross, fulfilled and thereby abolished, the Old Testament shadows? And if even the divinely established dietary regulations had lost their validity, was not the same true, in fact more decisively, with respect to all man-made rules that had been embroidered upon them?

---

371. Or: who wavers.

True indeed, but this legitimate inference was not drawn by every believer in Christ. Many, especially in Jerusalem and vicinity, but also in Rome and probably elsewhere, held fast to their "traditions."

Now as long as no saving significance or merit of any kind was ascribed to the perpetuation of such rules and regulations, and no offense was given, such persistence in clinging to the old could be tolerated. The adherents must be treated with love and patience. This was true especially during what might be called "the period of transition."

However, in mixed communities problems immediately presented themselves. Customs—Gentile versus Jewish—were bound to clash. The fact that the law of ordinances had been nailed to the cross, and along with it all man-made regulations had also become logically extinct, had not become clear to every believer in Christ. And the further and closely related fact that "in Christ" the wall of separation between Jew and Gentile had been broken down, never to be rebuilt, was frequently ignored, as it is even today in certain circles!

2. *What the two groups—the strong and the weak—*
had in common:

a. The members of each group must be regarded as genuine believers (Rom. 14:1-4, 6, 10, 13).

b. Each group was critical of the other (14:3, 4, 13).

c. Each group will have to give an account of itself to the Lord (14:11).

3. *The points with respect to which the two groups differed:*

a. The strong believed that they were permitted to eat anything (meats as well as vegetables); the weak were vegetarians (14:2).

b. The strong regarded every day as being "good." The weak regarded one day as being better than another (14:5). The emphasis falls on a.

4. *Paul's attitude toward the two groups and his admonitions addressed to the*
groups and to the congregation in general:

a. In at least one important point Paul agrees with the strong, namely, in believing that nothing (no food) is unclean in itself (14:14, 20; 15:1).

b. He admonishes each group not to look down on the other (14:3, 5, 19).

c. He is especially emphatic in denouncing the attitude of some strong people toward the weak (14:14-21), and he admonishes the strong lovingly to bear with the failings of the weak (15:1).

d. He stresses the fact that the matter of eating and drinking is not nearly as important as that of being a citizen of the kingdom of God, for the essence of that kingdom is not "eating and drinking but righteousness and peace and joy in the Holy Spirit" (14:17).

e. He admonishes both groups—*in fact, the entire congregation*—to pursue those things that lead to peace and mutual edification (14:19; 15:2, 3).

f. He points to the example of Christ, who did not please himself, and was willing for our sake, and to the glory of God, to suffer reproach (15:3-6).

g. He summarizes his exhortations by pleading: "Accept one another, then, just as Christ accepted y o u, to the glory of God" (15:7). He shows that, in Christ, Jews and Gentiles attain their unity. He states, "Christ has become a servant of 'the circumcision' (i.e., of the Jews) for the sake of God's *truth* . . . but the Gentiles glorify God for the sake of (his) *mercy*," quoting passages from the Old Testament to prove what he had just now said with respect to the Gentiles (15:8-12).

h. He closes this section—and in a sense, the entire letter up to this point— with the beautiful prayer-wish, "May the God of hope fill y o u with all joy and peace, in the exercise of (y o u r) faith, so that by the power of the Holy Spirit y o u may overflow with hope" (15:13).

5. *Similarities and differences between Paul's teaching (with respect to diets and days), a. in Romans, and b. in other epistles:*

There are resemblances and there are also differences between that which Paul says about this subject here in Romans, on the one hand, and what, on the other hand, he says about it in I Corinthians, Galatians, and Colossians; differences not in doctrine but in approach and style.

a. *Romans and I Corinthians*

Both here in Romans and in I Cor. 8:1-13; 10:14-33 Paul teaches that the church—and of course also believers individually—*should treat with consideration and tenderness* those who are *weak*; that is, who are, or seem to be, unable to grasp the significance of Christ's death on the cross for daily life. The strong and the weak should treat each other with kindness.

"Let not him who eats look down on him who does not, and let not him who does not eat judge him who does, for God has accepted him" (Rom. 14:3). "Be careful, however, that the exercise of y o u r freedom does not become a stumbling block to the weak" (I Cor. 8:9).

In the *Corinthian* passages Paul speaks about food that had been *offered to idols* (I Cor. 10:20, 28). This feature is not *mentioned* in Romans, though it may be implied. Also, in Romans (14:5 f.) there is a reference to the observance of *special days*. This item is absent from I Corinthians.

b. *Romans and Galatians*

Also between what Paul says here in Rom. 14:1-15:13 and what he says in *Gal.* 4:10, 11 there is a resemblance. In both letters reference is made to the observance of certain special *days*. But the manner in which the apostle refers to these days differs widely in these two epistles. In Galatians the reference is to sabbath-days, days of the new moon, festival seasons belonging to the Jewish cycle, and either (1) the sabbath and jubilee years, or (2) the New Year (Rosh Hashana) on the first day of the month Tishri. Paul is saying that strict observance of such days and festivals has nothing whatever to do with securing divine favor. As a foundation upon which to build one's hope of being justified in the sight of God such observance is merely a superstition. It is utterly futile, nothing but sinking sand. Paul, as it were, shakes his head in utter disgust when he reflects on the fact that rigid, painstaking adherence to the Mosaic law regarding stated days was actually being substituted for simple faith in Jesus Christ. He even states, "I am afraid about y o u, lest somehow I have labored among y o u in vain" (Gal. 4:11). Here, in Rom. 14:5, Paul simply says, "One person regards one day as being better than another; another regards every day as being good. Let each one be fully convinced in his own mind." The sharply critical and denunciatory style that characterizes the Galatian passages is completely absent from Romans, the reason being that by the weak brothers in Rome the observance of certain days was not viewed as having anything to do with obtaining salvation. So in Rom. 14:1, 5, 19; 15:1, 7 the apostle expresses himself in a very gentle and subdued manner.

c. Romans and Colossians

There are also similarities and differences between Rom. 14:1-15:13 and *Colossians*. In Col. 2:16, 17 Paul writes, "Therefore allow no one to pass judgment on y o u by what y o u eat or drink, or with respect to a (religious) festival or a New Moon celebration or a sabbath day." And in 2:20, 21 he asks, "If with Christ y o u died to the rudiments [or: basic principles] of the world, why, as though y o u were still living in the world [or: as though y o u still belonged to the world], do y o u submit to its regulations 'Do not handle! Do not taste! Do not touch!' "?

It is clear that here, in Colossians, Paul again sharply rebukes those whom he addresses, the reason now being that these people were giving heed to false teachers who were telling them, "Faith in Christ will not give y o u fulness of knowledge, wisdom, power, salvation. Therefore y o u must follow our rules concerning days and diets." At bottom this was an attack on the supremacy and all-sufficiency of Christ, "in whom all the fulness of the godhead dwells bodily" (Col. 2:9).

As has been indicated, the treatment of the same general theme—days and diets—in *Romans* differs sharply, since the *weak* ones addressed in this epistle did not attach any saving significance to their eating, drinking, and abstaining, and to their observance of certain special days.

1. Him who is weak in faith accept, but not with the idea of passing judgment on (his) opinions.[372]

---

372. προσλαμβάνεσθε (14:1 and 15:7), 2nd per. pl. pres. mid. imperat. of προσλαμβάνω, to take to oneself; hence, to accept, welcome. Note the third per. s. aor. mid. indicat. of the same verb in 14:3 and again in 15:7.

διακρίσεις, nom. and acc. pl. (here acc. after εἰς) of διάκρισις, a distinguishing or judging. Cf. I Cor. 12:10 (ability to distinguish or judge between).

διαλογισμῶν, gen. pl. (here objective gen.) of διαλογισμός, opinion, thought, reasoning. On this word (s. and pl.) see also N.T.C. on Mark, pp. 282-286. In nearly every instance the deliberations or reasonings are of a sinful nature. See the following passages: Matt. 15:19; Mark 7:21; Luke 5:22; 6:8; 9:46, 47; 24:38; Rom. 1:21; I Cor. 3:20; Phil. 2:14; I Tim. 2:8; James 2:4.

Paul is telling the members of the Roman church, whom he regards as being "strong"—he evidently is thinking of the majority—that they must not commit the moral error of passing judgment upon those who are "weak" in faith, must not condemn them for refusing to eat any meat.

The "weak" members probably reasoned as follows: "In this pagan city how do we know whether any meat at all is really 'clean'? How do we know whether the animal from which it came was actually a 'clean' one? How do we know whether it was slaughtered in the prescribed manner? And how do we know whether it was not first of all offered to idols?"

The apostle reasoned that as long as the vegetarianism of these people did not result from the conviction, "By becoming vegetarians we are putting God in debt to ourselves," they must be viewed as believers, brothers and sisters in Christ. They must be fully "accepted," that is, not only should they be formally recognized as members in good and regular standing of the church but they must also be heartily welcomed into daily fellowship with all other believers. From every aspect the welcome extended to them must be warm and genuine. The very suggestion of "accepting" (?) them with the purpose of adversely criticizing them for their "opinions" (or "scruples") must not even occur to anyone.

2, 3. One person believes he may eat anything, but another, being weak, eats (only) vegetables. Let not him who eats look down on him who does not, and let not him who does not eat judge him who does, for God has accepted him.

One person, namely, the strong, is convinced that there is no valid restriction on the kinds of food he may eat and enjoy. Another person, being weak—for explanation of "strong" and "weak" see p. 453—eats only vegetables. The strong one, or eater, should not look down with contempt on the weak one, or abstainer.

Nevertheless, this is exactly what the strong one would be inclined to do. As was explained earlier (p. 452) the strong ones or eaters were mostly converts from the world of the Gentiles, and in the church of Rome constituted the majority (pp. 21-23). "Why bother with those few vegetarians?" might well be their contemptuous outcry—the Jerusalem Council had been far more conciliatory (Acts 15:20).

The weak or abstainers, on the other hand, might be tempted to derive satisfaction from the very fact that they were in the minority—is not *one* on God's side a majority?—and might therefore begin to pass judgment on the eaters.

The apostle condemns both attitudes, that of *contempt* and that of *condemnation*. Though he desires that the rights of the weak shall be fully respected and that the vegetarian shall be treated with sympathetic regard and genuine deference, he is no less insistent on demanding that the weak refrain from condemning the strong, the eater, stating as his reason "for God has accepted him." It should be clear that in the present context the pronoun "him" can refer only to the eater, the strong one.[373] This view receives further confirmation from the next verse:

4. Who are you that you dare pass judgment on someone else's servant? To his own master he stands or falls.

The form of the question reminds us of 9:20, "But who are you, O man, to talk back to God?" What Paul is saying is that the eater or strong one is answerable only to "his own master," namely, the Lord Jesus Christ; just as, by way of illustration, a servant or slave would be answerable only to his own master. The eater is certainly not obliged to give an account to the abstainer. The latter has no right to condemn him. Paul continues: **And he will stand, for the Lord is able to make him stand.**

It should be borne in mind that the "eater" or "strong one" is the person who has, by God's sovereign grace and the enlightening power of the Holy Spirit, gained an insight into the meaning of Christ's death for daily living. Better than the "weak" person or "abstainer" he has grasped the truth expressed so beautifully in Col. 2:14, namely, that Christ "blotted out the handwritten document that was against us, which by means of its requirements testified against us, and he took it out of the way by nailing it to the cross."

The question, then, is this, "When a person, by the grace of God, has taken this lesson to heart, will he surrender this precious jewel?" To be sure, he cannot remain standing in his own power. But he has a Savior who said, "My sheep listen to my voice, and I know them, and they follow me, and I give them everlasting life, and they shall certainly never perish, and no one shall snatch them out of my hand" (John 10:27, 28). Or, as Paul expresses the same truth here in Rom. 14:4, "And he will stand, for the Lord is able to make him stand." The further question, namely, whether the term "the Lord" refers, in the present instance, to Christ, or to God, is academic. A good answer might well be, "It refers to Christ, and therefore to God."

In the introduction to this chapter—see above, p. 453—we took note of the fact that in addition to a difference of opinion, between the strong and the weak, with respect to *eating*, there was also a difference with respect to the observance of *special days*. Turning now to this subject Paul says:

5. One person regards one day as being better than another; another regards every day as being good.[374]

What was the day which "one person," that is, this or that convert to Christianity, regarded as more sacred than another day? According to some

---

373. For the opposite view see Käsemann, *op. cit.*, p. 369. Unless there is a good reason to do otherwise, the pronoun (here αὐτόν) should be interpreted as referring to its nearest antecedent, which in the present case is τὸν ἐσθίοντα.
374. Though textual support for the conjunction γάρ at the beginning of this sentence, so that it would read ὃς μὲν γὰρ κρίνει, etc., is rather strong, the context makes clear that if this γάρ is authentic it cannot very well be interpreted as indicating cause but must be viewed as continuative. Whether it is regarded as continuative or as unauthentic, in either case it can be omitted in translation.

it must have been the seventh day of the week, the Jewish sabbath.[375] Even though such an individual would join with the other members of the church in worship on the first day of the week (cf. Acts 20:7), he would close shop and cease to work on Saturday. Other commentators, however, call attention to the fact that the law of Moses not only distinguished between meats as being either clean or unclean, but also prescribed the observance of certain specific days as religious festivals. So, these people would continue to adhere to the Mosaic legislation on this point.[376] Again, since the very subject of *foods*, to which Paul made reference in verses 2-4, brings up that of *fasting*, it has been suggested that the apostle is here referring to days of fasting, after the manner indicated in Luke 18:12.[377]

On the other hand, the idea that in the present context Paul was distinguishing between *lucky* and *unlucky* days[378] must be rejected. If that had been the case Paul would certainly have condemned such a practice in no uncertain terms. He would not have written, **Let each one be fully convinced in his own mind.**[379]

Also, since the New Testament does indeed ascribe very special significance to the first day of the week (Matt. 28:1; Mark 16:2, 9; Luke 24:1; John 20:1, 19; Acts 20:7; I Cor. 16:2; Rev. 1:10), it is indeed very doubtful that the apostle would have expressed himself in such moderate terms if the "weak" members of Rome's church had been indifferent about setting this day apart from all the others (as far as practical in those days) as a day of rest and worship.

We must admit that we cannot now determine in what sense the weak members of the Roman church regarded one day as being better than another, while they still observed and honored the Lord's Day, that is, the first day of the week. That this ignorance on our part is not very serious is shown by the fact that, after verses 5, 6, in this entire epistle the apostle never again refers to this difference about *days*. He does insist, however, that "each one be fully convinced in his own mind" that what he is doing is right. No one must do what is contrary to the dictates of his own conscience as illumined by the Word! Let not the weak condemn the strong; but also, let not the strong look down on the weak; for:

6. He who regards one day as being special, does so in honor of the Lord; and he who eats does so in honor of the Lord, since he gives thanks to God. And he who abstains does so in honor of the Lord and gives thanks to God.

As a comparison with verse 5 shows, "He who regards one day as being special" is the weak person. Now Paul states that the person who makes this

---

375. So, for example, Lenski, on this passage.
376. C. Hodge, *op. cit.*, pp. 660, 661.
377. See Ridderbos, *op. cit.*, p. 306.
378. A view favored by Käsemann, *op. cit.*, p. 370.
379. I fully agree, accordingly, with Cranfield (*op. cit.*, p. 705) on this point.

distinction between days, a distinction which strong persons would not make, must not be looked down upon for doing so, for he does so with the purpose of honoring the Lord.[380] Similarly, the one who eats, paying no attention to the Mosaic distinction between clean and unclean, cannot be accused of being indifferent to the will of God. On the contrary, he too honors the Lord by doing what he does. Both the weak and the strong, in this matter of indifference, are honoring the Lord; the weak, by giving thanks to him for their vegetarian meal; the strong, by giving thanks for their meat, etc.

7-9. For none of us lives to himself alone, and none of us dies to himself alone. If we live, we live to the Lord; and if we die, we die to the Lord. So then, whether we live or whether we die, we are the Lord's. For to this end Christ died and lived, that he might be Lord of both the dead and the living.

Note the following:

a. "For none of us lives to himself alone," etc.

The fact that "we," both kinds of Christians, the strong and the weak, behave as we do, is because none of us lives a self-centered life. On the contrary, while still alive on earth we live for the Lord Jesus Christ. Cf. Phil. 1:21. Our basic aim is to please him. When we die we strive, even by means of our dying, to glorify the Lord.

b. "So then . . . we are the Lord's."

It is, after all, this Lord whose servants we are, and to whom we belong. Did he not purchase us with his precious blood? (I Cor. 6:20).

c. "For to this end Christ died and lived . . ."

Not here "lived and died" (Phillips), as if "lived" referred to Christ's life on earth before his death by crucifixion, but "died and lived." He died, and afterward, having risen from the dead, he went to live in heaven. Note the parallel:

	Christ *died* and *lived*
that he might be Lord of both	the *dead* and *the living*.

As our Mediator, Christ secured the indisputable right to exercise lordship over both those believers who have already died and those who are still alive on earth. This mediatorial lordship was the reward for the price he paid, the death he died. By means of his substitutionary death, followed by his intercessory life in heaven (Heb. 7:25), he sees to it that whatever he has merited for us, his children, is bestowed on us. Cf. II Cor. 4:10, "We always carry around in our body the *death* of Jesus, so that the *life* of Jesus may be revealed in our bodies." Cf. Rom. 6:4; Phil. 3:10.[381]

---

380. Literally "to the Lord." Such a *dative* can be viewed as one *of advantage*.

381. First of all see above, p. 221, footnote 192. The textual tradition of Rom. 14:9 is by no means uniform, but ἀπέθανεν καὶ ἔζησεν has the strongest support. Someone has tried to change the text by substituting ἀνέστη for ἔζησεν. There is also a variant that substitutes ἀνέζησεν for ἔζησεν, and there are variants that have all three verbs. Sometimes the sequence in which ἀπέθανεν and ἔζησεν follow each other has been reversed. The logic of the passage favors the already indicated parallel: *died* and *lived* followed by *the dead* and *the living*. It is

10-12. But you, why do you pass judgment on your brother? Or why do you look down on your brother? For we shall all stand before the judgment seat of God. For it is written,
" 'As surely as I live,' says the Lord,
'Before me will every knee bow down,
And every tongue will acclaim God.' "
So then each of us will give an account of himself to God.

In verse 3 Paul had warned the strong not to look down on the weak, and the weak not to condemn the strong. That this was nevertheless actually occurring and is an inexcusable sin he makes clear in verse 10, where, in reverse order (now referring to the weak first of all) the apostle accusingly asks why one church member is sinning against another. These critics should bear in mind that the one whom they condemn or despise is, after all, *a brother*. Note how this term of endearment, which has not been used since 12:1, indicates the seriousness of the sin that was being committed. See further on pp. 52, 214, 215.

Also, those who are passing judgment, or are looking down on a brother, must remember that not they are lords, but Christ is the Lord; and accordingly, that not they are the legitimate judges, but Christ is the Judge. They are therefore arrogating to themselves a prerogative that belongs to Christ and to God alone.

Says Paul, "We shall all stand before the judgment seat of God." In confirmation of this fact he quotes from the Old Testament. As happens frequently, so also here, the quotation is composite: the first part, " 'As surely as I live,' says the Lord," may be regarded as taken from Isa. 49:18 (cf. Num. 14:28; Deut. 32:40; Ezek. 33:11); the rest of the quotation, "Before me will every knee bow down, and every tongue will acclaim God," is from Isa. 45:23, according to the LXX text, with transposition of two words,[382] but without change in meaning.

The quoted words do indeed confirm the thought Paul has expressed, namely, that in the end every person, without exception, will pay homage to God (cf. Phil. 2:10, 11), recognizing him as Sovereign over all, and acclaiming him as being the righteous Judge of all.

That there will indeed be a universal judgment is the teaching of Scripture (Eccl. 12:14; Eph. 6:8; Rev. 20:11-15). That believers as well as unbelievers will stand before the throne of judgment is also clear from Acts 10:42; I Cor. 3:8-15; 4:5; II Cor. 5:10, and from the teaching of Jesus (Matt. 16:27; 25:31-46). That it is, indeed, God who through Christ will judge is taught in Matt. 16:27; 25:31-46; John 5:22; Acts 10:42; I Cor. 4:5; II Cor. 5:10. It

---

clear, of course, that the words "Christ lived" imply his resurrection. The possibility that ἔζησεν is an ingressive aorist, and means "became alive" or "began to live" must be granted. But the obvious parallel noted above seems to require "died and lived." It is because of Christ's death and because of his life in heaven that God's children are living to the glory of God.

382. LXX: ἐξομολογήσεται πᾶσα γλῶσσα; Paul: πᾶσα γλῶσσα ἐξομολογήσεται.

is as stated in Rom. 2:16 (see pp. 98, 99), "God, through Jesus Christ, will judge men's secrets."

Repeating the thought of verse 10 ("For we shall all stand before the judgment seat of God"), Paul concludes his reflection on this theme by stating, "So then each of us will give an account of himself to God." Note: *each* of us! Not a single one will be exempted. Also, the account will have to be given not to men but to *God*, the *Omniscient*, the *Holy* and *Righteous* One, who is also the God of *Love*.

Summarizing the main idea of verses 10-12—and in a sense even of 1-12 (see especially verses 1, 3, 4, 10-12)—Paul, addressing both the strong and the weak (note: "on one another"), but probably especially *the strong*, and drawing a conclusion, continues with the following exhortation:

13. Therefore let us stop passing judgment on one another; but rather, let this be y o u r judgment, namely, that y o u should not put any stumbling block or obstacle in y o u r brother's way.

Note the word-play: *passing judgment* . . . y o u r *judgment* or decision.[383]

Paul urges the weak to stop criticizing the strong, and the strong to cease finding fault with the weak. Both parties should decide not to place any hindrance in the way of their brothers. On the contrary—for the negative implies the positive—each group should help the other to become a more effective witness for Christ.[384]

In view of the fact that both parties love the Lord, repose their trust in him, and wish to walk in his way, it would be wrong to hurt one another's feelings by insisting that there be absolute unanimity with respect to every aspect of the practice of religion.

If, on a Sunday evening, perhaps after the church service, you invite six people to your home, but you happen to know that three of them have objections to the singing of a certain hymn, then, even though the other three plus yourself consider that hymn unobjectionable, you are not going to include that particular number in your evening social program. Instead, you are going to see to it that everybody receives a blessing and is happy. The same principle should be applied to ever so many similar situations. If an important religious principle is at stake, you are not going to be silent

---

383. Greek μηκέτι . . . κρίνωμεν, Let us pass judgment no more. ἀλλὰ τοῦτο κρίνατε, but decide this.

384. πρόσκομμα, in addition to its occurrence here in Rom. 14:13, is found also in Rom. 9:32, 33; 14:20; I Cor. 8:9; and I Peter 2:8. Meaning: (a) *literal*, a rock or other hard object against which a person may strike his foot, causing him to stumble or even to fall; (b) *figurative*, an occasion to take offense, an obstacle to the development of spiritual life or happiness, an incentive to sin.

σκάνδαλον, also in Matt. 13:41; 16:23; 18:7; Luke 17:1; Rom. 9:33; 11:9; 16:17; I Cor. 1:23; Gal. 5:11; I Peter 2:8; I John 2:10; Rev. 2:14.

Meaning: (a) *literal*, the bait-stick in a trap or snare; (b) *figurative* (about the same as πρόσκομμα), obstacle, that which causes opposition, resentment, offense, sin. On πρόσκομμα and σκάνδαλον see also G. Stählin, Th.D.N.T., respectively, Vol. VI, pp. 756, 757, and Vol. VII, pp. 352-358.

about your convictions, but in all circumstances you will observe the rule: "In things essential unity; in doubtful (or indifferent) liberty; in all things charity" (identity of the author of this motto not entirely certain). See also what has been said about Paul's flexibility (pp. 12, 13).

The substance of this exhortation is certainly entirely in line with, and may even have been induced by, the teaching of Christ (Matt. 18:1-9; Mark 9:42-48; Luke 17:1, 2).

14. I know and am convinced in the Lord Jesus that nothing is unclean in itself ...

Paul's language is very emphatic.[385] His conviction is firm, deep, and unshakable Cf. Gal. 5:10; Phil. 2:24; II Thess. 3:4; II Tim. 1:5, 12. It amounts to a persuasion that is based not only on the teaching of Jesus but also on the apostle's spiritual closeness to his Lord and Savior. For the teaching of Jesus on this subject see Matt. 15:10, 11, 16-20; Mark 7:14-23. For Paul's similar teaching see also I Tim. 4:4 "Everything God created is excellent, and nothing is to be rejected if it is received with thanksgiving." Add Titus 1:15, "All things are pure to those who are pure."

Accordingly, the impurity pertains not to the food as such but to the person who questions whether or not he should eat it: **but if anyone considers something to be unclean, then for him it is unclean.** This does not mean that sin is wholly a matter of subjective opinion or of conscience. No, there are indeed many things that are definitely forbidden. No mere opinion on man's part, or even the silence of conscience, can make right what God has declared to be wrong. But it does mean that even a human activity—in the present case eating meat a person considers to be unclean— is wrong for those who consider it to be wrong.

By expressing himself as he does the apostle accomplishes two things: (a) He encourages the strong by clearly showing that he takes their side; see verse 14a; (b) he helps the weak by reminding the strong that the weak are right in refusing to eat that which *they* (the weak) consider to be unclean (verse 14b). Should not this consummate, exquisite tact be a lesson for everyone; especially also for every pastor? What a loving heart, this heart of Paul, and how wise a disposition! No wonder that he continues as follows:

15. For if your brother is seriously upset because of what you eat, you are no longer walking in love.

The word "For" shows that the clause it introduces links with verse 13b rather than with verse 14. (Verse 14 can best be regarded as a parenthesis.) So what Paul is saying is really, "... Do not put a stumbling block or obstacle in your brother's way, for if your brother is seriously upset,[386] you are no

---

385. πέπεισμαι, 1st perf. pass. indicat. of πείθω, to persuade. To add strength to the expression this verb is even preceded by οἶδα.

386. λυπεῖται, 3rd. per. s. pres. pass. indicat. of λυπέω, to cause serious grief or distress. This verb occurs also in Matt. 14:9; 17:23; 18:31; 19:22; 26:22, 37; Mark 10:22; 14:19; John 16:20; 21:17; Eph. 4:30; I Thess. 4:13; I Peter 1:6; and frequently in II Cor., beginning with 2:2.

longer walking in love." Paul now uses the 2nd per. sing., you, driving home this urgent lesson, impressing it upon each of the addressed, one by one. He returns to the very subject, *love for one another*, on which he had expatiated with such warmth and eloquence in 12:9, 10; 13:9, 10, and even earlier (I Cor. 13). Love was the theme close to the heart not only of Paul but also of Peter (I Peter 4:8) and of John (I John 4:8); of God (John 3:16) and of Christ (I John 3:16)!

Paul continues: **Do not by your eating destroy your brother for whom Christ died.** The apostle is, as it were, saying, "Consider what you are doing! So dear is that brother of yours to Christ that he died for him. Nevertheless, you, by means of your unbrotherly conduct, are treating him in a manner which, were it not for God's irresistible grace, would destroy him. Immediately stop doing what you are doing, and do the very opposite!"

16. Therefore do not allow that which for you is a good thing to become an occasion for slanderous talk.

Paul realizes that if in the presence of the weak a strong individual eats that which by the weak is considered "unclean," he will be hurting that weak person. This would be even more true if, due to the insistence of the strong, the weak fellow-Christian would finally surrender and do what his conscience forbids him to do. Moreover, open quarrels between the two groups would certainly result in slanderous talk on the part of outsiders.

So the apostle warns the strong that they should not allow that which for them is "a good thing" to become an occasion of slanderous talk. But what is meant by "a good thing"? Opinions differ widely, as the footnote shows.[387]

What, then, does Paul mean when he, addressing the strong, says, "that which for you is a good thing"? In view of the immediately preceding con-

---

387. See General Bibliography.
The references are to the *commentaries* written by the following:

Commentator	Theory
	1
Calvin, p. 506	
Harrison, p. 148	
Käsemann, p. 376	Christian liberty: freedom from
Murray, p. 193	ceremonial observance
Sanday and Headlam, p. 391	
Van Leeuwen & Jacobs, p. 263	2
	the kingdom (or kingship) of God
Greijdanus (*Kommentaar*), Vol. II, p. 605	3
Lekkerkerker, Vol. II, p. 165	
(mentions both salvation and	
evangelical freedom)	
Lenski, p. 839 (the whole Christian faith,	salvation
our whole salvation, the gospel)	
Luther, *Works*, Vol. 25, p. 504	
Ridderbos, p. 312	
Cranfield, Vol. II, p. 717	4
Hodge, pp. 667, 668	the gospel

text, the natural answer might seem to be "your Christian liberty." The possibility that this answer is correct must be granted. Nevertheless, a good argument can be advanced for No. 4, the gospel. *Would an outsider not be more likely to slander the gospel itself than to take sides in this debate between the strong and the weak?* Besides, the apostle certainly regards the gospel as being a very good thing indeed. He uses the term "gospel" about 60 times in his epistles. He is so fond of it that he calls it "*my* gospel" (Rom. 2:16; 16:25), and even tells us that he is willing to put up with anything rather than hinder the gospel of Christ (I Cor. 9:12). What he considers a good thing for himself he must also have considered a good thing for others.

As to answers 2 (the kingdom or kingship of God) and 3 (salvation), if the correct answer is "the gospel," this surely is "the gospel of salvation," and if we look carefully at the meaning of the term "kingdom" or "kingship," as defined by Paul himself in verse 17, namely, "righteousness and peace and joy in the Holy Spirit," we will probably have to conclude that this description makes "kingdom" (or "kingship") of God equivalent to "salvation."

There is merit, therefore, in all four answers, though personally, if a choice must be made, I would still give a slight edge to "the gospel of salvation"; that is, of the realization of the kingship of God in the lives of God's children.

Having said, "Do not by your eating destroy your brother for whom Christ died. Therefore do not allow that which for you is a good thing to become an occasion for slanderous talk," the apostle continues,

17. For the kingdom of God is not eating and drinking but righteousness and peace and joy in the Holy Spirit;

The essence of God's royal reign, the evidence of that blessed reign in your midst, says Paul, as it were, is not affected by the kind of food a person consumes, whether ceremonially clean or unclean, whether only vegetables or also meats, but is attested by one's possession of the state of *righteousness* before God, consciousness of *peace* with God, a peace resulting from reconciliation with God (5:1, 10). It is characterized by the experience of Spirit-wrought *joy*, a joy inexpressible and full of glory (I Peter 1:8).

It is immediately apparent that this answer is in complete accord with the words of Jesus, "The kingdom of God does not come with outward display; nor will people say, 'Look, here (it is)!' or 'There (it is)!' for, note well, *the kingdom of God is within* y o u" (Luke 17:21).[388]

18. for anyone who serves Christ in this way is pleasing to God and respected among men.

Note: "serves Christ *in this way*"; that is (as the preceding verse makes clear), in the consciousness of having been justified by God, having peace with God, and experiencing the joy that was imparted to him by the Holy Spirit.

Such a person is, first of all, "pleasing to God." He is truly living for God, to God's honor and glory. See 14:6-8 and earlier, 6:22.

---

388. See also N.T.C. on Matthew, pp. 249, 250.

ROMANS 14:18-20

Note also the phrase, "and respected[389] among men." Those who say, "I don't care at all what people think of me," may be guilty of an other-worldliness that is not exactly pious. Paul had already written, "Always see to it that y o u r affairs are right in the sight of everybody" (12:17b). Calvin was certainly correct when, commenting on Rom. 14:18, he wrote, "That man is acceptable to God, because he obeys his will; he testifies that he is approved by men, because they cannot do otherwise than bear testimony to that excellence which they see with their eyes; not that the ungodly always favor the children of God; on the contrary, when there is no cause, they often pour forth against them many reproaches . . . but Paul speaks here of honest judgment, blended with no moroseness, no hatred, no superstition."

19. Let us then pursue the things that lead to peace and to mutual edification.[390]

Note the following:

a. *Peace* is a gift which God in Christ imparts to the church (John 14:27; 16:33; 20:19, 21, 26; Rom. 15:33; 16:20; II Cor. 13:11). He is "the God of peace" (Phil. 4:9; I Thess. 5:23; II Thess. 3:16). Therefore genuine peace is "the gift of God" (Phil. 4:7).

This does not mean, however, that we can take this peace for granted. On the contrary, here in 14:19 we are being reminded that it is our duty to "pursue the things that make for peace." This is in line with the thinking of Peter (I Peter 3:11), of the author of the epistle to the Hebrews (12:14), and, much earlier, of the Psalmist (34:14).

b. *Mutual edification.* This expression shows that Paul conceives of the church as being *an edifice.* This implies that it is a united body. However, this edifice or building must not be thought of as being finished. No, it is constantly rising (Eph. 4:16). Even the individual stones are anything but static. If matters are as they should be, the stones are in the process of being made more and more beautiful. Moreover, they are *living* stones! (I Peter 2:5).

The main building material is *love* (Eph. 4:16). This is even more important than *liberty.* "Be careful that the exercise of y o u r liberty does not become a stumbling block to the weak" (I Cor. 8:9). In fact, love is even better than *knowledge.* "Knowledge puffs up, but love builds up" (I Cor. 8:1).

20. Do not tear down the work of God for the sake of food. Everything, indeed, is clean, but it is wrong for a person to eat anything that causes (someone else) to stumble.

---

389. δόχιμος, approved, respected, esteemed. See also Rom. 16:10; I Cor. 11:19; II Cor. 10:18; 13:7; II Tim. 2:15; James 1:12.

390. Though the reading διώκομεν instead of διώκωμεν has strong support, it cannot be accepted. The transition from a conjectural, "We are pursuing the things that lead to peace . . ." (verse 19) to "Do not tear down the work . . ." (verse 20), would be very unnatural and abrupt. Besides, as it is true that didactic style predominates in the earlier part of the book of Romans, so hortatory style can be expected in the latter part. See, for example, 14:13. For the rest the reader's attention is called to footnote 140, p. 168.

We have already taken note of the fact that in verse 16 Paul was addressing the strong. There is no reason to believe that in the immediately following verses—including verse 20—he is directing his words of warning and exhortation to a different group. The first part of the passage causes no difficulty. Paul returns to the second person singular, last used in verse 15. This increases the forcefulness of his admonitions.

Having just a moment ago encouraged the work of *building up*, the apostle now warns against engaging in its very opposite, namely, *tearing down* or *destroying* (cf. Matt. 5:17; 24:2; 26:61; 27:40; II Cor. 5:1; Gal. 2:18). Such tearing down is all the more wicked because it concerns *the work of God* in the heart and life of the weak brother, and doing this for the sake merely of something material, namely, food!

And if someone objects that it is perfectly proper for the strong person to eat whatever he likes to eat, since everything in the line of food is clean, as Paul has himself admitted (14:14; cf. Mark 7:19-23; 1 Tim. 4:4), the answer is, "Everything, indeed, is clean, but it is wrong—or bad, evil—for a person to eat anything that causes (someone else) to stumble."

However, in the original this final clause of verse 20 is compressed into very few words: "but wrong for a person the eating with a stumbling block [or: with offense]."

The question arises, "Does Paul mean that the *strong* person should be on his guard lest by his eating he is giving offense to the weak brother?" Or is he saying, "It is wrong for the *weak* person to eat with a troubled conscience"?[391] For the first alternative see Robertson, *Word Pictures*, Vol. IV, p. 415; and Cranfield, Vol. II, pp. 723, 724. For the second, Murray, Vol. II, p. 195. Of these two, the first, as this interpreter sees it, deserves the preference. Reasons: (a) Not only in the immediately preceding but even in the immediately following context (verse 21) Paul is addressing the strong. It is natural, therefore, to assume that also here in verse 20 he does so. (b) This conclusion brings the present passage into harmony with verse 13b, where Paul admonishes the strong to cease finding fault with the weak. (c) Elsewhere, in a similar context, the apostle declares, "Therefore, if what I eat causes my brother to fall into sin, I will never eat meat again, so that I will not cause him to sin" (I Cor. 8:13).

After having stated what is *wrong*, a statement about what is *right* follows very naturally: **21. It is better**[392] **not to eat meat or drink wine or to do anything else that will cause your brother to stumble.**

It is not the apostle's intention to "lay down the law" with respect to eating and drinking. He is not issuing an order; rather, in a fatherly manner he is

---

391. The original reads, ἀλλὰ κακὸν τῷ ἀνθρώπῳ τῷ διὰ προσκόμματος ἐσθίοντι. Here the phrase διὰ πρ. expresses accompaniment or attendant circumstance.
392. That which is recommended as being "good" or "better" is expressed by means of an infinitive (in the present case articular), which forms the subject of the clause. Cf. I Cor. 7:1, 8, 26; Heb. 13:9.

urging the strong person voluntarily to curtail the use of his freedom, to do this out of regard for his weak brother in Christ. In the presence of that weak person let him forego the privilege of eating meat.[393] The same Paul who in verse 15 was saying, "For if your brother is seriously upset because of what you eat, you are no longer walking in love," is speaking here in verse 21.

There are three things from which, according to verse 21, the strong person is advised to refrain, out of consideration for those who are weak:
a. eating meat
b. drinking wine
c. doing anything else that will cause "your brother" to stumble.[394]

As to (a) refraining from eating meat, this follows naturally from the thought expressed in verses 2, 15, 16, 20.

As to (b), abstaining from wine, without additional information it is probably impossible to determine exactly why Paul adds this. According to some—see Cranfield, Vol. II, p. 725—this does not imply that the weak actually abstained from wine, but is simply mentioned because in verse 17 Paul made reference to eating *and drinking*. On the other hand, Murray's view (Vol. II, p. 195), shared by many other commentators, namely, that drinking wine was involved in the scruples of the weak, impresses me as being preferable. The reason for this abstinence is not given. Is it possible that the weak abstained from the use of wine because wine was used as a libation in animal sacrifices? We just do not know, but see also Dan. 1:8, 16.

As to (c), the apostle "is simply commending to others what has for some time been the rule for himself" (E. F. Harrison, *op. cit.*, p. 149). Cf. I Cor. 8:13.

The apostle was certainly giving excellent and inspired advice when he stated: **22. Whatever you believe (about these things) keep between yourself and God.** Note strong emphasis on the pronoun *you*, in the original occurring at the very beginning of the sentence. It is as if Paul, in his imagination, is listening to a "strong" believer; one, however, who delights in hearing himself talk. That loud talker is saying, "*I insist on my* freedom; and *I* say that *I* will not allow anyone to interfere with that unrestrained freedom of *mine*," etc. So Paul, as it were, answers, "*You* better keep between *yourself* and God that conviction *you* have!" He adds, **Blessed is the person who does not need to condemn himself over what he approves**; meaning, Inwardly happy is that person—namely, that "strong" believer—who *avoids* bringing God's judgment upon himself by insisting on the exercise of his

---

393. Here not the more general βρῶμα (verses 15, 20) or βρῶσις (verse 17), but κρέα, pl. of κρέας, "flesh-meat," as in I Cor. 8:13, the only other occurrence of this word in the New Testament. Cf. pan*crea*s; lit., all flesh.
394. On the assumption that the Nestle-Aland text is correct, something like ἄλλο τι ποιῆσαι (to do anything else) must be supplied in thought.

"liberty" even though such insistence results in harming his "weak" fellow-believer.

Over against the person who does not need to condemn himself stands the one who "has misgivings," and accordingly "is condemned." Says Paul: **23. But the one who has misgivings when he eats is condemned, because (his eating does) not (spring) from faith . . .** The "weak" believer—that is, the person who is not sure that he is doing the right thing but "wavers" (cf. 4:20) when he eats (meat)—stands condemned. This is true because his eating "does not spring from faith," that is, "is not in harmony with an *inner conviction that what he is doing is in line with his Christian faith*."

This person is sinning because he is trying to silence the voice of his conscience. He is convinced that what he is about to do is wrong, yet he does it. Accordingly, he is sinning. Says Paul: **and everything (that does) not (spring) from faith is sin**; that is, whatever thought, word, action, etc. does not spring from the inner conviction that it is in harmony with a person's faith in God; or, stating it differently, whatever action is contradicted by one's Christian conscience, is sin. To be sure, a person's conscience is not the Final Judge of his actions, whether past, present, or contemplated. That Final Judge is God, or, if one prefers, the Word of God. But this does not alter the fact that even for that individual who may not have become fully informed about the will of God as revealed in his Word it is wrong by means of his actions to oppose the voice of his Christian conscience.

15 1 We who are strong ought to bear the failings of the weak and not to please ourselves. 2 Let each of us please his neighbor for (his) good, with a view to (his) edification. 3 For even Christ did not please himself but, as it is written,
"The reproaches of those reproaching thee fell on me."
4. For whatever was written in former times was written for our instruction, in order that, through patient endurance and the encouragement of the Scriptures, we might have hope.

5 May the God (who is the Source) of patient endurance and of encouragement grant y o u to live in harmony with one another, in accord with Christ Jesus, 6 so that with one heart and mouth y o u may glorify the God and Father of our Lord Jesus Christ.

7 Accept one another, then, just as Christ accepted y o u, to the glory of God. 8 For I declare that Christ has become a servant of the circumcised for the sake of God's *truth*, to confirm the promises made to the fathers; 9 but the Gentiles glorify God for the sake of (his) *mercy*; as it is written:
"Therefore I will praise thee among the Gentiles,
and sing hymns to thy name."
10 And again, it says,
"Rejoice, y o u Gentiles, together with his people."
11 And again,
"Praise the Lord, all y o u Gentiles,
let all the peoples praise him."
12 And again, Isaiah says,
"There will spring up the root of Jesse,
he who arises to rule over the Gentiles.
In him shall the Gentiles hope."
13 May the God of hope fill y o u with all joy and peace, in the exercise of (y o u r) faith, so that by the power of the Holy Spirit y o u may overflow with hope.

G. *What Should Be the Attitude of the Justified Believer*
Toward the Weak and the Strong
(continued)
"We who are strong ought to bear the failings of the weak
and not to please ourselves"
15:1-13

The opening of chapter 15 looks like a new beginning. Actually the apostle summarizes what he has been saying about the weak, and indicates what should be the attitude of the strong toward them. But the opening does not stop here. It soon broadens in scope and fixes the attention of the entire congregation—and of all who will subsequently be brought into contact with this letter—on Christ, whose example of self-sacrifice in the interest of others should be followed by weak and strong alike.

1. **We who are strong ought to bear the failings of the weak and not to please ourselves.**

When Paul says, "*We* who are strong," he classes himself with the strong. When he continues, "ought to bear the failings of the weak," he means, "A moral-spiritual obligation rests on us strong ones; namely, not to think only of ourselves but also of the needs of others, in the present case the needs of those who are weak." See I Cor. 10:33.

What Paul is saying here in Rom. 15:1 cannot be far removed from his exhortation found in Gal. 6:2, "Bear one another's burdens, and so fulfill the law of Christ." The expression, "*bear*" the failings, does not merely mean, "tolerate" or "put up with" those failings, or even "bear with" them and "exercise patience" with those who have them. It means, "*We should put our shoulders under* these failings, and meaningfully *help* our weak fellow-believers *to carry* them."[395]

Noblesse oblige! People of high birth should behave *nobly* toward others. This well-known motto, when applied to the present situation, would mean that those highly privileged people who are endowed with clear insight into the liberating significance of the death of Christ for daily living, so that they are correctly called "the strong," are under obligation to deport themselves in a manner that is in keeping with their high privilege. Hence, they should

---

395. The verb βαστάζω—here βαστάζειν, pres. act. infin.—occurs more than 25 times in the New Testament. It is especially common in the Gospels and in Acts. It means: *to carry* (a water-jar, Mark 14:13; Luke 22:10), stretcher (Luke 7:14), stones (John 10:31), money (i.e., carrying it away, stealing it, John 12:6); also *to carry* (a corpse, transferring it from one place to another, John 20:15), a yoke (Acts 15:10), a man, Paul (Acts 21:35), a woman (Rev. 17:7). In Gal. 6:2 and also here in Rom. 15:1 it can best be interpreted in the figurative sense *to bear* or *carry* the burdens, cares or scruples, griefs or failings, of another person or of other persons. For a somewhat different meaning see Gal. 5:10 (*to bear* a person's judgment = to pay the penalty); and Rev. 2:2 (*to tolerate*, put up with). In Matt. 20:12 the sense is: *to endure*; and in John 16:12 and Gal. 6:17, *to bear*.

ἀσθενήματα, pl. of ἀσθένημα, in the New Testament occurring only here, means weakness, failing. In the present context the word refers to the scruples of those whom Paul describes as being "weak." The literal meaning of ἀσθενής is "without strength."

vigorously, generously, and cheerfully help the (in a sense) less privileged persons, the "weak" individuals.

When Paul adds, "We who are strong ought . . . not to please ourselves," he does not mean, "We, the strong, should never do anything to promote our own interests." Pleasing God above all (Rom. 8:8), and, while doing so, also pleasing God's image-bearers, including even ourselves, is the very purpose for which God created and redeemed us (Matt. 22:37-39; Rom. 13:9; I Cor. 10:33; Titus 2:9). *It is the pleasing of ourselves regardless of how this pleasing affects others that is here condemned.*

However, the divine approval does not even necessarily rest upon every attempt to please the neighbor. As Gal. 1:10 indicates, there is an attempt to please the neighbor that is evil. One who, being "nice" with a selfish purpose, trims his sails to every breeze of opinion or bias is acting wickedly. The person who, "with ulterior motive" (cf. 12:8), strives to please others is condemned. A vivid example is that of Absolom:

"Whenever anyone came with a complaint to be placed before the king for a decision, Absalom would call out to him, 'From what town are you?' He would answer, 'Your servant is from this or that tribe of Israel.' Then Absalom would say to him, 'Your claims are valid and proper, but there is no representative of the king to hear you.' And Absalom would continue and say, 'O, if only I were appointed as judge in the land! Then any man with a complaint or a case would come to me, and I would see to it that he gets justice.' "

"Also, whenever anyone approached him to bow down before him, Absalom would reach out his hand, take hold of him and kiss him . . . And so he stole the hearts of the men of Israel" (II Sam. 15:2b-7).

As has now been indicated, it is not only *the deed* but *also*—perhaps even *more* so—*the motive and purpose* that count. It is for this reason that Paul states,

2. Let each of us please his neighbor for (his) good, with a view to (his) edification. In other words, *with a view to the spiritual advantage of that neighbor.*

Now doing good for the benefit of others immediately reminds Paul of Christ (II Cor. 8:9), whose example we should follow. Therefore he continues,

3. For even Christ did not please himself but, as it is written, "The reproaches of those reproaching thee fell on me." Ps. 69:9.

Meaning: Christ is addressing God, and is saying, "For the sake of my people I am taking upon myself the reproaches leveled against thee."

The main lesson Paul is conveying is this: *If Christ, the Holy One, was willing to take upon himself so much suffering, in the form of insults hurled at him by his enemies, then should not we be willing to sacrifice just a little eating-and-drinking pleasure for the sake of our fellow-believers?*

Now for the details:

a. As often—see I Cor. 11:1; II Cor. 8:9; 10:1; Eph. 5:1, 2; Phil. 2:5 f.; Col. 3:13—Paul directs the attention of the addressed to Christ. In doing this, was he not copying Christ? See Matt. 11:29; 16:24; 20:27, 28; Mark 10:42-45; John 13:15. For Christ, as our Example, see also Heb. 3:1; 12:2; I Peter 2:21.

In connection with this subject two extremes should be avoided: (1) that of denying the truth that *first and most of all* Christ is not our Example but *our Savior*; and (2) that of denying that there is a sense in which our Savior Jesus Christ is indeed also our Example. Of course, he cannot be our Example unless he is first of all our Savior!

b. The words "Christ did not please himself" are a remarkable litotes or understatement for his marvelous and wholehearted self-sacrifice in the interest of sinners. See especially Isa. 53; Matt. 20:28; Mark 10:45; II Cor. 8:9; Phil. 2:5 f.

c. When the question is asked, "Why did the apostle refer to the insults or reproaches that were heaped upon Christ by *men* rather than to the far more terrible wrath of *God* which he suffered?" the answer might be that in so doing Paul makes his argument all the more effective, because the insults flung at Christ by *men* were heard, discussed, and remembered, but the wrath of *God* remained unseen.[396]

d. Paul quotes Ps. 69:9b. The words quoted are found in that exact form in LXX Ps. 68:10.

Psalm 69 is one of six Psalms most often referred to in the New Testament, the others being Pss. 2, 22, 89, 110, and 118.[397]

e. According to Ps. 69:9b, interpreted in light of the immediately preceding context, namely verse 9a, it was "zeal" for God's house that consumed the Speaker, namely, Christ, as pictured in this Old Testament passage. The implied lesson is that also the "strong" believers of the new dispensation should be filled with zeal: they should be eager to make sacrifices for the sake not only of their "weak" fellow-believers, but also, and most of all, for God. They should strive to promote his glory.

f. The eyes of those who maintain that Ps. 69:9 simply records the outcry of a devout child of God, and has nothing to do with the Messiah, are covered with a veil (II Cor. 3:14). These people are forgetting two things: first, the unbreakable bond existing between the old and the new dispensation (Luke

---

396. For a different answer, one worthy of serious consideration, see Cranfield, *op. cit.*, Vol. II, pp. 733, 734.

397. Other New Testament quotations from Ps. 69 are as follows:

Psalm 69 Verse(s)	New Testament
4	John 15:25
9a	John 2:17
21	Matt. 27:34, 48; Mark 15:23, 36; Luke 23:36; John 19:28, 29
22, 23	Rom. 11:9, 10
24	Rev. 16:1
25	Acts 1:20
28	Phil. 4:3; Rev. 3:5; 13:8; 17:8; 20:12, 15; 21:27

24:27, 44; John 5:46; I Cor. 10:1-4); and secondly, the indissoluble tie between Christ and his true followers (Acts 9:4; 22:7; 26:14; Col. 1:24).

The propriety of appealing to Scripture, as Paul does frequently and has done just now, is based on the principle embodied in verse

4. For whatever was written in former times was written for our instruction, in order that, through patient endurance and the encouragement of the Scriptures, we might have hope.

A very practical and unforgettable passage! In brief it informs us that if religion is going to mean anything to us we must practice it. Whatever was written in the Scriptures—which for Paul meant what we now call The Old Testament—was written "for our instruction."

As often, so also here, that word "instruction" indicates far more than impartation of *intellectual* knowledge. The emphasis, in fact, is on *practical* knowledge, knowledge that can be, and should be, applied to living the life of a Christian.

Two things are necessary if the sacred writings are going to be of benefit to us:

a. *patient endurance.* Anyone who diligently studies Scripture, asking God to apply its teachings to his heart and life, will be hurt by it again and again, for he will become more and more conscious of the fact that the distance between his own conduct and the ideal held before him in Holy Writ is great indeed. Nevertheless, he must pray for *strength to persist* in this study, learning more and more how to apply it to his life.

b. *the encouragement of the Scriptures.* Those who by God's grace and power persist in such a practical study will discover that these sacred writings, written in former times, not only hurt but also heal. In fact, they are filled with *encouraging* promises, which, when accepted by God-given faith, result in the birth and growth, within men's hearts, of firmly rooted Christian *hope*. See on verse 12.

What Paul is saying therefore is that the way in which Scripture will become a blessing for ourselves and through us also for others, is to put it into practice.

In a thrilling conclusion to his book[398] Col. E. W. Starling emphasizes that for the sake of the welfare of ourselves and of our nation we must begin to take to heart that *Christianity is* not just a theory to be believed but *a living force*.

5, 6. May the God (who is the Source) of patient endurance and of encouragement grant y o u to live in harmony with one another, in accord with Christ Jesus, so that with one heart and mouth y o u may glorify the God and Father of our Lord Jesus Christ.

---

398. *Starling of the White House*, Chicago, p. 327.

In the present passage the two concepts "patient endurance" and "encouragement" are taken up again from verse 4. The apostle, addressing the membership of the Roman church and all others who then or later would be made acquainted with the contents of this epistle, utters the solemn prayer-wish that, through the practical and devotional use of the Scriptures, the addressed, being made the recipients of the aforementioned two precious blessings, may reach the goal of living in harmony with one another. Cf. 12:16.

He adds a phrase about which there has been much controversy, but which can probably best be rendered "in accord with Christ Jesus." Just what does he mean by this?

Some interpret the little phrase to mean "in accord with *the will* of Christ Jesus."[399] Others, "in accord with *the pattern or example* of Christ Jesus."[400] If a choice has to be made between these two my preference would be for the latter, since the context twice refers to Christ as the believers' example (verses 3 and 7). However, is it not possible that "in accord with Christ Jesus"[401] is broad enough to comprise both ideas? Does it not mean, "in accord with that which Christ Jesus has revealed concerning himself both by precept and example"? To the present interpreter it would seem that Murray is correct when he states that what is after Christ's example must always accord with his will.[402]

Accordingly Paul is expressing the prayer-wish that true believers everywhere and of every variety, whether "strong" or "weak," may strive to reach the goal of living in harmony with one another and thus also with the example and will of Christ Jesus.

It is not necessary that Christians think exactly alike on every subject. But it is necessary that in the lives of all God's children the love of Christ Jesus be reflected and his will be done. Thus all will become truly united into one holy and powerful fellowship, one *body*. Cf. Eph. 4:1-6. Thus, and thus alone, the stated purpose will be realized, namely, that "with one heart and mouth (cf. Acts 1:14; 2:46) y o u may glorify the God and Father of our Lord Jesus Christ." On glorifying God see also Ps. 150; John 17:1; Rom. 11:36; I Cor. 10:31.

The expression "The God and Father of our Lord Jesus Christ" (cf. II Cor. 1:3; 11:31; Eph. 1:3; I Peter 1:3) should present no difficulty. The title "*God* of our Lord Jesus Christ" places the emphasis on Christ's *human* nature, and "*Father* of our Lord Jesus Christ" calls attention to the Son's *divine* nature, for not nativistic but trinitarian sonship is referred to here, a kind of sonship in which Christ, by whatever name he is called, is placed on a par with the

---

399. Cranfield, p. 737; Michaelis, Th.D.N.T., Vol. I, p. 669; Käsemann, p. 383.
400. Harrison, p. 152; Greijdanus, Vol. II, p. 621; Ridderbos, p. 322.
401. Original κατὰ Χριστὸν Ἰησοῦν.
402. Vol. II, p. 201.

Father and the Spirit. For more about this see pp. 253, 254 on 8:9-11; and
p. 315 on 9:5. See also Matt. 27:46 (=Mark 15:34) and John 20:17.

If we should stop at this point, we still would not have done justice to the
wonderful prayer-wish found in verses 5 and 6. To catch the true meaning
of the passage it should be brought into relationship with the person of Paul,
the apostle; that is, with his actual situation at the time he dictated this
epistle.

As was shown earlier (pp. 14, 15), when Paul composed Romans he was
working in Corinth. He was by no means living on Easy Street in that city;
not now (Acts 20:3), nor earlier. For the earlier situation in Corinth see Acts
18:6, 12; cf. I Cor. 1:11 f.; 2:3; 3:1; 5:1 f.; 10:14; 11:20 f. Besides, even
before composing Romans the apostle had experienced a series of afflictions
(see pp. 11, 12) so sharp and bitter that we may well ask whether under
comparable circumstances many a present-day pastor would not have sent
in his letter of resignation.

Nevertheless, so firmly fixed is Paul's resolution to continue, come what
may, that he even rejoices in the Lord, and here in Rom. 15:5, 6 speaks of
God as the source of the believers' "patient endurance and encouragement."
Moreover, when he thinks of the Savior his enthusiasm knows no bounds,
so that his language builds up to the striking climax: "Christ" (15:3), "Christ
Jesus" (verse 5), "our Lord Jesus Christ" (verse 6). What a marvelous Christian leader, this man Paul! Rather, what a marvelous God, this Source of
patient endurance and of encouragement, this God and Father of our Lord
Jesus Christ!

**7. Accept one another, then, just as Christ accepted y o u, to the glory
of God.**

In connection with this passage the question has been asked, "Does 'to the
glory of God' modify 'Christ accepted y o u,' or does it go with 'Accept one
another'?" The right answer is probably, "In a sense it modifies both." What
Paul is saying amounts to this, "Just as Christ accepted y o u in order that
by means of that acceptance God might be glorified—for he certainly is
glorified by the hearts and lives of the accepted ones—so, and with the same
ultimate purpose in mind, y o u should accept one another."

The high ideal expressed in verses 5 and 6, namely, to live in harmony
with one another and with heart and mouth to glorify God, here (in verse 7)
becomes the basis for the exhortation that the addressed should accept one
another. See what has been said with respect to this acceptance in connection
with 14:1 (including footnote 372). However, here (15:7) the *reciprocal* character of this acceptance is stressed. Not only should the strong accept the
weak (as in 14:1), but the weak must also welcome the strong.

Before leaving this passage it should be pointed out that between (a)
Christ's deed of accepting sinners, transforming them into beloved sons and
daughters, and (b) the believers' acceptance of one another there is an almost
infinite qualitative difference. For Christ to be able to accept sinners meant
nothing less than leaving the glories of heaven, entering into the miseries of

earth, and undergoing a death so agonizing that words are lacking to describe it. For saved sinners to accept one another implies no such sacrifice. Hymn writers have given expression to the contrast between the divine sacrifice and human sacrifices; see especially Frances Havergal's "I Gave My Life for Thee" and Isaac Watts' "When I Survey the Wondrous Cross." And as for the ultimate purpose of all human activity that is acceptable to God see Fanny Crosby's "To God Be the Glory."

The duty of Jew and Gentile to live in harmony with each other to God's glory is re-emphasized in verses:

8, 9a. For I declare that Christ has become a servant of the circumcised for the sake of God's *truth*, **to confirm the promises made to the fathers; but the Gentiles glorify God for the sake of (his)** *mercy* . . .

Verses 8, 9a indicate that not only for the Jews (lit. "for the circumcision"; cf. 3:30; 4:12; Gal. 2:7-9; and see footnote 119 on p. 149) but also for the Gentiles Christ has become and continues to be a "servant." Cf. Isa. 42:1. It was to the Jews that, during his public ministry, Jesus turned his attention first of all (Matt. 10:5, 6; 15:24; John 1:11). To them he *ministered*; i.e., rendered humble, personal service (Matt. 20:28; Mark 10:45; Luke 22:27).

He did this in order *to confirm God's truth*, his reliability, his *faithfulness* to the covenant promise, the promise made to Abraham (Gen. 12:1-3; 15:1; 17:7; 18:19; 22:18), Isaac (Gen. 26:1 f.), Jacob (Gen. 28:13-15; 32:28; 46:2-4), and Israel as a people (Exod. 20:1; 24:8). Christ *confirmed* the promise by again and again causing it to be realized in hearts and lives. Note the plural, "promises," indicating *the various affirmations* of the one central promise.

However, not only Jews but also Gentiles were blessed by the work of Christ, for from the very start it was the divine intention to gather his elect also from the latter. See Rom. 4:9 f., pp. 149-152; and 9:23 f., pp. 330.

Therefore, though, strictly speaking, God originally established his covenant with Abraham, Isaac, Jacob, the people of Israel, all of them Jews, nevertheless his *mercy* extended also to the Gentiles; in fact, "to the ends of the earth" (Isa. 45:22; 52:10), to all its "families" (Gen. 12:3).

> For the love of God is broader
> Than the measure of man's mind;
> And the heart of the Eternal
> Is most wonderfully kind.
> —from *There's a Wideness in God's Mercy* by F. W. Faber

So, in connection with the work of Christ for *Israel* it is especially God's *truth, his covenant faithfulness*, that stands out; and in connection with his work among *the Gentiles* it is predominantly his comprehensive, condescending *mercy* that shines forth.

It has been suggested that the reason Paul makes this distinction between Israel and the Gentiles is that he is still thinking about "the weak" versus "the strong," the former being mostly Jews, the latter mostly Gentiles. That suggestion may well be correct. But was there not, perhaps, a more basic reason for the distinction Paul draws? *To be sure, no one is saved except through God-imparted, personal faith in the Lord Jesus Christ!* (John 3:16; 14:6; Acts 4:12). But the *approach* to one group differs from that to the other. The distinction clearly spelled out here in Rom. 15:8, 9a must not be ignored.[403] Contrast Peter's *covenant-promise* appeal, as recorded in Acts 2:38, 39, with Paul's appeal to *the kindness or mercy of God* as described in Acts 14:17 and 17:24, 25. Both Peter and Paul were right in speaking as they did, but Peter was addressing a predominantly Jewish audience, while Paul, both at Lystra and in Athens, was speaking to Gentiles.

Before conversion has occurred the initial approach to Jews differs from that to Gentiles, though Acts 4:12 holds for both. But when Jews and Gentiles have become believers, they are *one* people, as Paul clearly teaches (Rom. 10:11, 12) symbolized by *one* olive tree (11:17 f.).

In view of Christ's mediatorial work, there is now *one* body of believers. The cementing of this unity (see verses 5-7) was one of the chief goals of this missionary to the Gentiles. See p. 23. Through the work of Paul and others God saw to it that also the Gentiles would be *glorifying* God, as 15:9b-12 is about to show.[404]

9b-12. as it is written:
"Therefore I will praise thee among the Gentiles,
and sing hymns to thy name."
    And again, it says,
"Rejoice. y o u Gentiles, together with his people."
    And again,
"Praise the Lord, all y o u Gentiles
let all the peoples praise him."
    And again, Isaiah says,
"There will spring up the root of Jesse,
he who arises to rule over the Gentiles.
In him shall the Gentiles hope."[405]

---

403. For more on this see my little book *The Covenant of Grace*, especially pp. 9-11; 39-76.

404. It is probably best to regard both Χριστὸν . . . πατέρων and τὰ δὲ ἔθνη . . . θεόν as being directly dependent upon λέγω. So construed note contrasting parallels:

Jews	Gentiles
truth	mercy

405. *Details respecting the Greek text:*

Verse 9b
This is taken from what is Ps. 18:49 in our English Bible. In the Hebrew Bible it is found in Ps. 18:50; and in the LXX in Ps. 17:50. Paul's text here in Rom. 15:9b is in complete accord with the masoretic text. The LXX text adds the word κύριε (O Lord) after ἔθνεσιν (Gentiles, nations). See also II Sam. 22:50.

Verse 10
This is an exact quotation of the LXX version of (part of) Deut. 32:43.

Verse 11
This reflects what is Ps. 117:1 in our English Bible; LXX Ps. 116:1.

LXX (translated into English):	*Paul (word for word):*
Praise the Lord, all y o u Gentiles	Praise, all y o u Gentiles, the Lord
Praise him, all y o u peoples.	And let praise him, all the peoples.

Again, as so often, Paul appeals to Scripture for corroboration of what he has just now said (see verses 8, 9a). He quotes four very appropriate passages. The first and third are from the book of Psalms; the second is from the Law; the fourth, from the Prophets, so that the three main divisions of the Old Testament are all represented here. Note "as it is written"; also "And again *it* says," where "it" means Scripture.

The four quotations are not selected at random, but form a striking climax.[406]

In the first quotation (verse 9b; cf. Ps. 18:49) the Psalmist states that *he* will declare God's name among the Gentiles. In the second (verse 10; cf. part of Deut. 32:43) *the Gentiles are summoned to join* in praising God. In the third (verse 11; cf. Ps. 117:1) the Gentiles are called upon *independently* to praise God. And in the fourth (verse 12; cf. Isa. 11:10) the attention is fixed upon the (Shoot springing up from the) Root of Jesse, who will rule over the Gentiles, and in whom they will *hope*. He is the One apart from whom the promises made to the fathers (verse 8) would remain unfulfilled, and without whom the Gentiles (verse 9a) would never be able to glorify God.

With Paul "hope" is *justifiable expectation*. It is *the solid foundation for future bliss*. It is the mainspring of the believers' courage and stick-to-it-ive-ness. Not only for the writer of the letter to the Hebrews but certainly also for Paul Christian hope is "an anchor for the soul, firm and secure, and entering into the inner sanctuary . . . where Jesus is" (Heb. 6:19, 20). This very Jesus is the One apart from whom the promises made to the fathers (Rom. 15:8) would remain unfulfilled, and without whom the Christians from among the Gentiles (verse 9a) would never be able to glorify God.

It is not surprising, therefore, that *hope* is a subject on which Paul loves to dwell (Rom. 4:18; 5:2, 4, 5; 8:20, 24, 25; 12:12; 15:4; II Cor. 3:12; Gal. 5:5; Eph. 1:18; Col. 1:5, 23, 27, etc.). In fact, in the very next verse the apostle directs the attention of the hearers and readers once more to hope and to its Source.

13. May the God of hope fill y o u with all joy and peace, in the exercise of (y o u r) faith, so that by the power of the Holy Spirit y o u may overflow with hope.
Note the following:
a. Another earnest and impressive prayer-wish. Cf. verse 5.
b. "the God of hope."
This "hope" does not indicate a weak aspiration but a firmly rooted expectation. See Heb. 6:19, 20. The phrase "the God of hope" means: the God who is the Source of hope and imparts it to those who trust him.

A comparison of Paul's text with that of the LXX will show that he has made three minor changes: a transposition in the first line; and in the second the addition of "And" plus the substitution of the third for the second person.
Verse 12
For the quotation from Isa. 11:10 Paul follows the LXX text, but omits ἐν τῇ ἡμέρᾳ ἐκείνῃ (in that day).
406. So also Ridderbos, p. 326.

c. The object of this hope is God Triune as revealed in the Shoot springing up from the Root of Jesse; in other words, as disclosed in the Lord Jesus Christ. See also above, on verse 12.

d. "joy and peace." This is the "joy unspeakable and full of glory" (A.V. I Peter 1:8), and the "peace of God that surpasses all understanding" (Phil. 4:7). See pp. 169, 249.

Paul was well aware of the fact that *in the presence of such joy and peace no room would be left for quarrels between "the weak" and "the strong."*

e. "in the exercise of y o u r faith."

Faith is God's gift, indeed, but that does not cancel the fact that man must exercise it. See Luke 8:50; Phil. 2:12, 13; II Thess. 2:13.

f. Though it is man who must exercise faith, he cannot do so by his own power but "by the power of the Holy Spirit."

g. "y o u may *overflow* with hope."

In Paul's writings we find a constant emphasis on the *overflowing* or "super" character of redemption in Christ. See Rom. 5:20, p. 184; further also II Cor. 7:4; Phil. 4:7; I Thess. 3:10; II Thess. 1:3; I Tim. 1:14; etc. In our present passage note

"fill . . . all . . . overflow."

h. "with hope." See above, under b.

And will Christian hope "be emptied in delight"? Will it vanish at the moment when the soul enters heaven? The answer is found in I Cor. 13: "Now *abideth* faith, hope, and love, these *three* . . ."

What a marvelous prayer-wish!

Practical Lessons Derived from Romans 14:1—15:13

Verse 14:1

"Him who is weak in faith accept, but not with the idea of passing judgment on (his) opinions." Time flies. Elimination of quarrels about non-essentials would conserve time and energy for proclaiming the good news of salvation to a world lost in sin. Also, if you wish to cure a person of his error, first of all make him feel "accepted." If his error is not basic, he may see it and, with the help of God, correct it before you even mention it.

Verse 4

"Who are you that you dare pass judgment on someone else's servant?" See also Matt. 7:1. That brother on whom you pass judgment is *not your servant but God's.* Besides, it is God alone who knows all that needs to be known before a judgment can be pronounced. We have no right to try to play God!

Verse 15a

"For if your brother is seriously upset because of what you eat, you are no longer walking in love." Always bear in mind: One loving deed is more valuable than a hundred correct opinions.

Verse 15b

"Do not by your eating destroy your brother for whom Christ died." Remember: that brother whom you are offending is a very valuable person. He was bought with Christ's own blood! Be careful, therefore, how you treat him!

Verse 19

"Let us then pursue the things that lead to peace and to mutual edification." Before I make an attempt to argue with my brother about eating and drinking or any other matter of secondary religious significance, I should ask myself the following questions:

a. Am I sufficiently well-informed about this matter?

b. Will this debate be helpful to the brother? Will it really *edify* him?

Verse 21

"It is better not to eat meat or drink wine or to do anything else that will cause your brother to stumble." What you are doing or are about to do may be ever so *lawful*. The question, however, is, "Is it *helpful*?" See I Cor. 6:12; 10:23.

Verse 15:7

"Accept one another, then, just as Christ accepted y o u, to the glory of God."

A very appropriate text for a sermon . . . on any Sunday of the year, but perhaps especially at the beginning of a new year.

Theme: ACCEPT ONE ANOTHER
1. Universal Need
2. Generous Provision
3. Resulting Obligation
4. Ultimate Purpose

The first two points would be mainly introductory. See Rom. 3:10, 23 for point 1; and 3:24 for point 2. The main thrust of the sermon would center on point 3 (see Rom. 15:7a) and point 4 (see 15:7b).

Verse 13

"May the God of hope fill y o u with all joy and peace, in the exercise of (y o u r) faith, so that by the power of the Holy Spirit y o u may overflow with hope."

Even though, strictly speaking, this is not a prayer but a wish, this wish can easily be changed into a prayer, since it certainly implies the prayer, "O God of hope, fill us with all joy and peace . . . so that by the power of the Holy Spirit we may overflow with hope."

Note the following:

a. What kind of joy and peace? See I Peter 1:8 and Phil. 4:7. Why are these gifts very important? See 15:13d.

b. How are these blessings obtained? Answer: by exercising faith, which implies the work of the Holy Spirit in our hearts.

c. How generously are they supplied? Note: "fill," "all." In fact, God grants us even more than we ask. We ask for joy and peace. He grants us joy and peace *and hope*; in fact, a hope so abundant that it *overflows* the boundaries of our hearts and minds . . . and will never cease to do so. In this connection see my book *The Bible on the Life Hereafter*, pp. 70-74.

Summary of Chapter 14:1—15:13

This can be found on pp. 453, 454.

Outline (continued)

Practical Application

Conclusion

Closing Commendation and Explanation of Boldness in Writing
"I myself am convinced, my brothers, that y o u yourselves are rich in
goodness . . . Nevertheless, I have written to y o u rather boldly . . .
because of the commission God in his grace has granted me, to be a
minister of Christ Jesus to the Gentiles"
15:14-16

Review of the Past
"From Jerusalem all the way around to Illyricum, I have fully proclaimed
the gospel of Christ"
15:17-22

Plan for the Future
"Now . . . I am on my way to Jerusalem, in the service of the saints. . . .
When I have completed this task . . . I will go to y o u
on my way to Spain"
15:23-29

Prayer Request
"I exhort y o u, brothers, by our Lord Jesus Christ and by the love of the
Spirit, to join me in my struggle by praying to God for me"
15:30-33

Commendation of Phoebe. Paul's Own Greetings and Those of All the Churches
"Greet Prisca and Aquila, my fellow-workers in Christ Jesus"
16:1-16

Final Warning
"I exhort y o u, brothers, to watch out for those who cause divisions"
16:17-20

Greetings of Friends
"Timothy, my fellow-worker, greets y o u"
16:21-23

Doxology
"Now to him who is able to establish y o u in accordance with my gospel
and the proclamation of Jesus Christ . . . be glory forever
through Jesus Christ! Amen."
16:25-27

CHAPTER
15:14—16:27

14 I myself am convinced, my brothers, that y o u yourselves are rich in goodness, amply filled with knowledge, and competent also to admonish one another. 15 Nevertheless, I have written to y o u rather boldly on some points, so as to remind y o u of them again. (I have done so) because of the commission God in his grace has granted me,[407] 16 to be a minister of Christ Jesus to the Gentiles, with the priestly duty of proclaiming the gospel of God, in order that the Gentiles might become an offering acceptable (to him), sanctified by the Holy Spirit.

Conclusion
Closing Commendation and Explanation of Boldness in Writing
"I myself am convinced, my brothers, that y o u yourselves are rich in goodness . . . Nevertheless, I have written to y o u rather boldly . . . because of the commission God in his grace has granted me, to be a minister of Christ Jesus to the Gentiles"
15:14-16

Approaching this part of Paul's Epistle to the Romans we should by all means avoid the mistake of thinking that what is found in 15:14—16:27 is *only* a conclusion, a kind of P.S., or Appendix, which, with very little loss, one could well afford to skip. On the contrary, neglecting or even underestimating the importance of 15:14—16:27 would amount to missing a very important part of the application of the doctrine of justification by faith.

We should bear in mind that the person who composed this letter had experienced, and was experiencing, the effects of this very basic doctrine in his own life. What kind of a person resulted? By means of the very spirit that is revealed in Rom. 1:1—15:13 Paul has already told us something about himself (see, for example, chapter 12), as he has done also in such individual passages as 1:8-16; 7:7-25; 8:38, 39; 9:1-4; 10:1; 11:1. Nevertheless, it must be admitted that by far the most of 1:1—15:13 is *doctrinal* in character. However beginning with 15:14 Paul becomes intensely *personal*. In a very natural—one might almost say unintentional—manner he shows us, by his own example, what kind of a person *he*, this justified-by-faith individual, has be-

---

407. Literally: because of the grace given me by God.

come. In reading even the opening verses of this Conclusion we are arrested by his *tact, modesty, prudence, humility, and concern for the feelings of others.*

Consequently here, indeed, is sermon material! Are not such qualities—in association, of course, with all-important trust in God—the very ones which should be in evidence in our lives? And if a minister should be afraid to dwell on these virtues, because he knows that in *his* own life these traits are not exactly outstanding, is not his very awareness of this fact all the more a reason why he should proclaim their necessity loudly and clearly. so that both his congregation and he himself may receive a transforming blessing?

As we read this Conclusion we are reminded of 1:5, 8-16. In the earlier verses Paul gave expression to his yearning to visit his friends in Rome. That thought returns here (15:23, 24, 32). In 1:5 he made mention of his "gift of apostleship." In 15:15 he again refers to this "commission which God in his grace has granted" him. Were we astounded by the depth of Paul's humility revealed in his earlier statement, "I am yearning to see y o u . . . in order that we may be mutually encouraged by each other's faith . . ." (1:11, 12)? We are no less astonished by his boundless generosity as he now writes, "I myself am convinced . . . that y o u yourselves are rich in goodness, amply supplied with knowledge, and competent also to admonish one another" (15:14).

But though what Paul writes in 15:14 f. is a somewhat amplified restatement of what he had written in the earlier part of his letter, there are also differences. In 1:13 he had merely stated that until now he had been prevented from visiting his Roman friends. Here, in 15:19-23, he gives at least a partial answer to the question what it was that had prevented him from coming. Moreover, in this later section he is far more explicit in revealing his traveling plans (15:23-29) than he had been earlier (1:8-15). Note also the prayer request now added (15:30 f.).

14. I myself am convinced, my brothers, that y o u yourselves are rich in goodness, amply filled with knowledge, and competent also to admonish one another.

Paul does not make use of flattery. He feels, however, that in view of the fact that he has pointed out certain weaknesses pertaining to groups and individuals within the church, he should now emphasize that these blemishes do not diminish his high regard for the church as a whole. He says, "I myself am convinced that y o u yourselves are *rich in goodness*"; that is, in kindliness, generosity of heart and action (cf. Gal. 5:22; Eph. 5:9; II Thess. 1:11). He adds, "filled with knowledge," practical discernment of every kind. He even credits them with being able independently—that is, without the help of Paul or anyone else—to caution one another against specific faults.

Today the word "counseling" is heard again and again. Ever so many books and articles have been written about it. Well, the apostle here reveals that also in this respect "there is nothing new under the sun." There was mutual counseling already in his day, and it was of a high character. By and large the members of the Roman church were *"competent* to admonish one another."

What makes Paul's remark even more heart-warming is the fact that in making it he addresses the members as being his "brothers." For this term of affection see on 1:13 (p. 52) and 7:1 (pp. 214, 215). Note strengthening modifier "my" ("my brothers") here (15:14), adding to the cordial nature of a passage which shows how filled to overflowing with love was this heart of Paul; better still, how rich were the fruits of the operation of the Holy Spirit in his life.

Paul continues: **15a. Nevertheless, I have written to y o u rather boldly on some points, so as to remind y o u of them again.**

The apostle had issued warning against such evils as antinomian tendencies (ch. 6), arrogance on the part of some (11:20, 21; 12:3), opposition to governmental authorities (13:2), the strong ridiculing the weak, and the weak condemning the strong (14:1 f.). Mercifully he adds, "so as to remind y o u," as if to say, "Of course, y o u knew all these things, and needed only a reminder."

What Paul is saying is not entirely the same as, but nevertheless reminds one of, lines in Pope's *Essay on Criticism*:

> Men must be taught as if you taught them not,
> And things unknown proposed as things forgot.

15b, 16. (I have done so) because of the commission God in his grace has granted me, to be a minister of Christ Jesus to the Gentiles, with the priestly duty of proclaiming the gospel of God, in order that the Gentiles might become an offering acceptable (to him), sanctified by the Holy Spirit.[408]

Note the following:

a. Paul has been outspoken not because he is unkind but because of his sense of duty as a minister of Christ Jesus to the Gentiles.

b. When the apostle says that he has written in this manner as "a minister of Christ Jesus to the Gentiles," does he not imply that most of the addressed were believers from the Gentiles?

c. ". . . with the priestly duty of proclaiming the gospel of God, in order that the Gentiles might become an offering . . ."

---

408. διὰ τὴν χάριν, because of the grace; that is, the *gift* imparted to me by God's grace. For more on χάρις see N.T.C. on Luke 2:40, p. 181.

With λειτουργός (here acc. s. -v) cf. "liturgist." Others to whom the word "minister" is applied, either literally or by implication, are Zechariah (Luke 1:23), the "prophets and teachers" of Antioch (Acts 13:1, 2), holy angels (Heb. 1:7, 14), and even Jesus himself (Heb. 8:2, 6). In a somewhat broader sense the word is applied to those who contribute to the cause of Christian benevolence (II Cor. 9:12). For its use in connection with tax-collectors see on Rom. 13:6, pp. 436, 437.

ἱερουργοῦντα, acc. s. masc. pres. participle of ἱερουργέω, to perform priestly duty, offer as a priest; in the New Testament here only.

προσφορά (cf. Acts 21:26; 24:17; Eph. 5:2; Heb. 10:5, 8, 10, 14, 18). The noun is derived from προσφέρω, to bring to or forward.

Does Paul mean that by proclaiming the gospel to the Gentiles he himself, in such cases where the message was accepted by faith, has brought these Gentiles to God as a sacrifice? Or is he saying that the Gentiles offered themselves to God as a sacrifice?

The first interpretation would seem to be paralleled by a passage from Isa. 66:20, "And they will bring all y o u r brothers, from all the nations, to my holy mountain in Jerusalem, *as an offering to the Lord*." Since it has become evident again and again that Paul was thoroughly acquainted with the Old Testament—certainly also with the prophecies of Isaiah!—this may well be the correct interpretation.[409]

Of course, even then, Paul is not forgetting that these converted individuals would also offer themselves "as sacrifices, living, holy, and well-pleasing to God ..." (Rom. 12:1).

d. Such sacrifices are "acceptable" (cf. I Peter 2:5) to God, being "sanctified by the Holy Spirit."

---

17. In Christ Jesus, then, I have the right to glory with respect to my work for God. 18 For I will not venture to speak of anything except that which Christ, in leading the Gentiles to God, has accomplished through me by what I have said and done. 19 (He accomplished it) by the power of signs and wonders (performed) through the power of the Spirit. So, from Jerusalem all the way around to Illyricum, I have fully proclaimed the gospel of Christ. 20 But it has always been my ambition to preach the gospel where Christ was not known, that I might not be building on someone else's foundation. 21 Rather, as it is written,

"Those who were not told about him will see,
and those who have not heard will understand."
22 That is why I have often been hindered from coming to y o u.

Review of the Past
"From Jerusalem all the way around to Illyricum, I have fully proclaimed
the gospel of Christ"
15:17-22

17-19a. In Christ Jesus, then, I have the right to glory with respect to my work for God. For I will not venture to speak of anything except that which Christ, in leading the Gentiles to God, has accomplished through me by what I have said and done. (He accomplished it) by the power of signs and wonders (performed) through the power of the Spirit.[410]

Note the following:

a. The connection between this verse and the immediately preceding context is immediately clear. Paul has described himself as "a minister of Christ Jesus to the Gentiles." So he now continues, "In Christ Jesus, then, I have

---

409. The idea that people can be presented to the Lord as a spiritual sacrifice was not strange to the Jews. See, for example, also S.BK. I, p. 84; III, p. 153.
410. Variants, such as πνεύματος θεοῦ and πνεύματος ἁγίου are probably the result of scribal addition. There does not seem to be a good reason to reject the shorter text.

the right to glory," etc. Exultation is in order; that is, exultation "in Christ Jesus," not self-glorification.[411] Cf. I Cor. 1:29-31; II Cor. 10:17. Note Paul's humility. He does not say, "For I will not venture to speak of anything except that which I have accomplished through Christ," but "For I will not venture to speak of anything except that which *Christ . . . has accomplished through me* by what I have said and done."

b. *"Christ . . .* has accomplished . . . through the power of *the Spirit."* Equal honor and credit is ascribed to both. For more on this see p. 253.

c. "He [Christ] accomplished it by the power of signs and wonders."[412] Both "signs" and "wonders" are *miracles,* supernatural deeds. A miracle is called a "wonder" when the emphasis is on the effect it has upon the beholder, causing him to be filled with the sense of wonderment and awe. On the other hand, when the miracle points away from itself and *signifies* the qualities (power, wisdom, grace, etc.) of the One who performs it, it is called a "sign."[413]

d. By far the best commentary on this statement of Paul, in which he reviews his past labors for the Lord, is certainly the book of Acts. It is strange that even some of the finest books on Romans fail to refer to Acts in this connection. Nevertheless, without thoughtfully reading what Luke in that book tells us concerning the signs and wonders which accompanied Paul's labors we are in danger of missing the real meaning and importance of the apostle's statement.

These "signs and wonders" were great in number and enormous in effect. At this point the reader should turn to Acts and read the following sections: 13:6-12; 14:1-3; 14:8-10; 16:16-18; 16:25 f.; 19:11-16. As a result of the first of these miracles ". . . when the proconsul saw what had happened he believed . . ." And as a result of the last ". . . the name of the Lord Jesus was magnified."

However, as Paul makes clear, many of the miracles that occurred during his lengthy pre-Romans ministry were the immediate results of *preaching* (note "by what I have *said* and done") applied to hearts and lives by the Holy Spirit. These successes were "gospel triumphs." Cf. II Cor. 2:14. In fact, in the book of Acts the emphasis is placed on these *spiritual* victories. See the following passages; Acts 13:42-44, 48, 49; 16:5, 14, 15, 32-34; 17:4, 11, 12; 18:4, 8, 27, 28. In spite of fierce opposition from the side of both Jews and pagans, even the enemies had to admit that Paul and his companions "were turning the world upside down" (Acts 17:6). The apostle's own inspired phraseology is much better: "Christ was leading the Gentiles to God."

---

411. The word καύχησις, glorying, boasting, reason for glorying, right to boast, pride (exact meaning here, as always, depending on the specific context), was used earlier in 3:27, and occurs also in I Cor. 15:31; frequently in II Corinthians, beginning with 1:12; and also in I Thess. 2:19 and in James 4:16. For the verb καυχάομαι and related forms see pp. 100-102, including footnotes 62-64.

412. Cf. II Cor. 12:12, "signs and wonders and mighty deeds."

413. In the original a *miracle* or *work of power* is a δύναμις a *wonder* is a τέρας, and a *sign* is a σημεῖον. For more information on this subject see R. C. Trench, *op. cit.,* par. xci.

19b-21. So, from Jerusalem all the way around to Illyricum, I have fully proclaimed the gospel of Christ. But it has always been my ambition to preach the gospel where Christ was not known, that I might not be building on someone else's foundation. Rather, as it is written,

"Those who were not told about him will see,
and those who have not heard will understand."

The expression "from Jerusalem all the way around to Illyricum" will have little meaning to the present-day reader unless he has a map or sketch of the indicated region in front of him. See it on p. 489. Note especially the line extending from Jerusalem in the southeast to Illyricum (Yugoslavia and Albania, p. 24) in the northwest. Although the book of Acts does not mention any missionary activity in Illyricum, Paul may have entered that territory, or may have reached its borders, on one of the occasions when he was in Macedonia; see especially Acts 20:2.

Why does Paul mention Jerusalem as the starting point for missionary activity? In view of the fact that all three great missionary journeys started out from Syrian Antioch (Acts 13:1-3; 15:40, 41; 18:22, 23), why does he not rather say, "from Antioch" instead of "from Jerusalem"? Was it because some of his early—though not the earliest—preaching had been done in *Jerusalem* (Acts 9:26-29)? Or because (after the first missionary journey) the leaders of the *Jerusalem* church had enthusiastically endorsed Paul and Barnabas as missionaries to work among the Gentiles (Gal. 2:9; cf. Acts 15:1-35)? Or, perhaps, because while praying in the *Jerusalem* temple the Lord had appeared to Paul and had told him, "Go, for I will send you far away to the Gentiles" (Acts 22:17-21)?

All of these facts are important, and one or more of them may have been part of the reason why Paul wrote as he did. Nevertheless, the main reason was probably the fact that not Syrian Antioch but Jerusalem was the southeastern limit of the region covered by the apostle on his journeys.

It will be recalled that the first journey covered a relatively small territory: Syrian Antioch to the island of Cyprus, to a group of Galatian towns;[414] and then, after virtually retracing his path through these towns, returning by sea to Syrian Antioch (Acts 13:1-14:26).

On the second journey Paul proceeded from Syrian Antioch via Galatia and Troas to Macedonia. Then turning toward the south and somewhere crossing the Jerusalem-Illyricum diagonal, he went to Athens and from there to Corinth. Later, by way of Ephesus and Caesarea he in all probability visited the church in Jerusalem,[415] and from there returned to Syrian Antioch. Thus on this trip he actually "went around" the diagonal (Acts 15:36—18:22).

The third journey outward bound somewhat resembled the second. This time, however, the apostle, again starting out from Syrian Antioch and revisiting the Galatian churches, entered Macedonia via *Ephesus, where he re-*

---

414. See N.T.C. on Galatians, pp. 4-14.
415. If, "the church" in Acts 18:22 means "the Jerusalem church," as is probable).

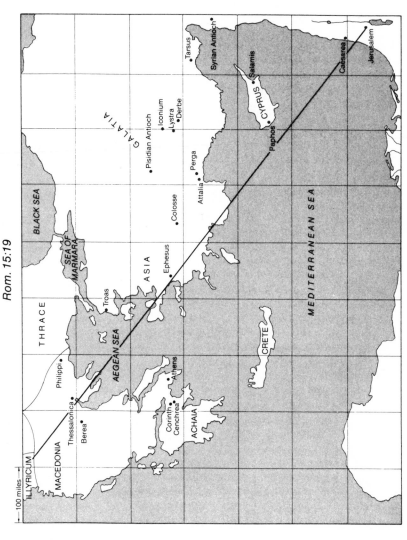

"From Jerusalem all the way around to Illyricum"
Rom. 15:19

mained for a long time, instead of via Troas (as on the second trip). From Macedonia he proceeded to Corinth, where he is now, composing and dictating his epistle to the Romans (Acts 18:23—20:3a).

From this rapid review, accompanied by sketch, the expression "from Jerusalem to . . . Illyricum" is readily understood. In an age when travel was much slower than it is today, the area covered by Paul and his companions was certainly amazing in its extent.

Looking back, Paul is able to say, "I have fully proclaimed the gospel of Christ." This has been interpreted to mean, "In my gospel proclamation I have not omitted any important doctrine." In the present context that is, however, probably not the meaning, at least not the full meaning, the apostle is trying to convey. As will become clear in a moment, he is beginning to state the reason why he did not make an earlier visit to Rome. At least in part what he is saying amounts to this, "At an earlier time I would not have completed my gospel-blazing circuit. Now I have fulfilled or completed it." Verse 23 contains Paul's own explanation, "In these regions there is no longer any place for me to work."

Paul considered himself to be a trail-blazer for the gospel, a pioneer missionary, a founder of churches. He *planted*. Now let an "Apollos" come to *water* the seeds! See I Cor. 3:6. That this basic program did not in any way prevent the apostle from visiting an already flourishing congregation in order to enjoy and impart the blessings of Christian fellowship and even to preach a few sermons there, must be granted. But the apostle's main aim was to proclaim the good tidings to those who had not yet heard this uplifting message. His ambition was to establish new foundations (churches), not to build upon someone else's foundation.

He justifies this method of operation by very appropriately quoting Isa. 52:15, according to the LXX text, which in this case is a faithful rendering of the original Hebrew.

This portion of Scripture deserves a more detailed consideration than is generally given to it. It should be borne in mind that the fifty-second chapter of Isaiah immediately precedes Isaiah's most famous and familiar chapter, the fifty-third. The chapter division between 52 and 53 is not a happy one. Better would have been making the new chapter begin at 52:13. That new chapter (what is now 52:13-53:12) could then be given the title "From Suffering to Glory in the Life of the Coming Messiah." What are now the closing verses of chapter 52 contain a brief summary of this path from Humiliation to Exaltation, and what is now chapter 53 develops this theme in far greater detail.

There can be no question about the fact that, according to the New Testament, this prophecy refers directly to Jesus. See John 12:37; Acts 8:26-35; Rom. 10:16; I Peter 1:11; 2:24. In fact, Jesus himself so regarded it (Luke 22:37).

In describing Messiah's humiliation Isa. 52:14 predicts that "many will be appalled at him because of his disfigurement." Fulfilment: the physical abuse and mockery suffered by Jesus. But this humiliation gives way to exaltation: "He will be raised, lifted up, highly exalted." Think of Christ's resurrection, ascension, and coronation (taking his seat at the Father's right hand in heaven). Isa. 52:15 shows that many nations will marvel because of his glory. Out of respect and reverence for him kings will keep silence before him. What follows is quoted by Paul here in Rom. 15, namely, "Those who were not told about him will see, and those who have not heard will understand."

That was the glorious prediction. Though many of his own people would reject the Messiah, Gentile kings and nations would listen to the wonderful tidings of salvation and would, by God's sovereign grace, hear and understand.

What Paul is saying, then, is that his prediction was being fulfilled in his own day; even more, that an important element was being realized in him as "the apostle to the Gentiles."

The question remains, "What was it that enabled Paul, writing from Corinth, after the completion of the first part of the third missionary journey— the part from Syrian Antioch, by way of Galatia, Ephesus, and Macedonia to Corinth—to believe and to state that he had now finished the great task of planting the gospel in the Jerusalem to Illyricum part of the Roman Empire? What was it that made it possible for him to say this *now* and not earlier; for example, after the completion of the second missionary journey? This belief and statement must have resulted from that which was accomplished on the third journey, during *the lengthy ministry at Ephesus*. It was from Ephesus that, by means of Paul *and his helpers*, one of them being Epaphras (Col. 1:7), the gospel had spread to the surrounding cities and towns; in all probability to Colosse and the other places located in the Lycus Valley, about 100 miles east of Ephesus (see the sketch), and to "the seven cities" mentioned in Rev. 1:11.

It would be difficult to exaggerate the results of the work of these church planters during this three-year period: "All the residents of [the province of] Asia heard the word of the Lord, both Jews and Greeks" (Acts 19:10. "In this way the word of the Lord spread widely and grew in power" (Acts 19:20). Not until this had been accomplished did Paul feel free to go to Rome. Or, in the words of Paul himself:

22. That is why I have often been hindered from coming to y o u.

23 But now that in these regions there is no longer any place for me to work, and since I have been longing for many years to see y o u, 24 (I plan to do so) when I go to Spain. I hope to see y o u in passing and to be helped forward by y o u after I have enjoyed y o u r company for a while. 25 Now, however, I am on my way to Jerusalem, in the service of the saints. 26 For Macedonia and Achaia have been pleased to make a contribution for the poor among the saints at Jerusalem. 27 They were pleased to do it and, indeed, they owe it to them; for if the Gentiles have come to share in the Jews' spiritual blessings, they owe it to the Jews to share with them their material blessings. 28 When I have completed this task, and have sealed this fruit to them, I will go to y o u on my way to Spain. 29 I know that when I come to y o u, I will come in the fulness of the blessing of Christ.

Plan for the Future
"Now . . . I am on my way to Jerusalem, in the service of the saints. . . .
When I have completed this task . . . I will go to y o u
on my way to Spain"
15:23-29

23, 24. But now that in these regions there is no longer any place for me to work, and since I have been longing for many years to see y o u, (I plan to do so) when I go to Spain. I hope to see y o u in passing and to be helped forward by y o u after I have enjoyed y o u r company for a while.
Note the following:

a. Paul mentions two reasons for his plan to visit the Roman church; the first relating to his task as a pioneer missionary; the second, to his love for the Roman Christians. The first: "there is no longer any place for me to work" (already explained); the second, "I have been longing for many years to see y o u." Cf. 1:10, 11.

b. the words "(I plan to do so) when[416] I go to Spain" show that visiting Rome's congregation is not the apostle's ultimate goal. That would be in harmony with his basic principle as expressed in verse 20. Nevertheless, visiting his Christian friends in Rome was certainly something to which he looked forward with eager anticipation.

c. Did Paul ever reach Spain? A definite answer cannot be given. We do, however, have the following early testimonies:

"Paul, having taught righteousness to the whole world, having gone to the limits of the West, and having given testimony before the rulers, thus was removed from the world and taken up into the Holy Place, having become the outstanding model of endurance" (Clement of Rome, I Corinthians V.vii). The expression "the limits of the West," most naturally refers to the western part of Europe; and in the present context, probably to Spain. This is especially true when, as in the present case, such a statement is made by someone who is writing from Rome.

"Luke relates them [these events] for the most excellent Theophilus because in his presence the individual events transpired, as he clearly declares by omitting the passion of Peter as well as the departure of Paul when the latter proceeded from the city (Rome) to Spain" (The Muratorian Fragment).

d. The words "I hope to see y o u in passing" should not be interpreted as if the apostle intends to rush through the city on his way to Spain. This expression simply reinforces the thought that Paul's ultimate destination is not Rome but Spain. That he intends to remain in Rome a while is clear from the very next line. Moreover, 1:11, 12, 15 show that the apostle looked

---

416. Greek ὡς ἄν = ὅταν followed by the pres. mid. subjunct. πορεύωμαι, "whensoever I go," indefinite; cf. "when I go to Spain, whenever that may be."

forward to enjoying sweet fellowship with the membership of the Roman church, and even to preaching the gospel in Rome.

e. "and to be helped forward by y o u." What does this imply? At this point some commentators restrict the meaning of the verbal form used by Paul[417] to *being commended to the grace of God* by the members of Rome's church (Acts 14:26; 15:40; implied in Acts 13:1-3). To be sure this is basic. Nevertheless, in accordance with the use of this verb elsewhere, some or all of the following items were probably also included: to be furnished with information, guides, provisions, money for the journey. The comprehensive meaning of the verb becomes clear when the following New Testament passages in which it occurs are read in light of their specific contexts: Acts 15:3; 20:38; I Cor. 16:6, 11; II Cor. 1:16; Titus 3:13; III John 6. See also Practical Lessons on Rom. 15:24, p. 524.

However, the addressees must not begin to think that Paul is about to make a straight course for Rome:

25-27. Now, however, I am on my way to Jerusalem, in the service of the saints. For Macedonia and Achaia have been pleased to make a contribution for the poor among the saints at Jerusalem. They were pleased to do it and, indeed, they owe it to them; for if the Gentiles have come to share in the Jews' spiritual blessings, they owe it to the Jews to share with them their material blessings.

Even though Paul regards preaching the gospel his main task (verses 16 and 20), he is deeply conscious of the fact that there is another very important obligation resting upon him, one that has to be discharged before he can wend his way to Rome, namely, that of helping to relieve the poverty of the Jerusalem saints. He knows that not only the soul but also the body must receive nourishment. The same Lord Jesus Christ who preached the Sermon on the Mount also fed the five thousand and the four thousand. The Savior's words recorded in Matt. 25:35, 36 are unforgettable.

Besides, the apostle remembered that some years earlier James, Peter, and John, leaders of the Jerusalem church, while extending to him the right hand of fellowship, in approval of his mission among the Gentiles, had added the words, "Only be sure to remember the poor," referring, of course, especially to the poor believers in Jerusalem.

This was also exactly in line with Paul's own thinking and planning (Gal. 2:10). He wanted to do it because he was a person with a loving heart, one who was eager to do something in return for the manner in which the Lord had blessed him. Besides, having himself been reduced to poverty again and again (II Cor. 11:27; Phil. 4:12), he was able to sympathize with those similarly afflicted. Last but not least, being a very practical person, he hoped that a gift coming from the Gentiles would contribute to the realization of his glorious purpose, namely, to break down once for all the terrible barrier

---

417. προπεμφθῆναι, aor. infin. pass. of προπέμπω, to send or help forward, to escort.

existing between Jew and Gentile, and to establish one holy universal church. Cf. Rom. 10:12; Eph. 2:14, 18; 4:4.

It deserves special attention that Paul tells the Romans that Macedonia and Achaia (see the sketch on p. 489)—meaning the Christians living in these provinces—*have been pleased* to make a *contribution*; that is, to give material expression to their participation in Christian *fellowship* with the believers in Jerusalem.[418] Though this was indeed a fact, it is worthy of note that Paul very generously omits to point out that he himself, by means of earnest and urgent exhortations (I Cor. 16:1-4; II Cor. 8 and 9), had contributed substantially to making it a fact.

The apostle points out, moreover, that the action of the Gentiles in relieving the need of Jerusalem's poor must not be viewed as cause for self-congratulation ("what good persons are we!") but rather as a moral obligation. The Gentiles have begun to share the Jews' spiritual blessings, those resulting from the acceptance of the gospel. Then should they not do their utmost to lighten the material burden under which their donors are groaning? In reality do not the spiritual blessings outweigh anything of a material nature that could be offered in return?

28, 29. When I have completed this task, and have sealed this fruit to them, I will go to y o u on my way to Spain. I know that when I come to y o u, I will come in the fulness of the blessing of Christ.[419]

The words, "When I have completed this task . . . I will go to y o u on my way to Spain" are clear. The explanation is found in verses 25, 26. See also Acts 24:17.

However, the expression "and have sealed this fruit to them" is among the most controversial in Romans. Rather than bother the reader with a description of all kinds of theories which I, along with many others, cannot accept, let me immediately present the view which strikes me as being the most reasonable.[420]

A church had been established in Jerusalem. By far the majority of its members were, of course, Christian *Jews*. They had accepted Jesus Christ as their Lord and Savior. For them it was difficult, however, fully to agree with the doctrine of "freedom in Christ." When they knew that Gentiles were no longer compelled to submit to circumcision or to avoid foods which in the law had been declared "unclean," some objected (Acts 15:1, 5). See what

---

418. It is interesting to observe that the word used in Gal. 2:9 to indicate *fellowship* is the same as that which here in Rom. 15:26 indicates a *contribution*. That Greek word—*koinonia*—has become so familiar in our circles that it is listed as an English word in Webster's Third International Dictionary.

419. εὐλογίας Χριστοῦ, supported by the leading MSS should be preferred to the expansion τοῦ εὐαγγελίου τοῦ Χριστοῦ, supported by later witnesses.

420. My view has much in common with that of the following authors:
    S. Greijdanus, *op. cit.*, Vol. I, pp. 649, 650.
    E. F. Harrison, *op. cit.*, pp. 158, 159.
    H. Ridderbos, *op. cit.*, pp. 337, 338.
    G. B. Wilson, *op. cit.*, pp. 239, 240.

has been said about this earlier, in connection with the subject of "the weak" and "the strong" (pp. 452-454). Besides, when these people noticed that the Gentile churches were rapidly increasing in membership, while they—their Jerusalem churches—were hard pressed to hold their own, they began to look askance at what was happening in the Gentile world.

There was really no excuse for their hesitancies, scruples, criticisms, and doubts. Had they only accepted *all* the teachings of Jesus, there would have been no problem. Had not Jesus pronounced a blessing upon the centurion, who did not belong to the people of the circumcision (Matt. 8:5-13)? And had not the Lord pronounced all foods "clean" (Mark 7:14-19)?

Now one of the reasons for organizing the drive for assistance to Jerusalem's poor saints had probably been to convince the Jerusalem Jews and others who agreed with them that they should accept Gentile Christians as equals. See Acts 10:1—11:18. When, therefore, the apostle now describes the contribution or collection as "fruit," he probably means that it must be regarded as a product of the Gentiles' genuine faith and of their sincere gratitude for the willingness of the Jewish believers to share with them their faith in Christ.

The gift from the Gentiles proved that the gospel was having a beneficial effect in their lives. It was the visible evidence of the operation of the Holy Spirit in the hearts and lives of the donors. And the handing over of this gift sealed or certified this gratifying fact to the Jewish recipients. Cf. Eph. 1:14, and see also N.T.C. on Philippians, pp. 61, 62, 208.

Do the words, "I know that when I come to y o u," etc. imply that Paul realized that the Romans might be somewhat disappointed about the news that he could not come to them directly but must first visit Jerusalem? However that may be, he now assures them that when he does come he will arrive "in the fulness of the blessing in Christ."

In view of 15:24 and also of 1:11, 12, 13b, 15, he must have had in mind such blessings as the joy of meeting and conversing with one another, his preaching in their midst, their listening to the apostle's report about divine blessings in other congregations, together planning the trip to Spain, etc.

When Paul was writing this, he had no way of knowing that his actual meeting with his friends in Rome would take place a few years later (see Acts 24:27; 28:11) than he had expected, and that he would be arriving as a prisoner. But even then a hearty welcome was in store for him (Acts 28:11-15), and he would receive much encouragement (Phil. 1:12-14), though some of the conditions in the Roman church would prove to be of a disappointing nature (Phil. 1:15a, 17).

---

30 I exhort y o u, brothers, by our Lord Jesus Christ and by the love of the Spirit, to join me in my struggle by praying to God for me, 31 that I may be rescued from the disobedient in Judea, and that my ministry to Jerusalem may be acceptable to the saints, 32 so that by God's will my coming to y o u may be a matter of joy, and that together with y o u I may be refreshed. 33 The God of peace be with y o u all. Amen.

Prayer Request
"I exhort y o u, brothers, by our Lord Jesus Christ and by the love of the
Spirit, to join me in my struggle by praying to God for me"
15:30-33

What we have here is (a) an appeal, (b) a description of the character of
the prayer requested by Paul, (c) an indication of its contents, and (d) of its
purpose. All this is climaxed by (e) an appropriate and concluding prayer-
wish.

A. *The Appeal*

**30. I exhort y o u, brothers, by our Lord Jesus Christ and by the love
of the Spirit . . .**
The very wording indicates that Paul is deeply conscious of the need of
the prayers of the church for him. Note the solemnity of the expression,
"by our Lord Jesus Christ," referring to the Savior in all the fulness of his
being and meaning for the church. Note especially "our," for he is both
Paul's Lord and the Lord of the addressed.

Paul appeals to "our Lord Jesus Christ" because it was that same Lord
who had sacrificed himself for Paul out of love for him (Gal. 2:20), and who
had personally appointed him to be the apostle to the Gentiles (Acts 22:17-22).

He appeals also to "the love of the Spirit," probably indicating (though not
all agree) that very love which the Spirit has poured out into the hearts of
all those who belong to Christ (Rom. 5:5) and who therefore can be expected
to pray for one another.

B. *Description of the Character of the Requested Prayer*

. . . to join me in my struggle by praying to God for me . . .
There is nothing superficial about genuine prayer. Isaiah describes it as
a *taking hold* of God (64:7). For Jacob—that is, "Israel"—it was a *wrestling*
with God (Gen. 32:24-30). And Paul here similarly calls it a *struggle*. Cf. Col.
2:1; 4:12. The apostle desires that the Roman believers join him in an intensely earnest and yearning petition.

C. *Its Contents*

The first requested petition is:
31a. that I may be rescued from the disobedient in Judea . . .
He refers here to the opposition he expects from the side of the unbelieving Jews in his own country. He calls them "disobedient" because of their
refusal to subject themselves to the will of God as revealed in the gospel
(Rom. 10:21; 11:30). That these Jews bitterly opposed Paul was made very
clear when he was about to sail to Syria on his way to Jerusalem, and a plot
by the Jews against his life was discovered. As a result traveling plans were
changed, the apostle instead going to Jerusalem by way of Macedonia (Acts

20:3). Moreover, he had not forgotten that earlier too the Jews had made an attempt to murder him (Acts 9:29, 30). See also Acts 20:22, 23; 21:4, 10, 11, 27 f.

The second requested petition is:

31b. and that my ministry to Jerusalem may be acceptable to the saints.
Paul had worked long and hard for this "collection" or "contribution" from the Gentiles for the poor saints in Jerusalem. Nevertheless, he was afraid that those for whom it was intended might not even be willing to accept the gift. He knew but too well that, in spite of the decisions of the Jerusalem Council (Acts 15:19-29), opposition to himself and his gospel of freedom in Christ had never ceased. See Acts 15:1, 5; Gal. 3:1 f., 17; 5:1-4; 6:12. That explains his request for this earnest petition.

D. *Its Purpose*

32 . . . so that by God's will my coming to y o u may be a matter of joy, and that together with y o u I may be refreshed.
The prospect here visualized is very pleasing: the plots of the Jews are foiled, and the Jerusalem saints, emancipated from their prejudices, not only welcome Paul but are also delighted with the "benevolence" he brings. As a result Paul, filled with joy, heads for Rome, where he finds refreshment in the company of his dear friends!

But that is not entirely what happened. In some repects the very opposite occurred. We are reminded of the adage, "Man proposes; God disposes"; expressed just as succinctly in German: der Mensch denkt, Gott lenkt; cf. the Dutch: de mens wikt, God beschikt.

What actually happened is recorded in Acts 21:17—28:16. What should be emphasized, however, is that Paul submits himself, with body and soul, for life, death, and eternity, to the wise and sovereign will of God. He writes "by God's will." In the present context God's decretive will is indicated. Result: even though events turned out in a manner Paul could not have anticipated, after he had been in Rome for a while he was able to write, "Now I want y o u to know, brothers, that the things that have happened to me in reality turned out to the advantage of the gospel . . ." (Phil. 1:12).

E. *The Prayer-Wish*

33. The God of peace be with y o u all. Amen.
Note the following:

a. Paul has been speaking about the Roman congregation, Jerusalem's Judaizers, the people of Macedonia and Achaia, his own traveling plans, etc. All of these are subject to change. Contingency is the universal rule. Stability is nowhere to be found. Nowhere? No, nowhere . . . except in God! That is why the present passage fits so neatly into this context; yes, *especially* here, where the apostle has just now revealed his uncertainty with reference to what might or might not happen to him in Jerusalem. Besides, in the immediately preceding line he has made mention of God's will. So also for this reason a reference here to "the God of peace" is very appropriate.

b. The expression, "the God of peace" must mean "the God who is the Author of peace," that is, who imparts peace. See II Thess. 3:16. Apart from close communion with him there is no peace.

c. The expression "the God of peace" is found also in Rom. 16:20; II Cor. 13:11; Phil. 4:9; I Thess. 5:23; and Heb. 13:20; the very closely related "Lord of peace" occurs in II Thess. 3:16.

d. The meaning of the word *peace* has been explained in connection with earlier passages (for example 1:7; 2:10; 5:1; 8:6; etc.). Basic to it is reconciliation with God through the death of his Son. As a result the person who has been thus reconciled has the inner assurance that past sins are forgiven, present events are being overruled for good, and in the future nothing will be able to separate him from the love of God in Christ. Consequently this person has received the richest blessing of all: salvation full and free, "prosperity," shālōm in its most comprehensive, religious sense, including serenity, the confidence: all is well.

e. When the apostle now expresses the prayer-wish that this God of peace be *with* those whom he addresses, he means that his inner desire—a desire to be realized in all who love the Lord—is that this God of peace may come so close to them that they may experience his peace in their lives, may meditate on it, possess it, rejoice in it. Compare the title *Emmanuel*, that is, "God *with* us," with the sick to heal them, with the hungry to feed them, and over-arching everything else, with the lost to seek and save them. See N.T.C. on Matthew, p. 141.

f. The apostle concludes this prayer-wish by adding the word of solemn affirmation and enthusiastic approval *Amen*. Cf. 1:25.

---

16 1 I commend to y o u our sister Phoebe, who is (also) a servant of the church at Cenchrea, 2 I ask y o u to extend to her a welcome in the Lord that is worthy of the saints, and to give her any help she may need from y o u, for she has been a helper to many people and to me personally.

3 Greet Prisca and Aquila, my fellow-workers in Christ Jesus, 4 who risked their necks to save my life, and to whom not only I but all the churches of the Gentiles are grateful. 5 (Greet) also the church (that meets) at their house. Greet my beloved Epenetus, who is Asia's firstfruits for Christ. 6 Greet Mary, who labored much for y o u. 7 Greet Andronicus and Junias, my fellow-countrymen and (former) fellow-prisoners, who are outstanding among the apostles and who were in Christ before I was. 8 Greet Ampliatus, my beloved in the Lord. 9 Greet Urbanus, our fellow-worker in Christ, and (greet) my beloved Stachys. 10 Greet Apelles, who is approved in Christ. Greet those who belong to the household of Aristobulus. 11 Greet Herodion, my fellow-countryman. Greet those of the household of Narcissus who are in the Lord. 12 Greet Tryphena and Tryphosa, who labor in the Lord. Greet Persis, the beloved, who has labored much in the Lord. 13 Greet Rufus, the elect in the Lord, and his mother and mine. 14 Greet Asyncritus, Phlegon, Hermes, Patrobas, Hermas, and the brothers (who are) with them. 15 Greet Philologus and Julia, Nereus and his sister, and Olympas, and all the saints (who are) with them. 16 Greet one another with a holy kiss.

All the churches of Christ extend greetings to y o u.

Conclusion

Commendation of Phoebe. Paul's Own Greetings and Those of All the Churches
"Greet Prisca and Aquila, my fellow-workers in Christ Jesus"
16:1-16

For the integrity of the text of Rom. 16:1-23 see Vol. I, pp. 26-28. On verse 24 see footnote 437, p. 513. As to the authenticity of 16:25-27 see Appendix, pp. 521-523.

A. *Commendation of Phoebe*

1, 2. I commend to y o u our sister Phoebe, who is (also) a servant of the church at Cenchrea. I ask y o u to extend to her a welcome in the Lord that is worthy of the saints, and to give her any help she may need from y o u, for she has been a helper to many people and to me personally.

The list of greetings is preceded by a note in which a certain lady named Phoebe is introduced and warmly commended to the church at Rome. It is reasonable to believe that it was Phoebe who, in departing for Rome, carried Paul's letter with her and delivered it to its destination. Some manuscripts even make mention of this in a subscript. We can easily understand that a note or letter of commendation, serving as a credential, was of great value both to the bearer and the addressed. Cf. II Cor. 3:1.

The lady's name *Phoebe* means *bright, radiant*. It is derived from pagan mythology, being another name for Artemis, the bright and radiant moon goddess, identified with the Roman goddess Diana. There are those who think that Phoebe must have been a Gentile Christian because—so they reason—Jews would certainly not give their children pagan names.

That reasoning may well be open to question, however, We should bear in mind that, as a result of Alexander the Great's conquest, with its accompanying spread of Hellenistic culture, names of Greek-pagan origin became popular all over the empire. Jews too soon adopted the habit of giving their children Greek names, just as even today Christian parents do not hesitate to name their children Dennis, Dion, Diana, Isadora, etc. And does anyone bother to change the pagan names of the days of the week?[421]

When Paul calls Phoebe "our sister," he means "our sister in the Lord." He continues, "who is (or "who is also")[422] a servant of the church at Cenchrea." Cenchrea was Corinth's seaport looking toward Asia. It was situated on the Saronic Gulf. See the sketch on p. 489. A few years earlier Paul had sailed from this port on his way from Corinth to Ephesus (Acts 18:18).

By calling Phoebe a *servant* of Cenchrea's church Paul probably means that she occupied a stable position, performed a definite and important function, in and for that church. She is accordingly called a *diakonos* of that

---

421. For more on this subject of pagan names see N.T.C. on Philippians, pp. 138, 139, footnote 116.
422. Whether καί is authentic is uncertain.

congregation. In Rom. 15:8 Christ was described as having become a *dia-konos*, that is, a *servant*, of the circumcised. To them he *ministered*. However, the word *diakonos* can also be used in a more specialized or technical sense. In Phil. 1:1 and I Tim. 3:8 it refers, in the plural, to deacons.

If that technical sense pertains to the word as used here in Rom. 16:1, then Paul is calling Phoebe a *deaconess*. Now it must be granted that in a later century the ecclesiastical office of deaconess was not unknown.[423] The question, however, is "Does *the New Testament* either here (Rom. 16:1) or anywhere else, refer to such an ecclesiastical office, namely, that of deaconess?" On this subject there is a division of opinion. For details see footnote 424.

The absence of any mention of deaconesses in the rest of the New Testament is a fact. For I Tim. 3:11 see N.T.C. on Timothy, pp. 133, 134; and for Titus 2:3-5 see N.T.C. on Titus, pp. 364-366.

In order to discover what kind of specific function Paul has in mind when he calls Phoebe a *diakonos* of the church at Cenchrea, we should pay close attention to what he says; namely, "Extend to her a welcome in the Lord that is worthy of the saints," meaning, such a welcome as would be fitting for saints to give. He adds, "Give her any help she may need . . . for she has been a helper[425] to many people and to me personally."

This may well be the key to the solution of the problem we are discussing. In light of the facts reported in 16:1, 2, what kind of help would Phoebe need when she arrived in Rome, which was clearly not the place of her residence? Would it not be protection and especially hospitality? And what kind of help did those travelers need who were passing through, and stopping over at, the seaport Cenchrea, Phoebe's home-town, proceeding from west to east or from east to west? Is it not a fact that even today such very busy junctions make strangers feel somewhat uneasy? Was not what they needed a cordial word of greeting, good advice, protection against danger, and frequently even a friendly home in which to pass the night, or even the

---

423. See *Apostolic Constitutions* II 26, 57; III 7, 15. On this subject also consult S.H.E.R.K., Vol. I, p. 245.

424. Among those who favor the rendering *deaconess* here in Rom. 16:1 are the following: C. Hodge, p. 704; J. A. C. Van Leeuwen and Jacobs, p. 279; R. C. H. Lenski, pp. 898, 899; C. E. B. Cranfield, p. 781; A. Schlatter, p. 396; W. Sanday and A. C. Headlam, p. 417; O. Michel, p. 377; A. F. N. Lekkerkerker, Vol. II, p. 187; and, most recently, R. Y. K. Fung, "Charismatic versus Organized Ministry," *EQ*, 4 (1980), pp. 195-237.

On the other hand, B. H. Beyer, in his article on this word (Th.D.N.T., Vol. II, p. 93), states that it is an open question whether Paul is referring to a fixed office or simply to Phoebe's service on behalf of the community. J. Denny, p. 717, regards the rendering "deaconess" as being "too technical." S. Greijdanis (Vol. II, p. 657) also rejects "deaconess." H. Ridderbos points out that if Phoebe ministers to the saints, as is clear from verse 2, she would be a *servant* of the church. What Paul stresses is Phoebe's importance for the church. That the word *diakonos*, as here used, refers to an ecclesiastical office of deaconess cannot be proved. Ridderbos adds that nowhere else does the New Testament make mention of deaconesses (pp. 341, 342).

425. προστάτις, fem. of προστάτης, one who stands in front, protector, helper.

days and nights until the next ship would leave harbor on the way to their destination?

In a word it was *hospitality* that was needed at very busy Cenchrea. And it was *hospitality* Phoebe knew how to offer. Is it not probable that, like Lydia (Acts 16:11-15, 40), Phoebe was a well-to-do Christian lady, blessed with an alert mind and with a heart overflowing with the spirit of kindness and helpfulness? Perhaps, also like Lydia, Phoebe was a businesswoman.

We can well understand that Paul must have referred many a "case" to Phoebe. For that reason, and probably also for other reasons, Paul is able to say, "For she has been a great help to many people and to me personally."

For a list of worthy women, including Phoebe, mentioned in Scripture, see N.T.C. on I Timothy, pp. 133, 134. The lesson is clear. Two extremes should be avoided: (a) that of ordaining women to an ecclesiastical office when there is no warrant for doing so in Scripture; and (b) that of ignoring the very important and valuable services devout and alert women are able to render to the church of our Lord and Savior Jesus Christ.

B. *Paul's Own Greetings*

In connection with the greetings (16:3-16a), the question, "How could Paul have known so many persons in Rome, since he himself had never been there?" has been answered. See p. 27 (under *3a*) and p. 28 (under *As to 3a*). The following facts should also be taken into consideration:

1. Several of these very names occur on inscriptions found in or near Rome (on tombstones, etc.). This does not necessarily mean that the same name refers to the same person. It does indicate that we can no longer be surprised about the occurrence of the name in Paul's epistle to the *Romans*.

2. Some of the names are definitely Latin: Junias, Ampliatus, Urbanus.

3. Mark, writing to the *Romans*, mentions "Simon, the father of Alexander and Rufus," as if to say, "people with whom y o u, in Rome, are well acquainted." Cf. Rom. 16:13, "Greet Rufus."

4. All the codices contain this list of names as part of Paul's epistle to the *Romans*.

Anent the reason for the inclusion of all these greetings, as was indicated previously (p. 28), the very fact that Paul had not been in Rome himself made it advisable warmly to greet those members of the congregation with whom he was acquainted, in order thus to gain an entrance into the hearts of the entire Roman church.

3-5a. Greet Prisca and Aquila, my fellow-workers in Christ Jesus, who risked their necks to save my life, and to whom not only I but all the churches of the Gentiles are grateful. (Greet) also the church (that meets) at their house.

Aquila was a Jew, a native of Pontus. We may assume that his wife, Prisca (in Acts called Priscilla), was also Jewish.[426] These two are always mentioned

---

426. Meaning of names: Aquila=eagle; Prisca=old woman; Priscilla =little old woman.

together. Their names are mentioned three times by Paul (Rom. 16:3; I Cor. 16:19; II Tim. 4:19), and also three times by Luke (Acts 18:2; 18:18; 18:26).

They were great travelers, moving often from one place to another, as has been indicated (pp. 16, 17). When Paul first met them they had recently come from Rome, having been expelled from that city by the decree of emperor Claudius, who had ordered all the Jews to leave Rome (Acts 18:2).

The two were tentmakers, as was Paul. Better still, they were Christians. Was it Paul who had been instrumental in bringing about their faith in the Lord Jesus Christ? Here in Rom. 16:3 Paul calls them "my fellow-workers in Christ Jesus." So all three—Paul, Prisca, Aquila—were partners both in daily vocation and in gospel proclamation. It is not surprising that in Corinth Paul had made his home with them (Acts 18:3).

When Paul, during his second missionary journey, homeward bound, departed from Corinth in order to make a quick stop at Ephesus, with a promise to return there later, Prisca and Aquila went with him. But when Paul departed from Ephesus and sailed to Caesarea, Prisca and Aquila remained at Ephesus (Acts 18:18-21). In that city there was work for them. It may be described as laying the foundation for the apostle's subsequent lengthy ministry in that city, described in Acts 19.

One day a famous and fervent preacher, an Alexandrian Jew, named Apollos, arrived in Ephesus. When Prisca and Aquila noticed that in spite of his eloquence and great learning there was something lacking in his knowledge of "the way of God," they invited him to their home and gave him further instruction (Acts 18:24-26).

It was toward the close of Paul's lengthy ministry at Ephesus that he wrote I Corinthians. Now he was with Prisca and Aquila again, as is clear from the fact that in his greetings he includes this item, "Aquila and Prisca greet y o u warmly in the Lord, and so does the church that meets at their house" (I Cor. 16:19).

Here in Rom. 16:3-5a Paul causes the salutation to Prisca and Aquila to be the first of a lengthy list. Not only is it the first, it is also the fullest and the longest of the greetings. It now appears that the couple had "risked their necks" for Paul; that is, had hazarded their lives for his sake. Did this happen during the riot at Ephesus described in Acts 19:23-41? Cf. I Cor. 16:9, 19; II Cor. 1:8-10. We cannot be certain about this. What is clear, however, is that the devout couple was and remained loyal to Paul to the nth degree.

Paul, in turn, was not slow in letting everybody know what Prisca and Aquila had done for him. Our passage shows that from all over, wherever Gentile churches had been established, messages of praise and gratitude poured in for this self-sacrificing loyalty of Prisca and Aquila. Note also that now the couple is back in Rome again, to which the apostle is addressing this letter. Once more, as in Ephesus, the home of Prisca and Aquila is a meeting-place for the congregation. On the subject of house-churches see pp. 22, 23. So Paul adds, "(Greet) also the church (that meets) at their house."

It appears from II Tim. 4:19 that at a later time the two left Rome once more and returned to Ephesus. The reason for this return may have been the Neronian persecution. It was from his prison in Rome that Paul, shortly before his death, sent one last greeting to these two loyal partners.

It is worthy of note that in two of the three instances in which Paul mentions this couple the name of Prisca occurs before that of Aquila. Similarly, in two of the three passages in Acts Priscilla is mentioned first. We wonder why this is so. Could the reason be that in this case the wife ranked even higher than the husband in her labors for Christ? However that may be, from the list of honorable women mentioned in Scripture Prisca (=Priscilla) must not be omitted. She deserves to be mentioned in one breath with Lydia, Phoebe, and all the others. And her husband too was fully committed to the cause of Christ.

It must have been with special emphasis—his heart probably throbbing a bit faster, his eyes brimming with tears of love and gratitude—that Paul wrote, "Greet Prisca and Aquila."

During his missionary career Paul had colleagues and fellow-workers. But he deemed it necessary to oppose Peter to his face (Gal. 2:11 f.). With Barnabas he had such a sharp disagreement that the two parted company (Acts 15:39). There was a time when Paul refused to allow Mark to remain one of his companions (Acts 15:38). He was going to reprimand Euodia and Syntyche (Phil. 4:2). And Demas was going to desert him (II Tim. 4:10). But even though Prisca and Aquila in a sense stood closer to him than any others—for they were his companions both in trade and in faith—as far as the record shows, between Paul, on the one hand, and Prisca and Aquila, on the other, there was always perfect harmony!

5b. (Greet) my beloved Epenetus, who is Asia's firstfruits for Christ.
Epenetus means praiseworthy.[427] It is fitting that Epenetus (or Epaenetus), who is Asia's[428] "firstfruits" or "first convert for Christ," is mentioned right after the greeting addressed to Prisca and Aquila, who were deeply involved in missionary activity carried on in that general region, the western part of Asia Minor, with its leading city Ephesus.

The very expression "firstfruits" implies that many others were to follow, which was actually what happened (Acts 19:10, 20). For the word "firstfruits" see also on 8:23 (p. 270) and on 11:16 (p. 369). Note "for Christ" because believers belong to him, since he has bought them with his precious blood (I Cor. 6:20; 7:23; II Peter 2:1), in order that they might glorify God.

It is easy to imagine that whenever Paul or any of his fellow-workers, such as Prisca and Aquila, looked back upon the tremendous expansion of Christianity in and around the Roman province of Asia, they must have said, "And it all began with Epenetus; he was *the firstfruits*." That may well have been

---

427. Cf. ἔπαινος, praise, Rom. 2:29.
428. not "Achaia's" (cf. A.V. "of Achaia"), for which there is no solid textual justification, and which probably arose because of confusion with I Cor. 16:15.

one reason why the apostle, his heart overflowing with profound emotion, writes, "(Greet) *my beloved* Epenetus." Of course, there may also have been other reasons why Paul makes use of the modifier "beloved" here and in connection with Ampliatus (verse 8), Stachys (verse 9), and Persis (verse 12), reasons which we cannot now discern.

6. Greet Mary, who labored much for y o u.

"Mary" (or Miriam) is a Semitic name borne also by several other women mentioned in the New Testament: the mother of Jesus (Matt. 1:16), the mother of John Mark (Acts 12:12), Mary of Bethany (Luke 10:42; John 11:1), the mother of James and Joses (Matt. 27:61; cf. John 19:25), and Mary Magdalene (Luke 8:2). How did Paul know that this particular Mary (Rom. 16:6) had labored much for the Roman church? The answer is found in Acts 18:1, 2, "After this, Paul departed from Athens and went to Corinth. There he met a Jew named Aquila, a native of Pontus, *who had recently come from Italy with his wife Priscill* because Claudius had ordered all the Jews to leave *Rome*." Paul did not remain uninformed about what was happening in the various churches. See also verse 19 and cf. 1:8.

7. Greet Andronicus and Junias, my fellow-countrymen and (former) fellow-prisoners, who are outstanding among the apostles and who were in Christ before I was.

An attempt should be made to answer the following questions with respect to which opinions vary:

a. Should we read Junias (masc.) or Junia (fem.)?[429] In the latter case Andronicus and Junia could be husband and wife.

b. Did Paul say, "my fellow-countrymen" or "my relatives"?

c. Does "who are outstanding among the apostles" mean "outstanding in the estimation of The Twelve" or does it mean, "who, as apostles, are outstanding"?

I suggest the following answers:

As to a. The continuation which can be rendered "men of note among the apostles" (R.S.V.) favors the conclusion that both were men.[430]

As to b. When for the first time in Romans the apostle uses the word in question,[431] namely, in 9:3, it must mean fellow-countrymen; that is, fellow-Jews. No good reason has been shown for adopting a different meaning for this word as used here in 16:7. It is hard to believe that Paul had three "relatives" (verses 7 and 11) in Rome, and three other "relatives" (verse 21) around him in Corinth. When Paul became a Christian, by far the most of his "relatives" must have given up on him. Cf. Phil. 3:7.

As to c. The Twelve are not in the picture here. Besides, in the New Testament the word *apostle* is used in a looser and in a stricter sense. According to the broader application of the term, such men as Barnabas, Epa-

---

429. That is, should we adopt the accentuation Ἰουνιᾶν or Ἰουνίαν?
430. The original reads ἐπίσιμοι ἐν τοῖς ἀποστόλοι.
431. the pl. of συγγενής.

phroditus, Apollos, Silvanus, and Timothy are all called "apostles." They all evangelize. They can be described as missionaries or itinerant Christian evangelists. What Paul is saying, then, is this:

Extend greetings to Andronicus and Junias, fellow-countrymen of mine; that is, fellow-Jews, former fellow-prisoners (cf. II Cor. 6:5; 11:23), men who are apostles, and as such, of note, and who were Christians even before I was."

The possibility must be allowed that what Paul meant was that the very fact that these men had embraced Christ even before he did made them outstanding among apostles.

8. Greet Ampliatus, my beloved in the Lord.

Ampliatus is a Latin name meaning *amplified*, enlarged. The name was common among slaves. Between Paul and fellow-Jews there was a strong attachment (9:1-4a), but between the apostle and fellow-believers the bond was far stronger. Ampliatus is Paul's "beloved *in the Lord*." Thus, in a sense, the attachment of the one to the other is similar to that between David and Jonathan (I Sam. 20:41, 42). In this connection see on verse 5b above, and by all means read II Cor. 6:14-18.

9. Greet Urbanus, our fellow-worker in Christ, and (greet) my beloved Stachys.

Urbanus, again a Latin name, means *urbane*, elegant, polite. Men of every social class bore that name. The fact that Urbanus is called "our" fellow-worker, in distinction from Prisca and Aquila who are called "my" fellow-workers (verse 3), may indicate that the relation between Urbanus and Paul was not as close as that between Prisca-Aquila and Paul. It should be recalled that the apostle had made his home with the two, but not, as far as is known, with Urbanus. Thus "our" may indicate that at one time this brother in Christ had been one of Paul's personal fellow-workers but was now a Christian worker in Rome; or it may simply indicate that since Urbanus is engaged in evangelistic work in Rome, a work which, wherever it was performed, was close to Paul's heart, he for that reason says, "*our* fellow-worker," a fellow-worker engaged in a cause that is *dear to all of us*.

"And . . . my beloved Stachys." Note again, as in verses 5, 8, and 12, that precious modifier, "beloved"; here, as in verses 5 and 8, even "*my* beloved." Stachys, meaning *ear of grain*, is a Greek name, but not very common.

10a. Greet Apelles, who is approved in Christ.

Apelles is a Greek name, borne also by Jews. Paul adds, "who is approved in Christ," meaning that amid difficult circumstances Apelles had remained true to the faith, dependable. It may be recalled that Paul was going to tell Timothy, "Do your utmost to present yourself to God *approved*" (II Tim. 2:15). See also I Cor. 11:19; II Cor. 10:18. An approved person is someone who, after thorough examination by the Supreme Judge, has the satisfaction of knowing that God is pleased with him and commends him. For the opposite of "approved"—therefore "unapproved, disqualified, rejected"—see I Cor. 9:27.

This is all we know about Apelles, but the manner in which Paul causes him to be greeted is certainly very encouraging.

10b. Greet those who belong to the household of Aristobulus.

Was this Aristobulus a grandson of Herod the Great? The expression "*the household* of Aristobulus" probably refers to the slaves of the person Paul has in mind. If the conjecture mentioned above should be correct, then it would seem that Aristobulus himself was not a Christian or that he had already died when Paul composed Romans. At their master's death these slaves were kept together and became the property of the emperor. This theory, in turn, might indicate that when Paul continues (in verse 11) by saying, "Greet Herodion," he is referring to a freed slave of Aristobulus or otherwise to someone whose name implies "associated with" or "having admiration for" the family of Herod. But this entire reconstruction[432] is full of hypotheses.

11a. Greet Herodion, my fellow-countryman.

Like Andronicus and Junias, Herodion was Paul's fellow-countryman, accordingly a Jew.

11b. Greet those of the household of Narcissus who are in the Lord.

The name Narcissus may remind us of (a) a bulb plant with smooth leaves and with clusters of orange, white, and yellow; or of (b) a beautiful (mythological) youth who pined away for love of his own reflection in a spring; and so also of (c) any person characterized by excessive self-love. But Paul's passage may especially remind us of (d) a freedman who, during the period when Claudius was emperor, became very rich and powerful. However, whether even this Narcissus was the man whom Paul had in mind cannot be established. All we can say is that the name sounds very natural in a letter directed to the church in *Rome*. Not all those who belonged to the household of Narcissus were believers, as is clear from the fact that Paul sends his greetings to those of this household who were "in the Lord."

12a. Greet Tryphena and Tryphosa, who labor in the Lord.

Tryphena (=delicate) and Tryphosa (=dainty, or perhaps luxurious), were they sisters? They may well have been; see, for example, also Mary and Martha (John 11:1); and today: Hilda and Mathilda, Ruth and Rachel, Joan and Jean. Parents often give their daughters like-sounding names.

But though Tryphena and Tryphosa may well have belonged to a family living on Easy Street, they themselves did not live a life of ease. Whenever Paul thinks of them his soul is filled with admiration. Therefore he makes sure that this high regard he has for them will be reflected in the greeting they receive; hence, "Greet Tryphena and Tryphosa, *who labor in the Lord.*" They were workers for the Lord to whom they had surrendered their lives.

12b. Greet Persis, the beloved, who has labored much in the Lord.

Persis=Persian lady. Like Ephenetus (verse 5), Ampliatus (verse 8), and Stachys (verse 9), this sister in the Lord is described as being "beloved." In

---

432. See also J. B. Lightfoot, *St. Paul's Epistle to the Philippians*, reprint Grand Rapids, 1953, pp. 172-175.

fact, in the present case, "*the* (not just *my*) beloved," perhaps stressing the fact that she is the object of God's love and of the love of the entire church. Like Mary (verse 6) she is described as one who "labored much." Does the distinction in tense:

Tryphena and Tryphosa *labor* (verse 12a)

cf.

Persis *has labored* (verse 12b)

indicate that the frailties connected with old age have caught up with Persis, so that no longer is she able to labor as diligently as was once the case? If so, Paul takes care that her past labors are not forgotten. A lesson for us all to remember!

13. Greet Rufus, the elect in the Lord, and his mother and mine.

This passage immediately reminds us of Mark 15:21, according to which the legionnaries, exercising their right of requisitioning, forced a Cyrenian, Simon, the father of Alexander and *Rufus*, to carry Christ's cross. Since Mark in all probability wrote his Gospel in Rome for the Romans, and since here, in Paul's letter to the Romans, a man by the name of *Rufus* is mentioned by name, the popular opinion, dating back to the early centuries, that the two sources refer to the same individual, *may* well be correct. We cannot be sure, however.

The interpretation of the phrase "the elect in the Lord" varies all the way from Cranfield's view that it does indeed mean "chosen by God, elect," to Lenski's that it has nothing to do with election unto eternal life but simply indicates that Paul regarded Rufus as being a choice Christian.[433]

It cannot escape notice that of Simon's two sons (Alexander and Rufus) only Rufus (=red) is mentioned by Paul. The reason for this *may* have been that, when the apostle composed Romans, Alexander had already died, or that this son of Simon was not living in Rome. Simon is also left unmentioned. Had he died?

There are, of course, also other possibilities. One of them is that while Alexander was not a Christian, Rufus was, and this not because of any innate goodness on his part but because he was "the elect in the Lord."

Also we should not forget that *whether Rom. 16:13 and Mark 15:21 refer to the same family is not at all certain.* Whatever be the truth in this matter, there would seem to be no good reason for interpreting the expression "the elect" in any sense other than it has elsewhere in Paul's writings (Rom. 8:33; Col. 3:12; II Tim. 2:10; Titus 1:1; and for the cognate verb see I Cor. 1:27, 28; Eph. 1:4). So the meaning "chosen by God, elect" must stand.

---

433. See Cranfield, p. 794; Lenski, p. 911. Murray (p. 231) also flatly states that "chosen in the Lord" does not refer to election in Christ, giving as a reason for his opinion that this would apply to all saints mentioned in this chapter. This argument is not very convincing, for one might also say that "beloved" would apply to all believers; yet the word is used only in connection with Epenetus, Ampliatus, Stachys, and Persis.

Note also "and his mother and mine," probably meaning, "and his mother (hence the wife or widow of Simon of Cyrene, *if* Mark 15:21 applies here), who has been a mother to me also." Exactly where and when it was that the mother of Rufus had mothered Paul we do not know. Fact is that here, as often, the apostle again proves that he appreciates what the female members have done and are doing for himself and for the church, to the glory of God.

14. Greet Asyncritus, Phlegon, Hermes, Patrobas, Hermas, and the brothers (who are) with them.

About these five men—were they slaves or freedmen?—we have no further information. The expression "and the brothers (who are) with them" probably refers to the other members of the same house-church.

15. Greet Philologus and Julia, Nereus and his sister, and Olympas, and all the saints (who are) with them.

Among slaves of the imperial household there were many named Philologus and Julia. These two may have been husband and wife, and the next two their children. "Olympas, and all the saints (who are) with them" may perhaps be considered to have been the other members of a house-church.

16a. Greet one another with a holy kiss.

There are three sets of passages in which the New Testament refers to the kiss or/and kissing.

The first is found in Luke 7:36-50, where Jesus tells his host, Simon the Pharisee, "A kiss you did not give me, but she (the penitent woman), from the moment I came in, has not stopped kissing my feet." The lesson is: not only should there be affection but it should be *expressed*. There should be a token of affection; for example, a kiss.

The second is described in Luke 22:47, 48 (cf. Matt. 26:47-49; Mark 14:44,45). Jesus says to Judas, "Is it with a kiss that you are betraying the Son of man?" Not only should love be expressed but this love should be *real*; the kiss should be *sincere*.

The third concerns the kiss interchanged between the members of the Christian community, the church. It is this kiss to which there is a reference here in Rom. 16:16 (=I Cor. 16:20) and also, with transposition of two words, in II Cor. 13:12. Not only should there be a kiss and not only should it be a symbol of genuine affection but it should also be *holy*. In other words, it should never imply less than three parties: God and the two who kiss each other. The holy kiss symbolizes Christ's love mutually shared.[434] It is indeed as indicated in I Peter 5:14, "a kiss of *love*," hence also a kiss of *harmony*, *peace*. If this is rightly understood believers will not deliberately omit kissing those whom they do not happen to like. They will *love* even those whom they do not *like*. The holy kiss is for *all* the members (I Thess. 5:26).

---

434. So also E. F. Harrison, *op. cit.*, p. 165.

Among the Fathers of the church it is Justin Martyr who first mentions this kiss. He indicates the very moment in the liturgy when this kiss was given, persons of the same sex kissing each other. He writes, "At the conclusion of the prayers we greet one another with a kiss."[435]

C. Greetings of All the Churches

16b. All the churches of Christ extend greetings to y o u.

On his travels from place to place Paul came into contact with ever so many churches. From them he would gather information to be passed along to others. It is reasonable to suppose that the churches visited by the apostle would ask him to transmit their greetings to the brothers and sisters in Christ he would meet elsewhere.

Paul was eager to comply with this request, for he himself, at every opportunity, was stressing the unity of all believers in Christ. See what has been said about this in connection with Rom. 9:24, pp. 330, 331.

Moreover, as an apostle of Jesus Christ he had been clothed with authority to promote this unity. "The entire Church of God on earth *one* body, with many members," was a theme on which he loved to dwell. The idea of keeping the various local congregations informed about each other, to encourage them to help each other in their respective needs, both physical and spiritual, and therefore also to forward the salutations of one congregation to as many of the others as possible, was in line with all this.

One day Rome was going to become the world's mightiest fortress of Christianity. For the purpose of welding together the various parts of that gradually arising empire, greetings, that is, tokens of loving concern reaching out from one division of that vast area to another, were effective tiebeams.

17 I exhort y o u, brothers, to watch out for those who cause divisions and put obstacles in y o u r way that are contrary to the teaching y o u have learned. Avoid them. 18 For such people are not serving our Lord Jesus Christ but their own bellies; and by smooth talk and flattery they deceive the hearts of the simple. 19 For the report of y o u r obedience has reached everyone, so that I rejoice over y o u; but I want y o u to be wise about what is good, and innocent about what is evil. 20 The God of peace will crush Satan under y o u r feet soon! The grace of our Lord Jesus (be) with y o u.

Final Warning
"I exhort y o u, brothers, to watch out for those who cause divisions"
16:17-20

17. I exhort y o u, brothers, to watch out for those who cause divisions and put obstacles in y o u r way that are contrary to the teaching y o u have learned. Avoid them.

435. *The First Apology*, Chapter 65, quoted from *The Fathers Of The Church* (tr. by T. B. Falls), New York, 1948, p. 105; also footnote 1 on that page. In the quotation of this sentence (concerning the holy kiss) as it appears in *The Ante-Nicene Fathers* (edited by A. Roberts and J. Donaldson), Vol. I, p. 185, Grand Rapids, 1950, there is a footnote informing the reader that the holy kiss passed into common Christian usage, was continued in the Western Church until the thirteenth century, and is still continued in the Coptic Church.

There are those who maintain that the passage, verses 17-20, cannot have been a part of Paul's epistle to the Romans because its tone is different from that found in the rest of this letter. They maintain that it is "out of context." (Something has been said about this on pp. 27, 28.) They ask:

"Since the apostle has been lavishing effusive praise upon the membership of the Roman church (1:8; 15:14), how could he then now, all of a sudden, be scolding them?"

Those who so reason should look again. On closer examination they will discover that what Paul says here in 16:17-20 is definitely "in context." In the preceding verse he has instructed the addressed to greet one another "with a holy kiss." This kiss was clearly a token of love, unity, harmony. So now in verse 17 he warns the congregation to watch out for people whose purpose it is to disturb this harmony and to create divisions. The connection is close.

Again Paul has just now referred to "all the churches of Christ." Is it even possible that, while reflecting on the conditions in these several churches, he could have dismissed from his mind the fact that some of them were being, or had recently been, disturbed by false teachers who followed him at his heels and did their utmost to overthrow the doctrine of salvation by grace alone? They were constantly causing divisions and putting *obstacles* (see on 14:13, p. 461, footnote 384) in the way, with the purpose of obstructing the true teaching the Romans had learned.

Nowhere does the apostle say or imply that these troublemakers were members of the Roman church. They were probably outsiders, traveling propagandists of error.

It is not necessary to believe that they were all of one kind. Some may have been legalists (Judaizers), others antinomians or perhaps ascetics, or advocates of a combination of two or more disruptive isms.

Paul does not say, "*Oppose* them"; for, though some of those whom he addresses might have been able to do this successfully, others could easily have been led astray if they had entered into a debate. Therefore Paul urges the *brothers* (on which see 1:13, p. 52; 7:1, pp. 214, 215) to *avoid* these dissenters altogether. He knew that the possibility that some of the members might otherwise have lost their bearings was real, especially in view of the clever methods employed by the propagandizers, as indicated in verse

18. For such people are not serving our Lord Jesus Christ but their own bellies; and by smooth talk and flattery they deceive the hearts of the simple.

The expression used in the original for "such people" in this case contains a touch of contempt. It could perhaps be rendered, "folks of this ilk," or "this sort of individuals." Paul clearly considers them to be imposters, quacks.

By stating, "For such people are not serving our Lord Jesus Christ but their own bellies," the apostle is, as it were, saying, "We either serve our Lord Jesus Christ"—note fulness of this glorious title—"or we serve ourselves. To do both at the same time is impossible. We pledge our allegiance to one or to the other." Cf. Matt. 6:24.

Thus within the compass of just a few words Paul exposes the basic error of the gang against which he is issuing a warning. Since in the case of these false teachers the first alternative, namely, serving our Lord Jesus Christ, is out, it must be that they are serving their own bellies. Cf. Phil. 3:19. Does "their own bellies" necessarily mean that these disturbers are all libertines, sensualists? Probably not, for in that case the warning would be directed against only one kind of troublemakers. The real meaning is therefore probably, "self-servers of any description, people who are slaves of their own ego." Whether they be Judaizers, antinomians, ascetics, or what not, how they love to hear themselves talk! They are filled with an exalted opinion of themselves (cf. Col. 2:18, 23). They are living "according to the flesh," allowing their lives to be determined by the cravings of their sinful human nature (cf. Rom. 8:4, 5).

That this is true follows also from the methods they employ to capture their audiences. They make use of smooth talk and flattery. Cf. Jude 16. They are what some would consider "eloquent orators," though in reality "slick shufflers." They are not really helping anybody, though they pretend to do so. They are deceivers, for they lead people away from the fulness of salvation in Jesus Christ. It is the hearts of the simple, unsuspecting, naive, gullible, that are led astray by these charlatans.

The question may be asked, "Is the warning of verses 17, 18 all that is needed in order to cause those addressed to continue to live lives to the glory of God the Father and the Lord Jesus Christ (15:6), lives rich in goodness (15:14), and in accordance with the teaching they have learned (16:17)?" Probably not. So Paul adds,

19a. For the report of y o u r obedience has reached everyone, so that I rejoice over y o u . . .

It is clear that the apostle is mentioning another incentive to Christian conduct: departure from the path of faith and obedience would be a deep disappointment, and this not only to Paul himself but to believers everywhere. The faith of the Romans was being talked about throughout the entire world, so that the apostle is constantly thanking God for them and rejoicing over them (1:8). They certainly would not wish to stop this thanksgiving and rejoicing, and to spoil the reputation they now enjoy.

Note the words, "the report of y o u r obedience." *Obedience* is a term of which Paul is fond (1:5; 6:16; 15:18; 16:26).

In order to make it easier for the hearers-readers to continue in the right path, the apostle lays down a simple yet comprehensive rule, namely,

19b. but I want y o u to be wise about what is good, and innocent about what is evil.

This passage immediately calls to mind several other Pauline texts; such as, I Cor. 14:20; Phil. 2:15; and I Thess. 5:21, 22; as well as the familiar saying of Jesus, "Therefore be keen as the serpents, guileless as the doves"

511

(Matt. 10:16), which, however, does not mean that Paul was necessarily quoting Jesus.

The wisdom Paul here advocates is more than knowledgeability. It is a spiritual as well as a mental quality. Cf. 11:33. It results from sanctified experience. Paul wants the Romans to live in such a manner that they will be equal to the task of choosing what is good in the eyes of God, and that they will be innocent or guileless[436] about what is evil. They should be wise for the purpose of doing and promoting what is right, and should not get "mixed up" with anything that, in God's sight, is wrong.

In verses 17-19 Paul has been telling the Romans how they should conduct their lives. That is very important. In ever so many passages Scripture stresses *human responsibility*. But *divine sovereignty* must not be ignored. In fact, man can do nothing apart from the strength imparted to him by God.

An instructive example of giving due recognition to both of these truths is found in the life of the youth David:

"David said to the Philistine, 'You come against me with sword and spear and javelin, but I come against you in the name of the Lord Almighty, the God of the armies of Israel, whom you have defied. This day the Lord will deliver you into my hands . . . that all the earth may know that there is a God in Israel.' . . . Reaching into his bag and taking a stone, he slung it and struck the Philistine on the forehead. The stone sank into his forehead, and he [Goliath] fell facedown on the ground" (I Sam. 17:45-49, quoted in part).

David did not forget to ascribe all the glory to God . . . but neither did he forget to sling the stone! Conversely, here, in Rom. 16:17-20 Paul exhorts *those whom he addresses* to do the following: watch out . . . avoid . . . obey . . . be wise . . . and be innocent. In other words, *Shoulder y o u r responsibility!* But he follows this up immediately by emphasizing that if there is going to be a victory—and yes, there will be one—it is *God*, he alone, who will achieve it:

20a. The God of peace will crush Satan under y o u r feet soon!

God will exercise his sovereign will in the interest of his people! For the term "God of peace" see on 15:33, p. 498. The apostle has been speaking about those who cause divisions, disharmony, strife. Over against them stands the Almighty, who is "the God of peace." In connection with that which this God of peace will do three items are mentioned:

a. He will *crush* Satan. In other words, he will fulfil the promise of Gen. 3:15. Not Satan but God is Victor.

b. He will crush him *under y o u r feet*. Those who are co-heirs (8:17) are also co-conquerors. The saints will participate in God's victory over Satan. See Rev. 19:13, 14.

c. He will do so *soon*. In a sense it is true that God is crushing Satan right along. A most decisive victory was won on Calvary. There can be no doubt about it, though, that the present passage has reference to the final, escha-

---

436. ἀκεραίους, ἀ-priv. plus κεράννυμι, to mix; hence, unmixed, unadulterated.

tological victory of God over Satan, a victory that will take place in connection with Christ's glorious return (II Thess. 2:8). That this great blessing for the elect will indeed be imparted to them *soon* no longer creates any real problem. See above, on 13:11, pp. 444-447.

d. God's triumph over Satan proves that for his people he is "the God of peace," that is, of complete salvation.

20b. The grace of our Lord Jesus (be) with y o u.

Note the following:

a. *Grace* is God's unmerited favor. For a word-study of this concept see N.T.C. on Luke, pp. 181, 182.

b. Here "our," not just "the" as in I Cor. 16:23. "Our" is here the word of trustful self-appropriation.

c. "Lord Jesus." Jesus means Savior, but in order to be our Savior he must be acknowledged as our Lord, the One who, having purchased us with his blood, owns us, and whose sovereignty over us we acknowledge with joy.

d. the word "be"—in "(be) with y o u"—is not in the text but is understood. The benediction is not a mere wish. It is a promise which becomes a reality in the lives of those who have embraced "our Lord Jesus" with a living faith. Cf. the Aaronitic benediction, to which is added, "So shall they put my name upon the children of Israel, *and I will bless them*." For more on this see N.T.C. on I Thess. 1:1, pp. 42-45. Other Pauline benedictions can be found in I Cor. 16:23 (already mentioned); II Cor. 13:14; Gal. 6:18; Eph. 6:23, 24; Phil. 4:23; I Thess. 5:28; II Thess. 3:18; I Tim. 6:21; II Tim. 4:22; Titus 3:15; and Philem. 25.

e. It is surely remarkable that in God's providence Paul's epistle to the Romans has come down to us in such a manner that while in 15:33 we have a prayer-wish, and here in 16:20 a closing benediction, the glorious doxology, certainly very appropriate for such a basic and marvelous epistle, is saved for the very last few verses (25-27). For more on the genuine character and placement of these verses see Appendix, pp. 521-523.

21 Timothy, my fellow-worker, greets y o u; (so do) Lucius and Jason and Sosipater, my fellow-countrymen. 22 I, Tertius, who wrote down this letter, greet y o u in the Lord. 23 Gaius, who is host to me and to the entire church, greets y o u. Erastus, the city treasurer, and our brother Quartus, greet y o u.[437]

Greetings of Friends
"Timothy, my fellow-worker, greets y o u"
16:21-23

The sending of personal greetings is resumed at this point; with this difference, that the previous greetings were Paul's own (verses 1-16a) and those

---

437. Verse 24 "The grace of our Lord Jesus Christ be with y o u all. Amen." is not adequately supported by textual evidence.

of "all the churches of Christ" (verse 16b) while, by contrast, the present greetings (verses 21-23) are those from individuals who, in one way or another, were associated with the apostle.

There certainly is not any good reason to find fault with this arrangement. In fact, one might even argue that grouping together all the greetings, so that what is now found in verses 21-23 would have followed immediately upon verses 1-16, with the painful warning of verses 17-20 introducing the doxology of verses 25-27, would not have been any improvement. The arrangement as we now have it is surely the best.

21. Timothy, my fellow-worker, greets y o u; (so do) Lucius and Jason and Sosipater, my fellow-countrymen.

Among those who are sending greetings Paul mentions Timothy first of all. A most remarkable person was Timothy or Timotheus. His character was a blend of amiability and faithfulness, in spite of natural timidity. It was concerning him that, a few years later, Paul was going to write, "I have no one likeminded . . . As a child (serves) with (his) father, so he served with me in the gospel" (Phil. 2:19-22). The apostle was going to call Timothy "my beloved child" (II Tim. 1:2). That Paul, writing from Corinth, would make mention of Timothy as one who was in his company, is not surprising. From the book of Acts we learn that on the second missionary journey, outward bound, Paul and Silas, having arrived at Lystra, took Timothy with them. On that same journey Timothy, having been separated from Paul for a little while, joins him again at Corinth, the very city from which the apostle, on his third journey, is now composing Romans. It is not strange, therefore, that also at this time Timothy was with Paul and sending greetings. For more on Timothy see N.T.C. on I Timothy, pp. 33-36. By calling Timothy "my fellow-worker" Paul was making a true statement. It was, however, an understatement. Timothy was indeed a fellow-worker, but to Paul he meant far more than that.

Another person who sends greetings is Lucius. There is no valid reason to identify this person either with the Lucius mentioned in connection with the church of Syrian Antioch (Acts 13:1) or with Luke, though Luke seems, indeed, to have been with the apostle at this time. See Acts 20:5 f. But nowhere does Paul call him "Lucius." See Col. 4:14; II Tim. 4:11; Philem. 24.

The Jason mentioned here could be the one to whom reference is made in Acts 17:5-9, and the Sosipater may be the Sopater of Acts 20:4. The apostle calls Lucius, Jason, and Sosipater "my fellow-countrymen." In other words he describes them as being Jews (one more reason for not identifying the Lucius of this passage with "the beloved physician"). For justification of the rendering "fellow-countrymen" instead of "relatives" see on verse 7, p. 504.

22. I, Tertius, who wrote down this letter, greet y o u in the Lord.

For an author of a letter to have a secretary was not at all unusual. That Paul also had one and would at the very close affix his own signature, at times even adding a few words, is clear from Gal. 6:11; II Thess. 3:17. See also I Cor. 16:21; Col. 4:18.[438]

In the present case the secretary, Tertius, being himself a Christian—Paul certainly would not entrust this kind of task to an unbeliever!—feels the need of adding his own personal greeting, a greeting definitely, like all the others, "in the Lord," that is, expressed as one who is included in that mystic and marvelous fellowship which unites all believers with Christ.

It is the Lord alone who knows how greatly indebted are writers of letters *and/or of books* to their faithful and competent Christian secretaries!

23. Gaius, who is host to me and to the entire church, greets y o u. Erastus, the city treasurer, and our brother Quartus, greet y o u.

This Gaius may well be the same person as the one mentioned in I Cor. 1:14. He should not be identified with the "Gaius from Derbe" of Acts 20:4. When Paul calls Gaius his *host*, he probably means that, since Prisca and Aquila were no longer in Corinth, it was this very man, Gaius, with whom the apostle was making his home. The added expression, "who is host . . . to the entire church" probably does not mean that from every section of Corinth believers crowded into the home of Gaius to attend the worship services. It may simply mean that Gaius was always standing ready to offer hospitality to any believer in need of it. We are thinking especially of travelers. This does not exclude the possibility that the home of Gaius may also have served as a house-church for *part* of the congregation.

"Erastus, the city treasurer." Much has been written about him. Some authors, and even translators, identify him with the man of the same name who on a Corinthian inscription is called *aedile*; that is, commissioner of public works. Such an officer was in charge of buildings, roads, public games, etc. But an *aedile* is not the same as an *oikonomos*, which is the term used here in Rom. 16:23. Cf. the English word *economist*, which causes one to think rather about a *treasurer*. Those who cling to the translation "commissioner of public works" will sometimes answer that Erastus could have performed both functions, that of commissioner of public works and that of city treasurer. But even if this be granted, does it justify any rendering other than "city treasurer" here in Rom. 16:23?

To identify the present Erastus with the one mentioned in Acts 19:22, connected with Ephesus, is also difficult. Or, perhaps, with the Erastus mentioned in II Tim. 4:20? On this see N.T.C. on II Timothy, p. 331, footnote 184.

About Quartus we know nothing beyond what is found here. He is called "our brother," which is certainly a term of endearment, in the present context meaning "our fellow-Christian." Probably Quartus had acquaintances in Rome, and accordingly sends Christian greetings.

---

438. Also A. Deissmann, *op. cit.*, pp. 171, 172.

25 Now to him who is able to establish y o u in accordance with my gospel and the proclamation of Jesus Christ, in conformity with the revelation of the mystery hidden for long
ages past 26 but now manifested, and in accordance with the command of the eternal God
clarified through the prophetic Scriptures in order to bring about obedience of faith among
all the nations, 27 to the only wise God, through Jesus Christ, (be) glory forever! Amen.

Doxology
"Now to him who is able to establish y o u in accordance with my gospel
and the proclamation of Jesus Christ . . . be glory forever through Jesus
Christ! Amen."
16:25-27

This is a lengthy doxology. Nevertheless, the New Testament contains
other doxologies equal in length (Rom. 11:33-36; Heb. 13:20, 21). Even those
of Eph. 3:20, 21 and Jude 24, 25 are not exactly short.

For exegetical purposes the paragraph may be divided into two parts:
verses 25, 26; verse 27.

**25, 26. Now to him who is able to establish y o u . . . in order to bring
about obedience of faith among all the nations . . .**

Various concepts introduced in the opening of Romans (see 1:1-11; especially 1:1-5) return here in 16:25, 26; such as:

a. establish or strengthen (16:25), cf. 1:11;

b. my gospel (16:25), cf. the gospel of God (1:1);

c. the mystery hidden for long ages past (16:25, 26), cf. the gospel which
he promised beforehand (1:1, 2);

d. through the prophetic Scriptures (16:26); cf. through his prophets in
(the) sacred Scriptures (1:2);

e. to bring about obedience of faith among all the nations or Gentiles
(16:26 and 1:5).

But even though the connection between the present passage (16:25-27)
and the beginning of the epistle is close, that between the present passage
and verses 17-20 is also close. Note especially, in verse 19, the expression
"the report of y o u r obedience" and here in 16:26 "In order to bring about
obedience of faith."

In connection with verses 25, 26 note the following:

a. "Now to him who is able to establish y o u"

As in 1:11 so also here Paul is referring to spiritual strengthening, not to
the impartation of any specific charismatic gift, such as speaking in tongues.

b. "in accordance with my gospel"

As in 2:16 and II Tim. 2:8, so also here, Paul has a right to describe the
good news as being "my gospel," for it had been revealed to him by the
Lord; and he, Paul, loved it (cf. I Cor. 9:16), proclaimed it, and was trying,
by God's grace, to show its effect in his own life. See also I Cor. 15:1; Gal.
1:11; 2:2, 7; Eph. 3:6, 7. For "our gospel" see II Cor. 4:3; I Thess. 1:5;
II Thess. 2:14.

c. "and the proclamation of Jesus Christ"

What Paul meant was "my gospel, that is, the proclamation of Jesus Christ."[439] It was by means of the good news, as loved and proclaimed by Paul, that God was able to confirm the addressed.

d. "the *proclamation*"

True preaching is the earnest and enthusiastic outcry of *the herald* as he announces the coming and arrival of the King, and as he urges the people to welcome him with joy and to be in subjection to him. See what has been said on this subject in connection with 10:14, 15, p. 350. As the apostle sees it, it is in connection with, and by means of, such a gospel proclamation that God is able to establish those who are here being addressed. It is that kind of *good news* to which Paul gave the name *my gospel*.

e. "in conformity with the revelation of the mystery hidden for long ages past but now manifested"

A *mystery*, as the apostle uses the term, *is something that*—in some cases even someone who—*would have remained unknown if God had not revealed it*; or, if the mystery is a person, if God had not revealed *him*.

The apostle is going to say three things about this mystery: first, that it was hidden for long ages past (verse 25b); secondly, that it has now been made manifest (verse 26a); and thirdly, that, in accordance with the command of the eternal God, it was being clarified through the prophetic Scriptures, in order to bring about obedience of faith among all the nations or Gentiles (verse 26b).

f. The essence of the mystery was this, that one day the Gentiles would not only be entering God's kingdom in large numbers but would be fellow-sharers, participants on equal terms, with the elect from among the Jews. "Christ in y o u, the hope of glory" (Col. 1:27) would be the solid basis for present salvation and future eschatological glory for *everyone*, regardless of race, who would, by God's sovereign grace, place his trust in the Savior. On this see also Eph. 2:11-22.

It was this mystery that had been hidden for long ages past, for though the decision had been made in God's eternal plan and though even during the old dispensation there had been foreshadowings of the realization of God's promise of salvation for both Gentile and Jew, the period of fulfilment on any large scale had not been reached until now. But *now*, the new dispensation having arrived, and the gospel being proclaimed far and wide, this mystery was being made manifest, was becoming abundantly clear. It was being manifested in *the fulfillment* of prophecy. Think of Gen. 12:3; 22:18. For more on this see N.T.C. on Eph. 3:5, 6, pp. 154, 155.

Was not this very epistle being addressed to a church consisting of both Jews and Gentiles, *unitedly* serving God? Think of Pentecost and its significance (Acts 1:4-8; ch. 2).

---

439. "of Jesus Christ" = "concerning Jesus Christ" (objective gen.).

But not only did the facts of salvation shed light upon ancient prophecies; in turn, these prophecies were now clarifying salvation truths and salvation events. A believer who would now turn to Isa. 53 and read about Messiah's substitutionary sacrifice and its meaning for his (the believer's) life would certainly exclaim, "Now, in light of Isa. 53, I see far more clearly than ever before what Messiah's death means for me!" See also Eph. 1:9-14; 3:1-13.

g. "to bring about obedience of faith among all the nations (or Gentiles)"

That was the purpose or goal of the indicated clarification. God delights to see in any person the kind of obedience that is based on childlike trust in him. For the concept "obedience of faith" see p. 45 (on 1:5). Note also "among *all* the nations," understandable in light of 10:12 and of Matt. 28:19; John 3:16; Acts 2:21.

Paul concludes this paragraph, this chapter, and in fact, the entire epistle, with the words of verse

27. to the only wise God, through Jesus Christ, (be) glory forever! Amen.[440] Here the thought of verse 25 is resumed; hence, "Now to him who is able . . . to the only wise God," etc.

When Paul reflects on what, by inspiration, he has composed, he is filled with amazement. So he must needs add this concluding line to his doxology.

He has been speaking about a love of the Holy One for those who in and by themselves are completely unworthy; a love of the Self-sufficient One reaching out toward those who are thoroughly unable to give anything in return that would enrich the Giver; a love of One who did not wait to extend help until those desperately in need of this love would be favorably disposed to him but who anticipated their love; a love altogether sovereign, unique: "But God demonstrated *his own love* for us in this, that while we were still sinners Christ died for us" (Rom. 5:8). Cf. II Cor. 5:19-21; I John 4:10.

What fills the apostle's soul with astonishment, as he concludes his epistle, is the fact that God was able to rescue *such* sinners; in fact, not only to *rescue*

---

440. Literally what Paul writes is, "to the only wise God, through Jesus Christ, to whom (be) glory forever." That is what he writes *if* ᾧ is authentic. So interpreted, the glory would seem to be ascribed not to God but to Christ, and the first part of the sentence, referring to God, would be "hanging in the air." Now it is true that Paul at times starts a sentence without immediately completing it; e.g. in Rom. 5:12 and in Eph. 2:1. But in such instances he takes up the thought again a little later, so that it is not left incomplete. In the case of Rom. 5:12 he does this in verse 18 of that chapter; and for Eph. 2:1 see 2:5. In the present case, however, he would have completely forgotten the thought with which he began. That can hardly be true. It is therefore far more reasonable to believe that the relative pronoun, if authentic, refers to God. Nevertheless, because of the position of the pronoun in the sentence, where it immediately follows the designation "Jesus Christ," a translation into English that retains the word-order of the original would cause the apostle to ascribe the glory not to God but to Jesus Christ, and would leave the sentence unfinished.

Therefore the translator might just as well omit the relative pronoun entirely, as happens in several published translations.

The 26th edition of Nestle-Aland *Novum Testamentus Graece*, Stuttgart, 1979, places brackets around all of verses 25-27, with explanation of these signs on p. 44* of the Introduction. For the reason to believe that it was Paul himself who was responsible for the closing doxology see the Appendix of the book you are reading, pp. 521-523.

them but to open for them the gateway to everlasting glory and to bring them inside . . . and at such a cost (Rom. 8:32)!

It is with all this in mind that Paul concludes his strikingly beautiful and impressive epistle by exclaiming, "To the only wise God, through Jesus Christ, (be) glory forever!" The fact that God was able and willing to rescue such sinners fixes Paul's attention on the divine *wisdom*; that is, on God's ability to employ the best means for the attainment of the highest goal, namely, the glory of God being ascribed to him by the hearts, lives, and lips of the redeemed. For more on this concept of *wisdom* see on 11:33, p. 386. See also I Cor. 2:6-13.

Note the exact wording: "To the only wise God, through Jesus Christ, (be) glory forever!" It was indeed through Jesus Christ (his departure from the realm of everlasting delight and honor, his self-sacrifice even unto death, death on a cross, victory over death and hell, etc.) that sinners were, are, and are going to be saved. And it is also "through Jesus Christ" that the redeemed ascribe never-ending praise to their Benefactor, God Triune. To him, therefore, be the glory forever. For other ascriptions of glory to God see 11:33-36; Gal. 1:4, 5; Eph. 3:20, 21; Phil. 4:20; I Tim. 1:17; I Peter 5:11; and Jude 24, 25.

As he had done before, namely, at the conclusion of Part I of this letter (11:36), so also now, at the close of the entire letter, Paul adds the word of solemn and enthusiastic affirmation and approval, AMEN.

APPENDIX

in connection with 16:25-27

Did Paul write 16:25-27? That he did not is the view of many New Testament scholars. That he did is vigorously defended by others.

Because of their anti-Rome and anti-Old Testament bias Marcion and his followers were not favorably impressed with references to Rome in 1:7, 15, and to the Old Testament in 15:4, 8, 9 f. Some believe that it was Marcion himself who mutilated the text of Romans. It was Origen who stated, "Marcion, by whom the evangelical and apostolic writings were falsified, removed this section [16:25-27] completely from the epistle, and not only so, but deleted everything from that place where it is written, 'whatsoever is not of faith is sin,' [14:23] right to the end."[441]

But whether the removal of the final two chapters of Romans was done by the heretic himself, as Origen believed, or by others, makes little difference.

As a result, in part, of manipulation some manuscripts bear witness to the existence, at one time or another, of a Romans in 16 chapters, some to a 15-chapter epistle, and some to one containing only 14 chapters.

A suitable *conclusion* was considered necessary for most of the editions. As many see it, such an ending was composed by an editor or by an editorial committee. It was then attached to several editions. However, there still remain some rather early witnesses which attest to the complete omission of the doxology (our 16:25-27); also some in which this passage occurs twice; that is, first after 14:23, then after 16:23 (24).

The result was the coming into existence, at one time or another, of the following five groups of textual witnesses:

a. doxology after 16:23 (24): ℵ B C D E 81 436 630 1739 1962 2127 syr^p cop vg, etc.

b. doxology after 14:23: L Ψ 181 326 330 451 460 614 1241 1877 1881 1984 1985 2492 2495 *et plur.*[40] syr^h goth[41], etc.

c. doxology after both 16:23 (24) and 14:23: A P 5 17 33 104 109.

d. doxology after 15:33: p^{46}.[442]

e. no doxology: G F 629 g E 26 Marcion, etc.

---

441. *Commentaria in epistolam ad Romanos* (re Rom. 16:25-27), in Migne, *Patrologia Graeca* XIV, 1290 AB.

442. This is the famous Chester Beatty Papyrus dating from around the beginning of the third century.

There have been scholars who, while crediting Paul with the composition of all 16 chapters, defended the thesis that it was he himself who was responsible for the appearance of this epistle in a longer and in a shorter form. According to this view the apostle realized that by far the most of what he had written in this letter—that is, everything with the exception of chapters 15 and 16—was of importance to every church and could therefore serve as a kind of circular letter. So he himself made his Romans available in two editions, one containing 14, the other 16 chapters.

The insuperable objection is, of course, that by so doing the apostle would have sliced in half the argument of 14:1-15:13 (concerning the strong and the weak). That theory must therefore be rejected.

There have been many other theories, equally objectionable, for which consult the older commentaries.

All of these studies have, however, become somewhat outdated by the appearance of a doctoral dissertation (revised) by Harry Gamble, Jr., namely, *The Textual History of The Letter to The Romans*, Grand Rapids, 1977. We shall now direct our attention to that work.

The dissertation is written in excellent style. The author, though handling a difficult subject, has thoroughly mastered the art of capturing and holding the attention of the reader from the very beginning to the end of his book. Moreover, the arrangement of the material is logical. Gamble presents a good deal of valuable information; for example, with respect to the Hellenistic letter-writing pattern and its influence upon the authors (including Paul) of the New Testament books.

On p. 92 and elsewhere he shows that only if what we now recognize as The Epistle to the Romans was actually addressed to the Romans—not, for example, to the Ephesians—does the peculiar character of the greetings of Rom. 16 make any sense. In fact, as the reader can see for himself by making a comparison, some of Gamble's arguments in favor of a Roman (not Ephesian) address for the letter are substantially the same as those found on pp. 27, 28 of the commentary he (the reader) is now studying.

On pp. 15-55 Gamble examines the textual evidence for the three major forms in which Romans has appeared: the 14-chapter, 15-chapter, and 16-chapter form. He concludes that the 16-chapter form is authentic.

Another excellent feature of the dissertation is that it defends the position according to which Romans is not a general letter, that is, one which could just as well have been addressed to any other church, but that its author reveals specific knowledge about the situation *in Rome*, p. 136.

And on p. 53 he presents a very fair appraisal of the Chester Beatty Papyrus, and maintains that it cannot be regarded as proving that the 15-chapter book of Romans was the original text.

With respect to one important point Gamble's dissertation has failed to convince me. Let the reader by all means check on this item for himself. Let him not just depend on my criticism.

It is Gamble's position that the passage, Rom. 16:25-27, is unauthentic. The reasons he gives are as follows:

a. The testimony of the manuscripts favors the placement of the doxology after chapter 14, not after chapter 16. The conclusion of a letter with a *doxology* stands in clear contrast with Paul's habit of concluding with a *grace benediction* (pp. 67, 123).

b. In agreement with Harnack, Gamble believes that the doxology is constructed with a certain *awkwardness* and pleonastic style (p. 108).

The answer to this might be as follows:

How do we know that the original did not contain the doxology at the end of the letter? At any rate the Alexandrian witnesses staunchly favor this position. And as to Paul's habit of concluding an epistle with a grace benediction, in I Cor. 16:23 the grace benediction does not occupy the final position, as Gamble himself admits. Also some of the other New Testament books do not end with a benediction. II Peter closes with a doxology; so does Jude.

It is very clear that Paul's epistle to the Romans is divided into two large sections: chapters 1 through 11, *doctrinal*; chapters 12 through 16, *practical*. The first large section definitely ends with a doxology (11:33-36), one of (about) 52 words. Then why should not the second large section similarly end with a doxology (16:25-27), of about the same number of words? Must we really take for granted that Paul would close his epistle—in which he sets forth the unmerited grace of Christ in such marvelous terms—with "Erastus, the city treasurer, and our brother Quartus, greet y o u"? Would not that be *awkward?*

For the rest, barring a few passages in which Gamble casts doubt on the authenticity of Colossians and II Thessalonians, without furnishing proof for the legitimacy of this doubt (p. 80), I recommend the reading of this very informative and interesting dissertation.

Practical Lessons Derived from Romans 15:14—16:27

CHAPTER 15
Verse 14

"I myself am convinced, my brothers, that y o u yourselves are rich in goodness, amply filled with knowledge, and competent also to admonish one another." The apostle has pointed out certain weaknesses characterizing the members of the Roman church. Therefore all the more he is quick to mention also their virtues. If that method would be adopted in every church today, would it not result in blessings for many and better relations all around?

Verse 15

"Nevertheless, I have written to y o u rather boldly on some points, so as to remind y o u of them again. (I have done so) because of the commission God in his grace has granted me ..." In our democratic society we are apt to look down on ideas such as "office," "authority," etc. Such an attitude is clearly in conflict with Scripture. The person who has been invested with an office should faithfully discharge the duties pertaining to it and should, by God's grace, adorn that office with a godly life. And, on the other hand, church members benefited by the institution of this office should honor the office-bearer, remember him in their prayers, and wherever possible co-operate with him.

Verse 24

"I hope ... to be helped forward by y o u ..." Paul had the right idea, namely, to get the membership of the Roman church to become involved in the glorious work of Christian missionary endeavor. People will become enthusiastic about a cause to which they themselves have contributed.

Verse 27

"... if the Gentiles have come to share in the Jews' spiritual blessings, they owe it to the Jews to share with them their material blessings." In order to receive a blessing one should strive to be a blessing!

Verse 31 (and 16:19)

"(Pray to God for me) that I may be rescued from the *disobedient* in Judea ... For the report of y o u r *obedience* has reached everyone ..."

In a day in which so much emphasis is placed on *freedom* of thought, speech, and action, it should not be forgotten that God requires *obedience* to his commands. It is our *duty* to love and worship God. To be sure, it is our privilege to do this, but it is also our obligation. We sometimes hear, "We do not try to influence our children with respect to their religion. We leave that entirely to them." Is that course really the right one? The Word of God teaches differently. See Gen. 18:19; Deut. 6:4-9; Eph. 6:1-4. Such *obedience* should spring from love and gratitude.

Verse 30

"the love of the Spirit ..."

For that *Holy* Spirit to dwell in our sinful hearts he must be loving indeed! Note also:

a. The Father loves us (I John 3:1)

b. The Son loves us (Rom. 8:35)

c. The Holy Spirit loves us (Rom. 15:30)

And these three are ONE. What a blessing! And what an inducement in return to love The Triune God!

CHAPTER 16
Verse 12

"Greet Tryphena and Tryphosa, who labor in the Lord." With respect to them note the following:

a. They are women, perhaps sisters. They may even have been twins. Kingdom work needs women as well as men.

b. These women not merely worked, they labored, worked hard, toiled.

c. Similarity in name is interesting. Similarity in religious ardor and devotion is best of all.

Verses 19b, 20a

". . . I want y o u to be wise about what is good, and innocent about what is evil. The God of peace will crush Satan under y o u r feet soon!"

The Practical Lesson: give both human responsibility and divine sovereignty their due; see the illustration, found on p. 512.

Summary of Chapter 15:14—16:27

In close connection with the immediately preceding prayer-wish Paul assures the Romans that he recognizes their excellent spiritual qualities. Nevertheless, he has at times felt it necessary to express himself rather boldly for their own benefit, exercising his duty as a minister of Christ Jesus to the Gentiles, his aim being to bring the Gentiles to God (15:14-16).

In pleasing humility, ascribing all the glory to God alone, the apostle describes *not* what *he* has done but what *Christ* has accomplished through him in leading many Gentiles to God. He had been privileged to proclaim the gospel of Christ all the way from Jerusalem round about to Illyricum (Yugoslavia-Albania). By means of signs and wonders, performed through the power of the Holy Spirit, that work had been signally blessed. Paul had been a trail-blazer for the gospel. From the very beginning his purpose had been to proclaim the gospel in places and regions where Christ was not known (cf. Isa. 52:15). That explains why he had not been able to make an earlier visit to Rome (verses 17-22).

Paul informs the Romans that since his work of establishing churches in the eastern part of the Roman Empire is finished and since for many years he had been yearning to visit his fellow-believers in Rome, he plans to do so on his way to Spain. However, he cannot come immediately, for he must first of all supervise the handing over of a generous bounty which the Gentile believers of Macedonia and Achaia had been collecting for the needy saints in Jerusalem. He adds, "They were pleased to do it and, indeed, they owe it to them; for if the Gentiles have come to share in the Jews' spiritual blessings, they owe it to the Jews to share with them their material blessings. When I have completed this task . . . I will go to y o u on my way to Spain. I know that when I come to y o u, I will come in the fulness of the blessing of Christ" (verses 23-29).

In need of the intercession of the church, Paul asks the Romans to remember him in prayer:

a. that he might be rescued from the plots of the unbelieving Jews;

b. that his ministry to Jerusalem—a ministry of benevolence—might be acceptable to the Jews, so that

525

c. his coming to the Romans might be a matter of joy, and, together with them, he might be refreshed.

This prayer was certainly answered, though not, in every respect, in a manner Paul had been able to foresee.

As to a, there was indeed a plot against his life by the Jews, but it was discovered in time, so that traveling plans were changed (Acts 20:3);

As to b, Acts 21:17 reports that the brothers in Jerusalem did indeed extend a hearty welcome to Paul and his companions, and glorified God when they heard Paul's report about the results of mission work among the Gentiles. Whether the Jerusalem saints also received the generous collection with grateful enthusiasm is not reported.

As to c, that petition too was granted, though not at the time and in the manner Paul had envisioned. But see Acts 28:11-15; Phil. 1:12.

The little paragraph ends with the prayer-wish of verse 33 (verses 30-33).

The apostle warmly commends to the church Phoebe, a servant of the church at Cenchrea, a seaport of Corinth. In all probability she was the lady who delivered the letter to the Roman Church.

Next, he extends his own greetings to many persons—men and women, Gentile and Jewish believers—members of the Roman Church and known to Paul. The list of individuals to whom greetings are sent begins with Prisca and Aquila with whom Paul had made his home when this couple was still living in Corinth. They were tent-makers as was Paul. But of even greater importance was the fact that they were "fellow-workers in Christ Jesus." So very loyal had they been to Paul that once they had even hazarded their lives for his sake. That may have happened during the riot of Ephesus described in Acts 19:23-41. But we cannot be certain about this.

Paul adds, "(Greet) also the church (that meets) at their house." It seems that wherever Prisca and Aquila were living—whether in Corinth, Ephesus, or Rome—they were always inviting their fellow-believers to meet with them for the worship service.

Next, Paul sends greetings to Epenetus, "Asia's firstfruits for Christ." Among several others to whom greetings are extended is also Rufus. Paul adds, "and his mother and mine," indicating that the mother of Rufus had been a mother to the apostle also; that is, had rendered motherly service to him. This Rufus reminds us of the Rufus mentioned in Mark 15:21, but whether the same person is indicated in both places is uncertain. At the conclusion of the list Paul writes, "All the churches of Christ extend greetings to y o u" (16:1-16).

Paul now tells the Roman church to watch out for false teachers. Let the members be on their guard, and this especially for two reasons: (a) by means of smooth talk and flattery these troublemakers try to deceive the hearts of the unsuspecting; and (b) the Roman believers should not spoil the good reputation (for obedience to the truth) they have gained everywhere. Using an expression that reminds us of a saying of Jesus (Matt. 10:16), the apostle adds, "I want y o u to be wise about what is good, and innocent about what is evil." In addition to placing emphasis on the *responsibility* the Romans should shoulder, he comforts them by reminding them that God, in the exercise of his *sovereignty*, will crush Satan under their feet soon. He adds, "The grace of our Lord Jesus (be) with y o u" (verses 17-20).

The greetings which friends are sending to the Roman church follow. The greeters include Timothy, a very dear friend and fellow-worker of Paul; Tertius, the apostle's secretary, to whom the apostle had dictated the letter; and Gaius, at whose home Paul was staying and who was ever ready to reveal his hospitality in the interest of the entire church (verses 21-23).

By means of a very impressive doxology, one which in many ways reflects the opening verses of the epistle, Paul brings his marvelous epistle to an appropriate close (verses 25-27).

BIBLIOGRAPHIES

Select Bibliography on Romans 9—16

A. *On Romans 9*

Bavinck, H., *The Doctrine of God* (translation of *Gereformeerde Dogmatiek* Vol. II, pp. 1-425), Grand Rapids, 1955; Edinburgh, 1979; see especially pp. 337-407.

Berkhof, L., *Systematic Theology*, Grand Rapids, 1949, pp. 100-125.

Calvin, J., *Commentaries on the Epistle of Paul the Apostle, to The Romans*, translated and ed. by J. Owen, Grand Rapids, 1947, pp. 332-380.

_____ . *Institutes of the Christian Religion*, translated by John Allen, Philadelphia, 1928, Vol. II, pp. 140-149.

Klooster, F. H., *Predestination: A Calvinistic Note* (Perspectives on Evangelical Theology), Grand Rapids, 1979, pp. 81-94.

Murray, J., *The Epistle to the Romans* (The New International Commentary on the New Testament), Grand Rapids, 1959; Vol. II, pp. 1-45.

B. *On Romans 11*

Lenski, R. C. H., *The Interpretation of St. Paul's Epistle to the Romans*, Columbus, 1945, pp. 678-743.

Robertson, O. P., *Is There a Distinctive Future for Ethnic Israel in Romans 11?* (Perspectives on Evangelical Theology), Grand Rapids, 1979, pp. 209-227.

C. *On Romans 10, 12-16*

Calvin, J., *Romans* (for full title see under A.), pp. 381-407; 449-556.

Cranfield, C. E. B., *A Critical and Exegetical Commentary on the Epistle to the Romans* (The International Critical Commentary), Vol. II, Edinburgh, 1979, pp. 512-542; 592-814.

Murray, J., title as under A.; Vol. II, pp. 46-64; 109-268.

General Bibliography

Aalders, G. Ch., *Het Boek Genesis* (Korte Verklaring), 2 vols., Kampen, 1949.

Abelard, P., *Commentarii super S. Pauli epistolam ad Romanos* (Minge, Patrologia Latina), Paris, 1844-64.

Althaus, P., Der Brief an die Römer, Göttingen, 1949.

Ambrosiaster, *Commentaria in XIII spistolas beati Pauli* (Minge, Patrologia Latina), Paris, 1844-64.

Ante-Nicene Fathers, ten vols., Grand Rapids, 1950, for references to Irenaeus, Origen, Tertullian, etc.

Asmussen, H., *Der Römerbrief*, Stuttgart, 1952.

Augustine, *Epistolae ad Romanos* (Minge, Patrologia Latina), Paris, 1844-64.

Barclay, W. *The Letter to the Romans* (Daily Study Bible), Edinburgh, 1957.

Barret, C. K., *A Commentary on the Epistle to the Romans* (Black's New Testament Commentaries), London, 1957.

Barth, K., *Der Römerbrief*, Zürich, 1954.

_____. *A Shorter Commentary on Romans* (tr. of *Kurze Erklärung des Römerbriefes*, 1956), London, 1959.

Batey, R. A., *The Letter of Paul to the Romans*, Austin, 1969.

Bavinck, H., *Gereformeerde Dogmatiek*, 4 vols., Kampen, 1918.

Beck, J. T., *Erklärung des Briefes an die Römer*, 2 vols., Güterslo, 1884.

Beet, J. A., *A Commentary on St. Paul's Epistle to the Romans*, London, 1902.

Berkhof, L., *Systematic Theology*, Grand Rapids, 1949.

Berkhouwer, G. C., *Dogmatische Studiën* (the series), Kampen, 1949, etc.

Best, E., *The Letter of Paul to the Romans* (Cambridge Bible Commentary), Cambridge, 1967.

Black, M., *Romans* (New Century Bible), London, 1973.

Boylan, P., *St. Paul's Epistle to the Romans*, Dublin, 1934.

Brakel, W. a, *Redelijke Godsdienst*, 2 vols., Leiden, 1893.

Bruce, F. F., *The Epistle of Paul to the Romans* (Tyndale Bible Commentaries), Grand Rapids, 1963.

Brunner, E., *The Letter to the Romans* (English tr. of *Der Römerbrief*, 1956), London, 1959.

Burton, E. D., *Syntax of Moods and Tenses in New Testament Greek*, Chicago, 1923.

Buttz, A., *Epistle to the Romans in Greek*, New York and Cincinnati, 1876.

Calvin, J., *Commentaries on the Epistle of Paul the Apostle, to the Romans* (tr. and ed. by J. Owen, Grand Rapids, 1947.

_____. *Institutes of the Christian Religion* (tr. by John Allen), Philadelphia, 1928.

Chamberlain, W. D., *The Meaning of Repentance*, Philadelphia, 1943.

Cranfield, C. E. B., *A Critical and Exegetical Commentary on the Epistle to the Romans* (The International Critical Commentary), 2 vols., Edinburgh, 1975, 1979.

Denney, J., *St. Paul's Epistle to the Romans* (The Expositor's Greek Testament), Vol. II, Grand Rapids, n.d.

Dibelius, M., *Die Geisterwelt im Glauben des Paulus*, Göttingen, 1909.

Dodd, C. H., *The Epistle of Paul to the Romans* (Fontana Books), London, 1959.

Doekes, G., *De Beteekenis van Israëls Val*, Nijverdal, 1915.

Donfried, K. P., (ed. & contributor), *The Romans Debate*, Minneapolis, 1977.

Erdman, C. R., *Epistle of Paul to the Romans*, Philadelphia, 1925.

Flynn, L. B., *Did I Say That?*, Nashville, 1959.

Foakes Jackson, F. J., and Lake, K., *The Beginnings of Christianity*, Vols. IV and V, Grand Rapids, 1965, 1966.

Fraser, J., *A Treatise on Sanctification*, London, 1898.

Fuchs, E., *Die Freiheit des Glaubens: Römer 5-8 ausgelegt*, Munich, 1949.

Gamble, H., Jr., *The Textual History of the Letter to the Romans*, Grand Rapids, 1977.

Gifford, E. H., *The Epistle of St. Paul to the Romans*, London, 1886.

Gispen, W. H., *Exodus* (Korte Verklaring), Kampen, 1932.

ROMANS

_____. *De Spreuken van Salamo* (Korte Verklaring), Kampen, 1954.

Godet, F. *Commentary on St. Paul's Epistle to the Romans* (tr. from the French), 2 vols., Edinburgh, 1880, 1881.

Gore, C. *The Epistle to the Romans*, London, 1907.

Greijdanus, S. *De Brief van den Apostel Paulus aan de Gemeente te Rome* (Kommentaar op het Nieuwe Testament), 2 vols., Amsterdam, 1933.

Haldane, R., *The Epistle to the Romans*, London, 1966.

Hamilton, F. E., *The Epistle to the Romans*, Grand Rapids, 1958.

Harder, R. C., a chapter in *De Heilige Geest*, ed. by J. H. Bavinck, P. Prins, and G. Brillenburg, Wurth, Kampen, 1949.

Harrison, E. F., *Romans* (The Expositor's Bible Commentary), Grand Rapids, 1976.

Hendriksen, W., *Beginner's Book of Doctrine*

_____. *Israel in Prophecy*

_____. *More Than Conquerors* (on the book of Revelation)

_____. *New Testament Commentary*: a volume on each of the four Gospels, and volumes on all of Paul's Epistles (except I and II Corinthians)

_____. *Survey of the Bible*

_____. *The Bible on the Life Hereafter*

_____. *The Covenant of Grace*

_____. *The Doctrine of God* (my translation of H. Bavinck's *Gereformeerde Dogmatiek*, Vol. II, pp. 1-425)

Place of publication of all the above: Grand Rapids

_____. The Meaning of the Preposition ἀντί in the New Testament (unpublished dissertation, Princeton Seminary, 1948).

Hodge, C., *A Commentary on the Epistle to the Romans*, Grand Rapids, 1886 (reprinted 1950).

Hoeksema, H., *God's Eternal Good Pleasure*, Grand Rapids, 1950.

Huby, J., *Saint Paul: Épître aux Romains*, Paris, 1957.

Hunter, A. M., *The Epistle to the Romans* (Torch Bible Commentaries), London, 1954.

Jowett, B., *The Epistles of St. Paul to the Thessalonians, Galatians, and Romans*, London, 1855.

Käsemann, E., *An die Römer* (Hand buch zum N.T.), Tübingen, 1973; English translation, *Commentary on Romans*, Grand Rapids, 1980.

Kelly, W. *Notes on the Epistle to the Romans*, London, 1873.

Kirk, K. E., *The Epistle to the Romans* (Clarendon Bible), Oxford-1937.

Klooster, F. H., *Predestination: A Calvinistic Note* (Perspectives on Evangelical Theology), Grand Rapids, 1979.

Knox, J., *The Epistle to the Romans* (The Interpreter's Bible), New York, 1954.

Kühl, E., *Der Brief des Paulus an die Römer*, Leipzig, 1913.

Kümmel, W. G., *Römer 7 und die Bekehrung des Paulus*, Leipzig, 1929.

Kuyper, A., *Het Werk van den Heiligen Geest*, Kampen, 1927.

Lagrange, M. J., *Saint Paul: Épître aux Romains* (Etudes Bibliques), Paris, 1950. This book contains a long list of commentaries of the Greek and Latin church-fathers.

Lange, J. P., *The Epistle of Paul to the Romans*, tr. from the German (Lange's Commentary on the Holy Scriptures), Grand Rapids, 1869.

Leenhardt, F. J., *The Epistle to the Romans*, tr. from French, London, 1961.

Lekkerkerker, A. F. N., *De Brief van Paulus aan de Romeinen*, 2 vols., Nijkerk, 1971.

Lenski, R. C. H., *The Interpretation of the Acts of the Apostles*, Columbus, 1944.

_____. *The Interpretation of St. Paul's Epistle to the Romans*, Columbus, 1945.

Liddon, H. P., *Explanatory Analysis of St. Paul's Epistle to the Romans*, London, 1893.

Lietzmann, H., *An die Römer* (Handbuch zum N.T.), Tübingen, 1933.

Lightfoot, J. B., *Notes on the Epistles of St. Paul: The Epistle to the Romans*, chapters 1-7, London, 1895.

_____. *St. Paul's Epistle to the Philippians*, Grand Rapids, 1953.

Lloyd-Jones, D. M., *Romans* (Exposition on Romans 3:20-8:39), 6 vols., Grand Rapids, 1971-1976.

Loane, M. L., *The Hope of Glory (an Exposition of Romans 8)*, London, 1968.

ROMANS

Luther, M., *Lectures on Romans*, tr. by W. G. Tillmanns and A. O. Preus (from German, Weimar edition of Luther's works, Vol. 56), Volume 25 of *Luther's Works*, ed. by H. C. Oswald, St. Louis, 1972.

Manson, T. W. *Romans* (Peake's Commentary on the Bible), London, 1962.

Meyer, H. A. W., *The Epistle to the Romans*, tr. from German, Edinburgh, 1884.

Michel, O., *Der Brief an die Römer* (Kritisch-exegetischer Kommentar über das N.T.), Göttingen, 1966.

Moule, H. C. G., *The Epistle of Paul to the Romans* (The Expositor's Bible, Vol. 5), Grand Rapids, 1943.

Murray, J., *The Epistle to the Romans* (The New International Commentary on the New Testament), 2 vols. Grand Rapids, 1959.

Nygren, A., *Commentary on Romans*, London, 1952.

Parry, R. St. J., *The Epistle of Paul the Apostle to the Romans* (Cambridge Greek Testament), Cambridge, 1912.

Ridderbos, H., *Aan de Romeinen* (Commentaar Op Het Nieuwe Testament), Kampen, 1959.

Robertson, A. T., *The Epistle to the Romans* (Word Pictures in the New Testament, Vol. IV, pp. 320-430), New York and London, 1931.

Robertson, O. P., *Is There a Distinctive Future for Ethnic Israel in Romans 11?* (Perspectives on Evangelical Theology), Grand Rapids, 1979.

Robinson, J. A. T., *Wrestling with Romans*, Philadelphia, 1979.

Sanday, W. and Headlam, A. C., *A Critical and Exegetical Commentary on the Epistle to the Romans* (International Critical Commentary), Edinburgh, 1911.

Schlatter, A., *Gottes Gerechtigkeit: ein Kommentar zum Römerbrief*, Stuttgart, 1952.

Schmidt, H. W., *Der Brief des Paulus an die Römer* (Theologischer Handkommentar zum N.T.), Berlin, 1962.

Steele, D. N. and Thomas, C. C., *Romans, an Interpretive Outline*, Philadelphia, 1963.

Taylor, V., *The Epistle to the Romans* (Epworth Preacher's Commentaries), London, 1956.

Thomas, W. H.G., *St. Paul's Epistle to the Romans*, Grand Rapids, 1956.

Trench, R. C., *Synonyms of the New Testament*, Grand Rapids, 1948.

Van Andel, J., *Paulus' Brief aan de Romeinen*, Kampen, 1904.

Van Leeuwen, J. A. C., and Jacobs, D., *De Brief aan de Romeinen*, Kampen, 1932.

Vaughan, C. J., *St. Paul's Epistle to the Romans*, London, 1880.

Vine, W. E., *The Epistle to the Romans*, London, 1957.

Volbeda, S., *De Intuitieve Philosophie van James McCosh*, Grand Rapids, n.d.

Von Hagen, W. V., *The Roads that Led to Rome*, Cleveland and New York, 1967.

Vos, G., *The Pauline Eschatology*, Princeton, 1930.

Warfield, B. B., *Biblical and Theological Studies*, Philadelphia, 1954.

Wilson, G. B., *Romans, A Digest of Reformed Comment*, Edinburgh, 1977.

Wood, L. J., *The Prophets of Israel*, Grand Rapids, 1979.

Zahn, T., *Der Brief des Paulus an die Römer* (Kommentar zum Neuen Testament), Leipzig, 1910.